S0-ARJ-041

HOLLYWOOD'S CENSOR

THOMAS DOHERTY

HOLLYWOOD'S CENSOR

JOSEPH I. BREEN

& the Production Code Administration

COLUMBIA
UNIVERSITY
PRESS
NEW YORK

Columbia University Press
Publishers Since 1893
New York Chichester, West Sussex

Library of Congress Cataloging-in-Publication Data

Doherty, Thomas Patrick,
Hollywood's censor : Joseph I. Breen and the Production Code Administration / Thomas Doherty.
p. cm.
Includes bibliographical references and index.
ISBN 978-0-231-14358-5 (cloth : alk. paper)
1. Motion pictures—Censorship—United States—History. 2. Breen, Joseph Ignatius, 1890–1965. I. Title.

PN1995.62.D64 2007
791.430973—dc22 2007026146

Columbia University Press books are printed on permanent and durable acid-free paper.

Printed in the United States of America

Designed by Lisa Hamm

c 10 9 8 7 6 5 4 3 2 1

FOR SANDRA, AGAIN

CONTENTS

OPENING CREDITS

What follows is not a biography of Joseph I. Breen but a cultural history of Hollywood and America with the life and character of Breen as the spine of the story. Along the way, Catholic priests, Jewish moguls, visionary auteurs, studio hacks, hardnosed journalists, and bluenose agitators will be clashing over the great art of the twentieth century, classic Hollywood cinema, during its high renaissance between the arrival of sound and the rise of television.

Though not certified by a Code Seal, the following production has an extensive credit list. Two players warrant top billing: Mary Pat Dorr, Joseph Breen's granddaughter, who graciously shared her memories of a doting grandfather and generously granted permission, with no strings attached, to quote from his private correspondence; and Barbara Hall, head of Special Collections at the Margaret Herrick Library of the Academy of Motion Picture Arts and Sciences, a fellow "Breeniac" who shared her unmatched expertise in matters Production Code. Martin S. Quigley, Pat Breen, Albert Van Schmus, and Monsignor Francis Weber patiently answered questions about the man they knew. Leonard Leff offered advice and research materials. Charles Maland lent his keen eye to the manuscript.

A number of kind scholars, researchers, and archivists provided invaluable guidance: Gregory Beal, Bob Dickson, Shawn Guthrie, Kristine Kreuger, and Linda Mehr at the Margaret Herrick Library and AMPAS; Nicholas B. Scheetz and Scott S. Taylor at Special Collections at Georgetown University; Rev. William Mugan, S.J., Nancy Merz, and Mary Struckel at the Midwest Jesuit Archives; Don H. Buske at the Historical Archives of the Archdiocese of Cincinnati; Julie Satzik at the Archdiocese of Chicago's Joseph Cardinal Bernardin Archives and Records Center; W. John Shepherd at the Catholic History Research Center and University Archives at the Catholic University of America; Sean Delaney at the British Film Institute; Pat McAvinue at the Drexel Library at St Joseph's University; Patrice M. Kane at Fordham University Library; Benjamin Singleton at the Newsfilm Library at the University of South Carolina; Matthew J. Olsen at the National Archives and Records Administration, College Park, Maryland; Patrick McNamara at the Archdiocese of Brooklyn Archives; Neil Bethke, at Archives and Special Collections at Loyola Marymount University; David Pavelich at the Special Collections Research Center at the University of Chicago; Wayne Dowdy at the Memphis Public Library; Colin Varga and Shawn Weldon at the Archdiocese of Philadelphia Archives; Rev. Joseph Bongard at Roman Catholic High School in Philadelphia; Ron Simon at the Paley Center for Media; and Madeline Matz, Rosemary Hanes, and Joe Belian at the Motion Picture Division of the Library of Congress. At Columbia University Press, Jennifer Crewe and Roy Thomas guided the manuscript and encouraged the author.

I also deeply appreciate all the friends who kibitzed, criticized, listened with good grace, and allowed themselves to be exploited for off-the-cuff research assistance: Matthew Bernstein, Sheri Chinen Biesen, Devin Carney, Julia Crantz, Lisa Debin, Andrew Hudgins, Rick Jewell, Ross Melnick, John Raeburn, Luke Salisbury, Maayan Zack, and all my colleagues at Brandeis University, especially Jacob Cohen for his thoughtful comments. Again, and above all, I owe my wife Sandra more than I can express.

Finally, I'd like to thank the members of the Academy for an Academy Film Scholars Grant and the opportunity to say the first part of this sentence.

HOLLYWOOD'S CENSOR

PROLOGUE
Hollywood, 1954

On March 25, 1954, from the stages of the RKO Pantages Theater in Hollywood and the Center Theater in New York, the Academy of Motion Picture Arts and Sciences presented its annual award ceremonies—the Oscars, live, on television. For only the second time in the Academy's twenty-six-year history, video was crashing the party, and NBC had sent out open invitations courtesy of another dream factory ("Oldsmobile brings you the famous Academy Awards Presentation!"). The come-on blurb in a new weekly publication called *TV Guide* had already realigned its screen priorities: "Jack Webb of *Dragnet* will be among those presenting the Oscars."

Viewed via the washed-out kinescope that has preserved the evening, and measured against twenty-first-century standards of global saturation and glitzy excess, the festivities in 1954 look dressed-down and low-tech, the production numbers mechanical and martial, short on sizzle and skimpy on skin. The musical highlight was a modest vignette in a faux dinner club, featuring Dean Martin crooning a bourbon-smooth version of "That's Amore" from *The Caddy* (1953), the latest box office hit from the golden comedy duo of Martin and Lewis. (Dino's jukebox evergreen lost out to the treacly "Three Coins in a Fountain.") In terms of sheer tonnage, the most elaborate choreography was reserved for a chorus line of behemoth Oldsmobiles parked on stage for the live commercials.

No matter. Still entranced by the novelty of bicoastal telecasts transmitted direct into the living room, Americans were thrilled to peek through the keyhole of the camera and spy on the glamour of a legendary Hollywood ritual. Of course, within the executive suites at NBC, the motives were less starstruck: advertising revenues might not recoup the costs of mounting the extravaganza, but the medium was selling more than any individual show. It was selling itself, betting on dividends down the line from a long-term investment in a blue-chip futures market. For the television industry, the Oscar ceremonies were a prize catch. For the motion picture industry, the incursion of video was a portent of things to come.

A dollop of controversy shadowed the telecast—not over the nominated films, or a scandalous gown, or an incendiary acceptance speech, but over the very fact that the hottest ticket in Hollywood was being squandered on the archrival. "I rushed home last night to watch this great show on television," confessed a depressed motion picture exhibitor the next morning. "I'm sure that millions of people (this morning's papers say about 43,000,000) did the same thing. Certainly the empty seats in the theaters across the country prove that these figures are correct." Not so long ago, the moving-image competition had been derided and disdained. "Television is nothing *but* rehearsals," the effete theater critic Addison DeWitt scoffed in Joseph Mankiewicz's *All About Eve* (1950), summing up Broadway's, and Hollywood's, high-hat attitude to the small screen. But with Milton Berle's madcap variety hour and the Friday Night Fights (also known as *Texaco Star Theater* and *The Gillette Cavalcade of Sports*) beaming topnotch, no-cost entertainment into private homes and public bars, the lofty superiority and smug complacency soon gave way to frayed nerves and furrowed brows. To the theater operators who manned the front lines and endured personal rejection at the box office window, ushering television into the Oscar ceremonies was the moral equivalent of trading with the enemy. Ornate motion picture palaces and 600-seat theaters alike—venues once filled to the rafters with sniffling matrons, snuggling couples, and popcorn-munching moppets sitting rapt before a women's weepie, a screwball comedy, or a matinee shoot-'em-up—were left sparse and vacant, shells of their former selves. Why give lapsed moviegoers another reason to stay home and watch movie stars on television—for free!—instead of making them pay for the privilege down at the local Bijou?

Worse, Hollywood's most exclusive soiree was not just shown on television, it was staged *for* television. The second Oscar telecast "marked the first time the Academy Awards was fashioned to be run off with the TV cameras always in mind," revealed the *Hollywood Reporter*. "The RKO Pantages audience, star-studded and glittering in evening dress, was passed up for the millions of more simply dressed home viewers." The *Los Angeles Times* rubbed salt in the wound: "Unlike last year's stuffy affair where the TV cameras were treated as intruders, this year the cameramen, decked out in white ties and tails, will have places of honor right on the stage." During rehearsals a symbolic turf war erupted between the old Hollywood pro Mitchell Leisen, director of the Pantages stage show, and NBC's William Bennington, director of the television show. "Let me rehearse, then you can try out your damn cameras!" an exasperated Leisen bellowed at the upstart. Think of it: the Academy of Motion Picture Arts and Sciences taking direction from the National Broadcasting Company.

Singer, dancer, funnyman, and shameless ham Donald O'Connor hosted the ceremonies, riffing off his persona as the goofy second banana in the splashy Technicolor musical *Singin' in the Rain* (1952), the big hit, though Oscar underachiever, from the previous year. A masterpiece of industrial craftwork from MGM's famed "Freed unit," the tightly knit team of artists supervised by unit producer Arthur Freed, *Singin' in the Rain* was a nostalgic homage to the early talkie era, when the quiet realm of silent cinema was shattered overnight by the thunderclap of sound, the last time Hollywood had faced a technological revolution upending the old order. The good-humored glance back at the glitches and scratches of the late 1920s offered reassurance that Hollywood would surmount an even greater threat in the early 1950s.

This night, the charmed entry in the list of Oscar-nominated films was *From Here to Eternity* (1953), directed by Fred Zinnemann from the James Jones novel ("the boldest book of our time . . . honestly, fearlessly, on the screen!"). Set on a hardtack, hot-blooded Army post in Hawaii in the days before Pearl Harbor, the khaki-colored melodrama devoted less screen time to close-order drill on the parade ground than to close-quarter tensions behind bedroom doors. Already iconic, emblazoned on one-sheet posters and spread across huge billboards, was an image of luxuriant sexuality: the glistening bodies of Burt Lancaster and Deborah Kerr, clad only in bathing suits, entwined on a beach as the surf rolls in and licks their lithe limbs, the couple a single organism horizontal in the sand. The film won eight Oscars, including Best Picture.

If the suave Dean Martin stole the musical portion of the show, a singer with a more intimate vocal style provided the note of highest drama. The award for Best Supporting Actor went to Frank Sinatra, the heartthrob of the wartime bobby-soxers, whose downward career spiral in the postwar era was reversed by his fierce performance as Maggio, the doomed rebel in *From Here to Eternity*. When actress Mercedes McCambridge read his name, the auditorium erupted in rapturous applause: Hollywood loves a comeback. "The ovation and enthusiasm," sighed the normally reserved *Variety*, itself reduced to a bobby-soxer swoon, "was of the gloss of which showbiz stardust is made." An overjoyed Sinatra sprinted up the aisle and graciously accepted his statuette, joking that he had *not* been asked to sing one of the nominated songs that year.

Taking over from Donald O'Connor to preside over a spate of more mundane award presentations was producer and screenwriter Charles

Brackett, president of the Academy. Brackett owned a shelfful of Oscars himself, the most recent received just that evening for *Titanic* (1953), and the most notable earned in collaboration with his longtime partner Billy Wilder for *Sunset Blvd.* (1950), coincidentally, or not, another resonant meditation on the lost glory of Hollywood's silent era. In his introductory remarks at the top of the show, Brackett put forward a brave face for the battered industry. "Tonight we celebrate a single year—1953. We celebrate it exultantly, as a year of rebirth, revitalization, new techniques, new dimensions," Brackett insisted. "As to the audience, it hasn't drifted, it has surged back—but with a new look, a more knowing eye, an insistence on showmanship, a demand for balanced perfection in every department of picture making."

To Brackett fell the task of bestowing the honorary Oscars, a category devised to give due, often overdue, recognition to motion picture insiders, technical wizards, and neglected old-timers, the heavy lifters around town who were eminently regarded if woefully bereft of star voltage. Though good public relations and obligatory business, the honorary awards segment of the Oscars presaged a slump in the proceedings, the chance for the ladies to scurry to the powder room or the men to wander into the lobby for a smoke.

The roll call of honorary recipients began with Pete Smith, a former press agent who since 1935 had produced and narrated a popular series of short films for MGM called the "Pete Smith Specialties," a monthly issue of whimsical vignettes with titles like *Romance of Radium* (1937), *Lions on the Loose* (1941), and *Movie Pests* (1944). Clocking in at ten to twenty minutes, the short or featurette had long been a staple entry on the program of newsreels, cartoons, singalongs, and sundry appetizers that unspooled before the main course of the featured attraction. Smith's shorts often played better than the films they preceded, but in 1954, with no captive audience and no sure profit margin, even the brand name extras weren't paying their rent. Smith had already announced his retirement, and the next year his unit closed up shop.

Also honored was producer Darryl F. Zanuck, president of Twentieth Century-Fox and the dauntless visionary behind CinemaScope, the new widescreen process designed to lure audiences away from the very medium they were watching. "You can see it without glasses!" exclaimed taglines, to prevent CinemaScope from being confused with the headache-inducing, and already fading, gimmick of 3-D cinema. After rolling the dice on CinemaScope, Zanuck was enjoying a huge payday with *The Robe* (1953), a biblical spectacle that earned three Oscars that night and accrued the highest

Hollywood, 1934: Breen, on the town with comedian Joe E. Brown.

(URBAN ARCHIVES / TEMPLE UNIVERSITY)

grosses of any film that year. To cap his introduction of Zanuck, Brackett wittily turned his note card lengthwise to mimic the elongated shape of the CinemaScope screen.

Sandwiched between the awards to Pete Smith and Darryl F. Zanuck—whose names the well-informed, or at least older, moviegoer would surely have recognized—was someone whose name, at best, rang only a dim and distant bell.

Brackett read the commendation. "The motion picture Production Code is a strong protection against self-appointed, wildcat censorship groups," he declared by way of preamble. "For his conscientious, open-minded, and dignified management of a difficult office, the Academy's board has voted an honorary award to the administrator of the Code—Mr. Joseph Breen."

On cue, a man walks forward from the wings: white-haired, well-fed, stiff-necked, barrel-chested, the very picture of a venerable Irish-American patriarch, a gentleman accustomed to the comforts of life and the respect of his peers, of his needs being met and his words being heeded—perhaps a police captain looking forward to a cushy pension, or a ward politician with a lifetime of favors in his pocket, or a monsignor from a prosperous parish with a case of twelve-year-old whiskey stashed back at the rectory.

After twenty years at the helm of the Production Code Administration, Joseph I. Breen was stepping down from the post he had forged, commanded, and cherished.

In retrospect, and set in relief against the rest of the program that evening, the curtain bow from Joseph I. Breen may be why so much about the twenty-sixth Academy Awards ceremony plays more like a grim wake than a joyous celebration. The controlling gaze of television, the extinction of the short film, the risky gamble on CinemaScope, and the retirement of the long-serving chief of the censorious Production Code Administration—all seemed to punctuate the end of a Golden Age, a shimmering epoch when Hollywood held a monopoly over the moving image, when throwaway shorts garnished a bountiful motion picture menu, when the square-shaped motion picture screen was plenty big enough, and when the moral universe projected by the medium was patrolled by a watchful sentinel.

As Breen walked across the stage to accept his trophy, the orchestra struck up an apt tune: "Don't Fence Me In." At the podium, a brief exchange occurs between Brackett and Breen, but the words, muttered away from the microphone, are barely audible.

"Joe—" begins Brackett.

"Thank you very, very much," Breen interrupts, speaking over the greeting.

"Say a word," urges Brackett.

But Joe Breen has already grabbed his trophy and is turning away, without saying a single word to either the home or the Hollywood audience. Taken aback, Brackett shrugs, the audience heeds the applause sign, and the orchestra, caught off guard, misses its cue to reprise the strains of "Don't Fence Me In." The camera cuts to a quick shot of Breen striding offstage, cradling his Oscar—the last glimpse of a man who, more than any actor, director, or producer in the room, had stamped his vision on Hollywood cinema.

1

THE VICTORIAN IRISHMAN

The signature at the bottom of the stationery read Joseph I. Breen, the firm hand a fair index to the man holding the pen. Face to face, however, the name was always Joe Breen, the consummate insider, backstage operator, and go-to guy. For twenty years, from 1934 until 1954, he reigned over the Production Code Administration, the agency charged with censoring the Hollywood screen, an in-house surgical procedure officially deemed "self-regulation." Though little known outside the ranks of studio system players, this bureaucratic functionary was one of the most powerful men in Hollywood. His job—really, his vocation—was to monitor the moral temperature of American cinema.

"Unless you are in the motion picture industry, you never have heard of Joe Breen," *Liberty* magazine proclaimed in 1936, dragging the publicity-shy player on stage. Breen "probably has more influence in standardizing world thinking than Mussolini, Hitler, or Stalin. And, if we should accept the valuation of this man's own business, possibly more than the Pope." The subject of the profile would have conceded his obscurity, resented the comparisons, and grimaced at the glib line about the Holy Father. Yet *Liberty* was right to hype its scoop and pump its angle: Joe Breen was big Hollywood news that never made the fan magazines.

A former journalist, consular officer, and public relations man, Breen was first brought to Hollywood in 1931 by Will H. Hays, president of the Motion Picture Producers and Distributors of America (MPPDA). Hays needed a well-connected and media-savvy Roman Catholic layman to mollify the most formidable constituency assailing Hollywood for purveying sin and profiting from its wages. By February 1934 Breen had wrangled control of the Studio Relations Committee (SRC), a weak-kneed advisory body tasked with enforcing screen morality. On July 15, 1934, he formally took charge of the Production Code Administration (PCA), the implacable new regime that replaced its toothless predecessor. Where the Studio Relations Committee made suggestions, the Production Code Administration gave orders.

Though popularly known as the Hays Office, the PCA was Breen's domain. It was he who vetted story lines, blue-penciled dialogue, and exercised final cut over hundreds of motion pictures per year—expensive "A"-caliber feature films, low-budget B-unit ephemera, short subjects, previews of coming attractions, even cartoons. "More than any single individual, he shaped the moral stature of the American motion picture," *Variety* reflected upon his death in 1965. "He was the most powerful censor of modern times, but he never looked upon himself as a censor, and, in truth, he wasn't really a censor."

In truth, he was—perhaps not in a strict legal sense, but for all practical purposes. Empowered by the MPPDA, fortified by a support system of millions of like-minded Catholics, Breen wielded a two-sided gavel forged of executive power and moral intimidation. Under the law school definition of censorship (a restriction on freedom of expression enforced by a state power), Breen was not a censor: he was an employee paid to maintain quality control by a consortium of private corporations. According to Will Hays and the studio chieftains, the review process overseen by Breen was an altruistic act of self-discipline, a solemn agreement among public-spirited businessmen that showed how seriously they took their great public trust, how they endeavored, always, to improve and uplift the American moviegoing public, upwards of 90 million customers per week, who sat spellbound and impressionable before the motion picture screen. "It is a mistake to think of the Production Code Administration as a form of censorship, a sort of policeman patrolling a beat," insisted Arthur Hornblow, Jr., producer of *Gaslight* (1944), who likened the filmmaker's fealty to the Production Code to the doctor's to the Hippocratic Oath or the lawyer's to the Canon of Ethics. "We are responsible members of a responsible profession, and the Code is the articulate enunciation of the ethical standards we have set up for ourselves."

To modern ears, the hiss of pure gas leaks from such pronouncements, the prattle of coerced businessmen spouting the cant of the times, the cynicism laced with a generous dose of self-deception. Yet the insistence on terminology is more than a matter of semantics. The word *censor* conjures the image of a narrow-minded prude, a purse-lipped matron or stone-faced minister squeezing the life and pleasure out of art. The best-known cutters have lived up to the mirthless portrait: Thomas Bowdler, the British physician who sanitized Shakespeare and lent his name to the prissy editing that denudes literature of eros and spice, or Anthony Comstock, the anti-vice crusader of the Progressive Era who sniffed through the U.S. mail to confiscate, eliminate, and prosecute senders and receivers of birth control pamphlets or underwear catalogues.

Breen's imprint on the Hollywood films he censored—or regulated—went deeper. No mere splicer of the negative, he was an activist editor with a positive goal for the motion picture medium. Bringing a missionary zeal to his custodial trust, he felt a sacred duty to protect the spiritual well-being of the innocent souls who fluttered too close to the unholy attractions of the motion picture screen. Yet mere inoculation was never his sole mission—always he sought to instruct, to shape, to nurture. Breen's legacy rests not in what he tore out of but in what he wove into the fabric of Hollywood cinema.

Like Thomas Bowdler, who became a dictionary verb, the head of the Production Code Administration also lent his surname to the language. Though never part of the civilian vernacular, the word was *lingua franca* around the company town in the Golden Age of Hollywood. "Breening" was the process whereby a film was cut to fit the moral framework of Joseph I. Breen.

CATHOLICITY IN PHILADELPHIA

For all his prominence in the annals of Hollywood, relatively little is known of Breen: he left behind no authorized biography, no unpublished memoir, and no central repository of papers. Though a seasoned journalist, a devoted correspondent, and a tireless memo writer, he maintained a low public profile during his tenure and kept his mouth shut in retirement. For Breen, a scandalous tell-all book (and he would have had much to tell) was unthinkable. In a city lit by flashbulbs and swept by searchlights, he shunned the glare, seldom making the scene or being mentioned in the seen-around-town columns. More unusual for an A-list Hollywood power broker, he slid under the radar of official government surveillance: at the Federal Bureau of Investigation, the keeper of thick files on countless second-tier screenwriters and bit players, Breen was barely a blip on the screen.

Out of camera range, Breen was impossible to miss. Even in a business of puffed-up egos and outsized personalities, he dominated the rooms he walked into, the full force of his charisma needing to be felt up-close, nose to nose. "Breen was the kind of person who, if you had dinner with him, you would know it," understates his friend Martin S. Quigley, editor of the trade weekly *Motion Picture Herald* from 1949 to 1972.[1] Sociable and loquacious, Breen was a lively raconteur who delighted in telling colorful anecdotes—some of them true—of his salad days as a newshound or his epic fights—some of them physical—with uppity directors. Yet he avoided the limelight the rest of the town craved. "Incredible as it may seem, and despite the fact that I come from Hollywood, I have no picture of myself to send you," he informed an admiring Catholic journalist in 1944. "I am probably the only person connected directly or indirectly with the motion picture industry in Hollywood who has not, at some time or other, sat for a photograph." His life must be pieced together from official records, trade press accounts, private letters, oral histories, Hollywood memoirs, and the occasional interview or written statement of principle. Above all, a sense of the man is best gleaned from the correspondence, memos, and documents contained in what is his chief legacy in print, the files of the Production Code Administration, a treasure trove of backstage infighting and evidence aplenty of Breen's extraordinary impact on the main currents of American cinema.

Given the territory, the temptation to filter Breen's life story through the lens of a vintage Hollywood biopic is well nigh irresistible. Streetwise and tough, unabashedly ethnic and intermittently corny, the first treatment bows to formula and traffics in clichés: the two-fisted Irishman going Hollywood to take center stage in a gruff Warner Bros. melodrama. Certainly he would be wrong for the starring role in the classy Great Man paeans from MGM or the spicy scenarios favored by the European refugees over on the Paramount lot. Cast the genial Pat O'Brien in the lead, not James Cagney (too edgy) or John Barrymore (too wasted) or Edward G. Robinson (too Jewish), and watch for shades of gray and moody undertones beneath the surface.

Joseph Ignatius Breen was born in Philadelphia, Pennsylvania, on October 14, 1888, six years before the official birth date of the movies and nine before radio.[2] His was the last generation of Americans whose childhood was not flooded with a torrent of projected images and broadcast sounds, the last generation to reach adulthood before the Great War shattered the hubris of Western civilization, the last generation whose public morals and formal manners were literally Victorian. It was never an age of innocence, but it was an age of fixed boundaries and firm lines, straight-laced and stiff-

1. Martin S. Quigley should not be confused with his father, Martin J. Quigley, the founding editor of *Motion Picture Herald* and coauthor of the Production Code.

2. Many profiles and biographical entries give Breen's date of birth as October 14, 1890. Conforming to local custom, he shaved a couple of years off his age after settling in Hollywood.

necked, of women encased in corsets and bound in stockings, of gentlemen adorned in greatcoats and top hats, of watchful chaperones supervising chaste courtship rituals before the automobile propelled young lovers down a bumpier road. Well into the 1950s, decades behind the fashion curve, Breen cradled his keys on a chain suspended from his vest pocket.

Breen traced his roots to the West of Ireland, his father, Hugh A. Breen, immigrating to America "in his manhood, after a stretch of curious activity which found no favor with the British Constabulary," as his son wryly put it. Bypassing Boston and New York, the elder Breen found his wife, Mary Cunningham, in West Hoboken, New Jersey, and continued inland to settle in Philadelphia.

Though not as polyglot as New York or as Irish as Boston, Philadelphia in the last quarter of the nineteenth century was an urban melting pot where the Irish mingled with an exotic mix of Italians, Poles, Jews, and more traditional stocks. A skeptical native son, Breen despised the corrupt Republican machine that ran Pennsylvania and lamented the bovine complacency of the electorate that tolerated it. "Nearly everybody in Philadelphia votes the Gang ticket," he observed in adulthood, and "cares nothing whatever for the character of its municipal government." Still, in a moment of W. C. Fields–like reverie, Breen admitted that "Philadelphia is not quite so bad as it is represented to be."

Know-Nothing nativism: a contemporary illustration of the anti-Catholic riots in Philadelphia in 1844.

Industrious and ambitious, Hugh Breen made the transition from shanty to lace curtain Irish in one generation, accumulating a modest fortune, said his son, "by way of the barter and sale of real estate in the up-and-coming community which goes by the name of West Philadelphia." Settling in the respectable Fairmount Park district of the city, the Breens were prominent enough to welcome as dinner guests such local luminaries as Kid Gleason, the second baseman for the Philadelphia Phillies (and later heartbroken manager of the infamous Black Sox in the 1919 World Series) and the sports journalist and humorist Arthur "Bugs" Baer.

By Irish immigrant standards, Hugh and Mary Breen raised a medium-sized family. Joe was the youngest of three sons—his eldest brother, Francis A. Breen, entered the priesthood and for forty years devoted himself to the Society of Jesus, including service as treasurer both at St. Joseph's College and on the Jesuit weekly, *America*. James J. Breen entered another text-intensive profession and became a prominent Philadelphia attorney and local politician. Two sisters—Marie, who never married, and Catherine, who wed a prosperous Philadelphia businessman named Thomas Quirk—completed the Breen family. With equitable symbolism, the career paths of the Breen boys traced the three main-traveled roads for upwardly mobile Irish-Americans in the twentieth century: religion and education (Francis), law and politics (James), and media and culture (Joseph).

The progress of the Breens up the ladder of success was smoothed by earlier arrivals forced to claw their way on to the first rung. Though the Irish had been flocking to America since the famines of the 1840s, led by their stomachs to build the railroads, run the saloons, and swell the enlisted ranks of the U.S. Cavalry, the settled population resisted the influx of emaciated refugees. Pamphlets denounced the Irish as vile "bog trotters" and editorial cartoons portrayed bewhiskered hooligans tumbling into paddy wagons after drunken donnybrooks. In the 1850s, the Native American Party, the so-called Know-Nothings, thrived on an anti-immigrant platform synthesized in a popular acronym for both the preferred employee and citizenship pool: NINA—No Irish Need Apply. The Irish, the Know-Nothings knew, were not bred for "the moderation and self control of American republicanism."

More than the land of origin, however, the resilient Catholicism of the Irish was the true stain of un-American-ness. "Popery is opposed in its very nature to Democratic Republicanism," wrote Samuel F. B. Morse, sending out a common message. Adherents of a creed cloaked in black robes and reeking of papist intrigue, Catholics pledged a treacherous allegiance to the foreign flag of the Vatican. Convents, seminaries, the parochial school system, and Catholic fraternal societies were under constant attack as incubators of Jesuitical subversion and nests of perverse sexuality.

Repudiating its Quaker roots, the City of Brotherly Love spawned one of the most spectacular outbreaks of anti-Catholic violence. In 1844, nativist mobs ("inflamed by the spectacle of many flourishing Catholic congregations in the city and its environs") ran riot in the streets, burning to the ground two Catholic churches and a convent. "The Irish Catholics were the foreigners against whom the opposition was directed," wrote Father Joseph L. J. Kirlin, the official historian of the archdiocese, in *Catholicity in Philadelphia* in 1909, himself still inflamed by the abuse hurled at his people ("Irish papists," "the miscreant Irish," "the degraded slaves of the Pope"). Breen grew up hearing tales of anti-Catholic mobs torching convents and seeing Thomas Nast cartoons depicting Catholic prelates as ravenous crocodiles invading the shorelines of Anglo-Protestant America.

The Civil War tempered some of the nativist bile. Mustered out of the Grand Army of the Republic, returning East or going West, Irish veterans claimed payment on the investment made in blood. Across New England and the Midwest, they waved the bloody shirt at election time and seized power from the older Northern European stocks. Exploiting a fluency in English and a familiarity with Anglo-Saxon jurisprudence often gained from the wrong end of the law, the Irish prospered in politics, business, and journalism.

The ascent of the Irish met periodic waves of backlash from inheritors of the Know-Nothing tradition, who might overlook the home country but never the faith. The 1890s witnessed a spike in nativist sentiment against Irish Catholics, in no small part because avid hustlers like the Breens were making it in America, scrambling up the economic ladder and nudging aside—leaping over—the underachieving sons of the genteel Protestant establishment. "One Irish name equaled a Catholic and that equaled mud," recalled a man who was both in 1890s America. From everyday social slights to official sanctions, Irish Catholics had reason to feel themselves a subaltern people in a rigged caste system.

Ambitious Irish-Catholic families like the Breens channeled their energies into religion, education, and politics, which were often the same thing. Insular by necessity, and perhaps instinct, they closed ranks in parochial schools and Jesuit universities, at the Knights of Columbus and the Ancient Order of Hibernians, in Ladies Sodalities and Catholic Women's Clubs—the institutions and associations that served as boot camps and officer's candidate schools for Breen's generation of Irish Catholics, a cohort who shaped more than their share of American culture in the next century.

As a full-blooded member of the tribe, young Joe grew up according to a strict ethno-religious catechism—literally so, the *Baltimore Catechism*, the basic training manual for American Catholics, having just been published in 1891. In Philadelphia, he attended Gesu Parish School through the eighth grade and then made the natural transition to the Roman Catholic High School for Boys, the archdiocesan free school. Popular, athletic, and a quick study, Breen was early pegged as a most-likely-to-succeed at Catholic High. He played basketball for Billy Markward, the beloved dean of Philadelphia basketball coaches, and was elected class president his senior year. The Fairmount parish produced a bumper crop of great basketball players, "stars in their days," as Breen later reminisced to a friend from the neighborhood, winking that "my well known modesty forbids me mentioning any names in this connection." By his own account, however, his most influential coaches were off the court. "Whatever formal training I have had, I got entirely from Catholic schools," he recalled, "aided, I am happy to say, by a fine old Irish Mother and an Irish Grandmother."

Whether at school, at home, or from the pulpit, the training sessions inculcated the same lessons: the primacy of the faith, the deference to priestly authority, and the absolute need for self-control in thought, word, and deed. The teachings of the one, holy, and apostolic Church being universal, the orthodoxies were drilled into Catholic schoolchildren everywhere, but the indigenous variation was uniquely unyielding. "The Irish developed a militant and vigorous catechistic religious style that matched anything stiff-necked Protestantism could produce," wrote Dennis Clark, the historian of the Irish in Philadelphia, speaking specifically of Breen's generation and archdiocese. "Peculiarly Victorian in its characteristics," American Irish-Catholicism cultivated a personal code of conduct that was "both strenuous and stoic, in a tight middle class image," with "stifling standards of propriety." Breen was a pure product of the domestic vintage.

Upon graduation from Catholic High in 1906, Breen followed the path of his brothers into the all-male classrooms of St. Joseph's College, Philadelphia's flagship Jesuit university and the house college for the Breen boys, all of whom maintained lifelong links with their alma mater. Founded in 1851, St. Joseph's was an ardent proponent of a rigorous Jesuit curriculum and a fierce propagator of the faith. According to its official historian, "a militant Catholicism, often typical of the Jesuits, was evident during the college's earlier decades, when Catholics found themselves a somewhat spurned minority in an overwhelmingly Protestant nation."

The militancy came with a chip on its shoulder. Though the worst of the anti-Catholic fevers from the 1890s had abated, nothing is a distant memory for the Irish, a people known not just to harbor but to treasure a grievance. Breen never lost his bitterness for the "stupid and ill-informed people" who considered Catholicism an alien infestation plotting to subvert American democracy and establish "a sort of tenth-century unholy alliance between Church and State, with the Church, in the person of the Pope, riding in the saddle and holding controlling reins." As much as anyone in his generation, he worked to erase the slander and bridge the divide between the Church of Rome and the United States of America, to make piety and patriotism one doctrine, indivisible.

In 1908, more restless than his brothers, Breen left St. Joseph's without graduating, a detail glossed over in later biographical entries. For the next six years, he worked as a beat reporter and feature writer for the *Philadelphia Record*, the *North American*, and other local newspapers. It was a storied age for big city journalism, a fast-talking, corner-cutting period immortalized by Ben Hecht and Charles MacArthur in their hit 1928 play *The Front Page*, where gruff editors yelled "Stop the presses!" between gulps of whiskey, and unscrupulous newshounds snatched pictures from the homes of grieving relatives to scoop the competition. "According to tales told by old Philadelphia newspapermen, Breen was a local Charley MacArthur, Ben Hecht, and Gene Fowler all rolled into one," recalled the journalist John J. McCarthy, himself a veteran of the glory days. The most oft-told tale of Breen's reportorial exploits—doubtless embroidered by former colleagues jealous that he had left the ranks of ink-stained wretches for the sweet life in Hollywood—concerned a breaking news story that was news to him. Bored by the drab city beat at the *Philadelphia Record*, Breen bunked off to see a musical comedy on tickets cuffed from the paper's drama critic. While he enjoyed the show, an oil refinery caught fire downtown, engulfing a block of businesses and illuminating the entire north end of the city. The conflagration was clearly visible from the editorial offices of the *Philadelphia Record*. "The city editor and the rewrite men were in a frenzy," chortled a veteran Philly journalist. "Some two hours later when the fire was out, and the show was over, Breen called the office and reported, 'Breen, downtown, talking. As usual—nothing doing.'"

If true, it was one of the few times Breen was caught flat-footed. Certainly the practical Mary Dervin, a lace curtain girl from the neighborhood ("the eldest daughter of the Fairmount Avenue Dervins"), would not have encouraged a suitor who was not dependable and diligent. Sweethearts from childhood, the couple married in February 1914. A daughter, Helene, followed the next Christmas Eve, the first of six children—three boys, three girls.

From the rough and tumble of big city journalism, Breen moved into the more secure ranks of government service, joining the U.S. Consular Service in 1914. An index card in the State Department archives describes the applicant as a "writer of 'special' articles. Engaged in general newspaper work 6 yrs" and notes a facility in French and Spanish (Breen could also claim a working knowledge of an older diplomatic tongue, Latin). Postings at U.S. consulates in Panama, the ports at Brest and Le Havre, France, and Queenstown, Ireland, followed.

On April 16, 1917, just as America was entering the Great War, Breen was appointed vice consul in Kingston, Jamaica, a tour of duty he would recall ever after as a bucolic interlude in a frazzling work life. "There is no spot in all the world half so beautiful as the British Isle of Jamaica," he remembered, waxing poetic over "this gem of the Caribbean where life is easy and love is a thing of long summer twilights." Transported by his own reverie, he sighed: "For those of us who care little for the flight of time and less for the machinations of trade and the mart, there are to be found in Jamaica vast stores of the stuff out of which dreams are made and fashioned."

That last bit was sheer blarney: Breen was not the stuff of which dreamy beachcombers are made. Driven and determined, what today would be diagnosed as a "type A" personality and manic workaholic, he craved action, thrived on competition, and kept a keen eye out for the main chance. He was a hard-nosed Irishman who kept his nose to the grindstone, often multiple grindstones.

A growing family to support on a meager government salary compelled another career shift. With the 1920s about to roar, a vista of possibility beckoned for a man of the world with a gift for fraternal camaraderie, a talent for prose on demand, and the capacity for dawn-to-dusk toil. When his next posting in Toronto, Canada, proved less congenial than balmy Jamaica, he abruptly resigned from government service.

In 1918, settling in New York, Breen was back behind a typewriter. By the fall of 1919, he was employed "as a 'feature writer,' so called," for "the big daily newspapers in New York." Keeping up the Catholic connection, he also served as secretary to Father Edward Tivnan, president of Fordham University, like St. Joseph's a Jesuit institution. He described himself in those days as "an overworked newspaperman with a houseful of babies to feed, clothe, and keep warm."

In 1920, Breen joined the International News Service and was dispatched overseas to cover the roiling political turmoil of postwar Europe.[3] The so-

3. Founded by William Randolph Hearst in 1909, the International News Service (INS) was a perennial third-string also-ran to the higher prestige and better-funded Associated Press and United Press agencies. Biographical entries on Breen often credit him as being an AP reporter, but AP has no payroll record for a Joseph I. Breen. In 1958, INS was bought out by United Press and subsumed under the renamed United Press International.

journ as a foreign correspondent would later give rise to colorful tales—that Bolsheviks in Hungary had sentenced him to death, that the British had kicked him out of Ireland—which have eluded verification in the historical record. One epochal historical event he did witness was the shedding of first blood in the long struggle between Soviet communism and Western democracy. "I was there, on the ground, in the midst of it all," when the Poles "saved all of Europe from the menace of Bolshevism," he wrote proudly years later, of his beat in Warsaw covering the Russo-Polish War in 1920. "It was the Poles who stood at the outposts of European civilization and fought back the hordes of wild men out of Russia." While a foreign correspondent, he forged friendships with luminaries of the European church, including a papal attaché in Warsaw named Achille Ratti, the future Pope Pius XI. "When I knew the Holy Father, he was simply Monsignor Ratti," he could not resist bragging to a Jesuit friend upon hearing of the promotion.

The frustrations of working unbylined for a corporate news provider drained his creative juices and wounded his ego. "By the time your story is rewritten, cut, or padded, or thrown out in toto, you wouldn't recognize it anyway," he complained, echoing the grievances of Hollywood screenwriters to whom he would do likewise. Still, like most newspapermen, he took a wry pride in his status as a lowly scrivener toiling in "the most forlorn business on earth." Ever after, he would relish a good scoop, seek out the company of newspapermen, and affect the swagger of the hard-bitten beat reporter. "There has always been a sort of glamour about newspapermen—the adventurous—the courageous—'the devil may care, but I get the dope style' style—and believe me he is it!" gushed an admirer in 1934, more than a decade after Breen had filed his last breaking news story.

In May 1921, trading on his proficiency in domestic Catholicism and foreign affairs, Breen secured a position as European Representative at the Bureau of Immigration at the National Catholic Welfare Conference (NCWC), a private relief agency and protean political action committee. "Mr. Breen has had extensive Consular work in Europe, has a good personality and judgment, and seems to appreciate the needs for Catholic welfare work," wrote the bureau's director, after Breen nailed the interview. Though dedicated to all things Catholic, the NCWC focused on immigration and overseas charity work. Breen's job was to survey the plight of European Catholics, suggest the best means of relief, and facilitate the emigration of worthy Catholics to America.

Sailing immediately for the free city of Danzig, Breen spent the next year observing the rural poverty and blighted cityscapes of a continent still shell-shocked by the Great War. He was deeply disturbed by the despair and

Catholic envoy to Europe: Breen, joking around with Rev. Richard H. Tierney, S.J., editor of the Jesuit magazine *America*, near Innsbruck, Austria, in June 1922.

(SANTA CLARA UNIVERSITY ARCHIVES)

poverty he witnessed. "I am one of those who, one year ago, frantically denounced our government for its European loans," he confessed in 1922. "Now I take it all back. The truth is, I am ashamed of myself."

For over a year, Breen crisscrossed the capitals of Europe, drawing on his background in the consular service to help Catholic immigrants from Belfast to Budapest fill out immigration forms with the answers that would satisfy the gatekeepers at Ellis Island. According to Breen, European Catholics were threatened by more than hunger and indigence. U.S. Protestant organizations, he warned the home office, were disseminating "strong anti-Catholic propaganda . . . under the guise of charitable work and otherwise."

The Bureau of Immigration had two agendas: first, to help destitute European Catholics keep body and soul together; and second, to transform fresh-off-the-boat Catholic immigrants into red-blooded Americans. "We seek to promote all these things among our people as a pledge of our Catholicity and our Americanism," Breen told a delegation of Catholic women in 1922. "We stand for the preservation of the faith among our Catholic foreign born who come here among us. We stand for loyalty and devotion to America, its government, its institutions, its ideals." The two allegiances affirmed a single faith—to America and to the Catholic Church. In his work, as in his life, Breen yoked together "a love for America and a devotion to our Catholic ideals of staunch citizenship and sturdy faith."

In 1922, Breen returned stateside to work at the NCWC's home office in Washington, D.C., where he directed the Publications Office and advocated the Church line in the *National Catholic Welfare Council Bulletin*, the official monthly magazine of the NCWC, which he edited from May 1923 to March 1924. Two themes dominate his unsigned editorials in the *Bulletin*: derision of the Ku Klux Klansman and any other "anti-Catholic bigot who has the misfortune to be at the same time brainless," and condemnations of the emergent menace of Soviet communism. "This philosophy is not socialism, but the rankest kind of perversion," he wrote in 1923. "It is Godlessness run to chaos." Only his last editorial offers a hint of the destiny on the horizon. "In all our work we have sought to help, in a practical fashion, the films that are worthy and to shun those which are offensive or ill conceived," he declared. "Good films, and even great films, may be produced without recourse to the offensive, the vulgarly suggestive, or the inane."

Manning the desk at NCWC headquarters, Breen watched the clock and cooled his heels, "hanging about here and doing little besides drawing my pay and collecting expenses." Always scrupulous in money matters, he was troubled when less punctilious staffers treated the collection plate as a slush fund. "This outfit, organized and functioning as it now is, is not only doomed to failure, but is guilty of a grave injustice," he confided to a Jesuit friend, disgusted that funds earmarked for charity had been squandered on comforts for the clergy. No more impressed with the civic polity of Washington than with Philadelphia, he described the capital as "the world's greatest rendezvous for get-rich-quick schemers, quack reformers, bunko-men, press agents, pious profiteers, claims-against-the-government beggars, and common thieves."

In April 1924, disillusioned with the backroom wheeling and dealing of Potomac politics, Breen resigned to take a job custom-made for his singular skills: overseeing the sales campaign of a book project entitled *Catholic Builders of the Nation: A Symposium on the Catholic Contribution to the Civilization of the United States*. Published by the Boston-based imprint Continental Press, Inc., and edited by C. E. McGuire, the massive five-volume compendium was a celebration of Breen's twin faiths. "In these remarkable volumes there is told for the first time the wonderful story of the part played by American Catholics, in various walks of life, in the upbuilding of this nation," read the ad copy. "The story they tell is a striking one which will fill you with justifiable pride in the superb achievements of Catholic Americans in the face of bitter opposition, misunderstandings, doubts, and no little irreligious animosity."

As Breen stepped from public service to private business and back, he acquired a set of strong opinions he was not shy about sharing in conversation or published commentary. On the evidence of his chatty letters and erudite essays printed in top-line Catholic periodicals, a fusion of religious conservatism and progressive ideology shaped his outlook on the great issues of the day. He detested the Eighteenth Amendment, and the long dry Sahara of Prohibition would stick in his craw ever after as an assault on the folkways of his tribe and the rituals of his church. Returning religious prejudice in kind, he derided the teetotaling churchwomen and abstemious ministers of the Christian opposition as a "horde of female fanatics" and "Protestant 'gentlemen of the cloth'" who "seem to be ever-ready to poke their noses into the other fellow's business." He was an Al Smith Democrat and a melting-pot assimilationist. He supported a minimum wage, open immigration, and universal education. He assailed the Ku Klux Klan, Bolshevism, the British Empire, and any other menace, foreign or domestic, to the Catholic Church.

Like most intellectuals of the 1920s, Breen was traumatized by the carnage of the Great War, "the Grand Fracas of 1914–1918," which he had witnessed as a consular officer, and whose grim aftermath he had surveyed for the NCWC. "I have no brief for militarism and I hate keenly the sight of a soldier of any kind," he wrote. "To me, the soldier stands for waste, for destruction, for guns, and trenches and bloodshed and death." He felt heartsick too at another by-product of war, "the steady stream of unhappy women made derelict by the business which sustains the solider," whom he saw cruising "the streets of Vienna, Berlin, Budapest, Bucharest, Rome, Paris, Brussels, and London." There but for the grace of God, and country, he thought to himself, might go the virginal schoolgirls cared for by the nuns of Philadelphia, condemned to the same sordid fate.

By mid-decade, though never straying from the orb of Irish Catholicism, Breen had roamed far beyond the clan to mingle with all strata and most species of American and European society. After peregrinations as a consular officer, foreign correspondent, and envoy with portfolio, he boasted "a general knowledge of Europe from Dundee to Sofia and from Gibraltar to Petrograd."

Yet however much the passport stamps betokened a cosmopolitan gentleman of broad experience, the holder was not exactly broad-minded. Nursed on the *Baltimore Catechism*, shaped by parochial schools, and guided to maturity by the Jesuits, he embodied the restraint, repression, and rigidity of a personality type known as the Victorian Irish. "The Irish have been called 'Queen Victoria's most loyal subjects' because in modern times they have sometimes been—paradoxically given their earlier history—associated with prudishness and sexual repression," the cultural historian Thomas Cahill observed in his partisan guidebook *How the Irish Saved Civilization*, a title Breen would have savored. The Irish-American character—or at least this Irish-American character—is defined neither by leprechaun charm nor whiskey-soaked gloom, but by a sober vigilance over the self and a brisk readiness to perform the same service for others, solicited or not. Despite being less popular on the vaudeville stage and the silent screen, and less endearing than the stock company of a Finley Peter Dunne column or John Ford film, the unsmiling face of stern reprimand plays a dominant role in any portrait of Irish-American life in the twentieth century—the cop with a billy club, the nun with a yardstick, the foreman with a mean streak. If a Hollywood biopic must select from a rack of ethnic stereotypes to clothe the figure of Joseph I. Breen, the Victorian Irishman makes a comfortable fit.

THE XXVIII INTERNATIONAL EUCHARISTIC CONGRESS (FOX–CATHOLIC CHURCH)

As the Roaring Twenties reached cruising altitude, Breen had earned a seat in the front pews of American Catholicism—rubbing shoulders with an elite brethren of politicians, businessmen, and clerics, men who if not ordained Jesuits tended to be Jesuit-educated or Jesuit-fixated. The Jesuits, or "Jebbies" to their familiars, were the shock troops of the Catholic clergy, an exclusive fraternity within an exclusive fraternity, priests with a special devotion to higher education, the Virgin Mary, and the propagation of the faith. As an honorific, the initials S.J. (Society of Jesus) were harder to earn and, among Catholics, more revered than a Ph.D.

Two of Breen's most helpful mentors in the priesthood were Wilfrid Parsons, S.J., editor of the Jesuit weekly *America*, a sort of *New Republic* for the Catholic intelligentsia, and Monsignor W.D. O'Brien, editor of *Extension Magazine*, a slick Catholic monthly. Throughout the 1920s, under the pen name "Eugene Weare," Breen contributed numerous articles to both publications on a mélange of political and cultural issues: immigration, Catholic education, communism, social welfare, private charity, and the blighted condition of postwar Europe. In a more lighthearted vein, he tried his hand at the occasional shaggy-dog piece ("I Sing of Hams and the Man"), whimsical profile ("When Al Smith Came to Fordham"), or blithe lyric ("Little fairies, blue and gold/let us sweet communion hold"). The true identity of the prolific Eugene Weare was an open secret to in-the-know Catholics, but the pseudonym was a convenient cover for a journalist who was also working as a press agent. The alter ego Eugene Weare allowed Joseph Breen to sound off and to double dip—using his articles to plug a project, sting an opponent, or flatter a client. By way of fair exchange, he gifted the servants of the

Church, bestowing sweets and groceries on the nuns, Notre Dame tickets and Irish whiskey on the priests.

In 1925, years of Catholic networking were rewarded with the brass-ring assignment that launched Breen into his life's work: his appointment as publicity director for the 28th International Eucharistic Congress, a worldwide gathering of the Roman Catholic faithful to be held in Chicago from June 20 to 24, 1926. The job offer came at an opportune moment. The sales campaign for *Catholic Builders of the Nation* was winding down, and Breen was coming off a long convalescence, his first bout with the stomach ailments that would plague him the rest of his life. "I'm looking for a job, this time in earnest," he told Father Parsons before the call came from Chicago. "The family treasury is getting low and I'm feeling well again."

The Eucharistic Congress had been lured to the heartland by George Cardinal Mundelein, archbishop of Chicago, a dynamic power broker in the nation's most Catholic city. Cardinal Mundelein had promised Pope Pius XI the awe-inspiring spectacle of one million communicants kneeling in Chicago, and the Cardinal was not a man to renege on a deal with the Pope.[4] The gathering would be the first Eucharistic Congress convened in the United States, and American Catholics planned a lavish coming-out party for the faithful. "The Holy Father knows that America does things," said the Cardinal, a true son of the city. "If it cannot be done in Chicago, it cannot be done anywhere."

Not since the storied World's Columbian Exposition of 1893 had the Second City hosted such first-class festivities. Already home to 880,000 Catholics, over 500,000 pilgrims swarmed into Chicago to attend the rituals and receive the sacraments—bunking with relatives, clogging cathedrals, and straining city services. Local dignitaries feted the papal delegates with a grand parade through the Loop, merchants festooned storefronts with welcoming signs and bunting, and the entire city bathed in the incense-scented pomp and ceremony of the Church of Rome. "Chicago has never been more bedecked with colors," marveled *Variety*, covering the religious pageant as the grand theater it was. "The streets are literally swathed in the silver and gold of the Pope's insignia with flags of practically every other foreign nation mingled with the Stars and Stripes." No Chicago politician with ambitions to higher office failed to corral the cardinals and bishops for a group photograph with himself grinning in the center. At Orchestra Hall on Michigan Avenue, a wily motion picture exhibitor mixed profit and propa-

4. Irreverent parishioners joked that for an encore Cardinal Mundelein was negotiating an exclusive Chicago booking for Judgment Day.

gation by booking *The Miracle at Lourdes* (1926), a French import dramatizing the visitation of the Virgin Mary to the peasant girl Bernadette.

From the Headquarters Office that served as command central in Cathedral Square, Breen oversaw the thousands of commercial and logistical details attendant to the Congress—galvanizing the tom-tom network of Catholic newsweeklies from Boston to Los Angeles, planting stories in secular newspapers and magazines, credentialing hordes of international journalists, and certifying truckloads of commemorative buttons, pennants, postcards, picture books, and votive candles. When the papal delegation arrived stateside, Breen assumed duties as protective press handler and shielded the cardinals from blundering into domestic controversy. At a press conference at the Drake Hotel in Chicago, he cut off a Spanish cardinal who was about to reply to a question about the League of Nations. Politics, he barked at the reporters, was strictly "out of order."

On the payroll and off the cuff, Breen also worked as Cardinal Mundelein's personal PR man, ghostwriting his pastoral pronouncements and showering him with plaudits. "Chicago's Cardinal Archbishop is the foremost ecclesiastic dignity of his day," he wrote in a pseudonymous profile of his employer, "an outstanding prelate" known far and wide as "a fine cultural ecclesiastic with the face of an esthete and the bearing of a prince." Breen referred to the great man as "George William"—but only behind His Eminence's back.

After the Congress hit town and the reviews came in, Breen could not have written more favorable notices himself. Predictably, the Catholic press gave the show rave reviews. "The most impressive religious spectacle the world has witnessed, perhaps since the Savoir was put to death on Cavalry," opined the *Brooklyn Tablet*. Less predictably and more gratifyingly, the secular newspapers were just as awestruck, celebrating the Eucharistic Congress with reverent front-page coverage, charting parade routes, listing mass schedules, and publishing special supplements for what the *Chicago Tribune* hailed as "the most colossal prayer meeting and song service in the authentic annals of Christendom." No glitches, no fatalities, and no discordant notes marred the four-day pageant—not when 62,000 parochial school children sang the twelfth-century "Mass of the Angels" in perfect harmony, not when rain threatened to dampen a parade of 30,000 exotic Catholics of Chinese, Indian, and Eskimo lineage, and not when an estimated one million communicants, delivered as promised, congregated for an open-air mass on the outskirts of the city.

For American Catholics, the 28th International Eucharistic Congress was more than a celebration of faith. It was a graduation ceremony. The phenomenal success of the jubilee—not only with Catholics but with

Americans of all creeds—confirmed the breaking out of Catholicism from the sectarian margins to the religious mainstream of American culture. Even as the Ku Klux Klan, lately revitalized by D. W. Griffith's *The Birth of a Nation* (1915), was allocating a third of its energies to the deviant brand of Christianity (a popular jest translated the initials as "Koons, Kikes, and Katholics"), Catholics were flexing their political muscle and cultural power, asserting full membership rights in a club heretofore closed to all except Anglo-Protestants. Catholics had first landed on North American shores in 1513, but in Chicago in 1926, they truly arrived.

Civic-minded Chicagoans noticed something else. As the Catholic multitudes sang and prayed, as the venerable men in medieval vestments marched in solemn procession, the city underwent its own kind of transubstantiation. For four days, the notorious epicenter of gangsterism was lauded nationwide as a "City upon a Hill," the home of "Scarface" Al Capone, bootleg booze, and sputtering tommy guns remade into a model of Christian charity. "The fact is that presently Chicago is really the wonder-city of the world," Breen exulted, surrendering fully to the boosterism of the inhabitants of the nominal Second City.

Breen had reason to crow: for him, the Eucharistic Congress was a career maker. The publicity he garnered for his job of publicity propelled the second-string player into the big leagues. A high-profile follow-up project further burnished the reputation of the point man. Papal legate John Cardinal Bonzano's last blessing in Chicago was not the signal for Breen to stand down. The work of the Eucharistic Congress was to be continued in a new medium with as yet untapped missionary potential.

To cultivate a prized demographic, two newsreel outfits, International Newsreel and the Fox Film Corporation, had given blanket coverage and marquee honors to the Eucharistic Congress. After the Congress, both companies arranged private screenings of the footage for the Church hierarchy. "Marvelous, marvelous," beamed a gleeful Cardinal Bonzano as the cameras panned the vast throngs of worshippers. Patrick Cardinal O'Donnell of Ireland bestowed his blessings and a blurb. "The newsreels have done the world a great service by bringing before us the greatest religious service ever held." Both companies also prepared special prints with Italian intertitles for Pope Pius XI.

Fox outdid the competition, however—not only by bankrolling a feature-length documentary of the Eucharistic Congress, but by donating exclusive copyright and all profits from the film to the Catholic Church. Founded by William Fox, the studio was run by Winifred "Winnie" Sheehan, who was one of only two Irish Catholics with operational control over a major motion picture studio (the other was Joseph P. Kennedy, president of FBO, the

Film Booking Office of America). Fox's gesture was a down payment on a long-term investment. For both sides of the hyphen, the shared production credit ("Fox–Catholic Church") promised mutual benefits.

The deal between Fox and the Catholic Church was brokered by Martin J. Quigley, the editor and publisher of *Exhibitors Herald* (after 1931, *Motion Picture Herald*), a trade weekly second only to *Variety* in circulation and influence. Founded in 1915, the magazine provided independent motion picture exhibitors with advice on programming and publicity. Unlike the sardonic, money-minded *Variety*, the must-read show business bible, *Motion Picture Herald* meshed exploitation tips, film reviews, and business forecasts with a faith-based editorial stance. Commerce and morality, Quigley believed, were not mutually exclusive, even in the motion picture business.

Like Breen, Quigley was a devout Irish Catholic and the product of Catholic, but not Jesuit, higher education, a graduate of Catholic University. Emblematically enough, it was *The Birth of a Nation* that inspired Quigley to cultivate the niche market of motion picture journalism and build an empire of trade publications with "special consciousness of the intimate concern of the customers of the box office and the exhibitor who served them." The publication lifeline of *Motion Picture Herald* traces the arc of classical Hollywood cinema: thick, lushly illustrated volumes in the 1930s and 1940s, thinning down as circulation faded in the 1950s and 1960s, and finally closing up shop in 1972. For Quigley, the movies were not just a business proposition, but a moral mission. A motion picture commemorating the Eucharistic Congress was the ideal admixture of his trade and his faith.

Quick to recognize the value of a 35mm pulpit, Cardinal Mundelein signed on at Quigley's first pitch. After all, figured His Eminence, the cinema was "bound to become a most powerful agent for good or for evil; and had we failed to use it, we would have convicted ourselves either of culpable oversight or deliberate neglect." The project was more momentous than the cardinal anticipated: the men who were to remake Hollywood into the second most Catholic city in America first joined forces around the production and marketing of *Eucharistic Congress*, the movie.

Sparing no expense, Fox meticulously preplanned the project. Under the supervision of veteran newsreel editor Ray L. Hall, a team of twenty cameramen recorded the progress of the Eucharistic Congress from send-off in Rome to fade-out in Chicago (where, walking among the crowds while slumming as a film critic for the *Chicago Daily News*, poet Carl Sandburg observed "the omnipresent camera boys on foot, in motor cars and in airplanes taking negatives"). Having pioneered the use of newsreels for propaganda as editor of the Official War Reviews of the Committee on Public Information during the Great War, Hall brought lofty ambitions and a penitential temper to his peacetime assignment. He envisioned no mere "super-newsreel," but an organic narrative with dramatic thrust and inspirational power. The film would be, he vowed, "perhaps the first deliberate attempt to [portray] a great historical event, recording not only the events as they occurred but also the spirit of the occurrence, the personalities of those who participated, and the emotional reaction of great throngs of people stirred by the deepest and most instinctive spiritual hunger of mankind." *Eucharistic Congress* fulfilled Hall's dreams. A cinematic landmark, the documentary is the first premapped feature-length record of an unfolding historical event, the prototype for a durable motion picture genre.

In the weeks after the Congress, Quigley and Breen worked frantically to wrap the project, Quigley on the production, Breen on the publicity. "There is a great amount of wonderful material and [I] believe the picture will be the greatest thing of its kind ever attempted," Quigley told Monsignor C. J. Quille, general secretary of the Congress. Breen was equally upbeat. "Very busy here with details of New York opening," he wired headquarters in Chicago. "Terribly difficult but outlook promising."

On November 8, 1926, the eight-reel, 96-minute devotional epic was presented in a manner befitting its aspirations at a venue built for another kind of icon: a gala premiere at Al Jolson's Theater in New York. The mouthful of a title card read: *His Eminence George Cardinal Mundelein Archbishop of Chicago Presents the Pictorial Record of the XXVIII International Eucharistic Congress Produced for him by Fox Film Corporation.* A full orchestra was on hand to perform the musical score composed by Erno Rapp, a symphony that mixed ringing cathedral bells, well-known hymns, and mass scores. Invited dignitaries and a sell-out crowd of 1,770 packed the house. Acting as master of ceremonies for the evening's entertainment, Monsignor Quille thanked William Fox and Winnie Sheehan for the means to spread the gospel "to the furthermost corners of the world." To speak before the screening, President Calvin Coolidge dispatched Secretary of Labor J. J. Davis to deliver a special message. More wisely, Hollywood sent its top man, MPPDA president Will H. Hays.

Hays came to sermonize for two causes. "It is well that so universal an event should have so universal a medium of expression," he declared, linking the power and glory of the two spectacles. "With the motion picture, the Eucharistic Congress will go to the farthest corners of the earth and the message of faith, the voice of religion, will be carried to those who could not attend but who will nevertheless see and participate in the very action itself." Not that Hollywood played denominational favorites. "The motion picture stands always at attention to cooperate to the fullest with all religious bodies, irrespective of creed or denomination." After Hays pontificated, Monsignor Quille picked up the ecumenical theme. Noting that theater manager Samuel L. ("Roxy") Rothafel and many of the musicians in the pit were Jews, he expressed his gratitude to Roxy and the boys for staging the live prologue and donating their time. Certainly Roxy's sense of showmanship was not restricted by creed: his prologue dramatized the birth of the baby Jesus at Bethlehem.

At the conclusion of the long warm-up of speeches and prologue, the lights went down, the orchestra sounded, the curtain opened, and the main event unspooled. Instinctively, some in the crowd crossed themselves as the light from the projector first hit the screen.

The rapturous audience in the Jolson Theater sang "Holy God We Praise Thy Name" in time with the on-screen choir and intoned "Amen" on cue, but the glacial pacing of the trip from the Vatican to the Loop must have been tough going for even the most devout moviegoers. The bulk of the running time of *Eucharistic Congress* is as tedious as a droning homily—static camera placements framing elderly clerics posing for pictures, trudging up cathedral stairs, and blessing the crowds. However, in the long third act, a dawn-to-dusk chronicle of the four-day celebration in Chicago, the film ambles into a state of cinematic grace. As the crowds of worshippers jam Michigan Avenue, pack Grant Park, and flow into Soldier Field (a sports arena transformed into "a great outdoor Cathedral"), the sheer size of the multitude seems to stagger the filmmakers. Slowly, the camera pans the congregation, lingering over the swarm of humanity, a cast of hundreds of thousands that, declares a title card, "dwarfs into insignificance the screen's greatest man-made spectacle."

The dogma unfurled in Chicago was not exclusively Catholic. Though ordered from Rome, the Eucharistic Congress proudly wore a "Made in America" label. American flags and patriotic bunting share the altar with medieval vestments and papal iconography. Commenting on the official emblem of the Congress, a fusion of the Stars and Stripes with the papal colors, the *New York Times* drew the correct conclusion: "It is an expression of two loyalties which the sound sense of the nation has accepted as compatible despite recent attempts [by the KKK] to inoculate Americanism with the spirit of religious bigotry and hatred." As Cardinal Bonzano walks to the altar to celebrate mass in Soldier Field, a huge American flag flaps in the wind. The camera pans and holds on a shot of the great altar framed by three more American flags, screen left, center, and right. "Never in America

Catholicity and Americanism: Old Glory dominates the skyline at Soldier Field, Chicago, during the Eucharistic Congress, June 20–24, 1926.

(CHICAGO HISTORY MUSEUM)

has so great a congregation assembled for so splendid a service," reads the title card, without exaggeration—and never on screen had the union of Catholicity and Americanism been consecrated so seamlessly.

Blessed by the auspicious send-off at the Jolson Theater, *Eucharistic Congress* seemed poised for what the Church's new partners would call boffo box office, especially with Fox picking up the tab for a publicity campaign worthy of a studio epic. Reviewers and advertisements gamely stressed the interfaith crossover appeal ("A Picture for All Humanity!"), but the ballyhoo targeted the obvious core constituency. Cooperating fully with the campaign, the church hierarchy stopped just short of promising penitential indulgences for Catholics attending *Eucharistic Congress*. "As absorbing and compelling a picture narrative as has ever been thrown on the screen," decreed Cardinal Mundelein, sounding like an ad-pub man for Fox. In archdioceses across the nation, bishops, monsignors, and priests were recruited to shill for the film, lobby cards were displayed in church alcoves, and flyers were included in prayer materials and parish mailings.

It fell to Breen, a novice in the motion picture trade if not sales and publicity, to put the show on the road. After the New York premiere, operating from the Chicago office, he coordinated playdates for *Eucharistic Congress* with Fox's regional distributors. Often, he used an exhibition practice known as "four-walling," wherein a neighborhood theater in a likely Catholic parish was rented out for captive audiences of parochial school children. "I am trying to be a real honest-to-goodness movie magnate," Breen joked to a friend. "It is a great life."

While peddling *Eucharistic Congress*—hitting the jackpot in the Catholic big cities, flopping in the Protestant heartland—Breen got his first education in the demographics of moviegoing. When the head count in the hinterlands failed to measure up to the standing-room-only crowds in the big cities, he had a ready explanation. "You know there is a little anti-Catholic bigotry prevalent in certain parts of this country," he commiserated to a Fox distributor in Colorado who played to an empty house, "and, shameful as it is, we are compelled to face the fact."

Breen also learned about the shadier sides of a cash business. Unbeknownst to Quigley or Breen, an independent filmmaker named A. Teitel had taken color motion pictures of the Eucharistic Congress. Marketing the knock-off under the title *Faith of Millions*, Teitel siphoned off revenue from the Church by sneaking the unauthorized version into towns ahead of *Eucharistic Congress*. "It is not by the wildest stretch of the imagination a better picture to show than the film offered by the Fox Film Corporation," Breen lectured a priest tempted to book the competition. "What you want is a motion picture of the Eucharistic Congress and not merely a series of attractive shots of the Congress." Backed by George William's lawyers, Breen threatened litigation and quashed the bootleg version.

By year's end, the motion picture of the Eucharistic Congress of 1926 had left a profound impression not only on its Catholic acolytes but on a tougher crowd. Just as the event overwhelmed America with the majesty of Catholic ritual and the volume of Catholic numbers, the release of the motion picture stunned Hollywood with how an energized Catholic clergy filled theater seats. In New York, ten thousand people were turned away from the doors of the Jolson Theater. In Chicago and Boston, audiences packed the house and stood ten deep on opening night. Surveying the long lines and SRO crowds, *Moving Picture World* commented that the throngs "gave veterans of show business something to think about." *Variety* agreed, predicting that the Fox–Catholic Church coproduction "certainly tied up the picture business for all time with the churches."

In retrospect, *Eucharistic Congress*, the premiere and the film, seems prescripted for symbolic foreshadowing: Joseph I. Breen, Martin J. Quigley, and Will H. Hays, seated under the same roof at the Al Jolson Theater, watching a motion picture homage to American Catholicism, preceded by a theatrical prologue on the birth of Christ choreographed by Roxy Rothafel. "I rejoice in the enterprise inaugurated tonight," Hays said before the screening, more prophetically than he knew.

For Breen, the selling of *Eucharistic Congress* was not just an experience "both novel and interesting," but a means to propagate the faith. "George William, when it is all done with, will probably make enough out of the film to pay the expense of the Congress," he calculated, with enough left in the till to funnel thousands of dollars into his favorite collection plate (the nuns). Not that Breen didn't sweat for every penny. "Don't let anyone tell you that marketing a movie is easy," he groused when, a year later, the film had finally played out. "It's the toughest job I've had in years and I have had all I want of it."

2

BLUENOSES AGAINST THE SCREEN

Though now an endangered species, virtually extinct, a creature known as the bluenose once roamed in vast herds through the landscape of American culture. "A prude; prig, self-appointed moral arbiter," explains the *Dictionary of American Slang*, tagging the type as a busybody sniffing out indecency in ordinary enjoyments, decadence in harmless diversions. Hollywood stuffed and mounted the bluenose in the fussbudget fluttering of the character actress Margaret DuMont, dowager foil to a leering, slouching Groucho Marx, a battle-ax matron always shocked, ever harrumphing, succumbing to the vapors at the slightest scent of impropriety.

A code word for lewdness since the nineteenth century, "blue" gained its suffix in the 1920s, a decade that spawned plenty that was blue to see red about. Besides a generation uninhibited by Prohibition, what put bluenoses most out of joint was the unconcealed delight avatars of the Jazz Age took in the tweaking. In the *American Mercury*, the house organ for the opposition, H. L. Mencken tarred the Philistine swarms with the derisive taxonomy *bubous Americanus*. "Heave an egg out of a Pullman window, and you will hit a Fundamentalist almost anywhere in the United States today," rasped Mencken in 1925, winding up for the pitch. "They are everywhere that learning is too heavy a burden for mortal minds." Though a gadfly by profession and disposition, Mencken expressed a widespread indignation at the musty Victorians bent on banning alcohol, evolution, and entertainment. In the Marx Brothers comedies, after all, audiences side with Groucho's mobile eyebrows, not DuMont's flaring nostrils.

Yet if the bluenose represented the extreme version of the spoilsport chaperone, another branch of the family tree occupied a position closer to the center of cultural gravity: the moral guardian. Smarter than Mencken's *bubous Americanus*, more open-minded than the corseted Victorian, and more sophisticated than the blinkered censor, the moral guardian was a force to be reckoned with. Where the bluenose was ridiculed, the moral guardian was respected. Where the outraged squawks from the bluenose were ignored or resisted, the reasoned opinion of the moral guardian was heeded and solicited. All bluenoses considered themselves moral guardians, but no moral guardian considered him- or herself a bluenose.

Throughout the first half of the twentieth century, bluenoses, moral guardians, and variants of each invested enormous energy in appraising and restricting the most visible and visceral projector of values, the motion picture medium. Whether the surveillance took the form of nonbinding grades from an educational board of review or coercive cuts dictated by a state censor, the custodial oversight was deemed a social good and a kindly stewardship, even a Progressive cause. Suspicious of a flickering amusement that mesmerized the commonest of folk and the dullest of immigrants—the first core audience for the movies—reformers of all stripes viewed the motion picture as a gateway to personal damnation and social deviance. Almost to a man—and, more importantly, woman, the fair sex being invested with the greater portion of custodial capital—Progressives believed that the motion picture medium, if left to its own devices, was more liable to pollute and degrade than refine and uplift. Just as a single lustful spasm in a brothel might sow the seeds of disease and dissipation, a brief session at a nickelodeon might undo years of educational guidance and moral instruction.

While all right-thinking Americans accepted the wisdom of censorship, the alliance was split on the applicable criteria. No two cities, counties, or states agreed on the bounds of propriety and the regions beyond the pale. Myriad flashpoints (drinking, blasphemy, dancing, civil strife, loose women, bungling policemen) and catchall categories ("vulgarity," "lowness," "affront to common decency") shifted with each point on the compass. Oklahomans gulped at liquor, Chicagoans frowned at Keystone Kops, and Dixie abided no ruffling of Jim Crow's feathers.

Filmmakers protested the cuts in the product and the banishment from whole markets not as violations of inalienable First Amendment rights but as wasteful business expenses. With so many quirky censors abroad in the land, no film was sufficiently sanitized not to run afoul of someone, somewhere—an ambitious councilman, a mayor's wife, or the sundry buttinskies, cronies, and hacks who sat on the numerous state and municipal censor boards.

Fed up with the costly cuts, one enterprising company sued a state censor board, taking the case all the way to the Supreme Court. The litigation backfired with explosive impact. In 1915, in *Mutual Film Corporation v. In-*

dustrial Commission of Ohio, the Supreme Court ruled that the movies were not a revolutionary new communications medium but "a business, pure and simple, originated and conducted for profit, like other spectacles, not to be regarded . . . as part of the press of the country, or as organs of public opinion." Being a commercial enterprise, motion pictures could be regulated by the states—and by logical extension the federal government. "[Motion pictures] may be used for evil," intoned Justice Joseph McKenna, gaveling down his film criticism with a flat statement that in 1915 was plain common sense. "Besides, there are some things which should not have pictorial representation in public places and to all audiences." Theoretically, under the Constitution, the U.S. Congress possessed the power to set up a federal agency regulating the content of the motion picture industry the same way the recently established Food and Drug Administration regulated the ingredients ground up in meatpacking plants. Cinema or sausages, each was fodder for the interstate commerce clause.

Backed by the highest court in the land and freed from pesky First Amendment considerations, state and municipal censor boards proliferated.[1] The membership screened, cut, and certified every frame of celluloid projected within local borders, tormenting motion picture distributors with an obstacle course whose hurdles stretched from state to state, city to city. Expensive film prints were shredded, confiscated, and banished. Worse, filmmakers had to pay for the trouble. Besides protecting indigenous morals, the censorship boards pumped up tax revenues and greased local palms by levying taxes on each print processed and purified.

For the first two decades of the twentieth century, pioneer filmmakers were too busy with their own cutthroat competition to muster organized resistance to the confiscatory censors. In 1921, however, a series of made-for-tabloid scandals put Hollywood square in the crosshairs of an angry army of moral crusaders still flush from their victory with the Eighteenth Amendment. Famous directors turned up dead, matinee idols shot heroin (and each other), and doe-eyed ingénues were rousted from sordid love nests. In the most lurid incident, the corpulent comedian Fatty Arbuckle was accused of the brutal rape and murder of a party girl named Virginia Rappe at a drunken weekend orgy. Arbuckle's three trials solidified Hollywood's reputation as a sun-drenched Sodom luring Midwest farm girls to a fate worse than waitressing.

---

1. The number of state censorship boards fluctuated over the years, but the six best-funded, longest-lived, and most troublesome resided in Kansas, Maryland, New York, Ohio, Pennsylvania, and Virginia. Upwards of 250 city boards also operated, in addition to the hundreds of marshals, ministers, and matrons who censored the local Bijou as a point of personal privilege.

Spurred into collective action, the major studios closed ranks and formed a defensive perimeter. On March 5, 1922, the Hollywood moguls and the New York moneymen who financed them organized their first professional consortium, the Motion Picture Producers and Distributors of America, Inc. (MPPDA), and an aligned though legally autonomous organization, the Association of Motion Picture Producers (AMPP).[2] The official purpose of both groups was "to foster the common interests of those engaged in the motion picture industry by establishing and maintaining the highest possible moral and artistic standards of motion picture production." To lead the MPPDA, the moviemakers turned to a non-pro: Will H. Hays, an Indiana lawyer and ace Republican operative serving as Postmaster General in the administration of President Warren G. Harding. The game plan for the MPPDA and the appointment of Hays as umpire was modeled after Major League Baseball and its first commissioner, Judge Kenesaw Mountain Landis, who had been brought in to clean up the game after the Black Sox scandal in 1919, a betrayal that had discredited an American pastime more sacred than moviegoing.

Slight, saucer-eyed, and purse-lipped, Hays was an easy man to underestimate. Born in Sullivan, Indiana, in 1879, of sturdy Scot-Irish stock and rock-ribbed Republican lineage, Hays grew up in a home suffused—so said his memoirs—"with the kind of spiritual 'air conditioning' in which it was a joy to live," where "the Christian life meant the Ten Commandments, self-discipline, faith in time of trouble, worship, the Bible, and the Golden Rule." In 1920, as chairman of the Republican National Committee, he had orchestrated the first modern media campaign for the presidency, planting the handsome but character-deficient Senator Harding on the front porch of the Harding mansion in Marion, Ohio, and having the candidate hold forth from a rocking chair while looking ruggedly presidential. "There were no gala tours, no whistle stops, but there were lots of pictures and movies," remembered the seasoned trade journalist and pioneer film historian Terry Ramsaye. After the stage-managed landslide victory, President Harding rewarded his media Svengali with the job of Postmaster General. When the studios beckoned, Hays jumped from Washington to Hollywood at pre-

2. Due to the fact that the membership of the two organizations overlapped (all members of the AMPP belonged to the umbrella organization, the MPPDA), the MPPDA and the AMPP are often conflated. Perhaps the clearest way to distinguish between the two groups is by personnel and location: MPPDA (moneymen, New York) and AMPP (moguls, Hollywood). The corporate distinction is crucial for an understanding of the evolution of Hollywood censorship: the ineffectual Studio Relations Committee operated as an on-site arm of the AMPP in Hollywood whereas the Production Code Administration derived its ultimate authority from the MPPDA in New York.

cisely the right moment, before any residue from the chicanery soon swirling around the Harding administration clung to the upright Hoosier. Shrugging off his timely exit, Hays always denied any premonition of the indictments on the horizon. "If correct, this was the first and only time he was ever in a state of such unawareness," Ramsaye dryly commented.

For the next twenty-three years, Hays served as fixer and figurehead for all things Hollywood. His first task was to sweep out the offal and declare the stables under new management. "The old careless, helter skelter days are over," Hays assured the public. "The chieftains of the motion picture now realize their responsibilities as custodians of not only one of the greatest industries in the world but of possibly the most potent instrument in the world for moral influence and education, and certainly one of the most universal mediums of artistic expression." Quickly tagged the "czar of the movies," the semiknown ex-cabinet officer became a household name.

For fronting for the Hollywood moguls, Hays received an annual salary of $100,000 with income tax paid, plus an additional $15,000 for living expenses. He was worth every cent. Just as Judge Landis cleaned up the athletic field of dreams, Hays guided the motion picture dream factory through a nasty stretch of bad publicity into the major leagues of corporate America. "The greatest reform ever created in the film trade came with the advent of big bankers into the business with their money, thereby pushing out the wildcatting promoter, tricky producer, and other easy money getters," *Variety* observed in 1926. "There isn't much question but that the association of Will Hays with pictures has had much to do with the confidence of large bankers in the industry."

Besides his high-level access to Wall Street and Capitol Hill, Hays possessed another requisite credential: unassailable probity. He was a nondrinker, a nonsmoker, and a Presbyterian Church elder, the last of which was not incidental—not just because he was not Jewish, like most of the Hollywood moguls, but because robust Protestantism was still the driving engine behind official morality in America, the best proof of which was the "noble experiment" in behavior modification currently undergoing disappointing field tests, Prohibition.

A lawyer by trade and a mediator by temperament, Hays looked upon the show business of motion pictures as more business than show. He brought to the job the style of an aloof executive who sets the tone for the office but keeps his distance from the salaried underlings. No micromanager, never starstruck, he spent more time in New York, Washington, D.C., or his home in Sullivan, Indiana, than in Hollywood. Though known to bristle at silent melodramas depicting stone-hearted plutocrats tormenting

Presbyterian probity and Republican connections: Will H. Hays, president of the Motion Picture Producers and Distributors of America, shakes hands with actor Frank Hopper, in costume as Teddy Roosevelt for Paramount's *The Rough Riders* (1927). Paramount studio head Jesse L. Lasky looks on.

the virtuous working poor, Hays mainly steered clear of intervention into storylines unless public outrage was loud enough to disturb his serenity. "Will Hays is a politician by instinct, training, and in his heart," *Variety* noted approvingly in 1927.

Nonetheless, a good part of Hays's workday involved the recitation of platitudes about the pious motives of the motion picture industry. In this regard, his most important public relations gesture was the establishment of the Studio Relations Committee (SRC) in 1926 and the promulgation of the first written rules for motion picture content. On June 8, 1927, at a special meeting of the Association of Motion Picture Producers in Hollywood, Colonel Jason S. Joy, a Hays functionary who headed the SRC, delivered a lengthy summation of cinematic trouble spots, an itemized list that ran to several hundred "censorable or objectionable scenes, captions, etc." The actionable material included whole scenarios, specific images, and offensive language, both printed (in the title cards of the silent cinema) and "spoken" on screen (and interpreted by aghast lip readers). After Joy's humorless presentation, the AMPP distilled the list and passed a resolution pledging to abide by the guide and abjure indecency. The injunctions became known by the prim title of the "Don'ts and Be Carefuls" or the "Do's and Don'ts."

Of course, a posted list of rules was all well and good, but for the moral guardian who still saw—and, after 1927, heard—a screen racing headlong into perdition, Hays and his "Don'ts and Be Carefuls" did not do the job. A singsong, childlike list of bromides and taboos failed to address the real threat and promise of the motion picture medium. That missionary work required men of a different temperament—and faith.

BANNED IN CHICAGO

Four cities can claim a controlling influence in the rise of American cinema: Hollywood, which manufactured the product; New York, which bankrolled the business; Washington, which (mainly) had sense enough to butt out; and, Chicago, which shaped the character of the medium in its prime. Ironically, the city notorious as the lawless playground for American gangsterdom exported to Hollywood a set of stiff bylaws. In the 1920s, as scar-faced bootleggers and corrupt pols worked the rackets that made the contraband flow, Chicago nurtured the personalities, the philosophy, and the power behind the Production Code.

Afflicted since 1907 with the nation's oldest censorship statute and home to an especially rock-headed crew of political hacks and activist cranks, Chicago was a treacherous port of call for the motion picture industry. Between the anti-vice-minded police commissioner William F. Russell and the Chicago Board of Censors, Hollywood ran a gauntlet as eccentric as it was severe. Doubtless the board's primitive technical facilities abetted its erratic judgment calls. Two years after the *The Jazz Singer* (1927), sound projectors had yet to be installed in the screening room in City Hall. Board members watched the talkies silent and read the dialogue from a printed text. The *Chicago Tribune* labeled Commissioner Russell "a moral Simple Simon" and the Chicago Board of Censors "a stupid nuisance," but the editorial writers didn't have to answer to the clubwomen, the clerics, and the electorate. For its part, Hollywood could not afford to write off the second most populous urban market in the nation. Banned in Boston alliterated, but banned in Chicago decimated.

Two local civic leaders sought a better working relationship, an arrangement that would allow Hollywood easier access to Chicago while granting Chicagoans prior restraint over Hollywood. Having absorbed the lessons of the Eucharistic Congress film, Martin J. Quigley and Joseph I. Breen figured that both cities, and one faith, should continue to benefit from privileged communications and mutual cooperation.

Breen was certainly predisposed to repay the city that had been so good to him. His salesmanship for Catholicity in Chicago had brought him to the attention of men with more secular interests and bigger pockets. In April 1928, he was hired to shill for another high-profile pageant, the Chicago World's Fair, conceived as a sequel to the landmark Columbian Exposition of 1893 and slated to open in 1933. (The theme was a Century of Progress and the timing was awful: by 1933, the nation was suffering through the fourth year of a Decade of Depression.) Breen's task was to coordinate the prepublicity campaign by lining up sponsors and beating the drum, "to get hold of some money and, incidentally, ascertain whether or not Chicago really wants a celebration in 1933." He hoped to get $15,000 or $18,000 a year for the job; he took $12,000.

Breen uprooted the family, now at full strength, with three boys and three girls, from Washington to Chicago. Mulling over the fortunes of the Breen clan down through the generations, he reflected, "I have, myself, this family weakness for the West and all things of the West"—still thinking Lake Shore Drive not Hollywood Boulevard.

Breen sold the World's Fair with characteristic tenacity—boosting the project in print, speechifying at luncheons, and collaring local businessmen for financial commitments. To attract free ink, the advance team staged a public debate on the question "Will the World's Fair Prove a Benefit to Chicago?" Breen, cajoled into playing devil's advocate, argued against the proposition he was paid to support. Facing off against a Jesuit professor from Loyola University, the St. Joseph's alum without a diploma let his competitive instincts override his self-interest: he won the decision hands down. As the crowd cheered and laughed, the flummoxed flack blushed beet red.

In June 1929, with the Chicago World's Fair a done deal, Breen become an assistant to Stuyvesant Peabody, president of the Chicago-based Peabody Coal Company. Peabody was an industrial magnate of the old school, as devoted to horse racing as coal mining. Though employed mainly in public relations, Breen performed "a gamut of duties which ranged from the settlement of strikes in Illinois and Kentucky coal districts to shipping strings of horses in and out of the Hawthorn and Churchill Downs race tracks." After having toiled for so long against looming deadlines in pressure-cooker atmospheres, he found the regular hours of an office job leisurely by comparison. "I have more time to do a little writing in my present post," he told Father Parsons. "I am not hard pressed, as I was on the publicity jobs." Of course, like the rest of his bullish generation, he was oblivious to the ticker-tape countdown to the Stock Market Crash marked on the calendar that October.

While savoring the tranquility of a solid income and a manageable workload, Breen remained devoted to Catholic actions and ethno-religious mixing, notably with Quigley, his partner in charity during the run of the Eucharistic Congress film. In 1929, Quigley hired him as an editor and writer for the *Chicagoan*, a fortnightly magazine conceived to be for the Second City what the *New Yorker* was for the first. While working for Peabody and continuing to represent Cardinal Mundelein, Breen wrote profiles and articles for the *Chicagoan* under a variety of whimsical pen names (Simon L. Rameynn, Shan Van Vocht) as well as a media-watch column entitled "Newsprint" under his initials "J.I.B." One counterintuitive assignment for the future censor was a profile of Little Egypt, the scandalous belly dancer of the 1893 Chicago World's Fair, now a respectable but still nimble restaurateur. "She was not so much *ambidextrous* as she was *tummydextrous*," Breen joshed, playfully coaxing her into a private show. Little Egypt gamely obliged. "What a dance!" he exclaimed. "No wonder the Columbian Exposition drew great crowds!"

In July 1929, while working for Stuyvesant Peabody, Martin Quigley, and Cardinal Mundelein—the trio being a neat index to the worlds of business, media, and religion that Breen straddled personally and professionally—the disparate strands meshed into a single cord. The epiphanic moment was later to be the stuff of legend, or at least an oft-told anecdote with shifting details. Daniel E. Doran, an Irish-Catholic journalist and Breen crony, related a version burnished by blarney, but credible enough in the outlines.

At Loyola University, Chicago's prestigious Jesuit university, several prominent Catholic laymen, including Quigley and Peabody, served on a special Administrative Council. Breen typically sat in on the meetings for his boss, who preferred to spend his leisure time at the racetrack. Among the clerical members of the council was the Rev. FitzGeorge Dinneen, S.J., pastor of St. Ignatius Church on Chicago's North Side.

Father Dinneen barged into a council meeting, apoplectic about an early talkie, *The Trial of Mary Dugan* (1929), currently playing to a packed house in Chicago's downtown Loop. A stagebound courtroom drama, the film exposed no visible sins but verbally flaunted the mercenary trade of the winsome defendant, a serial mistress in the docket for the murder of the last in a string of well-heeled lovers.

Already a local cause célèbre, *The Trial of Mary Dugan* was a case study in the quirks of the Chicago Board of Censors. When first previewed, the film had earned a "pink-ticket" (an "adults only" classification). Then, bowing to bluenose pressure, the board banned the film completely. Next, bowing

The film that started it all: serial mistress Mary Dugan (Norma Shearer) on the stand in Bayard Veiller's *The Trial of Mary Dugan* (1929).

to pressure from more open-minded constituents, the board reversed itself *again* and gave the film clear passage. "[That gives you an] idea of how the local censor board functions," grinned *Variety*, correctly predicting *The Trial of Mary Dugan* would be a "sure winner after [the] flock of publicity."

Father Dinneen was livid at the wishy-washy Chicago Board of Censors, his fury inflamed by the marquee exploitation of a wayward lass with an Irish surname. "I'm going to teach some people in this town a lesson," he vowed. "I'll stop these filthy motion pictures from coming into my parish if we have to clean out every alderman on the North Side." Breen described the priest as "all het up about it and looking for blood."

Being the only person in the room who knew anything about Hollywood, Quigley patiently explained the problems with Dinneen's brand of hot-headed activism: that protest campaigns only succeeded in creating controversy and increasing box office, that ad hoc agitation against a single transgression never solved the long-term problems, and that government censors applied no guiding (that is, Catholic) vision to motion picture content. Quigley had a better idea, a plan for cinematic morality he had been contemplating for years.

As Quigley talked, Breen listened.

HOLY WRIT: THE PRODUCTION CODE, 1930

The Production Code, the founding document of Hollywood censorship, was adopted in 1930 and operated, with varying degrees of coercive power, until 1968. Conceived in faith and invested with a sacred aura, the Code would be likened to another text, the Bible, and metaphors of print-based religiosity would waft around it like incense: the commandments, the tablets, the gospel. Like different translations of scripture, the verses of the Code might be refined and rephrased but the fundamentals were eternal and unalterable. "The more I thought about it, the more it seemed to me to be an *inspired* document," Breen recalled years later, italicizing his reverence.

Like a Hollywood script, composed in the collaborative sweatshops of the studio system by the lowly scriveners Jack Warner called "schmucks with Underwoods," the Production Code is a screen credit with several authors claiming the lead byline. The final document was amended, revised, polished, and tweaked by many hands, making precise authorship of each line, each word choice, hard to determine. Nonetheless, in any contract dispute mediated under the bylaws of the Screenwriters Guild, the proprietary credit would read: "The Production Code by Martin J. Quigley and Rev. Daniel A. Lord, S.J., based on an original idea by Martin J. Quigley."

According to Quigley, the origins of the Production Code began with himself. "Out of considerable experience with the status of pictures, and the industry's efforts to provide adequate regulation in a moral sense," he explained, writing in the regal third person, "Martin Quigley, in the summer of 1929, reached the conclusion that, while in certain quarters there was ample will to do the right thing, adequate measures and procedure were not available." Quigley resolved to correct the oversight by bestowing on Hollywood "a reliable yardstick and document of guidance to the appreciation of American mores and American decency." As his friend Terry Ramsaye corroborated, "the Production Code, and the considerations before it, with it, and behind it, [began] in the mind of Mr. Martin Quigley, who conceived it, nurtured it, and gave it to the industry" to assure that "the screen shall survive, and prosper, as a factor in civilization."

Quigley had long pondered a rudimentary Code of Ethics for the unruly medium he had reported on since 1915. Though an ardent foe of government censorship, he believed firmly in voluntary self-control and professional standards. Along with Terry Ramsaye, his longtime editor at *Motion Picture Herald*, Quigley hectored Hollywood to worship more than mammon, using his formidable publishing empire to advocate the adoption of the Production Code, demand the enforcement of the Production Code, and defend the Production Code from all enemies.

Besides the dictates of a Catholic conscience, Quigley was spurred into action by Father Dinneen's indignation over *The Trial of Mary Dugan*. Dinneen in Chicago and like-minded clerics and clubwomen in every parish and town had never much liked what they had seen in the movies, but what they now heard pumped up the volume on their dudgeon. With the introduction of synchronous dialogue, suggestive gestures and mimed motions were replaced by whispered intimacies, zinging wisecracks, and vulgar vernacular. As bluenoses got an earful, outrage over Hollywood's loose tongues and lax morals escalated. Figuring Breen knew the Jesuit psyche, Quigley asked him to arrange a meeting with Father Dinneen to consider an alternative plan of attack that would be more effective and principled, Quigley thought, than church boycotts, censor board fiats, or legislative action.

On or about October 1, 1929, Quigley, Breen, and Dinneen met at the Chicago Athletic Club for a power lunch to plot an ambitious motion picture project. Quigley explained his idea for a program of industry self-regulation to be guided by a written contract. In a spirit of compromise, he suggested that one of Dinneen's fellow Jesuits collaborate in the composition of the document, Rev. Daniel A. Lord, S.J., of St. Louis, Missouri.

Father Lord was the Jesuit version of a Hollywood multi-hyphenate. In a lifetime spent propagating the faith, the prolific priest churned out twenty-five plays, thirty books, forty-eight children's books, and a raft of booklets, pamphlets, and speeches. He was also a gifted musician who, like some kind of ecclesiastical hybrid of Thomas Aquinas and Flo Ziegfeld, delighted in staging extravagant religious pageants and composing show tunes. If applied to the pursuit of earthly profits, Lord's talents might have made him a Broadway impresario, but he was called early to the priesthood and channeled his energies along a more celestial career path. "I never wrote without A.M.D.G. and B.V.H.M. on the page," averred Lord.[3] Perhaps the too-perfect surname—the tag of a lazy screenwriter with a penchant for sledgehammer symbolism—preordained his ordination.

It was Lord's musical talent that first cued him to the seductive strains of cinema. As a young seminarian, he improvised piano accompaniments for the silent movies that he and his cloistered brethren were treated to twice a year. Naturally, the films shown to the apprentice Jesuits needed prior clearance from the senior faculty, so the young Lord played for the complete program of entrees under review. Hands on the keyboard, eyes on the

3. For the Latin *Ad Majorem Dei Gloriam et Beatae Virginis Mariae Honorem* ("To the Greater Glory of God and the Honor of the Blessed Virgin Mary").

"Get me rewrite!": the Jesuit multi-hyphenate Father Daniel A. Lord, coauthor of the Production Code, in 1944.

(MIDWEST JEWISH ARCHIVES)

screen, he beheld the full majesty of a blossoming art while inhaling the twin thrills of cinema and censorship. "By ordination time, I found myself with a specialty both unexpected and unusual," he quipped.

Lord's first on-site encounter with Hollywood occurred in 1926 at the behest of Cecil B. DeMille, the producer-director who even then was making his name with biblical spectacles inspired by the public domain tales of the Old and New Testaments. DeMille planned to follow up his epic version of *The Ten Commandments* (1923), based on the steamiest passages and most awesome special effects in the Book of Exodus, with *The King of Kings* (1927), a retelling of the life of Christ taken from the Gospels. Hoping to cover all his theological bases, DeMille hired a Jewish rabbi, a Protestant minister, and a Catholic priest as technical advisers. Father Lord got the gig as DeMille's on-set Catholic.

Like many a Midwest transplant plunked down in Hollywood, the Jesuit caught the glitter bug. Hanging around the set of a garish faux Jerusalem, kibitzing over title cards, and rubbing shoulders with DeMille while screening dailies (the priest and the director developed a lifelong friendship), Lord came to fancy himself a Hollywood player. Life back in St. Louis with the Ladies Sodality must have seemed pretty tame after schmoozing with "C. B." in the Paramount cafeteria.

Two unglamorous years later, when Quigley called with the Production Code assignment, Lord leapt like a starlet getting her big break. "Here was a chance to tie the Ten Commandments in with the newest and most widespread form of entertainment," he rejoiced.

Hays's dumbed-down "Don'ts and Be Carefuls," Lord realized, were merely "things that must not be done, matters of good taste and common decency. There were isolated statements, unconnected, in no way complete or clear." The Quigley-Lord Code would not merely chisel a list of thou-shalt-nots onto stone tablets; it would articulate the tenets of a religio-filmic philosophy. A true motion picture code "must make morality attractive, and the sense of responsibility of the movies to its public [must be] clear and unmistakable," Lord believed. "It must be a matter of general principles and their immediate relationship to the practical plots and situations of a film."

The document drafted by Lord contained two sections, a philosophical justification entitled "General Principles," followed by a list of prohibitions entitled "Working Principles." In moving from the general to the particular, the Code followed the logical gridwork of a scholastic treatise. The first section of the original Code was later titled "Reasons Supporting the Code." The document that later became known as "the Code" was a summary of the original prepared at the direction of Will H. Hays, because, said Lord, "in the abbreviated form it was a more workable and convenient set of instructions." That is, even ill-lettered moguls could follow the printed instructions if not the Thomistic philosophy.

The first section laid out a theory of media that recognized the cathartic and escapist function of motion picture entertainment but deplored the photoplay that "*tends to degrade human beings.*" Italicized references to "*moral importance*" and capitalized imperatives that "the motion picture has special *Moral obligations*" animate every line of the text. A key passage asserts the profound moral obligation filmmakers have toward the young:

> In General: The mobility, popularity, accessibility, emotional appeal, vividness, straight-forward presentation of fact in the films makes for intimate contact of a larger audience and greater emotional appeal.

More than the literature and paintings the Church had been censoring for centuries, the motion picture was peculiarly accessible, hence peculiarly dangerous, and hence peculiarly in need of custodial oversight.

The second section ("Working Principles") contained a list of positive and negative injunctions, a list far more comprehensive and logically arranged than the "Don'ts and Be Carefuls" of the Hays Office. It reiterated the overarching philosophy ("no picture should lower the moral standards of those who see it"); provided specific instructions on "details of plot, episodes, and treatment"; and set down precise guidelines on flash points such as vulgarity, obscenity, and costuming. In later years, the taboos and prohibitions would be extended, sometimes directly into the Code, sometimes as addenda and resolutions with Code-like authority.

With the document edited and copied, Quigley set about securing signatures for the contract. He lobbied Hays in private, editorialized in his magazine, and stirred up the Catholic ranks. Breen did likewise, double-teaming Cardinal Mundelein with Quigley to persuade "George William" to support their scheme for self-regulation, not Dinneen's demands for boycotts and censorship. Prophetically, as early as October 1929, Breen understood that for the Code mechanism to work a preproduction editorial stage was crucial. "I want Martin to set up a sort of Board of Examination of MSS [manuscripts—that is, film scripts] to more or less pass on the scripts before they are accepted by producers," he informed Father Parsons at *America*.

Quigley, Lord, and Breen struck at a propitious moment. Hollywood was buffeted by what the MPPDA called "one of the worst epidemics in state censorship bills ever to confront the industry." Descending suddenly, the epidemic was incubated by two airborne conditions. First, by 1930 even the remotest neighborhood theaters had been wired for sound, and hinterland audiences blanched at the double entendres and fast-pitched wisecracks of the flippant talkies. Second, the Great Depression had dried up state tax revenues. Nine states, heretofore quiescent, were contemplating the creation of censorship boards, both in response to constituent outrage and to squeeze revenue from film producers, who were charged a fee to have their product censorsed.

In January 1930, the MPPDA in New York and the Association of Motion Picture Producers in Hollywood met to discuss the Quigley-Lord Code, with Quigley traveling to Hollywood to deliver his case in person. On February 17, 1930, at the annual meeting of the AMPP, Hays, representing the moneymen in New York, came in to close the deal. The next day, the MPPDA officially released the text of the Production Code, and on March 31, 1930, the Code was formally ratified at the annual meeting of the MPPDA, a gathering officially described as "the most agreeable and pacific meeting the directors of this organization ever held." Smelling a rat behind the closed doors and tight lips, *Variety* wasn't buying. "While the assistant moguls were in annual gab-fest [in] the sound-proof compartment in which the lovely time, as reported was being held," its savvy reporter knew the "meeting's most important work was to ratify the newest Hays code for making pictures perfect."

The name—the Hays Code—stuck. Wary that the Code was cowritten by "a Catholic priest, and a Jesuit at that," Hays concealed the Catholic choreography and penmanship. "Mr. Hays rightly felt that it was most effective if the spontaneous nature of the Code was stressed, the fact that it grew out of the will of the industry," Lord noted, adding laconically that the MPPDA president "was later willing to let the Code be called the Hays code."[4] Quigley, Lord, and Breen suffered the Presbyterian's credit-hogging with Catholic forbearance. "The recollection of your colleague, W.H., also is not very correct about this development [the origins of the Code]," Quigley once told Breen, "but the purpose in this case, is, of course, obvious."

At this stage, the adoption of the Code was a public relations gesture designed to placate the bluenoses and to curtail agitation for state censorship. No one in Hollywood really knew what had been agreed to. On paper, producers were required to submit every picture to the Studio Relations Committee for approval before the negative went to the laboratory for final printing. If the SRC detected a violation of the Code, the producer had the right to appeal the decision to the 15-member committee of the AMPP, whose secretary would appoint a three-man board to hear the complaint. If the three-man board upheld the decision of the SRC, the producer might then push his appeal further up the chain of command, over the heads of the AMPP in Hollywood, to the Board of Directors of the MPPDA in New York. Only then would the decision be final.

Though theologically sound and culturally expedient, Quigley and Lord's blueprint had two structural flaws. First, no standardized procedure existed for the preapproval of motion picture scripts. Sometimes studios submitted scripts as a courtesy, sometimes producers shared dailies or rough cuts, but basically the Studio Relations Committee depended on a spirit of willing cooperation. Often, the SRC reviewed finished prints and only then noted violations and suggested deletions. Thus, the act of censorship required costly rewriting, reshooting, and reediting. Even presuming a producer acted in good faith, the expense of compliance created a built-in incentive to resist alterations and defy the SRC.

Second, the jury pool was tainted. If a producer appealed a decision by the SRC, three of his fellow producers were assigned to decide the case. Although the three-man Producers Appeal Board could not include a producer from the studio whose film was under review, the men who sat in judgment of each other knew when to nod and when to wink. Mutual back-

---

4. For his part, Lord was willing to let the Code be called the Lord Code. In later years, Lord and Quigley would bicker over billing and authorship, with Quigley prepared to gainsay the claim of the Jesuit for top billing. "The idea and plan of a production code was mine and first outlined by me to Will Hays and later presented by me to meetings of the Association of Motion Pictures Producers, Inc., in Hollywood, in January 1930," Quigley told *New York Times* film critic Bosley Crowther in 1955. He could, he added testily, provide witnesses and, if need be, affidavits. In Lord's mind, he was the author; to Quigley, the priest just happened to be around when he yelled "Get me rewrite!" In fairness, Quigley always conceded that Father Lord "prepared the original draft of the Motion Picture Production Code."

scratching, not impartial enforcement, was the rule; the studio paymasters, not the regulatory hirelings, had the final say.

With no cost-efficient review process on the front end, and a kangaroo court on the back end, the Production Code looked good on paper but crumpled in practice. No sooner had the Code been adopted than the signatories began to violate it. "Studios are more and more openly ignoring that Hays Code of ethics (morality)," *Variety* noted in September 1930, labeling the Producers Appeal Board "a fixing bureau whereby material that had been ordered out could be returned."

Meanwhile, in a related move, the MPPDA had negotiated a highly consequential arrangement back in Chicago. Through dint of his own moxie and the good offices of Quigley, Breen had parlayed his Catholic credentials and public relations skills into regular consulting work as the MPPDA's man on the scene. "The specific job assigned to me was a sort of 'peace-maker' and a producer, and establisher, of good will," he recalled. "I was specifically charged with the task of seeing to it that no serious, unjustified or unwarranted or unwise statements [about Hollywood films] got into the daily newspapers." In modern parlance, Breen's job was damage control: to calm the clerics, massage the moralists, and douse the fires of controversy before the box office receipts got burnt.

Breen and Hays had first met during the premiere of *Eucharistic Congress* (1926) at the Al Jolson Theater. The two had since crossed paths at the Peabody Coal Company, which was represented by Hays's law firm. Hays had been favorably impressed with Breen after seeing him conduct a round of bare-knuckled negotiations with the leaders of a coal miners union. "Whether Will Hays recognized some resemblance in truculent coal miners to peeved movie moguls has never been established, but the fact remains that after he had witnessed Breen competently handle a strikers protest meeting, he offered him a job with the Hays organization in Hollywood," reported the journalist John J. McCarthy.

While working in Chicago on consignment for the MPPDA, Breen juggled several other employments—publicity man for hire, freelance writer, and utility player for the Peabody Coal Company. His work product from the period reflects his frantic multitasking, with correspondence from one job hastily written on the stationery from another job.

By then, a man with a wife and six children had serious reason to hustle. With the Roaring Twenties having screeched to a halt, Breen grabbed at any extra income in reach. He was also angling for a permanent position with the MPPDA for the most understandable of motives. "Business is not picking up," he worried in the bleak summer of 1930, lucky still to be on the payroll at the hard-hit Peabody Coal Company. "There is widespread unemployment with no hopeful outlook in sight."

While looking for an escape hatch, Breen noticed what seemed to be an exception to the Great Depression rule. Even "in these hard days when, seemingly, almost everybody is out of a job," one business seemed relatively unscathed—or at least was putting up a good front. "The show houses offering talkies are pursuing the even tenor of their way despite all the calamity wailing about hard times and bad business," he observed, eying the lavish advertising for "the latest offerings of this newest of the arts to be commercialized." Unlike coal mining or magazine publishing, Hollywood seemed not to be "frightened by any loose talk of industrial depression or curtailed buying power."

Conveniently too, and notwithstanding the Great Depression, Breen's Catholic kinsmen were still steadily employed in God's work against Hollywood. As the lewd testimony in *The Trial of Mary Dugan* proved, the talkies had added a new sensory range to a sacrilegious clamor. Worse, the vaunted Production Code had done nothing to lower the volume. Increasingly beset by meddlesome priests, Hays required a full-time associate with a dual expertise in public relations and Catholic theology. On July 14, 1931, the MPPDA announced Breen's appointment as an assistant to Will Hays. Soon after, the adopted Chicagoan was called out to the site of production.

To Breen, the fateful summons would later seem ordained by a power higher than Will Hays. Stepping aboard the Twentieth Century Limited for the trip west, the man who had helped transform Chicago, for several days anyway, from a haven for gangsterism into a cathedral for American Catholicism envisioned working a similar transformation on another city notorious for trafficking in violence and vice—the true "wonder-city of the world," Hollywood.

3

HOLLYWOOD SHOT TO PIECES

In the summer of 1931, Hollywood was, for once, in perfect synch with the rest of the nation: the city shivered in the grip of a cold gnawing fear. The Great Depression that had extinguished industrial fires and eroded farm prices, broken banks and killed stockbrokers, consigned workers to breadlines and tossed families onto the streets, had also crushed the spirit of a business built on ballyhoo. Hale and hearty from birth, peddling a commodity of addictive potency, the motion picture industry had always prospered, swatting aside economic downturns while other enterprises faltered or went bust. Now, for the first time in its history, Hollywood knew red ink, black moods, and hard times.

Apocalyptic headlines in the trade papers ("Film Stocks in Sharp Drop," "Theatre Chains in Red") screamed the grim tidings. The old hands couldn't remember a worse time and even a newcomer felt the panic in the air. "The whole town is completely and entirely upset," Breen observed in the catatonic winter of 1932. "Everybody seems to be suffering from the DTs. Morale is shot to pieces."

Ironically, Breen's personal fortunes had never been brighter. He had not just landed on his feet, he had pole-vaulted into a rarified bubble of luxury and privilege. Blessed solvency—actually damn good money—was his happy lot during the downbeat decade.[1] As major studios teetered on the edge of ruin, Breen was flush with cash and showered with perks. He rated a chauffer-driven car, and soon a Beverly Hills address and Malibu beach house were among the compensations of doing God's work in sunny

---

1. Breen was hired by the MPPDA at $18,000 a year. By 1941, he was getting $1,000 a week. While Hays's kingly salary was public record, Breen's pay envelope was an "official secret" on the theory that the moguls would be less deferential to a man they exponentially out-earned.

California. "I must confess that the living out here is very agreeable," he admitted, settling into the sweet life in 1932. "I have a lovely house, costs are down, the climate is perfect, Mary and the kids like it, and the school here, in the Jesuit parish, is a dandy."

Away from the Jesuit parish, the living was not so dandy. One third of the nation, to take FDR's conservative estimate, was ill-housed, ill-clothed, and ill-fed, and the better portion of the remainder a precarious paycheck away from upping the percentage. Breen was lucky, and smart enough to count his blessings. "I manage to get to 7:15 mass at least four mornings a week and I pray for you and that U.S. Steel stock," he wrote Martin J. Quigley. "What more can I do?"

The MPPDA berth may have rescued Breen from the manic hustle and icy winters along Lake Michigan, but the job tested his patience and tried his soul. In bedazzling Hollywood, he entered a habitat stranger than gritty Philly, balmy Jamaica, war-ravaged Europe, or big-shouldered Chicago. "From a newspaper or publicity standpoint, this burg is probably the mad house of the universe," he wrote in a dispatch from the front in 1931, a first impression he was never really to modify.

Shortly after assuming his MPPDA post, Breen traveled to Hollywood for a preliminary site visit—to size up the major players, pick the brains of the local journalists, and get the lay of the land. From his plush quarters in the Roosevelt Hotel on Hollywood Boulevard, he typed out an eight-page, single-spaced report to Will Hays, a "statement of the general condition here."

The general condition was discouraging in the extreme. To the former big city reporter, consular officer, and foreign correspondent, the lifestyle of the locals was generally mystifying and sometimes appalling, "the most astounding thing of its kind I have ever heard about." Shocking tales of decadent behavior left him stupefied and scandalized. A glamorous screen siren openly bragged to the press that she was a lesbian, a prominent producer caught in flagrante with another man's wife was nearly shot by his own wife, and, at one Hollywood soiree, he was reliably informed, "the name cards at the dinner were *condrums* [*sic*] for the men and *cotex*, on which was a dash of ketchup, for the women." In this den of inequity, the task ahead would challenge the noblest character and the purest soul. However, "the right stuff in the right man will form an amalgam that will surely crystallize into a huge achievement worthy of a real Crusader." Of course, Breen knew just the man to play white knight.

Breen's official MPPDA title was "assistant to the president," meaning that he was at Hays's beck and call for emergency management. When the exorbitant salaries of pampered stars riled the down-and-out hoi polloi,

Breen was pegged to staunch the public relations problem. "We had just managed to smooth out the trouble caused by the publicity that a star was getting $30,000 a week [Constance Bennett at Warner Bros.], when [news of child star Jackie Cooper earning $7,500] came up," he groaned to a group of studio press agents. In 1932, when the kidnap-murder of the Lindbergh baby horrified the nation, it was Breen who announced that the plot device would be banned from all future crime films. When the studios tightened up standards for press credentials, Breen issued the precious green cards to the legitimate Hollywood reporters and told the freelancers, scam artists, and bootleggers, "No more."

Breen being Breen, he was not content to scurry about as an aide-de-camp. The Crusader had come to Hollywood with his own ideas for reform. "Bear in mind that your humble servant is pretty much a tyro in *matters movie* and considerable of an *auslander*," he informed MPPDA vice president Maurice McKenzie before submitting a five-page, single-spaced set of suggestions. Speaking for the alienated ranks of intellectual moviegoers who "have the impression that all pictures are trite, inane, dull, and unattractive when they are not sexy, jazzy, or suggestively offensive in other ways," he urged the production of "films of a higher order." Breen may have been a novice from another land, but he was not shy about instructing the natives in their own tradecraft.

Breen's chief responsibility was to maintain friendly relations and cordial lines of communication with the Catholics. Linked by faith, tribe, and career to the powerful cardinals, scribbling priests, and activist laypeople whose short fuses always threatened to explode into fiery opposition, he was the ideal envoy, a trusted kinsman fluent in the language and customs of his brethren. No one short of the pope could make the Catholics dance to his tune, but as a mediator Breen could stave off trouble and as an early warning system he could alert Hollywood before an attack was launched.

The MPPDA's pipeline to the Catholics came at a price. Breen was also their inside man. As Breen reported to Hays on the Catholics, the Catholics tapped Breen to read and squeeze Hays—while Breen, in turn, worked both sides of the street, cannily fortifying his position as the indispensable man in the middle. He was not a double agent on an undercover assignment. His affinities and associations were common knowledge, indeed his decisive job qualification. Still, the bankers and moguls paying his salary would have been surprised to learn how cozy and conspiratorial were the back-channel communications, how comfortably Breen nestled with the clerics. The MPPDA only provided his day job; the Church of Rome held his immortal soul. He would render unto Hays due service, but his true mission was to convert Hollywood.

In Breen's eyes, the place was in dire need of regeneration. Hollywood *after* the Code was sinning more damnably than Hollywood before the Code.

PRE-BREEN HOLLYWOOD

Pre-Code Hollywood is the marquee name for a brief period in motion picture history, a privileged zone of relative screen freedom, dating from (roughly) 1930 to (precisely) July 15, 1934. The phrase evokes a time when trigger-happy gangsters, wisecracking dames, and subversive rebels, male and female, ran wild through the lawless territory of American cinema. To survey the titles is to register the temperature of the times: *Red Headed Woman* (1932) and *Baby Face* (1933), where predatory trollops went horizontal for upward mobility; *Little Caesar* (1931) and *Scarface* (1932), where charismatic killers murdered with seditious relish; *I Am a Fugitive from a*

Pre-Code profligacy: mercenary vixen Lily (Barbara Stanwyck) listens as her mentor Adolph (Alphonese Ethier) reads from Nietzsche's *Beyond Good and Evil* in Alfred E. Green's *Baby Face* (1933). The sequence was mauled by both the New York State Censor Board and the Studio Relations Committee.

Chain Gang (1932) and *Heroes for Sale* (1933), where legal authority warrants only contempt; *Skyscraper Souls* (1932) and *Employees Entrance* (1933), where ruthless capitalists violated business ethics and female chastity at will.

Though later lauded for its frank sex and bared skin, pre-Code Hollywood was driven by economics not erotics. Scarred by the beaten-down quality of the harshest years of the Great Depression, the films careen through a universe cut loose from sure moorings and friendly ports, adrift and unanchored. Where the Jazz Age screen reveled in tweaking Victorian decorum with the shenanigans of wild youth, dancing daughters, and "It" girls, the pre-Code screen bespeaks more than a generational spat over manners and morals, bobbed hair and bathtub gin. In its most radical guise, pre-Code Hollywood denied the bedrock verities of American life, knocking down the pillars of Christian justice, capitalist progress, and constitutional democracy. While the world outside the theaters twisted in convulsions, the world inside spun its own topsy-turvy tales.

Consider pre-Code Hollywood's most extreme manifestation of Depression-bred hysteria, *Gabriel Over the White House* (1934). Directed by Gregory La Cava, bankrolled by William Randolph Hearst, and released by MGM, the film imagines a parallel universe where a dictatorial president possessed by the spirit of Abraham Lincoln rules as a messianic demagogue who abolishes Congress, declares martial law, and liquidates gangsters by firing squad in the shadow of the Statue of Liberty. The fascistic scenario is meant not as dystopic fantasy but as sound social policy. Even the madcap comedy teams, like the Marx Brothers in *Duck Soup* (1933) and Wheeler and Woolsey in *Diplomaniacs* (1933), seemed bent on fomenting serious anarchy, not just spraying seltzer bottles at upper-class swells but blasting to smithereens entire geopolitical systems.

The edgiest pre-Code films flashed the shield of Warner Bros., the studio that had its fingers closest to the pulse of the working-class, or no longer working class, public, that specialized in slum-pent melodramas with low-rent characters—bootleggers, boxers, convicts, taxi drivers, waitresses, stenographers, and working girls plying the oldest of professions. Of all the major studios, Warner Bros. stuck most in Breen's craw. "Warners makes a cheap low-tone picture with a lot of double meaning, wise-cracks, and no little filth which they think is funny," he said, calling them "the lowest bunch we have."

But Warner Bros. had competition in the race to the bottom. Frantic for patrons, every studio risked a "pink-ticket" or police raid to lure an audience whose spending was no longer discretionary, who were sometimes choosing between food and film. Paramount ventured *The Story of Temple*

Drake (1932), based on William Faulkner's *Sanctuary*, a lewd tale of rape and promiscuity from a prestige author. "The highlight of this particular story," Breen recalled years later, still not fully recovered from the trauma, "is a scene in a corn crib wherein a perverted criminal *attacks a young girl by injecting into her cloaca an ear of corn*." Fox managed to tart up the rural Americana of *State Fair* (1933) with a randy romance between the male ingénue and a fairground acrobat and some barnyard humor involving the prize hog Blue Boy and the flirtatious sow Esmeralda. Even MGM, the Tiffany studio with high-hat pretensions, bankrolled a project as bizarre as any in Hollywood history—Tod Browning's *Freaks* (1932), a circus-set netherworld where amputees, pinheads, Siamese Twins, monkey boys, bearded ladies, midgets, and dwarves rise up and overturn the natural order, murdering the strong and mutilating the beautiful.

Fueling the raw material of the pre-Code screen was the combustible advertising that served as kindling. "Gossip! Scandal! Shame!" promised *The Story of Temple Drake*. "I, Temple Drake, am guilty of love! I don't dare marry, I can't trust myself! I've done things no self respecting girl would dream of doing!" Being "too much of a woman to lead a one-man life," the frisky temptress in *Frisco Jenny* (1933) took "her happiness in one night stands." The publicity flyers for *Unashamed* (1932) trawled for a body double as uninhibited as its protagonist:

> $100 will be given to the girl or woman who is UNASHAMED to play the part of Lady Godiva and ride around the Public Square on a white horse stark naked at day break, Thursday, August 25 [1932]. All applicants must state age, whether married or single, name and address.

The come-on was a con, but in such stricken times more than one poor girl must have been tempted to answer the ad and trade her modesty for a fast buck. "You can't make a picture as bad as the ads lead you to believe it is," joked humorist Will Rogers, but Hollywood was doing its best to live up to the one-sheets, lobby cards, and taglines.

For bluenoses and moral guardians—a slice of the demographic more liable to loiter around the theater front or scan the newspaper ads than sit through a Warner Bros. double bill—the lurid posters and leering taglines sent out neon danger signs. To reel in the target audience, the ad-pub boys had to cast a line wide enough to alert the untargeted to what was going on beyond the lobby. In 1931, Breen reminded Maurice McKenzie that the MPPDA received "not merely so many complaints about *the picture* as about the advertising, because these people who complain *rarely go to the pictures*. They are moved to protest because of the *advertising*." The Hays Office condemned "the shovelers of print filth," but the scandalous ads were mocked up by the studios and distributed in official press materials.

One tightly wrapped package lived up to her advertising. Sailing atop the pre-Code tide as both siren on the rocks and admiral of the fleet was the auteur-cum-agent provocateur Mae West. Like Breen, West was a creature of the 1890s, but the only thing Victorian about her was the hourglass figure no corset could contain. A superstar of the vaudeville stage in the 1920s, she honed an act that flashed her cheek as a wordsmith, not fleshpot, earning notoriety in the Jazz Age for a series of burlesque farces climaxing with *SEX* (1926), which named the antecedent Hollywood insinuated with *It* (1927). Only with the arrival of dialogue could West go Hollywood. Her real effrontery was not protruding from her body (any Warner Bros. chorine showed more skin) but rippling from her voice. In her eyebrows, in her smirk, in the lilt of her husky contralto, she dared speak the unspeakable: her all-capitals delight in "it," SEX. "The wages of sin," she drawled, "are not always death." Of that, Mae West was living proof.

Having come to clean up the town, Breen felt humiliated by his failure to shut down the lurid red-light district. As Hays's assistant, he might yell and cajole and threaten the signatories to the Code, but he lacked a club to enforce his will. Some fellow Catholics whispered that, being on the payroll of the vice merchants, he was now in their pocket. "I hardly know what to say to you about this whole situation here," a mortified Breen wrote Father Parsons. "For the first time in my life, I have been stumped. It is all very strange and very curious. I fear, however, that all that we did about the Code [in 1930] was far-fetched."

Since the moguls were beyond redemption, Breen blamed his sponsor for lacking conviction and guts. "Hays, I am convinced . . . sold us all a pig in a poke," he fumed. "He raves and rants *at us* but seems to have an abject fear of certain of the executives of our member companies. . . . Under fire, Hays crawls." Yet however guilt-stricken and morally compromised, a man with a wife and six children could not live on faith alone. "These are no days to quit a job," Breen muttered in 1932, in the darkest days of the Great Depression.

Fortunately, at least for the cause of censorship, Breen's rage at pre-Code Hollywood was shared in parishes across America. Livid that the moguls who had gone to confession in 1930 had refused to do sincere penance, Catholics seethed with a righteous fury stoked by the embers of trust betrayed. The good padres felt duped by the wily moneychangers in Hollywood. The Christian injunction to turn the other cheek soon yielded to the Irish inclination to lash out with the back of the hand.

LEGIONS AT THE BARRICADES

To a grand alliance of moral guardians, the trademark transgressions of pre-Code Hollywood—the coarse wisecracks, the mercenary trollops, the chronic cynicism and snide contempt for stuffed shirts and lawful authority, all ballyhooed by lurid posters and drooling taglines—were no mere Hollywood hijinks but a grave threat to the moral fiber of the nation. More than in 1922, when the moguls had formed the MPPDA to put the best face forward, and more than in 1930, when the MPPDA had acceded to the Code to muffle the protests stirred by sound, Hollywood in 1934 incited a withering barrage of righteous anger and moral opprobrium. The product line was damned from the pulpit, condemned by editorialists, and denounced by politicians.

No one was more appalled by pre-Code Hollywood than the coauthor of the Production Code. In 1934, voicing the simmering anger of the hoodwinked Catholics, Rev. Daniel A. Lord, S.J., issued a pamphlet entitled *The Motion Pictures Betray America*, a slashing jeremiad accusing Hollywood of "the most terrible betrayal of public trust in the history of our country." As ever, his scholastic mind distinguished the venial from the mortal sins. "It is no longer a matter of single scenes being bad, of occasional 'hells' and 'damns,' or girls in scanty costumes," wrote Lord, but "a whole philosophy of evil . . . depicted with an explicitness that [has] excited the curiosity of children and the emulation of morons and criminals." The saddest proof of the mendacity of the moguls was their refusal to inoculate the innocent from harm—to assume the custodial responsibility of a moral adult to an infant soul a-borning.

A regular moviegoer in the early 1930s didn't have to be a Jesuit priest to notice a screen world that was more immoral in temper, more insurrectionist in impulse, and more contemptuous of time-honored truths than at any time in cinematic memory. Nor were Catholics alone in resenting the double-cross by the moguls and moneymen. "The Hays Morality Code acted as a kind of shield, protecting the dirty, filthy, vile minds of some of the producers in Hollywood," charged Pete Harrison, editor of the influential trade newsletter *Harrison's Reports*. "Hays made promises to the church people that he would allow no dirt in pictures and failed to keep his promises—and failed miserably." To the injury of paving the road to pre-Code hell was added the insult of being suckered into a devil's bargain.

After more than three years of unholy and unwholesome screen fare, Catholics formed an organization to beat back the plague. Its official name was the National Legion of Decency—morally upright Protestants and Jews might enlist as well—but the group was known as the Legion of Decency or, more ominously, simply "the Legion." The adjectival Catholic was understood.

A notion that had percolated in Catholic circles for years, the Legion took formal shape in October-November 1933, after Archbishop Amleto Giovanni Cicognani, speaking at the National Conference of Catholic Charities in New York on the authority of Pope Pius XI, denounced "the incalculable influence for evil" exerted by the motion picture screen. "Catholics are called by God, the Pope, the bishops and the priests to a united front and vigorous campaign for the purification of the cinema, which has become a deadly menace to morals," said the bishop, whose rhetoric and fluent English had a suspiciously familiar ring. No wonder: the editorial pens of Martin J. Quigley and Breen had touched up his remarks, the pair having met with His Excellency to revise the script and sharpen his focus. With formal marching orders from the high command, a moral crusade against Hollywood spread from pulpit, to pew, to picket lines, and finally to political action.

Within a matter of weeks, the Legion of Decency congealed into the most feared of all the private protest groups bedeviling Hollywood. Backed by a coordinated network of Catholic weeklies whose front-page headlines, editorial broadsides, and scare-mongering cartoons fueled parishioner outrage, the Legion lanced Hollywood's hide with pitiless zeal. It had numbers, focus, energy—and a blunt instrument. "Worn out by promises, tricked by pledges, deceived by codes, and dismayed by filth, the Church has finally decided to take action in the one way left for it—boycott," warned Chicago's *New World*.

The Legion was as good as its word, and it put its word into writing with a brilliant tactical device, the Legion pledge. A prayer-like pact, the Legion pledge was a contractual avowal signed by parishioners and recited in unison at Sunday masses, Knights of Columbus meetings, Ladies Sodalities gatherings, and parochial school assemblies. "I condemn absolutely those debauching motion pictures which, with other degrading agencies, are corrupting public morals and promoting a sex mania in our land," affirmed the pledger. "Considering these evils, I hereby promise to remain away from all motion pictures except those which do not offend decency and Christian morality."

Copies of the Legion pledge were distributed wherever Catholics congregated: Sunday masses, parochial schools, and, to the horror of exhibitors, in front of motion picture theaters to patrons queuing in line. One copy of the signed pledge went to the priest; the other was kept by the pledger. The exact number of pledgers was hard to calculate, and the percentage of signers who kept faith with the contract impossible to monitor,

Toxic Waters: the Legion of Decency raises its sword against the tentacles of the Hollywood octopus in an editorial cartoon from the *New World*, Chicago's Catholic weekly, on September 28, 1934.

but as the campaign gained momentum, *Variety* warned that "fully half of the U.S. Catholic population of 20,000,000 can be counted upon as enlisted crusaders." In the choice between faith and film, enough Catholic moviegoers refused to gamble on salvation to deplete box office revenues from Boston to Los Angeles.

While the Legion of Decency marshaled the religious opposition, two like-minded forces attacked Hollywood along different fronts: the federal government and the learned professions. The more serious threat came from a reenergized federal government poised to enact legislation to tether Hollywood to Washington, D.C.

In March 1933, President Franklin Roosevelt hit the ground running with a New Deal to combat the Great Depression, initiating a massive migration of power toward Washington. Among the dozens of agencies and initiatives FDR promulgated in his dizzying First Hundred Days was a new shooting script for Hollywood. Like industry and agriculture, the amusement trades were to be regulated under the National Industrial Recovery Act (NIRA). Besides fear itself, Hollywood feared that government control would lead to the creation of a federal censorship bureau dictating motion picture content. Heeding the hue and cry from constituents, a broad bipartisan coalition in Congress was considering legislation to do just that. Under FDR's activist New Deal and a Supreme Court that still considered the motion picture medium "a business pure and simple," federal censorship was a distinct and looming possibility.

The canny Catholics abetted Hollywood's fears. In September 1933, while accompanying Will Hays on MPPDA business in New York, Breen caught the scent of New Deal intervention and spread the news. "An extraordinary situation has developed here in connection with attempt to formulate NIRA Industrial Code for our industry," he excitedly wired Bishop John J. Cantwell of Los Angeles. "There is more than a fighting chance to have Roosevelt assert himself and his power under NIRA along lines certain to win your approval." Bishop Cantwell picked up on the cue. "There is no knowledge of what the National Government, by way of the N.R.A. [National Recovery Administration], may do regarding the moral values of screen entertainment, though it is reasonable to expect the Federal Government will not shut its eyes completely," he warned. Neither man wanted New Dealers to do a job best left to Catholics, but the leverage was tactically advantageous.

At the same time, at this worst possible moment, another of Hollywood's vulnerable flanks was attacked by a group of social scientists working under the banner of the Motion Picture Research Council. With financial support from a philanthropic outfit called the Payne Fund, the council conducted an extensive investigation into the impact of motion pictures on children. Between 1929 and 1932, educators and social scientists quizzed, measured, and probed young moviegoers to gauge how celluloid imagery warped malleable minds. (Appropriately, the base camp for the investigators and the fieldwork for the study was Chicago, ground zero for motion picture censorship and a city ever jittery about crime-susceptible youth.) The Payne Fund Studies resulted in a 12-volume chronicle, buttressed with graphs, figures, and jargon. Where the Legion of Decency judged Hollywood culpable as a matter of faith, the Motion Picture Research Council had tested the hypothesis via the scientific method.

In 1933, an accessible synopsis of the Payne Fund Studies by journalist Henry James Forman was published under the bracing title *Our Movie Made Children*. The project marshaled the full weight of lab-coated social science to confirm the gut-level suspicion that the movies burrowed like termites into impressionable juvenile minds: girls took to rouge and tobacco, boys to backtalk and violence, and all to disrespect and deviance. Likening the flood of images to a poisonous reservoir, Foreman told readers to think of Hollywood as a toxic water source that, if unregulated and unfiltered, "is extremely likely to create a haphazard, promiscuous, and undesirable national consciousness." The title of *Our Movie Made Children* summed up the threat: movies were making and thus remaking young Americans, supplanting the traditional character builders of church, home, and school. Groaning, Hollywood dubbed the findings "the Payneful Studies."[2]

Reading the danger signs from three directions, *Variety* sent up a front-page flare. "Producers have reduced the Hays Production Code to sieve-like proportions and are deliberately outsmarting their own document," it warned. "No longer is the industry up against bluenose factions. Responsible people, lawyers, doctors, and other professionals are resenting the screen and lettering by the bushel about it."

In 1934, a mogul eyeing the armies bivouacked outside the studio gates beheld a fearsome coalition arrayed against him. The Church (the Legion), the academy (the Motion Picture Research Council), and the government (the New Deal)—the most hallowed, respected, and powerful institutions in American life—all agreed that Hollywood was, in turn, a moral blight, a social problem, and a political liability. Fenced in and outgunned, the MPPDA Board instructed Hays to hoist the white flag and negotiate terms for surrender.

Of all the forces bearing down on Hollywood, the Catholic Church alone was rallying millions of potential moviegoers to forswear cinema else risk their immortal souls. If the churchmen could be placated, the other threats might recede, maybe disappear.

Enter Joseph I. Breen, not so much waiting in the wings as orchestrating the action from offstage. On one side, the moguls of the Hollywood studios; on the other, the prelates of the Roman Catholic Church; and, poised between the two—himself.

SIGNED AND SEALED: THE PRODUCTION CODE ADMINISTRATION, 1934

On December 8, 1933, MPPDA president Will H. Hays, MGM's J. Robert Rubin, and Paramount's George Schaefer met in the White House with FDR and General Hugh Johnson, head of the National Recovery Administration (NRA), to voice concerns about the New Deal being dealt the motion picture industry. With the Democrats in power, the Republican bigwig

2. The MPPDA hired its own Ph.D., the philosopher Mortimer Adler, to refute the findings of the Payne Fund Studies. Adler, a scholar who worked at a more leisurely pace than a screenwriter on deadline, failed to deliver the rejoinder until 1937, by which time his points were moot.

Hays had suffered a humbling demotion in status. No longer privy to the inner sanctums of government, he came to Washington as a supplicant not a player. In fact, his cushy job was on the line. Back in Hollywood, the erstwhile savior of the motion picture industry was being blamed for the pre-Code firestorm. Hays, the thinking went, should have *forced* the studios to abide by the Code.

That same month, Dr. James Wingate departed Hollywood to attend a censorship conference in New York, leaving Breen in charge of the Studio Relations Committee. Since taking over the office from Colonel Jason Joy in 1932, the former New York State censor with the university degree and the impressive title had been outwitted by the streetsmart moguls. He was also outflanked by his associate. On February 5, 1934, Breen officially replaced Wingate as head of the Studio Relations Committee. Breen had basically been running the office since December 1, 1933.

By then, Hollywood had another Motion Picture Code to worry about—not the one written by Quigley and Lord, but the one enacted under the provisions of the National Industrial Recovery Act. Like other American businesses, the motion picture industry faced the dread prospect of regulation by Washington bureaucrats.

No official record exists of the conversation between FDR, General Johnson, and the emissaries from Hollywood, but trade press reports noticed that the motion picture executives "emerged [from the meeting] very glum" and that FDR, film fan though he was, felt that Hollywood fully warranted the "eagle eye" of federal oversight. In particular, "the subject of off-color films" was also reported to have "caused some disturbance at the White House."

The NRA divisional administrator appointed to regulate the motion picture industry was a loyal New Dealer named Sol A. Rosenblatt, a man whose mogul-like name belied any sympathy with the studios. Being focused on economic recovery not moral reformation, Rosenblatt was happy, initially, to keep Hollywood's Code separate from Washington's, but as the months passed and Hays's Code remained flaccid, the trade press detected a baleful change of heart. The "continual talk about making the Hays Code of Ethics part of the NRA Code" was growing louder and more insistent.

In January 1934, Rosenblatt traveled to Hollywood to explain the New Deal in person and to deliver an uncoded message. He reminded studio executives that the NRA's Code, unlike the MPPDA's Code, held the force of law, direct from Washington. "[The New Deal Motion Picture Code] will not bring the millennium, true," Rosenblatt told his nervous hosts. "But it will help, so we can go forward and wipe out the wrong practices." The wrong practices to be wiped out were business as usual—cutthroat competition against outsiders, cozy monopoly for insiders. Rosenblatt claimed not to be interested in "regulation, interference, or censorship," but the whole purpose of the New Deal economic codes was to regulate and interfere with normal capitalist practice.

On January 30, 1934, the MPPDA arranged a private meeting between Rosenblatt and the three men who best knew the operation of the Production Code—Colonel Jason S. Joy, Dr. James A. Wingate, and Breen. Like anyone who sat across a table from Breen, Rosenblatt was impressed: with his dynamic personality, his commitment to screen morality, and his grasp of the intricate gears of the studio machinery. Again, no transcript exists of this second pivotal face-off between the NRA and the MPPDA, but Breen certainly argued that the work of censorship should be a private affair, a matter of Hollywood self-regulation rather than Washington edict, and Rosenblatt certainly concluded that Breen was the man for the job.

That evening, speaking before the Western Association of Motion Picture Advertisers, Rosenblatt waved a New Deal carrot and stick. "I am opposed to government regulation of this phase of the industry [that is, the moral content of motion pictures] and I am opposed to the snooping activities of certain reforming organizations," he began encouragingly, before lowering the boom: "Yet unless the facts are faced and present indications are taken into account, the industry is set for plenty of trouble." And who, pray, might head off that trouble? "Breen was one of the few persons who strongly impressed Sol A. Rosenblatt when latter was here with his censor[ship expertise] and candid knowledge of working conditions and his familiarity with purposes and intent of the Code so far as moral cleanup is concerned," reported *Variety*, after the New Dealer had left town.

On February 5, 1934, less than a week after Rosenblatt's visit, Breen was formally appointed to head the Studio Relations Committee. The official announcement was made after the annual meeting of the Association of Motion Picture Producers and the wording ("Joseph I. Breen has been appointed to represent Will Hays and the Motion Picture Producers and Distributors of America on matters pertaining to the Production Code and the Advertising Code") indicated what was already afoot: a reorganization of the hapless Studio Relations Committee into a new, as yet unnamed and unformed agency, under the wing of the MPPDA, not the AMPP. Breen "was found by the producers group to be the most satisfactory person on the court to handle stories and scripts from a censorship angle," *Daily Variety* reported. "This finding was okayed by Sol Rosenblatt. It was pointed out that the means employed by Breen in selling a producer on the idea of elimination were forceful and effective." The weekly edition of *Variety* also directly linked Breen's promotion to Rosenblatt's pressure. "Breen's position [as head of the SRC] provides for his approving all scripts and films made by majors and indie producers. This is at the suggestion of Rosenblatt, who will insist that code enforcement be done [according to] the machinery set up by Breen. The administrator deems this the best method for carrying out the purpose of the code than if a commission be set up for the handling of the independent end of this matter." Breen now had two powerful backers in his corner: the Catholics and the New Dealers.

"I tried to evade this responsibility, chiefly because it is an almost impossible task, but Hays insisted," a disingenuous Breen told Bishop McNicholas. "He seems to feel that with what little worthwhile tradition and background I have, added to my well-known Gaelic disposition to strike out a bit vigorously, some headway can be made." Of course, Breen had been maneuvering for the job since arriving in Hollywood—seething at the insolence of the sacrilegious moguls, itching to launch some "real Catholic action."

Upon assuming control of the SRC, Breen immediately tightened the screws, signaling *finis* to the days of the flexible Colonel Joy or the feckless Dr. Wingate. "I am trying to do something under the Production Code, but the going is tough," he told Parsons. "I am hopeful of doing something, to lessen, at least, the flow of filth, but I have no illusions about the problem."

After only two months on the job, Breen had rejected six pictures—as many as had been rejected under Joy and Wingate together during the previous three years. Producers bowed to Breen's objections in four of the instances and appealed his decisions twice. In both cases, Breen was overruled by the Producers Appeal Board.

The first incident involved a Fox musical with the risible title *Bottoms Up* (1934). After Breen rejected the film, producer B. G. "Buddy" DeSylva appealed the decision to the three-man producers jury made up of his colleagues Jack Warner (Warner Bros.), Harry Cohn (Columbia), and Emanuel Cohen (Paramount). Closing ranks, the trio obligingly overruled the SRC and gave a thumbs up to *Bottoms Up*. (After winning the appeal, DeSylva, sensing the future downside to crossing Breen, decided voluntarily to eliminate the objectionable scene.)

The other, more consequential dispute erupted during January 1934 in the interregnum between Breen's de facto and de jure control of the SRC. The arena for the battle of wills was a lavish costume drama from MGM, *Queen Christina* (1933), a star vehicle for Greta Garbo directed by the Russian-born master Rouben Mamoulian and produced by Walter Wanger, a class-act impresario destined to tangle with Breen for the next two decades. The film featured the regal Swedish goddess playing a tomboy Swedish monarch who falls hard for a dashing Spanish envoy (John Gilbert), a star-crossed affair blocked by her malevolent ministers and xenophobic peasantry.

The morning after: Nordic monarch (Greta Garbo) and Spanish envoy (John Gilbert) bask in the glow of an illicit affair in Rouben Mamoulian's *Queen Christina* (1933), produced by Walter Wanger.

Plenty about the courtly intrigues warranted disapproval from the new management at the Studio Relations Committee: a male valet attends the queen at bed; the queen bestows a wet kiss on her lady-in-waiting; a buxom serving wench is groped by drunken soldiers; and an innkeeper moonlights as a pimp. Carefully drawing his line in the sand, Breen focused his objections on a sexy tryst between the queen and the envoy.

The coupling revolved around a bit of unlikely gender confusion when the chilly Swede, incognito both in status and sex, encounters the hot-blooded Spaniard in a snowbound inn. Clothed in mannish attire, she is mistaken for a young lad, so why shouldn't the youth and the envoy spend the night together in the only available bed in the inn? "Aren't you going to undress?" inquires the Spaniard, when the two are behind closed doors. "Yes," whispers his demure companion, who unbuttons her jacket to reveal her feminine contours. The Spaniard is momentarily startled—and then delighted.

The next morning, the couple snuggles in bed, concealed from view by bed curtains, but the elated voice of the Spaniard from behind the drapery makes clear he is not alone. In fact, the inn being snowbound, he is not alone for three days of very unwedded bliss. After the 72-hour sleepover, still ecstatic, Garbo slinks around the bedroom, glowing with postcoital rapture, caressing the furniture, to imprint every detail of the magic idyll in her memory. The extended foreplay and languid aftertaste—the couple entering the bedroom, the tango before disrobing for bed, the unveiling of the queen's true identity, the lovers hidden from sight but snuggling in bed the next morning, and Garbo's radiance while gliding around the love nest—pulsate with erotic heat.

Breen wanted the entire sequence left on the cutting-room floor. In italics, he told MGM to delete "all the intervening scenes, action, and dialogue which are played *in the bedroom*" and to make sure Garbo was "*kept away entirely from the bed.*" To Louis B. Mayer, Breen explained that the Gilbert-Garbo tryst was too guilt-free to stand. "Sexual immorality is here presented as 'attractive and beautiful' and is made to appear 'right and permissible,' and thus comes the definite Code violation."

Besides raising Breen's hackles, the case of *Queen Christina* highlighted the design flaws in the Code's mechanism. Though Wanger had dutifully sent a script to the SRC for review and politely listened to suggestions for revision, he had simply ignored the advice. "It is quite apparent from the examination of the files that Mr. Wanger paid very little attention to our several letters on this [bedroom sequence], or what was said at the conference between himself, Colonel Joy, or Dr. Wingate," Breen complained, after viewing the completed film, with the bedroom *pas de deux* intact.

With Wanger and Breen irreconcilable, the kabuki show commenced: Breen held *Queen Christina* in violation of the Code, Wanger appealed the decision, the AMPP appointed a producers jury comprised of Wanger's colleagues B. B. Kahane (RKO), Jesse Lasky (Paramount), and Carl Laemmle (Universal), and the jury overruled Breen. "Joe and I had hoped that the Jury would agree with us that some further deletions were necessary in the bedroom scenes, but we were satisfied [that is, resigned] to let the matter lie as is," Colonel Joy told MPPDA official Earl Bright. (By then, the amiable Colonel Joy had walked through a revolving door to work at MGM.) Actually, the end run around the Code was less kabuki show than bedroom farce: even before Wanger's appeal was decided by the producers jury, indeed even as Breen pleaded with Mayer to cut the picture, *Queen Christina* was playing a roadshow engagement at the Astor Theater in New York.

Despite his five-for-six average, Breen steamed over the film that had gotten away. "The task is really an impossible one, as we are now constituted," he realized. "I can scold and argue and coax and threaten *but I have no real authority* to stop the dirty pictures." However vigilant the SRC, the tight-knit producers closed ranks to block enforcement. "Our machinery calls for the right of appeal to a jury made up of three producers, brothers-in-arms to the guy whose picture I may reject," Breen explained to Parsons. "This jury, you may be certain, is not likely to concur in any decision of rejection." He knew that a self-regulatory system worthy of the name required a realignment of the command structure, away from the producers and toward the regulators. "As matters now stand," he concluded, "the appeal to a jury of *producers* simply [doesn't] work out. The producers are [not] willing to condemn a picture made by a fellow producer—and the dirty pictures continue to be made."

As Breen struggled behind enemy lines, his allies on the field launched an attack that, if not exactly instigated by Breen, went forward with his encouragement and worked to his advantage. Suddenly, Catholics seemed to be everywhere—except at the movies. In Chicago, Cardinal Mundelein warned Catholics that patronizing "debasing pictures" constituted "a grave offense against the moral law." In St. Louis, Bishop John J. Glennon urged membership in the Legion and called films "an education only in immorality, crime, and lawlessness." In Breen's hometown of Philadelphia, Denis Cardinal Dougherty ordered the faithful to boycott Hollywood films—not just the immoral films, but *all* films as "perhaps the greatest menace to faith and morals in America today." In every parochial school, every parish, and every diocese, Catholics read the pastoral letters and recited the Legion pledge. Enough of the chorus stood by the words to further drain an already parched box office.

Motion picture producers had weathered boycotts and brickbats since 1895, but the uproar later remembered as "the crisis of '34" or "the storm of '34" was unprecedented in single-minded ferocity and popular appeal. "One of the amazing features of the [Catholic] boycott campaign is the amount of publicity given the move by daily papers throughout the country," shuddered *Billboard*, the entertainment trade weekly. "It is doubtful any similar move ever received the unanimous cooperation of the press as this boycott." Moreover, "practically all Protestant and Jewish denominations have joined the move and expect to have as many signers as Catholics."

That last alarum was an exaggeration, but a shared hatred of Hollywood united Judeo-Christian congregations across religious lines. Not wishing to appear slackers in the great moral crusade, Protestants and Jews hastened to hurl their own invective at Hollywood. The Catholic crusade "has touched levels of conviction lying far below our religious divisions" judging from "the widespread response of both Protestants and Jews to the Catholic leadership," the *Christian Century* noted approvingly. Agreed the *Catholic Telegraph:* "A specially gratifying feature of the movement is the wholehearted cooperation of our Protestant and Jewish fellow citizens." The last time so many righteous citizens had gotten so agitated, the result was the Eighteenth Amendment to the U.S. Constitution.

As the Catholics turned up the heat, and Protestants and Jews gladly joined in, the moguls vacillated between bravado and panic. "We have them on the run, to be sure, but the running, so far, is only a dog-trot," gloated Breen, smelling blood in May 1934, "[but] they have not awakened fully to the seriousness of the situation ... we still have a long way to go."

In truth, Breen and the Catholics were within sight of their promised land. On June 21, 1934, a special conference of the Catholic Bishops Committee on Motion Pictures was scheduled to meet in Cincinnati, Ohio, to plan the next move in the hardball campaign. With box office hemorrhaging in the Catholic strongholds in the big cities and with the New Dealers contemplating an alphabet agency especially for Hollywood, Hays, Breen, and Quigley tossed out a lifeline to the moguls.

Prior to the Bishop's conference, on June 13, 1934, the Board of Directors of the MPPDA had met in New York and unanimously passed a resolution creating a new enforcement regime, the Production Code Administration, "to strengthen in every reasonable way the effectiveness" of the Code. Any member company of the MPPDA (all the major studios) and any producer using the distribution facilities of the majors (thus, any respectable independent) would be bound to process its product through "the Production Code Administration" and acquire a stamped "Certificate of Approval." A violation of the rules would incur a fine of $25,000 for "disrupt[ing] the stability of the industry and caus[ing] serious damage to all members of the Association." Breen (officially) and Quigley (unofficially) were tasked with selling the deal to the bishops in Cincinnati. Hays told the pair that "the Catholic authorities can have anything they want," which was hardly necessary for the Catholic duo wanted exactly what the bishops wanted, namely for Hollywood to clean house and Breen to hold the broom. "The stage is set for a magnificent piece of worthwhile Catholic action and achievement," exulted Breen.

Breen and Quigley got unwitting help from an unlikely source: Mae West. While the Catholics conferred in Cincinnati, the poster girl for pre-Code bawdiness was releasing her third smut-cracking comedy, a fin de siècle burlesque entitled *It Ain't No Sin*. Breen had wrestled with the project months before, deeming West's third strike "a vulgar and highly offensive yarn which is quite patently a glorification of prostitution and violent crime without any compensating moral values of any kind." On June 6, 1934, he reluctantly passed the film, whereupon the MPPDA pronounced it "completely clean and interesting entertainment." However, being preceded by West's reputation, the indefinite pronoun in the film title invited idle curiosity about the antecedent. "What ain't no sin?" queried the press, eyebrows arched. "It means nothing," West purred. Dirty-minded grammarians thought otherwise. That the new Mae West picture with the fill-in-the-blank title was slated to hit theaters during the bishops' meeting in Cincinnati was not the kind of publicity tie-in Paramount desired.

With Mae West in the headlines, Catholics at the barricades, and the New Deal on the march, the bishops held all the cards. Besides, Breen and Quigley were playing with their poker hands face up anyway. The four prelates at the table—Archbishop John T. McNicholas of Cincinnati, Bishop Cantwell, Bishop John F. Knoll of Fort Wayne, and Bishop Hugh C. Boyle of Pittsburgh—retired to Bishop McNicholas's residence to huddle with Breen and Quigley and cut the deal. In cloth and in mufti, the coreligionists approved a censorship regime that ceded dominion of Hollywood cinema to Irish-Catholic theology for the next twenty years.

Not about to be fooled again, the bishops carefully inspected the fine print. To all appearances, the MPPDA had locked the studios into an airtight contract. The Producers Appeal Board was eliminated: no longer would Jack Warner scratch the back of Harry Cohn who scratched the back

Pre-Code Hollywood's "smut-cracking" agent provocateur: Mae West, flanked by Paramount president Adolph Zukor (*left*) and director Leo McCarey on the set of what was still called *It Ain't No Sin* in 1934.

of Emanuel Cohen. To replace the discredited Studio Relations Committee, an entirely new agency was created: the Production Code Administration, the name underscoring the centrality of the document. A decision by the PCA could be appealed only to the Board of Directors of the MPPDA back in New York—away from the domain of the Hollywood moguls and into the sphere of the Wall Street moneymen. Defiant producers and member theaters were not only to be held in a kind of corporate contempt and fined $25,000, but the loans, investments, and promissory notes from the east that funded motion picture production out west would be tied to compliance with the self-regulatory system. Without approval from the PCA, the Hollywood studios forfeited financing and bookings.

Breen's regulatory authority would flow from New York, not Hollywood: no longer a factotum, he would sit at the table with the moguls as an equal partner—actually, more than equal. Without Breen, Hollywood could not do business.

The second key modification established a rigorous review process for film projects prior to production. "Certainly, if there is a censorship, it should be done at that time," figured W. R. (Billy) Wilkerson, the influential editor and publisher of the *Hollywood Reporter*, speaking for the consensus. "Once time and money have been expended in production, it is fatal to have that production sliced to ribbons by censors' shears, causing a destruction of thousands of dollars, money that could and would have been saved if the slicing had been done from the script." Before the cameras ever rolled, the fix would be in.

Taken together, the two design renovations—the transfer of power from producers to regulators and the application of the Code during the script phase of production—created a smooth, conveyer-belt system for the censorship of studio films. The mechanism served the needs of commerce and morality, art not being a party to the negotiations.

A third element, not written into the contract but a crucial part of the deal, was Breen himself. The bishops wanted a soldier from the Church militant to keep the moguls in line; the moguls wanted a man who knew the motion picture business. No rival candidate for the job, equally acceptable to the Church hierarchy and the Hollywood executives, was even considered. Three years after landing a full-time job with the MPPDA, Breen had made himself an indispensable man.

At the end of the conference, the victorious bishops issued a conciliatory statement expressing satisfaction that "the producer's jury in Hollywood, a part of the original machinery for enforcement of the Production Code . . . has been abandoned and that additional local authority [namely Breen] has been assigned to the Code administration." The boycott was not officially called off—Hollywood was still on strict probation—but tempers cooled, pickets dispersed, and parish priests stopped lurking around theater fronts.

After the deal went down in Cincinnati, Hays traveled to Hollywood to inform the AMPP of the fait accompli negotiated by the parent organization. On July 11, 1934, after a tense six-hour meeting, the AMPP formally acceded to the plan that had already been approved by the MPPDA and accepted by the bishops.

Scared straight by Legion boycotts and New Deal threats, the members of the MPPDA Board sent instructions back to the moguls to do absolutely nothing to queer the deal. "If Joe Breen tells you to change a picture, you do what he tells you," Harry Warner wired the studio he cofounded. "If any one fails to do this—and this goes for my brother—he's fired."

"We went [to Cincinnati] to explain our problems," Breen said afterward, for the record. "We would have been glad to get a truce, of course. [The bishops] heard us out and asked us many questions that showed they were men of unusual ability and understanding. After I had explained to Bishop Boyle of Pittsburgh the problems we face in censoring films, he said to me, 'I'm glad you have to do it and not I.'" So was Breen.

Breen now stood as supreme sentinel and inspector general of American cinema. Henceforth no Hollywood film received a visa for exhibition without meeting Code specifications as interpreted by Joseph I. Breen.

WILL HAYS THE SECOND, THE HITLER OF HOLLYWOOD, THE MUSSOLINI OF AMERICAN FILMS, THE DICTATOR OF MOVIE MORALS, ETC.

With the Code mechanism locked in place, and a vigilant watchman at the controls, the MPPDA launched a public relations campaign to persuade the editorialists, politicians, and priests that this time Hollywood—chastened and converted—had truly repented. "From the bottom of its trunk, Hollywood today dug up a tattered, forgotten code of morals and prepared to put it into effect Sunday [July 15, 1934]," read the lead from the United Press wire report, reflecting the wary wait-and-see attitude. To persuade once-burned skeptics that the Production Code Administration was not another cynical ruse by Hollywood hustlers, Breen was put forward as the front man for the newly firmed-up moral backbone—a brief twirl in the spotlight he would shun ever after. "To all intents and purposes, Breen will be built up as Will Hays the Second, First Keeper of Hollywood Morals," reported *Variety*. The buildup involved an elaborate multimedia strategy starring Breen in person, in print, on the radio, and on screen.

The campaign opened with a calculated piece of performance art. On July 9 and 10, 1934, Hays and Breen spent two days visiting the major studios—meeting with production heads, strolling through sound stages, and looking at dailies. Of course, the pair couldn't tell much from a quick walk-through of the sets or a once-over of the rushes; the purpose of the two-man tour was to demonstrate that Breen was Hays's enforcer and that both men meant business.

Over the next weeks, Breen granted numerous interviews to newspapers and magazines to expound on the PCA. In the future, "Hollywood will be very careful," he promised. "There is no excuse for the wrong kind of picture and we do make some which are the wrong kind. Every decent man and woman in the business deplores the wrong type and there is a definite movement within the industry itself to ensure reasonably acceptable entertainment." Breen was already casting himself in the dual role of people's guardian and filmmaker's friend, the impartial arbiter between two squabbling factions prone to misunderstand each other's motives.

Breen's media roll-out ran into a few bumps. Despite a lifetime in journalism and public relations work, he had never personally been under the intense magnifying glass focused on all things Hollywood. Thrust suddenly into the headlines, the loquacious Irishman sometimes spouted off imprudently. "Theodore Roosevelt coined the term 'lunatic fringe' for a certain type of reformer and politician, and the present [censorship] movement now seems to have attracted its share of that type," he commented in an unguarded moment. The Legion of Decency bristled at the "lunatic fringe" crack and the religious press snapped back. "Breen talks too much," chided *Christian Century*, and even fellow Catholics rapped his knuckles. "We think Mr. Breen has been unfortunate in his statements and to that extent has forfeited the confidence that was rallying around him and his office," said his kinsmen at Chicago's *New World*.

Breen hastily backtracked. The former PR expert realized he had walked onto a stage far more conspicuous than either the Eucharistic Congress or the Chicago World's Fair; any verbal misstep brought down a firestorm of recriminations. However intemperate Breen's tirades in letters and private conversations might be in later years, his remarks on the record were chosen with care. Generally, he simply kept his head down and declined to comment.

Not, however, until the sales campaign for the PCA was completed. On August 29, 1934, Breen entered the studios of Hollywood's main competition for the first of a series of four half-hour radio shows, two in the evening (for the widest listening audience) and two in the afternoon (for housewives and clubwomen). The forum came courtesy of NBC president M. H. Aylesworth, who donated the airtime.

On the first show, between musical interludes from Meredith Willson and his Orchestra and light banter with the actors Lionel Barrymore and Irene Dunne, Breen delivered a ten-minute spiel underscoring two points he would make for the next twenty years: first, that the PCA was *not* censorship but "self-regulation"; and second, that compliance with the Code would not mean a decline in motion picture quality—which, he insisted, was higher than ever—but an elevation of artistic standards. He drummed home the same message in his next three appearances (on August 31, September 5, and September 7), which teamed him in turn with comedian Joe E. Brown, actor John Boyles, and Mrs. T. G. Winter, formerly president of the General Federation of Women's Clubs and currently co-opted as a shill for the MPPDA. "Breen was talking on the air for the first time and gave an excellent account of himself," judged *Variety*. "His 'copy' was good and his delivery strong."

The final medium in the public relations blitz was, of course, film. Breen warranted a plum role reserved for only a select few in politics, business, and the arts—a direct address from the newsreel screen, a star appearance that showed how heavily the industry had invested in the PCA. Hays, who had gone before the newsreels to proclaim Hollywood's commitment to

As part of the MPPDA's public relations campaign for the Production Code Administration, Breen poses with Irene Dunne and Lionel Barrymore before their broadcast over NBC radio on August 29, 1934. The smudges and chalk lines on the photo are compositor's marks.

(URBAN ARCHIVES / TEMPLE UNIVERSITY)

morality in 1930, had been discredited by the next four years; a new face, unblemished by the pre-Code era, needed to front for the reformation. On August 24, 1934, Breen and his staff performed before a Fox Movietone camera crew, a session that resulted in two newsreel segments released the next month: one a direct address from Breen alone, the other a brief glimpse of the full PCA staff sitting around a conference table.

In both clips, Breen performed like a trouper. A practiced public speaker, he exhibits none of the stricken deer-in-the-headlights demeanor of so many non-pros on the newsreel screen. Framed in a single long take, maintaining eye contact and enunciating in a crisp tenor, he faces the camera and minces no words. "All of the motion picture production companies in the United States have joined hands in adopting what has come to be known as a Production Code of Ethics," he declared, not mentioning that the motion picture production companies had already joined hands once before in 1930 only to let go immediately afterward. A reasonable man facing reasonable people, he makes the case and explains the particulars:

> [The Code's] broad general purpose is to insure screen entertainment which will be reasonably acceptable to our patrons everywhere—entertainment which is definitely free from offense. Now of course this doesn't mean that we are to impose upon you any unreasonable restrictions in the development of the art which is the motion picture. This does not mean that motion pictures are not to deal with live and vital subjects, stories based upon drama which is vigorous and stimulating, as well as entertaining. Neither does it mean that we are to make pictures only for children.

Warming to his rhetoric, he closes with a sharp warning:

> But it *does* mean quite definitely that the vulgar, the cheap, and the tawdry is out! There is no room on the screen at any time for pictures which offend against common decency—and these the industry will not allow.

Two weeks later, the second newsreel segment hit screens, a vignette set at the Production Code Administration's offices. Center screen, in medium shot, now wearing eyeglasses, Breen is no longer the stern preacher but the kindly spiritual adviser. "It may interest you to sit in with us at a meeting of the Production Code Administration in Hollywood, where we are working for finer and better motion pictures," he suggests, a solicitous host to moviegoers awaiting the main feature.

A cut to a wide shot reveals Breen sitting at the head of a conference table before a phalanx of Code men, arranged evenly on each side of a table with Breen framed front and center. The staff, comprised of Dr. James Wingate, Geoffrey Shurlock, Douglas Mackinnon, Islin Auster, Karl Lischka, Arthur Houghton, and Jack Lewis, serves as wax mannequins, with no lines of dialogue or reaction shots. The star speaks:

> Our job, as I see it, is quite simple. Nobody expects us to impose upon the public motion pictures which are dull or are lacking in vitality or vigor. No intelligent person will argue that we are to make pictures only for children. We must have stories with power and punch and backbone. At the same time, we must be on the lookout for scenes, action, or dialogue which are likely to give offense. The responsible men in this industry want no such pictures and will not allow these to be shown.

The voice of sweet reason from the avuncular fellow continues:

> You will understand that our Production Code Administration is not a one-man censorship. It represents the considered judgment of many persons of wide experience and a sincere interest in making motion pictures. From the very beginning of the picture, we work with producers, authors, scenario writers, directors and all who are connected with the production to the end that the finished product may be free from reasonable objection and that our pictures may be the vital and wholesome entertainment we all want these to be.

Outtakes from the sessions show Breen obligingly reciting his lines, again and again, as the camera moves in for close-ups and coverage. He never flubs a line.

Looking at Breen's film debut, *Billboard* columnist Len Morgan thought the MPPDA had blundered by lending "the most valuable publicity medium, the newsreels, to their opponents," the clips being a tacit admission that the pre-Code era was every bit as corrosive as the moral guardians claimed. "In practically every theater in the country Joe's noble features will grace the screen and he will bring up the subject of taking salacious films from the theaters and with great gusto and gesticulation tell the movie public that the Hays organization will never, never tolerate the minds of this great commonwealth to be corrupted by dirty pictures." Morgan speculated that the cagey ex-newspaperman had let his vanity overrule his better judgment. "We can't understand why Joe permitted himself to be used as the newsreel spokesman for the industry. With all due respect to Joe, the camera does not do him justice. We caught his act in several theaters and there was no thunderous applause following his movie debut." Besides, jibed

Morgan, "we do not believe that Joe took a flyer in pictures in the hope that he might be picked up by Metro to play the lead with Garbo." The tyro actor got a kinder notice in the trade paper that mattered most. "Joe Breen's second subject on picture morality is better, technically at least, than the first," *Variety* opined. "He surrounds himself with his staff, and when he undergoes the close-up ordeal he gets over the fact that more minds than one make up the industry's self-censorship machine."

That last point needed to be emphasized because, on second thought, the Breen-centric buildup contradicted a central tenet of the MPPDA's public relations agenda: that the PCA expressed the considered judgments of a diverse jury of sound moralists, not the verdict of a single pair of eyes—especially not those of a militant Catholic dispatched from the incense-filled rooms of a bishop's residence in Cincinnati. In putting Breen so far forward, the MPPDA campaign was perhaps too effective. "Joe Breen is the banishing American," punned the syndicated columnist Sidney Skolsky, splashing the sort of ink that could make a man a household name despite himself.

In the long run, the PCA was not to be known by a face—not Breen's, not even Hays's—but by a sign. The visible mark of quality control was a quite literal Production Code Seal of Approval, an oval logo encircling the MPPDA's initials. Hays had promised the bishops' committee that an emblem would serve as certification of PCA-approved films and that Hollywood would "give wide publicity to the use of this emblem in its various announcements." Like the wax imprimatur affixed to books approved by the Catholic Church (*nihil obstat* read the Latin inscription: "nothing stands in the way"), the Code Seal stamped Hollywood cinema as fit for clear passage.

True to Hays's word, the studios prominently showcased the Code Seal on a separate frame prior to the title credits of the initial lot of certified films. Upon first sight of the sign, however, its ostensible constituency did not burst into applause. In more than one theater, audiences greeted the emblem with jeering, booing, and what the *Hollywood Reporter* called "a good community 'hiss.'" In 1935, the point made, and perhaps to silence the raspberries, the Code Seal was shrunk and mounted inconspicuously on the title credits, usually the technical credits, on the bottom left. The change, insisted the MPPDA, was "to obviate the extra running time required by having the seal on a separate frame."

Any grumbling from the groundlings was drowned out by the cheering from the box seats. Mrs. Eleanor Roosevelt devoted her debut broadcast as a radio commentator neither to New Deal policies nor European fascism, but to Hollywood's reformation. "I am extremely happy the film industry has appointed a censor within its own ranks, Mr. Joseph Breen, assistant to

The Code Seal: the full-frame imprimatur of the Breen Office, later shrunk to a small oval at the bottom of the screen credits.

(ACADEMY OF MOTION PICTURE ARTS AND SCIENCES)

Will H. Hays," Mrs. Roosevelt declared, not yet with the program in her word choice. "It has long been a question of great interest to women's organizations, particularly, of course, because of the fact that moving pictures are so popular with children."

Whether jeered or cheered, the Code, Breen, and the Code Seal were now an integral part of the motion picture program. Repeated in person and print, on the radio airwaves, and from the newsreel screen, the message sank in. "The one thing in his brief talk that stands out is that vulgarity is through in the picture business," concluded *Variety*'s man on the newsreel beat, who also noted that Breen's explanation of the PCA "was non-committedly received by Saturday matinee audiences" watching at the Embassy Newsreel Theater in New York. At least no one hissed.

4

THE BREEN OFFICE

After July 15, 1934, what was quickly dubbed "the Breen Office" became a transit point for Hollywood cinema as essential as the laboratories processing the 35mm film stock. Far from being an impediment, the in-house censorship regime facilitated the artistic creativity and industrial efficiency of the vaunted Golden Age of Hollywood. The Breen Office maintained the gold standard by helping the major studios refine the substance, polish the surface, and corner the market.

What fueled the studio system machine—and what validated the work of the Breen Office—was a sudden infusion of cash into corporate coffers. By the close of 1934, after four long years of lean harvests, box office revenues had surged upward. As if triggered by the launch date of the Production Code Administration, revenues reversed the free fall and soared into the black. Thereafter, almost alone of the major manufacturers stunted by the Great Depression, the motion picture industry flourished in its own bull market.

The turnabout from pre-Code penury to post-Code prosperity suggested an instructive cause and effect. Smug with vindication, moral guardians trumpeted the connection between cleaner motion pictures and robust box office. As grateful educators shepherded flocks of school children to *Little Women* (1933), *Treasure Island* (1934), and *David Copperfield* (1935), prestigious literary adaptations that earned profits while fostering good will, the moguls shrugged and admitted that business was up and trouble was down.

The baton pass between two female stars embodied the realignment. By year's end, six-year-old Shirley Temple had elbowed aside the forty-something Mae West as the number one box office attraction. Temple, whose very name shimmered with religiosity, was a phenomenon of unprecedented and still unrivaled magnitude in Hollywood history: presexual innocence and robotic talent, a celluloid wunderkind who, until undone by puberty, was the true golden girl of 1930s Hollywood, spawning a cycle of sure-fire musical-comedy-melodramas and a growth industry in ancillary marketing spin-offs, none more symbolic and desired than the must-have Christmas gift of 1934, the Shirley Temple doll. Eyeing the bottom line, the moguls figured better to cash in the easy way with the adorable moppet tap-dancing on the Good Ship Lollipop than the hard way with the wild West sashaying up a saloon staircase.

No wonder the early reviews of the Breen Office ranged from glowing to giddy. The two rotating front-page columnists at the *Hollywood Reporter*, editor-publisher Billy Wilkerson and veteran trade reporter Frank Pope, competed to give thanks and lavish superlatives. "Every producer in this village will agree that Breen has steered a marvellous, even course in administering his office," raved Wilkerson. "A man with less diplomacy, less tact, and no conception of the great essential of successful pictures—showmanship—would never have lasted a week in Breen's job." Agreed Pope: "Probably no one except Breen knows how he has had to fight, knows how much opposition he met, and he won't talk about it. But if ever the right man was placed in the right job, Joe Breen seems to be that man."

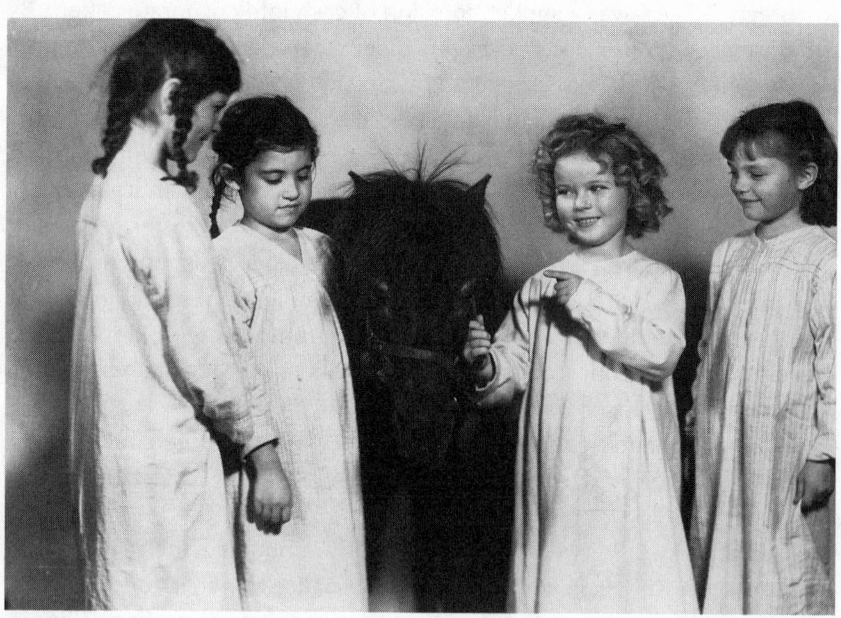

Out with Mae West: Shirley Temple, symbol of Hollywood's new morality, in a publicity shot from *Curly Top* (1935).

Other trade voices chimed in to praise the firm hand at the helm. "Few people realize what Mr. Breen has done for the motion picture industry unless they know the inside workings of the system," wrote Pete Harrison in his newsletter *Harrison's Reports*. "In less than six months time he has been able to do what Will H. Hays was not able to do, or at least he did not do, in twelve years. This statement may prove embarrassing to Mr. Breen but that is the way I feel about the matter." Even the sardonic *Variety* emphasized the connection between moral self-policing and economic self-interest. "It is difficult today, when one sees again the lines in front of box offices, and nearby parking spaces jammed, to appreciate how great was the fall and how high the rise has been," the editors recalled in 1936, looking back with dread on the "stormy days of 1932–33," the commercial nadir and immoral zenith of the pre-Code era. The showbiz bible attributed the reversal to the fact "that the quality of films has improved immeasurably, due entirely to intra-industry precautions and regulations [namely the PCA]."

The good news got better. The men in Washington no longer threatened the moguls in Hollywood with the sword of federal censorship. Reporting to FDR in 1938, the National Resources Committee showered praise on a medium so lately considered invidious. "At first, the motion picture was widely regarded as making for standardization at a vulgar level," concluded the New Dealers. "Now it is often hailed as a medium of cultural advance."

The state censors were also stymied by the sanitation job done at the source. A half dozen state boards still operated, and local philistines in places like Atlanta and Memphis still sliced and banned, but, crucially, the number of state boards did not grow and the trend line for the municipal boards was down. "Ever since the Joe Breen office on the Coast began to function and do a pretty thorough job of keeping films clear of any dangerous shoals, state censor boards all over the U.S. . . . have had less and less to do," *Variety* noted with relief in 1939. Once a chronic migraine, the censorship boards receded into a low-level headache.

The priests concurred with the press and the politicians. "The greatness of Joseph I. Breen's performance lies in this: not only has he wiped the screen clean of obscenities, but also—and the Legion believes this to be far more important—he has scotched the teaching of moral heresy," declared Breen's Jesuit support group at *America*, hammering home the core principle of Catholic censorship. "If the Catholic press, like *Time*, were picking the man of the year, it would doubtless hasten to name Joseph I. Breen, the enforcing agent of the Code."

Awash in black ink, no longer ducking brickbats as smut merchants and vice peddlers, skeptical studio executives became true believers. When first forced to submit to the Breen Office, a cigar-chomping mogul snarled, "You can't kick love, sex, and crime out of pictures and expect to get people into theaters." Yet people were mobbing the theaters—lining up for Code-approved pictures that caused no thorny controversy and garnered plenty of rosy bouquets. Had the lost audience returned to vote a mandate for cleaner, family-friendly pictures? Had the huge costs of retooling for sound technology in the late 1920s and the painful retrenchments of the early 1930s finally begun paying a return on investments? Had the same cultural impulse for stability and regulation that propelled FDR to Washington paved the way for the PCA in Hollywood? At the close of 1934, the reason was less important than the result. Profits and morality, cash flow and respectability—against all expectations, Hollywood was raking in the wages of salvation. Though born and billed as good for the soul, the Breen Office turned out to be very good for business.

OFFICE WORK

Located on the fourth floor of the offices of the Motion Picture Producers and Distributors of America at North 5504 Hollywood Boulevard, Hollywood 28, California, the Breen Office hummed with the ambient noise of a bustling bureaucracy in the middle third of the twentieth century, before Xerox, FedEx, and Microsoft had revolutionized document duplication and paper pushing.[1] In motion picture terms, the scene was less like the pressure-cooker bedlam of the newspaper racket in *His Girl Friday* (1941) than the steady rhythms of the insurance company in *Double Indemnity* (1944), where male executives gave dictation and the rat-tat-tat of manual typewriters clicked out fifty words per minute with sufficient force to penetrate two layers of carbon paper. The only shouting came from behind the door of the private office of the floor supervisor, when Breen was barking on the telephone to a producer as stubborn as he was.

Upon taking formal command, Breen's first order of business was strictly administrative: to put the internal bureaucracy into crisp working order. The old Studio Relations Committee, first under Colonel Jason Joy (1926–1932) and then under Dr. James Wingate (1932–1934) was underfunded, understaffed, and ill managed. Breen Office budgets were commensurate with the workload and importance, the lion's share of MPPDA dues going to the

1. In 1950 the Breen Office moved to the swank new headquarters of what was now called the Motion Picture Association of America, Inc., at 8480 Beverly Boulevard, Hollywood 48, California.

PCA. Like every department head, Breen complained about tight budgets and low salaries for himself and his staff, but with the PCA the MPPDA put its money where its rhetoric was.[2]

First and foremost, a tight ship meant the speedy turnaround of screen treatments and film scripts, a smooth conveyor-belt process moving the paper from in-basket to out-basket. Before 1934, on-site censorship was often performed only after the censors had eyeballed the film—an expensive and inefficient practice that squandered vast sums in postproduction editing and reshooting. The hassle and expenses assessed outside of Hollywood (banned screenings, restricted admissions, and shredded prints) were even more costly. To head off trouble, 35mm prints of likely controversies, such as Howard Hughes's *Scarface* (1932) and Walter Wanger's *Queen Christina* (1933), were sent to the state boards prior to release on a kind of preemptive censorship tour.

Under the Breen Office, the chosen medium for censorship was paper not celluloid. "Our *work*—the real work that we do—is concerned principally with the story, weeks and sometimes months, before the date on which the actual production of the film begins," Breen emphasized. "Three fourths of the time spent by the members of our staff have to do with the examination, study and discussion of story material before a move is made by the studio to cast the picture, or to start building the sets." He likened the sessions to university seminars in the close textual analysis of Hollywood literature. "And thus has come about a most intensive study of books, plays, original stories, and sometimes a simple idea that can be set down in 250 words or less."

The print-centricity was calculated to give New York, and therefore the Breen Office, tighter control over day-to-day Hollywood business. "A written record is essential," Hays's assistant Maurice McKenzie told Breen when the PCA opened for business. Carbon copies of all Breen Office correspondence with the Hollywood studios were sent to the MPPDA's offices to preempt any "attempt on the part of studio executives to keep from their company heads in New York knowledge of the true situation with regard to

2. The PCA was also funded by the fees assessed for a Code Seal: $50 for a new feature; $25 for reissues; $25 for shorts; and $25 for all foreign pictures. The fees escalated with inflation and a sliding scale was devised, calibrated to the film's budget. In 1954, for Class A films, where the negative cost exceeded $500,000, the fee was $1,150; for Class B films, where the negative cost was between $200,000 and $500,000, the fee was $1,000; for Class C films, where the negative cost was between $150,000 to $200,000, the fee was $600; for Class D films, where the negative cost was between $100,000 to $150,000, the fee was $300; for Class E films, where the negative cost $50,000 to $100,000, the fee was $150. Class F films, where the negative fee was anything less than $50,000, the fee was $100. All shorts were levied $50 for the Code Seal.

pictures and scripts within the studio." Three thousand miles was still a long way from the home office, but the paper trail put the remote production site on a shorter leash.

The preference for the printed page was reflected in the professional and academic backgrounds of the Code staff, many of whom were university-educated, an anomaly in a business dominated by uncredentialed self-made men. In 1934 an impressed Pete Harrison read the sheepskins of the first Code staff: Karl Lischka ("an exceptional linguist [who] has half a dozen college degrees. Previously to his joining Mr. Breen, he was Professor of History and of Educational Psychology of Georgetown University, in Washington, D.C."); Islin Auster ("a college graduate"); Dr. James Wingate ("a college graduate [who] was a member of the Board of Regents, Department of Education of the State of New York, [and] a high school principal for a number of years"); and Mr. Geoffrey Shurlock ("a college graduate, [who] early in his life served as literary secretary to a number of important au-

The original staff of the Production Code Administration in 1934: (*seated, left to right*) Geoffrey Shurlock, Breen, and James Wingate; (*standing, left to right*) Douglas Mackinnon, Carl Lischka, Islin Auster, Arthur Houghton, and John McHugh Stuart.

(URBAN ARCHIVES / TEMPLE UNIVERSITY)

thors, including Rupert Hughes"). Rounding out the first class were John McHugh Stuart ("a successful newspaper man for twenty years"), Arthur Houghton ("for twenty-five years he was connected with the New York legitimate theatre,") and Douglas Mackinnon ("Before joining Mr. Breen he was employed rather successfully, by the Educational Company and by a number of other companies in the production of short subjects.").

The other shared credential was fixed for the entire run of the Breen Office: the staff was a boy's club, woman's work being at the typewriter. The normative sexism of the age explains only part of the exclusivity. After all, women, not men, had long been hallowed as the true moral guardians of the nation. Just as the Women's Christian Temperance Union marched at the head of the parade for Prohibition, the General Federation of Women's Clubs was in lockstep with the National Legion of Decency on the issue of screen morality. Mrs. T.G. Winter, a past president of the General Federation of Women's Clubs, had been placed on the payroll of the Hays Office, pre-Breen. Moreover, women were almost always included in, and often chaired, censorship boards at the state and municipal levels. Even in the context of the 1930s—maybe especially in the context of the 1930s—a woman might have expected to have a reserved seat on the PCA's staff.

However, another Victorian attitude slammed the Breen Office door to female applicants. The hyper-masculinity of the PCA chief and the rough language bandied about the office during negotiations with foul-mouthed producers made the men squeamish about having a woman within earshot. Likely too, Breen avoided hiring a woman because female censors were associated in the popular mind with bluenose spinsters and prune-faced harpies. He referred to the schoolmarmish type as "the *mammon of censorship*, the leaders of Sunday-school groups, the women's clubs, the social welfareites and so forth." Breen and the boys were engaged in the serious business of making roughneck moguls submit to self-regulation—a man's job of work.

To process thousands of potential narratives—preliminary screen treatments, magazine stories, best-selling novels, and original screenplays—Breen set up an assembly-line system. On a typical morning, the day's work began with the staff congregating around a conference table for a "huddle" where projects were assigned, difficulties discussed, and troublespots flagged. Two men were given a copy of each script to read, mark up, make suggestions, and write the official memoranda. A third "outside reader" was consulted to make sure that the two-man team, after prolonged consultation with the filmmakers under review, had not gone native. Said Breen: "Our procedure is a sort of 'Irish Bull' procedure: where there is likely to be any difficulty, or trouble, we endeavor *to stop it before it begins*—"

After the lengthy and meticulous script review process, Breen and trusted members of his staff sat down for the final "print review" stage of the process. Only after eyeballing the final cut of the film, the version that would be released to theaters, would the Code Seal be formally issued. Sometimes, in order to help the studios lock in bookings with theaters committed to playing only PCA-approved films, the Code Seal was issued with a written stipulation that agreed-upon changes would be made prior to release—a token of the good faith and professional courtesy between two teams of serious players.

Breen closely supervised the work product of his staff, personally read all the troublesome scripts, and made the final decisions on policy matters when disputes arose in-house. In the early days, he worked a grueling schedule, poring over some one thousand scripts per year, often after hours at home, and personally examining the final cut of all the major feature films stamped with the Code Seal. "I am looking at pictures morning, noon, and night until I am almost frantic," he complained. As time went on, Breen delegated greater authority to trusted subordinates, particularly Geoffrey Shurlock, his second in command, but in the harried early days he personally shouldered the Herculean task of cleaning out all the important scripts—partly because it was in character, partly so bigwig producers would not browbeat less pugnacious underlings.

Whatever PCA staffer actually vetted the script, all communications to the studios went out under Breen's signature. In time, the staff learned to channel Breen's Victorian Irish sensibilities and his very thought and language patterns, making it virtually impossible to tell who wrote what memo and final draft of what letter.[3] Guiding all the philosophical discussions and executive actions was the text of the Code and an overarching principle summarized in a phrase (recited like a mantra by anyone who ever worked at the PCA) to make certain that Hollywood pictures would be "reasonably acceptable to reasonable people."

In any given year, the Breen Office vetted approximately 3,500 examples of story material—books, plays, novellas, and short stories, either original or culled from magazines. After the story treatment was cleared, the staff supervised successive revisions of the script and tracked the evolution through production. "Once the decision has been made by the studio to proceed with the development of the story, we receive and carefully study

3. Albert Van Schmus revealed to film archivist Barbara Hall that the tell-tale indicator of which staffer actually wrote which letter was a number at the bottom of the page after Breen's signature. For example, "2" denotes Breen's number two man, Geoffrey Shurlock.

the various drafts of the screenplay, the rewrites and the changes," Breen explained.

A controversial play, a scandalous novel, or a remake of a pre-Code film might require months, sometimes years, of review, revision, and refinement before the cameras were permitted to roll. In Breen Office-speak, a long-gestating project of dubious morality was called a "tough nut to crack." The repair work—salvaging studio investments in projects purchased before 1934 or rehabilitating dicey best sellers and sophisticated Broadway plays—justified Breen's power and pay grade. "Joe has saved the picture companies millions of dollars in stories they had purchased, and were ready to throw away because of their interpretation of the demands of the Legion of Decency," Billy Wilkerson reminded the moguls.

The bottom-line savings that most firmly cemented Breen's authority resulted from his efficiency and predictability. Unlike the state and municipal censorship boards, whose rulings were off-the-cuff and whose members rotated with election cycles, the Breen Office was an entrenched bureaucracy with transparent procedures, consistent regulations, stable personnel, and institutional memory. "These decisions, even as the decisions of public courts, have the force of law for the industry and are carefully considered in adjudicating subsequent cases," Breen noted. The legalistic cast to the language is telling: like an attorney mulling over case law for precedent, a producer might be able to slip through a loophole, but only if a prior ruling were on the books. In its penchant for precedent and process, the Breen Office resembled a court of appeals more than an autocratic star chamber. Over the years, with loopholes plugged and precedent established, the policies hardened and exceptions were exceptional.

Even so, the Breen Office was not a shadowy cabinet of faceless bureaucrats. Known by name and idiosyncracy, the chief and his subalterns kibitzed over the phone and schmoozed in person, making frequent site visits to the studios to view sets and costumes and to screen dailies, rough cuts, and final prints. In 1936, by one reckoning, Breen and his staff made 2,650 personal visits to the studios. To emphasize the assembly-line setup—and by way of promoting the office and himself—Breen issued weekly summations on Code-approved films and each year reviewed the work of the PCA in a comprehensive annual report.

Within less than a year of its inception, the Breen Office was running on all cylinders. "It may interest you to know that, at 'the close of business' last night [April 11, 1935], we did not have a single script on hand and not one pix—feature or short—waiting on our approval," Breen proudly informed Maurice McKenzie. "In other words, last night, for the first time in more than a year the slate of the PCA was absolutely clear. We have, at last, caught up with our work, which is a most distinguished achievement—one that I want you to know about."

As the Breen Office transformed the means of Hollywood production, the wraparound advertising underwent a selfsame change. Officially, the task of monitoring motion picture publicity fell outside Breen's purview to an administratively distinct branch of the MPPDA called the Advertising Advisory Council (after 1942, the Advertising Code Administration). The council oversaw ad copy, publicity stills, billboards, and press books. In 1933, even before the creation of the PCA, the Hays Office had given the council new power to clamp down on licentious ads.

Publicly, Breen deferred to the sister regulatory regime, denying any authority over 8x10 cleavage and gams, insisting that "supervision over the contents of still photographs resides in the department of the Advertising Advisory Council of the Hays organization." However, the tighter standards being applied to film content reined in the packaging as well. It figured: a man from the Advertising Council often sat in on the morning huddles and the two offices worked in collusion, literally side by side in the office space of both the East and West Coast offices of the MPPDA. Being in physical and ethical proximity, the Advertising Advisory Council kept a Breen-like oversight on cheesecake, pointed guns, and taglines. (From 1933 to 1937, the main office, based in New York, was run by yet another Irish-Catholic ex-publicity man, a well-liked insider named Jeff McCarthy, famed for devising the "road show" method of exhibition for *The Birth of a Nation* [1915], and tapped by Fox to work on the publicity for *Eucharistic Congress* [1926]. After McCarthy's death in 1937, the job was taken over by the less colorful Lester Thompson.)

Albeit distinct entities, the two regulatory branches of the MPPDA—the Production Code Administration and the Advertising Advisory Council—were subsumed in popular parlance under the marquee name of the "Hays Office," the all-purpose signifier for Hollywood censorship. Hays did not shrink from the credit. While Breen labored in-house to imprint his vision on Hollywood cinema, Hays remained the front man for the motion picture industry.

Though Breen's billing as "Will Hays the Second" could not have been a sobriquet appreciated by Will Hays the First, few turf wars erupted between the two most powerful non-moguls in Hollywood. Each kept clear of the other's sphere of influence. Morality, Hays conceded, was Breen's department. After the Breen Office had detected a "dozen basic factors, any one of which constitutes a Code violation" in Warner Bros.'s *Anthony Adverse* (1936), the studio tried to go over his head to Hays. "They have started working on the Boss, evidently to soften him up," Breen confided to Quigley, "and we had a frank discussion of the matter this morning [August 23, 1935] which, I think, will attend to that phase of the difficulty." It did.

Breen in turn knew where not to tread. For high-level liaisons, whether on the domestic or international front, Hays was the undisputed chief executive. (Breen referred to him as "the Boss" or "the Chief.") The difference between Hays and Breen was the difference between the political and the theological, the diplomatic and the confrontational, the dogged Midwesterner and the Bullish Irishman.

Officially, Breen was lower on the MPPDA hierarchy and pay scale, but Hays served at the pleasure of the moguls in Hollywood and the bankers in New York: he was their man doing their bidding. In 1935, when Hays's ten-year contract with the MPPDA came up for renewal, and with a Democrat in the White House, rumors swept Hollywood that the former Postmaster General would be replaced by the current Postmaster General, FDR crony James Farley. Hays dodged the bullet, but had he been replaced, the move would have been seen as a simple business decision.

By contrast, Breen enjoyed an independent power base as the Catholic envoy to Hollywood. If Hays were fired, there would be a few days of headlines. If Breen were fired, there would be hell to pay. "Mr. Breen, despite the difficulty of his work, commands the confidence of a large section of the American public, and if he were to give up his present job, [the MPPDA] could never find another man to command the confidence to an equal degree," cautioned Pete Harrison.

An early dustup between Breen and Hays over *The President Vanishes* (1934), a Paramount release produced by Walter Wanger, demarcated the spheres of influence. A loopy antiwar, anti–big business thriller, stoked by the backfire from the Great War and the social chaos of the Great Depression, the film depicts a cabal of sinister business tycoons conspiring to drag America into a European war. "Munitions is our business!" screech the carrion capitalists from industry, banking, and media. "And it's up to us to make it America's business!" In cahoots with a fascist paramilitary group known as the "grayshirts," the robber barons pull the strings in Congress and incite rioting in the streets. To prevent the stampede to war and the freefall into civic disorder, the president stages his own kidnapping and arranges the killing of his demagogic rival.

Detecting no moral lapses, Breen had approved the hysterical melodrama, but Hays declared, without explanation, that the film was "dangerous" and banned its release. "Mr. Hays's objections were prompted by a reprehensible, if understandable, Republican antipathy toward a film that gave the Democrats all the better of a political argument, and were not based on 'other' moral or artistic defects," observed the *New York Times*, nailing the difference in outlook between the politico and the moralist.

Wanger, typically, resolved to fight. Paramount, atypically, pledged to back Wanger.

"In going over Breen's head in the matter Hays has set a bad precedent," admonished Len Morgan in *Billboard*. "It will mean that Breen, who was supposed to have been judge and jury, will be considered a figurehead and rightly so." Morgan sagely predicted that "the producers as a group will override Hays in this instance, for they all realize that the country is watching the censorship angle and unless the producers back Breen to the limit there is going to be a decidedly adverse reaction."

After two weeks of turmoil, Hays backed off. The showdown was not just a personal victory for Breen, but a victory for the regime. *The President Vanishes* was released and promptly vanished.

Though the locals knew better, Hays was awarded the public laurels for rehabilitating Hollywood. MPPDA press releases and annual reports always lauded the diminutive "czar of the movies" as the animating visionary rather than the reactive vessel in the creation of the Production Code Administration. "By the spring of 1934, it had become apparent to Mr. Hays that the time had at last arrived when both the public and the industry would support a self-regulatory plan," read an official MPPDA history issued in 1936. "It was the realization of the goal toward which Mr. Hays had directed his efforts during the preceding 12 years." Breen warrants a single, cursory mention as an administrator whose "work has earned high praise."

For his part, Breen never contradicted the Boss in public or trespassed into his territory. When Twentieth Century-Fox hired stripper Gypsy Rose Lee (under her real name, Louise Hovick) for *You Can't Have Everything* (1937), the creative casting sparked concern that a chorus line of burlesque queens was shimmying into Hollywood cinema: MGM was checking out June St. Clair and RKO was auditioning Ada Leonard. Quizzed about the buttoned-down Code nuzzling up to the unzipped strippers, Breen replied, "That depends entirely on what is shown on the screen," before tossing the hot tomatoes back into the Boss's court. "At this time, this is not a Production Code matter, but, rather, might be a subject of industry policy for the attention of Mr. Hays."

By then, Hollywood knew full well which hands held which levers. Though Breen had been on the MPPDA's payroll since 1931, the raw power to enforce his edicts and the raw emotion he brought to his task gave him coequal status with the politician who outearned and publicly outshone him. In a town exquisitely sensitive to rank, the character, charisma, and commitment of the man turned "the Hays Office" into "the Breen Office."

Braced by vivid face-to-face encounters, trade press reporters highlighted the colorful personality at "the Breen laundry" or "the Breen plant."[4] For headline writers and columnists, the fortuitous single-syllable rhyme with "clean" was a ready-made pun and easy punch line ("Producers Scrub 'Em Clean Before Showing to Breen"). The neologists at *Variety* coined endless variations on verbs such as "Breens," "Breening," and "joebreening." In the national vernacular, Breen would never enter the dictionary of the American language but around Hollywood his surname was lingo and his word was law.

GOD'S WORK

Joseph I. Breen first glimpsed a rough draft of the Production Code at a luncheon with Martin J. Quigley at the Chicago Athletic Club in 1929. Years later, he recalled the Damascus moment in hushed tones. "The more I thought about it, the more it seemed to me to be an *inspired* document that fitted into the then current situation, having to do with motion picture entertainment, like a sharply cut figure in a colored picture puzzle," he marveled. "The Code . . . was, essentially, a moral treatise" whose "rules and regulations" stemmed from "the ancient moral law, which had been accepted by mankind almost since the dawn of creation." To Breen, the Code was less a collaboration between Martin Quigley and Father Lord than a tablet handed down from Mount Sinai.

The Code, said Breen, enunciated a set of eternal verities "rooted in the objective principles of morality as applied to public entertainment. These principles do not arise from timely, or geographic considerations. Such principles do *not* become outmoded." What was holy was forever holy, sinful eternally sinful. "Acts of immorality, at a particular time or place, may come into vogue. They may be widely and universally practiced. But this

4. Coinciding with the proliferation of the alphabet agencies of the New Deal and the bewildering array of "codes" promulgated by the National Recovery Administration, the Production Code Administration was liable to be confused with the myriad "code authorities" spawned under FDR's New Deal. Breen was sometimes misidentified as "NRA code administrator" and the Production Code Administration conflated with the NRA-mandated codes regulating pricing and economic practices in the amusement field. Irked by the confusion, the real NRA divisional administrator Sol A. Rosenblatt issued a statement declaring that "the code of ethics formulated by and for members of the Motion Picture Producers and Distributors of America has no connection with NRA."

does not alter the fact that such acts are *immoral*." Mere "*matters of convention*" changed with calendar and country, but certain principles "interpreted by intelligent and experienced people as being of immoral character" were timeless and transcendent. "*Conventions* change; moral *principles* do not." (Italics, needless to say, in the original.)

Like the line between mortal and venial sins in the Catholic catechism, the distinction between the philosophical core of the Code and the decorative frills was vital. To be sure, certain regulations arose from political compromise and commercial expedience. "We refrain from dealing with the traffic in illicit drugs, or with the white slave trade. We have an agreement not to deal with certain repellent subjects; another for the treatment of what we call 'national feelings': another for surgical operations, etc.," Breen admitted. "All these are important and should be retained, but I agree that these should not be treated as questions which arise under the Code, or questions which are to be handled by the provisions of the Code."

Breen's celestial vision and earthly tactics were guided by a due appreciation of the attraction of Hollywood's wares. Given "their widespread popularity, the vividness of their presentation, and the facility with which they never fail to impress and to stimulate," Breen believed that motion pictures "constitute a peculiar and powerful influence for good or evil, upon all who see them." In a magical, mysterious way, the seductive images convey "impressions which are formulative as to character and directive as to conduct. Not only to youth but to the public as a whole."

The last point—the custodial duty toward the young—weighed heavily on Breen and his generation of moral guardians. Children and young people, whose moral character had not yet been guided by religious training and civic schooling, were the unformed buds most perilously at risk from the visceral, stimulating spectacles beckoning from the screen. "Many realistic scenes and problems, not immoral themselves, but involving follies and vices of men and women, while suitable for adults, may be, and often are, harmful for children and adolescents because of the susceptibility, the ignorance, and the inexperience of youth." The universality of the motion picture medium, an entertainment with an open admissions policy for all ages and stages of moral development, not mature audiences only, was a self-evident argument for censorship. Quarantine being impossible, inoculation was essential.

The overarching mandate ("the cardinal principle of the Code") was that "*wrong must always be characterized as wrong, and not something else*." The motion picture spectator needed to know the moral score. "Sin is not a mistake but a shameful transgression. Crime is not an error of frailty but the breaking of the law. Wrong is not pleasant but painful, not heroic but

Condemned killer Rocky Sullivan (James Cagney) and two-fisted priest Father Jerry Connelly (Pat O'Brien) shake hands on a Production Code ending for *Angels with Dirty Faces* (1938).

cowardly, not profitable but detrimental, not plausible but deserving of condemnation." Eighty minutes of kinetic violence and lurid sexuality could not be redeemed by a stern monologue from a cleric or judge just before the end credits. Wise to "the subterfuge of attempting to wipe out a protracted wrong by one last line of dialogue affirming the right," Breen insisted on a bright line streaking across the narrative. "Our trouble usually comes when we have a leading character, portrayed as a criminal, who is made glamorous and who is glorified up to the last 75 feet of film." The "tone and atmosphere" must also reinforce the moral message. "Dialogue alone carries no conviction." The prime directive decreed "*that in the end the audience feels that evil is wrong and good is right*."

Under the Breen Office, the narrative trajectory of Hollywood cinema is not mystery solved, or success achieved, or boy-girl married, but morality upheld. Evil may exist, it may be portrayed vividly, and it may even tempt and torment the blameless and godly: but in the end the evil that men do must be outweighed by the ethical ballast, what Breen Office memo after Breen Office memo called "compensating moral values." In fact, evil exists to showcase good. Hollywood cinema under the Breen Office need not end happily, but it must end morally.

Enforced with unblinking vigilance, Breen's grand vision crystallized into a fixed set of thematic principles and content restrictions:

THE SACREDNESS OF THE BONDS OF MATRIMONY

The Code, wrote Breen, must "jealously guard marriage and firmly ward off from it [the] strongest standing threats against its stability." Of course, the greatest threat to the sacrament of marriage was the spouse who strayed outside of it. Adultery—the plot complication and narrative linchpin of comedy, melodrama, and mystery—could not be exiled from the screen, but it could be placed under strict surveillance and severe limitations, hinted at only if the "compensating moral values"—the sacredness of the institution and the wages of the sin—were boldfaced and dramatized. "The girls and boys of today are the fathers and mothers of tomorrow," Breen intoned. "And if our present day crop of youngsters are to be taught, by the cinema, that adultery is but a passing thing of fancy, that premarital indulgence is but an expression of natural 'love,' and that marriage is outmoded and stupid, how can we expect that respect for the seriousness and sanctity of the marriage state which is the very foundation of our society—and our Church?"

To Breen, there was no such thing as a bedroom farce. In literally dozens of memos to smirking filmmakers who thought otherwise, he decreed that adultery was no laughing matter. "The unacceptability of this story is suggested by the elements of illicit sex and adultery which are treated without sufficient compensating moral values," he lectured the producers of the British import *The Rake's Progress* (1945), whose title alone boded ill for monogamy. "You know, I think, there is no objection *per se*, under the Code to the treatment of illicit sex or adultery; but when such factors enter into a story to be treated under the Code, it is necessary that illicit sex and adultery be definitely and affirmatively shown to be wrong; the illicit sex and adultery must not be condoned—even by inference—or justified, or 'made to appear right and acceptable,' and the 'sinners'—those who engage in the illicit sex, and the adulterers—must be 'punished.'" Breen made sure they were.

THE SUPPRESSION OF THINGS OF THE FLESH

The corporeal body, both as a vessel of sexual pleasure and an organism with animal functions, must be hidden and denied. "Because of the natural and spontaneous reaction of normal human beings to sexual stimuli," Breen wrote, "the portrayal of definite manifestations of sex is harmful to individual morality, subversive to the interests of society, and a peril to the human race." A medium pulsating with erotic attraction and luxuriating in the allure of the image must pretend that the flesh it flaunts is not worth seeing and caressing, the body it frames not supple and desirable. Come, look and enjoy, says the screen siren, flirting and teasing, before her chaperone lowers the veil.

The naked body will not appear on screen, nor will its outlines be suggested to titillate: the Code will not abide a game of peek-a-boo. Occasionally, the partially clad body may be outlined, but in the mind only: the dancer who dresses behind a partition, the girl who slips into something more comfortable. An emblematic instance of faux-voyeurism under the Code occurs in Frank Capra's *It's a Wonderful Life* (1946) when Donna Reed, clad in a bathrobe, stumbles, loses her robe, and cowers behind a strategically positioned bush. Is she naked? Barely decent? Neither her date nor the spectator sees anything. Whatever the state of undress, the picture is for the mind alone.

A curvature impossible to conceal—female breasts—presented a uniquely tender topography for regulatory survey. "The nude breasts of the woman are out whether these be shown in travelogue pictures or the studio dramas," Breen decreed on his third day on the job. The nubile natives of Polynesian extraction who had lent pre-Code travelogues such ethnographic fascination were wrapped, blanketed, and saronged. The scandalous glimpse of a topless Jean Harlow in *Red Headed Woman* (1932), the jiggly buoyancy of the braless Clara Bow in *Call Her Savage* (1932), the nude underwater ballet with Olympic swimmer Josephine McKim body-doubling for Maureen O'Sullivan in *Tarzan and His Mate* (1934)—all became distant memories.

Sexual contact between males and females was limited mainly to osculation, an act placed under strict time and lip limits. Beginning in 1934, Breen issued a standard warning to dampen the ardor of Hollywood lovebirds:

> Please take specific note that we cannot approve scenes of *passionate, prolonged* or lustful or *open-mouthed kissing*. The injection of such scenes will cause a finished picture to be rejected.

The mouth-to-mouth restrictions were so well known that *Abie's Irish Rose* (1946) ventured a bit of self-reflexive ribbing: when a father spots his son and daughter-in-law smooching, he takes out his watch, counts three, and yells, "Time!"

As for the truly unspeakable sexual appetites, the carnal acts that were perverse and illegal, no explicit denunciations need sully the text of the Code.

"Sadism, homosexuality, incest, etc., should not even be hinted at in the motion pictures," Breen said. "The Code does not mention it, assuming of course, its obvious impossibility." The loves that dared speak their names in pre-Code Hollywood—the sadomasochistic shivers in *The Mask of Fu Manchu* (1932), the incestuous vibrations in *Scarface*, and the trilling homosexual waiters in *Call Her Savage*—were silenced, muffled, and closeted.

The performance of another biological function was more off-limits than sex. Breen evinced a personal discomfort—actually an obsessive aversion—to what he called "toilet humor," either by verbal reference or visual depiction. Under the Breen Office, the antiseptic erasure of bodily functions and excremental fluids on the Hollywood screen is even more total than the denial of sexual pleasure. However scatological Breen's own vernacular, excremental terms and actions were not just unheard, offscreen, and elliptical but utterly unimaginable.

Architecturally, the aversion to the carnal body, whether transportingly erotic or grossly corporeal, manifested itself in the heavy surveillance and freighted significance of the two household spaces designed for their retrospective activities: the bedroom and the bathroom. The famous twin beds that dominated the interior decoration of Breen Office bedrooms furnish the most obvious example. In the pre-Code *The Thin Man* (1934), wedded couple Nick and Nora Charles sleep in the same king-sized bed. In the Code-approved *After the Thin Man* (1936), the path to wedded bliss is blocked by a sturdy night table.

More unsightly than the bedroom was the bathroom. A marriage bed might be cut in half; a toilet must remain invisible. In the innocuous *Cheaper by the Dozen* (1950), a family comedy whose contempt for birth control Breen could only applaud, an innocent reference to the children needing to see "Mrs. Murphy"—that is, visit the bathroom—generated sheets of memos and countermemos between the Breen Office and Twentieth Century-Fox when Breen forbade the toilet, or lack of toilet, humor. Though acknowledging Fox's arguments were "not without merit" and that the film was "on the whole a pleasant, wholesome story of family life," the Mrs. Murphy scene went a bit too far. To approve it, wrote Breen, would "set a precedent that would threaten disaster for the future." A bath, a shower, or a sink might be shown, but a commode is not seen, a flush is not heard.

THE VENERATION OF WOMEN

Ideally, women were vessels of virginity or paragons of maternity. "To my way of thinking, the best feature of the Nineteenth Amendment to the Constitution is that our women, our good women, our mothers, wives, and sweethearts, may be moved to come to the rescue of the nation and State when the foes of liberty and justice seek to undermine our natural and civil rights," Breen wrote in 1923, after the nation had survived its first elections with women's suffrage. Yoking Victorian chivalry to the Catholic veneration of the Blessed Virgin Mary, the Breen Office upheld the view that women, though the weaker sex in custom and under law, were morally superior to brutish men, and thus the true protectors of what is best and holiest in American culture. Breen credited whatever success he had in life to the lessons learned at the knees of "a fine old Irish Mother and an Irish Grandmother." Of his Catholic education, he believed, "Out of it all, I should say that the best thing I got was a deep-set, inherent and instinctive *respect for women* and for the sanctity of the home and the imperishability of the Christian family. This is the best and finest thing I took out of the schools."

Like the celestial chiaroscuro in a Renaissance painting, the backlit halos and divine close-ups of the female face in Hollywood's frame bespeak a kind of religious adoration. Film critic Molly Haskell has characterized the shift from the awed perspective on women in classic Hollywood cinema to their manhandling in the postclassical tradition as a movement "from reverence to rape." The reverence flowed not only from Hollywood's desire to attract the female audience, its target of choice, but from the Victorian regard for the idealized female that Breen enforced under the Code. Roughing up women, even a slang term for a young girl, was intolerable under the Breen Office in its prime. A leading indicator of the waning of Breen Office influence was the blunt-force trauma done to women by abusive men in the film noir genre of the late 1940s and early 1950s.

THE RESPECT FOR AUTHORITY

On-screen insurrections against the forces of law and order—the clergy, the police, elected officials—were put down with lethal force. The institutions of social control are wise and salutary, the uniformed representatives stalwart and upright. An individual policeman may be corrupt but the police force is honest; an individual politician may be craven but the political system stands tall. If a minor official strays from his duty, his superior shows that whatever the flaws in a single link, the chain of command will hold firm.

The break with pre-Code notions of penology is best marked by the termination of the criminal-coddling gangster genre and the birth of a new police-friendly cycle of G-Men pictures: *Little Caesar* (1931), *The Public Enemy* (1931), and *Scarface* were transformed into *G-Men* (1935), *Let 'Em Have It* (1935), and *Public Hero #1* (1935). In 1932, even before the creation of the

Production Code Administration, Hays had squelched the trigger-happy gangster cycle with a ukase against storylines inspired by John Dillinger, the era's most notorious and admired gangster. Two years later, with symbolic dead aim, Hollywood's sympathy for colorful criminals was cut short subsequent to a screening of *Manhattan Melodrama* (1934), the gangster film Dillinger was watching before being gunned down by the FBI outside the Biograph Theater in Chicago.

Breen Office justice was just as swift and certain. The "G-Men" pictures, Breen proudly reported to Hays, "have the general thesis of glorifying the agents of the Department of Justice. The government men are the heroes." Where the gangster genre flaunted molls, flivvers, and tommy guns, the G-Men films stressed "the care with which the Government selects these men, the period of training through which the men are put, and the intelligence with which later they proceed with their work." After inspecting the G-man paean *Let 'Em Have It*, Breen felt a "most exhilarating" spirit of "fine uplift." "It made one feel that the Federal Government has approached the problem suggested by the nationwide crime wave in an intelligent, forceful, and vigorous manner. It made you feel proud to be an American."

Marriage, the body, the female, and the law were the four quadrants of imagery and values that Breen never took his eyes from. No matter how the studios squawked or the producers wheedled, the core principles were non-negotiable. This was understood, even conceded, by the studios. Yet not everything was conceded or unconditionally surrendered. Even under the intense gaze of the Breen Office, filmmakers found room to wiggle and play, subvert and defy.

5

DECODING CLASSICAL HOLLYWOOD CINEMA

As the Breen Office enforced the Code with iron fist and velvet glove, the landscape of Hollywood cinema underwent a seismic upheaval that soon settled into a placid equilibrium. At some mysterious point around the middle of the 1930s, filmmakers and audiences alike had mastered the grammar of a unique filmic language, a sophisticated dialect built on gentle implication, unspoken meanings, elaborate conceits, and winked signals. Always an act of imagination and interpretation, going to the movies became an exercise in deciphering and decoding allusions, nuances, and ellipses. Directors (the good ones) abided by the letter of the law while stretching its spirit. Audiences (the clever ones) read between the lines.

The fault line of July 15, 1934, marked so stark and sudden a fracture that the difference between the two screen worlds was best appreciated in retrospect. In 1935, the trade journalist Helen Gwynne attended a revival screening of MGM's pre-Code hit *Red Dust* (1932), not glimpsed since its original release. The steamy melodrama featured a bare-chested Clark Gable entwined in an adulterous romantic triangle with prim, married brunette Mary Astor, swept off her feet and onto her back, and randy platinum blonde Jean Harlow, squirming in his lap and sloshing naked in a rain barrel. Not until Gwynne looked at pre-Code Hollywood in a post-Code light did she realize how totally the curtain had been drawn over the flesh and flash so lately on view. "The only thing that's really shocking about the whole picture is that it couldn't possibly have been made in this year of Hays, 1935," she pined, blaming the wrong surname.

That same year, contemplating the transformation wrought by the Breen Office, producer Darryl F. Zanuck linked the shift in sensibility to the sound revolution that had shaken Hollywood in 1927. Whereas the switch to talking pictures "was a mechanical change and depended more than anything else on the perfection of mechanical devices," reflected Zanuck, "the present change is more difficult because it was psychological. It required no mere adaption to physical and mechanical appliances but an entirely new way of thinking." It also required an entirely new way of seeing.

The Code now served as a lens filtering the act of spectatorship. Before 1934, motion picture censorship was haphazard, regional, and capricious. Breen Office censorship was rigorous, universal, and predictable. The application of a standard rulebook ordained a new poetics for artist to master and viewer to apprehend. In 1953, moviegoers would be handed 3-D glasses to watch images lunge from the screen. In 1934, moviegoers were fitted with a prescription that kept images off the screen or out of focus.

A Hollywood filmmaker under the Breen Office might be likened to a poet struggling with the rules of a Shakespearean sonnet. The formal restrictions are preconditions for the creative act: fourteen lines, iambic pentameter, three quatrains capped by a rhyming couplet pithily wrapping up the package. Within the constraints, the poet is free to pick words and hone phrasing, to conjure imagery, symbolism, tone, and emotion—even, occasionally, to test the limits by squeezing in an extra syllable or sounding an off-note. The virtues of sonnet poetics are discipline, suspense, precision, and grace under expressive pressure. The flaws are stilted conventions, formulaic predictability, stale tropes, and suffocating rigidity. Also, attempts to vary the rhyme scheme with limericks, free verse, even Petrarchan sonnets, are strictly prohibited.

The great directors of the Golden Age of Hollywood had no choice but to sign up and compose on the dotted lines. Before the advent of auteurist privilege and the incentive of postwar capital gains tax law, no hired gun on the company payroll questioned the right of the owners to exert editorial control. The most intractable resistance to the Breen Office came not from directors, stars, or, needless to say, screenwriters, but from ruggedly independent producers like Sam Goldwyn, David O. Selznick, Walter Wanger, and Howard Hughes, obstinate cusses who resented the violation of their property rights, who wrote angry memos protesting that the film was *their* business, not Breen's.

Even so, Hollywood cinema was never purely by the numbers. Though the Breen Office counted the beats and measured the lines, expurgated the dictionary and dictated the syntax, artists exercised freedom of expression within the fixed limits. The Code regulated the spoken word and visible image, but the unsaid and the unseen lurk under the lilt of the dialogue and beyond the edge of the frame: the spectator has only to fill in the blanks. Listening to quick-witted couples whose verbal intercourse is never about the named nouns or topic at hand, watching the camera track over set design and fade to black, audiences learned to be cryptographers and connoisseurs, to read the signals and savor the delicacies. Some of the ciphers are child's play, others tougher to crack.

Except to the dim-witted or underaged, the neon-lit clues are giveaways. A shot of a couple embracing dissolves to ocean surf pounding against the shore; a camera pans laterally from couch, to rug, to fireplace. Often, after the elliptical pause, the viewer is then assured that the offscreen interlude had not, in fact, initiated what the mind's eye had just conjured. The couple is clothed and unruffled, not spent and satisfied. Perhaps they were only talking.

Of course, flirty wordplay and sly insinuation in Hollywood cinema predated the Breen Office. The banter in *The Thin Man* (1934), a pre-Code romantic comedy masquerading as a detective story, offers an exemplary instance. For reasons too convoluted to summarize, the police barge into the bedroom of the martini-swigging gumshoes Nick and Nora Charles (William Powell and Myrna Loy). It is nighttime, the couple are clad in pajamas, and a double bed looms large in the set design. Nick is pointing a handgun at an intruder.

"Haven't you two ever heard of the Sullivan Act?" snarls the cop.

"Oh, that's all right," coos Nora, mock-innocent. "We're married."

The punch line turns on a mature appreciation of three distinct acts, two legislative and one procreative: the Sullivan Act (illegal possession of a handgun), the Mann Act (transportation of an underage woman across state lines for immoral purposes—which impish Nora pretends to confuse with the Sullivan Act), and the sex act. Under the Code, only the Sullivan Act might be invoked, and not with so whimsical a witticism.

After the Breen Office zippered the lips of flippant screenwriters, elliptical language and shaded line readings served to juice up the erotic voltage word-wise. Consider *Desire* (1936), produced by Ernst Lubitsch, directed by Frank Borzage, and starring Marlene Dietrich as a slinky jewel thief and Gary Cooper as her smitten suitor. Conning a psychiatrist who knows far less about human sexuality than his patient, Dietrich pretends to be troubled by a husband who is—how to say?—no longer the man she married. All demure exterior, she purrs out her marital woes:

> DIETRICH: When we were married . . . [*meaningful pause*] he was such a strong, *virile* man . . . and now [*she looks up, bereft*]—oh, doctor—sometimes he imagines he's a schoolgirl running away from school. And do you know he has given up pajamas and taken to wearing nightgowns?

DOCTOR: I don't like that.

DIETRICH: I don't like it either.

Not to worry. Proper psychiatric care will "have him out of his nightgown and back in his pajamas in no time."

Continuing to press its luck, *Desire* ventures a less scandalous kind of nocturnal activity during a love scene between the two stars. The foreplay opens in a living room, where a drowsy Dietrich ("All I need is a nice soft bed.") lures Cooper to a balcony where she can shimmer in the moonlight. "You know, Mr. Bradley, the Spanish moon is very becoming to you," she volleys. Cooper returns the pass, whispering, "I never saw you in this light before." The clinch and the Hollywood kiss follow, with the soundtrack music swelling to the crescendo that the lovers must forgo. Next morning, the pair awake, conspicuously, in different bedrooms, but also, no less conspicuously, postcoitally spent. "Yes, dear?" sighs Dietrich, yawning and disheveled, when awoken by a friend.

Impotence, transvestitism, fornication—all were perfectly fine with the Breen Office, as long as Lubitsch and Borzage maintained plausible deniability. "It will be vital to avoid any suggestion that your two leads have been indulging in a sex affair during the week they have spent together," instructed Breen. "Their relationship should be portrayed as a clean love affair, devoid of any sex implications."

At once staid and steamy, *Desire* was held up as a model of Code compliance, "a praiseworthy example of how to instill a sex punch in a picture without offending anybody." That is, the sophisticated viewer read the signs, the simpletons gaped blankly. "The subtlety of [Lubitsch and Borzage's] scenes, say the censor contacts [Breen], keeps the children and the morons from surmising what has happened, and so their morals, the chief concern of censors, are protected," explained the *Hollywood Reporter*.

Tasked with spicing up the boy-girl wordplay while a chaperone from the Breen Office eavesdropped, Hollywood screenwriters perfected the art of two-tiered, double-meaning dialogue. To take a classic instance, in Billy Wilder's *Double Indemnity* (1944), from a screenplay by Wilder and Raymond Chandler, the extended motorway metaphor driven home by the slatternly Phyllis Dietrichson (Barbara Stanwyck) and the on-the-make insurance agent Walter Neff (Fred MacMurray) traffics in more than highway safety:

PHYLLIS: There's a speed limit in this state, Mr. Neff, 45 miles an hour.

WALTER: How fast was I going, officer?

PHYLLIS: I'd say around 90.

The master at work: faking a crying jag, director Ernest Lubitsch (*right*) hams it up with Evelyn Brent and Maurice Chevalier in a publicity shot for *Paramount on Parade* (1930).

Uncensorable subtlety: a sultry European jewel thief (Marlene Dietrich) snares an innocent American abroad (Gary Cooper) in Frank Borzage's *Desire* (1936), produced by Ernst Lubitsch.

WALTER: Suppose you get down off your motorcycle and give me a ticket?
PHYLLIS: Suppose I let you off with a warning this time?
WALTER: Suppose it doesn't take?
PHYLLIS: Suppose I have to whack you over the knuckles?

In the realm of verbal foreplay, a close runner-up to the speed trap in *Double Indemnity* is another stimulating conversation by way of Raymond Chandler, the extended racehorse metaphor between a coltish Lauren Bacall and the sure-footed Humphrey Bogart in *The Big Sleep* (1946), a flirtatious palaver that finds each jockeying for the inside track:

> BACALL: Well . . . speaking of horses, I like to play them myself. But I like to see them work out a little first, see if they're front-runners or come from behind.

Bogart is listening.

> BACALL: I'd say you don't like to be rated. You like to get out in front—open up a lead—take a little breather in the backstretch—and then come home free.

No slouch in sizing up horseflesh himself, Bogart returns the favor and rates the filly:

> BOGART: I can't tell 'til I've seen you over a distance of ground. You've got a touch of class, but I don't know how far you can go.
> BACALL: That depends on who's in the saddle.

Right on cue, crowds roared at Bacall's single-entendre comeback.

"I love Mr. Chandler because his dialogue is so warm, but I don't know how he gets away with some of the stuff that is served up for childish amusement in a gangster thing called *The Big Sleep*," a scandalized columnist in the *New York World-Telegraph* wrote. "Some of Mr. Humphrey Bogart's dialogue would have shocked a stevedore." Only a very prudish stevedore—and the stuff was served up for adult not childish amusement, which is why the Breen Office permitted the racy fare to come in under the wire.

Further up the scale in difficulty are the oblique references and offhand remarks that sail over the heads of the slower adult students in the audience. In John Huston's *The Maltese Falcon* (1941), when the faithless trollop Brigid O'Shaughnessy (Mary Astor) informs Sam Spade (Humphrey Bogart) that a paranoid male acquaintance spread crumpled pieces of newspaper around his bed at night to trip up intruders, she signals to Spade—and the listener quick enough to keep up with him—that she was sleeping in that same bed; otherwise how would she have known her companion's bedtime ritual?

Fair being fair, Breen realized that if a director obeyed the road signs and kept within the speed limit, he could not be pulled over and ticketed. "The boys hereabouts have come to know the Code pretty well and, consequently, they are injecting scenes into the pictures which are acceptable under the Code and which, because they are acceptable, we cannot reject," he wrote in 1941. "Many of these scenes seem not to be acceptable to some of our critics. Many are not what we would prefer them to be, but, when, in our judgment, they are acceptable under the Code, we feel we can do nothing except approve them."

Viewing almost any Hollywood film produced under the Breen Office cultivates a talent for decoding, but the free-fire zone of comedy was the true test for the razor-sharp mind and pricked-up ear. Whether sophisticated, screwball, or slapstick, screen comedy—the designated playground for subversion and transgression—was riddled with madcap pop quizzes. However, the advanced exam was the comedy of manners, a genre ever faithful to a plot complication that, said the Code, should always be handled delicately: adultery.

All the comedy directors who thrived in the 1930s, a pantheon including Howard Hawks, Gregory La Cava, Frank Capra, and George Cukor, learned to adjust their pre-Code friskiness to Breen Office reins. Indeed, the high renaissance of sophisticated screen comedy that blossomed after 1934 grew out of the tension between the strict limitations imposed from above and the subterranean stimulation churning up from below. Two gifted poets of comedy flourished under the creative controls: one, like Breen, was an Irish Catholic of conservative politics and priestly affinities; the other was a German Jew from the Weimar Republic, a man of epicurean mien and cosmopolitan outlook.

The son of a fight promoter, Leo McCarey failed at law and songwriting before finding his talent in Hollywood, where he quickly shot up the ranks from "script girl" to director. In the 1920s and 1930s, he collaborated with nearly every great name in the art of screen comedy, including Hal Roach (for whom he helmed over three hundred shorts), Laurel and Hardy (whom he teamed), Harold Lloyd (for whom he directed the once-great silent star's best sound film, *The Milky Way* [1936]), the Marx Brothers (for whom he served up *Duck Soup* [1933], the most unhinged of their pre-Code comedies), and Mae West (with whom he learned about post-Breen Hollywood when *It Ain't No Sin* turned into *The Belle of the Nineties* [1934]). Like not a few gregarious Irish funnymen, he had both a melancholy and a sentimental streak. McCarey's personal favorite among all his films was the all-out weepie *Make Way for Tomorrow* (1937), the heart-rending tale of an old couple abandoned by their ungrateful-brat children. The film was based on Josephine Lawrence's story "The Years Are So Long," which had been brought to his attention by a kindred spirit, Joseph I. Breen.

McCarey's *The Awful Truth* (1937) is a screwball comedy about a pair of seasoned combatants whose close-quarter infighting never precludes a below-the-belt punch. The ostensibly irreconcilable Jerry (Cary Grant) and Lucy (Irene Dunne) are the feuding spouses: each suspects the other of adultery, she because her husband has lied about his whereabouts on a business trip, he because his wife has spent a night away from home with her suave vocal coach. After the wife sues for divorce (the main bone of contention between plaintiff and defendant being the visitation rights to their hyperactive dog, Mr. Smith), the judge decrees that the divorce will become final at the stroke of midnight six months hence.

The comic ballet twirls around three stumbling blocks. First, McCarey must render the alleged adulteries by implication not explication. Second, he must preserve the sanctity of marriage by preventing the divorce. Third—the step that absolutely cannot be tripped up—he must maneuver the couple into a re-consummation of their marriage rites before the divorce decree becomes final. That is, Jerry and Lucy must be safely tucked into bed before the legal deadline at the stroke of midnight—literally, the first stroke, for when the bell tolls, Breen will swoop in like a sourpuss fairy godmother and bring the enchanted evening to a full stop.

To stage the conjugal curtain clinch, McCarthy winks at the fairy-tale backdrop to the midnight deadline. Determined to re-mate her spouse, Lucy lures Jerry to a remote cabin in the woods. Properly placed in adjacent bedrooms, the couple settles in to bed for the night. To keep the countdown in sight, McCarey periodically cuts to a cuckoo clock on the wall ticking off the time: two figurines, male and female, exit from adjacent doorways at the quarter hour to chime the time. The cutaway to the cuckoo figurines is the first leap into cartoonish fantasy in a comedy that for all its slapstick antics has so far been grounded in Newtonian physics.

Back in the real world, the door between the two rooms blows open. Jerry breaches the barrier. The couple converse about the spat that led to the divorce, but the sputtered wordplay is inconsequential. In a ventilated nightgown, Jerry stands agog and besotted at the sight of his wife in bed—a double bed, not incidentally. Under the warm covers, radiant in soft light, glowing with erotic allure, Lucy leans back into her pillow and bids Jerry a throaty "G'night." For the last time, the door slams shut behind Jerry.

Racing to beat the clock: Irene Dunne, director Leo McCarey, and Cary Grant in a publicity shot for their exquisitely timed screwball comedy *The Awful Truth* (1937).

McCarey cuts to the cuckoo clock chiming midnight. The male figurine turns on his heels and hungrily pursues the female through her doorway.

The Breen Office was amused and satisfied. "The last sequence, as written, seems possibly dangerous," Breen had warned during the script review phase. "Great care will be needed in shooting it, to avoid the sex suggestiveness that might lead to censor deletions which would ruin the end of your picture." Tickled at McCarey's clockwork timing, Code staffer Karl Lischka assured Breen that no prurient sex suggestiveness marred the conjugal *pas de deux*. "The good spirit and atmosphere of the picture," wrote Lischka, was irresistibly charming. "The bedroom scene in the cabin could possibly be suggestive, [but] only if it were not played in fine taste and for delicate comedy."

The exquisite sexual tension in the mating dance between Lucy and Jerry in *The Awful Truth* is the screwball comedy equivalent of director Alfred Hitchcock's ticking time-bomb formula for stretching out suspense: showing the tantalizing countdown to ecstasy is more stimulating than detonating a single loud bang. As the tick-tock, tick-tock of the cuckoo clock's minute hand inches ever closer to midnight, as the doorway of sexual opportunity threatens to close tighter than a chastity belt, McCarey slips Jerry and Lucy into the matrimonial bed with scant seconds to spare.

If Leo McCarey was the lyric troubadour of comedy under the Code, Ernst Lubitsch was its Shakespeare, the bard who made the rigid form supple and sensuous. His eponymous "Lubitsch touch" was a tag not only for his stylistic fingerprints but for how he caressed the outer edges of censorship.[1] A former clog dancer in German vaudeville, the agile Lubitsch sidestepped the danger zones to hit just the right mark—risqué but never vulgar, testing the elasticity of the Breen line while staying within bounds.

Breen first felt the Lubitsch touch during the script review process for *The Merry Widow* (1934), a spicy musical based on a German operetta. He knew "that Lubitsch would be a tough nut to crack," but after extensive consultations and repeated viewings of various versions of the film, he awarded it a Code Seal. On second thought, however, he concluded that it was the wily Lubitsch who had skipped past the Code. "The picture as it stands now is not the light, gay, frivolous, operetta which it is intended that it should be but rather the typical French farce that is definitely bawdy and offensively—in spots—suggestive," he wrote in a contrite memo to Hays, admitting that the Lubitsch touch had outsmarted his own.

The Merry Widow was Lubitsch's last pre-Code film, so dated, but not his last flirtation with the joys of sex outside and across the institution of matrimony. Breen notwithstanding, Lubitsch's romantic comedies—*Angel* (1937), *Bluebeard's Eighth Wife* (1938), *To Be or Not to Be* (1942), and *Heaven Can Wait* (1943)—treat marriage as an elastic band not a sacred bond, while even the nonmarried couples in *Ninotchka* (1939), a prophetic vision of the

1. As early as 1926, Lubitsch was known for his distinctive directorial style ("the Lubitsch quality"), but "the Lubitsch touch" became his trademark billing only after 1934.

victory of consumerism over communism, and *Cluny Brown* (1946), a satire of the British class system, require political or social complications to block the course of true lovemaking. In all Lubitsch's Code-approved work, he only pretends to heed the advice that the frigid Ninotchka gives to her capitalist suitor before her Siberian front melts: "Suppress it."

Released the same year as McCarey's *The Awful Truth*, *Angel* is a textbook index to Lubitsch tactility. Based on a randy play by Melchior Lengyel, the project had knocked around Hollywood for years, defeating the best efforts of both Irving Thalberg at MGM and Harry Zehner at Universal to fashion a Code-worthy film from a Code-defying play. "This play is definitely a violation of the Production Code, for the reason that it is a patent condonation of adultery," Breen wrote in 1934. "Part of the story is also played against the background of a Parisian brothel because the opening scene takes place in a Parisian brothel, which is, likewise, a subordinate Code violation."

John Hammell, assigned by Paramount to run interference with the Breen Office, felt sure that "with careful handling, the use of objectionable material may be avoided." After personal assurances from Lubitsch, Breen gave permission to proceed, the Code Seal being contingent, as ever, upon a review of the final print.

Lubitsch retained the brothel setting by retouching the interior decoration and whitewashing the nature of the business—though not so cryptically that a spectator of a certain age and sophistication couldn't translate the signage.

Angel opens with an establishing shot of Paris, always the site of illicit sex in the American mind, and then follows a beautiful, wealthy woman (Marlene Dietrich), who checks into a four-star hotel under a false name. Her enticing destination reads: "Club de la Russie, 314 Rue de la Tour."

The next scene gets the viewer there first. An elaborate, lateral tracking shot from outside a building, with the number "314" affixed above a Russian crest, peeks into five windows to spy upon a sequential series of pantomimed vignettes: (1) a well-dressed aristocratic matron, clearly the hostess-proprietor of the house, and a manservant, inspect a champagne bucket on a table in a private dining room; (2) in a larger gaming room, a quite attractive woman shows a ring to the matron, who appraises the bauble with an expert eye; (3) in the bar section of the room, crowded with convivial guests in formal wear, the woman pawns the ring to a cashier; (4) at the bar, a man approaches the matron and directs her attention screen right to (5) the object of his gaze, another quite attractive woman, whom the matron introduces to the man from the bar. With the visual montage complete, the dialogue track kicks in and a brief conversation ensues in which the matron is identified as a White Russian Grand Duchess, the celebrated hostess of an establishment dubbed a "delightful salon."

Cut to the exterior of the building where a man (Melvyn Douglas) enters and is told to cool his heels in a reception room. Dietrich then arrives for an intimate tête-à-tête with the Grand Duchess. Entering the reception lounge, Dietrich encounters Douglas, who mistakes the former employee for the present proprietor. He confides to her that a friend has suggested "for an amusing time in Paris go straight to the Grand Duchess and . . . and . . . here I am."

"So you want an amusing time in Paris?" she replies, pretending to misunderstand. Perhaps a visit to the Louvre, or the Eiffel Tower, or Notre Dame?

Perhaps, he parries, a party for two? Charmed, she agrees to an assignation.

The translation of Lubitsch's code is virtually word for word: a woman selling a precious possession (prostitution), arranged introductions (procurement), a "delightful salon" (brothel), the Grand Duchess (the house madam), and "an amusing time" (sex for hire).

"*Angel* has come out of the Lubitsch laboratory a creation of impeccable taste, yet tartly flavored with the risqué," declared *Variety*, which provided an instruction kit for how less nimble directors might skirt the Code while showing some leg. "Lines were rewritten, dishabille scenes adroitly shuffled, anatomy piquantly draped—but motivations in general remained the same and the fundamental triumph of virtue over vice was not disturbed." After the Breen pawing and the Lubitsch touch, the brothel became an "entirely innocuous setting that might have been a nitery, a gambling palazzo, or a rendezvous for a select clientele." Presumably, anyone who couldn't recognize the "delightful salon" as a high-class brothel had never patronized one.

Rival directors, more lead-footed than Lubitsch, were told by their studios to screen and study his films to learn how to tiptoe past the Code. "Many a good man went there, studied under him, copied him, but he always remained the master," wrote Billy Wilder and Charles Brackett in 1947, when Lubitsch died of a heart attack at age fifty-five. In a memorial tribute to their beloved mentor, the pair affectionately described the master's strokes:

> The pupils, confronted with the problem of putting a wedding night on the screen, tune it to violins. They write innuendoes and rogueries. They drown it all in blue moonlight and dissolve into dawn creeping through gossamer draperies. Not the professor, Lubitsch! He didn't give a hoot for the wedding night. He skipped it entirely. He photographed the lovers having breakfast. And he put more delightful connotations of sensuality in the bride cracking

the shell of a soft-boiled egg than could be evoked by the moistest of lips meeting the most censorable kisses.

Sharing the universal regard for Lubitsch's virtuosity, Breen granted the director the special dispensation due a genius. To Lubitsch's second-rate students, however, he issued a terse warning. "If at any time you are a bit foggy as to what constitutes honor, purity, and goodness or where sophistication stops and sin starts, I'll tell you." Like Wilder, Brackett, and the rest of Hollywood, Breen knew that Lubitsch was untouchable.

THE BREEN OFFICE SHUFFLE

In 1939, while planning *Rebecca* (1940), his American film debut, the British director Alfred Hitchcock had his first run-in with studio system censorship in the person of Joseph I. Breen.

In the languid drawl that would soon become the tonal trademark of Hollywood's most famous auteur and showbiz ham, Hitchcock confessed that he actually *enjoyed* his negotiations with Breen. The spirited give-and-take, said Hitchcock, possessed all the thrill of competitive horse trading.

"Breen wants Rebecca to die of cancer, and I want her to be shot with a gun," Hitchcock confided. Being the soul of reason, the director hit upon a compromise to end the impasse. "In the middle of the argument, I suggested that we get together on a hammer murder."

Rebecca's husband, Maxim de Winter, who in the novel shoots Rebecca, presented another problem for Breen, as yet unresolved.

"Would it be necessary to kill him?" asked a reporter.

"You mean Breen?" deadpanned Hitchcock. "I don't think so."

Not everyone in Hollywood felt so kindly. Whether considered a minor thorn in the side or a royal pain in the ass, Breen was suffered only because the alternatives of government censorship, Legion boycotts, and bluenose agitations were far worse. Depending on the project, and the filmmaker, the shotgun marriage between the censor and the censored might see the couple cordial, stone-faced, or bickering. Whatever the relationship, both sides were stuck with each other. No divorces were granted from the Breen Office.

In Breen's mind—producers disagreed—he was a model of sanity and serenity, not an imperious czar handing down harsh edicts, but a collaborator whose power derived from the consent of the governed. Censorship is a nettlesome but necessary job of work, boys, so let's all behave reasonably and make the best of things. Breen played with his cards on the table, not close to the vest: the deck was not stacked, but the house was going to win in the end.

Still, Breen never held all the cards. "We were in the business of granting seals," Geoffrey Shurlock emphasized. "The whole purpose of our existence was to arrange pictures so that we could give seals." The Code Seal could not be a rubber stamp, but neither could it be a cement roadblock. The goal for the regulators was to keep the game honest, for the producers to hide what was up their sleeves, and for each side to know when to fold and when to call.

To keep the betting honest, Breen maintained a complete blackout on information about productions under review. "As I told you in my last letter, we have to be scrupulously careful in giving any information whatever regarding unreleased pictures," he lectured Vincent Hart of the New York office, after Hart had blabbed about a screen treatment at MGM based on Sinclair Lewis's controversial novel *It Can't Happen Here*. "Our policy here is never to discuss with anyone the production plans of any of our member companies. In every instance when inquiry is made, we always refer the inquiry to the company."

Like any shrewd operator doing business with cagey customers, Breen made trade-offs, collected markers, and passed out chits. Having raised objections to the love scenes in a pair of Paramount confections, *Cafe Society* (1939) and *Zaza* (1939), he split the difference with the studio, relenting on the former, standing firm on the latter. "Cooperating with producers, the Joe Breen staff has agreed to relax a little on its requirements in cases where it is known the subject will be handled with finesse and good taste," the *Hollywood Reporter* noted in 1937. In exchange, filmmakers were expected not to abuse the leeway.

Besides making life easier all around, a collaborative spirit might pay unexpected dividends. As a former journalist who had also tried his hand at short story fiction in the 1920s, Breen relished his informal role as a script doctor and uncredited scenarist. "Breen today collaborates on more films than any dozen writers in Hollywood and gets none of the glory—or even screen credit," *Variety* revealed in 1935. Breen's touch-ups ranged from specific word changes to rough layouts of whole sequences. In 1934, Warner Bros., still in a pre-Code mentality, ended the melodrama *I Sell Anything* (1934) with the crooks making a clean getaway by fleeing to England by boat.

"The crooks must be punished," Breen ordered. "You can't make crime popular."

The studio complied by scripting a coda showing the crooks caught and jailed. The cost of shooting the new scene was estimated at $5,000.

"Why not just do it this way?" Breen suggested. "Just add one small scene of a police chief sitting at a desk. He orders a telegram sent to Scotland Yard to meet the boat when it docks at Southampton and fade your picture on that line."

The cost to the studio was $135 instead of $5,000.

"In two years [Breen] has written more sequences unaided, probably, than any one writer in the studios," claimed Douglas W. Churchill, the *New York Times*'s man in Hollywood. "With increasing frequency, [Breen] finds himself not advising but actually writing portions of the script. There is a sizable and embarrassing list of successful films for which he has written whole sequences: there is at least one in which he outlined the entire treatment." In 1939 the *Washington Post* also assigned the censor screen credit. "Studios say that scarcely a script is written without a few lines by Joe Breen. He doesn't just kill an unacceptable line; he offers a good substitute."

A frequently cited instance of Breen's creative input involved a delicate fault line that opened in MGM's earthquake-set *San Francisco* (1936), starring Clark Gable as reprobate saloon owner Blackie Norton, and Spencer Tracy as two-fisted priest Father Tim Mullen. Expecting furious resistance, the tremulous filmmakers—producer Bernard H. Hyman, director W. S. Van Dyke, and writer Anita Loos—pitched a curve ball to Breen.

"Now don't get mad, but we have an idea that will improve the picture a thousand per cent," they said. "Norton hits the priest—knocks him down."

Breen's reaction surprised the trio. "I see nothing wrong with that," he replied—so long as an earlier scene was inserted to show the priest outfighting Blackie in a boxing match. "If the clergyman accepts the blow with humility and doesn't strike back, you've got excellent drama, but if he retaliates, you will probably be in trouble." Sure enough, with the new scene as background, Father Mullen's turning of the other cheek to Blackie played as an act of Christian forbearance.

When a film with a Breen-altered script scored at the box office, producers might even appreciate the upside of censorship. "I have deep regard for Joe Breen and what he has done," said Arthur Hornblow, Jr., producer of the smash hit *Gaslight* (1944). "Oh, he has given me plenty of trouble, on occasion, in the way of making me change scripts to make them conform, but I find there is a great satisfaction in sweating through and getting the points made in the right way, instead of the easy way that is so often the wrong way." After wrangling for months with Breen over four drafts of the screenplay to *King's Row* (1941), the film version of Harry Bellamann's novel of incest, nymphomania, and syphilis (Breen's first impression: "If this picture is made, it is likely to bring down the industry as a whole"), Warner Bros. producer Hal B. Wallis conceded, "In the long run I felt it was all to the good:

audiences had a great deal to swallow in the picture, and too much grimness might have wrecked its chances at the box office."

Of course, not all collaborations were as affable. Especially in the early days, stormy story conferences, during which Breen shouted, pounded the table, and walked out, were frequent. When screenwriters-turned-producers Ben Hecht and Charles MacArthur were abusing mild-mannered Vincent Hart of the New York office during the production of their cold-blooded courtroom drama *Crime Without Passion* (1934), Breen told Hart to buck up and flail away. "The thing for you to do is to sneer back at these people—raise Hell with them—threaten to punch them in the nose—etc.," he suggested, giving a sense both of his modus operandi and mentoring style. "If you do this three or four times, I think you will have little trouble of this kind thereafter. The plan worked pretty well with me, and I think it will work with you."

As Breen's authority expanded and hardened, what rankled filmmakers most was his invasive scrutiny of the micro not the macro matters. All conceded that crime must not pay and that the wages of sin were death, but was it really necessary to eliminate the sight of a baby in diapers or the plosive sound of a street urchin blowing a "raspberry"? If in theory Breen expressed an open-minded willingness to finesse the tangential items, in practice he was seldom inclined to budge unless a producer had the gumption to push back. To Breen, the provisions of the Code had "an essential unity and coherence. One part cannot be ignored while another part is upheld and enforced. The Code may be likened to an arch of bricks, or mortar or stone, which is weakened and exposed to ruin by the removal of even a single stone." To take a tile from the foundation of the Code was to threaten the whole edifice with collapse. By fighting tenaciously not just for the Big Picture arc but the pea-brained minutiae, the Breen Office soon acquired a reputation not for grand vision but squinting myopia. It paid a scrupulous, not to say fetishistic, attention to the tiniest cinematic details.

It banned titles. Just as Mae West's first post-Breen release changed from *It Ain't No Sin* to *The Belle of the Nineties* (1934), Jean Harlow's mutated from *Born to Be Kissed* to *The Girl from Missouri* (1934). A hockey drama originally dubbed *Hell on Ice* melted down to *Idol of the Crowds* (1937). Neither *Wayward Girl* nor *Women of the Night* were upright enough labels for a dime-a-dance melodrama ultimately dubbed *Paid to Dance* (1937). In 1941, when the burlesque stripper Gypsy Rose Lee published a best-selling mystery novel called *The G-String Murders*, United Artists purchased the screen rights, figuring to translate the mention of an unmentionable into exploitable name recognition on a movie marquee. Breen ordered United Artists to slip on something less comfortable. "We are concerned about the prominent use of the object known as the 'G-String' as the murder weapon," he wrote. "It is our impression that the use of this extremely intimate female garment will be considered offensive, not only to the audience, but will undoubtedly be deleted in toto by censor boards." The film version was ultimately called *Lady of Burlesque* (1943). (Perhaps just as well: a poll commissioned by United Artists found that less than 30 percent of Americans knew what a G-string was.)

It demanded translations of all foreign words uttered, printed, or sung. The original German lyrics of "One Hour of Romance," a tune warbled by Kay Francis in *Confessions* (1937), had to be rewritten and sanitized in pure English. *Frankie and Johnnie* (1935), a costume drama based on the ballad about a two-timing cardsharp and his pistol-packing girlfriend, passed muster only because not a single bar of the universally known title tune was sung or hummed on screen. (Audiences must have been expected to walk *in* to the theater whistling the score.)

It blushed at the most innocuous exposures. A cameo appearance and product placement by Elsie the Borden milk cow in RKO's *Little Men* (1940) confirmed that breast oversight was not restricted to *homo sapiens*. "All this dialogue with regard to milking is highly dangerous, and must be handled so as to avoid vulgarity and otherwise unacceptable emphasis," Breen warned, causing city slickers and farmhands alike to guffaw when RKO leaked his memo to the press. "At no time should there be any shots of actual milking, and there cannot be any showing of the udders of the cow; they should be suggested rather than shown."

Inevitably, even the Breen Office nodded. Especially when Breen was away from the office on a business trip, a vacation, or in the hospital, the staff sometimes missed an insinuation, misunderstood a slang term, or simply got worn down and stopped arguing. In *They Drive by Night* (1940), when a trucker looks over the shapely Ann Sheridan (Warner Bros.'s "oomph girl" in contradistinction to MGM's "sweater girl" Lana Turner) and refers to a "classy chassis" with impressive "headlights," neither reference is to the equipment on an eighteen-wheeler. In *The Maltese Falcon* (1941), the word "gunsel" (archaic urban slang for homosexual) slipped by.

But far more contraband was confiscated than smuggled through. When a cheeky screenwriter described an ingénue in his script as "wearing a gown cut down to the Breen line," Breen penned in a marginal comeback: "If your Breen line is as low as I think it is, you'd better cut the dress two inches higher." The point wasn't where the line was but who would draw it. "Joe Breen has done an uncanny job at his censoring desk, and the longer he goes the more THEY respect him," said his boosters at the *Hollywood Reporter*, not needing to fill in the antecedent—the producers, directors, and screenwriters knew that looking over their shoulders was an alert inspector hard to distract and impossible to bribe.

Understanding that the Breen Office shuffle was a game of bluff and call, the wise filmmaker came to the table with surplus bargaining chips and a good poker face. Like Hitchcock trading murder scenarios for *Rebecca*, not a few players relished the bait and switch. "I used always to write three or four scenes which I knew would be thrown out, in order that we could bargain with Joe Breen for the retention of other really important episodes or speeches," recalled screenwriter Donald Ogden Stewart of his sessions with the "genial Irishman."

The Breen Office denied blackballing any individual project or author—presumably after suitable "breening" any book or play could be made fit for the screen—but in practice a few notorious titles, novels, and authors were put on the Breen Office equivalent of the Vatican index of banned books. The most marked of men was the hard-boiled novelist James M. Cain, a scarlet-letter name for much of the 1930s. In 1934, after paying $60,000 for the rights to Cain's steamy cauldron of adultery and murder, *The Postman Always Rings Twice*, MGM gave up on a film version for a decade, until, figuring *Double Indemnity* (1944) had opened the door on Cain material, the studio pitched the project anew.[2]

Having been kept out of the loop, Cain was surprised when MGM producer Carey Wilson ran into him on the Metro lot and excitedly announced, "You're going to say I'm crazy, but I am going to do your *Postman*."

"I don't say you are," Cain replied. "I say Breen is."

"He is not and I'm not. It's been lying around here for ten years, ever since we bought it off you and then the Hays Office got cold feet, but I say it can be done. And I'm not even worrying about Breen; I'm worrying about how to tell him. Just the same, I'm going to have some fun with him."

Breen figured Wilson would bring up the precedent of *Double Indemnity*, and Wilson figured Breen would figure as much. Playing cool, Wilson kept his mouth shut as he argued for *Postman*—leaving Breen ready with a counterpunch he was never required to throw.

"Why don't you say, 'What about *Double Indemnity*?'" Breen finally asked Wilson.

Because, said Wilson, "I know you're just sitting there with your right [fist] all cocked and ready to shoot it down when I begin, and I'm not going to give you the chance."

---

2. A treatment for *Double Indemnity* was first submitted to the Breen Office in 1935 and roundly rejected. Not until 1943 did a script finally pass muster.

The two players saluted each other's sagacity and the meeting finished with Breen giving his go-ahead and Wilson pledging, "It'll be a decent picture or my name won't be on it."

Cain wasn't as amused as Wilson by the friendly shuffle with "this jocund delightful fellow, this Breen person." Recalling that back in 1935 he could have gotten $25,000 from MGM for the screen rights to *Double Indemnity* had Breen not killed the project, he was forced to settle for $15,000 from Paramount in 1943.

"Now what I would like to know," asked Cain, dead serious, "is who pays me this $10,000?"

Cain answered his own question. "In my simple scheme of things, I think this jolly Irishman owes it to me, and if he should happen to read this, I would like him to know I still want it, and the passage of time hasn't mellowed my feeling about it in any way whatever."

THE ADVISORY FUNCTION

As the work of the Breen Office evolved, the regulatory apparatus came to operate along two separate tracks that, while distinct in theory, intersected in practice. The result was an exponential expansion of the scope and influence of the Breen Office—not under law but by custom.

Breen's first priority and formal responsibility was to enforce the letter of the Code. Gradually and unbidden, however, a second, parallel function emerged. As Breen and his staff mastered the censorship trade, they acquired a rarified expertise in the practices of the competition—the myriad censorship boards operating at home and overseas. Six states (Kansas, Maryland, New York, Pennsylvania, Ohio, and Virginia) and thirty-one major cites (Chicago, Atlanta, and Memphis being most troublesome) had permanent censorship boards, but the tally of local star chambers and bluenose satraps ranged from 200 to 250, a number that omitted the ad hoc censorship performed by mayors, police chiefs, and city councilmen.

After a Hollywood film stamped with a Code Seal lapped the theatrical release circuit, reports of its reception at the hands of local censors filtered back to the Breen Office for tabulation and review.[3] As newspaper clippings, censor board rulings, letters from clerics, clubwomen, and cranks

3. In the 1930s and 1940s, the theatrical lifespan of the average feature film might be eighteen months or more as it circulated from exclusive engagements and long runs in the big cities to wide availability in small hamlets at popular prices ("now playing at a theater near you!").

accumulated, the PCA's file cabinets came to hold a bulging archive on the quirks and qualms of censors far and wide, foreign and domestic, even what scenes were liable to infuriate which individual censors (Atlanta's rudderless Christine Smith and Memphis's irascible Lloyd T. Binford being the thorniest obstructions). Backed up by reports from the field, the Breen Office doubled as a vast central repository of censorable items. If a Code-approved film encountered trouble with the Ohio Board of Censors, the offense to the Buckeyes was noted, tabulated, filed—and remembered.

"The PCA acts in an advisory capacity in telling the producer, from lengthy experience in handling different subject matters and material, what may happen to the completed picture at the hands of certain state censor boards, boards in foreign countries, and different pressure groups," an unnamed source (doubtless Breen talking on deep background) explained to *Variety* in 1939. "The PCA merely advises the producer so that he will be informed what potential difficulties he faces. But the decision to alter a sequence, episode, dialogue, or action remains entirely with the producer."

Though not derived from sanctioned authority, the advisory role lent Breen de facto power over a wide range of matters that, by the book, fell outside the purview of the Code. As the foremost authority on what red flags not to wave before which state, foreign nation, or pressure group, Breen could suggest—disinterestedly, purely as a friendly caution—changes in film content he may also have desired but that he could not honestly credit to a Code mandate. Where Breen the Enforcer brooked no opposition, Breen the Adviser played the impartial arbiter and ex-officio helpmate. Like it or not, here's what those peculiar foreigners and hinterland yokels find objectionable in Hollywood cinema.

Given who was making the suggestions, the distinction between a cautionary advisory opinion (based on expertise) and a nonnegotiable ukase (based on the Code) tended to blur. When Fritz Lang's hit *You Only Live Once* (1936) inspired a spate of gritty crime films, Breen sent out a cautionary note reminding producers that such films "are certain to meet censorial and women's clubs objections." "Gangster Pic Cycle Nipped by Hays Ban," headlined the *Hollywood Reporter*. Likewise, in 1937, sober-minded women's clubs and temperance societies, down but not out after the passage of the Twenty-first Amendment, deluged the Breen Office with letters on the evils of the demon rum. Breen alerted studios that unless liquor was "absolutely necessary to the advancement of the story," pictures faced "increased cuts in some states and the possibility in others of being entirely thrown out." Though not himself averse to a scotch and soda, or two, he suggested that screenwriters "devise other means, other than drinking, to keep their characters busy." Headlined the *Hollywood Reporter*: "Hays Ban on Liquor."

Sometimes the advisory recommendations infiltrated the text of the Code as amendments or resolutions and took on the authority of the letter of the law. When the MPPDA included the liquor guidelines in an official version of the Code published in 1942, Martin J. Quigley lectured the custodians of his document that the copy in question was *not* the genuine article, but a "derivative document, most ineptly related to the instrument it is alleged to be." Hence, the "presumptuous" addition: "The use of liquor in American life, when not required for the plot or for proper characteristic, will not be shown."

Neither Quigley nor Father Lord had written those suspiciously Presbyterian-sounding words. "This might perhaps be an injunction of policy with respect to the nation's dry minority, but it is not a part of the Code and is not an issue of basic moral law," lectured Terry Ramsaye. Likewise, the "painfully specific" prohibitions on profanity such as "damn" and "hell" were cluttering a sleek catechism with excess verbiage. "It is a hell of a state of affairs," swore Ramsaye, when the Code is undercut by "attempts at the regulation of taste, which is quite distinct from morality—even if they are so often and tediously confused."

A set of concerns more incendiary than boozing or cursing also fell outside the sanctioned authority of the Breen Office. The momentous political issues confronting America during the Great Depression—calls for social and economic justice on the domestic front and alarms about the rise of fascism overseas—were nervously monitored by an industry ever wary of being on the wrong side of a divisive partisan debate. When a studio, usually Warner Bros., ventured into controversial thickets and dared to manipulate melodrama to denounce lynching, union busting, or fascist militarism, the MPPDA "on behalf of the industry" acted to stifle the preachments. Though the news might be delivered by the Breen Office, the policy came from upstairs, the MPPDA President and Board of Directors in New York, the real Hays Office.

The backstage dialogue over a film that was never produced illustrates the difference between enforcement and advisement—and between the moral purview of the Breen Office and the political sphere of the Hays Office. In 1936, MGM sent Breen a script based on Sinclair Lewis's dystopic antifascist novel *It Can't Happen Here*. A didactic mesh of real-life personalities and thinly disguised stand-ins for Huey Long, the late governor and self-styled "Kingfish" of Louisiana, and the fire-breathing radio priest Father Charles Coughlin, Lewis's speculative fiction conjured a not-too-distant future where a homespun demagogue brings storm troopers, book burnings, and concentration camps to an America whose vapid *demos* gets the government it deserves.

The sensitivity of the project warranted a detailed nine-page letter from Breen to MGM chieftain Louis B. Mayer. Breen frankly admitted: "The basic story, in our judgment, *is acceptable under the provisions of the Production Code,* but the story is enormously dangerous from the standpoint of political censorship, both in this country and abroad." Of course, MGM was free to handle a political time bomb, but the Breen Office was not responsible for defusing it.

> Before venturing to deal with the details of this story, we should like to state that the observations contained hereinafter are based *solely* upon our examination of the script from the standpoint of the Production Code and of political censorship. Because of the danger suggested by this script from the standpoint of *industry policy,* you will understand that nothing contained herein is meant to suggest any approval of this picture from the policy standpoint. The Production Code Administration has no responsibility for the policy angle which is inseparable from a story of this kind. The judgment ventured herein is not to be construed as having bearing whatever on this policy angle.

Along with a litany of Code-authorized mandates against brutality, violence, and blasphemy ("please eliminate the expression "Great God!"), Breen included a list of advisory cautions concerning the "political censorship" likely to result from fears about "general public disorder and rioting" should the film be produced.

> p. 72—Censor boards will surely eliminate the expression "with Prussic acid"—they will not allow the name of a specific poison.
>
> p. 83—Shad's line "I'd take him out and shoot him" will be eliminated by censor boards.
>
> p. 111—scenes 179 and 180—These scenes should be eliminated because of the definite detail of crime. Censor boards everywhere will eliminate it beyond any question of a doubt.

Breen signed off with an admonition that, he acknowledged, held no force of law:

> This story is of so inflammatory a nature, and so filled with dangerous material that only the greatest possible care will save it from being rejected on all sides . . . even [if] you do exercise the greatest possible care, the very nature

> of the picture is such as to subject it to the minutest criticism on all sides. This criticism may result in enormous difficulty to your studio if it does not result in the picture being denied permission to be exhibited publicly.
>
> We feel that you have a serious undertaking on your hands in launching a picture of this nature at this time. It is almost certain that the picture will be rejected pretty generally throughout the world, and it is more than likely that if it is permitted a permit for exhibition in this country, such permit will be obtained only after considerable negotiations and conferences with political censor boards everywhere.

Obviously, Breen personally frowned on a project as explosive as *It Can't Happen Here*, but he couched his objections as a courtesy opinion and kept to his side of the line of authority. Louis B. Mayer got the message: *It Can't Happen Here* did not happen.

Breen also regularly sent out warnings about the hurdles that might trip up provincial Americans in the overseas market. As Hollywood tightened its global grip over screen entertainment, complaints from foreign customers about Mexican banditos, Italian organ grinders, and Chinese coolies suggested that the stock stereotypes fit for domestic consumption traveled poorly in the countries of origin. Responding to angry letters with overseas postmarks and formal protests through diplomatic channels, the studios hired in-house advisers on foreign sensitivities to ensure, as *Variety* put it, that scripts "are not only joebreened for purity but also scrutinized by studio censors to be certain that nobody's toes are going to be stepped on." Of course, the person best qualified to "joebreen" the scenario was the man himself.

Breen's guidance on foreign affairs was especially valued for dealings with Hollywood's most important overseas market, the British Empire, an Anglophone preserve that included the United Kingdom, Australia, South Africa, and the colonies. Among other quirks, the reputedly bloodless British felt passionately about the neglect, cruelty, vivisection, medical experimentation, and other unethical treatments of animals, with no beast stirring more sympathy than the horse. Spurred to action by the equestrian carnage in Warner Bros.'s *The Charge of the Light Brigade* (1937), the British parliament empowered the British Board of Film Censors to ban any film implying cruelty to animals, a hard blow to the stampedes and rodeos in Hollywood westerns. To placate British sensitivities, the studios kept a more solicitous eye on horses than stuntmen, employing on-set observers and obtaining affidavits from humane societies.

The British had another aversion that Breen attributed to the inbred intolerance of the Protestant nation. "For your British print, we recommend that you shoot a protection shot of scenes showing characters making the sign of the cross," Breen suggested to David O. Selznick, referring to the Irish-Catholic plantation owners in *Gone With the Wind* (1939). "The action is acceptable pretty generally throughout the world except with the British Board in London."

Unlike Breen's edicts, Breen's advice might be rejected. After Paramount's success with Billy Wilder's *The Lost Weekend* (1945), the first Hollywood social problem film to depict the ravages of alcoholism, studios rushed into production a round of hard-drinking imitations. Breen tried to shut off the spigot with an admonition against exploitative "cycles" issued "for the good of the industry." Ignoring Breen's advice, Walter Wanger announced his own alcoholic melodrama, *Smash-up, The Story of a Woman* (1947). Breen tried again. "The 'use of liquor'—the scenes of drinking and drunkenness—which crowd this picture are proper and necessary," he admitted, but Wanger would do well to "dismiss this story from further consideration" because "showing a drunken woman moving about" is "both distasteful and repulsive; and the sound moral to your story will be forgotten in the reaction of disgust." Wanger went ahead anyway. He knew the ropes: as long as *Smash-up* did not violate the Code, Breen had no authority to block it.

Given the burden of his myriad regulatory and advisory responsibilities, Breen gladly relinquished authority over matters tangential to Catholic morality, domestic politics, or foreign sensitivities. Leo McCarey's *The Bells of St. Mary's* (1945) tolled a controversy not over the erotic sparks flying between Sister Mary Benedict (Ingrid Bergman) and Father O'Malley (Bing Crosby), but over the outmoded nineteenth-century treatment prescribed for tuberculosis, the novelistic malady that afflicts the beatific nun. "If only from a social welfare standpoint, we ought not to indicate in our pictures the wrong procedure for the treatment of such a widespread ailment as tuberculosis," Breen conceded when physicians bombarded him with second opinions. However, medicine was no more his specialty than Leo McCarey's. "We of the PCA have no authority in the matter, and it has been my experience that when we undertake seriously to suggest changes in films which are not strictly within our province, we get into trouble." Even for Hollywood's Supreme Enforcer and Advisor in Chief, enough was enough. "I think you know that I shudder at every suggestion made to impose further an additional responsibility on the shoulders of those of us who are of the PCA," he told the doctors. "We are already enormously overburdened."

6

CONFESSIONAL

As rendered in the purple prose of Hollywood memoirs and magazine profiles, the official portrait of Joseph I. Breen sketches a stereotype sent over from Central Casting: the bluff stage Irishman and the hard-nosed Mick, blarney and bluster, mixing the hearty congeniality of Pat O'Brien with the hair-trigger temper of James Cagney. "A man who could be as genial as a May breeze one minute and eruptive as a volcano the next," "gruff, hearty, and jovial," "a bull neck, a square jaw, and Irish blood," "one hard-boiled, two-fisted Irishman," and so on, as if taking dictation from the same studio press release. "Mr. Breen is a stocky, robust, and vigorous man with a dominating personality," was how the *New Republic* limned him in 1938. "His eyes are wide and candid, but his smiling mouth is tight in repose." In 1944, after a decade in harness, Breen may no longer have been in fighting trim, but neither had he mellowed. His MPPDA colleague Charles Francis "Socker" Coe described a man "silver-haired, florid of face, brown and wide of eye," who tends "just a little to avoirdupois but carries himself with a bustling erectness that mirrors a world of suppressed energy." The staff at the office concurred. "Joe was very . . . *positive* is putting it mildly," remembered Albert Van Schmus, who worked under Breen at the Production Code Administration from 1949 to 1954. "He was kind of . . . not bombastic, that's too extreme, but when he walked in to a room and started talking, people listened."

Acquaintances recall the personal magnetism, the boundless energy, and the easy eloquence of a born raconteur. "We were with him, chatted with him, interchanged ideas with him for over seven solid hours!" swooned a Catholic journalist in Chicago, who encountered Breen by chance outside an El station in 1930 and got the full treatment. "Never did hours flash by so quickly! Never did we hear a layman talk as he talked!" The talk was peppered with the erudition of a Jesuit education and the patios of a big-city reporter. "He is a newspaperman by profession, naturally gregarious, and having bounced about a lot, is no kill-joy," said a fellow newshound in 1938. "He sometimes conveys his ideas to the film panjandrums with colorful Celtic expletives—when the sound track isn't working."

Breen's use of Celtic, or rather Anglo-Saxon, expletives occasioned a good deal of wry commentary. Face-to-face, the man who fumigated screen dialogue was known to be foul-mouthed in his own conversation. Constrained from printing the unprintable in family forums, journalists made coy reference to the "colorful expletives" favored by the "two-fisted, leather lunged Joseph I. Breen." Breen's friend, the screenwriter and journalist J. P. McEvoy, regretted that in the prissy pages of the *Saturday Evening Post*, "I can't give you a verbatim report of one of Joe's sulphurous speeches explaining how he won't stand for sulphurous speeches." Tiptoeing around language that "would make a Billingsgate fishmonger blush," *Variety* observed, "It may sound paradoxical, but Hollywood is turning out cleaner pictures because of Joe Breen's profanity."

No verbatim transcript exists of the exact epithets and exclamations, but years later, when the usages could be typeset, longtime Code staffer Jack Vizzard emphasized Breen's saltier side in his R-rated memoir, *See No Evil: Life Inside a Hollywood Censor*. Vizzard relished the anecdote about the scatological one-upmanship in the first meeting between Breen and the noted vulgarian Harry Cohn, head of Columbia Pictures.

"What's all this shit?" scowled Cohn, when Breen presented him with his credentials.

"Mr. Cohn, I take that as a compliment," replied Breen. "My friends inform me that if there's any expert in this town on shit—it's you."

Geoffrey Shurlock, who knew Breen longer and more intimately, contradicted Vizzard's transcriptions. "Breen was not that type of man at all. Whatever coarseness and vulgarity he displayed—which was very rare by the way—was an act. He figured—with some justice—that when you got a script with coarse episodes in it, the best way to discuss the coarseness of the script was by using coarse language."

Breen knew that the coarse language was tactically advantageous, flustering the moguls who expected a genteel bluenose: here was no feminized censor, but a man's man, street-smart and not to be yanked around. "[The] Hays office['s] traditional silk glove tendencies have been changed to more virile tactics," reported *Daily Variety* in 1935. "Joe Breen brought the hemanism into the ultra-conservative confines of the office when he introduced the use of billingsgate [rough language, as above] in telling producers why this or that picture could not get by his purity seal."

The talk was backed up by intimidation tactics that were not purely vocal. "Equally as hardy with his hands as with his tongue, Breen, bespectacled, six feet tall and husky, too, has yet to lose a single fight-to-the-finish, verbal or otherwise, since he went on the spot last July [1934]," wrote an admiring journalist. That same year, when Pete Harrison visited the Breen Office for a firsthand look, he "heard stories about the battles [Breen] had fought with [filmmakers] that would make a genuine melodramatic thriller. . . . I learned that on several occasions he backed up a director, or a supervisor, or even a studio head, against the wall and threatened him with bodily injury because of some remark that cut Mr. Breen; for after all he is only human. And he has the physical ability to put his threats into deeds." Certainly, whether rhetorical or physical, doing battle with the moguls held no dread for a man who had emerged unscathed from the doctrinal infighting and personal grudges of the Catholic Church in America.

However acrimonious the dealings with the studios, Breen treated his staff with courtesy and good humor. He was happy to interrupt the business at hand with reminiscences from his salad days as a journalist or, in later years, from his early skirmishes in Hollywood, holding forth with anecdotes starring himself as the hero. He listened sympathetically and dispensed his sage advice on the proper handling of the temperamental artists and self-important martinets the staff had to deal with. To his equals, Breen was friendly and cheeky, to his superiors respectful but plainspoken. He and "Socker" Coe, who was appointed vice president of the MPPDA in April 1942, playfully called each other "Boss" because neither was sure who was higher in the chain of command.

Offstage and in private, the bright colors and airbrushed strokes of Breen's official 8x10 portrait begin to fray around the edges. Doing God's work at the Production Code Administration took an enormous personal toll. Breen possessed the fast-off-the-mark energies of a sprinter, but over the long run he got winded and faded. Though robust as a youth, he was often sickly in later life, afflicted with stomach, gall bladder, and intestinal ailments that regularly landed him in the hospital. From the mid-1920s onward, his letters complain of frequent coughing, vomiting, and intestinal pains, and his work life is interrupted by extended hospital stays and lengthy convalescences. "I remember sitting with him one August afternoon [in 1925] in the apartment of his brother, Jimmy, a Philadelphia lawyer, located in the Pennsylvania Hotel in West Philly," recalled the Catholic journalist Daniel E. Doran. "Joe was just recovering from a very serious illness which had lasted eight months and had reduced his 185 pounds of bone and muscle to about ninety-five pounds of skin and bones."

Late in 1925, when Breen signed on to publicize the Eucharistic Congress, he risked a relapse, but the importance of the work—and the need to support the family—overrode his misgivings. "If my health is good, I hope to get away with the job," he told Father Parsons, before leaving for Chicago. "Otherwise, I may be back East in short order." He soldiered on through the celebration of the Eucharistic Congress and the marketing of the documentary film, but while compiling the official history for a commemorative book, he collapsed under the weight of the work and was forced to relinquish his editorial duties.

Breen spent most of 1927 in Chicago and Philadelphia hospitals, visiting "one of my many doctors," or recuperating in Sea Isle, New Jersey, tormented by "some sort of an intestinal infection which the doctors have not been able to clear up. I've been flat [on my back] for two weeks with little hopeful prospects in sight." Two months later, still flat on his back, he informed a priest friend, "I have been seriously ill, and am still confined to St. Anthony's hospital, Chicago. I have had a serious infection in the gall bladder and my body is wasted and worn."

In between convalescences, Breen labored eighteen hours a day on the job of the moment, whether the Eucharistic Congress or the Chicago World's Fair. When he lacked an omnibus project to supervise, he compensated by taking on freelance work and charity projects for the Church.

In 1931, after moving to California, a new mission and a restorative landscape nourished the healthiest passage in Breen's life since his athletic youth. Pre-Code Hollywood may have been a moral blight, but the weather, the money, and the moderate workload were a salve to his physical well-being.

In February 1934, however, when Breen took over the Studio Relations Committee, he reassumed the breakneck pace and killing schedule that had repeatedly felled him in the 1920s. "Since I took over the administration of the Code—in addition to all else I have to do—I work seven days a week from about nine or nine-thirty in the morning until midnight," he wrote. "There were weeks when I hardly saw my babies from Sunday to Sunday."

Upon his appointment as PCA chief, the grueling regimen intensified. Even allowing for the puffery of a compliant Hollywood press corps, reporters who witnessed Breen at work in the 1930s were astonished at the volume of material flowing off his desk. "The task he has undertaken would have sent to the grave by this time ninety-nine out of each hundred of other persons who might have been appointed to the post, assuming these would want to do the work as conscientiously as Mr. Breen," said Pete Harrison.

Journalists were run ragged tailing Breen around on his daily rounds. They describe a dynamo, barking out dictation, coaching the morning huddles, and bolting out of the office to lower the boom, in person, on an uppity producer. "A husky citizen, firmly muscled, with iron-gray hair, he works at top speed, with five assistants, like a breaker boy in a mine, plucking slag and dirt from the run-of-the-mill films," ran a typical account. "He is a physical and mental personification of indefatigability," marveled another admiring reporter.

While reigning over Hollywood, Breen kept a low profile nationally and tried to live down his initial reputation as "the one man censor of the movies." Though by real-world standards he led a normal social life, by Hollywood standards he was a virtual recluse: granting only the occasional interview, shunning swank parties, and seldom appearing in the Hollywood gossip columns in man-about-town sightings. "He deliberately keeps in the background," reported *Liberty*. "He abhors publicity." Recalled Shurlock: Breen "didn't mingle too well [with the Hollywood crowd]" and socializing "just didn't work with this job." Besides, for a man with six children and a crippling workload, shyness was not the only reason to stick close to home.

Breen socialized on the fringes of what would later be called the Irish Mafia, the informal band of resident actors, directors, and screenwriters who shared an allegiance to the Pope, St. Patrick, and Johnnie Walker. Breen's mates were family men and churchman, like the actors Pat O'Brien and Frank Morgan, not the philandering boozehounds and Irish wastrels typified by the likes of John Barrymore, Errol Flynn, and screenwriter Gene Fowler. "I know Joe Breen, I have been with him in his home," wrote the English journalist William H. Mooring in 1934. "His family life is a model of family concord and married happiness." Twenty years later, Mooring still fondly remembered his first dinner as a guest of the Breens. It being Friday, Mary had prepared him a special meat dish, which was eyed enviously by the Breen children. "This was my first introduction to real, American family life," he recalled, by then a Catholic convert covering Hollywood for the Catholic press. "I have always remembered the squab, but even more clearly the Grace at table (which we skipped at home), the gaiety and games afterwards (our family was too small), and the atmosphere of this Catholic home which I may hope we have captured in our own."

Occasionally, Breen was spotted at a soiree or benefit, usually linked to the ethnography of the Emerald Isle: representing Hollywood at a St. Patrick's Day bash at the California Club with "those good sons or Erin" Pat O'Brien, director John Ford, and character actor Frankie McHugh or attending a benefit for the Abbey Players, visiting from Dublin. Mainly, though, he kept his shoulder to the wheel. "Clubs, golf, and other diversions have not taken much of his spare time and now that he is the busiest man in town they have no place at all in his daily routine," read a panegyric in the

Catholic press. Of course, one commitment outside the home was observed religiously. Every Sunday and Holy Day of Obligation, Joe, Mary, and the children attended mass at the Church of the Good Shepherd in Beverly Hills.

Inevitably, the dynamo wound down. "The job is a terrific physical trial, to say nothing of the mental and spiritual complications," Breen told Father Parsons after only a few months at the PCA. The pattern of the 1920s reemerged: he would work until exhaustion, convalesce, take a vacation, return to the desk rejuvenated, and then work until collapse. Again and again, he was hobbled by recurrences of the gall bladder and stomach maladies. "[My] doctor thinks it is all due to the terrific strain of the past year [1934] and he has hopes that a proposed trip will be just the thing to bring me around."

To leave the work at the office, Breen literally had to get out of town. In May 1935, Hays rewarded him with a two-month, all-expenses-paid European vacation, a hard-earned bonus and a long-deserved respite, said the *Brooklyn Tablet*, for "this excellent Christian gentleman who for months has labored fourteen and sixteen hours a day." Accompanied by Mary, he did the grand tour: Berlin, Carlsbad, Budapest, Vienna, Paris, and London, capped by a buoyant six-day road trip through Ireland. He gave movies and movie people a wide berth.

"I am simply *flabbergasted* because of [Hays's] kindness," Breen enthused to Maurice McKenzie, Hays's executive assistant. "I am to have a *two months* vacation *in Europe*, with the Boss paying all expenses for myself and Mary. I haven't recovered properly from the thrill of it all but the details will follow just as soon as I can gather my wits together."

On May 18, 1935, Breen left the office in the trusted hands of Geoffrey Shurlock and boarded the train to New York. *Variety*'s gossipy "Inside Stuff" column sent him off with a whimsical item:

> When Joe "Seal" Breen decided upon a trip to Europe, with a session at Carlsbad, he immediately picked up a string of advisors. For the next three weeks it became a daily battle of wills as to who would lay out his itinerary. . . . [Fox production chief] Winnie Sheehan and [MGM's] Louis Mayer were Breen's principal Coast counsel with [MPPDA Advertising Advisory Council head] Jeff McCarthy hollering from the East. The thing centered around whether Breen should start or finish in Carlsbad. Sheehan insisted the only logical schedule was to end the trip there, and Mayer agreed, but McCarthy, who arranged transportation, maintained he should make the resort his starting point over there.

Getting away from the Breen Office: Joe and Mary on vacation in Ireland, 1935.

(COURTESY OF MARY PAT DORR)

Like the Victorian gentleman he was, Breen sided with McCarthy and began the tour by taking the waters at the Bohemian resort:

> So Breen goes immediately to Carlsbad with a vow to keep all future plans a secret.

On July 30, 1935, after a joyous two months, Breen stepped off the train at Union Station, Los Angeles, where he told a waiting reporter that he hadn't given motion pictures a thought since leaving Hollywood. The next day, he was back at his desk, rested and ready to resume battle.

Upon return, Breen's mood swung upward: the indispensable man was back in harness, fighting the good fight. "I find the general outlook continues to be encouraging," he told Martin J. Quigley. "The boys in the studios, of course, tried to kick the traces over a little while I was away, but, fortunately, no serious damage seems to have been be done."

At least not to the Code; Breen was another matter. Once safely aboard the luxury liner *Manhattan* for the voyage to Europe, he realized the toll taken on his physical health and psychic equilibrium by the 18-hour days, the constant squabbling and screaming matches, the relentless deadlines and remorseless pressure. "I think [the trip] did me a lot of good, too because I was very tired when I started off and for the first two weeks after my departure from New York I slept many days as much as *15* hours!" he wrote Quigley. "All this seems incredible—because before I left here I seemed unable to sleep beyond two or three hours in the night. But now, thanks to the European trip, I seem to have difficulty in keeping awake."

The brusque and imperious façade Breen affected at work was consuming his inner life. Self-conscious enough to realize that the mask was becoming the man, he reflected on his psychic meltdown. "Along the first of the year I got to be as crabby as all hell—irritable, snooty, and dogmatic. What started out to be a pose—*hard-boiled* and *tough*—began to develop into a mode of living."

In offhand remarks to friends and in letters to confidantes, Breen expressed his discontent. Increasingly, he made noises about leaving the PCA.

Eager to keep their emissary at his post, Breen's fellow Catholics sought to soothe his misgivings with a full court press on his vanity and conscience. "You're not quitting are you? 'Say it ain't so, Joe,'" pleaded Patrick Scanlon, editor of the *Brooklyn Tablet*. "We don't want our Prima Donna to walk out, after all the rehearsal and just when the star performance is about to get going." Quigley chimed in to assure him that Hays "has always indicated a very hearty appreciation of you personally, and of your work." When Breen blustered, Quigley chalked it up to his "inalienable Celtic right of kind of blowing up every so often."

But Breen's irritability was more than Celtic venting. A sense of the personal cost of maintaining the bluff front, of wrestling with every producer in town, of being the designated whipping boy for the studios, the state censors, and the bluenoses, is reflected in the escalating desperation voiced in correspondence to his closest confidants.

By autumn 1937, Breen was at his wit's end. In an anguished letter to Quigley, he poured out his heart:

> Frankly, I'm terribly fed up [with] it and I want to get out. I've been at it now for three and a half years, day in and day out, and I'm beginning to feel the wear and tear of it. The constant quarrelling, fighting, arguing—the daily evidence that the sincerity of those with whom I have to contend assays about 10 per cent—the never-ending nervous tension which brings sleepless nights that are harrowing—is getting the better of me. I am convinced that, unless I find some miraculous way to completely change these people out here—*or get out of the job*—I am due for a nervous breakdown and an early grave.

Feverishly, he blurted out his torments:

> You have no idea what I have gone through. I have tried to "put on a good face"—to be courageous and "*gutty*" about it all, but I'm afraid I can't stand it much longer. And this, mind you, despite the fact that the difficulties are infinitely less today than they were, say, three, or even two, years ago. But three years ago, we were *fresh*—we hadn't been fighting the fight (good or bad) for three years. I find, today, that a good scrap that I should—and did—take "in my stride"—as a mere detail in the day's work three years ago, upsets me terribly. I worry ceaselessly.

The pressure, he believed, was literally eating away at him:

> The constant drive has me upset *internally*. I seem always to be in a state of *internal foment*. I can hardly sit in a chair for more than a few minutes and my digestion has gone to pot. I frequently vomit without any seeming cause at all. I do not get sick at the stomach and I don't get dizzy—symptoms usually associated with some illness of the digestive organs. I just vomit. When it is over, I seem, for an hour or two, to be allright again. I sleep very fitfully. I never get more than four or five hours sleep unless I get myself fatigued physically.

Financial worries—how would he take care of Mary and the children if he did quit?—added to his woes:

> The fact that Hays very generously gave me a substantial boost in salary served to keep me on, but I fear that I must now take some steps to remedy the situation. I am almost certain that, unless Divine Providence intervenes, I shall be a nervous wreck within a year—if I don't chuck the whole thing overboard.

The masculine stoicism bred into his tribe and generation aggravated the condition:

> So, you see, I am all worries—and so it is that I vomit. . . . I have not mentioned a word of this to *anyone*. Mary hasn't the slightest notion of what the real condition is. And neither has Hays.

Travel—his preferred restorative—soothed some of the tension. Throughout the 1930s, Breen crisscrossed the country on official and quasi-official business, by train in the days of luxury railroad travel, meeting with Jesuit friends in St. Louis and Chicago, stopping to visit brother James in Philadelphia, taking a side trip with Mary. In the summers of 1937 and 1938 he sailed to Europe, mixing a bit of MPPDA business with pleasure and relaxation. He also sought sun and a slower pace on vacations to Mexico and Panama. In 1939, for their twenty-fifth anniversary, he took Mary back to their beloved Jamaica for a second honeymoon.

As Breen's mood pitched and yawed, his Catholic sponsors grew alarmed. The concern resulted in a remarkable 12-page document, a diagnostic chart tracking Breen's psychological state, written in confidence by Rev. Gerard B. Donnelly, S.J., to Rev. Wilfrid Parsons, S.J., Breen's old friend and editor of *America*. In January 1936, Donnelly visited Breen in Hollywood, sized him up, and sent back to Parsons a white paper describing the subject's mental health. The report reads like a Jesuit version of an FBI profile or Freudian case study, with Donnelly the undercover agent-cum-therapist.

Donnelly's report opens with a joshing promise to Father Parsons to deliver in person the "interesting bits of my tour of the studios and the latest dope about Thelma Todd and Mae West." The priest then settles down to business. "I wanted in this letter to pass on the news, about Breen since that is what you and Quigley are most interested in."

Accompanied by Father John Devlin, the Legion of Decency's Hollywood chaplain, Donnelly happened to arrive at the Breen Office during one of the regular morning huddles. The title on the table was Sinclair Lewis's *It Can't Happen Here*, and the question was whether the antifascist tract and two similar stories should be approved for production. Though not strictly by the book, Breen solicited Donnelly's opinion. The priest argued that the upcoming presidential election and the foreign market in Italy and Germany made such provocative ventures unwise. After letting Donnelly say his piece, Breen revealed that the staff had just written a letter to MGM advising against the project for the same reasons. As Donnelly was sizing up Breen, Breen was psyching out the priest: moral minds think alike, Father.

Breen, Donnelly, and Devlin then went to lunch. Without prompting, Breen announced that he was quitting the job. "The more [Breen] talked the more I felt that he was fed up with the continual fights and cursing and yelling and with being made the goat," wrote Donnelly. "He was 'the target for all the hoots and jeers of all the critics.' He was 'carrying the whole burden alone.' The Code Administration after two years 'was running along nicely and was well established, functioning 100%'; so he was going to get out and let somebody else do the job. He made a good case for being depressed and sick of the whole thing."

Knowing Breen's volatile mood swings, Parsons and Quigley had instructed Donnelly to buck up their boy—partly by massaging his ego, partly by tugging at his Catholic conscience. The priest had prepared two rebuttal points. First, the PCA would collapse without Breen, who "was the one man in the country fitted by training and temperament—with the moral philosophy and the spirit to fight—to carry on the job." Second, Breen's work since 1934 had been a uniquely effective piece of Catholic action. Without his dynamic leadership, all that the PCA had accomplished would be lost.

Flattered but unpersuaded, Breen insisted that he was sick of the grind, that the PCA could muddle on without him, that he was throwing in the towel. Crestfallen, Donnelly went away from the lunch convinced Breen had abandoned his priestly calling.

However, over the next four days, during two dinners and two subsequent meetings at the PCA, Donnelly saw a different man. "As a result of these other two visits, my first impression underwent a complete change."

Donnelly now concluded that Breen "was certainly not sick of his job. He is enthusiastic about it. He talks of nothing else. He told story after story of his fights with producers and writers and quite obviously took a huge delight in the yells and threats and cursing. He was jamming unpleasant news down the throats of the studios—and loved it. He was dictator and from the spirit in which he talked I could see that he still got a big thrill out of enforcing his decrees."

Not least, Breen held a due regard for his own importance. "Again and again he told me how he was sitting at the top regulating the entertainment and moral thinking of 200 million people. He had stopped dirt and filth and outrageous ideas from getting to millions of impressionable young people."

Having examined and probed the patient, Donnelly gave his considered diagnosis. "I soon woke up to the fact that he was wholly convinced of the tremendous importance of his job, that he really felt he was doing a real bit of Catholic action, and that contrary to his own statements to me he was enjoying every minute of it."

Donnelly consulted Father Devlin for a second opinion. "You are absolutely right," agreed Devlin. "Breen sometimes gets depressed, and he talks a lot about quitting. But he does not intend to quit at all. He is completely sold on the idea of doing a tremendous moral job. He's too Catholic to quit."

7

INTERMISSION AT RKO

On April 25, 1941, a banner headline in the *Hollywood Reporter* broke startling news: "Breen Quits Hays Office Post." "Taking the industry entirely by surprise, Joe Breen resigned his post at the Hays office yesterday, offering no explanation except that he is 'tired,'" revealed the motion picture daily. Will H. Hays was to have made a formal announcement, but the news leaked out in New York and streaked west across the wire. "The story of Mr. Breen's resignation is correct," snapped Breen, bushwhacked by a trade reporter. "There is no comment!" Later, in a better mood, he pledged to soldier on at the Production Code Administration "until they can break in another boy." Ultimately, his resignation did not become effective until June 17, 1941.

Breen left his priestly work for a bigger payday and, he hoped, fewer headaches and less indigestion. Lured by nearly double his PCA salary (from around $50,000 to $100,000), he stepped down from the perch of the regulator to join the ranks of the regulated as general manager of RKO Studios and vice president of RKO Pictures. Instead of cutting the raw material, he would spin out the whole cloth of American cinema. It was not a felicitous career move. By May 1942, sullen but grateful, he was back at his desk in what was once again the Breen Office.

Breen's abrupt departure from the PCA, his truncated tenure at RKO, and his swift return to square one have always been something of a mystery. What compelled him to jump ship at just this moment when he had been complaining for years about the crushing workload and bitter battles of the censorship grind? Was it the serendipity of a job opening meeting the tipping point of total burnout? And why did Breen fail so abysmally as a would-be mogul? Was he simply promoted to his level of incompetence or did he fall victim to studio intrigue and corporate backstabbing? In retrospect, Breen's intermission at RKO calls to mind a man in midlife crisis—a husband leaving his frumpy wife for a more attractive partner only to slouch sheepishly back home once the passion is spent.

Not that RKO in 1941 was an enticing prospect for a randy fling. Formed in 1929 from a serpentine stock deal brokered by financier Joseph P. Kennedy (then involved with Hollywood filmmaking and silent star Gloria Swanson) and David Sarnoff, the broadcasting wizard and president of the Radio Corporation of America, RKO was the largest subsidiary division of RCA but the smallest and shakiest of the "Big Five" Hollywood studios. In 1933, its finances dried up by overproduction and theater acquisitions, the studio went into receivership, a notch away from bankruptcy, only to roar out of the Great Depression slump with Merian C. Cooper's blockbuster *King Kong* (1933) and prosper with a frothy franchise of Art Deco musicals starring Fred Astaire and Ginger Rogers. Nonetheless, compared to the powerhouse lineups at MGM, Twentieth Century-Fox, Warner Bros., and Paramount, the creative highs were built on a precarious corporate foundation, "a backdrop of management so fickle that one had to think like a Rockefeller to know who was in command or what the company policy was," observed film historian and Hollywood blueblood Betty Lasky in *RKO: The Biggest Little Major of Them All*, her inside-dopester account of the three decades of financial tumult and "wholesale firings and/or walkouts" that lent RKO "the image of a down-in-the-mouth studio." While brand name moguls like Jack Warner and Louis B. Mayer held sway like titled nobility, the executive ranks at RKO experienced an alarming turnover rate. "During the past five years, the RKO front office has been a veritable revolving door, with the boys whirling in and out at breakneck speed," wrote trade reporter Harold Heffernan in 1941. Fortunately, economic stability has never been a necessary precondition for artistic excellence in Hollywood. Coincidentally, as Breen was plotting his exit from the PCA, RKO was releasing its greatest motion picture, Orson Welles's *Citizen Kane* (1941).

For his part, Breen had good reason to seek more job satisfaction. With the big battles won and the machinery of self-regulation humming along, day-to-day life at the PCA had settled into a dull routine punctuated by low-level guerrilla warfare. After spending the second half of the 1930s in docile compliance, the turn toward the 1940s marked a measurable uptick in insolence and resistance from filmmakers. No one sought to overthrow the regime, only to sidestep and subvert it, to test the limits, gingerly and incrementally, torturing Breen—repayment in kind—with a thousand cuts. The incorrigibly recalcitrant became more openly rebellious; the reliably quiescent began to champ at the bit.

At the top of the list of malcontents was a pair of independent producers, each with a neck as stiff as Breen's and the financial wherewithal to go nose to nose. When the Breen Office pushed, David O. Selznick and Howard Hughes pushed back.

Selznick was the more respectable of the troublemakers. The grand impresario of *Gone With the Wind* (1939) was still chafing from his maddening skirmish with Breen over the wording of the curtain line snarled by a fed-up Rhett Butler at a stuck-up Scarlet O'Hara: "Frankly, my dear, I don't give a damn." The Breen Office had suggested that Rhett's kiss-off be changed to a less damnable valediction.

An exasperated Selznick took his case to the MPPDA Board, arguing that Rhett's retort was not only a "dramatic necessity but the best remembered line in the most beloved book of our generation." He won the appeal. "Can you imagine how silly Rhett would have sounded if he had said to Scarlet, 'Frankly, I don't care'?"

That, at least, is the oft-printed legend. In fact, the scuffle between Breen and Selznick was more complicated. On September 9, 1939, Selznick previewed *GWTW* to a surprised and (nearly four hours later) ecstatic crowd at Riverside, California, with Breen's substitute "I don't care" line. According to Selznick, the swooning audience felt cheated only by the deletion of a phrase "remembered, loved, and looked forward to by millions who have read this new American classic." The producer sought an exemption from Breen, who was unable, on his own authority, to override an exception to an ironclad Code dictate. However, he sympathized with Selznick's point and well understood the industry's stake in the $4 million epic, which had been gestating since 1936 and shooting for nearly a year. "Our discussions on the point have been very amicable and quite informal," Breen told Hays. "I have stated to David that I have no objections whatever to his taking the matter up with you and that we have no irritation or ill feeling in the matter at all." On October 20, 1939, when the MPPDA Board met and approved Selznick's appeal, it did so not only with Breen's full knowledge and approval, but with evidence from his own case files.[1]

Acknowledging Breen's amicability, Selznick's official brief to the MPPDA was more conciliatory than his subsequent public statements. "This word as used in the picture is not an oath or a curse. The worst that could be said against it is that it is a vulgarism," he contended, noting too

1. As Breen Office files noted, the epithet was actually heard once before, in the Warner Bros. Technicolor short *The Man Without a Country* (1937), a dramatization of Edward Everett Hale's cautionary tale of exiled affections. Spoken by the prodigal Lt. Philip Nolan, the key line "Damn the United States!" was doubly blasphemous (to God and country) but because the statement that led to Nolan's banishment served history and patriotism, Breen permitted the exclamation. "After all, it would have been a little harsh on Nolan to have exiled him for saying, 'Doggone the United States!'" explained trade reporter Douglas Churchill.

that an exception in his case "would establish a helpful precedent, a precedent which would give to Joe Breen discretionary powers to allow the use of certain harmless oaths and ejaculations whenever, in his opinion, they are not prejudicial to public morals." Moreover, even as Selznick was preparing his appeal, Breen took the rare step of releasing a statement expressing the PCA's esteem for what had lately been derided as "Selznick's Folly." "However many Oscars *GWTW* captures, and it will bid for them all, there should be an extra one for David Selznick for his fight to make this picture, in the face of the most baleful prophecies in production history."

Regardless, the brouhaha over the mild expletive garnered sheets of publicity, all of it roundly boxing the ears of the Breen Office. Reporters seized on the fatuous instance of bluenose sensitivity, and Selznick pumped the publicity machine. He had pulled off an unprecedented coup, managing not only to use the word but to do so in seeming defiance of rather than in collusion with Breen. "When Hays Office purists saw the naughty, naughty word in the script they were aghast," scoffed Hollywood columnist Jimmie Fidler. "Joseph Breen, chief censor of the Hays organization and probably the only Irishman in history to be appalled by so mild an expletive, rushed [to Hollywood] from New York to strike the offending word from the scenario."

The statement, an angry Breen wrote Fidler, "is not only false but utterly ridiculous." Despite feeling double-crossed, Breen decided not to confront Selznick by going public with his version of events. In retrospect, the back-and-forth over a single "damn" spat out in the most popular Hollywood film of its time was more than a blip and almost a bellwether. As long as a decision seemed "reasonable to most reasonable people," the Code accrued moral capital. When the decision seemed silly and unreasonable, the Code depleted its reserves of good will. Resentment was endurable; ridicule was lethal. As the dead ends of the grim 1930s opened into the expanding horizons of the purposeful 1940s, Breen found himself lagging behind the cultural wave, not riding the crest. "There hasn't been any objection to the line by any person who has seen the film," Selznick asserted, clinching his case with an accurate reading of the public pulse.

Pressing the advantage, Selznick agitated for reform. Admittedly, the Code was a "fortunate thing" back during the crisis of 1934, but "its set rules have become dated and I think it is about time to bring it up to date at least." The Breen Office regulations "go beyond even the most conservative opinion in their present form." Selznick's sniping in the press was what more timorous producers were muttering in private.

Breen's other nemesis was Howard Hughes, whose challenge to the Code came from the unlikely genre of the western, not hitherto known for testing the frontiers of decency, and whose offense was not a single word but a matched pair. Less cinematically talented than Selznick, Hughes, a multimillionaire aircraft tycoon who had been dabbling on and off in Hollywood production since the aeronautical spectacle *Hell's Angels* (1930), compensated with deeper pockets and greater mule-headedness. In early 1941, Hughes launched a huge publicity buildup for his latest thespian protégée, Jane Russell, and the proscenium from which to gander her curvature, *The Outlaw* (1943). The case of Howard Hughes, Jane Russell, and *The Outlaw* would bedevil Breen for nearly a decade, spilling forth most conspicuously only after the war.

Though less expansive by the tape measure, similar outbreaks erupted from the same regions. Besides Jane Russell, a gaggle of pert "sweater girls"—Veronica Lake in *I Wanted Wings* (1941), Ann Sheridan in *They Drive by Night* (1940), and Lana Turner in anything—stretched Code corseting with the contents of their contour-clinging pullovers. "In recent months we have noted a marked tendency to inject into motion pictures shots of low-cut dresses and costumes, which expose women's breasts, as well as 'sweater shots'—shots in which the breasts of women are clearly outlined and emphasized," noticed Pete Harrison, one of the few male critics miffed at the marked tendency. "All such shots are in direct violation of the provisions of the Production Code, which states clearly that 'the more intimate parts of the human body . . . the breasts of women' . . . must be fully covered at all times; that these should not be covered with transparent or translucent material, and they should not be clearly and unmistakably outlined by the garment." Citing the provision, the Breen Office notified studios that "sweaters that are too revealing, or outlining woman's breasts" must be put in mothballs.

Just as Margaret Mitchell's readers snickered at the delicate ears singed by *Gone With the Wind*, the Victorian dress code at the Breen Office incited hoots of derision. Joining in the "barrage of nationwide laughter and criticism," *Newsweek* reported that during the filming of *Henry Aldrich for President* (1941), Paramount kept its own in-house censor on set "watching scenes with nervous eyes to see that the girls didn't appear in the sweaters that are part of their everyday off-scene wardrobe." At *Motion Picture Herald*, the prudish Terry Ramsaye refused to join in the smirking, harrumphing that while "no point in the Production Code" required "that the screen shall indicate that women have no breasts," a firm policy existed against "making breasts into selling points." He intended no pun.

While the Code's not-so-dirty laundry was being aired in public, a string of unpublicized interoffice squabbles also frazzled and embittered Breen. The open defiance of Selznick and Hughes was the exception. Like manipu-

The original sweater girl: schoolgirl Lana Turner in *Dancing Co-Ed* (1939), with windbag teacher (Monte Woolley) and smitten boyfriend (Richard Carlson).

lative children, most producers preferred passive-aggressive resistance to noisy tantrums.

The favorite ploy was to ignore a few—not all, but a few—of the suggestions made by the Breen Office staff during the all-important script review phase. Later, when the review print was screened for what should have been a final pro-forma approval, the alert staffers noticed the original violations, left intact, and red-flagged them again. By then, however, corrective action required expensive postproduction editing and reshooting—whereupon the put-upon producer pleaded prohibitive costs and pressing release deadlines ("Be reasonable, Joe!"). The hurried last-minute negotiations and compromises meant that a process designed to be deliberate and smooth was rushed and pressured, resulting in a finished product that sometimes strayed over the Code line. Such knavery was not the usual Breen Office shuffle where both sides bobbed, weaved, and angled for advantage—it was cheating on the rules of the game.

By playing the postproduction change-up, veteran producer Hal Roach outfoxed Breen with the gender-bending comedy *Turnabout* (1940), a loopy farce in which a husband (John Hubbard) and wife (Carole Landis), cursed by a mischievous genie, switch bodies. As a satire on the divinely ordained immutability of sex roles, the plot twist already courted a misdemeanor arrest, but the cross-dressing antics (the actors don each other's clothing while lip-synching each other's dialogue track) risked a felony conviction. Whereas actress Landis is manfully restrained in her male guise, actor Hubbard flamboyantly embraces his inner female, flouncing about in a nightgown with exaggerated girly gesticulations that, given his visible male-ness, appear not female but effeminate. Equally scandalous to a Breen Office always on vigilant gender patrol was the trilling and sashaying of a prissy secondary character, played by Franklin Pangborn, a character actor whose shtick in trade was "pansy comedy." "This characterization of Mr. Pangborn as a 'pansy' is absolutely unacceptable, and must be omitted from the finished picture," Breen demanded. "If there is any such flavor, either in casting, direction, or dialogue, we will be unable to approve the picture." Sensing what was afoot, Breen underlined his demand in a second letter forbidding *"any action whatever* that might give a 'pansy' flavor" to scenes between Hubbard and Pangborn.

Sidestepping the Breen Office shuffle: (*clockwise*) William Gargon, Adolphe Menjou, Mary Astor, Joyce Compton, Berton Churchill, Donald Meek, and John Hubbard in Hal Roach's gender-bending comedy *Turnabout* (1940).

Shockingly, however, the pansy flavor perfumed the entire scenario. Pangborn and Hubbard bond during a cozy session of girl talk, cuddle with sisterly intimacy, and coo over the sheerness of a pair of nylon stockings. Bidding farewell, Hubbard tweets "Thank you again, and au revoir—Allen" and Pangborn tweets back "Toodle-oo, Timmsy." Roach's final cut contained "innumerable scenes with the Pangborn character, which suggested inescapably, sex perversion," bemoaned Breen.

The last line in *Turnabout* was more of a stunner than anything uttered in *Gone With the Wind*. Unbeknownst to the husband, his wife (whose body he inhabits) is pregnant. When he discovers his delicate condition, the couple pleads with the genie to restore their minds to their true bodies. The genie complies—overlooking one detail. "I've made a terrible mistake," he confesses. As the astounded husband moans in horror, the thrilled wife squeals: "Tim is going to have a baby!"

Roach told Breen he was "hard pressed financially" and needed to release the picture "promptly in order to get returns as soon as possible." Breen lectured Roach that "while the picture might be within the technical provisions of the Code," it was "highly unpleasant and likely to be received as such by my motion picture patrons." Roach claimed preview audiences were laughing their heads off.

Perhaps—but when *Turnabout* went into general release, bluenoses accused the Breen Office of being asleep at the switch.

"Two of our boys, here, followed [*Turnabout*] as best they could, in many instances getting a few pages of script *after* the material was shot," Breen explained to Martin J. Quigley, who wondered how in the name of Adam and Eve the gender twisting had slipped under Breen's nose. "We never received a complete script of the picture," Breen explained defensively. "There was a lull in our day-to-day receipt of pages, when, suddenly, the finished picture was submitted for our viewing." An old pro, Roach had knowingly violated the basic tenet of the review process, censorship in the script phase. "When our boys went to see it, they were, of course, amazed at the *then* ending," Breen shuddered.

In the juggling act that was self-regulation, Breen was bobbling the ball—in part because the center of cultural gravity had shifted. As wartime mobilization heated up, the equipoise between the normal temperature of the popular audience and the boiling point of the bluenoses became harder to calibrate. Ivan Spear, who covered the Hollywood beat for *Box Office*, sympathetically described the plight of the middleman censor. "Breen, in an effort to cooperate with producers, permitted dialogue and situations to stand which, a year or two ago, would have been summarily deleted," he explained. Besides *Turnabout*, the surge in borderline material "in which the dreaded *double entendre* was allowed to rear its ugly head" included *Arise, My Love* (1940), *The Philadelphia Story* (1940), *Comrade X* (1940), *That Night in Rio* (1941), and *Honeymoon for Three* (1941). "So, competent and hard-working Mr. Breen was squarely in the middle."

By 1941 the squeeze was tight enough to push Breen out the door. That spring, two films refused seals by the Breen Office, Fox's *Tin Pan Alley* (due to the diaphanous costuming of a chorus of harem girls) and Hughes's *The Outlaw* (due to "unacceptable breast shots" of Jane Russell) were appealed to the MPPDA's board in New York. Though the board upheld Breen in the first case, and finessed a deal in the second, the fact that producers were going over his head as a matter of course infuriated the man whose word alone had long been law. "This type of maneuvering and constant sniping at his work finally is reported to have prompted [Breen] to another post," concluded *Variety*. Sickly and weary of the torments, Breen finally decided that "his health was not being improved by the constant bickering." Figuratively and literally, a lack of intestinal fortitude caught up with him. He quietly handed his resignation to Hays and the decision was kept in-house until the *Hollywood Reporter* broke the news.

Soon afterward, rumors that Breen was being courted by RKO began circulating. Though Breen had been spotted dining with RKO president George J. Schaefer, he denied ongoing negotiations. *Variety* wasn't persuaded. "In trade circles, however, it is reported [Breen and Schaefer] have been talking—and not about the weather."

On May 16, 1941, an official statement from RKO formally announced the open secret. "Mr. Breen will take over his new duties shortly," the studio promised. Breen's official title would be General Manager in Charge of the Studio, with his formal election as a company vice president to take place at the next meeting of the RKO board that summer in New York.

In the midst of the transition, an intriguing rumor swept the industry: that Breen would bypass the post at RKO and replace Hays as president of the MPPDA. Hays was a sick man, still recuperating from major heart surgery. Perhaps more to the point in the war-shadowed summer of 1941, Hays's oft-expressed view of Hollywood as a mere entertainment machine was out of step with the job of propaganda on the horizon. "Washington is said to favor [Breen] and to look upon Hays with cold eyes," said the *Hollywood Reporter*, stoking the rumor mill. "Breen says nothing and looks bewildered by the cross-currents of pressure being brought to bear on him." Whether a trial balloon or wishful thinking, the buzz lasted less than twenty-four hours. As announced, Breen would go to RKO.

From his home in Sullivan, Indiana, Will Hays issued a terse expression of regret and appreciation. Breen's "signal ability, indefatigable energy and complete devotion to the principles upon which the Code is based enabled him to perform a very difficult task in a truly masterful manner. The entire industry is under a great obligation to him," Hays declared. "All wish him the greatest success in his new connection." Other industry voices were more full-throated in praise. Billy Wilkerson reminded Hollywood of a stunning set of statistics—that since 1934, Breen had vetted more than 50,000 scripts, books, and plays, and stamped the Code Seal on some 4,200 features and 12,000 shorts. "Wherever Breen goes, whatever he does, he will take with him the thanks of everyone connected with the making of pictures here for a tough job well done," said Wilkerson. "And he deserves the best he can get."

THE PCA IN LIMBO

As news of Breen's defection spread through executive boardrooms and studio cafeterias, speculation about a successor started immediately. To the motion picture industry, the head of the PCA was more important than any single studio mogul. He kept the state censors at bay, mollified the Legion of Decency, and marginalized independent productions by maintaining MPPDA control over exhibition venues. Breen's track record set a high bar: moral probity was the least of the job's qualifications. His successor had also to be an administrator of boundless energy and crisp efficiency, else the conveyer belt of studio production break down and unravel. Hundreds of films per year needed to be sorted, sanitized, and sealed.

Around Hollywood, Breen's departure was not greeted with the expected chant (while the cat's away, the mice will play), but by a rueful caution (the devil you know is better than the devil you don't know). After all, Breen was nothing if not predictable. Whatever resentments producers harbored against the Breen Office, the man in charge lent stability and certainty to the necessary business of censorship. Among studio executives, the desire for more liberating elbow room was balanced by the fear of bumping into damaging controversy or suffering an incompetent bluenose. "Now Hollywood *really* has Breen trouble," wrote a bemused Adela Rogers St. Johns, the diva of studio-smart journalism. "Whom are we going to get to replace the wise, experienced, diplomatic, tolerant, yet stern and rockbound Mr. Breen?"

No less anxiety-inducing was the prospect of a destabilizing rules change under a new regime. "No matter who is chosen, interpretation of the industry's film code is bound to differ from Breen's administration excepting on ironclad definitions such as nudity and obscenity," speculated *Variety*. Other predictions were more alarmist. "Without the guidance and moral force of its director, Joe Breen," the PCA might well become "a complete farce," worried Pete Harrison. "There is no other person in the industry who can give to the Production Code Administration the dignity and effectiveness that Joe Breen has given it." Perhaps not, but a capable substitute needed to be brought on board, and fast.

To calm the jittery moguls, Hays offered reassurances that "the work of the Production Code Administration is so organized that it will continue to function effectively with its present staff until the post of a director is again filled." Hinting that the Breen-centricity of the past was not to be the practice of the future, he reminded producers that "the Code Administration operates as a board with a director who is the presiding officer"—an administrative detail overlooked under the Breen regime.

The early handicapping on a replacement for Breen favored Francis S. Harmon, the head of the two-man branch of the PCA in New York since 1937. This was news to Harmon, who claimed to know nothing of the rumors. As a potential Code chieftain, however, Harmon had two drawbacks: first, he was not a Catholic, a virtual job qualification; second, he was already overburdened with other demanding duties. In addition to his Code work, he served as an executive assistant to Hays and as Coordinator of National Defense Activity for the Motion Picture Industry, a post assuming growing importance with war raging in Europe and looming for America.

The logical successor and heir apparent was Breen's longtime right-hand man, Geoffrey Shurlock, a master of both the requisite bureaucracy and theology. A holdover from the old Studio Relations Committee, the English-born literary editor by trade had been in harness since 1932. Like Harmon, however, Shurlock was not a Catholic; he was an Episcopalian. He was also considered a little too soft-spoken and genteel to grapple in the pit with the gruff studio heads. Contradictorily, the moguls wanted someone compliant, but not *too* compliant, for the job: someone strong enough to keep those other guys in line.

As the MPPDA board in New York and the moguls in Hollywood weighed the options, the line of succession was debated beyond studio gates—not just in the trade press and the civilian newspapers, but as far away as the chambers of the U.S. Senate. Sen. Gerald P. Nye (R-ND), cultivating his reputation as the most noxious antisemitic isolationist on Capitol Hill, accused Harry M. Warner of blackballing the candidacy of an unnamed member of the House of Representatives [John Costello]. "Mr. Warner is alleged to have most emphatically told his associates that this particular candidate would not be considered for a moment [to replace Breen] since he, Mr. Warner, had learned this candidate had voted against [FDR's] Lend-Lease bill [to aid Great Britain]," Nye charged.

Naturally, the palace guard to the PCA claimed a priority interest. Nervously eyeing the situation and kibitzing from offstage, the Catholics nominated two favorite sons, both of whom, *mirabile dictu*, shared a common religion and ethnicity: Rep. John Costello (D-CA) and U.S. District Court Judge J. F. T. O'Connor. The Catholics wanted if not a militant crusader then at least a weekly communicant who could be counted on to continue their privileged back-channel access. "As yet, we do not know who will take [Breen's] place, but we hope that he will be a Catholic of strong character," prayed Bishop Joseph T. McGucken of Los Angeles.

In fact, with Breen out of the picture, the Catholic auxiliary soon detected signs of backsliding. A mere four months after Breen's exit, *Variety* registered "a feeling in Catholic circles that films have undergone something of a 'moral deterioration' since the resignation of Joseph I. Breen as censor for the MPPDA." Of course, the notion that screen morality had deteriorated so rapidly was nonsense: all the films then in release had been vetted by the Breen Office. Apparently, the mere thought that the watchman was no longer at his post was sufficient to make the current Hollywood lineup look more squalid.

Coincidentally, or not, a post-Breen release emerged as Exhibit A in the Catholic case against creeping Episcopalianism at the PCA. MGM's off-pitch screwball comedy *Two-Faced Woman* (1941) gave Geoffrey Shurlock a bracing lesson in the travails of a censor's life in the crosshairs. "Do I remember it?" he blurted out to an interviewer decades later. "I nearly got fired over [that] film."

A would-be follow up to Ernst Lubitsch's luminous *Ninotchka* (1939), *Two-Faced Woman* reteamed Greta Garbo and Melvyn Douglas under the direction of George Cukor, who not only lacked the Lubitsch touch but had lost his own deft hand for screwball antics on view in *The Philadelphia Story* (1940). A mean-spirited comedy of ill manners, the film features Douglas as a neglectful, narcissistic husband to his new bride, Garbo, a rosy-cheeked ski instructor. With the honeymoon over, he abandons her at a ski lodge, returning to his high-powered media job in the big city and the affections of a comely playwright (Constance Bennett) determined to sink her claws into the married man. Desperate to rekindle the conjugal fires, Garbo arrives in town and pretends to be her own high-living, gold-digging twin sister. Smitten by the wild, impetuous doppelganger of his safe, outdoorsy wife, Douglas woos the faux minx.

To the literal non-Catholic mind, the fact that the husband was trying to seduce his own wife would preclude adultery, but as a Jesuit-educated censor would have understood, sin is a matter of volition no less than action. In courting the look-alike trollop, the wayward husband commits adultery in

Condemned by the Legion: a wayward husband (Melvyn Douglas) lusts after the sexier version of his own wife (Greta Garbo) in George Cukor's *Two-Faced Woman* (1941).

his heart. (Later, a confidential PCA report on the uproar confirmed that "the original story was told verbally to Mr. Breen by [producer] Mr. [Bernie] Hyman of MGM, and rejected by Mr. Breen.")

Released with a Code Seal in November 1941, *Two-Faced Woman* was condemned by the Legion of Decency for its "immoral and un-Christian attitude toward marriage and its obligations; impudently suggestive scenes, dialogue, and situations; [and] suggestive costumes." In a pastoral letter read at all masses, Archbishop Francis J. Spellman of New York warned that *Two-Faced Woman* was "a danger to public morality and, for Catholics, an occasion for sin." It was the first studio release to be condemned by the Legion—a box office death sentence that gave the moguls ugly flashbacks of the pickets and pledges of 1934.

"There is no exact science in the production of motion pictures," stammered MGM's Howard Dietz in response. "People do at various times differ as to the effect of a given line or scene, particularly in a picture such as this, which is a comedy, designed to amuse." Folding immediately, MGM cut *Two-Faced Woman* to Legion specifications—rebuilding sets already struck and calling Garbo and Douglas back for retakes "to make it clear in the minds of the audience that Blake [Douglas] knew Karin [Garbo] was his wife." After the face-lift, the film earned placement onto the Legion's less lethal B list ("objectionable in part for all"). Had Breen—or a good Catholic with close contacts at the Legion—been at the desk, the whole hassle might have been averted. Of course, that was just the message the Legion wanted to send.

Meanwhile, Shurlock ran the Hollywood office of the PCA, with a staff comprised of Addison Durland, Arthur Houghton, T. A. Lynch, Charles R. Metzger, Charles Pettijohn, Jr., and Harry Zehner. To signal the change of the guardian, Shurlock established a new credit line for the office stationery. Henceforth, all letters from the PCA to the studios would bear the imprint of the entire board. Rather than the personal imprimatur of Joseph I. Breen, the more modest autograph of Geoffrey Shurlock notarized all official PCA communications "for the board." Shurlock hoped to avoid bad blood by depersonalizing the process. Hays readily approved.

Shurlock's signature modesty notwithstanding, the moguls who took him for an easier touch than Breen were mistaken. Perhaps overcompensating for the shoes he was filling, the sweet-tempered Englishman played the part of the stubborn Irishman. "Shurlock can't be pushed around," reported *Variety*, itself somewhat abashed by his "surprisingly stern control." "[Shurlock's] definite 'no' on certain PCA topics has burned [the moguls] up. . . . His only reply to squawks is that [producers] won't get a Code Seal when his suggestions are ignored unless they want to carry the issue to the Hays directors, who always have sustained the PCA head." When producers tried to work the same hustle on Shurlock that had so beaten down Breen—ignoring PCA criticisms of the shooting script, filming the blue-penciled material, and then, when the final print was tagged for violations, pleading honest misunderstandings and the high costs of reshooting—Shurlock refused to roll over. "A couple of producers attempted to get by without making suggested revisions and wound up having to make the changes anyway on the completed picture. All of this has not set well," *Variety* continued. "Hence the clamor from producers for a new PCA chief."

Despite the dustups—the usual stuff, really—the PCA under Shurlock processed the incoming work punctually and guided studio releases through the pipeline on schedule. He had every reason to expect a permanent appointment. Yet as the weeks and then months dragged on, Hays and the MPPDA dallied, leaving Shurlock twisting.

On December 7, 1941, Hollywood woke up to more pressing business. After Pearl Harbor, Francis Harmon moved full time to coordinate the War Activities Committee (WAC) of the Motion Picture Industry, the wartime successor to the peacetime National Defense Coordinating Committee. On the West Coast, Shurlock was given full supervisory authority over the Code, but still no formal appointment. Asked if he wanted the job, Shurlock claimed to be content to play understudy. "Not for all the tea in China," he said. "Life's too short and I'm too weak. The sooner they get someone else to take over the berth, the better I'll sleep at night. Yes, the money's good, but not that job for all the gold in Kentucky."

THE CENSOR AS MOGUL

Hiring a censor to nurture creativity might seem counterintuitive, but George Schaefer's selection of Breen to oversee production at RKO was no roll of the dice or off-the-wall curve. Breen was an executive of proven ability and diligent habits; he understood the production process from first pitch to final cut; and he knew the plots, formulas, and genres of Hollywood as well as any man in town. What looked like an eccentric gambit on first blush might, on second thought, seem a stroke of genius. "Further proof of the sagacity of [RKO's] leaders is their installation of Joseph I. Breen in the top production job," gushed "Phil. M. Daly," the eponymous trade columnist for the *Film Daily*. "For eight years he has read every script the Coast has made. Obviously, as a result, he has the broadest possible knowledge of the job at hand."

As RKO's general manager, Breen was given, on paper, overall authority of the entire studio, except for the actual online supervision of pictures, the job of individual unit producers. Unlike the forceful studio heads at Warner Bros., MGM, and Columbia, whose tentacles stretched into every budget line and casting decision, the position of studio chief at RKO was more grand schemer than floor manager. The dizzying rate of turnover at RKO's highest executive ranks had ceded a good deal of operational control to middle management. The result was a studio style and ethos far more eclectic (*read*: scattered) than the personal imprint on production bequeathed by the likes of Irving Thalberg at MGM or Ernst Lubitsch at Paramount.

Breen took his time cleaning out his desk at the PCA. He was having trouble letting go. Even while traveling from Hollywood to New York for his first formal meetings with RKO executives, he made time to stop in Chicago to meet with Hays and Francis Harmon to discuss the transition.

Not until June 18, 1941, at the RKO sales convention at the Waldorf-Astoria in New York, was the former censor and tyro mogul formally introduced to the company's stockholders. As Breen sat on the dais, Schaefer spoke words aimed to please his new hire. RKO would never "swerve from the path of decency and wholesomeness," Schaefer pledged, before milking

RKO–Catholic Church: Breen, Auxiliary Bishop Joseph T. McGucken, Mary Breen, and RKO casting director Ben Piazzo at the Los Angeles premiere of the March of Time's special feature *The Story of the Vatican*, November 1, 1941. The woman on Breen's right has eluded identification.

(COURTESY OF MARY PAT DORR)

a likely metaphor. "If we have troubles at the box office, I do not believe that an under-sized sweater on an oversized girl is the solution," he jested. "Our troubles will be solved by the flexibility of the industry and not by the flexibility of the sweater."

After his official induction, Breen did something he had not done since 1934: he held a full-dress press conference. Exuding brisk confidence in his new role as studio mogul, a voluble Breen promised to shake things up at RKO with new talent and fresh ideas. "One thing wrong with the business is too many bad pictures are being released," he declared. "I won't make that kind." Asked what would happen if the PCA rejected one of *his* pictures, Breen chortled. "Those guys hadn't better monkey with me—I know all the answers." He also confessed his reason for bowing out: "I was punchy after eight years at it."

Reporters were impressed with a performance conducted with what the *New York Times* called "amazing candor and disarming frankness." *Box Office*'s Ivan Spear saw a changed man. At the PCA, Breen "barricaded himself behind a formidable secretarial wall. Few indeed were the newsmen who scaled the barrier to be permitted a few words with the censor-in-chief and even fewer were the morsels of information forthcoming when such rare interviews were granted." Breen's press conference revealed "a very sincere, interesting, and likeable gent, rather than the dour ogre which his former apparent allergy to newshawks indicated."

Once on the job at RKO, however, another species of shark circled around the new fish. When Breen sought to implement a reorganization of RKO production (a scheme involving three divisional operating heads answerable to him, with Sol Lesser responsible for the studio's "A" films, J. R. McDonough in charge of "B" films, and Reginald Armour acting as studio administrator), RKO higher-ups in New York balked. Wary of so fundamental an overhaul on site, the board of directors obstructed Breen's ambitions to consolidate his power.

Breen was more successful stroking the egos of his stable of artists, foremost among them the polymath genius Orson Welles. After watching the dailies of *The Magnificent Ambersons* (1942), Breen sent Welles a glowing note. "I have not been so impressed in years," he enthused. "The material we saw was really excellent, and although you know me to be a chronic kicker, in this instance I have naught but praise—from my heart. God love you." Welles's snowbound version of the Booth Tarkington novel, set in the lost world of Victorian America in the 1890s, was Breen's kind of picture. Breen also courted director John Ford, trying to lure his friend away from Fox for a unit production deal at RKO, and the New Deal documentarian Pare Lorentz, whom he feted at a special dinner at RKO studios.

Breen had to deal with another headache attendant to studio operations—the Production Code Administration. Despite the delicious irony in the role reversal of the former censor being censored by the censors, Code staffers never cracked a smile in their official correspondence to Joseph I. Breen at RKO. "Going through the script in detail, we call your attention to the following points," began a communication about RKO's wartime musical comedy *Four Jacks and a Jill* (1942), which cautioned Breen about burlesque bumps, plosive raspberries, and risqué lyrics ("I'm feeling as bare as an aspirin" would have to be cut from the song "I Haven't a Thing to Wear"). Still, Shurlock and his boys must have savored the chance to warn their former boss about the dangers of "illicit sex affairs" and suggest that on Catholic matters he "avail [himself] of the services of Rev. Father Devlin." Except for the impersonal signature at the bottom of the page, the letters from the PCA to Breen at RKO are indistinguishable from the letters Breen sent to RKO from the PCA.

The Code, Breen could handle; Machiavellian corporate intrigue, at least in a non-Catholic context, was a different story. By November 1941, Breen was flying to New York to meet with RKO's board of directors in order to underscore the terms of his contract: carte blanche in studio operations. Notwithstanding, as early as December, with four and a half years left on his five-year contract, Breen's star had so dimmed that the press had spotted the telltale signs of a fade-out. "Don't be surprised by an overnight announcement that Joe Breen is pulling out of an executive post at RKO to resume his old censoring role at the Hays Office," entertainment reporter Harold Heffernan revealed. Heffernan's scoop was premature, but that rumors of Breen's demise were floated so early meant that the knives were out. A face-saving cover story was already being fabricated: that Breen would ride to the rescue of a troubled PCA not be pushed out the door at RKO. "Plenty of pressure is being brought to bear on him for just such a move. The picture business has been in a jam over questionable scripts, etc., ever since Breen left six months ago," said Heffernan.

On December 16, 1941, RKO president George J. Schaefer moved to streamline operations and realign responsibilities by naming N. Peter Rathvon to a vice presidency. A financier of broad international experience who sat on RKO's board, Rathvon was already plotting to unseat an RKO executive higher up the ranks than Breen, namely Schaefer himself.

Though Breen could hardly be held responsible for the studio's track record in 1941, the dismal year-end report on RKO's investment portfolio did not burnish his image. RKO was still "the problem child of Hollywood" and the "weakest of all the companies for permanent star listing," *Variety* decreed in its annual postmortem on industry trends. "Maybe better luck in 1942."

Yet next year too the luck of the Irishman was all bad. First, Sol Lesser and J. R. McDonough resigned, contributing to the atmosphere of rudderless instability. Lesser was a name talent with a proven track record. McDonough had been with the studio for nine years. Breen had asked both men to delay a final decision until after he consulted with Schaefer, but both insisted on leaving immediately. Accustomed to a large measure of personal autonomy, Lesser and McDonough bridled at Breen's plans to centralize production and economize on small unit budgets. Another well-regarded associate producer, Howard Benedict, also bailed.

By the end of February 1942, "reliable reports" agreed that Charles W. Koerner, currently operating head of RKO Theaters, was in line to replace Breen. In a last-ditch effort to salvage the arrangement, Breen, Koerner, Schaefer, and the upper echelons of RKO retreated for a conclave in La Quinta, California, deep in the Mojave Desert, to try to iron out difficulties away from the prying eyes of the Hollywood trade press. Perhaps Koerner and Breen might split responsibilities, with Koerner as general manager and Breen staying on as vice president in charge of production? After a week of tense meetings, the only point of agreement was that Breen would clear out of town for a vacation.

Exhausted and defeated, Breen fled to Mexico. "I am very much under par and I feel the need of some relaxation," he wrote Bishop McGucken, not telling the half of it. "Plenty of fresh air and frijoles should make a new man of you," replied the Bishop cheerfully.

A new man was just what RKO had in mind, and he was not Breen. On March 9, 1942, Koerner took over as general manager of RKO, ostensibly to hold the post only until April 6, when Breen was slated to return from his extended siesta in Mexico. Officially, Koerner's duties were deemed temporary and "experimental," but Breen's days as a mogul were numbered. Having cut his teeth in the exhibition end of the business, Koerner was considered closer to the paying customers queuing at the ticket window. He was also immensely likeable and hugely popular on the lot. "[Koerner] was endowed with more warmth, charm, and generosity than anyone who had ever headed a studio during my time," recalled the actor Pat O'Brien.

The next week, Schaefer and members of RKO's board of directors visited the RKO lot to check out the setup under Koerner. They liked what they saw. Breen must have winced as he read the writing on the wall in Ivan Spear's column in *Box Office*:

> With competent Charles Koerner, who brings a practical, successful showman's viewpoint to the problem of production, sitting in the driver's seat (temporarily according to official communiqués—but permanently according to all indications) it is entirely reasonable to assume that the studio will soon have its own, internal filmmaking program on a comparably solid basis. So there is every sign that the Gower Street film foundry [the location of RKO's executive offices], long the overworked patsy for film capital rumor mongers, is finally off on a long end run.

Perhaps the quick quietus was a blessing in disguise. Martin J. Quigley, who well knew the temperament, and temper, of his friend, understood that the mantle of mogul was a bad fit for Breen. As far back as 1935, when Breen first talked about bolting the PCA, Quigley cautioned him against ever entering "one of those mad houses which are called studios." "I wonder very much how you would react to the political turmoil which exists, in one degree or another, in all of these studios [and] . . . I have a pretty definite picture in my mind as to how you would undoubtedly react to the bombastic mutterings of some of these tin gods who momentarily hold czaristic sway in the studios."

The tin god Breen rubbed the wrong way was N. Peter Ravthon, who by June 1942 had also edged out Schaefer, Breen's sponsor, to become RKO president. "I asked [Breen] about the RKO story," says Albert Van Schmus, who was hired by Breen as a production clerk at RKO in 1941 and later worked under him at the PCA from 1949 to 1954. "And he said he got into a controversy with N. Peter Ravthon. . . . And he said, 'we could not come to terms. We could not agree.' So he said, 'I'm leaving.' And he went back to the Code. At the Code they said, 'Any time you want to come back, you can come back.' "

Actually, Breen's soft landing back at the PCA was not a done deal. Initially, as the dream job at RKO fell apart, Breen played hard to get, insinuating his "disinclination to rejoin the Hays Office as Production Code authority." Besides pride, the main sticking point was money. Breen's old salary at the PCA was $50,000; his present one at RKO was $100,000. As Breen angled to split the difference, the MPPDA rather publicly interviewed a quite credible substitute, Judge Stephen S. Jackson of New York, who was a triple threat—a sitting judge, a crusading censor, and a practicing Catholic.

Breen swallowed hard and sent out availability signals. "[It is] understood that Breen is ready and willing to administer the Production Code again," *Variety* reported on March 23. He would return at his old salary, with RKO settling his contract with a generous severance "so that he can return to his old berth at the Hays Office." On May 15, 1942, Hays formally announced that the deal was closed, and a week later Breen was back behind his old desk at the Production Code Administration, mogul no more, censor again. "He might have been just on vacation as far as anyone was concerned," said Shurlock, relieved to be out of target range.

In a high-pressure, fast-paced working life, Breen had emerged unscathed and triumphant from the unforgiving precincts of tabloid journalism, government service, big business, and the Roman Catholic Church. He came undone and returned defeated only from the job of running a major Hollywood studio. "Not half a dozen men have ever been able to keep the whole equation of pictures in their heads," wrote F. Scott Fitzgerald in *The Last Tycoon*, thinking of MGM's maestro Irving Thalberg. Breen would not be numbered among them. The advanced calculus was beyond his skill set. The man who, at the PCA, left his imprint on hundreds of films, made barely an impression on the product line from RKO.

8

AT WAR WITH THE BREEN OFFICE

On December 7, 1941, at 7:50 a.m., the bulletin that would live in infamy rippled out from the Pacific. Radio, not cinema, transmitted the news, barked in tense, panicky tones broken up by the crackle of shortwave static. Later, memory, myth, and Hollywood remembered the thunderclap moment as the disruption of a pastoral idyll—returning from Sunday mass to huddle anxiously around a wood-paneled Philco, as in *The Sullivans* (1944), the heartbreaking tale of the five brothers from a single Iowa family killed by Japanese torpedoes in the waters off Guadalcanal, or having a warm celebration cut short by an icy threat, as in *They Were Expendable* (1945), John Ford's elegiac combat film. The blast from Pearl Harbor was a wall of demarcation between a secure existence and an unknown country, the open-ended phrase "for the duration" expressing the uncertain future.

From Pearl Harbor to V-J Day, Washington and Hollywood were entwined more tightly than ever before, or since. It is a familiar, oft-told war story—Hollywood's favorite, its own. Syncopated to the swing of Glenn Miller and the harmonies of the Andrews Sisters, the screen unreels the upbeat movies-go-to-war montage: dolled-up ingénues dancing with smitten GIs at the Hollywood Canteen, stars hawking war bonds at massive rallies, and actors and actresses pleading with moviegoers to donate blood, enlist in the WACs, work in a defense factory, save scrap metal, conserve gas, watch the shoreline, plant a Victory Garden, and seal loose lips. "Hollywood Does Its Bit!" exclaimed the newsreel intertitles, protesting a bit too much that pampered stars and wealthy executives were *not* soaking up the sun and lapping up the sweet life around swimming pools while less glamorous recruits sweated at Fort Benning or died on Bataan.

For the motion picture industry, no less than for the rest of America, World War II wrought a material and moral transformation. It meant not merely the enlistment into uniform of bankable leading men, brilliant A-list directors, and thousands of skilled craftsmen and technicians, but the conscription of the entire ideological apparatus of Hollywood cinema. Heroism was redefined, genres realigned, styles redesigned, happy endings forestalled, and boy-girl closure denied. "The problems of three little people ain't worth a hill of beans in this crazy world," the reformed isolationist Rick (Humphrey Bogart) tells Ilsa (Ingrid Bergman) in *Casablanca* (1942) before sacrificing his true love for the true glory.

Once enlisted in the crusade, Hollywood cinema underwent a metamorphosis as visible as the wardrobe change from civilian clothing to military dress. Casting off its prewar garb of frothy escapism and suiting up for an earnest, full-dress didacticism, the screen dedicated itself to basic training and drill instruction. After 1941, a chorus of stern exhortation and a tapestry of patriotic bunting telegraphed the messages of America at war.

The wartime telegrams delivered another message. Hollywood cinema had always been packed with subterranean meaning and laced with overt moralizing, but WWII thrust the cultural power of the medium straight to the surface. A collateral and unintended consequence of the up-front admonitions of the war years was the exposure of the hidden agendas of the Production Code. Where the Code Seal was a tiny oval, seldom noticed, in the lower left corner of an opening frame, a more prominent logo stamped on the end credits was hard to miss: the American eagle and the slogan "Buy War Bonds."

For Joseph I. Breen, WWII brought the dreadful prospect of literal telegrams from the War Department: his three sons were all serving in uniform, in the combat zones. In purely professional terms, however, the mobilization of the studio system meant his demotion from the ranks of Hollywood's General Staff. Not seeing, or refusing to see, that the event convulsing American culture was transforming Hollywood cinema, he upheld the Code and protected his turf as tenaciously as ever, oblivious to the present emergency. Breen was not a slacker or a saboteur; he was simply beside the point, irrelevant to the essential work performed by Hollywood at war.

SHATTERING THE MYTH OF MERE ENTERTAINMENT

"If you want to send a message, use Western Union," snapped Sam Goldwyn, or maybe it was Harry Warner. Whoever first spoke the words Hollywood lived by, the epigram masked the extent to which motion pictures had always been telegraphing messages and, in fact, had codified them. Before WWII, Hollywood's official stance was that motion pictures were escapist fantasies and fluffy diversions, soothing entertainments that massaged the stressed-out mind and lent surcease from the sorrows of the world beyond the theater lobby. "To reflect contemporary thought in motion pictures is treading on dangerous ground insofar as film audiences are concerned," *Variety* lectured in its issue of November 9, 1938. "Of the 85,000,000 people who attend pictures every week in the United States are found millions of varied beliefs" who "deeply resent any intrusion of 'enlightenment,' no matter how subtly interwoven into the story." The punctuation and the dateline are noteworthy: the snide quotation marks around the word *enlightenment* in an editorial written mere weeks after the Munich Pact and on the very day that the Nazi pogrom known as *Kristallnacht* ran riot across Germany.

Admittedly, the rise of Nazism and the conflagration in Europe were hard to ignore, but the business of Hollywood should always be entertainment "that serves the important purpose of complete relaxation, that shouts no message, points no moral, or teaches no lesson," declared Will Hays in 1939. Accused of war mongering and message sending, Hollywood pleaded dumb and innocent and pledged to remain so, come what may. The "wholesome function of recreation" was Hollywood's stock in trade, Hays reiterated in the summer of 1941, maligning the preachy filmmakers who would use the screen to "muse rather than amuse."

For a time, not even Pearl Harbor derailed the one-track mindset. On December 8, 1941, while FDR was addressing a joint session of Congress to demand a declaration of war against Japan, Hays wired the White House on behalf of the Motion Picture Producers and Distributors of America. Hollywood, he promised, would "maintain the continued flow of wholesome entertainment as an essential contribution to military and civilian moral and national spirit." With the war barely twenty-four hours old, Hays can be forgiven for still being in thrall to an antebellum mentality. Overnight, the 1934-minted pledge of "wholesome entertainment" had become an outdated commitment.

Hays was not alone in his fidelity to an obsolete ethos. "Under the circumstances [that is, WWII], the trend in production would seem to be toward high-class comedies, the best of film musicals, and every type of picture that will reflect the high optimism, courage, the loyalty to country, [and] the belief in ideals that have characterized the American people since the birth of this nation," Breen, still an executive at RKO, declared shortly after Pearl Harbor. Neither man yet realized that the nostrums that had served Hollywood so well in peacetime sounded like prattling nonsense during wartime.

In June 1942, settling back into his post at the Production Code Administration, Breen continued to exhibit a severe case of target fixation and cultural lag. The present emergency, he stubbornly insisted, would have no impact on his office work. "The war simply does not affect the Code or its application," he declared in his first interview back at what was again the Breen Office. "It has raised no issues or questions that were not present and covered by the Code in peace time."

Even the obliging yes-men at *Motion Picture Herald* seemed a bit stupefied by that pig-headed pronouncement.

"Is the screen going to let down its standards a bit, as radio is doing, to permit a strewing of 'hells' and 'damns' through the dialogue of war subjects for purposes of patriotic emphasis?" Breen was asked.

"It is not," he replied tightly.

"But doesn't this mushrooming crop of war films coming up present some questions of policy which you haven't had to deal with before?" pressed the reporter.

"Not at all," Breen responded. "We have always had war films. We have always had soldiers, sailors, and marines in pictures, and we have always had pictures utilizing training bases, battleships, and military installations of all kinds as settings. There has always been a requirement for military approval of these pictures and a standing routine for meeting this requirement has been in effect for years." WWII may have increased the percentage of military-minded motion pictures, but it certainly need not change the house rules at the Breen Office. "It does not parallel or conflict with our function. Today there are more films of that kind. That is the only difference."

To the accusatory question that vigilant patriots asked the home front slacker ("Don't you know there's a war on?"), Breen seemed to be replying, "Yes, but that's not my department."

But if the Breen Office had made a separate peace, then whose department was it? Neither Hollywood nor Washington knew for sure. Among the myriad agencies springing up to fight WWII, propaganda was the shared bailiwick of a convoluted flow chart of overlapping bureaucracies, both civilian and military. Every branch of the armed services operated its own publicity unit; every civilian agency, New Deal or war-born, wanted a piece of the action. However, the highest-profile agency assigned to the job was the Office of War Information (OWI).

Formed in June 1942 under the directorship of CBS news analyst Elmer Davis, the OWI was tasked with coordinating wartime propaganda across the civilian media. Realizing the vital importance of motion pictures, the OWI established a special unit to tutor Hollywood, the Motion Picture Bureau, headed by a cinema-impaired factotum named Lowell Mellett. To guide the incorrigible civilians in the motion picture colony, the OWI published a 50-page booklet entitled *Government Information Manual for the Motion Picture Industry*. Hollywood now operated under the eyes of two supervisory agencies (the PCA and the OWI) with two different guidebooks (the Production Code and the *Information Manual*). Inevitably, the moral vision of the Code collided with the wartime values of the *Manual*.

In a broad sense, the outlook of the two guidance systems was compatible. The PCA mandate that good (us) triumph over evil (them) certainly accorded with the OWI's mission. In matters micro and macro, however, the moral fixations of the Code pulled Hollywood cinema away from the practical needs of WWII. To the standard prewar arguments against the Code—that it shackled creativity, that it insulted the audience, that it wasted resources on costly rewrites and reshooting—was added the more searing criticisms that it lulled the home front, that it impeded the war effort, even that it was unpatriotic. In peacetime, the Breen Office shuffle over double entendres, twin beds, and sweater girls played out as petty squabbles for small stakes; in wartime, the disputes over language, images, and values had potentially lethal consequences.

The official MPPDA line, affirmed for the duration, was that "the motion picture industry is as much a war asset as munitions plants," and that "the Code was even more vital in wartime than in peace." But how much of an asset was a wartime plant that fired blanks? How vital was an instructional manual that did not teach the skills and values necessary to win the war? In 1943, Charles Francis ("Socker") Coe, vice president and general counsel of the MPPDA, boasted that "criticism of the moral values of our product is virtually at a vanishing point." Coe was right: but moral values were not the same as military virtues.

From this vantage, the wartime service record of the Breen Office was less than honorable for two reasons. First, the conveyer-belt bureaucracy that operated so smoothly for in-house censorship was an active impediment to martial instruction—squandering time, setting up roadblocks, and sugarcoating harsh lessons. Second, and more blameworthy, the Code qua Code contributed nothing to a lucid understanding of how and "why we fight"—the methods and meanings of a multicultural democracy engaged in mortal combat with ruthless totalitarian regimes in two theaters of operation. In Catholic terms, the sins of omission were more serious than the sins of commission.

The blinkered perspective of the Breen Office was nowhere more evident than in the skirmishes over screen dialogue. Always an irritant likely to bring a snort of derision from all but the bluest noses, the penchant for euphemism and the deletions of the mildest epithets seemed, in wartime, silly and schoolmarmish. Deaf to the clamor for change, the Breen Office still winced at vernacular that was being typeset in popular magazines and heard on the radio.

The British import *In Which We Serve* (1942) and a feature-length *March of Time* production, *We Are the Marines* (1942), precipitated an early linguistic clash over the utterance of the mildly profane "hell," "damn," and "bastard." Those three words on screen incited thousands of words in memos, letters, and policy statements from the Breen Office.

Written by and starring Noël Coward, and directed by Coward and David Lean, *In Which We Serve* exalts the gallant crew of a British naval vessel and the women back home who do more than watch and wait.[1] Though the stiff-upper-lipped message of *In Which We Serve* was impeccably British, the language was bluntly Anglo-Saxon. "Hell," "damn," and "bastard" (or, as the Breen Office termed it, "profanity and vulgarity in flagrant form") were spat out with a fluency unknown in Hollywood's Navy. Imported stateside by United Artists, the film was flagged for obscenity by the New York office of the PCA, then being supervised by Charles Francis Coe, Francis Harmon having assumed full-time duties as head of the War Activities Committee of the Motion Picture Industry.

Being on site, Coe argued the case for the defense team when UA protested the decision. With Breen's input and advice, he composed a nine-page brief in defense of the decision to censor a patriotic service film from a wartime ally. Doubtless *In Which We Serve* was a worthy motion picture and doubtless Noël Coward was a great artist, but "in the entire brief, appellant gives no substantial reasons why the Code should be altered to accommodate the current situation. One may presume he bases his exceptions on changes in custom flowing from the war." To this, Breen and Coe asked by way of reply: "To accommodate a war time tendency are the permanencies of years of progress in the motion picture industry to be incinerated on the winged oath of an individual [Coward] enamored of his own production?" The pair tossed out a series of contemptuous rhetorical questions: "Are we to conclude that the height of dignity is achieved by that person who calls another person 'bastard'? Is it the essence of creative art to hurl 'hell' and 'damn' at children in motion picture theaters?" To answer in the affirmative "would reduce the motion picture to the moral standard of the New York stage in its lowest form of expression." In late 1942, with the Allies still on

1. Coward's own attitude toward kid-glove treatment of the Nazis was summed up in his sardonic tune "Let's Don't Be Beastly to the Germans."

the ropes in two theaters of war, the Coe-Breen brief then printed the stunning line:

> The function of the Production Code is not to be patriotic, it is to be moral.

Astonishingly, the Breen Office was not second-guessed further up the ranks of the MPPDA—at least publicly. Despite the admitted tendency of combat terrors "to invite some use of strong language," studio chieftains went on record opposing "any lowering of the bars against profanity in pictures made by members of the Hays organization." Gossip columnist Hedda Hopper also backed the establishment. "I'm with Hays and his two assistants, Socker Coe and Slugger Breen," wrote the queen bee of Tinseltown babble.

Yet almost everywhere else the Breen Office was scoffed at as prissy and effete. The GI attitude was voiced in a handwritten inquiry mailed to the MPPDA from an APO address overseas:

> Gentleman:
> What do *you* call the bastards?

As sarcastic protest letters poured in from moviegoers in uniform, Breen tried to explain the constraints on home front vocabulary to an infantry lieutenant. While acknowledging that soldiers, "especially those under great emotional stress, indulge, occasionally, in language which is strong and forceful and picturesque," he reminded the peeved officer that the kind of language acceptable in a barracks or foxhole "may not be acceptable coming from the motion picture screen to mixed audiences in theaters. . . . It is our thought that the motion picture screen would do a very definite disservice to the growing boys and girls of America if we were to accustom them to harsh vulgarities, or worse, in screen dialogue."

After much wrangling, a compromise was reached that reasserted the power of the Breen Office to zip loose lips. "The use of the words 'hell' and 'damn' [is] permitted at the sole discretion of the Code administration when used by men in military services or portraying such persons in active duty under pressure of great dramatic force apparent on screen whose pictures are produced cooperatively with or under sponsorship of government where words are not offensive per se." Having won the point, however, Coe and Breen relented on the cases in question—not out of magnanimity but expedience. Censoring Rhett Butler in *Gone With the Wind* was fatuous; censoring real-life Marines in a *March of Time* tribute was indictable. "We went through 'hell' to save 'damn' and only as it applies to this one picture,"

Coe joked, when he announced that the men in *We Are the Marines* might speak like leathernecks. "We voted to uphold the Production Code, but we relaxed its provisions in this case because of the nature of the scene in which the words were used." *In Which We Serve* was also given conditional dispensation (yes to *hell* and *damn*, no to *bastard*). Generally, though, the "sole discretion" of the Breen Office meant that, for the duration, combat-hardened soldiers spoke, as Warner Bros. producer Hal Wallis groused, "like choirboys."

However exasperating, the purgation of epithets was a sideshow. Far more serious were the obstacles to basic training put up by the Breen Office. For the Hollywood feature film, the most significant wartime service involved the creation of a dynamic and durable new film genre, a military-minded hybrid of fraternal melodrama and battlefield action that thrived long after 1945: the WWII combat film. For this crucial war work too, Breen and the staff were normally either fouling up the situation or AWOL.

Though soon to calcify into cliché, the tropes of the combat film were fresh and vital at birth, the purpose deadly serious: to maximize survival in the crucible of combat and to inculcate the essential albeit unromantic skills needed to win victory. The genre taught that the most important quality of the modern warrior was not physical courage but cooperative fellowship. Following the map laid out by the OWI's manual, Hollywood awarded its highest medals to the soldier who displayed maturity, tolerance, and brotherly love. While condemning the master-racism of Nazi Germany and Imperial Japan, the WWII combat film celebrated the motley ingredients of the American melting pot.

No longer a gallant lone ranger riding in to save the schoolmarm, the featured hero was suddenly plural, the rescue mission a group project. A united, coordinated squad of hyphenated ethnicities and regional eccentricities equipped with complementary occupational skills, the champions in the ranks were Jewish, Irish, Italian, WASP, Polish, Iowa farm boys, Texas cowhands, Brooklyn cabbies, navigators, bombardiers, rear gunners, radiomen, mechanics, pilots, and copilots, all forged to function as a well-oiled military machine. The very titles of the WWII combat films elevate cohesive action over singular valor, denoting units (*The Flying Tigers* [1942], *The Fighting Seabees* [1944]) or battles (*Wake Island* [1942], *Bataan* [1943], *Thirty Seconds Over Tokyo* [1944]), not individual heroes. Even the five ill-fated brothers who inspired *The Sullivans*, the only major WWII combat film titled after a surname, comprise a protean squad.

A fit, maybe the fittest, example of the war-tempered genre is Warner Bros.'s *Air Force* (1943), directed by Howard Hawks, written by Dudley Nichols, and produced by Hal Wallis. The star of *Air Force* is the crew of a

B-17 Flying Fortress named the *Mary-Ann*, the message that every airman is a vital link in the chain of command. The narrative takes an embittered lone wolf who has washed out of pilot training and folds him into the pack; the theme insists that each man has a job, no one more important than the other, and that the pilot, the glamorous cock of the air before 1941, is only one of the engine parts needed to keep the *Mary-Ann* soaring. The cinematic apparatus reinforces the message: Hawks's framing emphasizes group compositions, and the cast is an ensemble of sturdy character actors, not high-intensity stars.

At Warner Bros. the crew assembling *Air Force* was committed to doing OWI's work. "Dudley Nichols wrote a fine script involving characters that were a cross section of the Allies: an Irishman, a Pole, a Swede, a Jew, a Welshman, and an Englishman," Hal Wallis recalled, reciting the Central Casting roll call. The filmmakers also heeded government guidelines for the depiction of the Japanese enemy. To portray him as too powerful was to sow the seeds of defeatism; to portray him as too weak was to foster complacency. The Japanese, insisted Wallis, must appear "as well-trained, highly intelligent men, neither pushovers nor invincible."

Group heroism: even in the kangaroo courtroom of the Japanese enemy, the WWII combat unit stands firm in Lewis Milestone's *The Purple Heart* (1944).

As producer Wallis, director Hawks, and screenwriter Nichols struggled to inculcate the skills and values needed to wage WWII, *Air Force* endured the usual script review process at the Breen Office. Breen demanded changes that Wallis found alternately "amusing" and "maddening." A mild joke about a dog being housebroken was flagged for "vulgar connotations," and the expression "hold your hats, boys" was scratched. He also banned the remark, "My mother was scared by the Empire State Building," a phrase with phallic connotations Wallis missed.

Jack Warner intervened to plead with Breen for special "consideration [for] our scene in *Air Force* where [actor John] Garfield sees Pearl Harbor burning and says 'Damn 'em.'" "Being strictly a man's picture we want to keep this in the picture and if necessary will put it up to the [MPPDA] board of directors but hope this won't be necessary as I know you realize the importance of this picture which was made with the cooperation of our Air Force."

Air Force cooperation or not, Breen told Warner to remove the expression. Citing the decision of *In Which We Serve*, he viewed the matter as a settled issue. Warner, of course, was free to appeal, but given the precedent, such an appeal would not be sustained. "In the face of all this, you had better find some substitute words to put into Mr. Garfield's mouth." Warner neither appealed nor complied: with the Air Force in his corner, he knew he could win the game of bluff in the court of public opinion. So did Breen, who on second thought exercised his "sole discretion" and permitted the words to come from Mr. Garfield's mouth.

The wartime files of the Breen Office are filled with such idiocies. In *Casablanca* (1942), Rick was not allowed to shoot the Nazi Major Strasser in cold blood; he had first to be provoked. "We had taken the risk of shooting the scene without an official approval from Breen, and had to reshoot it in its entirety," remembered Wallis, who should have known better. Likewise, the Breen Office demanded, as per prewar policy, that the killer of a Nazi agent in playwright Lillian Hellman's wartime melodrama *A Watch on the Rhine* (1943) be punished under law. The nonplussed Hellman responded with an acid note inquiring whether "the Hays Office was aware that killing Nazis was now a matter of national policy." National policy or not, even a Nazi could not be slain unless he shot first.

Given wartime realities, the linguistic expurgations and narrative roadblocks from the Breen Office were not merely derided as sissified but condemned as obstructionist. Filmmakers who had long chafed under the Code now had powerful ammunition and well-placed allies. "If any censor should interpose his prewar rules, he should be told to climb up a tree and stay there for the duration," wrote Pete Harrison in 1942, calling for gutsy war films that neither sheltered home front civilians nor insulted the frontline veterans. Long a staunch defender of the Breen Office, Harrison now declared, "Let the war censorship board determine what is right or wrong in pictures for the duration."

In fact, despite Breen's best efforts, Hollywood's moral universe was clouded by the fog of war. For the first time since 1934, an alternative vision was available in American cinema. It came not from the Hollywood feature film, but from two items on the screen menu not under Breen Office oversight: newsreels and combat reports.

Officially, due to the time-sensitive nature of a format with journalistic-like status, the newsreels were not subject to censorship by the Breen Office. Restrictions by the Code would have been redundant for the most timorous of news outlets anyway: throughout the 1930s, commercial constraints and political censorship had prevented the newsreel from sounding a discordant note over the motion picture bill. During WWII, however, with patriotism trumping escapism, combat footage taken by military photographic units projected a shocking contrast to the soundstage images vetted by the Breen Office. As unspooled by the five commercial newsreels and the long-form combat reports produced by the various branches of armed forces, documentary footage of war showcased images of brutality, carnage, and death never before seen on the American screen. While the Breen Office still controlled 90 percent of the motion picture program—the cartoons, the comedy shorts, and the feature film—the newsreels and combat reports on the very same bill were a (comparatively) free-fire zone. Increasingly, as the war ground on, a home front hardened by casualty figures and inured to harsh newspaper reportage faced flashes of the horror of war on the motion picture screen. "There is no need further to sugarcoat the pill, and in this connection there will be another slight change in policy," announced Stanton Griffiths, head of the Domestic Film Bureau of the Office of War Information, in 1944. "Hereafter, in war footage, if a lot of Americans were killed too, you will see them as well as the enemy dead. There will be no pulling of punches in this respect."

Actually, punches were pulled: the worst of the combat footage, of American and enemy dead alike, was cut by military censors in Washington, so as not to undermine morale. Still, in the context of a Hollywood sealed by the Code, the newsreels and combat reports were a bracing, sometimes sickening, gut punch.

Living up to its recruitment posters, the U.S. Marine Corps issued the harshest up-close looks at combat and its casualties. In *With the Marines at Tarawa* (1944), the camera lingers over tableaux of Japanese incinerated by flamethrowers and grisly vistas of dead Marines bobbing in the surf and strewn in the sand. "The real thing at last," promised the ads, eyeing the unreal things on the rest of the motion picture bill. "No punches pulled, no gory details omitted!"

Code-sheltered home front audiences flinched at the sights. "Dead bodies of Marines on the beach, washing back and forth with the surge of the seas, is not exactly entertainment," complained a Midwest theater manager, distressed at "the stunned reaction that comes from those people who have relatives in the service." Gradually, though, scenes that might have nauseated audiences just months before were faced with stoicism. Gainsaying exhibitor opinion, a hardened reviewer for the *Hollywood Reporter* opined, "It is doubtful that [*With the Marines at Tarawa*] will cause many abdominal nip-ups, for audiences are becoming accustomed to seeing the dead."

As the war wore on, as newspaper coverage, *Life* magazine photographers, and newsreels shed more blood and fewer tears, even the Breen Office was compelled to move its goalposts. In 1944, after the War Department released suppressed details of the Bataan Death March, Robert E. Sherwood, head of the overseas branch of the OWI, decreed an end to the "silk glove treatment of the Nazis, Fascists, and the Japs [that] has been apparent on the screen and in other communications media." No official ukase announced a loosening of Code standards, but the harder hearts and thicker skins of a nation at war worked to dim the sunshine patriotism.

To modern eyes, the Hollywood version of WWII seems a sanitized scrapbook of evasions and euphemisms filmed to the tune of OWI propagandists and Breen Office prigs. "In the 1940s, cinema delineated little but a fairy tale world of uncomplex heroism and romantic love, sustained by toupees, fake bosoms, and happy endings," remembered cultural historian Paul Fussell, himself a grizzled combat veteran, looking back with bile. "It was a medium whose conventions equipped it perfectly for the evasion of wartime actualities, and it adapted to its new requirements without in any way changing step."

Wartime moviegoers disagreed. In the context of the strict imagistic and tonal surveillance of Hollywood under the Code, American cinema during WWII was unvarnished and unnerving. Infused with a deep, inconsolable sorrow, somber wartime melodramas like *Happy Land* (1943), *The Human Comedy* (1944), and *The Sullivans* no longer warranted the condescending prewar moniker of "women's weepies," the three-hankie films made for a good cry. During the wrenching "telegram scenes"—when the death notice from the War Department via Western Union comes to the door—home front theaters were wracked by sobs, and some moviegoers, overcome by grief, bolted for the exits. In the grim textures of late-war combat films like *A Walk in the Sun* (1945) and *The Story of G.I. Joe* (1945), a genre designed for Americanized esprit de corps ended in the equality of the grave.

No wonder even the Code-sealed feature films of the last two years of the war jarred audiences who came to the theater for escape and confronted a memento mori. Trade press critics wanted it both ways: on the one hand, shouting "there is no room for sissy stuff in war pictures!" and on the other complaining "let us spare the public's feelings!" In *Thirty Seconds Over Tokyo*, the true story of Captain Ted Lawson, a flyer in the Doolittle raid on Tokyo who lost a leg after ditching his B-24 over China, an amputation scene proved too much for the home front. "The public is in no mood to accept scenes depicting a fighting man's sufferings," lectured Pete Harrison, who after three years had reconsidered the box office downside of verisimilitude. "Sending people out of a theater in an unhappy frame of mind helps neither their morale nor the theater attendance." Without nudging

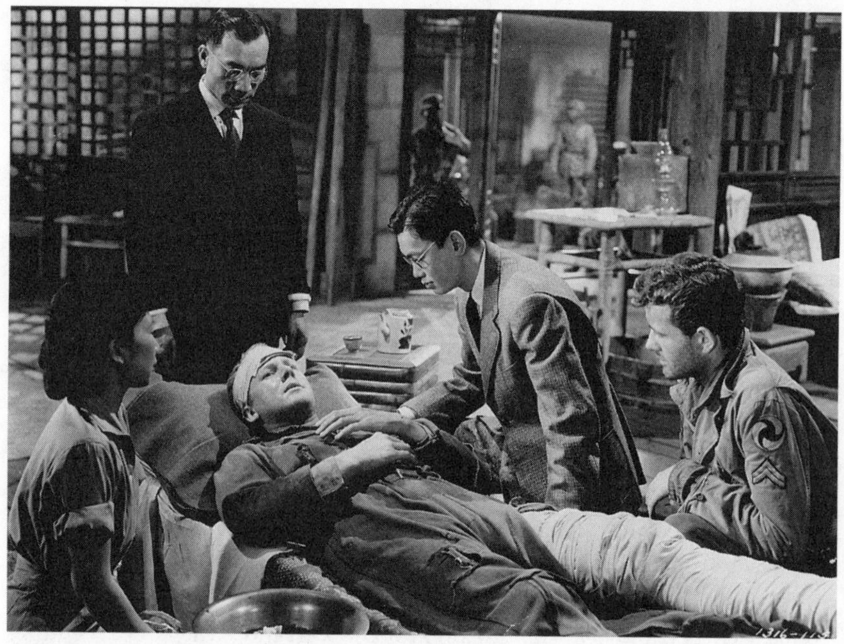

Grim realism: hidden in the home of a Chinese merchant (Ching Wah Yee), wounded Doolittle raider Lt. Ted Lawson (Van Johnson) is treated by a young Chinese doctor (Benson Fong) while his crewman (Robert Walker) sits vigil in Mervyn LeRoy's *Thirty Seconds Over Tokyo* (1944). For a Code-sheltered home front, the amputation scene was hard to stomach.

from either the Breen Office or the OWI, MGM toned down the trauma in subsequent release prints.

Some requests for surcease were impossible not to take to heart. After an anguishing moviegoing experience, a grieving Gold Star mother appealed to the syndicated columnist Walter Winchell to sensitize Hollywood:

> I lost my own son less than four months ago in the Pacific. He was 19. Last week was the first time (since receiving the tragic news) that my husband and I went to a movie theater. So we chose one we thought would give us a lift. It was *American Romance*. The scene where the parents read the telegram from the War Department was almost more than I could bear, as it almost paralleled our own grief. Then we saw *Janie* and it was full of similar misery for us all and, I am sure, other parents whose sons have been killed in action. Why doesn't the movie industry consider all of us and not open wounds again and again?[2]

The wounds opened by wartime cinema would never totally heal over: too much carnage had been seen, too much heartbreak endured. At the end, though, it was the awful denouement that surpassed all imaginings. In the first week of May 1945, the newsreel record of the Nazi concentration camps was screened to a shocked and disbelieving home front. "Don't turn away! Look!" orders Ed Herlihy, the narrator of the Universal Newsreel issue "Nazi Death Mills," rebuking faint-hearted spectators who averted their eyes, sickened at the sight of corpses, fetid and rotting, piled in mounds, stacked like cordwood, incinerated in ovens. Herlihy knew his audience.

"SEÑOR PRESIDENTE"

"We continue to have serious problems," Breen wrote Father Lord in 1943. "The war has us spinning around like a top." The dizziness was professional not personal. "I fought the battle of Beverly Hills," more than one fortunate veteran of the Hollywood home front would say self-deprecatingly in later years. For Breen, who since 1937 had resided on a gorgeous palm-lined street on Ridgedale Drive, off Sunset Boulevard, just north of the Los Angeles Country Club, the mock-brag was literally true. Better: on weekends, he

---

2. Directed by King Vidor, *An American Romance* (1944) was a Technicolor epic depicting the rags-to-riches trajectory of a hustling Hungarian immigrant. Directed by Michael Curtiz, *Janie* (1944) was a juvenile romantic melodrama whose effervescence was tempered by a wartime intrusion.

and the family, with Mary at the wheel of a prewar Cadillac, would drive up the Pacific Coast Highway to their beach house in Malibu, where soldiers drilled in the sands and airplanes patrolled the skies, protecting a mainland still jittery about Japanese bombardment. Washing in with the California surf, the sounds of Saturday night dinner parties trickled down the beach, a privileged comfort zone in a world at war.

Breen's work life officially joined the war effort in only one way. In 1943, Nelson Rockefeller, of the Office of Inter-American Affairs, approached Will H. Hays about making the PCA chieftain a special consultant on motion pictures. The plan was to borrow Breen for three months, during which time he would develop ways to use motion pictures to shore up Pan-American relations and undermine Third Reich infiltration into Latin America. "Rockefeller was most insistent that the undertaking was of very great importance, and that Breen was the one man to do the job," stated a confidential MPPDA memo.

Breen balked. In his mind, it was not that Code work took precedence over war-related work, but that Code work was the best kind of war-related work. Hays informed Rockefeller that "Breen would be willing to do whatever he could in the matter that would not seriously interfere with his work on the Production Code." To abandon the office for three months in Washington was out of the question.

After being approached directly by the Rockefeller Committee, however, Breen wrote an advisory memo setting forth his opinion on Latin American film relations. "The big job to be done is to endeavor to improve the general moral tone of our pictures as viewed from the standpoint of the folks in Latin America," he wrote. The prevalence of violent crime in Hollywood cinema "must present our American people in a very curious light to the people of Latin America." Moreover, the epidemic of "casual drinking is not good for Latin American consumption." Finally, against the backdrop of a war-ravaged world, Breen suggested that "we might make a special effort to watch more carefully the costuming of our women in motion pictures" and "be particularly careful in the treatment of such subjects as marriage and divorce." He concluded his to-do list with the comment "that if this is the kind of propaganda which the Coordinator's Office would subscribe to, [I feel] that a good job could be done," but that "to indulge in political propaganda in entertainment films would be bad." That is, at the height of World War II, when the central purpose of the Washington-Hollywood alliance was to inject propaganda into entertainment films, Breen argued against the entire rationale.

Breen's aversion to propaganda was the legacy of the previous world war. Like many intellectuals of his generation, he harbored a deep antipathy to government-orchestrated persuasion, a distrust derived from his revulsion at the jingoistic campaigns by the British Ministry of Information and the Committee on Public Information in America during the Great War. The "clever, insidious and incessant" war propaganda, Breen wrote in 1928, had drawn America into the carnage in Europe, especially the "series of lies purposely manufactured and cleverly circulated by professional British propagandists." Being "the most gullible people on earth," good-natured Americans were easy marks for the wily Englishmen. "[Propaganda] plunged us into the greatest war in all history and it may do so again," he warned. World War II notwithstanding, Breen resisted signing up for a practice with so disreputable a lineage.

Breen went further: the propaganda seeping into wartime Hollywood cinema struck him as suspiciously subversive. The OWI, he felt, was a nest of revivified Popular Fronters.

Dormant during the Hitler-Stalin Pact interregnum of 1939–1941, the romance of American communism bloomed afresh with the Soviet-American alliance against Nazism. Now that the Soviet Union was an honored ally and "Uncle Joe" Stalin was on a first-name basis with FDR, the popular arts threw garlands at the Red Army and spouted the party line. Hollywood films such as *Mission to Moscow* (1943), a starry-eyed whitewash of Stalinism, and *Song of Russia* (1944), an anthem to the noble heart of Mother Russia, were celluloid testimony to the affection between Hollywood and Moscow, something that before the war would have been unimaginable, and would be so again soon after.

Breen had been an ardent anticommunist since the Bolshevik revolution. In the 1920s, both as the editor of the *National Catholic Welfare Council Bulletin* and as an essayist for *America*, he had warned of the menace of communism and chronicled its anti-Catholic depredations. In 1937, when he accepted an honorary degree from Loyola University of Los Angeles (later Loyola Marymount University) and delivered the commencement address to recipients of the Jesuit sheepskin he skipped out on at St. Joseph's College, it was Soviet communism not German fascism that was on his mind. Introduced as "a cultured Christian gentleman with an agile mind, determined will, and courageous heart," Breen dispensed the soporific bromides demanded of the occasion ("As Jesuit trained students you are looked upon with respect by the world.") and veered into current affairs only once. "Do what you undertake to do so that when a crisis comes—such as Communism—the United States of America will have trained men to go forth like our forefathers to preserve all that we honor and cherish."

Like many conservative Catholics, Breen spied a hammer and sickle behind the emblem of the wartime Popular Front. In 1943 his animosity led him to spout off imprudently during an interview with Marcia Winn in the *Chicago Daily Tribune*. The OWI had set "out to use the screen to propagandize for selfish if not sinister purposes," he charged. The personnel was dominated by "the short haired women and long haired men type."

What, asked Winn, did he mean by that?

"Pink," Breen replied, a color that smeared both the sexual and political orientations of the OWI staffers.

Ultimately, though, not even Breen could deny the call of country in WWII. In 1943, pressed by Hays and courted by Rockefeller, he agreed to go to Washington for two months to work as a special consultant on motion pictures to the Coordinator of Inter-American Affairs, popularly known as the Rockefeller Committee. Characteristically, once on board, Breen spoke with pride of "the extent of the importance of the work which Nelson and his group have in mind" and gloried in his subsequent election as president of the Motion Picture Society for the Americas.

Chartered on March 21, 1941, the Motion Picture Society for the Americas was a nonprofit corporation established "to bring about a closer cultural relation between the United States of America and other American Republics" by fostering educational exchange, commercial trade, and mutual understanding, "especially in relation to the motion picture." During the war, the society worked in liaison with the Council of Inter-American Affairs, the government entity charged with coordinating propaganda south of the border. Amid the tangle of competing agencies, the Motion Picture Society for the Americas (private and Hollywood-based) was easy to confuse with the Motion Picture Division of the Council of Inter-American Affairs (government and Washington, D.C.-based).

Upon assuming office, Breen centralized command authority under his own name, instructing Francis Alstock, his opposite number in government, to make sure that all correspondence be addressed personally to Joseph I. Breen "and *not* to individuals employed by the society." Alstock complied, good-naturedly addressing Breen as "Señor Presidente." Breen kept the office in good order and reformed budgetary practices, refusing to spend money not allocated up front. C. O. Rowe, Rockefeller's executive assistant, complimented Breen on his "outstanding work." "We have received reports from persons conducting business with the Society that you are doing a wonderful job."

Breen's service with the Motion Picture Society for the Americas did not change the order of battle in WWII. His job was to facilitate coproductions, to welcome visitors from South America, and to keep Hollywood productions from insulting Latin sensibilities. Though the appointment of a high-level MPPDA official showed how important Washington and Hollywood

Not changing the order of battle in WWII: Breen, in his role as president of the Motion Picture Society for the Americas, meets Venezuelan Consul Alberto Posse-Rivas in 1944.

(COURTESY OF MARY PAT DORR)

took relations south of the border, the solicitous attention was more a diplomatic gesture than a military necessity.

Dusting off his rusty skills as a consular officer, Breen guided Hollywood filmmakers through customs, permits, and tariffs. As part of the hands-across-the-border efforts, James A. FitzPatrick, producer-narrator of *FitzPatrick's Traveltalks*, a popular series of travelogues released by MGM from 1930 to 1955, was dispatched to Central America to chronicle the happy locals in exotic costume. Breen's hands-on attention extended to the special permits for gasoline and tires for FitzPatrick's equipment truck, ordering underlings that the necessary arrangements "be gotten under way pronto!"

Even the Victorian Breen was amused at the prudish customs south of the border. "Curiously enough, we have repeated protests against the showing of young women in public places, and *hatless*," he puzzled. "For a long while we wondered about this, until we discovered that, pretty generally throughout Latin America, women do not go about with nothing on their head—unless they are women of loose morals."

Meanwhile, on his own home front, Breen experienced few material discomforts. In the Malibu beach home, Mary entertained regularly and, in the context of wartime rationing, lavishly, hosting friends, servicemen, and Catholic charity groups. "Things, generally, with me are going along better than I have any right to expect," Breen wrote Bishop McNicholas in 1943.

"Two of my girls are married and engaged in the very serious business of raising families. My three boys are all in the service—two in the Marine Corps, and one in the Army." Of course, for a family with three blue stars in the window of their Beverly Hills home, the Breens counted their blessings every day a telegram did not arrive with tidings of a gold. An unexpected knock on the door meant a tense intake of breath and anguished looks between husband and wife.

However, few American families with three sons serving overseas went untouched by a casualty report. In a single week in 1944, Western Union knocked twice. Joseph, Jr., the eldest son, had been wounded in Europe. Tommy, the youngest, an enthusiastic surfer, had lost a leg on Guam. Later, a form letter from the Navy addressed to "Mrs. J. R. Breen [*sic*]," with blanks filled in, informed the family that

> your son, *Thomas E. Breen, PFC, USMCR*, entered the Naval Hospital, Mare Island, California, on *29 October* 1944 for *AMPUTATION, TRAUMATIC, RIGHT LEG*. His condition is not serious at this time. You will be notified by telegram of any serious change in his condition. He has been advised to write you at this time.

Soon after, news arrived that the middle son, James, stricken with malaria in the Pacific, would also be routed home to recuperate.

"We have two of our Marines home from the South Seas—one [James], on a convalescent leave, after having had recurrent malaria, and Tommy, from the hospital at Mare Island," Breen wrote Father Lord a few days into 1945. "Both are making great strides, and both will, I am sure, be all right—all in good time. They are both in fine spirits and, believe it or not, anxious to go back into combat." Upon hearing of Tommy's injury, Bishop McGucken expressed his sympathies and offered comfort in an affectionate letter. "I am sure that [Tommy] is happy and confident, and that you, too, will realize that God will take care of him so that his injuries will not be a handicap which he cannot overcome," said the bishop, dwelling on "the happiness of having the brave young marine at home with you who has made such a heroic sacrifice for his country."

While the three Breen boys all served well up in the front ranks during the war years, Breen's sideline status is reflected in the way his name, since 1934 the stuff of headlines and bad puns, disappears from the Hollywood trade press. For the duration, he was a top-billed player no more. His fixation on the Code to the exclusion of all else—his refusal to face the real Big Picture—infuses the lengthy letter on PCA policy he composed for MPPDA official Arthur E. DeBra in 1944. Tasked with community liaison,

DeBra had requested orientation on the operation and philosophy of the Breen Office. In the entire 52-page document Breen wrote in response, not once does he mention WWII. As a father, he had almost lost two sons, and he had seen all three suffer from their tours in the combat zone. However, in his official capacity as head of the Production Code Administration, the Second World War might never have happened for Joseph I. Breen.

9

IN HIS SACERDOTALISM

"You know, I don't want to discourage you, but in a way you should be a Catholic to be a member of the Code staff," the veteran Breen officer Eugene "Doc" Dougherty told Albert Van Schmus. Out of work and on the market in 1949, Van Schmus, a former production clerk at RKO, was angling for a staff position at the Production Code Administration. When Van Schmus landed the job, Dougherty took the avowed Congregationalist under his wing. "He kept telling me I could do it," Van Schmus laughingly recalled. "He was very encouraging, but he said, 'I have to be honest with you, I think that's what a member of the staff *needs* to have. They've got to understand that kind of morality.'" Fortunately, Van Schmus was a quick study. Once tutored in the catechism, the good-natured Dutchman was soon interpreting the Code like a right-handed Irishman.

"A Jewish-owned business selling Roman Catholic theology to Protestant America" is the wry definition of classical Hollywood cinema, an ecumenical division of labor that, in terms of motion picture content if not front-office personnel, grants one religion special dispensation. After July 15, 1934, Roman Catholics exerted a virtual veto power over the visible universe of Hollywood's Golden Age—and the man wielding the gavel was no lackadaisical Midnight-Mass-at-Christmas Catholic but a self-described soldier in the "the Church Militant."

The Jewish imprint on Hollywood has been widely chronicled by film historians, most notably in Neal Gabler's 1988 tribute, *An Empire of Their Own: How the Jews Invented Hollywood*, a work whose subtitle spotlights the religion Gabler ranks first. However, a defender of another faith might argue that Catholics promulgated their own kind of Holy Roman Empire in Hollywood. The doctrinal pedigree of Frank Capra, John Ford, and Alfred Hitchcock, three of the greatest directors from Hollywood's classical era, neatly represents the dominant strands of Italian, Irish, and Anglo-Catholicism respectively. No one needs a parochial school education to detect the Catholic affinity for dutiful self-sacrifice in Capra's *Mr. Smith Goes to Washington* (1939) and *It's a Wonderful Life* (1946), the veneration of Madonna figures in Ford's *How Green Was My Valley* (1941) and *They Were Expendable* (1945), or the guilty conscience gnawing at Hitchcock's *Saboteur* (1942) and *Spellbound* (1945). Moreover, the theology is often practiced by the dramatis personae. Murmuring in Latin, clutching rosary beads, and making the sign of the cross, priests, nuns, and pious parishioners walk in procession through soundstage after soundstage, genre after genre. No wonder devout Catholic moviegoers of a certain age still catch themselves genuflecting while exiting a row of theater seats.

If Catholics on screen were close to legion, Catholics behind the screen were nearly almighty. One of the more curious phenomena in the history of American popular culture, the dominion of the minority religion over the mass medium was achieved by a web of Catholic faithful, ordained and lay, whose long tentacles and precision coordination might confirm the darkest Protestant suspicions about Romanish intrigue: Daniel A. Lord, coauthor of the Production Code, a Jesuit priest; Martin J. Quigley, creator and defender of the Code, a graduate of Catholic University; and Joseph I. Breen, Jesuit-educated from boyhood, Jesuit-related by blood (his brother Francis was a Jesuit priest), and Jesuit-fixated by inclination (all the Breen boys were schooled and nurtured by his beloved "Jebbies").

A review of the secret communications and backstage scheming among Breen, Quigley, and a phalanx of Catholic clerics in 1929–30 (when the Code was first conceived, composed, and adopted) and in 1933–34 (when the screws were applied and tightened) reads like an after-battle report on a covert action behind enemy lines. The maneuvering is at once a proof of Catholic clout and a mark of residual insecurity about the recent promotion from scorned cult to cultural powerhouse. Even as Catholics flexed their muscles and pushed their weight around, the main players preferred to work behind the scenes, to show one face to the Anglo-Protestant majority and another *intrafamilias*. In 1930, when Breen coaxed George Cardinal Mundelein of Chicago into giving his blessings to the Code, one statement was released to the secular press, another to the Catholic press. "We could get the Cardinal to spill [the first] statement to the tune of the photographer's click," advised Breen, ever the sly press agent.

Wary of a backlash, the authors of the Code initially shunned their byline. Lord's role was not publicly revealed until May 1934 when *America*, the Jesuit weekly, bragged that the "the so-called Hays code of morality was written by Father Daniel Lord, S.J." Non-Catholics read the news in the secular pages of *Variety*, which also noted that Lord's authorship was "kept more or less a secret even from the average member of the film trade by the Hays organization during the [four] years the Code has been in effect."

When Lord was first mentioned as the brains behind the Code, Martin J. Quigley, the true idea man, bit his tongue. Later, Quigley sought to allay the impression that the document was the result of dictation from the Catholic Church, not wanting to "increase the fears and apprehensions of non-Catholics and strengthen the opposition to the Code operation." Quigley repeatedly asked Father Lord, who was not bound by a Franciscan vow of humility, to stop showboating. "It is most undesirable that the Code and the Legion of Decency should be confused, [to imply] that the idea of the Code did not originate in the industry but was, seemingly, imposed on the industry by a Jesuit priest who came to New York and made the company heads take it," he scolded. For the record, Quigley stated that "the Hays Office did not ask the Church in which Father Lord was a priest, or any other Church, to draw up a Production Code." If the Code must be known as a Catholic production, better to presume it arose from the faithful in the pews, not the uniformed ranks. "I asked to be kept out of it," Quigley recalled in 1948, when he first revealed his authorship to the mainstream press, "because I figured it should not be known as the work of one man; that it should be considered as having spontaneously arisen from the conscience of the industry."

Of course, there was nothing spontaneous about the Code, and the conscience it arose from was as invincibly Catholic as the man who enforced it. Though a minor player in the machinations that led to the adoption of the Code in 1930, Breen was a chief architect of the enforcement regime designed for what he called "some real Catholic action." As he told Rev. FitzGeorge Dinneen, S.J., in 1934, his purpose was the establishment of "an overall authority *which would function on a platform of Catholic understanding and interpretation of moral values*." When Breen cozily referred to "our Production Code" and in the next breath scowled at "the so-called Hays Moral Code," he left no doubt about who really owned the Code and who merely got top billing.

The official Hollywood line on the theology behind the Code—mouthed by Hays, Breen, Quigley, Lord, and anyone else speaking on behalf of the motion picture industry—was that the document embodied a consensual Judeo-Christian amalgam. "The Code was not to be an expression of the Catholic point of view," insisted Father Lord in 1946, sticking with the cover story. "It was to present principles on which all decent men would agree. Its basis was the Ten Commandments, which we felt was a standard of morality throughout the civilized world." He modestly conceded that the document "happens to have been written by a Catholic priest," but stated flatly that "the Motion Picture Production Code is not the product of the Catholic Church." In so saying, Father Lord broke what, in the Catholic Decalogue, is the Seventh Commandment.

THE CATHOLIC PROHIBITION MOVEMENT

Just as immigrant Jews got in on the ground floor of a business aborning in the early 1900s, the rise of Hollywood as a mature oligarchy in the 1920s was coincident with the emergence of Catholicism as a centerpiece religion in American culture. The Eucharistic Congress of 1926, event and film, was the ritual celebration of that coming of age. Settling into the exalted status it would enjoy for the balance of the century, the Church grew more confident about venturing beyond its own cloistered walls and preaching to a nationwide congregation. Catholics were well prepared to deliver a homily on what became their preferred topic. Turning to Hollywood cinema, they could draw on over sixteen hundred years of intellectual firepower and ecclesiastical expertise in the criticism of public art.

The motion picture medium caught the eyes of American Catholics immediately, and for good reason. The Church of Rome demanded stern sacrifice, deferred gratification, and days of obligation; the palaces of Hollywood (the very architecture wallowed in pagan Orientalism and Egyptomania) promised visceral thrills, instant pleasure, and voluptuous leisure. The flesh of man being weak, the priests gave the devil his due. "So great is the power of the motion picture to impress the youth of the land that one hour spent in the darkness of a cinema palace, intent on the unfolding of the wrong kind of story, can, and frequently does, nullify years of careful training on the part of the church, the school, and the home," declared Bishop John J. Cantwell of Los Angeles. Breen, who was serving as the bishop's ghostwriter, solemnly agreed with himself, warning that "one dirty film, in less than two hours, can nullify all the work of the schools." Apparently, the line between salvation and damnation was so thin that a guileless child might plunge into perdition in the space of a matinee, might have years of parochial school education and priestly guidance wiped out by seven reels of celluloid. The looming threat was literally of biblical proportions. "Herod is abroad!" cried out the Jesuits at *America*, reaching into the gospels for a comparison a Jewish mogul might well ponder. "The slaughter of the innocents has begun."

However, as imminent as the danger was, the Catholics would not rush headlong into the fray. Understanding the spiritual power of the medium, they paused to lay the groundwork with argument and exegeses. Experienced in working the levers of power, they would then apply pressure to the most sensitive nerve endings. Finally, and most decisively, the Catholics knew better than to fight the war for motion picture censorship with the tactics that had proven so disastrous in the last great moral crusade launched in America.

"Censorship is just as stupid an institution as Prohibition," editorialized *Billboard* in 1933. "It was born in the bat cellars of ignorance and was nursed in the bigotry of the Dark Ages." Maybe so, but if the two great American prohibition movements in the first half of the twentieth century share a common cradle, the crusade to dry up alcohol and the crusade to purify the screen were destined for very different outcomes. Both aimed to regulate a mood-altering diversion and both sought to enforce a sectarian creed on a polyglot nation, but while the Protestant experiment in behavior modification was an utter catastrophe, the Catholic action was a smashing success.

Of the many hallowed institutions discredited by Prohibition, none was brought lower than the dry, evangelical Protestant churches. On January 17, 1920, the Eighteenth Amendment set the noble experiment in motion, an empirical trial that quickly blew up in the laboratory of American culture. "In 1929, there was liquor in half the downtown offices, and speakeasies in half the large buildings," reported F. Scott Fitzgerald, a Catholic who sometimes practiced civil disobedience. No less in tune to the times than the drinking public, Hollywood flaunted the scofflaws and mocked the teetotalers: flasks and spiked drinks, speakeasies and bathtub gin, tipsy flappers and drunk drivers careen through Jazz Age cinema. By the early 1930s, watching defenders of Prohibition fulminate about the demon rum in the sound newsreels, thirsty moviegoers jeered and hissed.

The loudest heckling came from the ethnic groups that packed the cavernous cathedrals in America's big cities—the French, the Italians, the Poles, and especially the Irish, all peoples not known for a native aversion to alcoholic beverages. Fair being fair, the bad odor from Prohibition did not linger over the Catholic campaign to prohibit the intoxicants of the motion picture screen.

The old-time Protestant religion carried other baggage into the 1920s and 1930s. The new communications media could be unkind to the evangelists who pioneered its exploitation. As transmitted via radio and newsreels, the shrill voices and the spastic gesticulations of pulpit-pounding sermons made the preacher men—and, in one oddball case, woman—seem more like snake oil salesmen than ministers of the faith. In June 1926, as the Eucharistic Congress convened in Chicago for an inspiring outpouring of faith, Aimee Semple McPherson, the most colorful and eccentric of the mass-com evangelists of the Jazz Age, emerged from a bizarre disappearance (was it a kidnapping? a love nest getaway?) to provide a front-page contrast between Protestant chicanery and Catholic solemnity.[1] In 1927, Sinclair Lewis smote the money changers with *Elmer Gantry*, a roman à clef of evangelist Billy Sunday that forever branded the tent-show revivalist as a Bible-thumping charlatan hustling god-fearing rubes.

With Protestantism discredited by Prohibition and sullied by hucksters, Catholicism seized the inside track in the race to imprint a moral vision on the most visionary of the new media. Adorned in plain black suits for daily life and regal vestments for ritual occasions, the solemn dignity of the Catholic hierarchy offered a reverential contrast to the braying antics of the Protestant evangelicals. Happenstance or not, the repeal of alcohol Prohibition in 1933–34 coincides punctually with the onset of Production Code prohibitions.

Heeding the backwash from Protestant activism, the Catholics behind the Code took pains to distinguish between the voluntary self-regulation adopted by the motion picture industry and the coercive morality mandated by the Eighteenth Amendment. In the 1920s, when an Irish Catholic had to break the law to quench his thirst, Breen had railed against the "narrow-minded, bigoted, and thoroughly illogical Evangelical Protestants" whose agitation brought about "what is unquestionably the greatest menace to which this nation has ever been subjected." The Anti-Saloon League was a "despicable lobby" and the Women's Christian Temperance Union a band of "fanatical" fakirs. "The great and unpardonable sin of this day and generation is to drink liquor or use tobacco in any form," wrote Breen, who partook of both, in 1928. In later years, he was more diplomatic but no less dogmatic about the difference between Protestant-style Prohibition and Catholic-style self-regulation. "This philosophical theory of reformation by legislation—the attempt to make people good and righteous by legislative fiat—is no new thing in American legislative annals," he asserted. "Prohibition is the Exhibit A in this kind of thinking."

Thus, contrary to expectations, the founding fathers of Hollywood censorship—Hays, Breen, Quigley, and Lord—were all ardent and eloquent opponents of government censorship. Though adopted under coercion, the PCA was not seen by its creators as a craven capitulation to bluenose agitation but as a responsible arrangement between private businessmen and citizen-activists. "Here was a program of *self*-regulation, for *self*-control" by

1. In the 1930s, Father Charles E. Coughlin gave Protestant radio demagoguery a Catholic accent but not a run for the money: the funds that poured in to the Shrine of the Little Flower in Royal Oak, Michigan, fed his ego but not his wallet.

"those best qualified, it seemed to me, to undertake such a program and to see to its successful conduct," Breen believed.[2] The distinction between what they called "political censorship" and their own brand of internal discipline was not, for once, Jesuitical. "Official censorship has never worked anywhere it has been tried," Breen declared when he began the work of unofficial censorship at the PCA. "It seems to me that official censors are always getting righteously indignant about the wrong things."

Breen and the Catholics got righteously indignant about the right things—the Big Picture morality. In 1930, after Quigley briefed Hays on his plan for a Motion Picture Code of Ethics, the Presbyterian elder failed "to understand just what it was all about," Breen recalled. Hays "was prone to measure morality merely by police statistics and was overly concerned with such trivialities as whether film characters might smoke cigarettes, drink liquor, and say 'damn,'" wrote the Rev. Gerard B. Donnelly, S.J. Thankfully, once shown the way by the Breen Office, Hays "gradually abandoned the meaningless and trivial standards mentioned above and adopted instead true and noble concepts of cinema morality"—by which, of course, Father Donnelly meant Catholic concepts.

Fortifying the clout of the Catholic Church was its hierarchical organization and general staff—tactical advantages the statistically more numerous Protestants lacked. Where the power of Protestantism was diluted across denominations and divided by doctrine, class, and region, every congregation its own synod, Catholics were one big flock, a huge unified parish under the guidance of an organized priesthood with a martial command structure. Protestantism was from the pews, congregational, and dispersed; Catholicism was top-down, universal, and cohesive. Swelled with first- and second-generation immigrants predisposed to defer to priestly authority, Catholics comprised a precision-guided pressure group of awesome effectiveness. "Satisfying one church group is good reason for another being dissatisfied," figured a Hollywood executive in 1930, what with "two hundred denominations and each being suspicious of the other." Two hundred Protestant denominations perhaps—but only one Holy Roman Catholic and Apostolic Church.

For Hollywood moguls apt to see Christians as a monolithic entity, the difference between obstreperous Protestant diffusion and obedient Catholic solidarity was difficult to grasp. The resident expert explained the doctrinal nuances in yet another Code creation story. Breen's friend, the journal-

2. I don't think it's so good to be called a self regulator," PCA staffer Morris Murphy once confided to Jack Vizzard. "It sounds like someone who plays with himself."

ist and screenwriter J. P. McEvoy (who claimed to have heard the exchange), related his version in 1938, before too much time for embellishment had elapsed.

The scene takes place in late 1933 when the picketing and pledging from the Catholics first rattled the studio gates. Breen warns a mogul that Hollywood can jerk around "the women's clubs, Y.M.C.A.s, Jews, Mormons, Quakers, and any other and all Protestants, but whatever they do, they are not to tangle with the Roman Catholic Church."

"What can the Catholics do to us that the Protestants can't?" asks the skeptical mogul.

"Keep their people out of the movie houses," Breen answers.

The mogul chuckles. "Do you mean to tell me that in this day and age, people will stay away from the theater because the Church tells them to?"

"Catholics will," insists Breen.

"I don't believe it."

"You boys will find out," Breen promises.

Besides a lifetime in the Church, Breen derived confidence from working both sides of the street. As early as November 1930, he had hatched plans to advance his position, and faith, within the MPPDA. A Catholic journalist who chanced upon "this champion of the Catholic Church in America!" on the streets of Chicago listened awestruck as Breen "unfolded his plans for Catholic Action on one of the most momentous matters ever faced by the Church in America, or any other country." Privy to inside information from Hollywood (by way of Martin J. Quigley and his own part-time job with the MPPDA) and Catholicism (by way of a lifetime moving and shaking within the hierarchy), he played the two sides off against each other—for his cause and career.

In January 1931, Breen seized an opportunity to do some Catholic action that would also do himself some good. Universal Pictures had recently purchased the screen rights to Charles Norris's novel *Seed*, a best seller with a sympathetic view of birth control. A "very dangerous book," judged Breen, "really sinister and insidious." Worse, the infamous birth control advocate Margaret Sanger was rumored to be among the cast. Assuming the overdetermined nom de plume "Walter White," Breen composed a call to arms in Philadelphia's *Catholic Standard and Times*, an editorial that alerted Catholics to Universal's plans and warned of "the suggestive filth that is inseparable from any discussion of Birth Control or to the dissemination of false prophecies and false teachings that threaten the very fabric of our civilization." All good Catholics were urged to express their outrage to Universal in a calm and reasonable manner. "Write a dignified protest to Carl Laemmle, Senior," he advised. Universal would, understandably, want to retain Norris's lascivious title because "it is of great value due to the widespread sale of the book," but "under Laemmle Senior's guidance" the objectionable elements would surely be eliminated. "But—whatever you do must be done today. The picture is now about to be filmed—and tomorrow it may be too late."

The editorial did the trick. Inundated with angry but sane letters, Laemmle hastily called upon Father Lord to vet the shooting script. "Frankly I am more than pleased with the treatment given to a very dangerous story," reported Father Lord, always glad to be back in show business. "There were infinite possibilities in the original treatment that would have caused much unpleasant controversy." In a repentant letter to the *Catholic Standard and Times*, Laemmle assured Philadelphia Catholics that Universal's version of *Seed* would have "no propaganda" for birth control and "would contain not the slightest offense to those of the Catholic faith." Also, Margaret Sanger would not be making a cameo appearance.

The scheme was a slick exercise in behind-the-curtain stage management. While galvanizing the Catholic troops, Breen took care not to insult Laemmle. While keeping faith with Catholic doctrine, he took care to appreciate Universal's financial stake in a hot property with an exploitable title. (Already too he understood that effective Catholic censorship needed to be applied during the script phase—before the shooting started.) The successful campaign to expunge the fulcrum plot point of the novel *Seed* from the film *Seed* (1931) foretold many similar disappearances and mutations in the transposition from page to screen during the PCA era. It also served as Breen's audition for the MPPDA—proof to the moguls of his pull with the Catholics, proof to the Catholics of his access to the moguls.

Upon arriving in Hollywood as assistant to Will Hays in 1931, Breen continued to scheme to lock in Catholic oversight, and the Catholics reciprocated by aiding and abetting their inside man. In 1934, in an internal report to the Episcopal Committee, Father Dinneen, the Chicago priest whose to-the-barricades zealotry had been a catalyst for the Code in 1929, described Breen as "a militant Catholic layman [who] will fight to exclude filth from the pictures." Dinneen advised that "pressure should be put on [Breen] directly from the Bishops and Catholic authorities, insisting on the enforcement of the Code adopted by the producers. This kind of backing would be his most effective weapon in his battle with the directors in the studios."

While urging his fellow Catholics "to keep suspended over the heads of the producers the sword which is now threatening to decapitate them," Breen stoked the paranoia. "I have not neglected the opportunity to encourage this fear [among the moguls] and to emphasize the dire disaster which lies ahead of the industry unless something, by way of cleansing process, is undertaken at once," he informed Bishop McNicholas. He signed his

MPPDA stationery to McNicholas and other bishops "your Excellency's most obedient servant."

Returning the compliment, Bishop McNicholas referred to Breen's service as "a priestly work," a calling just shy of ordination. The bishop was not alone in sensing a commitment that was more than secular. "The initials *I.H.S.* are familiar to millions, particularly when interwoven with the symbolic Cross of Christianity on the religious garments and church accessories of the Roman Catholic Church," explained the trade journalist Howard Hall in his newsletter *Cinema Hall-Marks*. "Summarily they stand for *In Hoc Signo*, a Latin phrase which is religiously interpreted 'By This Sign (the Cross) We Conquer.' However those initials at this time [August 1934] could stand for Joseph I. Breen, who, beyond any reasonable doubt, seems to be *In His Sacerdotalism*, or according to the dictionary, 'zeal for priestly things.'"

In his sacerdotalism, however, Breen could not seem too zealously priestly. Officially, he kept the Catholic hierarchy and especially the Legion of Decency at one degree of separation. "Joe picked one of the Catholic boys on the board" for "liaison with the Legion" to "avoid charges of being in cahoots with the Legion of Decency," recalled Albert Van Schmus. However, face-to-face conversations, telephone calls, and exchanges of letters kept up a constant murmur of back-channel communication. Breen always gave the Church a courtesy heads-up on Catholic-sensitive material and told studios to consult Father John Devlin, the Legion's designated "technical advisor" in Hollywood, on Church history, liturgy, and vestments. No motion picture project with Catholic content was approved without private consultations and informal vetting from Church authorities. In the early days especially, Breen regularly sent scenarios and screenplays to Father Lord and *America* editor Rev. Wilfrid Parsons, S.J. ("under strict confidence") for clearance and commentary. Father Lord boasted that "as late as 1953, I sat in with the board of the Breen Office to listen to scripts and to watch the formula that grew out of the Code applied to questionable situations."

Whenever priests visited Hollywood to inspect the mission, the junketeers received solicitous VIP treatment from the MPPDA and privileged access to the studio soundstages. Breen was never too busy to stroke an ecclesiastical ego, to introduce the good padres to a favorite star, or to arrange a private studio tour. He insisted only that the proper protocols be followed, meaning that the priests be routed via the Los Angeles archdiocese. "Any request from Your Excellency would be met with a prompt and whole hearted response on the part of our member companies," he assured Bishop Cantwell. "We stand at attention!"

Even the Catholic connection had its limits however. Breen refused to lean on producers when importuned by priests to help a favored parishioner with alleged star quality. "To attempt to assert myself in a matter of this kind, not only seriously interferes with the dispensation of my responsibility but likewise causes me great embarrassment," he explained to Bishop Cantwell.

Breen's most serious intra-Catholic squabbles were with his ostensible reserve troops in the Legion of Decency. Independent of the Breen Office, the Legion graded films along a sliding scale of morality from the wholly pure A-1 ("morally unobjectionable for general patronage"), to the slightly diluted A-2 ("morally unobjectionable for adults"), to the mildly toxic B ("morally objectionable in part for all"), to the deadly poisonous C ("Condemned"). A Catholic who willfully exposed himself to a Condemned film was placing his immortal soul in jeopardy. Hollywood thus had to pass inspection from two Catholic quality-control boards: the preproduction scrubbing of the Breen Office and the postproduction scoring of the Legion of Decency.

When the Legion had the temerity to condemn or B-rate a Hollywood film awarded a Code Seal, Breen bristled at the second-guessing. After 1934 he often considered the Legion "a pain in the neck." To Quigley, he confessed, "I am thoroughly disgusted with the Legion of Decency and more especially with that branch which holds forth on the South Shore of Lake Michigan [in Chicago]." The resentment was as much professional as personal. A bad grade from the Legion undercut Breen, whose job, after all, was to keep the Catholics quiescent. Usually, back-channel communications and the common bond of Catholic values prevented a split decision, but when the Legion's sense of decency conflicted with Breen's, the non-Catholics in Hollywood were understandably perplexed.

It was a measure of Catholic power—and the shudders evoked by memories of 1934—that when Breen's Code-approved films flunked the Legion test, the studios entered into private negotiations with the priests and edited the works to avoid the mark of the class C film. When Twentieth Century-Fox's *Forever Amber* (1947), a Technicolor costume drama featuring Linda Darnell as a scheming vixen who jumps via mattress from serving wench to royal mistress, was branded with the Legion's scarlet letter for "glorifying immorality," Fox meekly protested, and then knuckled under.

Under Legion dictation, *Forever Amber* was framed with a ham-handed prologue:

> This is the tragic story of Amber St. Clare . . . Slave to ambition, stranger to virtue . . . fated to find the wealth and power she ruthlessly gained wither to ashes in the fires lit by passion and fed by defiance of the eternal command . . . The wages of sin is death.

Also, lest the moral of the story be lost on latecomers, a spoken epilogue intoned the lines:

> In heaven's name, Amber, haven't we caused enough unhappiness? May God have mercy on us both for our sins.

Thus bookended by printed and spoken voices of morality, *Forever Amber* was reclassified to a B ("morally objectionable in part for all"). Ungracious in victory, the Legion huffed that the picture "still lacks the morally compensating values which should be present in a story of this kind."

For the Breen Office, a split decision with the Legion had one tactically compensating value. When the Legion condemned or B-graded a film sealed under the Code, the disagreement proved that Breen was not playing dummy to a Church ventriloquist. "While the head of the Code Administration is a Catholic, its membership, of usually nine persons, includes a decided range of faiths and religious viewpoints," Terry Ramsaye noted. "Also, as the records frequently indicate, the Seal of Code approval is not to be considered a pass and green light through the examinations of the Catholic Legion of Decency."

Edited by the Legion: saucy serving wench Amber St. Clair (Linda Darnell) hustles dashing Lord Carlton (Cornel Wilde) to the amusement of his pal Lord Almsbury (Richard Greene) in Otto Preminger's *Forever Amber* (1947).

As Breen presided over the Code and prospered in Hollywood, he accrued the tributes due a prominent Catholic layman, including honorary degrees from Loyola University of Los Angeles in 1937 and his nominal alma mater St. Joseph's in 1954. On July 14, 1938, in a ceremony in the Vatican presided over by his old acquaintance Pope Pius XI, Breen accepted the honor he most treasured, the designation as Knights Commander of the Order of St. Gregory, a coveted pontifical decoration bestowed for meritorious service to the Church. The man who had ridden into the mouth of the dragon in Hollywood had literally been dubbed a knight.

However, Breen declined more blessings than he accepted. "If, in a moment of weakness, I were to permit myself to have any part in your plans to honor me, I should be so conscience stricken that I would be afraid to go home to Hollywood," he telegrammed the Ladies Solidarity of St. Louis, who wanted to recognize him as "an outstanding Catholic American who is doing great things for our country" and publish his picture in the *Queen's Work*, their monthly journal. "I am so completely unworthy of such an honor that were I to lend any aid whatever to such an enterprise, I should thereby expose myself to the very valid charge that I am hardly more than a fraud and hypocrite. My neighbors out there, who know me well, would surely laugh at me and point me out as a kind of first rate fakir." As for the picture, he also demurred. "If you ever got a good look at me, you would not trouble very much about getting hold of my photograph. Frankly, I'm not much to look at. I'm built more for comfort than for style. I am certain that printing my picture in the *Queen's Work* will add no new names to your list of subscribers."

Predictably, as Catholics wielded the moral equivalent of final cut over Hollywood cinema, Protestants grumbled from the back pews. "The minority control of the most vital amusement source of the nation is one of the most astounding things in the history of the United States," protested the *Protestant Digest* in 1940. Secular critics were no less vexed by the overweening Catholicism or shy about naming the Vatican agent inflicting a plague of priests, nuns, and altar boys on Hollywood cinema. "Joseph I. Breen, a Catholic of Irish descent, is the one-man censor of the movies," complained the *New Republic*, whose film critic Otis Fergusan charged that "the Catholic machinery" had "stampeded the Protestants" and "captured the movies." Sometimes the tones of nineteenth-century anti-Catholicism seep in to the rhetoric of critics indignant that Hollywood trembled before "a single benighted individual" who was "a devout adherent of one of the narrowest of creeds," a religion built upon what an editorial in the *Harvard Journal* referred to as "an ichthyopathagic [fish-eating] concatenation of primordial superstitions." In a letter of complaint to Eric Johnston, who succeeded Will Hays as Breen's boss in 1945, a Methodist minister charged: "Let me again say that Mr. Breen is at the very center of the problem. Thousands of people believe he is where he is as the specific and particular agent of the Roman Church."

"I am constantly being charged with being 'an agent of the Pope,' 'a spy for the Papists,' etc.," Breen wrote Father Lord in 1937. "My mail, which comes to the office, is opened by two girls out in the file room who sort out the material I should see, personally, and undertake to handle the other stuff without bothering me. These girls read these 'protests' from the anti-Catholic bigots."[3]

Staying on message, the MPPDA stressed the ecumenical ethos and universal tenets of the Code. "The truth is Mr. Breen heads the Production Code Administration—a board whose eleven members include adherents of the Catholic, Protestant, and Jewish faiths, are of varying ages and widely different backgrounds and experience," explained Francis Harmon, Hays's assistant and head of the New York office of the PCA.

Though Hollywood filmmakers knew only too well which faith held controlling interest around town, only occasionally did the information leak out in a big way to the civilian press. In 1936 the Catholic power in Hollywood made headlines when a secular Irishman named George Bernard Shaw initiated a newsworthy donnybrook with the MPPDA. Shaw was a familiar figure to Americans, not just as a renowned Anglo-Irish playwright but as a star of the early sound newsreels, where the spry septuagenarian played the very picture of the eccentric literary Englishman—dapper, sardonic, game for anything.

In 1923, Shaw had written *St. Joan,* as reverent and orthodox a treatment of the Maid of Orleans as could be expected from an agnostic raised as a Protestant in Ireland. According to Shaw, the play was slated to be a Hollywood production until sinister forces intervened. On September 14, 1936, in a letter to the *New York Times,* Shaw accused an organization he dubbed "Azione Cattolica" of killing the project. Disabused of the notion that "the Hays Organization represented nonsectarian American decency," he lashed out at the "meddling by amateur busybodies who do not care that the work of censorship requires any qualification beyond Catholic baptism." Shaw was compelled to go public with his dilemma because "very few inhabitants of the United States, Catholic or Protestant, lay or secular, have the least suspicion that an irresponsible Catholic society has assumed public control of their artistic recreations."

3. Also in the mailbag were letters from antisemites accusing Breen of being an agent of the Jews.

Will Hays denied all of Shaw's charges: no screen treatment had been received by the PCA and hence no opinion had been tendered; no organization called "Catholic Action" existed; and, besides, no censorship existed in Hollywood; the proper term was "self-regulation."

Interviewed by the *New York Times* at his country home in Ayot St. Lawrence, the playwright responded in a suitably Shavian manner. "The whole thing is a muddle. I am in a muddle still," he confessed. "All I know is that the film business in America is in the grip of a Catholic censorship strong enough to intimidate an English producer into submitting a play for its approval; and its disapproval knocked the whole enterprise on the head although hundreds of thousands of dollars were blamelessly at stake."

"I never heard of the Catholic Legion of Decency, but what a splendid idea—more power to its elbow," he gibed. "I heard the name Breen, a good Irish Catholic name, but beyond wondering whether he was related to the famous Dan Breen, whose tactics played a part in the struggle for the Free Irish State, I had no idea where Mr. Breen came in." (Luckily for him, or Shaw, Breen was away on vacation when the brouhaha erupted.)

The reporter for the *New York Times* explained to Shaw the difference between Hollywood's in-house censorship regime and the ex parte ratings of the Legion of Decency: that the Breen Office reviewed scripts for the MPPDA and the Legion rated films for the Catholics.

Savvy to how the pincer movement worked, Shaw replied that "this amounts to telling Hollywood that if an improper or anti-Catholic film—say, Mark Twain's *Joan*—is produced, 20,000,000 Catholics in the United States will be told by their spiritual directors to boycott it." (Exactly.) "As Hollywood isn't expert in problems either of propriety or Catholic doctrine, it turns in panic to any one who professes such expertness for assurance that its scenarios are all right before it ventures $100,000 or so on each. There is always somebody ready to act as a censor in this way for due consideration." (Right again.)

What was he going to do now, asked the man from the *Times*.

"Nothing," Shaw shrugged. "Haven't I done enough?" After all, he had awakened the gulled and lulled Protestants of America. Before the firestorm over *St. Joan,* "not one American in 50,000 had the faintest suspicion that the film art for which his country is famous was, in effect, under a Catholic censorship, which was bound as such to operate as a doctrinal censorship as well as a common-decency censorship."

Shaw nailed it. The Code was no mere bluenose aversion to sex, drinking, swearing, and violence, but a force for Catholic orthodoxy. He may have been in a muddle about the mechanism, but he understood perfectly the catechism.

TWO-FISTED PRIESTS AND BEATIFIC NUNS

"A visitor from Mars, popping into a dozen cinemas at random, would be convinced that the United States is a Catholic nation," groused the *Protestant Digest*, which had its own notions about the religious roots anchoring the United States. "If Roman Catholic domination of censorship continues, the film screens of most of the world will be flooded with pictures such as *Going My Way* [1944], *The Song of Bernadette* [1945], and *The Bells of St. Mary's* [1945]."

The Protestant gripe list was too short. A preacher seeking to rid the screen of meddlesome priests might also have mentioned *San Francisco* (1936), *Angels with Dirty Faces* (1938), *Boys Town* (1938), *Knute Rockne, All American* (1940), *The Fighting 69th* (1940), *Men of Boys Town* (1941), and *The Keys of the Kingdom* (1944), in addition to dozens of prison and combat films where Catholic priests were the chaplains chosen to take the long walk to the chair with convicted killers or lend spiritual comfort to GIs in foxholes. "It's just that the Catholic mentions are remembered more, since the Catholic ritual is so much more dramatic than that of any other faith," replied a priest from the Legion of Decency, with the serenity of the elect.

The statistically disproportionate presence of priests, nuns, and Catholic sacraments in classical Hollywood cinema served multiple purposes: to attract a prime moviegoing demographic; to pet a cranky pressure group; to regale non-Catholics with the exotic rites of a mysterious faith; and, not least, to stroke the Catholic eminence at the Production Code Administration. How much of the celluloid Catholicity flowed directly from Breen defies precise measurement, but the deep sympathy to Catholicism, specifically its Irish branch, is more than happenstance. "Nearly everyone in Hollywood is perfecting an Irish brogue at the moment [August 1934] in the hope it will touch the heart of Mr. Breen," semi-joked the Hollywood journalist John C. Moffitt, emphasizing the lesser half of the equation. Whether or not filmmakers hoped to touch Breen's heart with a brogue or a blessing, they took care not to get his Irish up with a depiction of Catholicism that was anything less than worshipful.

Breen's public relations work on behalf of American Catholicism long predated his arrival in Hollywood. Throughout the 1920s, whether counseling immigrants for the National Catholic Welfare Council, peddling volumes of *Catholic Builders of the Nation*, or trumpeting the Eucharistic Congress, he sought not only to make Catholics into better Americans but to make America a better home for Catholics by educating the Protestant majority about Catholicism. "The great need of the Church in the smaller towns is active, open contact with those not of our Faith," Breen wrote in the Jesuit weekly *America* in 1929. "Once this is established, there is less of that irreligious animosity, that willingness to believe untruths about Catholicism, which is now the almost universal tendency in most of the smaller towns in the Hinterland." Breen helped bring Catholicism to small town America—the Bible belt citadels of the Deep South, the bulwarks of Protestantism in the Midwest, and the tony Episcopalian townships of New England—via the best of all distribution networks, the neighborhood motion picture theater.

In conversations and correspondence, Breen referred often to his Hollywood mission as a piece of "real Catholic Action" by a staunch member of "the Church militant." In 1934, while plotting to put teeth in the Code, he envisioned a screen world of "clean, wholesome entertainment based upon Catholic ideals of fun and entertainment and recreation. If we could provide some means for Catholic story tellers to tell—and write—stories based upon Catholic philosophy, is it unreasonable to expect that here, again, we shall see the influence of the movies showing itself upon audiences?"

Even before being put on the full-time payroll of the MPPDA, Breen knew the kind of theological intervention Hollywood required and how to reward it. After Carl Laemmle of Universal heeded the (Breen-orchestrated) howls of protests from Catholics about *Seed* (1931), the proposed film version of the Charles G. Norris novel about the "dirty business of birth control," Breen urged Bishop Cantwell of Los Angeles to send Laemmle "a formal word of evidence of our Catholic appreciation of this fine action. [Universal] did a very courageous thing and we must not allow the service to pass unnoticed." As he emphasized to the bishop, "the *fact* is that the Universal Company *did* accept our viewpoint—our Catholic viewpoint—against the sneers and slurs or the opposition" who counseled Laemmle against "permitting 'ignorant Papists' to tell him how to run his business."

If adherence to Catholic orthodoxy was Breen's highest praise for a motion picture producer, he ranked a motion picture imbued with Catholic doctrine as a sheer masterpiece. Paramount's *Cradle Song* (1933), a women's weepie set in a Spanish convent, brought tears to the eyes of more than its target audience. Directed by Mitchell Leisen, the maudlin tale of a selfless nun who becomes mother to an orphan girl left at the convent door was "the most exquisitely beautiful thing I have ever seen," Breen rhapsodized to Father Lord. "Every line, every sequence is thoroughly Catholic in both tone and spirit and the technical details are perfect." Not that he harbored any illusions about the commercial appeal of the Catholic faith served straight-up, unmixed with tonic. "Despite all of this, however, it looks to me to be headed for a box office flop," he surmised correctly. "It is probably too fine a thing for the mob and yet it is exactly the kind to thing which we ought to have."

However, only a few years later the moviegoing mob was drawn, in droves, to Catholicism—not as practiced by suffering Spanish nuns but as incarnated by charming Irish priests. The Hollywood padres belonged to an order of streetwise, multitalented, two-fisted Irishmen, affable guys from the ethnic enclaves of the big cities, not at all like the namby-pamby ministers of the genteel divinity schools of New England or the wild-eyed tent-show evangelists of the rural South. Sexually celibate though they were, they exuded virility and vitality, as surefooted on the boxing canvas as the marble altar. At their most charismatic and believable, they were played by Pat O'Brien, Spencer Tracy, and Bing Crosby, actors who had knocked around with, or been knocked around by, the type since childhood. In fact, in temperament and physique, the priests bore more than a passing resemblance to—Joseph I. Breen.[4]

From the packed gallery of priest-ridden, Irish-addled motion pictures produced under the Breen Office, a combat film released on the eve of World War II by Warner Bros., the most gruffly Jewish of all the major studios, may be the *ne plus ultra*. Besotted with near-toxic levels of blarney, brogues, and malarkey, *The Fighting 69th* (1940) divides humanity into two groups, the Irish and the proto-Irish, conjuring a cinematic old sod soaked with drinking, brawling, and absolutely no pesky colleens. Though precisely two decades would elapse before a prince of the tribe grabbed the greatest prize (the White House), *The Fighting 69th* exudes the swagger of an ethnic group in full command of the center stage in American culture.

Based on the exploits of the storied New York regiment, *The Fighting 69th* suppresses the memory of the Great War as a charnel house of meaningless slaughter to tell a tale of spiritual redemption, Irish-Catholic style. At the high end of the Irish chain of command is the real-life war hero William "Wild Bill" Donovan (George Brent), already a legend, the second-most-decorated veteran of the Great War after Sergeant Alvin York, himself soon to receive a commemorative biopic in *Sergeant York* (1941), which, contra *Protestant Digest*, was as favorable a depiction of evangelical Protestantism as Hollywood ever put on screen. Donovan is stern and sober, every inch the Victorian Irishman. Rounding out the trio are Father Francis P. Duffy (Pat O'Brien), the real-life regimental chaplain, and the fictional Jerry

4. Monsignor C. J. Quille, the Chicago priest who supervised the Eucharistic Congress, exemplified the type. "He learn[ed] to fight with his fists, not box, mind you, but *fight*; at eighteen years he [was] rated to be the best amateur lightweight in the Middle West," wrote Breen, in an admiring profile of Quille in 1929.

Plunkett (James Cagney), a brash guttersnipe whose bravado hides a yellow streak. Another Irish character type, the dreamy poet, appears in the person of Joyce Kilmer (Jeffrey Lynn), who composes verses on the march. The parade of ripe Irish stereotypes follows the usual rule for ethnic comedy: if performed by the clan in question (director William Keighley, actors Brent, Cagney, O'Brien, et al.), the latitude for stereotypical depiction is extended accordingly. (Through careful not to open the door to nastier epithets aimed at less assimilated groups, Breen permitted Cagney to utter a mild slur that would never have been permitted to escape from the mouth of a non-Irishman. "I don't like these flannel-mouth micks who go around singing 'Molly Malone' all the time," Plunkett informs Father Duffy.)

Like the three Breen brothers, the valorized Irish triad in *The Fighting 69th* follows the three main traveled roads to success in America: religion (Duffy), government (Donovan), and the arts (Kilmer). By contrast, the brash, volatile, and ill-educated Plunkett belongs to the Irish-American past, his very name an echo of the mid-nineteenth century where no Irish need apply, except to Plunkett of Tammany Hall. Only two interlopers breach the Hibernian ranks: the troops of an Alabama regiment, brought on screen for a melee of fisticuffs and a nod to regional diversity, and a

Irish-Catholicism ascendant: Father Francis J. Duffy (Pat O'Brien), Jerry Plunkett (James Cagney), and William "Wild Bill" Donovan (George Brent) in William Keighley's blarney-laden *The Fighting 69th* (1940).

Jewish-American imposter, who wants to join the ranks. Both are swept into the Irish tide.

The tie that most tightly binds the Irishmen of *The Fighting 69th* is not alcohol, fisticuffs, or poetry but religion. Father Duffy blesses the troops, says Midnight Mass, leads the men in the Lord's Prayer (the Catholic version), and delivers the last rites to dying soldiers of all faiths. Bathed in divine chiaroscuro while sermonizing in direct address, Father Duffy provides the moral backbone and narrative spine of the film. Under his guidance, the unregenerate Plunkett will find God, country, and courage, and learn that all three are one.

Whether for a feature-length homage or a walk-on bow, the doctrine, rituals, and uniformed personnel of the Roman Catholic Church were scrupulously monitored. "We would like, further, to recommend that you secure the services of a very competent Catholic priest, who will serve as technical advisor on this picture," Breen instructed Twentieth Century-Fox during preproduction on *The Song of Bernadette*. Yet Breen couldn't resist showing off how he had earned his stripes as a Knight of St. Gregory. "For example, it is noted more than once that the recitation of the rosary begins with the recitation of the Hail Mary. This may have been the proper procedure during Bernadette's time. It is not, however, the proper procedure at the present time. One who was to begin, properly, to recite the Rosary would begin with a recitation of the Credo." He continued with precise instructions on the doctrine of the Immaculate Conception and the sacrament of Extreme Unction.

With such expertise on hand in the Breen Office, Fox hardly needed to recruit an outside consultant for technical help. For the record, though, Breen referred producers to the official adviser on matters of faith on screen. "We strongly urge and recommend that you get into touch with Father Devlin (telephone number, Crestview 6-3726), who is the technical advisor appointed by Archbishop Cantwell for consultation with studies on all motion pictures having any bearing on Catholic matters," ran a typical admonition. However, the blessings of the in-house layman mattered more than the advice of the offstage clergyman. Impressed by the liturgical accuracy and clerical character of *Joan of Paris* (1942), a priest knew whom to thank. "I'm sure you have your strong Catholic hand in [it]," he guessed in a fan letter to Breen. "Believe me, it thrills a Catholic heart to see our faith getting that kind of publicity." Breen admitted, "you are correct in your assumption that we had much to do with the scenes dealing with the Catholic priest and his seven reel peregrination."

Easing Breen's qualms toward a Catholic theme was the affiliation and pedigree of the star, director, or screenwriter. A co-ethno-religionist such as the directors Leo McCarey or John Ford could be counted on for verisimilitude and reverence. Tipped off that McCarey's *Going My Way* would feature a romantic backstory for "the crooning padre" played by Bing Crosby, Bishop McGucken fretted over potential punctures in the wall of celibacy. Breen assured the bishop that neither McCarey nor he had taken complete leave of his senses. "There is no suggestion of a 'sex angle' in the picture," he promised. "The provisions of the Production Code do not permit any such treatment on the screen of Catholic priests. If a motion picture even remotely suggesting what is worrying [you] were to come along here, it would not be approved." Just to be sure, he advised McCarey that "wherever you show Jenny [the priest's girlfriend, pre-vocation] in company with the priest, that she have a companion with her, another lady possibly, who could be established as her secretary or maid," thereby allaying any implication that Father O'Malley would make a pass at, or intercept one from, his old flame.

After a decade of Breen Office nudging and supervision, Catholic clergy, rituals, and sacraments were as familiar to American moviegoers of whatever denomination as the cowboys, showdowns, and landscape of the Hollywood western. The screen sacerdotalism that began with *Eucharistic Congress* (1926), that advanced apace in the 1930s with the two-fisted priests from the seminaries at Warner Bros. and MGM, achieved its apotheosis in the late war–early postwar period from 1944 to 1946, an interlude that saw the release of *The Keys of the Kingdom*, a lush version of the A. J. Cronin novel about Catholic missionary work from Scotland to China; *The Song of Bernadette*, a pious dramatization of the visitation of the Virgin Mary to a French peasant girl at Lourdes; and—the films that marked the high crest of Hollywood-filtered Irish Catholicism—producer-director Leo McCarey's two-part fusion of piety and hokum, *Going My Way* and *The Bells of St. Mary's*.

The extraordinary ecumenical success of McCarey's back-to-back hits (the latter is not really a sequel, but a continuation of the musical ministry of the itinerant Father Chuck O'Malley) confirmed for Hollywood the wages of Catholic salvation: *Going My Way* took the year's top Oscars and box office spot with $6.5 million in gross receipts, and *The Bells of St. Mary's* paid even higher dividends, grossing over $8 million. (Each sum represented huge windfalls for the time.) True pop-cult phenomena, the two films soared on the need for religious solace in wartime, on McCarey's sure touch with the Irish-Catholic characters so close to his heart, and, above all, on the singular charm of the man in the collar, the versatile singer, radio personality, and motion picture star Bing Crosby. In Crosby's Father O'Malley ("just dial 'O'—for O'Malley"), Catholicism would never find a more congenial propagator of the faith.

Like Breen, Crosby was a dropout from a Jesuit institution of higher learning, Gonzaga University in Spokane, Washington, home to a more outdoorsy and laid-back order of padre than the Victorian Irish of the urban east. Crosby's performance style was constructed around a seemingly artless naturalism. Whether as an actor or a singer, he never seemed to be straining for a note, and when he donned the priestly collar for McCarey, he refused to stiffen his easygoing persona one notch. Slighter in build than Pat O'Brien and Spencer Tracy, he shunned the two-fisted approach (like Bing, Father O'Malley's game is golf), preferring gentle persuasion, usually set to music, to strongarm tactics. Like the cantor's son played by Al Jolson in *The Jazz Singer* (1927), religious scruples would not deny the crooning padre the rewards of American show business. (Jack Robin gets Broadway stardom, Father O'Malley scores a pop music hit.) Nor would moviegoers be denied the listening pleasures of Bing Crosby's gift from God. Sitting down at the piano, blessed with the voice of an angel, he was the life of the party, not the scowling chaperone. The silky-smooth, deep-bottomed baritone preached a sugarcoated, singalong-with-the-chorus gospel. "Swinging on a Star," the theme song from *Going My Way*, charted a painless stairway from earth to heaven, making of Catholicism a tuneful mix of spiritual transcendence and sweet harmony.

In *Going My Way*, despite first impressions, Father Chuck O'Malley is not the new kid on the block but the bishop's hired gun and a precursor to a figure Americans would get to know well in the postwar era, the efficiency expert. Porkpie hat in hand, he has come to update a shopworn institution, St. Dominick's Church, and its old-school (and just plain old) pastor, Father Fitzgibbon, played by Barry Fitzgerald (an alumnus of Dublin's Abbey Players—and a Protestant in Catholic clothing). With an empty poor box and an anemic collection plate, Father Fitzgibbon's parish needs an injection of new blood, a steady cash flow, and a firm hand to pull its juvenile delinquents off the streets and into the choir loft. As Father O'Malley makes his rounds, often wearing a baseball jacket that sports his rooting interest in (naturally) the St. Louis Cardinals, the Irish whimsy is poured on thick: Father O'Malley sings a drowsy Father Fitzgibbon to sleep with "Too-Ra-Loo-Ra-Loo-Ral" (". . . that's an Irish lullaby . . ."); Father Fitzgibbon nips from a bottle of Irish whiskey (improbably rationing himself to one bottle per year); and, in the eye-watering finale, Father O'Malley reunites the old priest with his frail, aged mother, brought over from Ireland.

The story element that worried Bishop McGucken—"the crooning padre's" pre-vocation backstory with a former girlfriend, now a famous opera singer—is handled with chaste delicacy, but not without sexual tension. Jenny (Risë Stevens) is still carrying a torch for the man she thinks is just plain "Chuck," his collar hidden by his overcoat. Bubbling with excitement at the reunion, she grabs his hand and drags him to her dressing room backstage at the Metropolitan Opera. As per Breen's suggestion, the former lovers are well chaperoned, doubly so, she behind a set of doors with her maid, Father O'Malley in an anteroom with the orchestra conductor, a slightly embarrassed witness to the miscues, for as Jenny babbles about Chuck's treasured love letters, he can see what Jenny cannot, that her "very old friend" Chuck is now a man of the cloth. Encountering her former beau in priestly garb for the first time, she smiles, comprehending more than their terminated correspondence. "*Father* Chuck—it'll take a little while to get used to that," she says wistfully.

The most honored and universally beloved musical-comedy-melodrama of its time, *Going My Way* scored not just in Catholic enclaves in the big cities (where priests and nuns herded parochial school students into matinees on field trips) but in the Protestant small towns. "A must for Catholics and a must-not-miss for all others," raved the *New York Post*. Pope Pius XII loved it.

If *Going My Way* struts the masculine side of Irish Catholicism, with St. Patrick as its patron saint, *The Bells of St. Mary's* tolls the feminine side,

The crooning padre: Father Chuck O'Malley (Bing Crosby) and his old flame (Risë Stevens) in Leo McCarey's *Going My Way* (1944).

with the Virgin Mary as its presiding icon. Upon arriving at St. Mary's, the parochial school run by an unnamed order of "good sisters," Father O'Malley is warned by the rectory housekeeper—a prune-faced harpy with a thick brogue and the not-accidental moniker of Mrs. Breen—that the previous priest was taken out in a wheelchair and that the present one will be "up to your neck in nuns." Though cloistered nuns, the belles of St. Mary's retain the power of their gender to discombobulate men.

Less buoyantly tuneful than *Going My Way, The Bells of St. Mary's* is more interesting because of the courtship between two A-list Hollywood stars whose trajectory, in any other milieu, would be into each other's arms. In truth, the magnetic attraction applies here too. No matter how many layers of black cloth and stiff white collars come between Sister Mary Benedict (Ingrid Bergman) and Father O'Malley, they are celibate lovers whose affection, simpatico, and longing for each other pulsates through the film.

Despite, or because of, the head-to-toe blanketing in black, Bergman was never more luminous: her flawless face framed by a nun's habit, her tresses never shown much less let down, her posture (straight-backed, hands folded) concealing the voluptuousness moviegoers had beheld from *Intermezzo* (1939) to *Spellbound* (1945). Playing a former tomboy with a flare for sports, the actress shows a gift for physical comedy heretofore untapped by Hollywood. In a marvelous bit of trademark McCarey shtick, she teaches a young boy the manly art of pugilism, tossing jabs and hooks, dancing the fancy footwork, and, for the topper, taking a sock on the the jaw—a two-fisted nun.

The emotional intimacy between the priest and the nun sparks across eyeline matches, medium shots, and verbal volleys. "Luther? How'd he get in here?" Father O'Malley jokes when Sister Benedict calls out a boy's name for classroom recitation. In a coy whisper, sharing her smile only with Father O'Malley, Sister Benedict joshes back, "We never knew." Bonding over work, the couple anxiously watches their children perform in the school nativity play, but the lovers also quarrel—substantively—over educational policy and academic standards, with Sister Benedict sticking to the rules and Father O'Malley willing to let standards slide. (In both films, McCarey's version of Catholicism winks at a little cheating; his God cuts everyone slack.) Being a Bing Crosby picture, music and song also binds the couple. In a callback to a similar vocal bond shared by Irene Dunne and Cary Grant in McCarey's *The Awful Truth* (1937), Sister Benedict coquettishly ends a Swedish folk song by lilting the final lyric into Father O'Malley's name.

Alas, no end-reel clinch can consummate the relationship. The romantic triangle, with the Church the immovable obstacle to the course of true love, cannot be resolved by Hollywood ingenuity. After a third-act diagnosis of tuberculosis, Sister Benedict must be exiled from her beloved St. Mary's. As she walks out of Father O'Malley's life forever, disappearing under the black capes of her sisters in Christ, the priest looks more stricken than Rick in *Casablanca*. Though this couple, like Rick and Ilsa, can cherish the memory of their brief encounter (they'll always have St. Mary's), the awful truth is that the denial of the love is all wrong cinematically, a sacrifice on the altar of dogma. In this, the film was more subversive of Catholic doctrine than Breen, if not McCarey, ever realized.

Leaving a preview screening of *The Bells of St. Mary's*, a hard-bitten trade reporter numbered himself among the audience members who "left the auditorium brushing unabashed tears from happy eyes." Perhaps the best tribute to the popular appeal of McCarey's religious pageants—and to how successful Breen had been in bringing to "the smaller towns of America" "an active, open contact" with Catholicism "with those not of our Faith"—came from the Italian-Catholic director Frank Capra, who bowed to McCarey during his own excursion into transcendently verified self-denial, *It's a Wonderful Life* (1946). In Capra's Christmas-season evergreen, after the

Unspoken love: chaperoned by Sister Michael (Ruth Donnelly), an adoring Father O'Malley (Bing Crosby) visits an ailing Sister Benedict (Ingrid Bergman) in Leo McCarey's *The Bells of St. Mary's* (1945).

holy hamlet of Bedford Falls degenerates into the hellish Pottersville, the local Bijou is turned into a bawdy burlesque house. When all returns to goodness and decency in the ur-American small town, the movie on the marquee is *The Bells of St. Mary's.* "Hello Bedford Falls!" shouts the ecstatic George Bailey (Jimmy Stewart). "Hello movie house!"

By 1946, even Leo McCarey and Bing Crosby felt that Hollywood's rampant Catholicism had reached a "saturation point." Wary of being typecast, Crosby unhooked his collar, McCarey returned to nonclerical comedy, and both called a halt to Father O'Malley's rounds. (When McCarey returned to Catholic themes in his fevered anticommunist melodrama *My Son John* [1952], the result was an artistic and commercial disaster.)

With every studio in Hollywood seemingly converted to Catholicism, Protestants could only sulk from the sidelines. "For years now, the custom has been to work Catholic churches, sacraments, charitable institutions, hospitals, schools, madonnas, altars, doctrine, and priests into pictures with or without a pretext," complained the ever-annoyed *Protestant Digest*, with rising frustration as the trend refused to abate. "Scarcely a week goes by without some vivid demonstrations of this."

Heeding the Protestant outcry, "our producers have tried continuously to get together stories showing Protestants in the same light as were Catholics with the production of such pictures as *Going My Way*, *Song of Bernadette*, and *The Bells of St. Mary's*, but other than the Warner production of *One Foot in Heaven* [1941] have uncovered no material that would lend itself to good entertainment. As a matter of fact, the Warner picture, guided throughout by a Protestant leader, was not too successful at the box office as compared to the other pictures, all of which were sensational," lectured Billy Wilkerson, an agnostic on box office tallies. "We doubt if there are a half dozen Catholics in our studios who are in a position to suggest, if they would (and they wouldn't) the production of a Catholic picture and have the authority to see it through. However, there's not one producer in our midst, Protestant, Catholic, or Jew, would wouldn't grab a *Going My Way*, *Song of Bernadette*, or *Bells of St. Mary's*."

Not until Breen retired from the PCA did the Christian competition feel the "time is ripe" to foment a reformation against Hollywood's "constant tendency to show all men of the cloth on screen as Catholic priests." In 1954, American Lutherans bankrolled a likely piece of counterprogramming, a biopic entitled *Martin Luther* (1954). "The Roman Catholic Church in my opinion has done a better job in encouraging the writers and producers to handle religious themes and to use stories in which priests and nuns appear," admitted Henry Endress, chairman of Lutheran Church Productions. "Apart from that, it's easier to obtain competent technical advice from the Catholic

Church; and"—no use denying it—"the color and drama of Catholic ceremony is attractive to film men working with a visual medium."

For twenty years, Breen made certain that Catholicism infused the main currents of Hollywood cinema, both as underlying vision (the Code) and visible presence (the two-fisted priests and beatific nuns). At times, the priestly work stirred in Breen an almost messianic zeal fired by the belief that he—this man, at this time—had been chosen for the errand into the Hollywood wilderness. In 1936, while visiting the PCA's office in Hollywood, Father Donnelly watched as Breen leapt from his desk, excitedly paced the floor, and fulminated on his favorite subject. "Anybody else in the job would be too polite, wouldn't fight, wouldn't curse; the studios would mistake politeness for weakness and ride roughshod over the Code," Donnelly reported, quoting Breen's spiel. "But he could fight, he could yell louder than [Jack] Warner or [Sam] Goldwyn; he was the one man who could thrust morality down their gullets. The hand of God had been there." Imagine "the horrible state of affairs that would be in existence if he, a Catholic, were not sitting at the bottle neck, the rotten filth that would be in the pictures. And more than that—the hand of God (he said) had been in this whole thing."

But if the Code was Breen's cross to bear, it was also a sword to smite the wicked. Said Father Donnelly, who was only the stenographer: "He was the one man in the country who could cram decent ethics down the throat of the Jews, make them like it, and keep their respect."

10

"OUR SEMITIC BRETHREN"

"These Jews seem to think of nothing but money making and sexuals indulgence," Breen fumed in a letter to the Rev. Wilfrid Parsons, S.J. "People whose daily morals would not be tolerated in the toilet of a pest house hold the good jobs out here and wax fat on it. The vilest kind of sin is a common indulgence hereabouts and the men and women who engage in this sort of business are the men and women who decide what the film fare of the nation is to be. You can't escape it. They, and they alone, make the decision. Ninety-five per cent of these folks are Jews of an Eastern European lineage. They are, probably, the scum of the scum of the earth."

Breen was just getting warmed up. The notion that "these dirty lice would entertain, even for an instant, any such procedure as that suggested by a Code of Ethics" was ludicrous. Gullible Will Hays might have trusted "these lousy Jews out here [to] abide by the Code's provisions but if he did then he should be censured for his lack of proper knowledge of the breed." Surely patriotic Wall Street financiers would not stand by idly as the nation was "debauched by the Jews. Some bankers may—some of the Jew Bankers. But you can't make me believe that our American bankers, as a general thing, have fallen so low that they will permit their money to be used to paganize this nation." To his friend and patron Martin J. Quigley, Breen also vented his loathing of the tribal degeneracy and rapacious greed of Hollywood Jewry. "The fact is these damn Jews are a dirty, filthy lot. Their only standard is the standard of the box-office. To attempt to talk ethical value to them is time worse than wasted."

In 1932 the sentiments and slurs Breen put to paper were not eccentric utterances. Before Nazi genocide made outspoken antisemitism déclassé in polite conversation and disqualifying for ambitious politicians, Breen's language—and worse—was, if not exactly consensus opinion, then not strikingly aberrant either. Vulgar and sophisticated, casual and dedicated, antisemitism was the second most acceptable prejudice in the catalogue of all-American bigotries.

By some reckonings, Hollywood's boom years during the Great Depression were boom times for antisemitism. Opponents of the New Deal derided FDR's economic programs as the "Jew Deal," Washington being a city almost as notorious as Hollywood for contributing Jewish surnames to newspaper headlines. From the airwaves, unfettered by the Roman Catholic hierarchy, the radio priest Father Charles E. Coughlin denounced Jews in tones of rising rabidity as the decade dragged on. (Hoping for a studio biopic, Father Coughlin held his fire at Hollywood, a natural target.) Inspired by the Fatherland, the German-American Bund parroted the Nazi party line for domestic consumption and circulated antisemitic leaflets donated by Joseph Goebbels's Reichsministry for Propaganda and Popular Enlightenment.

Yet just as the surge in prejudice against Irish Catholics in the 1890s can be seen as a frantic rearguard action from outpaced Anglo-Protestants, the antisemitism of the 1930s is a leading indicator of the forward momentum of a thriving 3 percent of the population. Even the phrase "Jew Deal" might be heard less as a bigoted hiss than a backhanded compliment to the Jewish brain trusters at the highest levels of the U.S. government. In politics, entertainment, sports, art, science, and business, Jews had never had so prominent a profile in American life—and compared to the lot of their kinsmen elsewhere were among the blessed of the earth.

Nowhere were the blessings bestowed more bountifully than in Hollywood, a city that by the 1920s vied with New York as the magnetic pole for nativist loathing of American Jews. Under the breath or smack in the face, the whiff of antisemitism permeated attacks on the motion picture industry. If only the crudest bigots came right out and said that Hollywood was a nest of swarthy Jews conspiring to blacken the purity of Christian America, the metaphors for damnation mirrored the Judeo-Christian divide, with the place names (Sodom, Gomorrah, Babylon) from the Old Testament symbolizing the decadence of Hollywood for believers in the New. Even the label for the Hollywood studio heads ("moguls") oozes the invasive orientalism of rug merchants haggling at a bazaar or moneychangers defiling a temple. For its Jewish founders, the creation of the Motion Picture Producers and Distributors of America in 1922 and the appointment of the ascetic Presbyterian Will H. Hays to the presidency was an act of cultural antidefamation no less than economic self-preservation.[1]

1. The first use of the word *moguls* to refer to the Hollywood studio heads is hard to pinpoint, but references in both the trade and civilian press were commonplace by the 1930s.

Yet to deny the obvious—that Hollywood was American Jewry's grandest stage—was to ignore a statistical anomaly that was at least interesting and perhaps meaningful. "The names of William Fox, Louis Mayer, Adolph Zukor, Marcus Loew, Samuel Goldwyn, the Warner brothers, Carl Laemmle, etc., are so permanently identified with the movie industry that the Jewish trademark on the movies is virtually indelible," conceded the *Kansas City Jewish Chronicle* in the touchstone year of 1934. "The Jewish angle is not being dragged into the movie issue; it exists, whether you like it or not." Drawing attention to that angle might be an impartial observation, a veiled warning, an antisemitic rant, or shades and gradations of each. To gauge how much of the outrage at Hollywood derived from antisemitism and how much from motives untainted by intolerance is sometimes difficult to calibrate.

Of course, sometimes it is not so difficult. "Pants pressers, delicatessen dealers, furriers, and penny showmen started in the picture business when it was in infancy and they are now the type of 'magnates' who preside over its destinies today," wrote Karl K. Kitchen in *Columbia*, the official magazine of the Knights of Columbus, in 1922. "If the Jews who shaped its policies were cultured gentlemen of taste and refinement there would be no occasion to find fault with them. But the men who control the motion picture industry are foreign born Jews of the lowest type."[2] For American antisemites, the moguls of Hollywood were the homegrown answer to the Elders of Zion or the agents of the Rothschilds. In 1930 Major Frank Pease, a Hollywood agent turned professional Jew-hater and red-baiter, accused Paramount's Jesse Lasky of two counts of treason by luring Soviet director Sergei Eisenstein stateside with a bourgeois motion picture deal. "What are you trying to do, turn the American cinema into a communist cesspool?" raged Pease, his nativist bile vacillating between anticommunism and antisemitism.

Pease's instinct for the link between the foreign tribe and the alien ideology was an inspired piece of xenophobia. Throughout the 1920s and 1930s, the slander that Hollywood worshipped at a "Bolshevik temple" did double duty: Jews and reds, Christ-killers and communists, one and the same. "Certain bigots representing malcontents who want to ruin what they cannot rule whisper that Hollywood is run by isms," Harry M. Warner replied in a speech to the American Legion in 1939. "I tell you that this industry has no sympathy with communism, fascism, Nazism, or any ism other than Americanism." He didn't mention the other ism hanging in the air, Judaism.

2. Despite his suspicious initials, Karl K. Kitchen was a real journalist, an occasional *Photoplay* contributor who covered the entertainment beat for the *New York World* and who, said the editor of *Columbia*, "knows the movie industry inside out."

For critics of Hollywood repulsed by the boorish bigots, who fretted over the moral threat from the motion picture screen not the tribal makeup of the movie colony, the Jewish angle might still offer room for leverage. Father Daniel Lord slyly played both sides of the religious card in his 1934 polemic *The Motion Pictures Betray America*. While reminding the former "pants-pressers" that America had lifted them "from $15-a-week jobs to the control of tremendous motion picture companies," he pleaded with the ingrates to clean up Hollywood "for the honor of the Jewish people (who are largely in control of the industry; though I personally blame fallen Christians more than I do their Jewish associates)." Labeling the moguls as apostate Jews who besmirched the good name of a noble people, he claimed common cause with the "Jewish societies which feel that the Jews engaged in the making of pictures in Hollywood have betrayed the fair name of the Jewish people which gave the world its basic Ten Commandments." At their most ecumenical, Catholics cast the crusade against Hollywood immorality as the kind of golden-rule missionary work that crossed religious lines. Even the Legion of Decency posed as a nondenominational body "neither Catholic, Protestant, nor Jewish but a composite of the best" and claimed to monitor Hollywood for the average moviegoer "whether he be Catholic, Protestant, or Jew who prefers decency and wholesomeness in his screen fare."[3]

Almost always, though, behind the proffered hand of friendship a rabbit punch was poised in reserve. The "school of vice" that was Hollywood, editorialized Philadelphia's *Catholic Standard and Times*, was run by men who "are by race and conviction, alien to the ideals of Christendom."

Particularly in intra-faith communications, Catholic crusaders against Hollywood minced no words, lashing out at "the Jews"—not "the moguls," not "the producers." "Jewish executives are the responsible men in ninety per cent of all the Hollywood studios," Bishop John J. Cantwell of Los Angeles noted in the *Ecclesiastical Review* in 1934. "If these Jewish executives had any desire to keep the screen free from offensiveness, they could do so. It is not too much to expect that Hollywood should clean house, and that the great race which was the first custodian of the Ten Commandments should be conscious of its religious traditions." Accused by a Jewish correspondent of flirting with antisemitism, Bishop Cantwell expressed condign amazement ("My Jewish friends in this city would not think for an instant that I should prepare an article condemnatory of the Jewish race") and raised the ante on competitive victimization ("I, too, have come of a race and faith that has suffered much persecution.").

3. Potential Jewish recruits may have balked at the line in the Legion pledge about staying away from all motion pictures that gave offense to "decency and Christian morality."

True enough. Bishop Cantwell would never have prepared an article condemnatory of the Jewish race. However, a friend of the bishop's was less circumspect in his language, the man who had, in fact, ghostwritten the bishop's essay, Joseph I. Breen.

IRRELIGIOUS ANIMOSITY

The uglier side of Breen's militant Catholicism first came to light in the work of two diligent film historians, Gregory D. Black in *Hollywood Censored: Morality Codes, Catholics, and the Movies* (1994), and Frank Walsh in *Sin and Censorship: The Catholic Church and the Motion Picture Industry* (1996). Culled from private letters written during the pre-Code era, the antisemitic language ranges from a handful of vicious screeds to numerous glib references to "the Jews" as shorthand for the moguls. Sometimes blithely, sometimes bitterly, Breen refers to "these Jews out here" and urges Catholic laymen "to get after the Jews in this business" and apply pressure "to bring to the Jews a realization of the danger which threatens them." In a two-page proposal for collective Catholic action against Hollywood, written in 1934 for Monsignor Hugh Lamb, Cardinal Dougherty's assistant in Philadelphia, and copied to Rev. Gerald Donnelly, S.J., of Chicago, he described a district manager for Warner Bros. as "a kike Jew of the very lowest type." If Breen's correspondents ever suggested he dilute his venom with the milk of Christian kindness, the admonitions are not extant in the archives.[4]

The antisemitic passages in Breen's private correspondence may be the most notorious words put to paper by the prolific journalist, essayist, and memo writer. Before the revelations from Black and Walsh, Breen, if known at all, was remembered as a hidebound bluenose. After the revelations, his portrait has assumed more sinister shadings. Today, film historians routinely label Hollywood's in-house censor an "extreme anti-Semite," a "rabid anti-Semite," and "notoriously anti-Semitic."

More than the character of the man is at stake in Breen's attitude to the Jewish moguls he worked shoulder to shoulder with for over two decades. A not-so-closet antisemite at the very top of the MPPDA's self-regulatory regime would surely have skewed the contours of Hollywood cinema during a crucial passage in American culture, a time when images of Jews car-

4. On the other hand, none of Breen's correspondents seems to have replied in kind. On the rare occasions the liberally minded Martin J. Quigley referred to the ethnicity of the moguls, he used the ironic-affectionate phrase "our Semitic brethren."

ried more significance than the foul words in some private letters. Whether by omission or distortion, Hollywood's picture of things Jewish in the 1930s is weighed against the starkest of stakes.

Two other points are worth considering. First, Breen wrote when blunt slurs were *lingua franca* at most levels of American society and, on the ear-witness testimony of every unexpurgated Hollywood memoir, at the highest echelons of the motion picture business. Whether in Yiddish or English, the Jewish moguls matched the Catholic censor in linguistic crudeness. In moments of anger, the foul-mouthed Harry Cohn, head of Columbia Pictures, did not refer to Frank Capra, his ace director, as a vertically impaired gentleman of Sicilian heritage. Nor was it unknown for religious prejudice to be returned in kind. According to Pete Harrison, Joseph M. Schenck—Loews Theater tycoon, founder of Twentieth Century Pictures, and Russian-born Jew—spat out an expression at the Roman Catholic Church "so foul that it cannot be printed" when the prominent Catholic lawyer Joseph Scott and the financier Dr. A. H. Giannini met with the Association of Motion Picture Producers in 1933 to warn about the storm brewing among the Catholics. Whatever the feelings of cultural marginality in a predominantly Christian nation, the Hollywood moguls were not delicate flowers cringing before a clerical Gestapo.

Second, rabid antisemitism is a full-time job. If Breen were a frothing bigot, if his hatred of Jews were passionate and pathological, the fever would infest his entire life and writings, not only a handful of letters written in the early 1930s.

A survey of the full record reveals that Breen's outbursts were neither all-consuming nor lifelong. The antisemitic bile erupted during the pre-Code era, when Breen, newly arrived in Hollywood, was shocked by the folkways of the locals and anguished by his impotence at the Studio Relations Committee. Prior to his pre-Code ravings, and after, Breen displays none of the obsession with Jews that defines the dedicated antisemite. In the 1920s, his attitude is impartial and respectful. After 1934, he is publicly and forthrightly *anti*-antisemitic.

Breen left a published record of his attitudes toward Jews in the numerous articles he wrote under the name of Eugene Weare for the Jesuit weekly *America* and the Catholic monthly *Extension Magazine*. Naturally, he weighed his words for typeset pages with a care he relaxed in private correspondence. Still, a Judeo-centric survey of his prose reveals no fixations or resentments. On the rare occasion the topic at hand leads naturally to a comment on the Jews, Breen is always temperate and usually admiring. In the context of the 1920s and the Catholic forums, his outlook is even-handed, good-natured, and open-minded.

For example, in 1922–23, while traveling for the National Catholic Welfare Conference, Breen wrote a series of commentaries for *America* on conditions in war-torn Europe. The impulse behind the articles is charitable, the common thread being that American Catholics, blessed by God to live in a land of plenty, have been negligent in their duty to feed, clothe, house, and comfort their brethren. To light a fire under the uncharitable, he raises the dread prospect of well-financed Protestant relief groups trawling for converts among destitute Catholics. For the Jews, however, he has only admiration. "The Jews, of course, are wonderfully organized and they aid their own people in an intelligent fashion" he observes, praising "the well-informed American Jews who direct and supervise the work of the Joint Distribution Committee [and who] will brook no interference from Methodists, Baptists, or the YMCA." He rebukes American Catholics for being outdone by Protestant and Jewish educational efforts, which have so far outstripped Catholic energies that the next generation of Europeans will be one "in which the only educated men and women will be Jews. American Jews, to their credit, are seeing Jewish boys are helped to go on with their studies."

In 1922, in a speech to a delegation of Catholic women, Breen again brandished the altruism of American Jews to rebuke the parsimony of American Catholics. "[Catholic] places [in European universities] have been taken by the Jewish boys and girls who are supported and maintained by the generosity of the ever-watchful, genuinely courageous American Jew who has made it his business to see to it that, despite all the misery and suffering which is so widespread in Europe, Jewish boys and girls shall not neglect the all-important training of higher education." Far from being a sinister cabal, the Jews offer a generous model that Catholics should emulate.

No Irish-Catholic intellectual could ignore the two most explosive ethno-religious issues of the 1920s: the revival of the Ku Klux Klan and the passage of the Immigration Act of 1924. For the KKK—whose acronym was glibly rendered as "Koons, Kikes, and Katholics"—Breen expressed withering contempt. For the Immigration Act of 1924, an exclusionary measure that severely restricted immigration by privileging applicants of European origins, he advocated a nuanced position—deriding "the '100 per cent Americans' of the Kukluxer type" and the "Nordic myth" that sparked the legislation, but recognizing the need for a common heritage "to be preserved and handed down intact to future Americans." Even so, he worried that America "will no longer be the refuge of the oppressed, the ambitious, the adventurous, the derelict, or the 'scum' [his quotes] of all nations."

Like every immigrant group, Jews encompassed all of the above categories. "Increasingly large numbers of our immigrants have been Hebrews," Breen observed. "The huge number of Jews who are coming here are said to be thoroughly undesirable from any standpoint"—and here the author inserts a demurral—"though it may be remarked, in passing, that a similar charge was made against the Irish and German immigrants of half a century back." Later, in the same article, he lauds the Jews for avidly assimilating into the American melting pot.

Neither Breen's private correspondence nor public commentary bespeaks a whisper of antisemitism—until he moves out to Hollywood in 1931 and begins to work with Jewish moguls and artists, a breed apart from any the well-traveled journalist and diplomat had ever encountered.

After July 15, 1934, secure in the authority of his office, and inured if not reconciled to Hollywood manners, Breen cooled off. No antisemitic screeds appear in letters to his intimate friends, and no insinuations are extant in his personal correspondence to MPAA officials. "These babies out here are difficult people to cope with" is how he put it to Hays's assistant Maurice McKenzie in 1935. More than discretion, the absence indicates a change of heart. By the end of the decade, both in public pronouncements and private correspondence, he had situated himself on the opposite end of the spectrum.

On the evening of April 26, 1936, Breen is found in interesting company for a worthy cause: cosponsoring an anti-Nazi banquet given at the swank Victor Hugo Cafe in honor of Prince Hubertus zu Lowenstein, a blueblood exile from Hitler's Germany. A leading Catholic intellectual and a fearless opponent of Hitler, Prince Lowenstein had brought together an unlikely mesh of Jews, Catholics, and Popular Fronters. At $100 a plate, a phalanx of Irish Catholics (besides Breen, actors Pat O' Brien and James Cagney, screenwriter Marc Connolly, director John Ford, Fox producer Winifred Sheehan, and, serving as honorary chairman, Bishop Cantwell) joined hands with Jewish producers Irving Thalberg, Jack Warner, David O. Selznick, and B. P. Schulberg. The organizers of the soiree were the agnostic wits Dorothy Parker and Donald Ogden Stewart, late of the Algonquin Round Table, and currently prowling the gilded cage of the screenwriters stable. A hot ticket for premature antifascists, the dinner was a rousing success.

The benefit for Prince Lowenstein was the starting gun for a wave of anti-Nazi activism that swept Hollywood in the late 1930s. Coordinating the campaign was an outfit called the Hollywood Anti-Nazi League for the Defense of American Democracy, formed in July 1936 to organize rallies, print pamphlets, and—covertly at first, more boldly as war clouds darkened—inject anti-Nazi propaganda into Hollywood cinema. Headed by A-list screenwriter, patrician reformer, and fellow traveler Donald Ogden Stewart, the Hollywood Anti-Nazi League was a classic Popular Front group, an alliance of liberals, leftists, and communists, with the grunt work performed by the communists and directional guidance from Moscow.

As long as communism was popular in the Popular Front, Breen, a fervent anticommunist since the Bolshevik Revolution, would not march in solidarity even had his politically sensitive position permitted him to do so. Nonetheless, he continued to lend his name to the Hollywood Anti-Nazi League, attending the first-year anniversary celebration—a dinner, dance, and entertainment bash held in the proletarian digs of the Fiesta Room of the Ambassador Hotel in 1937.

By late 1938, with the Munich Pact signed and violence against Jews mounting in Germany, Hollywood's anti-Nazi activism took more aggressive forms. So too, in Catholic circles, did a critique of antisemitism as an impulse incompatible with Catholic teachings. Beginning in July 1938, with escalating firmness and specificity, Pope Pius XI delivered a series of speeches and public statements assailing race hatred. "Catholic means universal and not racist, not nationalistic, not separatist," said the pontiff.

In 1938, two pamphlets issued by Father Lord's St. Louis-based imprint, The Queen's Work, attacked antisemitism from a Catholic perspective. Entitled *Why Are Jews Persecuted?* by Father Joseph N. Moody and *Dare We Hate Jews?* by Father Lord, the pamphlets were sold for ten cents and five cents, respectively, and distributed to Ladies Sodalities and catechism classes for study and discussion.

Father Moody's work is a history lesson on the rise of antisemitism in the Western world that roundly debunks the myths and blood libels. Father Lord's essay, characteristically, looks to the gospels for inspiration and authority. Both priests preach the orthodox Catholic view that hatred destroys the soul of the hater, both priests condemn the Nazi regime and its stateside fifth columns, and both priests argue that antisemitic persecution only strengthens the bonds of kinship and faith among Jews, whom Catholics seek to convert. Beyond the ken of the good padres is that the Nazis are bent not on persecution but annihilation.

Breen read the pamphlets closely and both left a deep impression. Moody's "very remarkable document" (Breen's words) spurred him to make inquiries about the author, a young professor at Cathedral College in New York. "I note what you tell me about Father Moody, the author of the very excellent pamphlet on the Jews," Breen wrote Lord. "It is, indeed, a splendid document, and quite so the best thing I have ever seen. I agree too, that it is important to stress the Catholic side and the Catholic viewpoint on this question, which seems to be of absorbing interest throughout the world at the present time." At the request of what he described as "a local non-sectarian group" (almost certainly the Hollywood Anti-Nazi

League), Breen negotiated a special deal with Lord to print 25,000 copies of Moody's pamphlet for distribution around town. He also circulated hundreds more on his own dime.

Breen's only qualm about the venture was that the pamphlets, aimed at a Catholic readership, might be more useful if couched in broader Christian terms. "It seems to be agreed hereabouts, that less emphasis on the Catholic viewpoint would bring more effective results among those who are not Catholics but who need to be enlightened on this important subject," Breen told Lord, adding "I have myself distributed more than a thousand of these pamphlets."

Breen had good reason to be mulling the topic of antisemitism. On October 1, 1938, *Box Office*, the glossy trade weekly, published an editorial entitled "Bigotry Stalks the Boxoffice," a statement occasioned by a crude antisemitic leaflet circulating around theaters in the Midwest. Closer to home, a pro-Nazi nutcase named Henry D. Allen had been flinging copies of the leaflet from the windows of office buildings in downtown Los Angeles. "Hollywood is the Sodom and Gomorrah where International Jewry controls Vice-Dope-Gambling," the leaflets read. "Where Young Gentile Girls are raped by Jewish producers, directors and casting directors who go unpunished." A caricature depicted a hook-nosed Jew despoiling a vessel of lily-white Aryan womanhood. By 1938, a trade press condemnation of Nazism's "lying and inflammatory literature" expressed mainstream opinion in Hollywood. However, the decision by *Box Office* to print a full-page reproduction of the leaflet was genuinely gutsy, and a gesture calculated to inflame emotions.

Two weeks later, after the letters and telegrams poured in, *Box Office* printed a generous sampling. Some correspondents requested that their names not be used; others *insisted* that their names be used. One writer who proudly signed his name was highlighted in a boldfaced, boxed-off column:

> I have myself received copies of this vicious and salacious leaflet. I understand also that untold thousands of these were dropped from a large office building in Los Angeles [the Garland Building] a short time back. The whole business is so revolting, and so thoroughly un-American, that I want to be the first, if possible, to lodge my protest against it.
>
> I stand ready to go the limit to help out in any way possible and I am hastening to tell you that you may count on me to do anything I can to run this vicious thing into the ground.
>
> —Joseph I. Breen, Production Code Administrator.

Christian Vigilantes Arise!

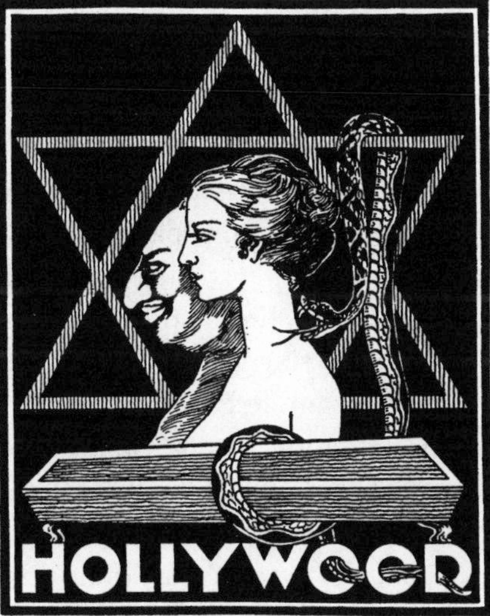

BUY GENTILE

EMPLOY GENTILE

VOTE GENTILE

Boycott the Movies!

HOLLYWOOD is the Sodom and Gomorrha
WHERE
INTERNATIONAL JEWRY
CONTROLS
VICE - DOPE - GAMBLING
where
YOUNG GENTILE GIRLS ARE RAPED
by
JEWISH PRODUCERS, DIRECTORS, CASTING DIRECTORS
WHO GO UNPUNISHED

THE JEWISH HOLLYWOOD ANTI-NAZI LEAGUE CONTROLS
COMMUNISM
IN THE MOTION PICTURE INDUSTRY

STARS, WRITERS AND ARTISTS ARE COMPELLED TO PAY FOR COMMUNISTIC ACTIVITIES

Domestic Nazi propaganda: the anti-Hollywood, antisemitic leaflet that circulated stateside in 1938.

The letter was a unique avowal of principle from a man who, since taking over the PCA, had scrupulously avoided public stances on politically charged issues.

On the evening of November 9–10, 1938, the Nazi pogrom known as *Kristallnacht* erupted across Germany, an outbreak of mob terror made vivid stateside by live radio reports, front-page headlines, and wire photos. For many Americans, and not just Jews, the event marked a tipping point. Two days later, on a special radio show commemorating the twentieth anniversary of Armistice Day, the singer Kate Smith debuted a song written during the last war with Germany, but shelved by composer Irving Berlin. The tune was "God Bless America." An overnight sensation, the patriotic anthem provided the soundtrack music for the nation's march from purblind isolationism to national defense.

Much of Hollywood had already made the transition. On November 18, 1938, 3,500 motion picture industry personnel packed a mass "Quarantine Hitler" rally at Philharmonic Auditorium in Los Angeles. In between impassioned speeches from actor John Garfield and director Frank Capra, and supportive messages from actress Joan Crawford and exiled novelist Thomas Mann, the crowd unanimously voted to send a telegram, signed by Breen and dozens of other prominent Hollywood personalities, to President Roosevelt:

> The Nazi outrages against Jews and Catholics have shocked the world. Coming on the heels of the Munich pact, they prove that the capitulation to Hitler means barbarism and terror. America as the foremost democracy has taken the lead in opposing this threat to civilization. We in Hollywood urge you to use your presidential authority to express further the horror and the indignation of the American people.

The next year, Breen lent his support and prestige to the Committee of Catholics to Fight Anti-Semitism, an organization spearheaded by Dr. Emmanuel Chapman, a professor of philosophy at Fordham University. According to its statement of purpose, the group took its inspiration from recent admonitions by the Catholic Bishops to "guard against all forms of racial bigotry, of which Pope Pius XI, speaking of a pertinent instance, said, 'it is not possible for Christians to take part in anti-Semitism.'"[5] Realizing that "the growing anti-Semitism in the United States is a serious threat to

5. The pope spoke the words to a group of Belgian pilgrims on September 6, 1938. "Spiritually, we are all Semites," he concluded, reportedly with tears in his eyes. Official Vatican news sources failed to report his words, but a Belgian newspaper quoted him at length. Pope Pius XI died on February 10, 1939.

the principles of democracy and of Christianity and that some Catholics too have been deceived into taking part in this campaign of hate," the committee planned an ambitious program of activities that included radio broadcasts, speaker's bureaus, and pamphlets to educate "our Catholic people to combat racial bigotry and antisemitism as opposed to Christianity and democracy." Along with predictable signatories such as Dorothy Day of the *Catholic Worker* and the progressive Catholic journalist Harry Sylvester, the two authors of the Production Code lent their names to the cause: Rev. Daniel A. Lord, S.J., and Martin J. Quigley.

The committee also issued a pamphlet articulating the Church's teachings on racism and tolerance. At Quigley's request, Breen gathered statements from prominent Hollywood Catholics, such as Warner Bros. producer Bryan Foy, MGM screenwriter James K. McGuinness, and actors Don Ameche and Irene Dunne (Spencer Tracy and Loretta Young being on vacation). "I am sure it would be helpful to the work if you would sign one yourself," suggested Quigley.

Breen not only signed the letter, he issued a statement, published in the *Voice*, the newsletter of the committee, and reprinted on the front page of *Hollywood Now*, the biweekly organ of the Hollywood Anti-Nazi League:

> It is my judgment that there is nothing more important for us Catholics to do at the present moment [July 1939] than to use our energies in stemming the tide of racial bigotry and hostility.

When a better-known Irish Catholic in the media—the radio priest Father Charles Coughlin—attacked the Committee of Catholics to Fight Anti-Semitism, the Hollywood Anti-Nazi League contrasted the "pro-fascist priest" with the pro-tolerance censor. "Outstanding leaders of the Catholic Church from all over the nation have joined the Committee pledging to fight anti-Semitism and bigotry," reported *Hollywood Now*. "Irene Dunne and Joseph Breen are among the leaders in the film colony here who are members."

Breen also contributed to the victims of Nazism in other ways. With fellow high-profile Hibernians Pat O'Brien and James Cagney and a diverse group of motion picture players that extended from Walter Wanger on the left to Walt Disney on the right, he attended a charity concert by violinist Mischa Elman to benefit Non-Sectarian German Refugee Relief. Elman was Jewish and the "non-sectarian" designation a conceit: the German refugees in need of relief were mainly Jewish.

Given the public record, Breen's surviving friends express surprise at his epistolary antisemitism and exasperation that the tirades would tar his reputation. "It is unrealistic to think that anyone who was antisemitic would be employed for years in the motion picture industry," Martin S. Quigley, who knew Breen well, states flatly. "I don't mean that in a moment of frustration that Joe didn't say or write something that, in the light of what good taste is now, should not have been said. But my personal view is there is no basis for calling Joe an antisemite. The best evidence is that Hollywood is a tight community and a person who was anti-Jewish couldn't have survived ten minutes." Former PCA staffer Albert E. Van Schmus, who was hired by Breen at RKO in 1941, worked for him at the PCA from 1949 to 1954, and remained a lifelong friend, agrees: "I can't recall Joe ever displaying any anti-Semitism."

Of course, Breen did display antisemitism in his letters of the early 1930s; but he did not embody it, and, well before the outbreak of World War II, he vehemently opposed it, in public statements in the press and private correspondence. Personal letters and published declarations, attendance at banquets and charity events, and involvement with the Hollywood Anti-Nazi League and the Committee of Catholics to Fight Anti-Semitism are heavy counterweights to a small cache of personal letters. A cynical reading would conclude that the Irish bigot was smart enough to keep his true feelings to himself and suck up to the men who were buttering his bread, but, on balance, the venom of the early 1930s seems an ugly spasm, the product of a hot temper and simmering frustration.

Besides, Breen could prove an equal-opportunity ethnic insulter. In 1934, writing to Father Lord, he ruminated that "in my brief experience in the motion picture industry the one thing that stands out in my mind is the total lack of what we call *bigotry*. The Jews are clannish just about as the Irish are clannish and they help one another in this business, just about as much as the Irish help each other,"—and here he paused—"which means very little." Continuing his ethno-religious musings, he observed:

> I have never seen, among the Jews, the slightest suggestion of anti-Catholic prejudice. Maybe it is because of racial or *ir*religious animosity; maybe it's because they feel our Catholic folk are pretty generally honest and reliable. But, whatever the cause, they really seem to be friendly to us. They are charitable, as you know, and good natured. They are, also, almost entirely without morality of any kind where the wife of the other fellow is concerned. At home they are, generally, good family men. . . . So much for *that*.[6]

6. Breen's partial italicization of the word "*ir*religious" to modify animosity toward the Jews is typographically significant—animosity against religion, he felt, being not religious but antireligious.

HOLLYWOOD'S RESTRICTED COVENANTS

If the answer to Breen's own Jewish question is, at least, complicated, the policy of the Breen Office toward Jews is straightforward enough. No antisemitism filtered into Hollywood cinema on Breen's watch. In fact, little that is Judaic registers at all. Basically, after 1934, Jews weren't vilified on the American screen; they just vanished from it. Only with World War II did Hollywood's emblematic ethnicity return to Hollywood's cast of characters.

The exclusion of high-profile Jewishness after 1934 marks a sharp break with earlier admissions policies. In the late 1920s and early 1930s, American Jews were vibrant presences in Hollywood cinema. The obvious landmark is Warner Bros.'s *The Jazz Singer* (1927), the epochal first sound film, a Jewish-centered yet all-American narrative complete with Yiddish vocabulary in the intertitles and an official program that included a Yiddish-English glossary for baffled gentiles. Later, in the talkative, wisecrack-crazy environs of pre-Code Hollywood, Jewish comics and character actors kibitzed and kvetched at will. Among the playwrights imported from New York to compose dialogue for the former mimes, Jewish writers (the original "schmucks with Underwoods" in Jack Warner's endearing phrase) tapped out ironic inflections and cynical slang that enriched the vernacular on both sides of the screen.

The strict enforcement of the Code stemmed the flow of Jewish-American characters and coinages. The Code's injunction against mocking foreign nationalities and showing due respect for religion toned down and eliminated the rawest portraits of non-WASP types. To modern eyes, classical Hollywood cinema can seem an inventory of jaw-dropping stereotypes, but under the Breen Office the motion picture screen was better mannered about ethnic portraiture than the vulgar, freewheeling realms of the vaudeville stage and the funny pages of the family newspaper. Jews, whose heavily accented inflections and malapropisms enlivened the octave range of early sound cinema, went mute after 1934. Even the federally regulated medium of radio proved more congenial to Jewish caricature: no Hollywood equivalent exists for *The Goldbergs*, the long-running radio program about the borscht-belted travails of a Jewish family in the Bronx.

Tragically, the Code was not Hollywood's only ethno-religious consideration. The absence of Jews on the American screen coincides, and not coincidentally, with the rise of Nazism in Germany. Within weeks of Hitler's ascension to power in January 1933, Hollywood films with identifiable Jewish content or prominent Jewish actors were denied entry into the Third Reich. After July 15, 1934, the erasure of things Jewish from the Hollywood screen was abetted by the certainty that Jewish content would be banned from the lucrative German market. Being rational capitalists, the moguls assumed that the Nazi fever would cool, that the sane, conservative Germans would eventually come to their senses and do business. In the meantime—with the crucial exception of Warner Bros.—best to hunker down and seek an accommodation.

In this context, a screen portrait of a Jew-qua-Jew was not just a political statement against Nazism but a self-inflicted commercial limitation. In accord with MPPDA policy, Breen advised against—but could not forbid—the insertion of an explicit political agenda into Hollywood cinema for fear of offending any domestic constituency or closing out any foreign market. In 1936, commenting on the wisdom of a proposed anti-Nazi film entitled *The Mad Dog of Europe*, he warned the moguls that "there is strong pro-German and anti-Semitic feeling in this country, and, while those who are likely to approve of an anti-Hitler picture may think well of such an enterprise, [you] should keep in mind that millions of Americans might think otherwise." It was sound commercial advice. As ever, the impulse was nonjudgmental and bottom line, the purpose to keep out of the crosshairs of political controversy at home and conduct business abroad.

By the late 1930s, however, as the Nazi bureaucracy of racism hardened and the rants turned to pogroms, antisemitism, once thought to be a temporary fever, emerged as a bedrock principle of the Third Reich. Moving at a glacial pace, taking the most timorous of steps, a few studio filmmakers confronted realities Hollywood officialdom thought best to avoid. In condemning mob violence and intolerance, melodramas such as *Black Legion* (1936), about a KKK-like band of costumed vigilantes, and *They Won't Forget* (1937), a veiled version of the 1915 lynching of Leo Frank, a Jew accused of the rape and murder of a factory girl in Atlanta, Georgia, played as transparent allegories against fascism and antisemitism.

However, not even allegory was committed lightly to the screen. The radioactivity of Jewish elements—indeed the very word "Jew"—can be detected in William Dieterle's *The Life of Emile Zola* (1937), a prestige biopic from Warner Bros., the most brashly anti-Nazi of all the major studios. The fulcrum event in the story is Zola's courageous defense of the French army captain Alfred Dreyfus, a Jew unjustly accused of treason and railroaded by antisemites on the General Staff. But how to render the motive without speaking it aloud?

The sleight-of-hand solution presupposes an alert spectator. As the French General Staff searches for a scapegoat in the ranks, Dieterle's camera pans down a list of inscribed names. Beside Dreyfus's name, under the column labeled "Religion," flashing by in the blink of an eye, is the scrawled word: "Jew." Given the historical context—not really 1894 but 1937—Warner Bros., the Breen Office, and the audience understood that the nation on trial was not France. Connecting the dots, Breen suggested that Warner Bros. soften the scenes where mobs of French citizens burn piles of Zola's pamphlet *J'Accuse!* as too "suggestive of recent activities in Germany" (namely, the book-burning bonfire in Berlin on the night of May 19, 1933, already an emblazoned newsreel image of the Nazi *Walpurgisnacht*).

Though not daring so much as to whisper the word "Jew," *The Life of Emile Zola* helped give voice to a muffled issue. By the late 1930s, films dealing with "hot" topics (meaning fascism, not sex) were "bringing picket lines in front of American theaters and causing foreign governments to ban pictures to an extent that alarms the whole industry," worried the *Hollywood Reporter* in 1938. Throughout this critical juncture, Hays kept his head in the sand and continued to prattle on about how Hollywood was mere entertainment, a harmless sedative to soothe the psyche of stressed-out moviegoers.

In late 1938, ignoring Hays's speechifying, Warner Bros. announced plans to produce *Confessions of a Nazi Spy* (1939), the first marquee spelling of the four-letter word that had made front-page headlines since 1933. The espionage thriller attacked the Nazis by name, but managed to avoid mentioning the pertinent three-letter word. Yet the film was a risky gambit—so much so that an alarmed Luigi Luraschi, the censorship liaison to the Breen Office at Paramount, took the unusual step of meddling in the business of a rival studio. "I feel sure that if the picture is made and is any way uncomplimentary to Germany, as it must be if sincerely produced, then Warners will have on their hands the blood of a great many Jews in Germany," he informed Breen. When an undaunted Warner Bros. submitted the script, Breen passed along an advisory caution, but the tone is pro forma, not like the stone-faced warnings he had issued a few years before when he steered studios away from film versions of *It Can't Happen Here* and *The Mad Dog of Europe*. "[The script] is *technically* within the provisions of the Production Code, but appears to be *questionable* from the standpoint of political censorship in this country and abroad," he told Jack Warner, both of whom knew that last bit was an understatement. At the same time Breen was reviewing the script for *Confessions of a Nazi Spy*, he had other reading material on his mind: the pamphlets by Father Lord (*Dare We Hate the Jews?*) and Father Moody (*Why Are Jews Persecuted?*) and the "vicious and salacious" antisemitic leaflets floating around Los Angeles.

On September 1, 1939, the outbreak of war in Europe closed out the German market and opened up Hollywood to a reconnection with its Jewish roots. Ironically, or appropriately, the most visible violation of the long embargo on Jews occurred in the Celtic regiment of *The Fighting 69th* (1940). In the whole Irish stew, the only exotic ingredient is played by character actor Sammy Cohen, a (literally) Central Casting Jew whose intertextual ethnicity stretched back to Raoul Walsh's Great War epic *What Price Glory* (1926), where he played a Jewish doughboy named Lipinsky. Set off among a sea of Irish faces, Cohen wears a visage of suspiciously non-Celtic heritage.

Observing Cohen's physiognomy, a dubious top sergeant accosts him in a lilting brogue: "Did you say your name was *Murphy*?" The soldier confesses he was born "Mischa Moskovitz" but has assumed the Irish alias to join the 69th. Unfazed by the infiltration, James Cagney's character strikes up a conversation with his comrade in arms, bantering with Cohen in (untranslated) Yiddish in a bit that recalls Cagney's pre-Code patter in a language the Irish-Catholic actor picked up as a boy knocking around Hell's Kitchen. (The Yiddish was translated and approved by the Breen Office.)

On the eve of America's entry into World War II, the most direct assault at Nazi antisemitism came from Hollywood's most renowned artist. To speak out against the Third Reich, Charles Chaplin succumbed to the revolution he had vowed to forever resist, synchronous dialogue, for his talky anti-Nazi satire *The Great Dictator* (1940). Chaplin's recantation was acclaimed by a fervent admirer. In a fawning effusion unique in the annals of Breen Office correspondence for a project not featuring a priest, nun, or saint, Breen showered praise on the act of comedy and conscience. During the script review phase, Breen seems almost embarrassed to bother the great Charles Chaplin with the petty details of the Code. "Your picture is so fine a piece of great screen art that to intrude with what is hardly more than a technical violation of our regulations seems to be small and picayune, but, as you will see from the attached resolution, we have no other alternative," he apologized to the liaison at Charles Chaplin Studios, before bowing to the ethereal Charlot. "May I take this occasion again to tell you how very, very much I enjoyed *The Great Dictator*. It is superb screen entertainment and marks Mr. Chaplin, I think as our greatest screen artist. More power to his good right arm!"

After Pearl Harbor, backed by the Office of War Information, Jews finally broke forever the restricted covenants of Hollywood cinema—usually as members of multiethnic military platoons marching alongside Irish roughnecks, Italian Romeos, and corn-fed WASPs. A telltale surname (Weinberg, Greenbaum), typecast character actor (George Tobias, Sam Levene), and a tandem sports allegiance (Brooklyn Dodgers) tagged the GI as the Jew on the team. For the slower students in the audience, the message of Judeo-

Christian harmony was spoken aloud. "Gee, you sing pretty good, Sammy," a soldier says to a fellow worshipper belting out the Protestant hymn "Rock of Ages" during the ecumenical deckside religious ceremony that opens the combat film *Guadalcanal Diary* (1943). "I should," he replies. "My father was a cantor."

After the Second World War, when the ethnic prejudices and racial bigotries that divided Americans no longer needed to be bottled up in the interests of wartime unity, Hollywood projected a more divisive picture of Judeo-Christian America. Jews were not merely breaking the restricted covenants, the covenants themselves were being exposed and attacked.

Crossfire and *Gentleman's Agreement*, the tag-team pair of righteous anti-antisemitic social problem films from 1947, are the canonical postwar landmarks, but a beloved comedy that no longer looked so loveable in the postwar atmosphere is a better zeitgeist avatar. A year earlier, in what seemed a sure-fire high concept, Bing Crosby Productions bankrolled an updated version of *Abie's Irish Rose* (1946), produced and directed by Edward A. Sutherland. Based on the hit play by Anne Nichols and previously filmed in 1928, the melting pot comedy-melodrama featured a pair of star-of-David–crossed lovers, he Jewish, she Irish Catholic. Lacing Irish whiskey with a borscht chaser had been a staple of Broadway and Hollywood since the 1920s: besides *Abie's Irish Rose*, *The Cohens and Kellys* (1926) and *Kosher Kitty Kelly* (1926) also stirred the Hebrew-Hibernian brew. In the 1930s, the Code and the overseas market conspired to snuff out the cycle, but in 1946, with the Nazis defeated and Jews back on screen, the timing seemed perfect for a revival of ethnic hybridity.

The updated *Abie's Irish Rose* opens in London, not New York, with a newsreel montage of V-E Day jubilation in Piccadilly Circus and Trafalgar Square. After G.I. Abie Levy (Richard Norris) and USO entertainer Rosemary Murphy (Joanne Dru) meet cute but chastely in a hotel room, a whirlwind romance leads to a civil marriage ceremony performed by a Protestant military chaplain, followed by a V-J Day montage that transports the couple to New York.

New York is the natural home for the shenanigans, but the unnatural dateline dooms the antique conceit. Whereas Abie, Rosemary, and every other character on screen have kept pace with the times, Abie's Jewish father and Rose's Irish father remain unreconstructed prewar bigots. Traumatized by the prospect of exogamous in-laws, each responds according to the faith of his fathers. The Jewish patriarch puts his head in his hands and moans "Oy vey iz mir!" The Irish patriarch puts his head in his hands and moans "Wurra! Wurra!" The thrifty Jewish father watches each nickel; the hot-tempered Irish father keens at high decibel. Undeterred, newlyweds Abie and Rosemary maintain ethno-religious equipoise with a Christmas tree in the parlor and a mezuzah on the apartment door.

No less evenhandedly, the Breen Office mandated a guiding principle for *Abie's Irish Rose*:

> It will be necessary to obtain proper technical advice regarding the characterization of the various clerics and ecclesiastics in this story, as well as any religious ceremonies which may be employed in the finished picture.

The Code staff also emerged from the morning huddle with a balanced cue sheet for both the Levys and the Murphys. "Patrick's line 'Huh!—the Jew Parson!' seems to us offensive and should be rewritten" (it wasn't) and "the reactions of the Archbishop should not be farcical" (they weren't).

Excepting the Jewish and Irish fathers, the cast of *Abie's Irish Rose* has learned the lessons of the Office of War Information, none better than the clergy. Friendly competitors for the souls of men, the official delegates of the Judeo-Christian triad are each imbued with the spirit of tolerance and

The Hebrew-Hibernian brew fizzles out: Jewish patriarch Solomon Levy (Michael Chekhov) refuses to tolerate Rosemary (Joanne Dru), the Irish-Catholic wife of his son Abie (Richard Norris) in *Abie's Irish Rose* (1946), the out-of-synch remake of Anne Nichols's Jazz Age chestnut.

professional courtesy: the Jewish rabbi is urbane, the Catholic priest is dignified, and the Protestant chaplain is an officer and a gentleman.

As in the Jazz Age original, the third act reconciliation is built around the grandfathers' acceptance of the twins born to Abie and Rosemary. Playing peacemaker, the priest corrals the kvetching Mr. Murphy for a visit to the couple's apartment. "Abie might be a direct descendent of the kings of Jerusalem," suggests the priest affably.

"No—just plain 'Jew'" interjects Abie, whose clipped pronunciation of a word so long unspoken on the motion picture soundtrack quiets the room.

Viewing *Abie's Irish Rose*, preview crowds reportedly "laughed lustily at the best gags and chuckled forth steadily between times," but sourpuss representatives from ecumenical review committees refused to crack a smile. "The worst sort of caricature of both Jews and Catholics—much worse than the 1928 original—and a film that sets us back twenty years in the work we have been trying to do in bringing the people of America closer together," declared a spokesman. "What may have been comical to the public in years gone by is no longer funny in these critical days," lectured Pete Harrison, who delivered a history lesson for good measure. "Having just emerged from a world conflict that was sparked by racial intolerance, the public is in no mood to find comedy in situations or characterizations that tend to degrade peoples."[7] Once viewed as light-hearted and progressive, now considered heavy-handed and retrograde, *Abie's Irish Rose* wilted in the postwar light.

A new Jewish type who was not a Jewish type at all filled the ethnic niche. Neither the vaudevillian Jew of the 1920s nor the wisecracking Jew of the pre-Code 1930s, but a full-blooded Americanized Jew, he was a character with no shtetl backstory, no ghetto roots, and no Yiddish inflections. He was Jewish because he, and the film, came out and said so.

The announcement was first made in RKO's *Crossfire*, directed by Edward Dmytryk, and produced by Dore Schary. Unlike Sam Goldwyn, Schary believed in the telegraphic power of Hollywood cinema. "In the purely escapist pattern lies oblivion," he said. "There are many intelligent, adult subjects not yet touched upon which have nothing to do with censorship." Schary was as good as his rhetoric, rushing out *Crossfire* six months ahead

7. As usual, Billy Wilder kept his sense of humor about the Irish-Jewish axis. In *The Lost Weekend* (1945), an alcoholic writer trudges all over New York looking for a pawnshop to sell his typewriter. Unfortunately, the pawnshops are closed because of Yom Kippur, even the Irish pawnshops. "We've got an agreement," explains a Jewish pawnbroker. "They keep closed on Yom Kippur and we don't open on St. Patrick's."

of the prestige entry in development at Twentieth Century-Fox, *Gentleman's Agreement.* A minicycle of two, the Judeo-centric social problem films had a short shelf life due not to timidity but to the limited cachet in preaching a message already heeded.

The ethnic content of both films coasted through the Breen Office, which focused more on sexual innuendo than progressive intentions. Having rejected the original version of the novel on which *Crossfire* was based, Richard Brooks's *The Brick Foxhole,* where the victim of a bigot was a homosexual, Breen warned against any "suggestion of a 'pansy' characterization about [the victim] in his relationship with soldiers." After the homosexual was transformed into a Jew, Breen objected to the ethnic slurs. "We recommend changing the expression 'Kikes,'" and "we suggest changing the expression 'Yid,'" Breen informed RKO executive Harold Melniker. The worst the killer utters is the relatively mild "Jewboy." The Irish-Catholic detective who leans into the camera to deliver a sermon on tolerance quotes worse invective tossed at his grandfather ("a dirty Irish Mick—priest lover—a spy from Rome"), who was killed by nativist thugs on the streets of Philadelphia.

Gentleman's Agreement, the certified barrier breaker, is a piece of naked Oscar bait whose romantic complications are punctuated by hectoring lectures. Based on the book by Laura Z. Hobson, directed by Elia Kazan, and produced by Nebraskan Methodist Darryl F. Zanuck, the film came to shore not a foot ahead of the postwar tolerance wave. To punch up a hard-hitting exposé on American antisemitism, magazine writer Philip Schuyler Green (Gregory Peck) poses as a faux Jew for six months, a metamorphosis achieved by changing his name to Phil Greenberg. A gifted supporting cast helps to disguise the creaky plot machinations: Celeste Holm as Phil's hip and open-minded coworker, fashion editor Ann Dettrey; John Garfield (the A-list star altruistically taking third billing) as Phil's close friend and for-real Jew Dave Goldman, a decorated combat veteran; June Havoc as Phil's catty secretary Miss Wales, an undercover Jew and closet antisemite (her sort of well-mannered Jew is okay, but best to keep "the kikey ones" from ruining things for the rest of us); and Dorothy McGuire as Kathy, a beautiful but backbone-deficient divorcée, Peck's designated love interest. ("She doesn't rate you," Ann tells Phil, in the most heartfelt line in all the didactic discourse.) During the course of his journey into Judaism, Phil gets a taste of the slurs, condescension, bad jokes, and discrimination endured by Jews who cannot revert to Gregory Peck at will. Mainly, though, antisemitism in America is a matter of restricted access to prime real estate: hotel rooms, country clubs, and suburban neighborhoods.

Unlike *Crossfire, Gentleman's Agreement* spews the worst of the slurs on the Code's index of forbidden words (*yid, kike, nigger*), a breach that had

"I'll become Jewish!": Philip Schuyler Green (Gregory Peck) tries to explain antisemitism to his son (Dean Stockwell) while Phil's mother (Anne Revere) considers his parenting in Darryl F. Zanuck's production of Eliza Kazan's *Gentleman's Agreement* (1947), from Laura Z. Hobson's best seller.

been negotiated in advance and which was facilitated by the literary prestige of the source novel, the good intentions of the film, and Zanuck's formidable clout within the industry. More audacious than the epithets was the naming of the names of a trio of crude antisemites in American public life: Gerald L. K. Smith, a radio demagogue born of the 1930s still ranting in the 1940s, and the two most notorious racist politicians serving in Congress, Rep. John Rankin (D-MS), who had been known to decry "kikes" from the floor of the House of Representatives, and his senior partner, the white supremacist standard bearer Sen. Theodore G. Bilbo (D-MS).

Though reconciled to the racial and ethnic slurs and even the names of the politicians, Breen fretted over the sympathetic portrait of a divorced woman. He cautioned against intimations of an "illicit sex affair between your two sympathetic leads," Phil and Kathy, and suggested that perhaps Kathy become a single girl in the transition from book to screen. Zanuck, who personally oversaw the production close to his heart, held his ground. "Kathy is a divorcée. Anyone who has read the book knows it is impossible to tell the story unless she is a divorcée. Your suggestion in this regard cannot be complied with." Breen also pressed Zanuck to deflect any suggestion of premarital intimacy. "My dear Joe," Zanuck wrote back wearily. "Phil and

Kelly are in love. They will behave on screen as well bred adults behave when they are in love."

Breen's education in the dialectics of Jewish representation ended with a revealing instance of cross-cultural miscommunication. Despite impeccable literary and cinematic credentials, the British import *Oliver Twist* (1948), directed by David Lean and produced by J. Arthur Rank, was denied a Code Seal. The problem was the depiction of Fagin. Based on the original illustrations by George Cruikshank and brought to menacing life by Alec Guiness, all nasal rasp and beetle-browed avarice, the Victorian caricature of the skinflint, hook-nosed Jew resembled a Reichsfilmkammer poster for *The Eternal Jew* (1940).

"We assume, of course, that you will bear in mind the advisability of omitting from the portrayal of Fagin any elements or inferences that would be offensive to any specific racial group or religion," Breen cautioned Rank when the project was first submitted in 1947. "Otherwise, of course, your picture might meet with definite audience resistance in this country."

A year later, having ignored Breen's warning, Rank ran into definite audience resistance from the Anti-Defamation League of the B'nai B'rith, whose members emerged from a private screening in a state of shock. Francis Harmon, head of the New York branch of the PCA, alerted Eric Johnston, pres-

From the pages of *Der Stürmer*: Fagin (Alec Guiness), brandishes a pitchfork-like implement at the street urchins in David Lean's *Oliver Twist* (1948).

ident of the Motion Picture Association of America, that the ADL considered the Fagin portrayal "a grotesque Jewish caricature stereotype which Julius Streicher's Nazis tried [to] impose on the world." Had *Crossfire* and *Gentleman's Agreement* been for naught? "In a world still smoldering with the hates and falsehoods stirred up by the most serious antisemitic pogroms of all history, one has a right to question the judgment and the logic of bringing Fagin to the screen at this time," scolded Dore Schary, now MGM production head, wondering what the Brits could have been thinking.

Slated for stateside release in 1948, *Oliver Twist* was shelved. Two years passed before the film obtained a distribution deal with Eagle Lion Classics, an outfit without studio affiliation that specialized in foreign film fare. When Rank applied for a Code Seal, Breen sided with the ADL. On November 22, 1950, he gave the bad news to Jock Lawrence, Rank's liaison with the PCA:

> Yesterday we viewed the Rank Production of *Oliver Twist*, and I am sorry to have to tell you that it is our considered unanimous judgment that this picture is not acceptable under the provisions of the Production Code, because of the element, in the picture, which definitely suggests a highly offensive characterization of a Jew.

Breen cited the pertinent chapter and verse:

> Under the general heading of "National Feelings," the Code provides that:
>
> "The history, institutions, prominent people and citizenry of all nations shall be represented fairly."

Given the pedigree of the film and the importance of the Anglo-American market, Breen offered the retrograde British a lengthy disquisition on the American, and the PCA, way:

> It has been the practice of the Production Code Administration to interpret this provision to include *races* as well as *nations*, and to insist upon it that all *races* "be represented fairly." We have repeatedly argued thus regarding the treatment of Negroes, American Indians, Germans, Japanese, and so forth, and we feel that the Jew, too, is entitled to be "represented fairly" in our films, and it is our judgment that in *Oliver Twist*, the offensive caricature might well be said to represent *unfairly* the Jewish race and people.

Eagle Lion Classics appealed Breen's decision to the MPAA Board in New York, declaring "it would be a gross injustice to deprive anyone of the privilege of seeing *Oliver Twist*." Alert to the political-cultural minefield, Eric Johnston personally attended to the matter. After viewing the original British version and having "a lengthy but calm discussion," the board shipped the film back to Breen for further examination. He was not overruled; he was simply asked to look again at the film and perhaps suggest a compromise solution.

Breen's compromise was to demand seventy-three cuts, mainly of "the close-ups on silhouettes of Fagin, which emphasizes his grotesque appearance." The deletions sliced the film's running time from 116 to 105 minutes.

After Eagle Lion cut the film to order, the MPAA Board met again to consider the reconsideration. Breen slipped quietly into New York for the second MPAA meeting on *Oliver Twist*. Eagle Lion had met his terms, but so volatile was the issue that the whole MPAA Board, rather than just Breen, went on record and voted to award the recut *Oliver Twist* a Code Seal. Even with the cuts the vote by the MPAA Board was not unanimous: three members still felt the film should have been rejected outright for an antisemitic odor that no amount of cutting could fumigate.

Afterward, looking back on the whole affair, Breen regretted the failure of Rank and Lean to heed his advice and dodge the controversy. "It seems to me that this fine picture could have been made in such a way as to escape the very clear offensiveness which is inherent in the portrayal of the character of Fagin," he told Jock Lawrence. "I seem to remember that twice before, our companies hereabouts made the picture with no unpleasant or unfavorable reactions of any kind."

Breen—so far behind the cultural curve on language, sex, and violence—was in perfect synch with the mood on race, religion, and ethnicity. American moviegoers winced at the portrait of Fagin in *Oliver Twist*, and Jewish exhibitors quietly refrained from booking the film. Just as the warm-hearted *Abie's Irish Rose* looked stilted in the postwar light, the villain from *Oliver Twist* looked more Third Reich Germany than Victorian England. Guinness's Fagin was "more a caricature than a character," lectured Red Kahn in *Motion Picture Herald*. "The overemphasis placed on Fagin's facial characteristics is in highly questionable taste and will prove offensive to any person of discernment."

Actually, not quite every person of discernment took offense. Breen's "suppression" of *Oliver Twist* was attacked from an unlikely quarter. "No Jew or group of Jews can speak for or represent the Jews of America," declared the American Council for Judaism, breaking ranks with the American Jews who opposed the British import and denouncing the Hollywood ally of the Anti-Defamation League, Joseph I. Breen, for his vigilance in expunging antisemitism from the American screen.

11

SOCIAL PROBLEMS, EXISTENTIAL DILEMMAS, AND OUTSIZE ANATOMIES

Two soldiers walk furtively up the steps of a darkened balcony. Sliding into a back row, they begin a hushed conversation about the night before, half-remembered through an alcoholic fog, a woozy flashback that starts with drinks in a bar and ends in a hot-blooded killing. From behind the men, a projection booth beams shards of light onto a motion picture screen, illuminating their faces in an eerie, flickering glow. The hour is late, well past midnight, but the neon sign above the ticket booth said "Open All Nite," a scheduling holdover from wartime, when round-the-clock factory shifts led to off-hour playtimes. With no kids or nuzzling couples in sight, the night-owl balcony is a lonely and forbidding place, a bit dingy, maybe a little dangerous, not like the friendly Bijou back home or the plush palaces of a bygone era. On screen, the sprightly fanfare and droning narration from a newsreel mixes into the whispers of drunkenness and murder. The GIs ignore the film; it has nothing to do with them. These moviegoers have seen things not allowed into the world of Hollywood cinema. That world is no longer their world.

The scene is from Edward Dmytryk's *Crossfire* (1947), the first Hollywood film to dare speak the name of homegrown antisemitism. Released six months earlier than Elia Kazan's higher-profile and higher key-lit *Gentleman's Agreement* (1947), the year's tandem exposé of un-Christian conduct in America, *Crossfire* is a hybrid of two telltale motion picture genres born of World War II, the film noir and the social problem film. Forced into union, the murky milieu and gloomy alienation of the film noir and the bright line of sight and crystal-clear vision of the social problem film spawn a mutant offspring—one strain is all nerves, the other knows all the answers.

In plot, in tone, even in the combat echo of the title, *Crossfire* signals the realignments in postwar American culture. World War II exposed tens of millions of uniformed servicemen and home front civilians to regimentation, rationing, and spasms of unholy terror. It made cynical hipsters out of country hicks, sophisticated ladies out of girls next door, and worldly wise veterans out of youngsters wet behind the ears. It gave a Depression-scarred generation hard-won confidence, marketable skills, and pocket money. It also killed over 300,000 Americans, without regard to race, ethnicity, rank, or virtue.

From a Big Picture perspective, WWII adhered to an orthodox Production Code scenario. Not only did Good triumph over Evil but the denouement drove home the morally compensating value of the great crusade, nowhere more starkly than in the motion picture medium itself. In early May 1945, the first Army Signal Corps newsreels of the Nazi concentration camps were released to appalled home front moviegoers. Images of man-made horror never before imagined, much less captured by the motion picture camera, unspooled at the top of a program designed for zany cartoons, upbeat travelogues, and chirpy musicals: mounds of rotting bodies bulldozed into mass graves, charred corpses packed into crematoria ovens, and columns of the walking dead, mutilated, skeletal, and tattooed. "Evil exists to showcase good," Joseph I. Breen had written, a faith hard to keep after 1945.

Like the rest of America, Hollywood sensed the dawning of a new day with V-J Day. On September 19, 1945, the MPPDA ousted the old boss and appointed an up-to-date executive model more in tune with the times. After some gentle nudging, Will H. Hays, the original czar and brand name logo, resigned to make way for Eric A. Johnston, president of the U.S. Chamber of Commerce. A well-known and well-liked spokesman for robust capitalism, Johnston was a good fit for the gray-flannelled cut of the postwar fashion, a suave organization man committed to foreign trade, labor-management cooperation, and nonpartisan civic-mindedness. "Call us progressives, or liberal progressives, or conservative liberals—such tags have lost their old meanings in the present crisis of growth and change," he declared in *American Unlimited*, a collection of his speeches published in 1944. Nodding in approval, *Variety* bestowed its benediction: "Johnston looks like the happy choice to grease the wheels and smooth the roads." One of Johnston's first initiatives was to pave over the name of the Motion Picture Producers and Distributors of America. As of December 12, 1945, Hollywood's official letterhead read: the Motion Picture Association of America (MPAA), the name it bears today.

High on the list of Johnston's cosmopolitan credentials was his Episcopalian heritage. Once again, the moguls had selected a gentile front for the Jewish-flavored business. Again too they had chosen a CEO with a hands-

No longer the Hays Office: *Motion Picture Herald* publisher and coauthor of the Production Code, Martin J. Quigley (*left*) sizes up the new president of the newly renamed Motion Picture Association of America, Eric A. Johnston, in 1945.

(QUIGLEY PHOTO ARCHIVE/GEORGETOWN UNIVERSITY)

off approach to the nuts-and-bolts toil on the factory floor: Johnston had been on the job for over a year before he found time for an on-site visit to a Hollywood soundstage. "Industry interests elsewhere have prevented me until now [March 1947] from getting around to the studios and becoming acquainted first hand," he explained.

Johnston's casual management style and open-minded outlook extended only so far. "The Production Code will be rigorously and religiously adhered to," he pledged upon appointment. No doubt: but the Christian rhetoric of moral probity—the dominant didactic mode of the 1920s and 1930s, expressed most rigidly in the Code itself—gave way to the fuzzier, less dogmatic language of liberal tolerance and nondenominational niceness. "An America divided will never lead the way to a world united," Johnston stated when he formally assumed what it took everyone a while to stop calling the Hays Office. "We cannot be good neighbors until we learn to get along ourselves."

The twists of fate and the turns in postwar history prevented the urbane, energetic, and progressive Johnston from healing a divided world with a global good-neighbor policy. In quick succession, he confronted a trio of threats more dire than the onslaughts that had compelled the creation of the Hays Office: the House Committee on Un-American Activities, the Department of Justice, and—the menace of all menaces—television. Johnston's responses were in turn craven, stoic, and sluggish.

In October 1947, the House Committee on Un-American Activities (HUAC) launched the first in a series of wildly publicized hearings into alleged communist subversion in the motion picture industry. Initially, Johnston showed backbone and pledged defiance, but under the heat of bad publicity, picket lines, and congressional subpoenas, the MPAA wilted. Pressured by panicky moguls, Johnston inaugurated the blacklist era by promising that the major studios would never "knowingly employ a communist." Neither the Production Code Administration nor Joseph I. Breen came under scrutiny during the investigations, a measure of the depth of ignorance in the halls of Congress about the true nature of the ideological apparatus dictating the party line in Hollywood.[1]

The next year, another branch of the federal government delivered a more crippling body blow when a long-litigated series of antitrust suits brought by the Department of Justice against the major studios concluded with what was for Hollywood the unhappiest of endings. In 1948 a judicial decision dubbed the Paramount Decree compelled the studios to divest ownership of their theater chains. The vertical integration of production, distribution, and exhibition—the sweet monopoly that had oiled the studio machine and crushed independent competition—was now a busted trust. By breaking the choke hold of studio control over exhibition, the Department of Justice gave theater owners more autonomy over booking and programming. Less dependent on Hollywood product, exhibitors became less bound by Hollywood codes.

Of all the postwar plagues to strike Hollywood, the most terrible was television. A shadow on the horizon since the early 1930s, the long-dreaded living room alternative took off as soon as V-J Day blew the factory whistle for postwar prosperity. With head-spinning speed, the small screen outpaced the dominion of the big screen, sparking a mass migration from public hives to home cocoons that ended forever the celluloid monopoly on moving picture entertainment. In 1946, 90,000,000 Americans every week went to the movies. In 1950 the number had dwindled to 60,000,000 and the trend line was all downward.

---

1. A few months after the 1947 HUAC hearings, a telling bit of industry gossip, perhaps passed along in jest, perhaps not given the temper of the times, appeared in the *Hollywood Reporter*: "Now that the Attorney General's office has placed the Progressive Citizens of America on its list of 'suspect' organizations, policy makers at the Production Code Administration are insisting that the full name of that group be used in all [newspaper] copy—not just the initials, PCA."

Rattled by Congress, the courts, and television, Hollywood struggled to regain balance and recapture the sure-footed swagger of its high-profit, high-prestige past. Yet its past was part of the problem. More than political turmoil, economic dislocation, and competitive pressure from a rival medium buffeted the front offices and backlots. In a not-unrelated development, fissures were also cracking open in the moral grounding of the industry.

At first, Hollywood hoped to partake of postwar prosperity with only minor adjustments to the practices perfected in the 1930s and mobilized during wartime. Certainly the 1934 design scheme for financial and cultural stability warranted no remodeling. With the changing of the guard from Hays to Johnston, the Breen Office offered a reassuring continuity both by way of bureaucracy and personnel. In recognition of his centrality, Breen received a promotion. Along with his title as director of the Production Code Administration, he was named a vice president of the MPAA, sharing billing on official stationery with Eric Johnston. Breen had already been granted the post by board resolution in 1944; his appointment under new bylaws was made official when Johnston assumed the presidency. Significantly, a condition for Johnston's appointment was that Breen retain the same degree of autonomy he had enjoyed under Hays, presiding over the PCA "without any interference or outside influence." The Hays Office may have vanished, but the Breen Office was installed more firmly than ever.

From his vice presidential perch, Breen dutifully blurbed the current motion picture roster. Touted in official MPAA press releases as "the man who for the past 15 years has seen practically all the pictures produced in Hollywood from early script to finished product," he played his part in the feverish boosterism so characteristic of postwar Hollywood. "In the last three or four months, there have passed through our office seventy or eighty pictures which compared favorably with the best Hollywood has produced in years," he declared in a letter—really a publicity release—to Johnston in 1949. "For sheer artistry, for variety of subject matter, I doubt if in many years we have had so fine a collection of motion pictures." True, the list of upcoming releases included some edgy material (*Intruder in the Dust*, *Madame Bovary*, and *All the King's Men*) and some future classics (*Battleground*, *She Wore a Yellow Ribbon*, and *I Was a Male War Bride*), but the usual chaff was also well represented (*And Baby Makes Three*, *The Fighting Kentuckian*, and *The Story of Sea Biscuit*). Overall, little in the preview of coming attractions threatened to drive protean tele-viewers away from the glowing box in the living room.

The blights conjured by the acronyms HUAC, DOJ, and TV were tangible enough, but something else—more amorphous and atmospheric—was knocking Hollywood out of frame and off its game. In a postwar world of Kinsey Reports and suburban affluence, of cocky ex-warriors and spunky career girls, the quaint decorum and stern catechism of the motion picture screen seemed at least one zeitgeist out of date. After four years of rationing and regimentation, few veterans of either front—secure in a steady paycheck, eligible for easy credit terms, tempted by hectoring advertising—felt obliged to defer gratification in matters of consumption. Increasingly, too, they were less willing to defer to moral guardians on matters of entertainment.

If, in the years after 1945, Hollywood appears caught in a cultural lag while stewing in an institutional funk, its own wartime service helps explain the disconnect. Every downtown palace and corner nabe had screened bloody newsreels and searing combat documentaries. In military classrooms, millions of soldiers had learned about the transmission of venereal disease and mastered how-to manuals in killing from 16mm screenings. Even the Hollywood feature film, scrubbed and brushed by the Breen Office, registered the trauma and tragedy of combat veterans and home front families whose wounds were beyond the consolation of a Production Code ending.

The postwar challenges to the Breen Office came from every motion picture front, but three genres launched the most serious assaults: the social problem film, the film noir, and the art film. In these theaters of operation, the secure moral universe of Joseph I. Breen was infiltrated and softened up—not overturned as yet, but undermined. Like the GIs in *Crossfire*, who instinctively sought shelter in a motion picture theater only to find that the interior was no longer as welcoming, the screen no longer as relevant, neither Hollywood nor its audience could return again to status quo ante.

THE GENRE WITH ALL THE ANSWERS

Mustered out of wartime service, filmmakers nurtured by the studio system and disciplined by the Breen Office returned to civilian employment committed to getting a piece of the action on screen. Always a purblind conceit, the Haysian myth of mere entertainment had evaporated under the heat of four years of combat-tempered celluloid. Even the House Committee on Un-American Activities understood that the motion picture medium was more than a wind-up toy.

For their part, moviegoers also seemed willing to forgo amusement to muse over messages on religious prejudice and racial bigotry, on psychological traumas and physical disabilities, on veteran readjustment and postwar alienation, and on the fallout from newly minted words like *neuropsy-*

chosis, blast radius, and *genocide.* With the enemy overseas vanquished, America and its cinema turned inward to ponder the domestic problems deferred for the duration. "That's history," insists the Voice of Morality (and Liberal Tolerance) in a lecture on bigotry in *Crossfire.* "They don't teach it in school, but it's real American history just the same." Actually, the place they didn't teach it was at the movies, but that was changing.

The instructional impulse was nourished by a therapeutic cycle of "psychiatricals" whose true repressed memory was the terror of the war: Mitchell Leisen's *Lady in the Dark* (1944), in which neurotic career girl Ginger Rogers is cured by psychoanalysis and marriage; Billy Wilder's *The Lost Weekend* (1945), in which alcoholism is a treatable delirium not a moral failing, and Alfred Hitchcock's *Spellbound* (1945), in which the pieces of a jigsaw dreamscape congeal to cure a sick mind. By the time of *Smash-up* (1947), *The Snake Pit* (1948), and *The Dark Past* (1948), American audiences were so well drilled in the techniques of Freudian psychoanalysis that the on-screen shrinks hardly needed to pause for a review session.

Being in the business of interpreting dreams, the staff of the Breen Office was savvy to the ways Hollywood's id surged beneath the Code's super-ego. Though the Code "has nothing to say about psychiatry, psychoses, fixations, complexes, psycho-analysis, introverts or extroverts, plain or fancy insanity," noted trade reporter William Weaver, sending out an alert on behalf of the Breen Office, "writers who interpret this fact as a swell new way to 'get around the Code' are in for enlightenment to the contrary, for the policy of the PCA with respect to this new variety of material is to be the same as that applied to the old, exacting of the psychiatrically motivated wrongdoer the same penalties that would be exacted of him if he weren't nuts." Slipping into a reference from Greek mythology the founder of psychoanalysis might have appreciated, Weaver warned: "There'll be no Trojan horsing of contraband under [a] Freudian banner."

Yet the Freudian banner *was* the contraband: the great denial of human responsibility and free will, the cornerstone of Catholic doctrine. Helplessly in thrall to irresistible impulses and unconscious motivations, characters acted out of compulsion not choice. Usurping what had so lately been the sole prerogative of the man of the cloth, the psychiatrist stepped forward as the secular priest in postwar Hollywood cinema, the couch and self-awareness replacing the confessional and penance.

Knowing that the war had let loose a host of monsters from the id, Breen sought to repress the discontented who might topple civilization. On March 20, 1946, in a conference with fifty executives from MGM, he began the first of a ten-day series of "refresher courses covering all points of the Code and censorship in various parts of the world." Breen emphasized "the need in these changing times for the greatest possible care in order that pictures may not be seized upon by critical censor boards at home and abroad as an excuse for curtailing the freedom of the screen." The war had opened up cracks in the Code; Breen knew he could not close them all back up, but he wanted to keep them from spreading.

Breen's reference to "these changing times" was a recognition that the postponed payments on a series of wartime promissory notes were fast coming due. Repressed for the duration, the inequities in American culture rushed to the surface after 1945—and unlike the psychic quirks of the individual patient, which could be cured by a wise shrink on a case-by-case basis, the maladjustments of the nation as a whole required collective action. When the pyschiatricals moved off the couch and into the world, Hollywood played against type and ventured into risky political territory. Having commanded a soapbox since December 7, 1941, filmmakers felt entitled to redress the grievances of the body politic in a didactic new motion picture genre, the social problem film.

The postwar social problem film had roots in the 1930s, when, almost single-handedly, Warner Bros. hazarded a gutsy series of polemical "preachments" (later dubbed "social consciousness films"), the least wishy-washy of which, no surprise, were released during the pre-Code era. In bitter, tight-lipped melodramas such as *I Am a Fugitive from a Chain Gang* (1932), *Heroes for Sale* (1933), and *Wild Boys of the Road* (1933), the studio gave voice to the injustices of the criminal justice system, the suffering of disposable war veterans, and the plight of juvenile runaways. After 1934, Warner Bros. struggled with the Breen Office to maintain the family tradition, denouncing labor exploitation, nativist bigotry, and homegrown fascism in, respectively, *Black Fury* (1935), *Black Legion* (1936), and *Confessions of a Nazi Spy* (1939). Whatever the gripe, the anger coursing through the social consciousness films of the 1930s derived from the chronic malignancy in the economy. By contrast, the postwar social problem films almost never had anything to do with money. The problems Americans now faced were psychic, social, and political.

Leading the pack was William Wyler's *The Best Years of Our Lives* (1946), a perfectly pitched melodrama tracking the rocky readjustment of three combat veterans to a civilian homeland that is sedate, prosperous, and oblivious to their harrowing backstories. Produced by Sam Goldwyn and written by Robert E. Sherwood from the novel by MacKinlay Kantor, the Best Picture of 1946 was also the first unblinking look at the anguish of a disabled veteran, played by amputee Harold Russell, a sailor whose hands had been burned off in a shipboard fire. The metal hooks that were now Russell's hands would not be made flesh in the last reel.

To Hollywood's surprise, along with the gold statues and critical bouquets, financial rewards accompanied the kind of somber, issue-oriented scenarios long deemed box office poison. "The idea that pictures on controversial subjects are questionable at the box office has been well beaten over the head by results to date on *Gentleman's Agreement* and *Crossfire*," reported *Variety*, tallying up the profits accrued from anti-antisemitism.

Of course, some subjects were more politically controversial and commercially dubious than others. Typically, by the time Hollywood got around to tackling a social problem, a national consensus had congealed around the solution or at least the correct attitude. A popular art, no matter how well intentioned, must ride the crest, not leap out ahead of a cultural wave. In one turbulent current of American life, however, Hollywood refused to play it safe. Where alcoholism, mental illness, veteran readjustment, and ethno-religious prejudice responded readily to the healing remedies from a wise psychiatrist, an understanding girl, or a righteous journalist, a deeper and more virulent affliction, not locked in the subconscious but carved into the skin, was resistant to the usual patent medicine: racism.

Though the defaming of African Americans on screen began with the birth of the nation's movies, the Breen Office lent the portraits a coast-to-coast consistency north and south, enforcing the racial laws written into the Code and practiced in American life with its characteristic attention to detail. In the context of an appalling picture book, however, the racial regulations put in place in 1934 actually *restrained* the most hateful and hysterical caricatures. Judged against the gallery of wide-eyed "spooks" and slack-jawed simians flaunted in the 1920s and the pre-Code era, the depiction of blacks under the Code as desexualized sideshows, shuffling about the fringes as neutered Stepenfetchits and nurturing Mammies, is a visible improvement.

The text of the Code addressed race in two sections, with divergent impulses. Under "Particular Applications," Part II, "Sex," section 6, the Code decreed:

> *Miscegenation* (sex relationship between the white and black races) is forbidden.

However, also under "Particular Applications," in the section called "National Feelings," the Code elsewhere insisted:

> The history, institutions, prominent people and citizenry of other nations shall be represented fairly.

In addition to the most-favored nations of Ireland and Italy, "other nations" might logically encompass the continent of Africa and the immigrants who came to America in chains. Thus, while the Jim Crow color line was encoded in "the miscegenation clause" (as it was called), the respect for national feelings (read: ethnic and racial sensitivities) was also mandated, a reflection of the schizoid disconnect in a nation that preached equality and practiced discrimination. The Code instructed Hollywood to be restrictive and open-minded, racist and tolerant.

A Haysian edit not a Jesuit edict, the miscegenation clause had been penciled in to the third draft of the Code in 1930 to placate Southern exhibitors. The tampering angered Martin J. Quigley and Rev. Daniel A. Lord, S.J., the original authors, who distinguished between "items of policy and expediency" edited in by anonymous MPPDA hands and the Catholic vision infusing the Code. The Haysians, Quigley complained to Breen, inserted "political considerations which have nothing to do with morality." Quigley was "absolutely infuriated all the time that I knew him with the original Code where it said that we could not treat a picture dealing with miscegenation," recalled Geoffrey Shurlock. "He thought it was outrageous and un-Christian." It was also economically expedient. A film that endorsed

Breaking the miscegenation clause, sort of: Granny (Ethel Waters) casts a wary eye on her mixed-race granddaughter (Jeanne Crain) and all-white beau (William Lundigan) in Elia Kazan's *Pinky* (1949).

integration between the races, much less countenanced miscegenation, faced a total blackout in theaters throughout Dixie.

As a consequence, under the Breen Office in the 1930s, Jim Crow fixed Hollywood's color line. In 1933, when MGM proposed a version of *Pudd'nhead Wilson*, Mark Twain's subversive satire on America's mixed bloodlines, first James Wingate and later Breen nixed the project. Yet because race was deemed a political not moral problem, Hays not Breen took point position on racially sensitive projects. "We will want to watch *Green Pastures* very closely from the viewpoint of Southern opinion and ideals," he cautioned Breen, speaking in code, when the popular all-black musical went into production at Warner Bros. Not to fear: in *Green Pastures* (1936) even the afterlife hued to a black and white color scheme. "I take it hereafter the Lord must be a colored man," Breen joked to Jack Warner.

During WWII, the "Americans All" rhetoric promulgated by the Office of War Information opened the eyes of the Breen Office to its racial blind spots. Stereotypes and caricatures that would not have been blinked at before the war came into sharp focus in the postwar light. In 1939, when Breen looked at John Ford's *Stagecoach* (1939), he fretted about the gold-hearted prostitute, the whiskey-drinking doctor, and the law-breaking sheriff. In 1950, when Breen looked at Ford's *Rio Bravo* (1950), the indigenous extras emerged from the background. "With respect to the portrayal of American Indians in motion pictures," he suggested a sensitivity session with the National Film Committee of the Association of American-Indian Affairs. "This organization is comprised of prominent serious-minded citizens, who are concerned that this minority group be fairly portrayed," he admonished. "It is our considered opinion that it behooves the industry to see to it that Indians in motion pictures are fairly presented."

The most conspicuous victims of unfair representations were also the most conspicuous beneficiaries of the postwar enlightenment. Once a fringe opinion, the notion of racial equality (though emphatically not interracial sexuality) was edging into the mainstream. The introduction of Jackie Robinson to the batting lineup of Major League baseball in 1947, the integration of the U.S. armed forces in 1948, and the consensus among progressive politicians and cultural elites, if not Southern senators and Dixie juries, that Jim Crow was an un-American activity, emboldened Hollywood to liberalize its own admissions policies.

If 1947 was Hollywood's year of the Jew on screen, 1949 was Hollywood's year of the Negro—and white actors passing as Negroes passing as whites. Like the social problem films bewailing antisemitism, the films against Jim Crow never dared propose a radical overhaul of American society or advocate federal legislation. Combating racism was a matter more of personal transformation than political reform, self-awareness not civil rights. As such, liberal bromides pervade the race-conscious social problem films—until a single word, common in conversation though not Hollywood's sound track, cuts through the mealy-mouthed blather and verbal mush: nigger.

Before 1934, the on-screen utterance of the most lacerating epithet in the American vernacular was a rarity but still a judgment call. In director Dudley Murphy's version of Eugene O'Neill's *The Emperor Jones* (1933), an independent production starring the regal singer-activist Paul Robeson, the word was heard in prints distributed in the South but "Negro" was dubbed in for prints distributed in the North and in Southern race houses. With the enforcement of the Code, under MPPDA fiat, the slur was forbidden by name. However demeaning the depictions of blacks on screen, however unsavory the minstrel antics of white actors in blackface, the Breen Office silenced the sounds of racist invective.

Appropriately, the Civil War super-production that replaced *The Birth of a Nation* (1915) as Hollywood's archetypal Confederate fairy tale incited a contentious preproduction squabble over the epithet. Although Rhett Butler's valedictory "damn" garnered all the verbal publicity for David O. Selznick's *Gone With the Wind* (1939), the more obscene word was also fiercely debated in the script review phase of the long aborning project. Readers dismayed at the promiscuous use of the word in Margaret Mitchell's book feared the worst and implored the Breen Office to keep the slur out of the film version. Speaking on behalf of his boss, Francis Harmon offered assurances that the "established practice of our Production Code Administration" was "to request the deletion of such expressions as 'nigger,' 'wop,' 'chink,' 'dago,' etc. [that are] derogative to any racial or national group."

True to Harmon's word, Breen Office staffers spent years sensitizing Selznick's script. "We urge and recommend that you have none of your white characters refer to the darkies as 'niggers,'" Breen advised Selznick in 1937. "It seems to us to be acceptable if the Negro characters use the expression; the word should not be out of the mouth of white people. In this connection you might want to give some consideration to the use of the word 'darkies.'" Two years later, victorious at last, the relieved Code staffer Islin Auster happily informed Breen that "Mr. Selznick agreed not to use the word 'nigger.'"[2]

After Pearl Harbor, when wartime unity mandated the whitewashing of divisive phrases and inconvenient facts from cultural consciousness, the word and what it echoed was not referenced or otherwise acknowledged.

2. The liberal Selznick was likely using the epithet as a bargaining chip for the expletive he really wanted on the sound track.

Nudged along by the OWI, Hollywood accorded blacks appreciably better screen treatment across the genres, notably in the ensembles of melodramas such as *Casablanca* (1942) and *Lifeboat* (1944) and combat films such as *Sahara* (1943) and *Bataan* (1943).

Once ethnic, religious, and racial slurs were broached in *Crossfire* and *Gentleman's Agreement*, the trigger word was cleared for a full hearing. In 1949 the detonation of "nigger" served as a kind of linguistic shock treatment in three of the year's four integrationist social problem films: *Home of the Brave*, *Pinky*, and *Intruder in the Dust*, with the more discreet *Lost Boundaries* stopping at "coon" and "darkie." In each case, the Breen Office proved eager to help the spokesmen for racial equality say their piece.

The first of the quartet to deal with what critics preferred to call "anti-Negro prejudice" was *Home of the Brave* (1949), produced by Stanley Kramer, directed by Mark Robson, and written for the screen by Carl Foreman and Herbert Baker. As performed on Broadway in 1946, the original play, by Arthur Laurents, lectured against an outbreak of antisemitism in a WWII combat squad. By 1949, however, with *Crossfire* and *Gentleman's Agreement* having soaked up the press ink on the antisemitic angle, Kramer injected fresh blood into the project by transforming the victim of GI prejudice from a Jew to a black. *Home of the Brave* thereby inverts the trajectory of *Crossfire*, which ratcheted down the controversy quotient by switching the homosexual in the novel to a Jew for the film. So swift was the pace of attitudinal change in postwar America that the Jewish hook had already lost the cachet of controversy.

As much a psychiatrical as a social problem film, *Home of the Brave* insists racism is all in the mind, and not only in the white mind. A black GI named Moss (James Edwards) is stricken with hysterical paralysis after returning from a combat mission on a Japanese-held island. The enemy is not the Japanese (who remain invisible) but the visible racism of the combat squad, heretofore a model of cohesive fellowship, now exposed as a unit whose camaraderie is only skin-deep.

According to *Home of the Brave*, interpersonal prejudice is not the logical expression of a racist system but the character flaw of a racist individual, the despicable T. J. (Steve Brodie). Baiting Moss with slurs and insults, he imitates the molasses-mouthed, slack-jawed stupidity of the character actor Stepin Fetchit, a self-reflexive jibe at Hollywood's role in perpetuating the imagery it is now condemning. Pitted against the vile T. J. is the solicitous shrink (played by Jeff Corey, whose manner and visage reinforces the already conventional linkage of Freudianism and Judaism), a sensitive soul who administers palliatives derived from Viennese techniques and American pharmaceuticals.

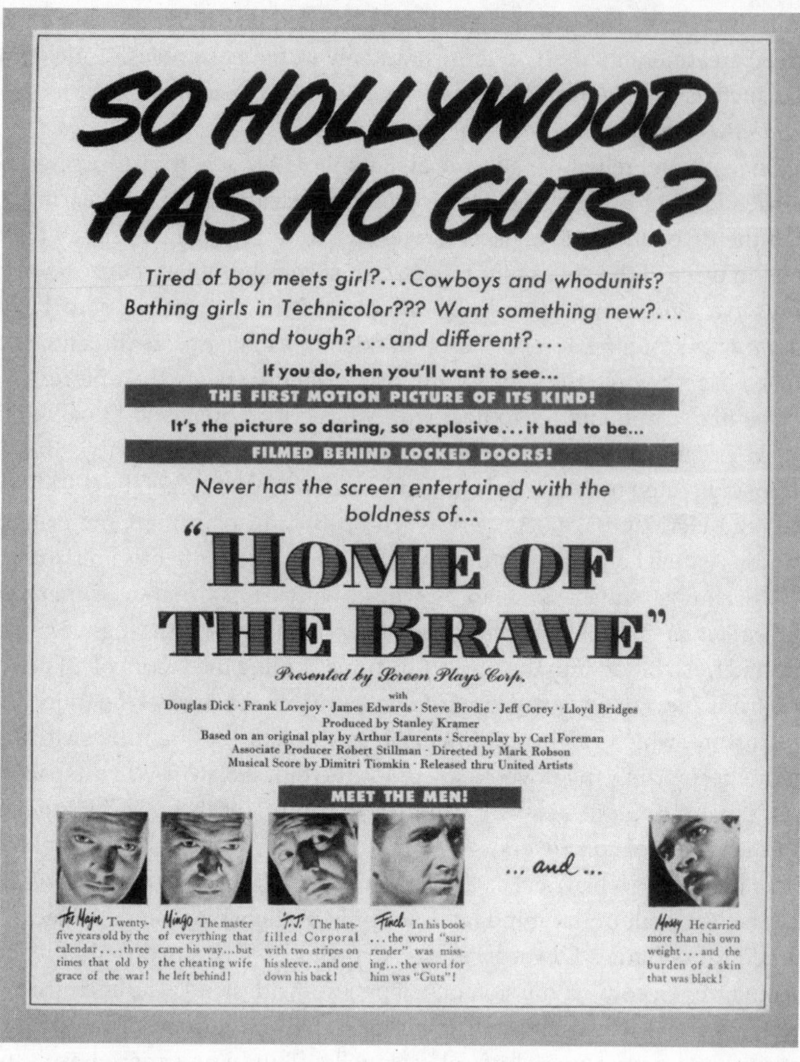

Ratcheting up the controversy quotient: an advertisement for Stanley Kramer's "psychiatrical" social problem film, *Home of the Brave* (1949).

Spoken first by T.J., next in fear and anger by Moss's friend, then screamed repeatedly by Moss himself, and finally, shouted by the shrink to jolt his patient into sanity, the trigger word crackles on the dialogue track, each actor sounding off like a child having just learned a nasty word. "There was a lot of discussion on whether we should use 'nigger,'" Kramer told the African American journalist Lillian Scott. "But it's as simple as this and there's no sense in making it involved: we're trying to do something real. This is a word used in a derogatory sense. We had to ask ourselves if this is a word that a person would use in this action? And how would the Negro react?" Kramer paused, embarrassed. "Let's face it, 'nigger' is a daily usage word. So we decided to use it, because we believe if you do something you feel is true and real, your dramas must have an honest basis."

Breen cautioned Kramer that the daily usage word, and similar slurs, be used sparingly and for morally compensating value. "While it is necessary that you build properly for the psychological climax, it is likewise important that you not offend by the quantity of insults," he advised. "Derogatory references to Negroes" were always offensive, and Kramer should know "the desirability of eliminating any such references possible." (By then, the Breen Office was also discouraging the use of the still-ubiquitous "Japs" for the former wartime enemy.)

To endorse racial tolerance, however, was not to sanction miscegenation. As in nineteenth-century American literature, postwar Hollywood cinema applied the one-drop rule: the offspring of an unholy union was permanently stained. The next two race-minded entries, *Lost Boundaries* and *Pinky*, acknowledge what miscegenation has wrought and concede the upside of passing for white, but neither can admit that love as well as sex may blend the bloodlines. Nor may the films portray interracial passion by casting mixed-race actors as what were still called mulattos. The solution was to cast white actors to front for the gradations of blackness.

In *Lost Boundaries* (1949) Melchoir Ferrer, Beatrice Pearson, Susan Douglas, and Richard Hilton (Caucasians all) play a black family passing for white. Produced by Louis de Rochemount, best known for the *March of Time* series and based on a true-life exposé from *Reader's Digest*, the tale, with an admirable lack of hectoring or histrionics, depicts the necessary compromises and hard choices of a promising young doctor (Ferrer) forced to choose between being true to his Negro self or practicing his profession. Given the chance to become the family doctor in the small New Hampshire town of Keenham, whose lily-white Currier and Ives snowscapes gleam accusingly in the mise-en-scène, he and his wife accept the one nonnegotiable proviso for employment.

When the secret of twenty years is forced out into the open, the traumatized son runs off to Harlem for a dark night of the soul, the ashamed daughter relinquishes her white boyfriend, and the racially recataloged family is shunned by former friends. After a sermon by the town's open-minded Episcopalian minister (the setting, remember, is New Hampshire), the family may stay in the community. However, if the son reunites with his blonde girlfriend or the daughter goes to the prom with her white beau, the reunions occur offscreen, outside the frame of the narrative. The boundary the film may not trespass is sexual.

Likewise, in *Pinky* (1949), Twentieth Century-Fox's extremely Caucasian ingénue Jeanne Crain played a nurse passing for white, the unlikely granddaughter of the coal-black actress Ethel Waters. Fortunately, after being bequeathed the estate of a cranky Southern dowager, Pinky sacrifices married life with an open-minded white doctor in order to uplift her race as a celibate schoolmarm. The corrupted bloodline will end with Pinky.

Strictly speaking, the circuitous conceit of white actors passing for blacks passing for whites was a violation of the Code's miscegenation clause. After all, textually, in the world of the film, the mixed-race characters engage in interracial, though not sexual, romantic relations. Extra-textually, however, the top-billed actors playing the racial shades are white. Thus, the more inviolable offscreen taboo policed by Jim Crow is unbroken. Though the fiction imagines a forbidden act, the casting obeys the law of the land.

Alone of the quartet, Clarence Brown's *Intruder in the Dust* (1949) dispenses with psychiatrical shock treatments or hypocritical casting. Shot on location in Oxford, Mississippi, and written by the soon to be blacklisted screenwriter Ben Maddow from the novel by William Faulkner, the tale is suffused with the past-is-present haze of Yoknapatwapha County, Faulkner's literary landscape. Importing Italian neorealism to grandiose MGM, Brown cast residents of Oxford for bit parts and as background extras. When the uppity black farmer Lucas Beauchamp (Juano Fernandez) is accused of killing a white man, the only question, so it seems, is whether his execution will precede or postdate his trial. Outside the jail, in the town square, the men, women, and children of Oxford mill about, itching for a lynching, reenacting a local ritual that, perhaps, a few of the playactors had participated in for real. Wisely, Brown and Maddow lob the trigger word in the opening moments of the film, quickly, matter of factly, knowing the utterance has lost its novelty. A masterpiece of Southern Gothic shadings, *Intruder in the Dust* confirms the truism that the minor works of great novelists make better movies than their masterpieces.

Though compromised by more than the Code, the race-minded social problem films were, in context, bold gestures. What plays as a cheap trick today packed a wallop in 1949. "It is in fact startling to hear many of the expressions, which are employed usually by the prejudiced, coming from the screen," commented *Motion Picture Herald*, forbearing to write the words. Watching a rough cut of *Lost Boundaries*, a teary-eyed Walter White, executive director of the NAACP, confessed to being profoundly moved. "One thing is certain—Hollywood can never go back to its old portrayal of colored people as witless menials or idiotic buffoons now that *Home of the*

Brave and *Lost Boundaries* have been made to be followed soon by other films from the studios of Twentieth Century Fox [*Pinky*], Metro Goldwyn Mayer [*Intruder in the Dust*], and others." Above all, the placement of the camera signaled a permanent break with the vision of the past: the close-up validation by a screen that no longer averts its gaze from the black visage, that insists on the shared humanity of beholder and beheld. The bearing of the dignified actor Juano Fernandez in *Intruder in the Dust* says it all: nothing is wrong with him; the social problem is out there on the streets of Oxford, Mississippi, not in his head.

Given the enforcement of the racial codes offscreen, Breen proudly claimed kinship with Hollywood's progressive wing. "Joe Breen says, and he oughtta know: '*Pinky* is possibly one of the most outstanding motion pictures ever made. This is motion picture drama at its best,'" reported gossip columnist Herb Stein, passing along a rare blurb from his source. When critics carped about the compromises in the messages and casting of the integrationist film cycle, Breen told the purists to look where the real censors operated. "We don't pass on subject matter. We pass only on treatment. If a subject is controversial—say a *Gentleman's Agreement, Home of the Brave,* or a picture on slum clearance—that is none of our business," he told the *New York Herald Tribune,* insisting that American cinema had more to fear from the state censors than from the Breen Office. "Many things come into my office that I'd like to see on the screen, but we can't under present conditions," he explained. "Personally, I'd say it's too bad we can't make these pictures, but we'd have the censors on us in every state if we made them indiscriminately."

Breen's point was underlined by the head of the Memphis Board of Censors, an irascible geriatric named Lloyd T. Binford, a Central Casting incarnation of the furrow-browed, narrow-minded bigotry that Hollywood faced east of the Breen Office. Born and bred in Reconstruction-era Duck Hill, Mississippi, Binford enforced an unreconstructed Confederate litmus test on Memphis-bound Hollywood cinema from 1928 until his retirement at age eighty-eight in 1955.[3] Of the many images that affronted Binford, none riled him more than touchy comminglings between blacks and whites. Binford's racism was a family inheritance: his father had written the Jim Crow laws for Mississippi, the model for Jim Crow laws throughout the

3. Binford first made national headlines when he banned Cecil B. DeMille's *The King of Kings* (1927), which Father Lord's technical advice notwithstanding, Binford called "a perversion of the true life of Christ and one of the one worst travesties on the Bible that I have ever seen." When Binford finally retired, *Variety* trumpeted the news with a classic headline: "Memphis Powders Blue Nose."

Deep South. Compared to Lloyd T. Binford, Joseph I. Breen was Eleanor Roosevelt.

As postwar Hollywood tilted more to integration, Binford became more notorious: he had more work to do to maintain separate but unequal screen space. Throughout the later 1940s, barely a week went by without a Binford outrage headlined in the Hollywood trade press. He banned from Memphis the sultry songstress Lena Horne ("the white people don't want to see her"), the fleet-footed bandleader Cab Calloway ("inimical"), and the comedian Eddie "Rochester" Anderson, Jack Benny's gravel-voiced, back-talking sidekick ("Rochester has too familiar a way with him for a Negro"). "Binfordized" was the name *Variety* gave to a film put through the racial wringer in Memphis, a process far worse than Breening.

Of all the Binfordizations, the most infamous was the banning of *Curley* (1947), a Hal Roach comedy featuring a spunky schoolteacher and her multiracial, Little Rascal–like gaggle of schoolchildren. "I am sorry to have to inform you that the Memphis Board of Censors was unable to approve your *Curley* picture with the little Negroes as the South does nor permit Negroes in white schools nor recognize equality between the races, even children," Binford informed United Artists, Roach's distributor.

The incident ballooned into a nationwide scandal tarring the city of Memphis—and a public relations coup for the MPAA. Here, at last, the

Better Breened than Binfordized: the notorious Lloyd T. Binford, septuagenarian head of the Memphis Board of Film Censors, in 1945.

Breen Office stood on the side of the angels. "We are against political censorship from outside the industry," Breen declared proudly. "Right now we are making a test case on censorship, the first since the United States Supreme Court upheld the constitutionality of motion picture censorship [in 1915]. Our case is based on the Memphis censor barring of Hal Roach's *Curley* in 1947 because it depicts Negro children playing with white children." (Despite the best efforts of the lawyers for UA and the MPAA, "political censorship"—the kind not performed by the Breen Office—remained the law of the land. In 1950, after a three-year court fight finally settled by the Supreme Court, UA and the MPAA lost the case against Binford on a technicality.)

Vying with Binford for capricious local color was Atlanta censor Christine Smith. Like Binford, Smith was a Dixiecratic film czar wary of all manner of interracial intercourse. As a good daughter of the Confederacy, she also cast a narrow eye on untoward aspersions on female sexuality. Smith was smart enough to ignore *Curley*, but she banned *Lost Boundaries* as a piece of racially combustible kindling that could only "adversely affect the peace, morals, and good order of the city." In *Pinky*, however, Smith detected no threat at all. "I think the picture will show the south that Negroes are different than they think they are and that Negroes are people and individuals," she said. Perversely, Binford passed *Pinky* too, commenting, "It's a peculiar kind of picture but we didn't find anything particularly objectionable in it."

Whether reversed or upheld by the courts, the whims and bigotries of local censors like Binford and Smith were reminders of the costly alternatives to the PCA. A Hollywood film bearing a Code Seal "should not have any other type of censorship imposed upon it," declared Universal president Maurice Bergman, outraged that "one gentleman in Memphis and one lady in Atlanta decide what their constituents shall see on the screen." Better that one gentleman in Hollywood—for the time being.

THE GENRE WITHOUT A NAME

At heart, the social problem film was Code friendly. Whether alcoholism or antisemitism, veteran readjustment or virulent racism, to expose the problem was to resolve it within the framework of American democracy and Hollywood dramaturgy. It was a conciliatory, therapeutic genre. Social problem screened; social problem solved.

At heart, film noir was Code splintering. The dark genre sabotaged the sunny optimism of Hollywood cinema with a gloomy weltanschauung smuggled in by foreign-born agents like Fritz Lang, Billy Wilder, Robert Siodmak, Otto Preminger, and dozens of refugee cameramen, set designers, and musicians, not from the USSR but Germany and Austria. Film noir was the un-American activity in Hollywood that the U.S. Congress should really have been investigating.[4]

"Down these mean streets a man must go who is not himself mean," noir progenitor Raymond Chandler wrote in an iconic evocation of the landscape, urban and moral, trod upon by the hard-boiled paladin in his tough-as-nails *oeuvre*, a line that from a Breen Office perspective had things exactly backwards: men might be mean and crooked but the streets must be fair and square. Though ever alert to "the subterfuge of attempting to wipe out a protracted wrong by one last line of dialogue affirming the right," Breen found the squalor in the noir atmosphere impossible to dissipate. The protracted wrong-ness seemed to soak into the very celluloid. No soothing Voice of Morality or lawful end reel wrap-up could wash away the grime of a netherworld that from studio logo to final frame smeared the entire running time.

The visual palette that gave the genre its name was the first tonal difference to catch the eye: the stygian blackness of night for night photography, the low-key lighting, and the expressionistic chiaroscuro, crisscrossed with looming shadows and cones of harsh, florescent light. Moviegoers dazzled by the celestial radiance of Hollywood's sparkling fantasy worlds had their faces rubbed in the muck of trashy back alleys, dead-end streets, foggy dockyards, and lowlife hangouts. Even the natural sunlight was pierced by Venetian blinds.

The world in the frame befit the candlepower: out of joint, vertiginous, and blurry. No longer bolted to the soundstage floor, the cameras pivoted, swiveled, and turned all a-kilter for canted angles and woozy lines of sight. Seen through a wide-angle lens, in monstrous close-up, the human face looked bloated and bestial; under a cold light, actors were exposed pockmarked and sweat-drenched while actresses looked sculpted and glacial, not at all like the beautiful stars made divine by awed backlighting.

The heroes—or anti-heroes, or villains—were a strange, un-American breed. Neither rugged individuals nor stalwart team players, they were hol-

4. The phrase *film noir* was coined by the French after WWII, and filtered into the discourse of film criticism sometime after the publication of Raymond Borde and Etienne Chaumeton's *A Panorama of American Film Noir* in 1955. Until then, American commentators struggled to describe a collection of films, dark in atmospherics and worldview, that looked and felt different but whose essential coloring eluded their critical spectrum. Various names were floated: crime films, crime mellers, and, in one dead-on designation, films of "masculine brutality." Two hawk-eyed critics who consistently spied something worth talking about in the unnamed genre were James Agee and Manny Farber.

Dead end: faithless hussy Anna Dundee (Yvonne De Carlo) and born patsy Steve Thompson (Burt Lancaster) meet their fate in Robert Siodmak's *Criss Cross* (1949).

low men, a lineup of none-too-smart losers caught in a web of determinism, backed into cul-de-sacs, sapped of all free will, figures at the whims of capricious gods from a Greek tragedy, not the covenant-bound deity of a Passion play. Narrated by doomed participant-observers in weary, detached voice-overs, their flashbacks bespoke the lack of choice and volition, the futility of escaping a destiny that has already happened. The film noir titles gave fair warning of the duplicity, brutality, and entrapment around the corner: *The Postman Always Rings Twice* (1946), *The Killers* (1946), *Out of the Past* (1947), *Kiss of Death* (1947), *Nightmare Alley* (1947), *Force of Evil* (1948), *Criss Cross* (1949), and *D.O.A.* (1950). Tapped out, the narrators embrace their doom, reading their bad hands and not even weeping. "I knew it would all fall apart," says insurance-agent-gone-bad Walter Neff (Fred MacMurray) as the blood leaks out of him in *Double Indemnity*. "It was in the cards," says drifter Frank Chambers (John Garfield), awaiting electrocution in *The Postman Always Rings Twice*. "It was in the cards—or it was fate—or a jinx—or whatever you want to call it," says the resigned patsy Steve Thompson (Burt Lancaster) in *Criss Cross*. What you did not call it was a moral universe.

Or maybe the landscape of the Greek tragedy was too well mapped: predestination is a kind of order, in Christian terms Calvinist not Catholic, but still a cosmic drama written by an Olympian God. Further out on the ledge of noirish pessimism lay an existential void with no moral calculus whatsoever, no natural law, pre-moral or amoral, a godless wilderness ruled by the base instincts of force and fraud. Neither Sophocles nor John Calvin but Thomas Hobbes is the philosopher-king of the film noir that casts man as a nasty and brutish creature disciplined only by the threat of violence. Again, the titles seal their fate: *Brute Force* (1947), *Gun Crazy* (1949), *They Live by Night* (1949), and, the noir with the most Hobbesian title of all, *The Asphalt Jungle* (1950).

Perhaps the most calloused of the postwar noirs was the punch-drunk cycle of boxing films. In the 1930s, when even a priest was two-fisted, the punches thrown on Hollywood's canvas were clean hits during sanitized two-steps. In *Body and Soul* (1947), *Champion* (1949), and *The Set-Up* (1949), the fights were brutal and bloody, the camera relishing close-ups of torn and bleeding eyes, pummeled bodies, and crushed knuckles. Mobile, lightweight cameras (another gift from WWII) pinned moviegoers against the ropes with the pugilists, giving a better-than-ringside seat as cameramen on roller skates bobbed and weaved with the action. Struggling for survival in the ring, the boxer was an urban everyman, the fight game a metaphor for other games, no less dirty and rigged.

Unlike the social problem films, prestige productions that flaunted their high seriousness and literary credentials, the film noirs tended to float under the radar of critical regard. What critics could not overlook were the dirty hits, low blows, and "unusually large number of scenes of violence and brute force" that had infiltrated Hollywood cinema. At *Motion Picture Herald*, reporter Fred Hift singled out *The Lady Gambles* (1949), where Barbara Stanwyck is beaten up and left unconscious; *Criss Cross*, where Burt Lancaster is wrenched from a hospital bed, the bones from his broken body cracking on the sound track; and *Manhandled* (1949), where a man is slowly crushed to death by a car. He might have added the sadistic glee of the cackling sociopath played by Richard Widmark, who pushes an old woman in a wheelchair down a flight of stairs in *Kiss of Death*.

Such cruel screen fare was enjoyed by only a certain kind of unsavory audience: men. Traditionally, women were Hollywood's target of choice; sell the girl or the wife and the exhibitor filled two seats, hers and the man she dragged along to buy the tickets. Film noir was encrusted with a violence "angled to sharpen it for appeal to the male audience," its "masculine brutality" and "unnecessary realism" conceived to lure the lone wolves. The rough edges, cold cityscapes, and raw nerves of the genre played poorly in

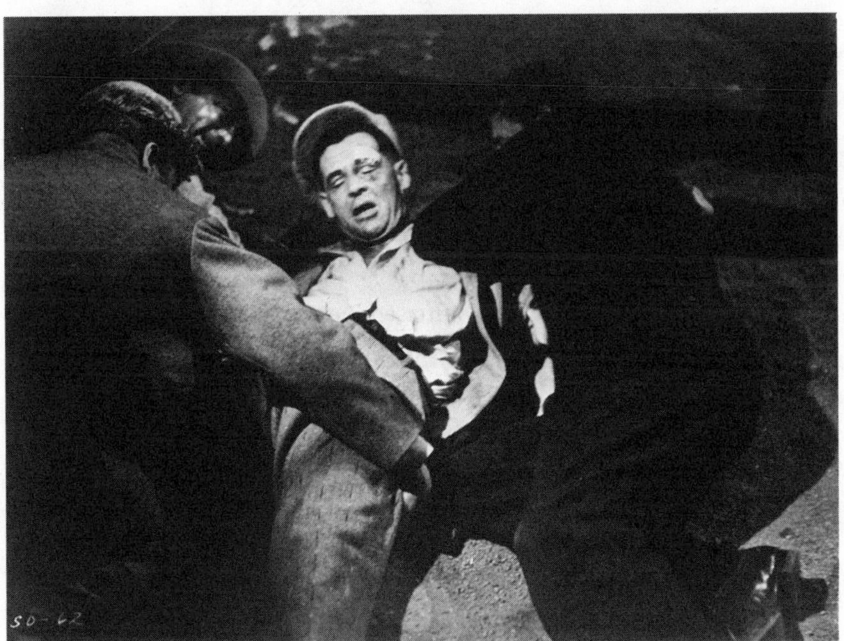

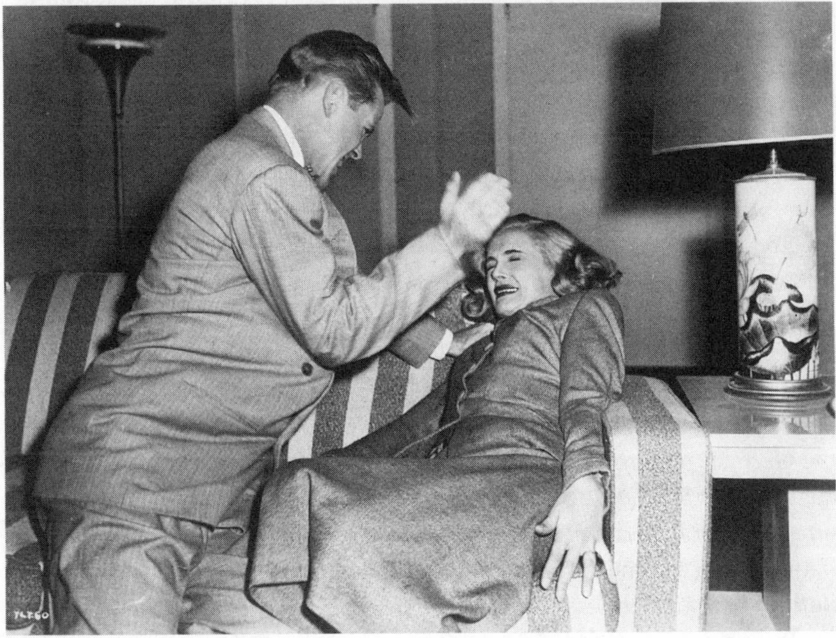

Masculine brutality: [*top*] a washed-up boxer (Robert Ryan) is pummeled in Robert Wise's *The Set-Up* (1949), and a thieving murderess (Lizabeth Scott) is slapped around by a hoodlum (Dan Duryea) in Byron Haskin's *Too Late for Tears* (1949).

the small towns and repulsed the female audience. The core demographic was men, single men, not on dates, maybe with a buddy, many presumably combat veterans whose pulses quickened at the sight of violence.

Commentators sensed that the dark films were spawned by the war, but they weren't sure why or what the phenomenon boded for the future. "Sadism . . . has been increasing in the films since the war. It is probable that it is in fact an aftermath of war," a sour Terry Ramsaye ruminated, dismayed that Hollywood had descended so low as to abandon "the great family entertainment of the millions" for "scenes of masculine brutality" and "all manner of hideous demonstrations intensified and presented as art." Fed on "a steady diet of violence and excitement . . . of 3,000 people drowning and the next day of hundreds dying in bombings, [audiences] become hard and tough," said MGM chief Dore Schary. "Naturally this is reflected in their entertainment tastes." William H. Mooring, the Legion of Decency's layman in Hollywood, understood that violence per se was not what haunted the genre but "violence of the human spirit." The Legion's "objections to pictures now are of a much graver nature than formerly," he said. "It's not the routine of bare legs and low-cut gowns, but offenses against basic morality."

The Breen Office also knew that film noir broke with the usual routine. After WWII, in film after film, staffers found themselves flinching before scenes of physical and psychic violence. "More will have to be done by way of toning down the brutality and gruesomeness before a finished picture based upon this material could be approved," Breen warned Harold Melniker, producer of the bare-knuckled boxing film *The Set-Up*, urging him to raise "wherever possible, the rather low tone of the story and eliminating to the greatest extent possible, excessive brutality and gruesomeness." A few frames of brutality were eliminated, but the low tone went the distance.

As sure as day followed night, Hollywood's dark brutality incited an upward spike in censorship battles with the state boards and city czars. The most litigious skirmish occurred while the smoke was still clearing from the rubble of World War II. Produced by Walter Wanger and directed by the German refugee Fritz Lang, *The Woman in the Window* (1944) and its quasi-sequel *Scarlet Street* (1945) rank among the blackest aces in the film noir deck. Both starred Edward G. Robinson as a milquetoast patsy, Joan Bennett as a femme fatale, and Dan Duryea as a flashy-dressing gunsel. Both were also relentlessly lurid and cruel. Breen had passed *The Woman in the Window* after a Code ending (it's all a dream!) that fooled no one. When the sordid *Scarlet Street* dispensed with the end-reel wake-up call, sterner censors outside the Breen Office placed the film off-limits.

Scarlet Street is the dead-end address of a henpecked husband and amateur painter named Chris Cross (Robinson), another born patsy led all too willingly into a life of adultery and embezzlement by a heartless floozy (Bennett), who cheats on him with an even more heartless two-bit hoodlum (Duryea). When Chris learns his dream girl is a faithless tramp, he grabs an ice pick and kills her.

The third act surprises by dragging the hoodlum to the electric chair for the murder ("Won't somebody give me a break?" he screams) and allowing the killer to walk free. But though Chris has beaten the rap, he is double-crossed by a guilty conscience. Homeless, deranged, he wanders the wintry streets, the voice of his dead mistress murmuring in his mind, oblivious to the thousands of dollars his paintings are fetching in the fancy art galleries.

Seeing that Chris's life was a living hell and assured by a Voice of Morality of a proper transcendent punishment, Breen passed the film. The grand dame of Atlanta censorship, Christine Smith, was less forgiving. She banned *Scarlet Street* from her domain, calling it "licentious, profane, obscene and contrary to the good order of the community." Out in Hollywood, Breen may have succumbed to the toxins of permissiveness, but Smith knew a series of blatant Code violations when she saw them. "The film deals with an immoral woman and illicit love, shows the enactment of a murder, and permits the man who commits the murder to go unpunished except by his own conscience," she said, citing chapter and verse.

Playing hardball and angling for publicity, Wanger and Universal, the film's distributor, took Smith to court. "We shall spare no effort to assure the people of Atlanta the right to see a picture which has already been shown in more than 180 cities throughout the country and which has been passed by every state board of censorship in the nation," Wanger promised.

To protect his own turf, Breen closed ranks with Wanger.[5] The producer and the censor coordinated a defense against what Breen called "the pot-shooting of crackpots, politicians, and misleading radio commentators who charge the industry is not competent to police its own morals." In an affidavit for Wanger's court case, Breen reiterated under oath his long-standing opposition to "political censorship from outside the industry" and argued that "to deprive art of dramatic license in choosing its own punishments, so long as the punishment is morally adequate, would mean to rob art of its contribution to progress. . . . All other ages have conceded art this prerogative." Sounding more like a civil libertarian than a Victorian Irishman, he testified: "It is my opinion that political interference with the exhibition of *Scarlet Street* is not only a contamination of the principle of free expression

5. The relations between the two had grown quite cordial since the long ago dustup over the bedroom ballet between Greta Garbo and John Gilbert in *Queen Christina* (1933).

Banned in Atlanta: Chris Cross (Edward G. Robinson), painted into a corner in Fritz Lang's *Scarlet Street* (1945).

to which we as a democracy are committed but that it is a public disservice." (Atlantans won the right to see *Scarlet Street* after a local judge overruled Smith and the censor board chose not to appeal the decision.)

Christine Smith was not alone in her revulsion at Hollywood's plunge into darkness. "There has been growing criticism of the movies—that they are packed with morbidity, violence, and crime, with a perceptible trace of immorality," worried Abram F. Myers, general counsel of the Allied States Association of Motion Picture Exhibitors. "Those of us who lived through the outburst against moral laxity on the screen in the early 1930s, and witnessed the skillful job done by Will Hays in putting out that fire, cannot help wondering why the situation was again allowed to get out of hand."

Breen didn't need anyone reminding *him* about 1934. "For all practical purposes, I am chiefly responsible for the day-by-day operation of the Production Code Administration—subject always, of course, to Mr. Johnston's supervision and guidance," he told Myers, noting that only two Code pictures in the last four years—the British import *Black Narcissus* (1947) and Twentieth Century-Fox's *Forever Amber* (1947)—had earned a C rating from the Legion of Decency. "It is not true to say that there has been any 'laxity in Code enforcement' or that there is any 'situation of indecency' in pictures," Breen insisted. Myers stood his ground: the point was not the number of condemned and controversial pictures but the general tone and atmosphere of Hollywood films. "If you are unaware of this, then you must live in an ivory tower," he told Breen.

The Breen Office was no ivory tower. The threat from the brutally masculine crime films required action—perhaps new addenda to the Code by the MPAA, but definitely a cautionary word to the studios.

On June 28, 1949, Breen called a full-dress meeting that brought together the PCA staff, representatives from all the major studios, and prominent independent producers. Attending for MGM, Robert Vogel reported the substance of Breen's remarks to studio head Dore Schary, who forwarded the memo along to MGM's stable of directors and producers. "Breen's office has been receiving tremendous amounts of mail from the public complaining about excessive brutality and gruesomeness in pictures," reported Vogel. "He feels that the volume and emphasis of complaints is so great that it becomes important for us to stop the hue and cry before we get into serious trouble." The regulators and the regulated agreed that violence was the life's-blood of drama, but "it is a matter of avoiding excesses—of omitting the last scintilla of brutality, which seems to be coming much too frequent." Surely, filmmakers understood the difference between the knockabout roughhousing in a western saloon where chairs crash and bottles break and the "sadistic overemphasis" infusing the current crop of crime films. Vogel closed his report with a congenial nod to the man who was watching their backs. "It should be borne in mind that Joe Breen is not setting himself up as dictating what must be done," wrote Vogel. "Very emphatically, he is trying to warn us friendlily of dangers that lie ahead."

Reflecting on the atmospheric shifts in postwar Hollywood, Breen conceded that the "biggest offense" was "excessive and unnecessary brutality," a quality not of the social problem film genre but from the shadowy genre as yet without a name. "It's a hangover from the war, when life was considered cheap," he said ruefully.

The war was always the usual suspect, the great divide between the serene Breen dawn and the squalid un-Breen twilight.

SHOOT-OUT OVER *THE OUTLAW* (1941–1949)

Social problem films and film noirs were full-blown genres whose entries collectively beat against the Breen Office and forced erosion by increments. However, the most explosive collision with Hollywood's sturdy censorship regime came from a star vehicle whose defiance was so egregious and whose circumstances so singular that it likely strengthened rather than weakened the wall it ran up against. Spanning the entire decade of the 1940s, the path of the film traces the prewar, wartime, and postwar valence of the Production Code Administration. Like an incubus in a recurring nightmare, Howard Hughes's mangy western *The Outlaw* reared up again and again to taunt and haunt Joseph I. Breen.

Breen's purgatorial travails over *The Outlaw* began in late 1940 when Hughes, the wealthy, misophobic industrialist and aviation wizard, renewed his dormant enthusiasm for the art of cinema. Hughes had operated a production company in Hollywood since 1927, his stock portfolio in oil drilling and aircraft manufacturing underwriting his name above an eclectic list of noteworthy titles, including the Great War aerial epic *Hell's Angels* (1930) and the pitiless gangster film *Scarface* (1932), both of which taught the locals lessons in showmanship, controversy, and profits. *Scarface*, a *film à clef* of the rise of Al Capone, was the most notorious of the bullet-ridden pre-Code gangster genre, a mélange of incest and insurrection that, as much as the leering wisecracks of Mae West and the insolent programmers from Warner Bros., led to the 1934 crackdown.

Hughes reveled in playing the wildcat flyboy to the fat-cat moguls and upsetting the clubby conservatism of the MPPDA. After *Scarface*, he baited the lax pre-Code regime with the smirking title and self-reflexive premise of *Cock of the Air* (1932), a film too lascivious even for the compliant Producers Review Board of the Studio Relations Committee, which assailed the entire production as "obscene and immoral in title, theme, and portrayal." Hughes appealed the ruling to the MPPDA Board in New York, the first time that a producer had bucked the decision of his fellow producers since the nominal adoption of the Code in 1930. New York backed Hollywood, and Hughes sheared a few frames but kept intact the title and the titillation.

In December 1940, after a prolonged hiatus from producing motion pictures, though not from bedding motion picture starlets, Hughes left the factory floor of his aircraft plants and returned to the soundstage not only to produce but direct a project close to his heart: a version of the life of Billy the Kid entitled *The Outlaw*, custom-fitted to showcase his protégée of the moment as the sexual sizzle behind the wanted poster.

To recycle the inevitable joke, the objectionable parts of *The Outlaw* were twofold: Jane Russell. The low-cut dress that clung to the buxom 19-year-old actress and the panoramic curvature packed into a cantilevered, push-up brassiere (a miracle of engineering designed by Hughes himself) breached the corseting of the female front mandated by the Code.

Pre-Code Howard Hughes: Chester Morris spanks Billie Dove in Hughes's bawdy *Cock of the Air* (1932).

Of course, the size, shape, contour, movement, and exposure of female breasts had figured as lively spheres of contention since Breen first unsheathed his tape measure in 1934. With dreary regularity, cautionary letters from the Breen Office recited a canned admonition that the secretaries could type from memory:

> We direct your particular attention to the need for the greatest possible care in the selection and photographing of the costumes and dresses of your women. The Production Code makes it mandatory that the intimate parts of the body—specifically, the breasts of the women—be fully covered at all times. Any compromise with this regulation will compel us to withhold approval of your picture.

To prevent surprises from popping out on screen, the Breen Office preapproved all borderline costumes by inspecting 8x10 still photographs of the actress in wardrobe. Whenever a sly producer tried to slip over the Breen line by submitting a photograph taken from an eye-level or low-angle perspective, Breen scrawled across the photo a request for the full-view, high-angle shot—knowing that the director would elevate his camera to shoot the lady for maximum exposure. As ever, the print review stage was usually pro forma, all disputes over décolletage, tight dresses, and bared legs having been smoothed over during preproduction.

When Breen and his staff sat down to review *The Outlaw* and beheld Jane Russell—bouncing on horseback, strutting in clinging blouses, and leaning over in plunging necklines to spill out the upper portions of her 38D–25–36 figure—the vista inspired the most goggle-eyed of all Breen outbursts over mammary excess. "In my more than ten years of critical examination of motion pictures, I have never seen anything quite so unacceptable as the shots of the breasts of the character of Rio [Russell]," he sputtered. "Throughout almost half the picture the girl's breasts, which are quite large and prominent, are shockingly emphasized, and, in almost every instance are very substantially uncovered." Without cuts—or more covering—the Breen Office absolutely refused to grant *The Outlaw* lawful passage.

Unlike Jane Russell, Hughes refused to bend. Vowing a fight to the finish, he appealed Breen's ruling to the MPPDA Board in New York. He also bankrolled a publicity push that splashed his pinup-able star over the pages of every American magazine with a pictorial section.

At that point, for the first time in a showdown between Breen and a producer, the MPPDA Board blinked. Partly because of Hughes's enormous financial resources, partly because of the ongoing "sweater girl" fiasco that had brought such ridicule upon "the Hays Office," the board tried to finesse the situation by officially reaffirming Breen's decision and then appointing a special mediating committee to negotiate with the mercurial tycoon—a committee that demanded forty feet of footage be cut ("Eliminate completely the business of Rio bending over the bed and exposing her breasts") but permitted a more ample view of Jane Russell than Breen thought proper. Hughes made the requisite eliminations and on May 15, 1941, after what was delicately termed "an amicable agreement on certain revisions," a Code Seal was issued. *The Outlaw* thus became the first studio film to outflank the Breen Office since 1934, a rebuff that helped propel Breen into his brief tenure as head of production at RKO.[6]

Rather than capitalize on the victory, however, Hughes quit the field. Despite clearing the MPPDA hurdle, he was still stymied by two formidable obstacles. State censor boards, given an advance peek at *The Outlaw*, de-

---

6. *The Aviator* (2004), Martin Scorsese's biopic of the Hollywood-period Howard Hughes, includes a fanciful reenactment of the MPPDA Board meeting over *The Outlaw*. The sequence depicts a stern-faced lineup of motion picture executives, with Breen (played by Edward Herrmann, an actor known for his patrician roles) counter-historically in attendance, tsk-tsking over Russell's ample cleavage, and Hughes (Leonardo DiCaprio) cordially greeting the censor he once tangled with over *Scarface*. If I am not mistaken, this is the first portrayal of Breen in a Hollywood motion picture—appropriately, the wry recognition came from Scorsese, a director who is also a film historian.

manded more cuts than the MPPDA. As a result, a skittish Twentieth Century-Fox balked at distributing the film. Frustrated by the roadblocks, Hughes withdrew the film to consider his options. Besides, with MGM releasing a Technicolor biopic of the penny-dreadful desperado entitled *Billy the Kid* (1941) and the B-grade programmer *Billy the Kid Wanted* (1941) also in circulation, the market for sociopathic teenaged gunslingers was glutted.

For nearly two years, Hughes kept the project in stasis. After Pearl Harbor, not even he was crazy enough to ignore the fortune to be made from contracts with the Army Air Corps.

Finally, on February 5, 1943, at 8:30 p.m., Pacific War Time, at the Geary Theater in San Francisco, Hughes premiered the long-rumored, long-gestating *The Outlaw*. To shill for the opus, he hired ace publicity man Russell Birdwell, a dapper huckster renowned as the magician who conjured front-page coverage for David O. Selznick's search for an actress to play Scarlet O'Hara in *Gone With the Wind* (1939). For his expertise, Birdwell commanded a consulting fee of $1,000 an hour—or so said his self-publicity.

The breast-beating ballyhoo Birdwell drummed up for *The Outlaw* has entered the annals of Hollywood legend. Taglines insinuated splendor in the hay ("Would you like to tussle with Russell?") and bosomy bounty ("What are the two best reasons to see Jane Russell in *The Outlaw*?"). One-sheet posters papered San Francisco and huge 24-sheet billboards distracted motorists with pictures of a languid, disheveled Russell stretched out in a haystack, packing a smoking pistol.

For the barrel-chested Joe Breen, the double entendres were not as galling as the bogus claims boldfaced in the advertising copy: "The Picture That Couldn't Be Stopped! Exactly as Filmed!" The second exploitation angle—that *The Outlaw* had eluded the high sheriff of the Production Code Administration—was a bigger provocation than the other two. Crowing about his alleged getaway, Hughes pledged "to the film public of the country that they would see" *The Outlaw* "as he made it or not at all." Providing an unobstructed view, said Hughes, was for him a matter of personal honor. "Not one inch of film has been removed and any efforts to delete a single piece of the film wherever it may play will be greeted with the toughest court fight that time and patience and resources can wage."

Of course, the bluster was a sham: *The Outlaw* had been granted a Code Seal back in 1941, over Breen's objections, after negotiations with the MPPDA Board, but still in accord with regulatory protocols. However, the prosaic facts were buried under Birdwell's avalanche of publicity, lending *The Outlaw* not just the taint of salaciousness but the banner of subversion.

Hughes and Jane Russell, Birdwell winked, had wiggled out of the Code girdle.

A rowdy premiere and sellout crowds for the exclusive run at the Geary Theater augured well for a box office windfall, but again the erratic Hughes stalled the forward momentum. Like most everything about *The Outlaw*, the problems came in twos. The first was aesthetic. Even with Jane Russell jiggling in the saddle, the turgid horse opera—complete with ludicrous feats of marksmanship, preternaturally intelligent horses, and idiotic Indians—made for hard traveling. In the director's chair, the cock of the air was a hamhanded amateur. Caught in a moment of unprofessional candor, Birdwell admitted the film was so bad it sent chills up and down his spine. *The Outlaw* reversed the "morally compensating value" exchange rate fixed by the Breen Office: moviegoers had to suffer through 120 minutes of arid melodrama and tepid dialogue for the visually compensating value of Jane Russell.

For male spectators, long blinkered by the Breen Office, the unequal bargain was considered a fair deal. As the featured topography on the frontier landscape, Jane Russell's outline paid out compensation in full. While diverted by the wolf whistles for Russell, however, no one noticed that the true romance in *The Outlaw* revolved around the three hombres: Sheriff Pat Garrett (Thomas Mitchell) is homoerotically obsessed with Doc Holiday (Walter Huston) and violently jealous of the cute young Billy (Jack Beutel), who has usurped him in Doc's affections.

The second problem was bad timing and, unlike the first, it was insurmountable. In 1943 the giddy indulgence surrounding *The Outlaw* was a rebuke to the wartime ethos of rationing and restraint, austerity and sacrifice. The Hughes-Birdwell ballyhoo (top-price tickets at $2.50, exorbitant exploitation costs, and a luxury press junket that transported a herd of Hollywood scribes up to San Francisco to be plied with booze and feted in plush hotels) seemed wasteful, frivolous, almost unpatriotic. Despite wartime restrictions on travel and accommodations, "the mob of about 50 trade and newspaper reporters found it easy sailing under the powers of Hughes's wide open bankroll," tut-tutted *Variety*. At *Motion Picture Herald*, the veteran trade reporter Red Kahn was frankly disgusted. "Chiefly atrocious was the smell of the entire enterprise," he commented afterwards. "There was a pre-war type of party at the Bal Tabarin [nightclub] after the debut. It was all free, in fact—food, liquor, and champagne. Any resemblance to the cold and hard realism of these grimly realistic days was not even coincidental." As if to remind the revelers there was a war on, the screech of air-raid sirens and a lights-out interrupted the festivities.

The tug of a guilty home front conscience was not the only reason to roll back the searchlights. "High places in Hollywood are visibly disturbed by all

Breast-beating ballyhoo: a fanciful advertisement from 1946 recounts the censorship history of *The Outlaw* according to ad-pub man Russell Birdwell. The film was completed in 1941 not 1944, premiered in February 1943 not June 1944, received a Code Seal in 1941, and was not presented "exactly as filmed."

of this [*Outlaw* ballyhoo]," warned Kahn. "One false step can crack the entire spinal column." The backbone in question was not, for once, the protection from political censorship afforded by the Breen Office, but the privileges the major studios enjoyed as a coddled wartime industry. With Hughes squandering energy on a smarmy vanity project, Hollywood's enviable access to scarce resources such as film stock, technical equipment, and gasoline might be called into question by less-favored home front industries. Wartime Hollywood staked its reputation on bond rallies and stars in uniform, on stirring flag-wavers like *Mrs. Miniver* (1942) and *This Is the Army* (1943), not garish premieres and lavish press junkets.

Again, *The Outlaw* went to ground. When Hughes released the film three years later, the postwar zeitgeist was ready to embrace its featured attractions.

In 1946, for the third time, Hughes fired up the publicity machine, again with Birdwell at the levers. The photo spreads and pinup pictures from 1941 and 1943 were republished, the double and single entendres were reprinted, and fresh stunts were cooked up especially for the re-release. Birdwell's most inspired brainstorm linked what Hughes and Russell were each best known for. With peacetime fuel to burn, the ad-pub wizard hired skywriting airplanes to buzz over southern California, writing out "The Outlaw," and then tracing two enormous circles with a dot in the middle of each.

Lip-smacking come-ons and outré stunts were venerable Hollywood traditions, but Birdwell's exploits went beyond anything the major studios had cooked up since the pre-Code era. "The whole campaign of this picture is a disgrace to the industry and I am on the verge of publicly attacking Howard Hughes with a blast in the newspapers," Darryl F. Zanuck wrote Breen. He and Breen had had their disagreements over the years, but the liberal producer and the conservative censor saw eye to eye on the ads for *The Outlaw*. "The major companies make many mistakes, but I have never seen any major company resort to such cheap vulgarity as this," groused Zanuck.

None of the taglines, photographs, or stunts had been approved by the Advertising Code Administration, a branch of the MPAA administratively distinct from the Breen Office but whose surveillance of hem and bust lines was no less rigid. What disturbed the MPAA—and infuriated Breen—was that Hughes's ad campaign repeated the false claims made in 1943 about *The Outlaw* being screened "exactly as filmed," without cuts, without deletions demanded by the MPAA Board.[7] Back in 1943, Breen and the MPPDA Board had let the matter slide: the slander became a moot point after Hughes withdrew the film and pulled down the advertising. Now Hughes was persisting in printing the calumnies in the revived publicity campaign. Breen could not suffer the defiance thrown in his face every time he looked at the newspaper ads—nor could the MPAA, whose self-regulatory regime depended upon the integrity of the Code Seal. Compelled to respond, the MPAA charged Hughes with highlighting "misleading statements to the ef-

7. Breen and Francis Harmon also suspected that Hughes was playing fast and loose with the print, sneaking in reels from the original unapproved print of *The Outlaw* with reels from the PCA-approved print stamped with the Code Seal in the titles.

Lawless territory: Jane Russell, in one of her more demure poses, with Jack Buetel in Howard Hughes's *The Outlaw* (1943).

fect that *The Outlaw* was finally approved under the association's Production Code with no deletion therefrom." Hughes was told to stop billing his Code-approved film as non-Code approved.

When Hughes refused to submit or reedit the ads, the MPAA held him in violation *not* of the Production Code, whose seal he had obtained in 1941, but of the Advertising Code, whose tenets he was violating in 1946. "Disapproved and unsubmitted advertising in exploiting *The Outlaw* . . . constitutes grounds for expulsion from the association [the MPAA]," the MPAA informed Hughes. It was Breen, however, who was given the privilege and pleasure of delivering the ultimatum:

> You are hereby requested to surrender immediately Certificate of Approval #7440 issued for *The Outlaw* [in 1941] and to remove the seal of the Association from all prints of the motion picture within seven days of this request.

With a deep stubborn streak backed by deep pockets, Hughes dug in his heals and lashed out with lawyers, suing the MPAA for $5,000,000 and triple damages, later upping the ante to $7,500,000. "The entire Hays Office, in its very essential fundamentals, is a group boycott, in restraint of trade, and in absolute violation of the anti-trust laws of this country," asserted Hughes, arguing a point that the Department of Justice was to win two years later. He then resigned from the MPAA, declaring "It was about time people quit trying to tell the American public what it can see, read, and listen to."

Though Hughes's inbred orneriness was reason enough to defy the MPAA, his grievances dated back to *Scarface* in 1932. "The Hays Office of that day [the Studio Relations Committee] demanded that I re-shoot a lot of the picture before they would give it a seal," he told Billy Wilkerson at the *Hollywood Reporter*. "I did [the re-shooting] at a cost of $150,000. The money meant nothing, but the story material eliminated on their order about wrecked my picture. I was willing to bow to their desires, but look what happened. Only a few weeks after the release of my picture, MGM released *Red Headed Woman* [1932], which made the original version of my picture look like a religious picture by comparison."[8] Now, Hughes felt, the double standard was being repeated with another red-headed woman, Rita Hayworth. "Have you read the ads for Columbia's *Gilda* [1946]?" he demanded. "There's hardly a line in any of my ads or a photograph as suggestive as those ads. So why pick on me?"[9] Replied the MPAA: "*The Outlaw* campaign differs from the others because it is the only one based entirely on nothing but the star's outsize anatomy."

For the multimillionaire tool-and-aircraft magnate to pose as the put-upon little guy battling the big bad majors may seem a stretch, but to Hollywood Hughes was the maverick outsider, dabbling in a sideline that was the bread and butter of the moguls and jamming up the works. Worse, besides disrupting normal business practices, a lightning rod like *The Outlaw* stalled any movement toward liberalization. When all was quiet on the censorship front, the Breen Office might relax its grip. When tabloid headlines stirred up the sleepy censorship boards and bluenoses, the Breen Office felt compelled to tighten the reins.

Thus, far from being lionized for defying the MPAA, Hughes was slammed for playing with fire. "It's not good showmanship or good business to disregard an entire industry's precepts in self-regulation," lectured *Variety* editor Abel Green in a rare bylined editorial headlined "Hughes Is

---

8. Hughes misremembered the pre-Code censorship process (no Code Seals were granted until 1934), but he had a point. Among the most scandalous sex farces of the pre-Code era, MGM's *Red Headed Woman* featured a slinky Jean Harlow seducing her way into furs and fortune. In the last scene, set in Paris, she cuddles with her latest sugar daddy in the back seat of a chauffeur-driven Rolls Royce—unrepentant, unpunished, luxuriating in the wages of sin. Before the fade-out, she winks into the rear-view mirror at her studly chauffeur.

9. Though no less voluptuous than the raven-haired Jane Russell, the red-headed Rita Hayworth delivered her smoldering gaze standing, not reclining, in a gown with décolletage measured to the Breen line, and the only cylinder smoking in her hands was a cigarette.

Wrong." Precisely *because* Hughes was identified with Hollywood in a way that the marginal independents weren't, his actions had "an invidious effect on the rest of the picture business." To Hollywood, Hughes may have been a troublemaking interloper, but to main street America he was motion picture royalty.

Hughes ignored the counsel to back down and play ball. Having blocked the MPAA with a court injunction, he launched *The Outlaw* into limited release.

As Birdwell fanned the flames, the MPAA and Hughes scuffled in the press and in the courts. In point of fact, the defendant had more to lose than the plaintiff. In 1946, with box office revenues soaring and theater attendance at 90 million per week, an endless flow of cash into studio coffers beckoned on the postwar horizon. As the strongest bulwark against state and federal censorship, the Code remained Hollywood's best insurance policy for continued prosperity. "The [MPAA] must protect its Code, must continue to control its producer members, for otherwise the whole foundation of the production of pictures will be kicked right out from under the industry," Billy Wilkerson reminded readers who understood that the grandstanding by the mule-headed Hughes threatened to ruin the racket for everyone. "It takes something like *The Outlaw* to start a crusade," warned Jack Bryson, legislative director for the MPAA, ever mindful of the last crusade.

Fortunately for Hollywood, Washington was willing to let the MPAA police its own. If the Breen Office was a conspiracy in restraint of indecent trade, that was okay with the U.S. Department of Justice, which "without question" backed the civic-minded, morally sound policy of self-regulation set up by the MPAA. "*The Outlaw* tends to encourage the evils being fought by the Department of Justice," a spokesman confirmed, perhaps under the illusion he was speaking about a crime film.

Yet except for the DOJ and the MPAA, Americans were having a roaring good time with the tussle over Russell. Headline writers bested Birdwell with salacious wordplay, comedians threw punch lines, and columnists smirked and rolled their eyes. Even the staid *Reader's Digest* joked about a quiz show contestant who replied to the question, "What are California's twin peaks?" with "Jane Russell." On the radio program *Ozzie and Harriet* six-year-old Ricky Nelson was growing up fast. "All right," says Ricky after reluctantly agreeing to loan some money to his nine-year-old brother David. "But I was saving it for something important. I was going to see Jane Russell in *The Outlaw*."

Hughes and his lawyers were not to join in the laughter, at least not in court. On June 14, 1946, Judge John D. Bright of the U.S. District Court in New York upheld the right of the MPAA to revoke the Code Seal for *The*

Outlaw. Writing in a dense legalese that trumped Birdwell's ad-pub lingo, he ruled:

> The advertising now in controversy consists of pictures, cut, and lithographs of the lady 'Rio' (Jane Russell), featuring more her breasts, legs, and positions than the saga of Billy the Kid, and using the words "Exactly as it was filmed—Not a Scene Cut."

Judge Bright gaveled down the obvious decision:

> As to the words "exactly as it was filmed—not a scene cut," I can see no fair reason for interfering with the rejection [of the Code Seal]. They are not true.

If Hughes wanted to retain the Code Seal, he needed to comply "with the conditions upon which the Seal was granted."

The defenders of the Breen Office were jubilant. Not only had the court case been won, but they could lord their superior wisdom over the MPAA, whose Board of Directors had made the devil's bargain back in 1941. "It is obvious that the compromise by which the Seal was issued, against the judgment of the Production Code Administration, should not have been made—that if it was made for the avoidance of controversy and litigation, it has failed," Terry Ramsaye gloated. Now that Hughes had reneged on the ill-advised deal, condign punishment demanded that the MPAA revoke the Code Seal—forthwith and permanently.

At this juncture, with *The Outlaw* controversy splashing across front pages from coast to coast, Hughes's aerial vocation broke into the action. On July 7, 1946, the tycoon-producer-pilot nearly died when the experimental plane he was flying crashed into a Beverly Hills neighborhood. Rescued from the burning wreckage, he walked into the emergency room of a nearby hospital and, without benefit of screenwriter, ad-libbed a memorable curtain line. "I am Howard Hughes," he gasped. He then collapsed.

After waiting a decent interval, the MPAA carried out its sentence. On September 13, 1946, acting on instructions from Eric Johnston, Breen notified Hughes that *The Outlaw* no longer possessed a Code Seal. The official reason was not Jane Russell's two good reasons but Hughes's refusal, in open defiance of MPAA regulations, to conform to the Advertising Code. That is, the advertising that falsely claimed the Code-approved film was not Code-approved rendered it non-Code approved.

"The only thing I have to say about *The Outlaw* is this: the censors may not like it but the public does," declared an unbowed Hughes. "If the Hays

Office is going to try to keep the American public from seeing this picture which the public wants to see, then it appears to me that the Hays Office is assuming a great deal of responsibility."

Stripped of the Code Seal, *The Outlaw* was too hot to handle for studio-affiliated theaters, but just the ticket for hard-pressed independent exhibitors. From big cities to remote backwaters, the film moseyed across the territories and made a killing. Backed by Hughes's checkbook, riding a wave of publicity, booked by exhibitors willing to risk studio ire and civic hassles for a surefire box office hit, the single deviance that was *The Outlaw* thrived, racking up a "terrific box office swell," said a chagrinned *Variety*, despite "being banned by censors and panned by critics."

Eventually, taking his own sweet time, Hughes made the film safe for the studio-affiliated houses too. In October 1949, after *The Outlaw* had played for years in independent venues, he resubmitted the film—and the advertising campaign—to the MPAA, whereupon its original Code Seal (PCA No. 7440) was reissued. Thus, the most notorious renegade film of the 1940s was finally roped and branded.

In the end, both sides could claim victory: Hughes because he secured over 4,000 playdates and grossed an estimated $3,050,000 for his non-Code film, the MPAA because it established its lawful authority both to issue and retract a Code Seal.[10] "If we stay within the boundaries of the Production Code, we need have no fear that our freedom of expression will be curtailed, but if we do not do so, there is no question at all that we will have censorship—Federal Censorship—thrust upon us," declared Eric Johnston, raising the familiar bugaboo. "With the whole world slipping down Laxity Lane, the screen must hold fast to its standards of decency and good taste."

Johnston's curious defense raised two impolite questions. If the whole world was slipping down Laxity Lane, why was the screen still holding fast to antique standards of decency and good taste? And how long before Hollywood too veered from the straight and narrow?

10. In 1950, *The Outlaw* broke into *Variety's* list of the top 20 all-time box office hits with gross receipts estimated at $5,075,000. In June 1951, Hughes formally ended his antitrust suit against the MPAA.

12

INVASION OF THE ART FILMS

In 1946, on the resonant date of July 15, Joseph I. Breen met the reliably irritable British press corps. He had traveled to London at the invitation of the British producer and corporate brand name J. Arthur Rank to expound upon the Production Code for the British Film Producers' Association. "I do hope it will be possible for you to spare him for this trip as our members would be glad to meet him and hear at first hand the principles and details of your Code," Rank cabled Eric Johnston, the recently installed president of the Motion Picture Association of America. The globally minded Johnston readily agreed, expressing confidence that "Mr. Breen's visit will serve further to strengthen the cooperation and friendly relations between the British and American motion picture interests." With the war over, both sides of the pond felt that a better understanding of Breen Office protocols would facilitate the trans-Atlantic motion picture trade. Moreover, by smoothing the entry of British films into the American marketplace, the MPAA hoped to forestall import quotas from an island chafing under Hollywood's heel.

As the most lucrative overseas market for Hollywood's product line, the British required special solicitude. Breen maintained a hectic schedule: granting interviews, visiting studios, and conferring with his British counterpart, J. Brooke Wilkinson, chief of the British Board of Film Censors. Basking in the glow of Anglo-American comity, the Hollywood envoy gave an informal once-over to a dicey project from Gainsborough Productions entitled *The Wicked Lady* (1946), a costume drama that had earlier been denied a Code Seal due to "the breasts of several of the women [being], in our judgment, unduly and indecently displayed." Breen reexamined the rippling bodices and suggested retakes with alternate camera angles. "You have a very good picture," he told his hosts. "If it can be made reasonably acceptable for the American market, you have a great money maker."

True to form, the Fleet Street regulars peppered Breen with hostile questions, resentful not just of Hollywood hegemony over the British Isles but suspicious that the Irish-American censor harbored a tribal antipathy toward British cinema. Pointing to Code-stretching material such as Preston Sturges's *The Miracle of Morgan's Creek* (1944), a wartime farce where a very pregnant party girl needs to snare a surrogate husband; Fritz Lang's *Scarlet Street* (1945), a sordid film noir trafficking in adultery, murder, and a cynical portrait of the sacred institution of marriage; and Tay Garnett's version of James M. Cain's *The Postman Always Rings Twice* (1946), an equally sordid film noir trafficking in adultery, murder, and a cynical portrait of the American legal system, the Brits claimed Breen blocked the door to imported labels that the domestic brand waltzed right through. Rank himself had recently been forced to shoot two endings to his thriller *Bedelia* (1945)—one in which the culpable heroine commits suicide (non-Code) and one in which she is punished by the authorities (ur-Code).

Breen patiently defended his decisions, placating if not exactly charming the British journalists. He bantered good-naturedly about *Forever Amber* (1947), Twentieth Century-Fox's forthcoming costume drama inspired by Kathleen Winsor's ribald novel about a saucy serving wench with ample charms and naked ambition.

"How can you make *Forever Amber*?" carped the Brits.

"I was afraid that was going to come up," Breen sighed. "Remember the chapters on the fire of London and the great plague?"

"But you wouldn't go to *Forever Amber* to see the fire of London or the plague," scoffed the reporters.

"Well, confidentially," Breen stage whispered, "that is what you're going to see."

"That's taking money under false pretences!"

"That's one school of thought," he grinned.

Despite the coyness, Breen was on his best behavior. He now wore two hats and had two agendas: advocate for America's morality as director of the PCA and spokesman for Hollywood's economic interests in his postwar role as MPAA vice president. "Nothing but good can arise from this frank exchange of views, especially since the American representative was of Mr. Breen's caliber," beamed Rank. Breen saluted Rank in kind. "Many of the details that were causing difficulty between the British and American industries were ironed out, and henceforth I am sure there will be a better understanding of each other's problems." Once explained, the Code made eminently more sense than the judgments rendered by the capricious British Board of Film Censors, which tended to base its decrees on vague upper-crust notions of "common decency."

A visit to the colonies: Breen with British actor James Mason and his wife, Pamela Kellino, on a film set at Denham Studios in Buckinghamshire, UK, August 3, 1946.

(GETTY IMAGES)

Back in the States, Breen repeated the old adage about the Anglo-American relationship being a tale of two peoples separated by a common language. "Certain expressions which are perfectly harmless over there have an altogether different meaning here," he observed, and vice versa. While the Yanks blanched at "damn" and "bastard," the Brits balked at "bum" and "bloody." In matters of film content too, British eccentricities perplexed the American. "In a picture going to England you can't show a doctor operating on a patient, nor can the Lord's prayer be said, nor can there be any scenes showing what they call sacramental ceremonies such as a priest hearing confession," he explained. Of course, that last peculiarity—the suppression of Catholic ritual by British censors—was a special irritant.

The Brits might have responded that their American cousins were also a bit queer: not only was the title of Rank's *The Rake's Progress* (1945) changed to *The Notorious Gentleman* for stateside marquees in 1946, but an entire scene needed to be refilmed to clear Breen Office customs. Playing a college prankster, Rex Harrison climbs a university tower and plants a chamber pot on the spire. "This enameled utensil should not be a chamber pot," ordered the ever coprophobic Breen. The scene was reshot with a top hat replacing the chamber pot.

Summing up his trip abroad, Breen expressed gratitude for his cordial reception and shrugged off the sniping from the British press. "I'm sure they were disappointed," he smiled. "I appeared miscast to them as a bluenose. I am too fat and too genial."

Yet on the personal front Breen was not playing the genial fat man. Soon after his return from Europe, he was racked by the intestinal ailments that had afflicted him since the mid-1920s, conditions aggravated by stress, overwork, and smoking. First in November 1946 and again in May 1947, he underwent major abdominal surgery. After his second setback, he made an urgent appeal to Eric Johnston for time off from the job. "Since last November [1946], I have made two trips to the hospital and have undergone two serious abdominal operations," he informed his boss. "I have come through it all, I think, with flying colors; but my doctors are of the opinion that, despite the fact that I feel well—and appear *to be* well—I ought to get away from here for a while." Breen requested a three-month sabbatical from Code work, not just for his own health but for the benefit of Judge Stephen S. Jackson, who had been brought on board in April 1947 to be groomed as successor.

On paper, Judge Jackson possessed an impressive résumé for a substitute Breen. A former justice of the New York Domestic Relations Court, the prominent, 48-year-old lawyer was considered an expert on the problem of juvenile delinquency, the up-and-coming social menace of the postwar era. His religious pedigree was also impeccable. A graduate of Holy Cross College and Harvard Law School, Jackson served as professor of social legislation at Fordham University and legal adviser for Catholic charities in New York. No ivory tower liberal, he had led campaigns against striptease shows and girlie magazines in Times Square. Credentialed in law, Catholicism, and media surveillance, Jackson seemed the perfect solution to the problem of succession at the PCA.

The plan was for Jackson, guided by experienced Code staffers, to ease into command by chairing the morning huddles and presiding over meetings with producers. Breen would rest up at home and check in as needed. Unfortunately, Judge Jackson was accustomed to aggressive cross-examination and gaveling down edicts from the bench. Having the statutes—that is, the Code—on his side, he assumed he could simply lay down the law rather than dance the Breen Office shuffle. The process of negotiation—the give-and-take during the script review phase, the mutual respect for each other's line of work, and the friendly horse-trading—was not suited to his judicial temperament. Producers grumbled that the new guy was not right for the job, that the office needed someone more flexible and film-smart, someone more like—Joe Breen. They preferred a fellow shyster to a hanging judge.

Asked by Eric Johnston how Jackson was faring at the job, Breen offered formal support ("I think he is doing very well") and hedged his bets. "The work, as you know, is not easy," he reminded Johnston. "The problems which come up from day to day are difficult, and involved, and confusing." Moreover, having long dealt with Breen, producers tended to look to him as final arbiter on close cases. Remembering how the moguls had once tried to go over his head to Will Hays, Breen backed Jackson—up to a point.

The point was *Letter from an Unknown Woman* (1948), a mawkish farrago of doomed/forbidden love, suitably punished, set in fin de siècle Vienna and elegantly directed by temporary French import Max Ophuls. Universal producer William Gordon had played by the rules and spent three years conscientiously shepherding the project though the Breen Office until hitting a brick wall with the intransigent Jackson. Unless the heroine recited verbatim a self-flagellating mea culpa, penned by Jackson himself, no Code Seal would be forthcoming. A livid Gordon called Breen, and Breen pulled rank and overruled the judge. "I have just talked with Mr. Breen about *Letter from an Unknown Woman*," a chastened Jackson informed Gordon. "He advised me that it is his opinion that we should not further persist in our objection to the picture. While that is not in accordance with my view, I, of course, yield to Mr. Breen's decision."

While the understudy garnered bad reviews, rumors of Breen's departure swirled around Hollywood, further unnerving an industry already battered by the House Committee on Un-American Activities, the Department of Justice, and television. With a crisis over censorship and succession the last thing the MPAA needed on its worry list, Johnston prevailed upon Breen to stay on. By mutual agreement, Judge Jackson would return to the less disputatious profession of law. Cornered by a *Variety* reporter in New York, Breen confirmed the good news. "I have no early plans to resign my office. Those reports you hear simply emanated from the fact that I've been sick for a while." Pressed to elaborate, Breen said only, "I'm getting pretty old." He was just shy of sixty.

In lending the reins to Jackson, Breen was not experiencing his second seven-year itch: he was genuinely unwell and, as usual, overworked. Moreover, intimations of his own mortality merged with suspicions that the Code regime was also losing stamina, weakening at the margins, its enemies making slow but steady inroads.

For Breen, the triumphant trip to Britain was a charmed interlude emblematic of the ordained imperial relationship: Hollywood, the power base for a great cinematic empire purveying Catholic morality; the rest of the world a colonial outpost teeming with paying customers and potential converts. At the same time, however, his diplomatic mission was also a recognition that the client states were getting restless. Though the superpower citadel was hardly under siege by foreign invaders, postwar Hollywood detected rumblings in the provinces and burrowings into the homeland. Long-dormant motion picture industries, overrun by Hollywood in the 1930s and flattened by war in the 1940s, began to awaken and stir. The upsurge in profile and profits from a once marginal market became serious competition—not just to Hollywood's box office receipts, but to the moral universe of the Breen Office.

THE SWANK APPEAL OF THE ART HOUSE

At first in a handful of theaters in New York, Chicago, and Los Angeles, and then slowly spreading into medium-sized cities and university towns, a new kind of exhibition venue sprang up on the motion picture circuit. Marketing innovation and lifestyle choice, the site was dubbed the art house. Described in the trade press as "small, intimate houses with low overhead where pictures are good for long runs," the art house catered to an upscale audience seeking "better" (or at least non-Hollywood) pictures on a single bill, without the wraparound clutter of newsreels, cartoons, and shorts. Often too the theaters were willing to forgo that other mark of Hollywood programming, the Code Seal.

Like a verdant oasis amid the arid monotony of Warners, Paramount, and Fox theaters, the art house blossomed in the postwar era. "Out-of-the-ordinary features are going into neighborhoods and towns where there was a prejudice against them hardly a year ago," *Box Office* reported in 1947, still tracking the phenomenon as a mild curiosity rather than worthy competition. By 1949, around one hundred art houses played foreign films exclusively and some 250 to 300 additional theaters booked the foreign labels intermittently. In a flush postwar economy, the demand for a diversity of consumer choices in motion pictures no less than in household appliances sustained a niche market for a product line manufactured outside of Hollywood.

Not since the silent era, which, at least linguistically, practiced no discrimination against foreign language cinema, had Hollywood faced competition from nonnative speakers. Though a small tangential trade in foreign cinema, mainly German and Yiddish language fare, defied the English-only policy, eking out an existence off the main distribution track and out of Code purview, even that limited market share shrank after Nazism extinguished the export market from Germany. The only players on the board were the occasional French *succès d'estime*, such as Jean Renoir's *Grand Illusion* (1937) and Julien Duvivier's *Pépé le Moko* (1937), or the more numerous imports from the Anglophone British, notably the distinctive *oeuvre* from a quirky Londoner named Alfred Hitchcock, himself imported in 1939 by David O. Selznick. Whatever the country of origin, the competitors were but gnats buzzing around the Hollywood behemoth.

After WWII, however, foreign films began to attract a growing audience of self-imposed exiles from the Hollywood imperium. Like so much else, the phenomenon was attributed to the backfire from the war: well-traveled veterans were less forgiving of soundstage re-creations of Paris, Berlin, and Rome, and war-tempered moviegoers of all ranks were less tolerant of Breen Office versions of heaven and earth. Having developed a taste for the rigors of the social problem film, a sizable minority was willing to forgo all-American accessibility to read subtitles, endure downbeat drama, and muddle through alien film formulas. Unlike the core audience for foreign cinema in the 1930s, the postwar art house crowd was not dominated by native speakers pining for the homeland tongue but by monolingual Americans seeking an alternative to a monotonic Hollywood sound track.

Predictably, the studio hands scorned the pretensions of the non–hoi polloi. Catering to a coterie of poseurs and critics was no way to sustain a vibrant industry. The art house was "built on longhairism and snobbery," wallowed in "social bellyaches in unhappy lands," and depended on "swank appeal," sneered Terry Ramsaye, defending the establishment, as usual. Unruffled, the art house crowd pled guilty as charged to being snooty connoisseurs. Unlike the common rung of doltish Hollywood fans who represented "an intellectual level closer to infantile mewling and puking than to adulthood," the art house "depends upon the above-average and mature audience" and never underestimates "the intelligence and taste of [its] patrons," drawled the manager of the Georgetown Theater in Washington, D.C.

As financial competition, foreign films were more annoyance than menace. The percentage siphoned off from the yearly domestic box office revenues never broke out of the low single digits. Demographically, the art house aficionado and the nabe regular may not even have overlapped. However, in the coin of cultural capital, foreign cinema threatened Hollywood's domestic tranquility simply by offering an alternative to the studio system monopoly—and an alluring, respectable alternative at that. An estimated 25,000,000 American "non-theatergoers" who turned up their noses at the set menu of the studios "may be snared by pix originating outside of Hollywood's domain," warned *Variety* in 1947. "Although foreign films still aren't getting much playing time in most cities, the fact that they [have] caught on to such a great extent in certain of the keys [choice metropolitan markets] indicates the public wants a change from the standard type of pictures now turned out in Hollywood."

At the art house, the gleam of status shimmered next to the beacon of art. The high-end imports were not seedy exploitation flicks from fly-by-night indies or dreary Soviet agit-prop screened by Communist Party study groups, but quality labels stylishly stitched with a chic European logo. The dribble of foreign films—first from Britain, then Italy and France, eventually Japan and Sweden—soon grew to a steady stream that rocked the complacency of planet Hollywood. "Times are certainly changing," declared *Box Office* in 1947. "Up to the time *Henry V* [1944; U.S. release 1946] demonstrated that it could make money without ever going near a first run theater, it was the practically unanimous verdict of distributors that Shakespeare was one of those luxuries that they could do without." In 1948 the British import *Hamlet* struck a body blow against the empire by garnering ecstatic critical praise, doing solid business on a hard-ticket basis, and grabbing the year's Best Picture Oscar. "Certainly the *Hamlet* award was a jolt to many of

Art house hit and Oscar winner: Gertrude (Eileen Herlie) and Claudius (Basil Sydney) hover over the melancholy Dane (Laurence Olivier) in Olivier's *Hamlet* (1948).

us," admitted studio loyalist Billy Wilkerson at the *Hollywood Reporter*, resolving to brush up his Shakespeare.

Even before the postwar wave, foreign cinema had confronted the Breen Office with unique problems. Where the processing of studio product was streamlined and standardized, the Code regulation of foreign cinema was clunky and haphazard. Unable to blue-pencil offensive material during the script phrase, the Breen Office did censorship the old-fashioned way: eyeballing the release print and ordering deletions. It could dictate but not guide; demand a scene be cut out, but not edited in. The impact of the Code on the moral universe of foreign cinema was all negative.

Back in the 1930s, with Hollywood set on the straight and narrow, Breen had hoped to remedy the foreign situation by expanding his hegemony beyond the three-mile limit. "The Code [should] be adopted and universally accepted throughout the world," he figured, in order to "bring about uniform standards of acceptability outside the United States." A British, French, or Chinese Joe Breen would give the Code a moral protectorate spanning the globe.

Needless to say, the scheme for world domination by the Breen Office was a pipe dream. Prevented from policing foreign morals in remote Hollywood, Breen made do with the role of customs inspector. In 1935 the MPPDA set up a branch office of the PCA in New York to handle American films produced on the East Coast and to clear foreign imports at the point of debarkation. A two-man shop originally staffed by Vincent Hart and James Wingate, the office facing Europe expedited the clearance process and, in some instances, preapproved British scripts. (In 1937, Hays's assistant Francis Harmon took over the East Coast branch of the PCA.) Even with the foreign film franchise, the New York branch carried a far lighter workload than the West Coast office, between 10–20 percent of the volume handled in the company town.

From a Breen Office perspective, the main trouble with foreign cinema was that it was, well, foreign. Dialogue, gestures, traditions—a whole range of censorable material whose contexts and insinuations were tagged by eagle-eyed and sharp-eared PCA staffers when reviewing Hollywood cinema—sailed over the heads of the culturally parochial Americans when looking at imported product. Even with freelance linguists hired to consult on films from France, Italy, Poland, or Sweden (in-house workhorse Geoffrey Shurlock was fluent in Spanish), the Breen Office confronted a barrier more than linguistic to ensure that certain meanings *were* lost in translation. Unlike Hollywood filmmakers, who abided by the Code as the price of doing business, foreign filmmakers had little incentive to work under the glare of a distant pair of American eyes. As a result, British comedies,

French costume dramas, and Italian neorealism trafficked in images, language, and values banished from the American screen since 1934.

Little matter. Before World War II, foreign films were too scarce and obscure to foment a moral crisis. Though deemed something of a "headache," the flow of imports into the heartland was a trickle, too minor to cause concern. Code-wise, the nation's borders were secure.

The singular, notorious exception was Gustav Machaty's *Ecstasy* (1933), featuring the actress Hedy Kiesler (soon to be rechristened Hedy Lamarr by a smitten Louis B. Mayer) streaking nude across the Czechoslovakian countryside and miming an ecstatic orgasm in close-up, a sight so unusual that *Variety*'s befuddled male critic failed to understand what the lady was so excited about.[1] "Usual close-ups of the heroine's face during her emotional stress are extremely audacious," he puzzled.

Ecstasy laid bare the latent attraction of foreign cinema for stateside art lovers. Foreign meant flesh—décolletage, thighs, and (with luck, before the cops closed in and confiscated the print) glimpses of nudity, white female nudity. Just as Victorian gentlemen had strolled through the museums of Paris to ogle the nymphs and nudes painted by the European masters, the postwar art house lover might scope out voluptuousness covered up, even in silhouette, by the Breen Office.

Ecstasy aside, the most closely watched foreign films came from Great Britain, the only significant non-American market since the onset of sound. Over the years, British filmmakers with an eye to export learned to navigate the shoals of Breen Office censorship by remote control. Most agreed with British producer John Maxwell, who figured that any film cleared at home would easily pass muster stateside because the British Board of Film Censors was "the most narrow-minded and rigidly Puritanical in the world." In fact, one of the trademark examples of the bluenose backwardness of the Breen Office—the twin beds in the bedroom of a married couple—was an advisory caution Breen passed on from the British. "The scene of the husband and wife sleeping together in the same bed will be deleted by the British censor board," he repeatedly reminded producers. "Accordingly, we suggest you protect yourself." As late as 1947, even the Breen-approved bedroom décor in the screwball comedy *Her Husband's Affairs* (1947) did not measure up to the building codes of the British censors, who insisted that the twin beds slept in by married couple Franchot Tone and Lucille Ball be at

1. Not until 1950, under the title *My Life* and with scenes reshot under the supervision of the Breen Office, was *Ecstasy* released with a Code Seal. Lamarr appears "in a bathing suit instead of the altogether," reported a disappointed reviewer.

least twelve inches apart. Two days of retakes cost $30,000—or $2,500 per inch.

Nonetheless, the postwar Brits were untwisting their knickers in other areas. Despite the smiles all around during Breen's London trip, British films were getting less chaste and more cheeky. "British pix are having some rough sledding at the Joe Breen office lately on their way to U.S. theaters," *Variety* reported in 1947. "The Anglo view of what's the right thing in a pic [continues] to vary widely with that of the Yanks—or at least to those manning the bulwarks of the Production Code." Among the provocations were *Pink String and Sealing Wax* (1946), a murderous lark that ended "without the surcease enjoined by the Code"; *My Heart Goes Crazy* (1946), a musical comedy that included a "pansy" vaudeville routine by comic Sid Field; and *Fanny by Gaslight* (1944), a costume drama featuring a scene in a brothel and whose title was changed to *Man of Evil* to preclude dorsal connotations stateside.

For the first time since 1934, however, sidestepping rather than surrendering to the Breen Office was a way to avoid clearing American customs. Not being chained to the major studios, the art house offered a safe haven where the Code Seal was not a precondition for exhibition. In fact, the lack of a Code Seal, the mark of American provincialism, was a magnet for the art house crowd. Who knew what those wanton foreigners might unspool?

More than a rival storefront selling offshore wares, then, the art house was an architectural stake into the heart of the studio system. Back in 1934, the original agreement setting up the PCA had stipulated that affiliated exhibitors who screened films without a Code Seal were subject to a $25,000 fine—a clause that made Breen a surly gatekeeper to the exclusive, members-only club that was the Hollywood oligopoly. In 1941, when the Department of Justice first deemed the cozy setup a violation of the Sherman Anti-Trust Act, the MPPDA was left in the untenable position of arguing that the Hollywood studio system was not what it manifestly was, a monopoly in restraint of trade. The $25,000 fine provision was a signed confession of the steel links binding production, distribution, and exhibition. On March 30, 1942, belatedly realizing its legal exposure, the MPPDA rescinded the $25,000 threat over exhibitors and applied it instead to the studios in their role as distributors.

Whether levied at exhibitors or distributors, the $25,000 question was a distinction without a difference.[2] For independents seeking to break out of the art house ghetto, a Code Seal was a transit visa into more desirable

2. When foreign films were imported by the distribution arms of the major studios, the Breen Office exacted the same control over foreign films as domestic films.

neighborhoods. As long as the studios controlled the exhibition chains—either through outright ownership or off-the-books pressure—foreign films bumped into a very low ceiling of profitability. "If foreign producers come over here and expect to do business with their films, particularly in the commercial houses, they'll just have to conform," said a smug MPAA official.

The power to deny access to the choice commercial houses was Breen's trump card against films, foreign or domestic, that snubbed a Code Seal. "In the case of foreign pictures, subject matter and treatment have been in violation of provisions of the Production Code due to the depiction of incidents ranging from condonation of lying to homosexuality, rape, and incest," he noted in an in-house memo to Johnston in 1949. "Nothing in reality stands in the way of Hollywood producers from producing pictures equivalent in subject matter and treatment to various of the foreign pictures which have gained some critical and public attention in the United States, other than the commercial realization that if such Hollywood pictures even doubled the gross income of equivalent foreign pictures the income would not be sufficient to repay the producer for half the cost of production." Although Americans seemed increasingly willing to read subtitles—and gawk at foreign flesh—the number of venues welcoming a non-Code infiltrator from abroad was limited.

Yet just as a handful of scrappy independent producers in the 1930s had defied the MPAA's monopoly, independent distributors and exhibitors of art films in the postwar era bridled at the studio chokehold. Arthur L. Mayer, manager of the Rialto Theater in Times Square and a pioneer importer of foreign films, had knocked heads with the PCA since the 1930s—not with Breen but with his opposite number on the East Coast, Francis Harmon. "As an independent distributor whose pictures have been occasionally denied bookings in affiliated theaters through the edicts of the Code Administrator, I cannot regard such boycotts with your cheerful faith in their divine origin, nor do I agree that my failure to secure a seal necessarily brands me as a lecherous old rascal engaged in peddling pornographic propaganda," he wrote when Harmon demanded that the moody French melodrama *Pépé le Moko* be cut before a Code Seal could be issued in 1941.

After 1945, however, the presumptive right of the Breen Office to regulate the flow of imports was challenged by a powerful and expanding constituency. The boom in the art house market and the respectability of the product stream created a movie-minded special-interest group that, while less regimented and more diffuse than the vast congregations of the Legion of Decency, was no less passionate about film. An elite regiment of critics, undergraduates, and upscale consumers was willing to march forth to defend the integrity of Laurence Olivier's *Hamlet* or Vittorio De Sica's *The Bicycle Thief* (1948) with a righteous zeal not inspired by Howard Hughes's *The Outlaw* (1943) or David O. Selznick's *Duel in the Sun* (1947).

Throughout the postwar high renaissance of foreign cinema, the weighty purpose and daring artistry of European sophistication was a favorite bludgeon for critics to hurl at the low aspirations and trite formulas of Hollywood fluff. The art film was Shakespeare and Dickens, social seriousness and political consciousness, eros and existentialism. When the movies became art, the bluenoses who had long been snickered at became philistines who had to be beaten back. More than the social problem film (which was Code-friendly) or the film noir (which floated under the radar of the postwar intelligentsia), foreign cinema galvanized opposition to the Breen Office and emboldened Hollywood filmmakers to mount rebellions closer to home.

THE REBUKE FROM ITALIAN NEOREALISM

Greeting the Christmas season of 1949 alongside frothy holiday fare like *Adam's Rib* and *On the Town*, the Italian neorealist masterpiece *The Bicycle Thief* (1948) unspooled as a surprise gift to American moviegoers. Directed by Vittorio De Sica, the minimalist chase film was the crown jewel of a cinematic style born in the ashes of postwar Italy, a stunning achievement that deeply moved almost everyone who saw it: audiences to tears, critics to superlatives, and filmmakers to imitation.

The path for *The Bicycle Thief* had been paved by Roberto Rossellini's *Open City* (1945) and *Paisan* (1946) and De Sica's own *Shoeshine* (1946), also from postwar Italy, also eye-opening slices of life and lessons in on-location, under-the-gun ingenuity. Collectively, in story and style, the neorealist films were the antithesis of studio-system quality control, a wrenching jolt from the gloss of the soundstage and the comforts of formula, all the more praiseworthy for having risen from the ruins. "We must blush at our Hollywood product when war-torn Italy sends us six fine, true films made by four new directors," lamented the *New Republic*.[3]

After surmounting the obstacles to motion picture production in war-torn Italy, neorealism faced barbed-wire barriers to motion picture exhibition in sealed-up America. Reviewing *Open City*, *Variety* neatly summa-

3. The Italian films that made the *New Republic* blush were Rossellini's *Open City* and *Paisan*, De Sica's *Shoeshine* and *The Bicycle Thief*, Luigi Zampa's *To Live in Peace* (1947), and Giuseppe de Santis's *Tragic Hunt* (1948).

rized the censorship gauntlet that a foreign film had to run before finding a place on domestic screens:

> Since [*Open City*] has no play dates in major houses requiring the Production Code Administration seal, pic has not been presented for approval to the Johnstonites. It's got plenty to make them blanch if and when it is shown them, although the New York State censor board okayed it with insignificant scissorings. Principal sympathetic femme character speaks openly of her pregnancy, although she's not wed, and the traitoress who leads to the capture and death of the partisans betrays them for a combination of cocaine and the love of a lesbo German spy. That's just a sample of the angles for the PCA to mull, while the handling of the priest will no doubt make the Legion of Decency gulp hard, although the film has been okayed by the Vatican.

Within *Variety*'s tally of tribulations was a ray of hope: the niche for foreign cinema as Hollywood counterprogramming. What repelled the Breen Office—drugs, lesbianism, and unwed motherhood—attracted the art house crowd. Also, reading the early signs of a future schism, the review discerned dissention within the censorship ranks. The New York State censors had passed *Open City* with "insignificant scissorings" and the Legion of Decency would give the film a B not a C rating. Rather than occupying the sensible center, the Breen Office stood at the extreme end of motion picture censorship.

Confounding the experts, *Open City* became a huge hit, the first of the subtitled postwar art films to demand Hollywood's attention. Playing for months, sometimes years, in a single art house, prospering through terrific word-of-mouth and the cachet of must-see status, Rossellini's behind-enemy-lines thriller, directed on location and under duress with such fidelity to time and place it was sometimes mislabeled as a documentary in soundstage-bound America, the film chronicled Italian resistance and collaboration in Nazi-occupied Rome, including the quiet courage of a priest, executed by the Nazis. Trying to account for the lucrative longevity of *Open City*, *Variety* noted the film possessed "angles to appeal to Catholics and Communists," a remark surely unique in postwar criticism.

Unlike *Open City*, *The Bicycle Thief* was not an obvious candidate for a nationwide controversy over freedom of expression. The plot is spare, the action simple, the style austere. Amid the economic and architectural devastation of postwar Rome, the unemployed sad sack Antonio (Lamberto Maggiorani, a nonprofessional actor De Sica plucked from the crowd) grabs a lucky break when his name is called for a plum job—to paste up movie posters on the facades around the city. After pawning the family's wedding linen to purchase the bicycle required for employment, the proud patriarch, now able to support his family, peddles home with his wife riding on the crossbar, astride their vehicle out of poverty.

The kernel of hope is crushed when, moments into Antonio's first workday, the bike is stolen. A pedestrian again, Antonio, with his doe-eyed son Bruno (Enzo Staiola) in tow, wanders the mean streets of the Eternal City in a frantic search for the bicycle thief.

Rome is all rubble and ruin, choking in the dustbin of its own history—crowded, claustrophobic, labyrinthine; the citizenry cold, irritable, or hostile. When the frantic Antonio looks around for help, the authorities he implores are bored, impotent, or distracted: the cops shrug, the union boss dithers, and the Church turns away. In the end, the thief escapes, the bike is lost, and the anguished Antonio, pushed beyond the limits of human suffering, becomes what he pursues and steals a bicycle. Now the slumbering mob springs to action and swarms around the cornered, cowering Antonio. Only Bruno's tearful pleas persuade the mob to release the abject bicycle thief: De Sica knows that to cart Antonio off to jail in the third act would be a blight too far, a downshift from neorealism into paleo-melodrama. The final shot shows Antonio and Bruno walking back into the belly of the city, swallowed up by the milling, uncaring crowd.

An instant classic, *The Bicycle Thief* played like a frame-by-frame refutation of the Hollywood tradition: harsh in look, downbeat in tone, bare-bones in scale, with no gorgeous stars, no happy ending, no justice on earth, and no compensating moral value.[4] In case anyone missed the point, the poster Antonio pastes to the walls of Rome advertises RKO's glitzy *Gilda* (1946), the fantasy alternative to the cosmos peddled by *The Bicycle Thief.*

As any experienced Breen watcher could predict, *The Bicycle Thief* skidded past two bright stop signs on the road to a Code Seal, each put up to deny the carnality of the body. At one point, Bruno walks into an alley to urinate against a wall, only to be interrupted before letting go. Later, Antonio bursts into what appears to be a brothel. Perhaps the brothel scene might be finessed (American moviegoers raised on Ernst Lubitsch films might not have recognized the drab décor and drabber occupants as belonging to a house of ill repute anyway), but the urination scene had to be eliminated in toto, the body being a vessel whose excremental nature was unmentionable and unsightly.

4. Decades later, the film was still doing emblematic duty as the noble art house alternative to crass Hollywood commercialism. In Robert Altman's *The Player* (1992), an idealistic screenwriter is murdered by a ruthless studio executive after a revival screening of *The Bicycle Thief.*

More bemused than outraged, De Sica refused to cut or reshoot. "[I] am astounded at the requested eliminations," he responded from Italy. In a cablegram ordering his domestic distributors to stand firm, the director referred to a well-known precedent serving as a fountain in Europe:

> As to Bruno's wall scene, once more its spirit and execution have been judged everywhere simply candid. STOP. May I recall that noble religious town of Brussels, Belgium['s] emblem is [a] boy in said circumstances whose statue stands in one of its squares. STOP.

In his face-off with the Breen Office, De Sica was fortunate in his choice of American business partners. *The Bicycle Thief* was distributed by Mayer-Burstyn, a partnership formed in 1936 between Arthur L. Mayer, operator of the Rialto Theater, a flagship art house in New York, and Joseph Burstyn, a veteran foreign film importer. Singularly and together, Mayer and Burstyn made the case for art house cinema in the press, before the MPAA Board, and eventually all the way to the U.S. Supreme Court.

Burstyn took point position for the partnership. Sensing the critical winds at his back, he waged a loud public relations campaign against the Breen Office on behalf of *The Bicycle Thief.* In private correspondence, he accused Breen of trying to "sabotage" foreign language imports to protect the major studios from international competition. "I have reluctantly come to the conclusion that there may be motives involved in your refusal to issue a seal of approval to this artistic masterpiece other than those mentioned in your [rejection] letter," he charged. "Utterly false," shot back Breen. "It is a foul and dishonest suggestion, which is unworthy of any responsible person . . . yours is the first and only charge of this nature which has ever been made against me or the integrity and honesty of the P.C.A." For the record, Breen issued a more temperate public response: "To suggest that the Production Code Administration's decisions are influenced in any way by factors other than the moral content of the pictures is sheer nonsense." He assured Burstyn that if De Sica cooperated, "the seal of approval of the PCA would be readily granted." Refusing to give an inch, Mayer-Burstyn appealed Breen's decision to the MPAA Board in New York.

Though an unlikely cause célèbre, Bruno's mimed micturation—no glimpse of genitalia or squirt of fluid soiled the screen—unleashed a torrent of headlines and commentary. Wags dubbed the vignette that Breen wanted cut and Burstyn vowed to preserve "the sacred wee-wee."

The balance of critical opinion weighed in heavily for Burstyn. Bosley Crowther, the senior film critic for the *New York Times* and a staunch champion of foreign cinema as the healthiest antidote to Hollywood pabulum, excoriated the Breen Office and the MPAA. Like Burstyn, he imputed commercial motives in Breen's suppression of "alien and adult artistry." After listing the prestigious awards won by *The Bicycle Thief*, including an Academy Award as the Best Foreign Film of 1949, he asked, "Could it be that the members of all these bodies have dirtier minds than the Code Administration and Mr. Breen?"

Fed up with all the squawking "in the name of high art and the right of a small boy to be pictured trying to wet on a fence," Terry Ramsaye dripped sarcasm over "the eternal loss to the traditions of our great art, and the scorn that the critics of the ages to come will have, if the ruthless Mr. Joseph I. Breen, Production Code Administrator, shoving his iron fist in the face of creative inspiration says 'that little boy shall not wet on the wall tonight or ever!'"

As the ink poured from the pages of the popular press, Mayer-Burstyn rode the wave of free publicity. The revamped advertising campaign for *The Bicycle Thief* showed pictures of little Bruno pleading with audiences "Please don't let them cut me out of *Bicycle Thief*!" and illustrations depicted him facing a wall, going about his business, boasting, "I'm the kid they tried to cut out of *Bicycle Thief* . . . but couldn't!"

On May 28, 1950, at a tense meeting of the MPAA Board in New York, Breen and Bursytn went mano a mano over the sacred wee-wee. Before the meeting, Burstyn telephoned Breen and "objected rather forcefully" [to the MPAA's appeal protocols] and indicated "to me that we, alone, were out of step in evaluating the general acceptability of this picture." On that, Burstyn had the Breen Office dead to rights.

Breen argued that first Bruno, then *le deluge*. "The motion picture screen will be flooded with similar scenes from now on," he claimed, straight-faced.

After viewing the picture and listening to the point-counterpoints, the MPAA Board voted to sustain Breen's decision. The Code was the law, and the tribunal could gainsay neither their enforcer nor their document, especially for a foreign import.

Again, Burstyn was urged to submit a revised version with the required deletions, whereupon a Code Seal would be promptly issued. The repeated gestures of accommodation indicate that despite public solidarity and official intransigence, Breen and the MPAA Board wanted to walk away from a losing hand. Nonetheless, De Sica and Mayer-Burstyn refused to compromise. Breen also stood pat. In the end, no Code Seal certified *The Bicycle Thief*, the most beloved art house hit of the day.

For Mayer-Burstyn, the principled stand exacted a price. "Original! Uncut! Uncensored!" bragged the ads, but the uncut and un-Sealed *Bicycle Thief* was restricted to the art houses and a handful of affiliated theaters willing to

The sacred wee-wee: an ad for Vittorio De Sica's art house cause célèbre, *The Bicycle Thief* (1948), published in 1950 at the height of the dispute between distributor Joseph Burstyn and the Breen Office.

risk the ire of the MPAA. "As a result [of having no Code Seal] . . . this world-famous picture grossed less than one-third as much as *Open City*," recalled Arthur Mayer years later, still bitter. Though Mayer-Burstyn and De Sica had won the laurels, and maybe even the argument, Breen had won the battle.

He had not, however, won the war. Art films of manifest aesthetic worth and moral sobriety, if not Catholic morality, tossed the "reasonable people" standard back in the lap of the man who had formulated it. Admittedly, the films were not suitable for children; admittedly, the films violated the Code; but (reasonable people agreed) these films were artistically and thematically substantive. *Open City* and *The Bicycle Thief* were not trafficking in Mae West's double entendres or Jane Russell's two good reasons.

Virtually alone of the agents of American censorship, Breen refused to grade foreign cinema on a curve. Even the Legion of Decency knew better than to condemn *Open City* or *The Bicycle Thief*, both of which were rated

"B," the equivalent of an "adults only" classification.[5] "All regulatory codes, particularly that of the Breen Office, are flexible to the extent that they must be interpreted," observed *Variety*, figuring that niche-market foreign films were entitled to "a freer interpretation of codes than . . . Hollywood product." Breen should follow the sensible example of his fellow censors, advised the trade paper. "Customs and state and municipal boards censors have been taking the broad view in recognition of the fact that the lingualers, playing art houses, appeal almost entirely to a sophisticated trade and get very little child attendance."

More than the social problem film or the film noir, the art film exposed the existence of a specialty audience for motion pictures—an audience not bound by the Code, an audience that sought out foreign cinema expressly to escape the Code. In calmer moments, Breen appreciated the dilemma. "If pictures cost less to make and were aimed at specialized audiences that would be a solution," he conceded. "I'd love to see that sort of thing—a chain of 3,000 to 4,000 theaters as a special outlet for adult audiences. Our trouble in this business is that we're so gaited that we try to be all things to all men—youngsters, adolescents and adults. We could treat certain themes in a more adult manner than we do now if it were not for our mixed audiences." As long as Hollywood defined itself as the consensus medium, the universal entertainment for all age groups, the Breen Office would continue to monitor and, when necessary, block the invasion of the art films.

Happily, however, even art house programming sometimes fell into line. While still licking his wounds from the bruising battle over De Sica's *Bicycle Thief*, Breen took solace from an art film with no controversial bathroom break and the best of all possible casting. "Young Tom, the baby—the boy who lost his leg at Guam—has just returned from a six-months jaunt to India," he bragged to Father Lord. "He has the star role in a Technicolor picture, directed by Jean Renoir, and carrying the title *The River* [1951]." Unaware of Tom Breen's Hollywood lineage, the great French director had selected him for the male lead in a languid colonial melodrama filmed on location in India, almost the way De Sica had plucked Lamberto Maggiorani from the streets of Rome. "Those who have seen the picture in the rough cut say it is not bad, and I hope that this report proves to be true," Breen reported with a father's pride. "Tom looks well and makes a fine appearance."

The River sailed through the Breen Office.

---

5. Despite "deceit sympathetically treated; excessive gruesomeness; suggestive costume and implications and use of narcotics," *Open City* was given the Legion's relatively lenient B rating due to Rossellini's sympathetic portrait of the heroic anti-Nazi priest Don Pietro (Aldo Fabrizi). Ultimately, the Breen Office also awarded the film a Code Seal after selective cuts, including the elimination of a shot showing an infant seated on a chamber pot.

INGRID BERGMAN: FROM ST. JOAN TO JEZEBEL

In 1948 the actress Ingrid Bergman, a luminous blend of exotic Swedish temptress and all-American corn-fed girl, was at the zenith of her Hollywood stardom. Introduced to American moviegoers in *Intermezzo* (1939), the Hollywood remake of her breakthrough Swedish film, the Nordic siren was graced with a fresh-faced beauty, natural charm, and lilting command of English that nabbed her showpiece parts in an eclectic range of A-list studio productions: the focus of WWII's most romantic love triangle in *Casablanca* (1942), the naive bride tormented by a homicidal husband in *Gaslight* (1944), the therapist with a warm beside manner in *Spellbound* (1945), the beatific nun in *The Bells of St. Mary's* (1945), and the not-really-bad girl who marries a Nazi for Cary Grant in *Notorious* (1946). With none of the glacial aloofness of her countrywoman Garbo, Bergman was the kind of girl men wanted to take home to mother—and to bed.

Not confined to the studio backlots, Bergman's incandescence also lit up the theatrical stage. For a six-month run beginning on November 18, 1946, she was Broadway's hottest ticket in a production of Maxwell Anderson's *Joan of Lorraine*, a play-within-a-play about an acting troupe rehearsing a performance of the trial and execution of the fifteenth-century French warrior-saint. Bergman was ten years too old for the role, but no one complained. Popular magazines showered her with adoring ink, and gruff theater critics swooned like smitten schoolboys. "She possesses that strange and inescapable radiance, that quality of shining honesty and unaffected warmth which adds a unique loveliness and an irresistible air of lyric simplicity and directness to everything she does," sighed Richard Watts, Jr., no easy touch, at the *New York Post*.[6]

Knowing the profit margin of celestial stardom yoked to Catholic piety, the veteran Hollywood producer Walter Wanger secured the film rights to *Joan of Lorraine*, ceding to Bergman, guided by her business-manager husband, the Swedish physician Dr. Peter Lindstrom, a goodly share of future profits. Wanger and director Victor Fleming jettisoned Anderson's artsy play-within-a-play structure for a straightforward hagiography highlighting the passion of St. Joan. As the project went into production, all the elements were in place for critical garlands and box office bounty: a beloved actress with a proven track record of saintly rectitude in two media, headlining a popular play that would be a holy obligation for millions of Catholic moviegoers.

---

6. All the male theater critics for New York's eight major daily newspapers employed the words "radiant" or "luminous" to describe Bergman's performance in *Joan of Lorraine*.

Breen was thrilled to learn that Wanger was backing a "five-million dollar Technicolor picture of St. Joan of Arc, with Ingrid Bergman as St. Joan." At a time when Hollywood was being led astray by femme fatales and buxom outlaws, a religious biopic in the spirit of *The Song of Bernadette* (1945) venerating two exemplary Catholic virgins, St. Joan and the Blessed Mother, seemed a punctual, even providential arrival. "We are all enormously interested in the undertaking, and I am hopeful that we will get out of the subject a great picture," Breen wrote to Father Lord. "Say a prayer that it comes out well."

Wanger's faith was not in the power of prayer but in what the *Hollywood Reporter* typeset as "$uper aleman$hip and $howman$hip." Under his supervision, *Joan of Arc* became the most expensive and extravagantly publicized Hollywood spectacle since *Gone With the Wind*.[7] Countless radio spots blared the news, *Life* devoted a full-color cover and ten-page layout to the film, and a blazing sign lit up Times Square with a gigantic image of Bergman, in armor as Joan, 80 feet high. Also, in what was both a coup and a portent, the gala premiere, slated for November 10, 1948, at the Victoria Theatre on Broadway, was to be telecast live by WIZ-TV.

Joan of Arc, boasted Wanger at a trade press confab prior to the official unveiling, "is not a Hollywood version of the Jeanne d'Arc legend but was made with respect to the archives and will stand the test of time." He then made an intriguing free-association. "If only J. J. McCarthy were still alive, he would know how to sell this picture to the hilt because of the spiritual message entailed." The legendary press agent Jeff McCarthy, who had supervised the Advertising Advisory Council from 1933 until his death in 1937, had also handled the publicity on a religious epic that debuted in New York twenty-two years earlier, almost to the day, *Eucharistic Congress* (1926).

Released to "a waiting world," *Joan of Arc* drew standing-room-only crowds at the recently restored 1,060-seat Victoria and settled in for a long run that would precede roadshow openings in other major cities. After a year of "hard-ticket" sales, if all went according to plan, *Joan of Arc* would then be released to the nabes "at popular prices."

Unfortunately, when the reviews came in, the New York critics were respectful but not enthusiastic. Yes, the ambition of the project was admirable, the Technicolor photography was dazzling, and the set design (clogged with a literal "cast of thousands") was astonishing—but something was missing. For all its earnestness, or maybe because of all its earnestness, *Joan of Arc* possessed neither the spirited fun of *The Bells of St. Mary's* nor the

7. The official negative cost was $4.6 million, excluding millions lavished on publicity.

spiritual uplift of *The Song of Bernadette*. Inconveniently too, the horrific ending was too emblazoned in sacred memory to be tampered with by a cliffhanger escape from the stake. Overall, the reviews were mixed enough to compel Wanger to edit the blurbs selectively in the advertising copy.

Breen's reaction was decidedly unmixed. So captivated was he—by the actress, by the saints she played for Leo McCarey and now Walter Wanger, by the prospect of a high-intensity Hollywood candle lit to female-centered Catholicism—that he broke his own house rule and shilled for the project. "Walter Wanger has recently completed the production of a motion picture based upon the life of Joan of Arc," Breen informed the syndicated columnist George E. Sokolsky, an influential political commentator greatly admired by the PCA chief. "It comes through on the screen as an utterly magnificent story of the unquestioning faith of an illiterate peasant girl who saved France from complete destruction." Perhaps, Breen suggested, Sokolsky might enjoy a private screening of the film, and "if you feel about it as I do, you could find it within the scope of your work to bring it to the attention of the readers of your daily column?"

Breen's pro bono return to flackery paid off. Sokolsky viewed the film and devoted his next column to a rave review. "As I cannot contain my emotional response to Walter Wanger's *Joan of Arc*, I have to tell you that never in all my days have I been driven to describe and praise an artistic work which, like all true art, carries with it an eternal message—the message of human liberty," wrote the tyro film critic. "Nothing that I have seen or listened to equals in beauty, in authenticity, in fine acting or emotional response of the audience to *Joan of Arc*."

"Simply magnificent!" exulted Breen in a letter of thanks to Sokolsky. "Everybody hereabouts is profoundly impressed with [your review], and it will help much, I think in the general effort which is constantly being made here by all of us to raise the tone of the pictures made in Hollywood, and to focus attention on the more important and worthwhile subjects." If *Joan of Arc* scored with Sokolsky, a rabbi's son, the Catholic-themed costume drama had all the makings of an interdenominational crossover hit, the New York critics be damned.

However, before *Joan of Arc* could be truly tested in the crucible of the marketplace, to the slack-jawed shock and heart-wrenching dismay of Wanger, Breen, and substantial portions of the American male demographic, the surefire package spontaneously combusted when the beloved star, to all appearances, took leave of her senses. In April 1949, as Wanger was nursing the release of *Joan of Arc* on a hard-ticket, roadshow basis, the halo around Ingrid Bergman dissipated under the heat of the most sensational scandal to rock Hollywood since the Fatty Arbuckle trials of 1921–22.

Saint: Ingrid Bergman in Walter Wanger's production of *Joan of Arc* (1948).

Bergman and the Italian director Roberto Rossellini were entwined in an extramarital and exceedingly public sexual affair. Intoxicated by *amore*, the lawfully wedded Bergman was making a forlorn cuckold of her devoted husband, the good Dr. Peter Lindstrom, and a motherless child of her adorable ten-year-old daughter, Pia.

Bergman had met Rossellini after writing him an effusive fan letter praising his *Open City* and *Paisan* and offering her services as "a Swedish actress who speaks English very well, who has not forgotten her German, who is not very understandable in French, and who in Italian knows only 'ti amo.'"

The Swedish actress's grasp of Italian improved markedly after Rossellini arrived in Hollywood, where he bunked at the Lindstrom's Beverly Hills home and dined out regularly with the lady of the house. Taken with the neorealist auteur as well as his aesthetic, Bergman signed on for Rossellini's next project, a stark and steamy melodrama set on Stromboli, a volcanic island off the coast of Italy. With Bergman a commodity of proven bankability, RKO contracted to finance the production and distribute the film stateside. Star and director then flew off to Stromboli.

Almost immediately, volcanic metaphors of seething passion and explosive eruption began to flow from the headlines of the tabloid press worldwide. Newspapers and magazines confirmed the unholy rumors with photographs of Bergman and Rossellini, lovebirds aglow, holding hands on Stromboli. "The star and the director looked happy indeed," winked a cutline in *Life*. Bergman denied a marital break, but the pictures didn't lie even if she did.

Walter Wanger was more concerned with his lost revenues than Bergman's lost honor. On the ropes after a string of financial setbacks, desperate to recoup an estimated $9 million investment, he watched in horror as the religious epic with the irreligious star stalled in its tracks. "One thing is pretty certain, the Bergman-Rossellini copy isn't helping *Joan of Arc*," clucked gossip columnist Herb Stein, telling Wanger nothing he didn't already know. "And who would ever have thought it of Ingrid?"

Certainly not Breen, who responded to the scandal as if Sister Benedict had doffed her habit to cavort on the burlesque stage. The Bergman-Rossellini affair, he wrote to a Jesuit friend in France, ranked as "possibly, the most shocking scandal which even Hollywood had had to contend with in many years. Miss Bergman, from the first day of her arrival here, has always conducted herself in a most commendable manner. There has never been even the slightest breath of scandal about her. She was regarded as a fine lady of unimpeachable character, a good wife, and a good mother."

Yet somehow the Italian cad had mesmerized America's adopted sweetheart:

> In some way, which nobody seems to be able to explain, immediately upon her getting into contact with Rossellini, she seems completely to have lost her head. Confidentially, I have reason to believe that, since she left here hardly more than six weeks ago, she has been living with Rossellini, and thus giving great scandal to people in all parts of the world.
>
> Her husband is utterly stricken. She sends no replies either to his letters, or to messages from her child, and frequently the report has been published that she proposes to desert her child, divorce her husband, and marry Rossellini. The whole thing is so utterly shocking that most of the people here in Hollywood are really speechless.

Breen pegged Rossellini as part mercenary Casanova, part demonic Svengali, "a thoroughly sinister character whose interest in Miss Bergman is prompted solely by the hope that, with her under his wing as a star, he can gather for himself a lot of money."

Breen beseeched his Jesuit friend on behalf of Wanger, Bergman's husband, and Bergman's attorneys to try and intervene—perhaps with the Italian government. "I dislike of course, to presume upon our friendship, to trouble you about this matter, but we are all sick and saddened about it."

On April 22, 1949, the same day that Breen tried to recruit the Society of Jesus to persuade the Vatican to strong-arm the Italian government (to do what? deport Bergman to Hollywood escorted by papal guards?), he wrote Bergman herself. Presuming to speak on behalf of the Hollywood community ("who have come to look upon you as the *first lady* of the screen—both individually and artistically"), hoping against hope that the press reports were "untrue and that they are, possibly, the result of some over-zealousness on the part of a press agent, who mistakenly believes these kinds of stories are helpful from a publicity standpoint," Breen warned Bergman that her wanton behavior could "very well *destroy your career as a motion picture artist*. They may result in the American public becoming so thoroughly outraged that your pictures will be ignored, and your box office value ruined."

Bergman's fall from grace genuinely anguished Breen. Unable to abide the thought of a wife and mother abandoning her husband and child for something as selfish as romantic love and base as sexual desire, he pleaded with the actress to assure the public—and himself—that "you have no intention to desert your child or to divorce your husband, and that you have no plans to marry anyone."

Breen closed with an impassioned plea:

> I make this suggestion to you in the utmost sincerity and solely with a view to stamping out these reports that constitute a major scandal, and may well result in *complete disaster to you personally.*
>
> I hope you won't mind my writing to you so frankly. This is all so important, however, that I cannot resist conveying to you my considered thought in the matter.

Hoping for the best, he signed off "with assurances of my esteem."

In a brief note of reply, penned in an elegant hand and datelined "Stromboli," Ingrid Bergman answered her heartsick correspondent ("Dear Mr. Breen!"). She thanked him for his "very kind letter," but sadly concluded that no statement could undo the harm already done. "I am deeply sorry to have hurt any friends involved in the pictures I have already made," she assured him. "I hope with all my heart they will not have to pay for my fault." Her valediction was gracious and affectionate. "My sincere thanks for your concern and kindness."

By the time Bergman's letter arrived on his desk, Breen had already gotten the bad news. Tired of the charade, Bergman had admitted the affair "with the stoical calm of Joan of Arc facing her destiny," as the *New York News* wrote, casting her lot "with the eccentric and unpredictable Italian movie director into whose hands she has tossed her Hollywood-built career as well as her life." When the news sunk in, a former fan, reeling from the incriminating photo layout, wrote *Life* to tell the editors, "You have disillusioned the whole of American manhood."

With Bergman unrepentant and soon divorced, pregnant, and married to Rossellini, *Joan of Arc* was a lost cause. However, *Stromboli*, the other motion picture top-lining the no-longer-sainted star, had accrued millions of dollars' worth of free publicity. Assuming the domestic release print cleared the Breen Office, perhaps *Stromboli* would recoup for Rossellini-Bergman what *Joan of Arc* had lost for Wanger-Bergman.

Despite a sense of almost personal betrayal, Breen maintained his textual fixation and issued a Code Seal to *Stromboli* after RKO obligingly cut the print to ribbons. "We saw the picture and said it did not exceed the Code," he explained stiffly. "If it was a mistake to make the picture, that is none of our business. We concerned ourself with the Code." RKO president Ned E. Depinet insisted that *Stromboli* had suffered "no major changes" despite the thirty minutes sliced from the original running time. An appalled Rossellini called the Code version a "laughable" hatchet job that made him "look like an imbecile."

Meanwhile, Bergman was being burned at the stake of American public opinion. In "the filthy loathsome pictures of Ingrid Bergman," Rep. John Rankin (D-MS) detected a plot to "destroy our American way of life." Senator Edwin C. Johnson (D-CO) branded Rossellini "an infamous Nazi collaborator," "a notorious cocaine addict," and "an associate of dope smugglers." Both politicians demanded that the MPAA amend the Production Code so films might be licensed according to the moral character of the screen performers. Unlike Representative Rankin, a fringe character reviled as a crackpot bigot, Senator Johnson wielded formidable influence as chairman of the Interstate Commerce Committee. He scheduled hearings for May 15, 1950, to probe Hollywood's morals with none other than Judge Stephen S. Jackson, bouncing back after his unfulfilling stint as Breen's heir apparent at the PCA, serving as committee investigator.[8]

For Hollywood, during the heyday of the House Un-American Activities Committee, yet another congressional circus was a must to avoid. "We are getting our ears beaten down by this terrible tragedy of Ingrid Bergman and

8. Breaking with his colleagues, HUAC member Rep. Richard Nixon (R-CA) deplored the Rankin-Johnson licensing schemes and praised the Code for having been "eminently successful in raising the moral standards of the films."

Rossellini," Breen said in the midst of the furor, his choice of words—not "scandal" or "controversy" but "terrible tragedy"—a window into his own personal distress.

On April 26, 1950, in a full-dress campaign to ward off yet more bad news from Capitol Hill, Eric Johnston, Francis Harmon, Breen, and a phalanx of studio executives conferred with Senator Johnson during a secret three-hour meeting at the MPAA's headquarters in Washington, D.C. After Breen explained the history of the Code and the ethos of self-regulation, an enlightened Senator Johnson agreed to a deal: the MPAA would adopt new advertising regulations and the senator would call off his hearings. The next day, Senator Johnson issued a statement conceding that the men of the MPAA shared his "deep convictions respecting the harm to the American people involved in the exploitation of immorality of motion picture performers." The men of the MPAA were described as "greatly relieved."[9]

On June 22, 1950, keeping its end of the bargain, the MPAA's Board of Directors met in New York and amended the Advertising Code to ban "the use of advertising that exploits the misconduct of screen personalities." Not being party to the Hollywood-Washington bargain, art houses publicized *Stromboli* with huge banners reading "Senators Say It Is Red Hot Lurid Sex!" However, despite its volcanic location and off-camera shock waves, *Stromboli* was dormant at the box office.

Also dormant was Ingrid Bergman's Hollywood career. Breen was right, at least for the short term, about the actress "ruining her box office value." Bergman was expunged from Hollywood so thoroughly that a clip of her death scene in *Joan of Arc*, included as a centerpiece moment in the industry short *History Brought to Life* (1950), was deleted after news of her affair broke.

Bergman's imported work also faced domestic barriers. "Any picture starring Ingrid Bergman and directed by Roberto Rossellini will not get a Johnston office seal," *Variety* declared, revealing that Breen had "reportedly" told distributors the ban was nonnegotiable. "Breen's refusal of a seal to any Bergman-Rossellini effort results, of course, from the bad public reaction generated last year [1949] when the actress left her former husband and daughter in Hollywood to go to Italy with the producer." Breen had no authority to deny a seal purely on the basis of cast and crew, but the pair's next collaboration, the somber but eminently uncensorable *Europa '51* (1952), was not released stateside until January 1954, in an English-dubbed

9. According to Jack Vizzard, Breen brandished a photostat of his letter to Bergman pleading with her to mend her ways, thereby convincing Senator Johnson that Hollywood had made a good-faith effort to save the wayward woman from herself.

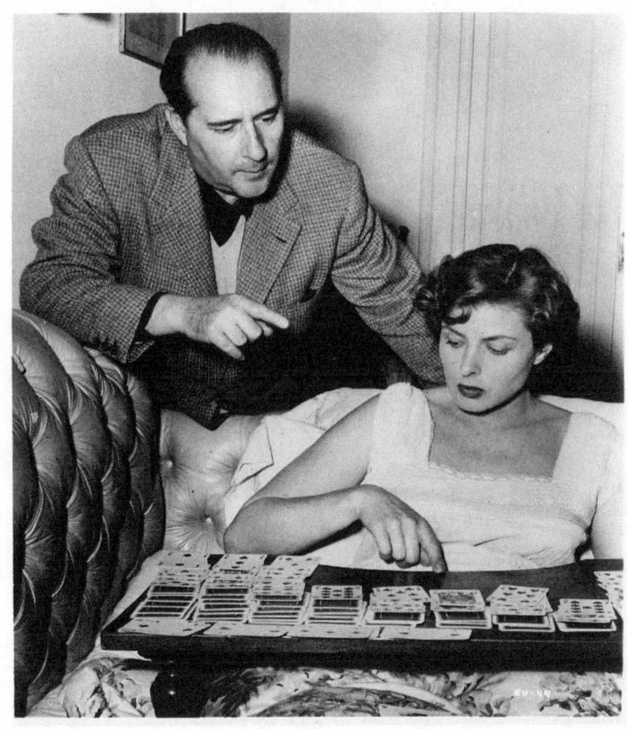

Sinner: Ingrid Bergman with director Roberto Rossellini, by then her lawful husband, on the set of *Europa '51* (1952).

version titled *The Greatest Love*, with a self-imposed "adults only" classification—and no Code Seal.

Not until 1957, after her comeback role as the sole surviving Romanov in *Anastasia* (1956), did Bergman return to America, coaxed back to accept the New York Film Critics award for Best Actress. She did not return in sack cloth and ashes. "I have never regretted the things I did," she said with her Joan-like "stoical calm." "I regret the things I didn't do." She also won the Best Actress Oscar from the Academy of Motion Picture Arts and Sciences at a ceremony she pointedly did not attend.

By then, America's rekindled infatuation with Bergman, on her own terms, was not so much an early warning sign of the breakdown of the old Hollywood codes as a confirmation of their collapse. In the intervening years, the Hollywood studio system and the moral consensus about motion picture content—the two main support beams sustaining the Production Code Administration—had each buckled. Ironically, neither the foreign film invaders nor the domestic fifth columnists had shattered the ancient regime. In fact, the lethal blow did not come from the motion picture medium at all, at least not the kind projected in theaters, art houses or otherwise.

13

AMENDING THE TEN COMMANDMENTS

In 1950 the Motion Picture Association of America minted a new slogan to herald the new decade and buck up the faint of heart. "Movies Are Better Than Ever!" crowed the taglines, all flop sweat and no stage strut. Alas, however good or bad the movies, business was worse than ever, confidence lower than ever.

The tally at the ticket window tracked the vertiginous slide into redder and redder ink: from a high of 90,000,000 theatergoers per week in 1946, Hollywood's last gilded year, to a tarnished average of 60,000,000 in 1950, to a leaden 45,000,0000 in 1954, the moviegoing audience sliced in half in less than a decade, with the trend line still heading south. Unlike the crises of the pre-Code era, Hollywood was not beset by an inert economy or bedeviled by out-of-joint bluenoses: it was ridiculed, shrugged off, and abandoned. Trade press pundits and studio producers puzzled over the "lost audience," as if the throngs so lately milling in lobbies and snaking around the block had simply been misplaced rather than seduced by amusements closer to home. "The swimming pools are drying up all over Hollywood," cracked screenwriter Herbert Clyde Lewis, taking solace in black humor. "I do not think I shall see them filled in my generation."

Backed up against the wall, Hollywood took defensive measures. Exhibitors built drive-ins to attract suburban families and entice that profitable, proliferating creature discovered during wartime, the teenager. Widescreen cinema was devised to humble the video square and coax back the lapsed millions with eye-popping spectacles and biblical grandeur. Bold and provocative storylines were ventured and hyped. Size or sensation were the two salvations for theatrical motion pictures: deliver what television could neither showcase nor say.

Like the motion picture industry, Joseph I. Breen spent the early 1950s off-balance and worn down: tired, defensive, his energy sapped and health

No longer in fighting trim: Breen in 1951, six months before being diagnosed with lung cancer.

(URBAN ARCHIVES/TEMPLE UNIVERSITY)

failing, his downward arc an index to Hollywood's own decline. In December 1951, decades of smoking yielded the grim diagnosis of lung cancer. Stricken while on vacation in Spain, Breen was rushed back home for treatment at Hollywood Presbyterian Hospital, where a tumor and most of his right lung were removed. Though soon reported "doing quite satisfactorily," he never regained the jaunty spring in his step, never again savored the jousts of a Knight Templar charging forth for some real Catholic action.

The Code certainly needed a champion on the field. Once the critics had nipped at its heels; now they went straight for the jugular.

The scrappy Sam Goldwyn drew first blood. In 1949, in an address to the Theater Owners of America, he condemned state censors and pressure groups ("petty, single-minded, single-tracked dirt-sniffers who feel they have to justify their official existence by using their scissors instead of their heads") and contrasted the onerous political censorship inflicted in primitive backwaters like Memphis and Atlanta to the "voluntary self-regulation and self discipline" practiced by the motion picture industry. "Once a picture has a seal from the Production Code, it is fit to be shown any place."

So far, so good: Goldwyn was parroting the MPAA party line. But the blunt-spoken, ruggedly independent producer was too attuned to the pulse of postwar moviegoing to serve up pabulum only. "Don't get the impression I am in complete agreement with everything in the Code and the way it is interpreted by my good friend and benevolent keeper of our conscience, Joe Breen," Goldwyn hastened to add. "It is my firm belief the time has come to bring the Code up to date, to conform to the changes that have taken place during the 19 years since it was first adopted. It needs overhauling, revamping, renovating."

Though Goldwyn's suggestion smacked of apostasy to the fundamentalists, Eric Johnston, the conciliatory president of the MPPA, appeared open to a negotiated settlement. However, Breen, the old Hollywood hand, pulled time in grade on the greenhorn. "I was here, on the ground, in Hollywood during the fatal years, 1931 to 1934," he lectured his nominal superior whenever a producer or critic floated a proposal to modernize—Breen hated the word—the Code. "If you will examine the files of our office in New York I think you will find much from which to draw a picture of those troublesome days. Better still, you might find time to talk with Mr. Hays." For the veterans of censorship wars past, merely to call up the traumatic memories of the pre-Code era was sufficient to silence the clamor for reform. At *Motion Picture Herald*, any proposal to tamper with the Code was compared, in all seriousness, to amending the Ten Commandments. "One does not consider it probable that even the dynamic Mr. Goldwyn would be trying to bring the Ten Commandments 'up to date,'" editorialized Terry Ramsaye. "Also, he can probably settle with his friend Mr. Joseph I. Breen easier than with Moses."

Not necessarily. Though no longer in fighting trim, Breen spent his last years in office holding fast to the original tablets. Whenever a producer, a screenwriter, or a critic had the temerity to suggest that the Code be modified, that filmmakers be allowed more leeway in dramatizing the realities offscreen, Breen's jaws clenched and his eyes narrowed. The Code required neither "relaxing nor tightening," he maintained. It was already a perfect fit. "Not only has there been no relaxation of the standards of good taste and decency represented by the Code, but there will be none," he pledged in 1952. "Hollywood, as it has done in the past, will continue to provide clean and wholesome entertainment." As long as Breen held the seal, the pagans under the Hollywood sign would not be dancing around a molten calf.

However, from both outside and inside the studio gates, a rising chorus of disapproval sounded off against the Breen Office. To a defiant cadre of critics, filmmakers, and moviegoers, the Code was no longer an infallible document fated to function in perpetuity. It was being questioned, taunted, and ignored. Some of the Code's "restrictions are as inappropriate as the bathing suits of 1927 would be on the beaches of today," wrote Ruth A. Inglis, a researcher for the Commission on Freedom of the Press and the author of *Freedom of the Movies*, in 1947, perhaps thinking of that skimpy fashion risk born of the atomic age. "Please bear in mind we cannot approve the Bikini type bathing suit," Breen frowned when Hollywood sought to import the beachwear from France. Insisted Inglis: "The Code was not divinely inspired or intended for all eternity."

Joseph I. Breen would argue on both counts. Increasingly, though, as the postwar 1940s slid into the Cold War 1950s, the keeper of Hollywood's conscience was no longer lauded as a gallant knight in a tournament for decency but derided as a doddering friar from the Dark Ages.

THE REVOLT OF THE ELITES

In 1950, as the MPAA unfurled its spiffy new slogan, the anthropologist Hortense Powdermaker published an ethnographic study of the tribal rituals of the motion picture industry entitled *Hollywood, the Dream Factory: An Anthropologist Looks at the Movie-Makers.* Based on interviews with some 300 native informants, from studio chieftains to soundstage pygmies, and conducted with the same scientific detachment that had informed her first book, a study of Melanesian islanders in the Southwest Pacific, Powdermaker's fieldwork uncovered scant difference between the Melanesians and the moguls, except, curiously enough, in their contradictory attitudes to certain superstitions. "The Hollywood taboos embodied in the self-imposed Production Code have the same psychological origin as do those of primitive man—fear," she scribbled in her notebook. "But they differ in that they do not represent the actual beliefs, values, or behavior of the people practicing them."

Powdermaker's sly conceit—treating the Hollywood community as an aboriginal "primitive society" giving lip service to Christian missionary positions—expressed the outlook of a new breed of postwar intellectuals who viewed the Code with cynicism and disdain. "The Code simply does not belong to this world," the anthropologist declared, which, the Catholics might reply, was precisely the point.

The antagonism to the Code marked an abrupt generational and cultural shift among what today would be called "opinion elites." Whether in the groves of the academy or the pages of the popular press, editors, professors, and commentators once prone to assail Hollywood for immorality now rolled their eyes at its hidebound Victorianism or waxed indignant at its fairy-tale illusions. A few went further, seeing dire consequences for a nation beclouded by the Code. "I believe that the Production Code, as it operates today, does actual, demonstrable harm to the community," asserted the media critic Gilbert Seldes in *The Great Audience,* his pioneering 1950 study of the popular arts. "Although I do not exaggerate the influence of the movies (or any other art) I think that the Code, its frivolous applications, and the evasions it encourages have become a dangerous and destructive element in American life." The journalists, scholars, and critics who had bolstered the Code regime in 1934 had switched allegiances and defected to the enemy.

More surprisingly, and ominously, the elite disdain was filtering into the mainstream. The organs of popular taste and consensus opinion—family magazines such as *Life, Look, Collier's*, and the *Saturday Evening Post*—mirrored the smart set's malaise about the movies and discontent with the Code. In 1949, *Life*, a reliable barometer of middlebrow sentiment, convened a round table of motion picture experts—critics, producers, and "average moviegoers"—to diagnose Hollywood's ills. Commenting on the Production Code, the critics hated it, the producers suffered it, and the regular Joes and Janes resented it. "I would like to see adult movies more adult and children's movies more childish," opined the obligatory small town housewife from the Midwest.

Compelled to respond to *Life*'s disgruntled panel, the MPAA convened its own group of experts: Eric Johnston, Paramount president Barney Balaban, RKO president Ned E. Depinet, Francis Harmon, head of the New York branch of the PCA, and Breen. "Never before have moviemen of their rank and influence met together to explain their industry to the public," boasted *Parade* magazine, the sympathetic forum chosen for a counterattack that was more defense than offense. No one in Hollywood, insisted Breen, "seeks to deny to the motion picture screen the right of discussion of problems which are valid," but some subjects are simply inappropriate "for mixed audiences for reasons of decency and good taste." Like a broken record—a shellac 78 from the 1930s—he played the same old song. "If you read the Code, you will find that it permits the widest possible freedom of expression."

Breen's entry into the public debate showed just how loud and acrimonious the postwar invective had become. Heretofore he had felt that the best response to criticism of the Code was silence. "It has been my experience that every time we become involved in any public discussion of censorship, we bring down upon our heads the wrath of every nut in the country," he explained. However, as the attacks intensified, Breen was forced to hit back. He spoke more frequently to the trade press, granted the occasional interview to the civilian newspapers, and, once, lashed out furiously at a loyal supporter who had the audacity to question his integrity. In 1952, conceding the need to play a more aggressive defense, he formally reversed the policy of aloof disregard and designated the voluble Jack Vizzard to respond to criticisms as official spokesman for the Breen Office.

A former seminarian with a master's degree in philosophy from the Gregorian University in Rome, Vizzard had been hired as a staffer in 1944.

Breen sized him up as "a fine, outstanding fellow with a real head on him, and he looks like a winner." As the public defender of the Code, Vizzard parried inquiries from reporters, issued press releases, and addressed business luncheons and university forums. The Code, he told audiences, was set up to "preserve on the screen the values of the Ten Commandments, lest pictures turn into an instrument for poisoning our culture." When director William Wyler declared that the Code was "due for revision" to nurture "more mature pictures," Vizzard replied, "It is difficult to see how Wyler, who is unquestionably a great director, has been hurt or seriously inhibited by the Code. He directed *The Best Years of Our Lives* [1946], which was the most richly rewarded film in recent times, walking off with nine Academy 'Oscars.'"

Trying to calm ruffled filmmakers all around, MGM's Dore Schary, Hollywood's house liberal, counseled moderation. "I can assure you I have never had any trouble with the Breen Office—that all subjects can be put on the screen under the Code provisions," said Schary. "I can't go along with the idea of a Code revision to bring it up to date. I happen to know how hard Joe Breen works, and how conscientiously he examines every questionable project to see what adjustments can be made. The Code is a most flexible instrument. Just look at our picture *Battleground* [1949]. Some time ago it would have been impossible to say 'Battling Bastards of Bastogne' on the screen. Today, Mr. Breen recognized that this nickname was necessary and in conformance with reality and he let it pass." According to Schary, the Code needed no updating because Breen was getting more up to date.[1]

Or maybe Breen was just getting worn down—by sickness, by the grind, by the ceaseless internecine bickering and escalating public denunciations. "I have seemingly, at least, recovered from my illness of a few years back, but I am getting old, and lazy, and I would like to retire, but, believe it or not, I just do not seem to be able to do it," he confided to Father Lord in 1950. "Confidentially, I have fear that if I did step out some things might happen with the organization hereabouts that would not be good." Lord knew what that meant: the hard-won dominion of Catholicism over Hollywood would be placed at risk.

Breen had good reason to fear the mounting attacks: the wrecking crew was not going after bricks, or even the support beams, but the very foundation, "challenging the Code as an institution." In 1950, pouring out his anxi-

1. At a preview screening of *Battleground*, the sudden verbal flexibility jolted unwary moviegoers. When the title card reading "Dedicated to the Battling Bastards of Bastogne" flashed on screen, the audience gasped.

eties to Father Lord, he compared the former vexations to the current attacks:

> Heretofore, back over a period of seventeen or eighteen years, the difficulties we encountered were suggested, pretty much, by disagreements with our *interpretation* of the Code. The charge would be made that we had the wrong slant on a given incident, or that the thing we were objecting to was a violation of the letter, but not the spirit of the document.

Nowadays, the criticisms struck at the heart:

> In recent years, however, there has been a growing disposition to seek to destroy the Code, to do away with it. . . . I have noticed since the war, a very positive development that suggests paganism. This manifests itself by the disposition to throw off all standards of decency, of honesty, of honor. Heretofore, as I have told you, they questioned our interpretation of the Code. Now they seek to repudiate the standards.

In fact, despite Breen's protestations of oaken intransigence, the original 1930 Code had been edited and revised several times over the years. Usually enacted without fanfare by a quiet vote of the MPAA Board in New York, and seldom a matter of common knowledge beyond the industry, the additions clarified or expanded on the Quigley-Lord text by listing the precise epithets or slurs banned from the screen or inserting a caution about alcohol use. Minor calibrations, the tampering was likened to adding a plank or two to the permanent structure by way of supportive upkeep.

There was one curious exception—not a design overhaul but a piece of detail work. On September 11, 1946, in response to the personal intervention of H. J. Anslinger, U.S. Commissioner of Narcotics, the MPAA Board voted to revise the ban against the drug trade in the 1930 Code to smooth the production path of an opium-themed thriller from Columbia Pictures titled *Assigned to Treasury*, later released as *To the Ends of the Earth* (1948). Less a commercial venture than a protection payment to Washington during the heyday of the House Committe on Un-American Activities, the film was a puff job meant to burnish the image of the narco squad at the Treasury Department just as *G-Men* (1935) had polished the badge of the Federal Bureau of Investigation.

Even so modest and sensible a revision unnerved the Legion of Decency and *Motion Picture Herald*, for whom any tinkering with the text was sacrilege. Quizzed by Martin J. Quigley about the policy reversal, Breen wired back, "I did not suggest or recommend [the] Code amendment but [I] did recommend several changes in language of [the] proposed amendment which was submitted here for our consideration." Not to worry, he assured his old friend: "We are unanimously of the opinion that the amended paragraph is all right inasmuch as it will permit the approval of stories dealing with certain phases of illicit drug traffic which are not likely to be seriously offensive." Unappeased, Quigley grumbled, "there is no immediate evidence of an artistic necessity or public demand for an excursion into the deliriums of drug addiction by the screen."

In December 1947 the MPAA subjected the Code to two other minor tweakings. Responding to public criticism, the body moved to tighten up the restrictions on salacious titles and crime scenarios.

The 1930 Code had said simply:

> Salacious, indecent or other obscene titles shall not be used.

Logically enough, the command was interpreted to mean that obscene titles per se were forbidden, an outlook that failed to reckon with the scarlet pages behind a pallid book jacket. Kathleen Winsor's ribald novel *Forever Amber* had an innocuous enough title and an innocuous enough screen version, so titled, released in 1947 with a Code Seal, but the film warranted a C rating from the Legion of Decency on the theory that spectators who had read the salacious novel could read into the unsalacious film salaciousness not evident on screen. The title alone seduced in-the-know moviegoers to imagine the worst.

To fill the loophole, the 1947 revision prohibited:

> Titles which suggest or are currently associated in the public mind with material, characters or occupations unsuitable for the screen.

"In effect, [the revision] makes it impossible—if the Production Code Administrator so chooses—to hang a title like 'Forever Amber' on a picture, even if the story itself is sapolioed sufficiently to get past Joe Breen's crew," explained *Variety*.[2] The titular overhaul also muted the unsavory echoes of the word "strange," as in *The Strange Affair of Uncle Harry* (1945) and *The Strange Love of Martha Ivers* (1946).

The same meeting laid down a new criminal code. Already burdened with twelve sections on crime, the MPAA decided to make it a baker's dozen by banning pictures dealing, by name, with the lives of notorious

2. "Sapolioed" was *Variety*-ese for censored or cleaned up. The term was derived from a once popular brand of soap.

criminals. The bill of attainder was probably added to forestall a biopic of the starstruck gangster Bugsy Siegel, terminated in his Beverly Hills home six months earlier.

The next round of revisions, undertaken on March 27, 1951, was more substantive, but still designed to fortify rather than remodel. With a watchful Breen in attendance, the MPAA's Board of Directors performed the most extensive repair work to date—mainly strengthening the Code, but inadvertently weakening it with one alteration. The main purpose of the meeting was to address three issues that had long gnawed at Breen's Catholic conscience: suicide, euthanasia, and abortion.

Unaccountably, back in 1930, Quigley and Lord had overlooked a cornerstone of Catholic doctrine. "The Code is silent on suicide," Breen admitted, an act he deemed "a violation of natural and divine law." Nonetheless, armed with an elastic interpretation of the Code's section on death scenes that tend "to lessen the regard for the sacredness of life," Breen waged religious war against the too-convenient plot device of having a fallen woman jump into a river rather than repent to save her soul. Forbidding what had earlier been merely "discouraged," the 1951 provision added the words:

> [Suicide] should never be justified or glorified or used to defeat the due processes of law.

Euthanasia was another troubling lacuna in the Code. "It is our judgment that 'mercy killing,' so called, is, in reality, *murder*, and, as such, must be treated under the provisions of the Production Code governing the treatment of murder"—that is, condemned at all times. "Who can tell what effect the telling of these stories may have on those who see them?" Breen worried. "Might it not be that some thoughtless *mother*, for example, with a crippled, or deformed, or underprivileged child may get out of such a story a quite definite suggestion as to how to evade her responsibility? Might it not be that a thoughtless *child* may get from this picture the suggestion of how to rid himself of a burdensome parent?"

Though lacking a specific mandate to ban euthanasia scenarios, Breen stretched his authority to encompass what fell outside his mandate. As he wrote in 1944, "the *policy matter* involved in stories of this nature is of sufficient importance to secure an agreement or understanding among all the producers which will *prevent* the telling of such stories on the motion picture screen." In the wake of Nazism, Breen won the point. The Code would not explicitly forbid references to the practice, but euthanasia would be subsumed, by common consent, under the rubric of murder.

As a potential plot point for screen drama, abortion was so beyond the ken of Lord and Quigley that the 1930 Code had omitted any reference to it. In practice, Breen had simply disallowed it. Now listed first in the original litany, the overlooked sin was named in the new provision:

> Abortion, sex hygiene, and venereal disease are not proper subjects for theatrical motion pictures.

By way of fair exchange, in a concession to studio pressure and law enforcement reality, the editorial meeting loosened the regulatory reins by granting more freedom to crime scenarios. The regulation stating "there must be no scenes at any time showing law-enforcement officials dying at the hands of criminals" was qualified with an open-ended escape clause "unless such scenes are absolutely necessary to the development of the plot."

Finally, in a chagrining reversal of recent policy, the Anslinger revision was re-revised and the ban on drug-related scenarios was reimposed. In the years since 1946, Anslinger had decided that a drug scenario, even an antidrug scenario, "kindles the curiosity of the susceptible." Thus, the amendment to the amendment:

> Neither the illegal drug traffic, nor drug addiction, must ever be presented.

At that, Martin S. Quigley, his father's son, could not resist an editorial I-told-you-so. "It was pleasant to discover eventually that Mr. Anslinger found that he was off on the wrong foot in his support of the weakening of the Code provision against narcotics."

For critics whose alienation of affections since 1934 was irreconcilable, the minor adjustments to the Code generated little notice or celebration. They saved their rejoicing for the reinterpretation of a far more historic amendment. In 1915 the U.S. Supreme Court had ruled that cinema was "a business pure and simple." In 1952 the nine uniquely influential opinion elites serving on the court reversed themselves on the question of motion picture censorship. Perhaps wary of giving Hollywood too much credit, the Justices turned to the art house to correct their mistake, selecting an Italian import to set American legal precedent.

In 1950 the French-Italian hybrid *Ways of Love* (1948) was released stateside, a trilogy of short films made up of *A Day in the Country*, directed by Jean Renoir; *Jofroi*, directed by Marcel Pagnol; and *The Miracle*, directed by Roberto Rossellini, the neorealist auteur notorious for luring Ingrid

Bergman away from husband, child, and Hollywood. Rossellini had directed *The Miracle* in his pre-Bergman days as a paramour of the Italian actress Anna Magnani. A spiritual allegory to its admirers and a shocking blasphemy to its detractors, the film told the story of a dim-witted peasant girl (Magnani) seduced and impregnated by a man she believes to be St. Joseph. Driven from her village, taken in at no inn, she gives birth alone in an empty church in the mountains.

Reading the writing in the Code ("No film or episode may throw ridicule on any religious faith.") and educated by his exasperating experience with *The Bicycle Thief*, the foreign film distributor Joseph Burstyn didn't bother to apply for a Code Seal. However, after approval from the Motion Picture Division of the State Department of Education (the New York State censors), *The Miracle* settled into an extended run at the Paris Theater, a premium art house in New York.

Whereupon all hell broke lose. *The Miracle* was condemned by the Legion of Decency. It was condemned by the American Legion. It was condemned by Francis Cardinal Spellman, archbishop of New York. It was condemned by every politician with an electorally significant Catholic constituency in the state of New York. Thinking better of its earlier leniency, the beleaguered New York censor board reversed itself and banned the film.

As politicians postured, churchmen fulminated, and critics rallied around the art house, the ruckus headed for court—with prints of *The Miracle* being pulled from theaters and screenings rescheduled with each new court decree as the case slowly wound its way through the American judicial system. Despite crushing legal costs, the tenacious Burstyn, an unheralded hero of freedom of expression for motion picture art, kept his case before the bar of justice. Officially the MPAA had no dog in the fight, but Breen, his antennae still acute, sensed ill omens in the air. "This whole business concerning Burstyn's latest attempts to stir up trouble is, in my judgment, very portentous," he confided to MPAA legal counsel Kenneth Clark. "He may yet get us into a situation by which we shall be made to suffer very much."

On March 26, 1952, in a unanimous decision with momentous import for the art of cinema, the U.S. Supreme Court ruled "that motion pictures are a significant medium for the communication of ideas" and thereby granted the moving image access to First Amendment protections. Speaking for the full court, Justice Tom C. Clark underscored the judicial U-turn: "We conclude that expression by means of motion pictures is included within the free speech and free press guaranty of the First and Fourteenth Amendments. To the extent that language in the opinion in the *Mutual* case is out of harmony with the views here set forth, we no longer adhere to it." *Stare decisis* notwithstanding, the 1915 Supreme Court ruling that defined motion pictures as a "business pure and simple" was now inoperative. Unlike the guardians of the Production Code, the Justices of the Supreme Court conceded the need to update the U.S. Constitution.

Responding to the rulings, the MPAA cheered from the sidelines. Eric Johnston hailed *The Miracle* decision as "a giant step forward toward removing the shackles of censorship from the screen," an overdue corrective that assured "the motion picture, like its sister medium the press, cannot under the Constitution be censored anywhere in the country." The nonvoting members of the Hollywood establishment professed to feel likewise. "Irrespective of how the winds blow in the troubled area of political censorship and judicial pronouncement," assumed Martin J. Quigley, "the American industry may well find cause for renewed rejoicing in its own Production Code." The MPAA and its supporters still held fast to the bright line distinction between political censorship and self-regulation, as if the decision striking down state censorship would have no impact on studio censorship.

THE REVOLT OF THE INDEPENDENTS

In 1948, in the *Screen Writer*, the in-house journal of the Screen Writers Guild, a classified ad appeared from a subscriber with a chip on his shoulder and time on his hands:

> Wanted, An Idea: Established writer would like a good up-to-date idea for a motion picture which avoids politics, sex, religion, divorce, double beds, drugs, disease, poverty, liquor, senators, bankers, wealth, cigarettes, Congress, race, economics, art, death, crime, childbirth, and accidents (whether by airplane or public carrier); also the villain must not be an American, European, South American, African, Asiatic, Australian, New Zealander or Eskimo. Noncontroversial even among critics, if possible. No dogs allowed.

Judging from the ripe sarcasm, not all the opinion elites in revolt against the Code were from outside the studio gates. A new breed of filmmaker, unwilling to kowtow to cobwebbed convention and ready to carry the flag for artistic integrity, emerged to challenge the indentured servitude to an industrial system on the downslide. "There is some sinister force at work hereabouts," Breen muttered to Quigley in 1949. "I just cannot put my finger on it, but I am satisfied in my own mind that this condition, which has come about in recent months, did not just 'happen.' There is an African in the woodpile!"

Not African but American in origin, the sinister force at work thereabouts was the postwar revolution in manners and morals that classic Hollywood reflected, fomented, and, eventually, was undone by. Yet the cultural dislocation that Breen intuited but could not quite put his finger on was prompted by a more tangible institutional convulsion. The Hollywood studio system was cracking up.

MGM, Warner Bros., Paramount, Twentieth Century-Fox, and RKO, the five major studios, "the Big Five," had become big by controlling the three tiers of the motion picture business: production, distribution, and exhibition. Either by outright ownership (the Warner Theater, the Fox Theater, the Paramount, and so on) or by a controversial, all-or-nothing practice known as block booking (which forced exhibitors to book a complete slate of studio films instead of single surefire hits), Hollywood cornered the motion picture marketplace. Pressing exhibitors further under the studio thumb was the need to obtain a Code Seal for their wares, else be slapped with a $25,000 fine levied by the MPPDA. Stipulated in the original agreement creating the PCA, the penalty lacked the force of law, but the hefty tariff made for intimidating leverage. "As you go along in your work, it might not be a bad thing for you to occasionally drop a hint to your people back there that such an arrangement is in effect, and that the $25,000 fine will be assessed against any company which violates our agreement," Breen suggested to New York–based Code staffer Vincent Hart in 1934.

The real danger for exhibitors wasn't the $25,000 fine, but an impaired relationship with the major studios, all of whom were signatories to the PCA and all of whom would blacklist exhibitors who played non-Code films. The whole scheme operated to crush independent competition and keep exhibitors in bondage to the major studios. In 1934, speaking before the newsreel cameras, Breen had blurted out the truth when he warned:

> The responsible men in this industry want no such [immoral, non-Code] pictures and *will not allow these to be shown*.

Note the language, italicized in Breen's original spiel: *not* refuse to produce films that violated the Code but, rather, refuse to permit theaters to show them.

For the majors, the system worked like a charm. By 1938 the MPPDA reckoned that fully 98 percent of films on American screens had been certified by the Breen Office. The deviant 2 percent made up a barely above-ground market of independent features, screened in unaffiliated venues or "grind houses," with titles like *Love Life of a Gorilla* (1937), *Assassin of Youth* (1937), and *Sex Madness* (1938), no-budget films either rejected by the Code or never submitted for approval and projected one reel ahead of the vice squad. Although only 2 percent of screen fare, the un-Sealed cinema accounted for 60 percent of the complaints logged by the Breen Office, which vainly explained that the trashy knockoffs were emphatically not the Hollywood brand, that the independent producers were slick hustlers and carny con men, never to be confused with the responsible, civic-minded burghers of the major studios. Regal Hollywood called the non-Code upstarts "bootleg pictures," as if they were violators of a protected copyright, which, in a sense, they were.

From its inception, therefore, the moral shield provided by the Breen Office served the not incidental purpose of tightening Hollywood's grip on the motion picture market. Whether from inside or outside national borders, alien and aberrant cinema was run underground or out of town. For the moralist, the Code was a public service. For the moneyman, the Code was the muscle behind a circular protection racket.

In 1948, when the Paramount Decree sought to bust the trust by delinking production from exhibition, the ruling also threatened to weaken the sovereignty of the Code Seal. "The big strength of the Code [is] due largely to major ownership of theater chains, which were a party to the agreement to support the actions of Joe Breen in the industry's self censorship of its product," the *Hollywood Reporter* explained. "When divorcement was ordered, there were many who thought the Code had the props knocked out from under it because the new owners of the theaters, so divorced, were not party to any Code agreement." True enough, in theory, but most exhibitors still refused to book non-Code films to avoid local censorship problems or bad relations with the studio signatories to the Code. "When we have committed ourselves to foreign films and other 'mavericks' of the trade, the majors seem to become right apathetic about letting us have any selected items from the Hollywood output," observed a rueful exhibitor in 1953. Even after 1948, Hollywood dominated the supply line, the distribution stream, and the show rooms—with the PCA turning the screws.

Unsurprisingly, the Code's role as an enforcer for the studio system infuriated the freelancers cut out of the sweetheart deal. "What right has Will Hays and the producers he represents to institute a censorship that smacks of monopoly?" demanded Pete Harrison, in *Harrison's Reports*, his weekly newsletter for independent exhibitors. Unlike Quigley's slick *Motion Picture Herald*, Harrison's one-man operation accepted no advertising and thus had no percentage in playing studio sycophant. Though an early Breen booster back in 1934, Harrison had come to suspect that the Breen Office gave slack to the majors and the shaft to the indies.

In 1946, Harrison used his editorial soapbox to lodge the direct accusation that the "independent producers are not given the same consideration by the Production Code Administrator as are the major producers." He quoted an independent producer who claimed that Breen had shrugged off the double standard by replying, "Well, the major companies have the means of treating such situations artistically." Harrison then goaded his target by name. "Where was Breen when Walter Wanger's script on *Scarlet Street* [1945] was submitted to his office?" Or *The Corn Is Green* [1945]? Or *The Strange Affair of Uncle Harry* [1945]?" he wondered, listing a trio of Code Sealed titles that had run into trouble with various state censors. "Mr. Breen swallows major camels but chokes on independent morsels."

Incensed, Breen lashed back. "How in the name of heaven, anyone making the slightest pretense to editorial integrity could launch upon such an attack *without first getting the facts,* is simply beyond my comprehension," he told Harrison. Umbrage ("What kind of responsible journalism is this?") followed umbrage ("You did not hesitate to accept the false story and use it to impugn my honesty, and characterize me as a crook.") before Breen capped his epistolary fit with an italicized denial that he had ever said the majors handled situations "more artistically" than the independents:

> I never made any such statement in my life. *The statement is utterly and unqualifiedly false.* In another part of your editorial you make the charge that "the Production Code Administrator does not give the same consideration to the major producers that he gives to the independents." There is not one scintilla of truth in it.

Wise to the tricks of the trade, the former newspaperman demanded of Harrison equal column inches and same-sized typeface: "I count on you to give this letter the same editorial consideration you gave to your attack upon me."

Harrison complied, publishing the complete "abusive and irascible" letter, interrupted by his own snippy comebacks, in a special four-page supplement to *Harrison's Reports.* "Just because Joe Breen has seen fit to resort to personal abuse and insult is no reason why I should stoop to his tactics," wrote Harrison, before stooping. First, he castigated Breen for being so thin-skinned:

> After all, he holds a political job and must learn to take criticism like a good politician without whimpering like a baby. But it seems to me as if he can't take it. He is your friend as long as you tell him what a great man he is, but he resents criticism of his work.

Not backing away from his charges, Harrison quoted a story editor:

> Breen gives the independents' scripts to his subordinates, who use microscopes in going over them, and keeps the major scripts for himself. How many scripts can he read? Besides the major studios send their slickest salesmen to him to convince him that everything in the script is as it should be.

Taking the editor's prerogative of getting the last word, Harrison headlined the exchange "Joe Breen's Temper."

Given the bad blood between the MPAA–PCA axis and the independents, a historic break with the Code would logically be instigated by an independent signatory at the end of its patience. The rebel was United Artists. Formed in 1919 by silent greats D. W. Griffith, Mary Pickford, Douglas Fairbanks, and Charles Chaplin, United Artists was the original case of the inmates taking over the asylum. It was not a studio with backlots and prop inventory, but a financing and distribution outfit whose client list was comprised of independent filmmakers. Though a member of the MPAA by necessity, real estate poor UA was a second-class signatory denied a seat at the executive table in New York. Mary Pickford, no shrinking violet on or off screen, chafed at the moral taxation without representation assessed by the MPAA, and often said so. As a creature of the majors, the PCA was "both Congress and the Supreme Court," she complained, with minor players like UA disenfranchised constituents.

UA's vice president Max E. Youngstein agreed with America's former sweetheart. On film content and advertising alike, the PCA and the Advertising Code Administration were using "a different yardstick" to measure the morality of the independents. "I am willing to comply with the Code in its spirit and its letter, but I must insist that the yardstick for the pictures distributed thru United Artists be the same as the one applied to every other company," an aggrieved Youngstein told Eric Johnston.

In 1953, after what UA felt was a long train of abuses by the Breen Office, the company sought to eclipse MPAA oppression with Otto Preminger's *The Moon Is Blue* (1953), a wink-wink comedy of manners that dangled the seduction of a precocious but as yet unbedded ingénue as bait. The film was denied a Code Seal for the general tone of lecherous prurience, but press coverage zeroed in on Breen Office objections to the proper dictionary entries "pregnant," "seduce," and "professional virgin." The "virgin" ban became the trigger word for a furious linguistic brouhaha that—more than the damning over *Gone With the Wind*, more than the breast gags trailing *The Outlaw*, and more than the smirks over "the sacred wee-wee" in *The Bicycle*

Thief—was a public relations fiasco for the Breen Office. Breen had seemingly chosen to go to the wall not over a cornerstone of the Code or even a brick, but a meaningless chip, a rock-headed decision that further squandered the fast-depleting moral capital of the PCA.

Preminger appealed the decision to the MPAA Board in New York, which, still chastened by the backfire from *The Outlaw*, sustained the decision. The Breen Office and the MPAA would hang tough together.

Then—amazingly—United Artists distributed the film anyway. In league with independent exhibitors desperate for a hit and itching for a fight, UA struck at the system many despised but few dared cross. Condemned by the Legion of Decency, uncertified by the Breen Office, *The Moon Is Blue* was thrown down like a gauntlet.

Motion Picture Herald was apoplectic. United Artists and the deviant exhibitors were "playing with fire" and showing "an astonishing contempt to audiences of the innumerable Main Streets that lie importantly between Broadway and Hollywood & Vine."

To its editorial dismay, however, the venerable trade journal was no longer a reliable roadmap to the American heartland. The low tone, the adjective, the verb, and even the noun ignited no firestorms on the main streets between the coasts. First at previews, then in regular playdates, capacity crowds chortled so loudly during *The Moon Is Blue* that the dialogue track was drowned out. Listening to the laughs and eyeing the till, Abram F. Myers of Allied Theaters couldn't figure out "why any grown-up should be protected against this film." The grown-ups agreed: the film grossed over $4 million, with savvy trade sources estimating that "sans controversy" the gross would have been a meager $1.2 million. For the first time, with a popular Hollywood film, not a subtitled art house import, the Code was out of line with the state censors, the trade critics, and, fatally, the mainstream audience. "The judgments of the Code's administrators would appear to have been way out of tune with the nonchalance of the public," exulted Bosley Crowther, the raja of 1950s film criticism, at the *New York Times*.

In tune with and worse than a nonchalant public was an activist judiciary. In the case of *The Outlaw*, the American justice system had been content to let the MPAA police the morality of its own. After *The Miracle* decision, however, state courts and city judges, taking the cue from above, began ruling against local censorship boards. The steady erosion of the power of the Bindfords, Smiths, and sundry local czars to slice up or shut down films set a cautionary precedent for the MPAA variation. "If the Production Code were law, it would be plainly unconstitutional," declared Judge Herman M. Moser of the Baltimore City Court, when he struck down the

Un-Sealed but approved: William Holden and Maggie McNamara in Otto Preminger's *The Moon Is Blue* (1953), the film that defied the Breen Office and helped break the MPAA's grip on exhibition.

banning of the *The Moon Is Blue* by the Maryland State Board of Motion Picture Censorship.

On May 12, 1953, by way of preemptive defense, the MPAA Board formally voted to reaffirm support for the Code and reassert the distinction between state censorship and private self-regulation. Denying rumors that a "watering down" was in the works, Johnston called the Code an inviolable "contract with the American people." However, the statement Johnston issued did not parse:

> There has been a feeling in some areas both within and without the industry that the Code or some parts of it are out of "style." It is a living and vibrant document that deals with principles of morality and good taste. These are ageless.

Of course, the document could not be both living and vibrant (and hence malleable) and "ageless."

As *The Moon Is Blue* darkened the skies, an old nemesis returned for a final tussle with the Breen Office. Howard Hughes, still bitter over his pre-Code treatment, buoyed by the success of *The Outlaw*, and now at the helm of his own studio, RKO, decided to combine a proven attraction in two dimensions with a technological innovation in three: a sexy musical featuring a scantily clad Jane Russell titled *The French Line* (1954), filmed in Technicolor and 3-D. In *The Outlaw* the "flat" version of Jane Russell had proven emergent enough; *The French Line* bid to inflate the curvature.

The Breen Office did not need 3-D glasses to fill in the picture. "Re-examination of the Production Code, in view of modern technological developments such as 3-dimension, is under way with the possibility that the provisions of the voluntary self censorship rulings may be revamped to take into cognizance the realism that the new systems impart to the screen," the *Hollywood Reporter* noted in 1953. "One meeting has already been held in the office of Joseph I. Breen to examine the application of the Code . . . to the new vistas opened up by the developments, especially in 3-D." A Code staffer, probably Jack Vizzard, observed that "what is acceptable in 2-D may be highly objectionable in 3-D"—a reference to that other expansion in the topography of Cold War America, the contours of the female breast.

"We assume the best of taste will be exercised in the selection of the decollete gown [for Jane Russell]," Breen wrote hopefully during the script review process for *The French Line*, but Vizzard, assigned as point man, had bad news about "breast shots in bathtub, cleavage, and breast exposure." During five separate screenings in the PCA projection booth, presumably with 3-D glasses in place, Breen and the staff confirmed Vizzard's depth perception. "The costumes for most female characters and especially Jane Russell, were intentionally designed to give a bosom peep-show affect beyond even extreme décolletage and far beyond anything acceptable under the Production Code," agreed another staffer.

Fed up with negotiations, Hughes dispensed with the Code Seal and ballyhooed the world premiere of *The French Line* at the Fox Theater in St. Louis, Father Lord's home base. It was the first time a Big Five studio, a signatory to the MPAA contract, had dared to distribute a film without a Code Seal, making RKO liable to a $25,000 fine. The fine was duly assessed; RKO duly refused to pay.

Dreading more controversy and derisive headlines, higher-ups in the MPAA sought to avoid a showdown. "If within the Code in a helpful and cooperative way, we could get a seal on *The French Line* it would be a tremendous thing all around especially for us," the MPAA's Kenneth Clark gently suggested to Breen. "I am convinced that if this could be done, it would be a long time before another serious break developed in Hollywood

A new dimension in censorship: Jane Russell violates dress and dancing codes in Howard Hughes's 3-D Technicolor musical *The French Line* (1954).

against the Code and our system of self regulation. It would be a lesson heeded by even the thickest skulls!"

Yet Breen's was the thick skull. In 1946, when Hughes had bucked the MPAA over *The Outlaw*, the trade press and the studios had rallied to support the self-regulatory regime. In 1954, even longtime loyalists parted company with Breen's line on *The French Line*. "The Breen edicts, painful at times, generally have rounded out a self-censorship of our product that has given strength to this activity throughout the land," commented Billy Wilkerson. "We've seen quite a few other pictures even more suggestive than what was complained of in the RKO picture: dances just as hot or hotter. We don't know what Breen ordered cut; however, we're certain the whole thing could have been avoided by a give-and-take agreement between Breen and Hughes without much damage to the picture." Perhaps: but the truculent Hughes and the intransigent Breen each refused to budge.[3]

3. Keeping to *The Outlaw* game plan, Hughes milked maximum publicity value out of the controversy before acceding, over a year later, to the cuts needed to obtain a Code Seal for *The French Line*.

As the designated defender of the Code, Vizzard predicted that the "glaring breast shots of Jane Russell and a dance sequence during her rendition of 'I Want Your Man' in the latter part of the picture will certainly bring the cops to any theater where it is shown." But who would call out the cops? "There was no unfavorable reaction to the controversial Jane Russell dance in the film," said a trade reporter, removing his 3-D glasses to observe the sellout crowds at the Fox Theater. "Audiences apparently just enjoyed it."

Openly defied with profit and without penalty in the back-to-back cases of *The Moon Is Blue* and *The French Line*, Breen was feeling the heat and wilting under the glare. "After twenty years of this kind of experience, one's hide becomes a bit tough," he had confided a few years earlier to his friend, MPAA legal counsel Sidney Schreiber. "I was going to say 'impregnable,' but that would not quite be the truth." From United Artists and Howard Hughes, his hide had taken the worst tannings yet.

Breen had never bounced back completely from his cancer surgery in 1951. "Since that time, I have been quite definitely under par," he admitted to Father Lord in 1954. "There was for almost two years the pain which seems to be inseparable from this kind of operation. Following this, I began to develop a few more ailments which, I suppose, are inescapable when a guy reaches my age!" Worn down by work, weakened by illness, mortified by the scorn of his peers and the nonchalance of the public, he signaled his readiness to retire from the field.

By then, the Code was also showing its age. The postwar revolutions in manners and morals, the legal expansion of the right of cinema under the First Amendment, and the competition from television had forced the MPAA to stretch the limits of its own rules. "Hollywood is taking a different view of screen 'morality' and, as a result, marked changes in [the] interpretation of the Production Code are on the way," *Variety* predicted in 1954. "In a sense, the picture business is embarking on a new era, for even the symbol of old-guard screen standards—Code administrator Joseph I. Breen—is doing a fade."

14

NOT THE BREEN OFFICE

It should have been an easy sale. In 1950 the irrepressible Martin J. Quigley approached the Motion Picture Association of America about sponsoring a short film to commemorate the twentieth anniversary of his most treasured byline, the Production Code. He had written a rough screen treatment extolling the virtues of custodial self-regulation. In his mind's eye, Quigley pictured a closing vignette almost poignant in its fidelity to the waning habits of a vanishing demographic. The last shot, he directed, would show "a group of eager, bright-faced men, women, and children entering a theater lobby, with sound track carrying a final message dealing with the protection, etc., which the Code helps to give all kinds and classes of people with entertainment hours."

Quigley's pitch was dead on arrival. In 1954, upon the twentieth anniversary of the Production Code Administration, he again peddled the project. Again, the MPAA passed.

What was once a shield of honor had become the rusted emblem of Hollywood past. With rising vehemence and contempt, critics and journalists, educators and academics, even city councilmen and suburban housewives looked upon the Code Seal as a relic of the time that spawned it, the distant, dusty, and best-forgotten 1930s. The certificate of safety and artistry had come to mean dated material and stale contents.

For studio accountants, the numbers in the ledger books were more worrisome than the text of the Code. So lately ascendant and unchallenged, the dominant, not to say only, moving image game in town, Hollywood was reeling from a humbling demotion in status and solvency. Television had supplanted its centrality, stolen its audience, and depleted its coffers.

The man who more than any mogul personified the ancient regime was also down and, soon, out. Though nominally still in harness, Breen was no longer at his desk every day, or even most days, easing himself out, and beginning, as Geoffrey Shurlock recalled, "to fade out of the picture." "Look, I've got to get out of here," he told Shurlock, his loyal factotum for twenty years. "I'm not earning my salary and it's not right."[1] At age sixty-six, a little forlorn and a lot burnt-out, he quit—for good this time.

The industry that had pleaded for Breen to ride to the rescue in 1934, that had welcomed his return from RKO in 1942, that had pressed him to stay on in 1948, did not protest the leave-taking. Sensing that the value of the Breen Office had reached the point of diminishing returns, the ranking studio heads had decided to expand the range of screen expression along with the size of the screen. Just as Breen's entry in 1934 heralded the clampdown, his exit in 1954 meant the release of the Victorian Irish grip on American cinema.

In keeping with local custom, a wrap party marked the close of production. At the Academy Awards ceremonies of 1954, Breen was given the Hollywood equivalent of a gold watch, an honorary Oscar, both retirement gift and official kiss-off. He had not been forced to retire; his health was poor and the fire in his belly had flickered out long ago. "I am anxious to get out now [August 1954], but I seem to be having difficulty in persuading [the MPAA] Board that I ought to leave," he told Father Lord.

On October 14, 1954, a weary Breen formally stepped down from his priestly work. The corporate farewells were dutiful, maybe a bit relieved. "Joe Breen has rendered this industry service of such importance that there is no way to properly appraise his contribution," said Y. Frank Freeman, chairman of the Association of Motion Picture Producers. "His job was not an easy one—we all had our differences and battles with him—but he administered the Code fearlessly, faithfully, and honestly." Along with the golden statue, Breen received a golden parachute in the form of a generous benefits package from the MPAA, which paid him $20,000 yearly until 1961 as an "emeritus advisor."

Geoffrey Shurlock, who had served the cause of self-regulation since 1932 and who had been denied a permanent appointment during Breen's hiatus at RKO, finally inherited possession of the Code Seal. In announcing the succession, MPAA president Eric Johnston praised Shurlock as an "extremely able, respected, and experienced executive." Wags joshed that Shurlock's background fit the job description: as a boy, he had operated the washing machines in the family laundry business.

1. Breen's annual salary by then was $65,000, which he voluntarily cut in half during the last six months in office.

The Shurlock Office in 1957: settling in for the print review stage at the MPAA's Beverly Hills headquarters are (*front row, left to right*) Albert Van Schmus and Harry Zehner; (*middle row, left to right*) Milton Holdenfield, Geoffrey Shurlock, and Morris Murphy; and (*back row, left to right*) Eugene "Doc" Dougherty, Jack Vizzard, and M. A. J. Healy. Secretary Laura Greenhouse sits at the desk, pen in hand, ready to jot down Code violations.

Ruminating over Breen's exit, the old-timers waxed nostalgic. "While Breen held the reins, it was commonly referred to as just the 'Breen Office' or the 'Breen seal,'" *Variety* reminisced. "With Geoffrey Shurlock taking over, it now should theoretically become the 'Shurlock Office.' It'll take some getting used to, after all these years." The new name never stuck. A few months later, editor Abel Green tried again. "The trade will have to get used to 'shurlocking' as it had to 'joebreening' as a synonym for Code Production cuts." That coinage never caught on either.

No fool, Shurlock pledged continued adherence to "the Breen principle" learned at the feet of the master. "In the classic phrase of Joseph I. Breen, the man who for 20 years guided the Code, its object is 'to make pictures reasonably acceptable, morally, to reasonable people.'" Continuity was the byword; no need to fix what was not broken. Even Breen's honorary Oscar was construed as a gesture of renewed commitment to the PCA, "a slap at those in and out of the industry who have been clamoring for drastic changes in the industry's self-censorship machinery," as the *Hollywood Reporter* tried to spin it.

Yet only the willfully blind or tone deaf refused to read the writing on the wall or hear the rustlings in the wind. In the 1930s, the Breen Office seized control and expanded its authority. In the 1940s, it guarded the perimeters, made a few tactical retreats, and beat back the major challenges. In the 1950s, post-Breen, the Shurlock Office waged a hopeless rearguard action against incursions from all sides: foreign and domestic, independents and majors, the intelligentsia and the vox populi. Year by year, piece by piece, compromise by compromise, the Production Code Administration backed off, ceded turf, and, finally, faded away.

CRACKING THE CODE

With the taskmaster out of the picture, the pent-up frustrations of two decades on a tight leash broke into open defiance. No sooner had Breen announced his retirement than producer Sam Goldwyn renewed his demand for the MPAA to "modernize" the Code. "The world has moved on in the years since the Code was adopted and I believe that, without departing from fundamentals, the motion picture industry should move with it," said Goldwyn, without malapropism. Actually, Hollywood needed to move with the audience or lose it.

The cantankerous generation of postwar intellectuals remained poised at the point of the spear. Before World War II, newspaper columnists and literary critics had held Hollywood in such low esteem that few considered the Breen Office a blight on artistic expression or political discourse. After World War II, the snide disregard turned to grudging respect. Like the rest of the nation, including the members of the House Committee on Un-American Activities, the eggheads of the liberal imagination now looked upon motion pictures as art to cherish and messages to heed.

In 1954 the syndicated columnist and New Deal standard-bearer Arthur Schlesinger, Jr., detected a "gathering revolt against the Motion Picture Production Code" and welcomed the barbarians at the studio gates. More audaciously, he blasted a lately unassailable party to the arrangement. "For nearly a generation, the movies of this country have been filmed according to the ground rules of a minority religious faith," charged Schlesinger, forgetting the role that his mentor FDR had played in brokering the deal. "The line should be drawn when it comes to imposing sectarian standards, whatever the sect, on our richly diversified American culture." Schlesinger had reduced the transcendent doctrines of the Catholic Church to the eccentric beliefs of a mere sect.

The New York–Washington corridor was backed by allies from Hollywood eager to spill inside information. In 1954 the journalist-playwright-screenwriter Ben Hecht published his acidic memoir *A Child of the Century*. Gaily throttling his paymasters, Hecht ripped into the clichés, stupidities, and falsifications of Hollywood under the Code—a never-never land teaching "that the most potent and brilliant of villains are powerless before little children, parish priests, or young virgins with large boobies; that injustice can cause a heap of trouble but it must always slink out of town in Reel Nine; that there are no problems of labor, politics, domestic life or sexual abnormality but can be solved by a simple Christian phrase or a fine American motto." Hecht paid no lip service to the lofty aspirations of the Code; he just fired away.

Once apostasy, Schlesinger's secular critique and Hecht's jaundiced contempt were becoming conventional wisdom. It was not only syndicated columnists and cynical screenwriters who derided the Code; the popular weeklies and daily newspapers joined in the jeering. In 1954, the tipping-point year, even the middlebrow *Life* lambasted the complacence of MPAA president Eric Johnston, "who recently likened the Breen Office code to the Constitution of the United States," and lectured: "The Code should be easier to amend than all that; and Sam Goldwyn is right—it now needs amending." Unlike the 1930s, when mainstream commentators and editorialists had excoriated pre-Code immorality and rallied to support the Production Code Administration, the Cold War critical consensus regarded the Code as outdated, repressive, and—the kiss of death—silly.

The game was truly up when the Code was snickered at from the motion picture screen. In the British import *The Captain's Paradise* (1953), a hilarious paean to unlawfully wedded bliss from Ealing Studios, Alec Guinness plays the double-dealing Captain Henry St. James, a packet boat captain with two wives in different ports, one a stiff British helpmate in Gibraltar, the other a hot-blooded spitfire in North Africa. To maintain Codely propriety, a written prologue and epilogue were appended to the bigamous farce. Unlike the voices of morality bookending *Forever Amber* (1947), however, the admonitions are fig leaves hiding nothing. With British tongue in cheek, a disclaimer written for the puritanical Americans, not the British Board of Film Censors, opened the film:

> There are many (mostly men) who may find the story that follows inspiring. There are others (mostly women) who will find it infuriating. Our condo-

> lences to the former and reassurances to the latter; the hero, Captain Henry St. James, never existed. The whole saga is, in fact, a fairy story. Relax and enjoy it.

The epilogue chuckled:

> Yes, we have to conclude that this is a fairy tale. It never happened. It couldn't happen. If it has ever occurred to you as a possibility, forget it. There are all kinds of laws, divine and human, against it. To say nothing of the scandal. Our considered advice is to go home now and have a hot cup of cocoa and bring a cup to your spouse—the only one you have.

The "fairy story" referred to is not *The Captain's Paradise* but the Production Code; the "laws divine and human" inscribed in its text, a polite conceit for the children and the bluenoses ("to say nothing of the scandal").

As the Brits were ridiculing the Code, the Supreme Court was revisiting the not unrelated issue of state censorship. Ohio had banned a re-release of Fritz Lang's classic *M* (1931), and New York had banned Max Ophuls's classic-to-be *La Ronde* (1950). Again, the court chose foreign cinema of unimpeachable moral seriousness and aesthetic value to broaden the umbrella of First Amendment protection and deny the constitutionality of pre-censorship by the state, the selfsame practice the Code performed for the studios. "Motion pictures are, of course, a different medium of expression than the public speech, the radio, the stage, the novel, or the magazine," wrote Justice William O. Douglas in a 9–0 decision handed down on January 19, 1954. "But the First Amendment draws no distinction between the various methods of communicating ideas. . . . In this nation, every writer, actor, or producer, no matter what medium of expression he may use should be freed from the censor."

Not everyone wanted to be freed from the censor in Hollywood. Director George Stevens reminded Sam Goldwyn that the Code "does less restraining on the general content of the film than any other governing or controlling device that has yet been presented." The most loyal constituency also stood firmly behind the regime it had helped bring to power. "The Code is as necessary in Hollywood as the camera and the makeup box," insisted the Catholic monthly the *Sign* in 1954, the year the Code seemed as superfluous as hand-cranked cameras and intertitles.

In fact, the unthinkable editorial presumption—amending the Ten Commandments—was not only on the table, it was a done deal. On September 13, 1954, the MPAA approved the first transformative amendments to the Code since its adoption in 1930. The revisions had been informally vetted a year earlier, but with the MPAA embroiled in the controversy over *The Moon Is Blue* (1953), the association chose to delay formal approval to avoid the appearance of concessions that smacked of "liberalization" under duress. Labeled "technical or clarifying," the revisions were proposed by Breen himself as a parting gift to his successor. Perhaps, with a tune-up, the machinery would be durable enough to weather the gathering storm.

By far the most noteworthy of the 1954 revisions was the abolition of the ban on miscegenation. Henceforth, interracial romance, congress, and marriage were classified among screen subjects to be treated "within the careful limits of good taste." The Jim Crow color line might now be crossed with the blessing of the Code, even if producers, fearful of exhibitor boycotts south of the Mason–Dixon line, waited over a decade to exploit the freedom full on the mouth with Stanley Kramer's *Guess Who's Coming to Dinner* (1965). The long lag time between permission and production is an instructive reminder that the Code was never the only factor inhibiting Hollywood from tackling controversial motion picture content.

In another sign of the times, the Code section entitled "Repellant Subjects" was retitled "Special Subjects," shifting the phrasing from the moral language of the 1930s to the neutral prose of the 1950s. The newly renamed section eliminated the bans on "branding of people or animals" and "apparent cruelty to children or animals." The former no longer presented a problem and cruelty to children or animals was, said Breen, "adequately covered by other provisions of the Code."

Liquor—which despite the repeal of Prohibition in 1933 had remained in the section for "crimes against the law"—was distilled into a habit to be portrayed "within the careful limits of good taste." Another holdover from the Prohibition era ("methods of smuggling should not be presented") was also eliminated. Neither anachronism had been updated in the intervening twenty years.

Finally, showing how hopelessly out of touch the Code had become by the ultra-hep year of 1954, a set of words and phrases long forbidden as vulgar or profane was given a fair hearing on screen: *hell, damn, fanny, hold your hat, nerts, tom cat* (applied to a man not a feline), and references to, though not the telling of, "traveling salesman and farmer's daughter jokes."

Un-blurtable without special signed permission even under the provocation of WWII, the long-deleted expletives of "hell" and "damn" warranted a clarifying paragraph:

> It should be noted that the words "hell" and "damn," if used without moderation, will be considered offensive by members of the audiences. Their use,

therefore, should be governed by the discretion and the prudent advice of the Code administration.

A verbal firewall breached only by the Warner Bros. short *The Man Without a Country* (1937), the MGM blockbuster *Gone With the Wind* (1939), and a handful of WWII combat films, "hell" and "damn" had generated reams of interoffice memos and press commentary. Only a year earlier the mild expletives had been stricken from producer Hal Wallis's *Cease Fire* (1953), a combat film shot in Korea, where the battling bastards of the peninsula were not permitted three utterances of "hell" and "damn." The Code being the Code, the Breen Office had refused a seal. When Wallis appealed, the MPAA Board backed the Breen Office, and Wallis reluctantly complied and deleted.

Expending moral capital on a pair of words that burned only the bluest of ears earned no credit and plenty of derision for industry self-regulation. Breen had long been seeking an opportunity to end the blanket prohibition and stifle the carping. He found the perfect vehicle in Columbia's *On the Waterfront* (1954), produced by his friend Sam Spiegel, directed by Elia Kazan, and written by Budd Schulberg. For the director and writer, both friendly witnesses before the House Committee on Un-American Activities, the neorealist melodrama shot on the docks of Hoboken was a metaphor for the plight of a good-hearted palooka caught between his better angels and tribal loyalty. For the performers, it was a proving ground for the emotional intensity of the Stanislavski Method. For Breen, it was a Catholic-conversion narrative, a tale of spiritual transformation, through suffering, facilitated by his most beloved screen character, the two-fisted priest.

The dialogue in question was snarled at the dockyard missionary Father Barry (Karl Malden) by the conscience-stricken laborer Terry Malloy (Marlon Brando):

> "You go to hell!" barks Terry.
> "*What* did you say?" responds the astonished priest.
> Terry repeats the phrase: "You go to hell."

The imperative was forbidden by the Code; the context—spat in the face of a Catholic priest—was incendiary.

Saving Spiegel the trouble of composing an appeal to the MPAA's Board of Directors, Breen wrote the brief himself—pleading the case that he *not* be required to do what he had always done unstintingly: enforce the letter of the Code. *On the Waterfront*, Breen wrote, was "an outstanding motion picture which deals, powerfully, with the problems of corruption among the waterfront unions in New York City, and the solution to these problems, largely through the leadership of a courageous priest." Admittedly, "we have here the question of a technical Code violation in the use of the word 'Hell,' over which the staff has no discretion." Nonetheless, the dialogue should "not be required [to be taken] out of the picture." Breen's Jesuit schooling in argumentation served Spiegel well:

> Although the letter of the law is violated, the intent of that section of the Code which deals with the use of the word "Hell" is not violated. The expression "Go to Hell" is not used in a casual manner, as a vulgarism, or as a flippant profanity. It is used seriously and with intrinsic validity and has the effect of a physical blow in the face, against the priest.

Harkening back to a happier time, he cited an apt precedent counted among his most felicitous script polishings:

> The overall shock-impact of the scene is not unlike that of the famous scene from the motion picture *San Francisco* [1936] in which Clark Gable strikes the priest, Spencer Tracy, in the face.

On the Waterfront ventured another linguistic violation that Breen was embarrassed to broach given the year, the stakes, and so worthy a Catholic-friendly picture: the use of the expression "hold your hats." Although the haberdasheryism was expressly forbidden by the Code, the staff felt that "the offensiveness of this phrase has long since disappeared, and is now quite acceptable in decent society." Hoping to head off the snide headlines, Breen counseled a policy of benign neglect. Since the phrase was included in the finished print anyway, "the Code Administration would like to be directed simply to ignore the point, and be empowered to issue the Code Certificate of Approval."

Understandably, Hal Wallis gave the Breen Office holy hell when he heard about the dispensation granted Sam Spiegel. "I am amazed and outraged at the approval of the phrase in the Columbia Picture," he wrote Breen. "Having gone through a series of meetings because the word 'Hell' was not permitted in our picture *Cease Fire*, even though spoken by actual soldiers on the real battlefields of Korea, it is exceedingly difficult to reconcile your approval of the more direct phrase 'You go to hell!' with the rejection of the use of the word 'Hell' as it was originally spoken in our scenes made in Korea." Nor was Wallis impressed with Breen's fancy rhetoric. "This is the most fantastic mumbo jumbo I have read or heard in a long time."

Playing smart, the fiercest defenders of the Code acquiesced to the revisions. "The energies of the PCA should be expended on essentials not trivialities," concurred the *Motion Picture Herald*, upholding the crucial distinction between "essential principles of the Code" and "certain regulations of policy and expediency." The latter were not "part of the Code proper, were not in the original document and have been introduced from time to time because of some real or imagined need." It was Will Hays and his minions, not Quigley and Lord, who had blacklisted harmless colloquialisms like "hold your hats" and "nerts to you."

In truth, at this stage, the moral foundation of the Code was not being eroded. Still, to use Breen's favorite metaphor, the revisions pulled out a few bricks in the wall of infallibility. "The Code's strength was in its overall impact, its integration as an inviolable whole," pointed out the veteran producer and screenwriter Virginia van Upp, a voice of prophecy. "When you start chopping up parts of it, you indirectly make all of it susceptible to attack."

Confirming the worst fears of the inerrantists, once the editorial itch was scratched, the impulse to paw over the document led to major revisions and redactions. Breen was a strict constructionist who looked upon the Code as a sacred text, handled with reverence; Shurlock was a liberal interpreter who looked upon the Code as an elastic document, infinitely malleable and amendable.

The boss was not gone long before Shurlock began to sound suspiciously squishy. The old concept of punishment for sin needed to be "modernized in harmony with common sense and sound psychological dicta," he declared. A good case in point was Nunnally Johnson's *The Man in the Gray Flannel Suit* (1955), whose well-tailored protagonist "expiates a moral fault [fathering an illegitimate child during wartime] by remorse or by assuming a neglected responsibility [child support payments], rather than coming to a violent end." Promised Shurlock: "As producers become interested in more stimulating and trailblazing stories, the Code will help them find more penetrating and solid methods of treating them."

The most stimulating and trailblazing story came at the Code from an unexpected flank (drugs not sex), though the man leading the charge looked familiar enough. The ever-pugnacious Otto Preminger, whose *The Moon Is Blue* had precipitated the 1954 revisions, again forced the MPAA back to the drawing board with *The Man With the Golden Arm* (1955). A psychiatrical in which a pharmaceutical was the social problem, the film featured Frank Sinatra as a heroin-addicted trumpet player, shooting up with needles and shivering in the throes of cold-turkey withdrawal, a jittery violation of the prohibition against scenes "which show the use of illegal drugs,

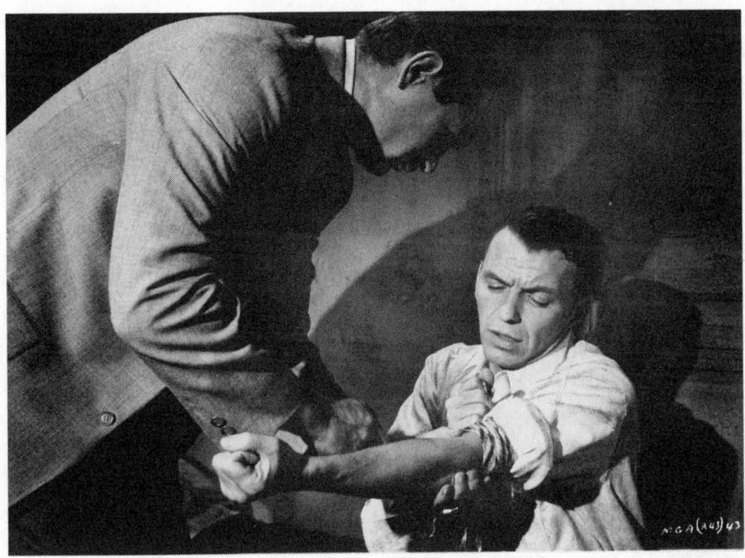

Shooting up: Frank Sinatra violates the Code's drug laws in Otto Preminger's *The Man With the Golden Arm* (1955).

or their effects, in detail." The regulatory road of Preminger's second color-schemed film title retraced the path of his first: denied a Code Seal, he appealed to the MPAA Board, which upheld the denial, whereupon Preminger and United Artists released the film anyway—to high critical praise and solid box office.

As the MPAA sweated through Preminger's drug-induced crisis, television, of all media, underscored the obsolescence of the 1930s-minted taboos. Though banned from the big screen, plotlines built around kidnapping and drug addiction had been overlooked when the National Association of Radio and Television Broadcasters adopted its own self-regulatory document, the Television Code. Thus, the living room screen was free to depict two controversial scenarios forbidden to the motion picture screen. In 1955, MGM purchased the rights to the kidnapping thriller *Fearful Decision*, already telecast by ABC's *The U.S. Steel Hour*. The Shurlock Office had no option but to derail the MGM project; crime stories based on kidnapping had been forbidden since 1932, in reaction to the national revulsion over the kidnapping-murder of the Lindbergh baby. MGM appealed to the MPAA Board, which overruled Shurlock "on technical grounds" (the kidnapping takes place before the story opens), but the rationale was a transparent cover story. With the living room medium having already telecast the scenario, what sense did it make to prevent the motion picture medium from screening same?

Similarly, Twentieth Century-Fox, which had purchased the screen rights to Michael Gazzo's hit Broadway play *A Hatful of Rain,* was facing a loss of $250,000 if narcotics-themed material remained unfilmable. In public the studio played the good soldier. "We will never make any picture at Twentieth that does not meet with Code approval," promised a spokesman. Behind the scenes, however, Fox joined the clamor for revision. At the *Hollywood Reporter,* Billy Wilkerson, midway into his third decade of Code-related commentary, felt entitled to offer some advice. "Because our producers are evidently of the belief that our product should be of greater adult approach . . . it could be that the Code as set up years ago should undergo some changes," he suggested. "If so, change it and stop pussyfooting with its current administration."

On December 11, 1956, the MPAA stopped pussyfooting. After nearly a year of behind-the-scenes brainstorming by a special committee comprised of Eric Johnston, Daniel T. O'Shea (RKO), Barney Balaban (Paramount), Abe Schneider (Columbia), and Martin J. Quigley, who served as special consultant, the Code was given not just a tune-up but a major overhaul. While the prohibitions on sexual perversion and venereal disease were retained, and the restrictions on crime scenarios were somewhat tightened, the flat bans on illegal drugs, abortion, white slavery, and kidnapping were rescinded.[2] Johnston assured the moviegoing public that the underlying moral principles of the Code were eternal, but "in the light of experience and present day conditions" the policy changes were desirable. Expanding on the expansion, he only muddled his case. "A few years ago I made the observation that the Production Code was intended to be—and has been—a flexible living document—not a dead hand laid on artistic and creative endeavor." Far from being a capitulation, the revisions were another demonstration of "our faith in and adherence to the voluntary system of self-regulation in the industry."

Tellingly, while loosening the plotline belt several notches, the 1956 revisions tightened the Code in one sensitive area of the Cold War body politic. Under the heading of "National Feelings," a new provision was added:

> No picture shall be produced that tends to incite bigotry or hatred among peoples of different races, religions or national origins. The use of offensive

2. True to the studio's word, Twentieth Century-Fox's *A Hatful of Rain* (1957), directed by Fred Zinnemann, was the first Code-approved film to deal directly with drug addiction.

words as chink, dago, frog, greaser, hunkie, kike, nigger, spic, wop, yid, should be avoided.

Johnston insisted that the caution against the new obscene words was in fact a "blanket prohibition" and conceded that under the new provisions *Baby Doll* (1956), released earlier that year, could not have received a Code Seal because of the use of the words "nigger" and "wop." Significantly too, miscegenation, forbidden in 1930, permitted if "treated within the careful limits of good taste" in the 1954 revision, went unmentioned in the 1956 revision. Apparently, the mere memory of the word, and what it said about the Code and America, had become as offensive as the more familiar epithets. To the satisfaction of Martin J. Quigley, the miscegenation clause was simply written out of the text.

The 1956 revision was the first step toward a true institutional crack-up. Unlike the entry of *hell, damn*, and *nerts to you*, topics like drugs, kidnapping, and prostitution were narrative themes whose editorial insertion could not be characterized as "technical or clarifying": it knocked down pillars from the rock-solid edifice.

As the PCA twisted to fit the new fashions, the Legion of Decency kept the faith, still refusing to grade on a curve with its A-B-C ratings, still formidable enough to force a studio to submit to an edit at gunpoint. Yet Hollywood's surrender was no longer instinctive and universal. RKO acceded to a Legion edit of the costume drama *Son of Sinbad* (1955) because of the too-diaphanous gowns worn by its undulating belly dancers, but elsewhere filmmakers refused to fold. Rhetorical or official, a rebuke or condemnation from the Legion might still slice revenues in certain markets, but the mark of C was not universally lethal, even among Catholics, who, like the rest of America, were motorized and mobile, who had only to drive to an adjacent city to avoid a glowering parish priest at the corner Bijou. The battalions of obedient parishioners who once fell out of line at the ticket window had dispersed—gone to the suburbs, still observing the faith but refusing to genuflect on command.

Moreover, with Breen gone, the PCA and the Legion soon found themselves singing from different hymnals. On December 16, 1956, Francis Cardinal Spellman of New York strode to the pulpit of St. Patrick's Cathedral and ignored the obvious homily topic on the nativity to lash out at *Baby Doll*, a lust-driven melodrama directed by Elia Kazan and written by Tennessee Williams. The Cardinal had not seen the film, but he had seen the advertising and heard about the story. An infantile teenage bride (Carroll Baker), underdeveloped mentally but not physically, pouts and preens through an unconsummated marriage with her scurvy white-trash husband

Passed by the Shurlock Office: the teasing teenage bride (Carroll Baker) and her frustrated husband (Karl Malden) in Elia Kazan and Tennessee Williams' lurid *Baby Doll* (1956).

(Karl Malden) while his sleazy Sicilian business rival Silva (Eli Wallach) seeks to claim the girl's virginity.

Baby Doll had already been condemned by the Legion of Decency but the cardinal felt so foul an offense required a pulpit-pounding denunciation and a call to 1934-style Catholic action. Good Catholics, said the cardinal, must stay away from the "contemptuous defiance" of God's law "at the pain of sin." Furthermore, he gave his own personal C rating to the lax and complicit Shurlock Office, the "so-called self-regulatory system of the Motion Picture Association of America."[3] Like Cardinal Spellman, the Legion did not hold Elia Kazan or Tennessee Williams most culpable. In granting a Code Seal to a patently prurient scenario, Shurlock and his staff showed "an open disregard of the Code." The relations between the PCA and the Legion had sometimes been snippy, but never rocky. *Baby Doll* led to an acrimonious divorce between the two senior partners of Hollywood censorship.

3. Episcopalian Shurlock was away in Europe when *Baby Doll* received its Code Seal under the aegis of the former Catholic seminarian Jack Vizzard. "It was I, as temporary Mexican General of the Code operation, who yielded and gave Gadge [Kazan] his sequence," Vizzard admitted years later, also confessing that he had totally missed the plain implication of oral sex between Baby Doll and Silva, something that the more worldly Catholics at the Legion discerned immediately.

Since 1922, compromise, capitulation, and abject fear had defined the relationship between Hollywood and the moral guardians of American culture; from the mid-1950s onwards, resistance, defiance, and cynical exploitation would be the rule. Producers and directors who had toiled obediently in the studio system and danced the Breen Office shuffle on cue, declared independence and practiced uncivil disobedience. "In this country, judgments on matters of thought and taste are not handed down ironclad from an unchallenged authority," director Elia Kazan informed Cardinal Spellman. "People see for themselves and finally judge for themselves. That is as it should be. It's our tradition and our practice." Of course, it was not the tradition and the practice; just the opposite. Even a few years earlier, Kazan's multiple presumptions—to lecture a Prince of the Church on values, to assert that morality was not ironclad, and to elevate individual choice over clerical command—would have been heretical.

Preminger, Kazan, and a legion of coconspirators, both studio-backed and independently financed, soon dared far more. Throughout the latter half of the 1950s, Hollywood cinema flaunts its Code-snubbing moments so brazenly the gestures might seem pre-Code were not the weight of the last twenty years hanging over the insolence. "It's open season on Hollywood's Production Code and the set of morality standards appears the target of brickbats from various directions," *Variety* noticed in 1957. "There have been pro and con about its functions in the past, of course, but rarely has there been such a concentration of expressions of concern about its values." United Artists vice president Max E. Youngstein was not conflicted. "The Code should go away," he said.

On second thought, the Code need not go away too quickly: too much fun was to be had poking at the old parchment. Like parochial schoolboys baiting the nuns, Hollywood filmmakers in the latter half of the 1950s razzed the Code with devilish impertinence. Freed from the need to horse-trade with Breen, the Roman Catholic Alfred Hitchcock took a front seat in the row of naughty boys. In *To Catch a Thief* (1956), when Cary Grant and Grace Kelly passionately embrace, Hitchcock cuts to fireworks exploding in a nighttime sky. In *North by Northwest* (1959), when Cary Grant and Eva Marie Saint passionately embrace, Hitchcock cuts to a shot of a train zooming into a tunnel. Where Lubitsch's delicate touch was sophisticated and lyrical, Hitchcock's orgasmic editing was bawdy and blunt.

Perhaps the best instance of Hollywood's twin impulses in the twilight of the Code era—the taking of the new liberties and the anxieties of the old influences—occurs in a film by, who else, Otto Preminger. In *Anatomy of a Murder* (1959), a taut courtroom drama about a man on trial for the murder

Cracking the Code, one word at a time: prosecuting attorney (George C. Scott), no-nonsense judge (Joseph N. Welch) and accused murderer (Ben Gazzara) in Otto Preminger's *Anatomy of a Murder* (1959).

of his wife's alleged rapist, Preminger, who had staked his career on cracking the Code, bows in homage to its impact. Since 1934, the entire Code edifice had seemed to stand or fall on the muting or muttering of a single trigger word, a metonymy for so much else—hell, damn, kike, nigger, virgin. In *Anatomy of a Murder*, the word is "panties."

In the rape case that provokes the murder, a "certain undergarment" emerges as a pivotal piece of evidence. However, before the garment may be introduced into courtroom testimony and cinematic dialogue, the defense and the prosecuting attorneys approach the judge's bench for a nervous, whispered conversation about vocabulary. Afterwards, the judge (played by Joseph N. Welch, the real-life counsel for the Army in the televised Army–McCarthy hearings of 1954) stands to deliver instructions from the bench that are also instructions to moviegoers raised on the Code:

> For the benefit of the jury—but more especially for the spectators—the undergarment referred to in the testimony was, to be exact, [the victim's] panties.

At the sound of the word, the courtroom gallery erupts in raucous laughter. The judge waits for the chuckling to subside. Stone-faced, he continues:

> I wanted you to get your snickering over and done with. This pair of panties will be mentioned again in the course of this trial, and when it happens, there will not be one laugh, one snicker, one giggle, or even one smirk in my courtroom. There isn't anything comic about a pair of panties which figure in the violent death of one man and the possible incarceration of another.

Properly chastened, the courtroom gallery—and presumably the galleries in theaters across America—settles down for the rest of the proceedings.

"PIOUS PLATITUDES TAKE IT ON CHIN"

The provocations of the 1950s were gentle nudges compared to the rude curtain-closer on Hollywood's moral universe, Alfred Hitchcock's patho-psychiatrical *Psycho* (1960). A seminal movie memory for generations cradled by the Code, Hitchcock's slashing ambush seems storyboarded for the express purpose of hacking apart all the conventions and expectations of American cinema since 1934.

The lurid plot and lacerating style are partners in the crime. After languidly fornicating with a divorced man, Marion Crane (Janet Leigh) absconds with $40,000 embezzled from her trusting employer. Driving through rainswept darkness to meet her lover, she stops to spend the night at a rundown roadside motel, managed by the amateur taxidermist and deranged mama's boy Norman Bates (Anthony Perkins). When Marion checks in, Norman goes to a peephole to check out Marion. Transfixed, his eye glistening with sexual arousal, the voyeur scans her naked body as she disrobes for a shower. Only later will the voyeurs watching *Psycho* learn the full story of what unreels. Dressed in his dead mother's clothing, Norman pulls back the shower curtain and stabs the beautiful young woman to death for an insane reason that has nothing to do with her crime, a transgression for which she has repented moments before.

The jagged incisions into the naked body of an innocent woman—with the knife thrusts shredding the victim's flesh in rhythm to the jump cuts—was a murderous frenzy without precedent in Hollywood cinema. Equally unprecedented was the first-act death of the top-billed actress Janet Leigh, a malicious severing of the spectatorial contract between Hollywood and its star-centric audience. Nor did Hitchcock fail to trespass against another forbidden zone in the bathroom of the Bates Motel. Before entering the shower, Marion flushes some bits of paper down the toilet—a jarring swoosh that mirrors the swirling vortex to come.

After *Psycho*, and kindred spirits in cinematic dislocation such as *The Manchurian Candidate* (1962), John Frankenheimer's conspiracy thriller about incest, assassination, and the illusion of free will, and *The Birds* (1963), Hitchcock's next flight into a moral void, Shurlock could only play a futile zone defense before shrugging and forfeiting the game. "There are now no taboos on subject matter," Shurlock admitted in 1963. "Movies have changed with the changes of civilization." The Code had changed too, from an ironclad contract to a scrap of paper.

That same year, Eric Johnston was fatally stricken by a cerebral hemorrhage. Leaderless and in crisis (again), the motion picture industry floundered, marking time with a caretaker interim president, MPAA vice president Ralph Hetzel, before turning, in April 1966, to Jack Valenti to pilot Hollywood to a safe port in the post-studio, television-dominated era. Valenti possessed the usual qualifications for the MPAA presidency: as a former trusted aide to President Lyndon Johnson, he was politically connected; as a former publicity man from Texas, he was media savvy; and as an Italian Catholic, he was not Jewish. Valenti was also an ardent opponent of censorship—federal, state, city, and (this was new) in-house.

"I did not become president of this organization to preside over a feckless Code," Valenti announced during his first site visit to Hollywood. Though implying he meant to put teeth back into the regime, he was actually planning to defang it. Valenti was determined to guide the industry away from an atrophied self-regulation into a more lenient corporate oversight. "It was plain that the old system of self-regulation, begun with the formation of the MPAA in 1922, had broken down," he reasoned. "From the very first day of my own succession to the MPAA President's office, I had sniffed the Production Code constructed by the Hays Office. There was about this stern, forbidding catalogue of 'Dos and Don'ts' the odious smell of censorship, I determined to junk it at the first opportune moment."

Two instances of PCA folly hastened the arrival of the opportune moment. The swan song controversies erupted over *The Pawnbroker* (1965), Sidney Lumet's version of Edmund Lewis Wallant's novel, and *Who's Afraid of Virginia Woolf?* (1966), Mike Nichols's version of Edward Albee's play. Both were respectable works drawn from esteemed literary sources, and both glimmered with an art house veneer of Serious Adult Cinema. Both were also clear violations of the Code—*The Pawnbroker* for image, *Who's Afraid of Virginia Woolf?* for language, a division of disobedience that neatly matched the sight-and-sound surveillance of the PCA.

The Pawnbroker was a harrowing tale of a Jewish Holocaust survivor who runs a pawnshop in Harlem, a man tormented by the past and stunted in the present. During a flashback to a concentration camp and in a sequence in his pawnshop, the film exposed two glimpses of female nudity, full shots of the female breast. Shurlock had no option but to deny the film a Code Seal because "indecent or undue exposure is forbidden." Back in synch with the PCA, the Legion of Decency condemned *The Pawnbroker* for the same reason. Bare breasts were never "necessary," said Monsignor Thomas F. Little, the Legion's executive director. "[The filmmakers] could have had the same scene and shot it from the back."

Whether the breast shots were necessary or gratuitous, the Legion's days of privileged access to Hollywood's editing rooms were over. Ely Landau, producer of *The Pawnbroker*, appealed Shurlock's decision to the MPAA Board, which, after a four-and-a-half-hour meeting, overruled Shurlock, leaving the breast shots intact and issuing a Code Seal. "The sole exception granted *The Pawnbroker* is to be viewed as a special and unique case and in no way as one setting a precedent," declared acting MPAA president Hetzel. Knowing better, *Variety* italicized the significance of the MPAA's "precedent-shattering step":

> *For the first time in the history of the Hollywood Production Code official recognition has been given to the good taste and artistic merit with which a subject is treated, not only to whether it hews to the current standards by which the Code is interpreted.*

In other words, the Code might brush aside moral standards in favor of artistic merit.

The next year, *Who's Afraid of Virginia Woolf?* answered its own question when Shurlock refused the film a Code Seal due to its no-holds-barred bouts of uneuphemized vernacular and salty poetry. Warner Bros., the film's distributor, was willing to eliminate "friggin'" and "screw you," but demanded to let loose two "screws" and a host of equally blunt phrases. Moreover, the studio announced that Code Seal or no Code Seal the film would be released with a self-imposed "adults only classification." Less shocked by language than image, the former Legion of Decency, now christened the National Catholic Office of Motion Pictures (whose acronym NCOMP sounded far less fearsome than "the Legion"), awarded the film a surprisingly lenient A-IV ("morally objectionable for adults, with reservations").

Confronted with a fait accompli, the MPAA Board voted again to overrule Shurlock and exempt *Who's Afraid of Virginia Woolf?* from the Code. As with *The Pawnbroker*, the art of the project outweighed the letter of the

Not a rhetorical question: Elizabeth Taylor, Richard Burton, George Segal, and Sandy Dennis in Mike Nichols and Edward Albee's *Who's Afraid of Virginia Woolf?* (1966).

law. In a feckless demurral that fell on deaf ears, the MPAA hastened to add that vulgar dialogue not as able as Albee's "would not be approved for a film of lesser quality, or a film determined to exploit language for language's sake." Also, for the second time, the board insisted the exception was a one-time thing. "This exemption does not mean the floodgates are open for language and other material."

True to its word, after a fashion, the MPAA was not opening the floodgates; it was dynamiting the dam. On September 20, 1966, Valenti unveiled a new Production Code that repudiated the old Production Code. The new text was not a revision of the old but a wholesale rewriting that deleted the stern Jesuit prose for a philosophy "permissive rather than prohibitive," as the *Hollywood Reporter* alliterated. Expunging the last vestiges of Quigley–Lord–Breen moral absolutism, the new document stressed opposition to "censorship and classification by law" and delegated the parents of America as the final "arbiters of family conduct." As a helpful guidepost, family-unfriendly fare was tagged with a warning label ("Suggested for Mature Audiences"), but not barred from production or exhibition. The official MPAA press release explained, "this revised code is designed to keep in closer harmony with the mores, the culture, and the moral sense and the expectations of our society." The old system of "archaic prohibitions" and "gauzily defined guidelines" was pronounced dead and buried. A good soldier, Shurlock claimed to be "delighted" with the "long overdue" new Code and pledged to "try to persuade the producers to be more reasonable in the type of pictures they are making." The headline in *Variety* summed up the turnabout: "Pious Platitudes Take It on Chin as Film Biz Rewrites Moral Code."

In shredding the old document, Valenti and the entertainment conglomerates that had supplanted the studio system were not calling for a screen world without limits or open admission for all moviegoers. "This is still self-restraint, self-regulation, and self-discipline," he maintained. "We want to make clear that expansion of the artist's freedom doesn't mean tolerance of license." But a Code that was a denial of its former self did, in fact, mean greater tolerance if not total license: "the expansion of the artist's freedom," after all, was the point. In the pre-Code era, Hollywood had defied a Code meant to bind. In the brief neo-Code era after 1966, Hollywood slipped into an elastic Code built for comfort. If the crosscut violence of *Bonnie and Clyde* (1967) and the cross-generational sex of *The Graduate* (1967) were worthy of a Code Seal, then the old stamp of approval really had melted into a rubber stamp. The dilemma for the MPAA was how to abandon the farce of self-regulation while still keeping a quarantine around film content deemed toxic for younger audiences. The solution was to rate rather than regulate.

Almost from the birth of the medium, the notion of motion picture ratings—classifying films according to content and restricting admission by age—had offered a middle ground between state censorship and the free market. Though a road not taken in Hollywood, state and city censorship boards often awarded exhibition licenses contingent upon "adults only" postings (dubbed "pink tickets"). Traditionally, the motion picture industry had rejected the "adults only" label due to enforcement difficulties at the ticket window and Hollywood's self-definition as an "art for the millions," accessible to all. "It is dangerous for Hollywood to classify pictures," *Variety* explained in 1934. "The industry not only stands to lose millions yearly in trade but the very tabbing of a picture in front of a box office is an invitation and incentive for lawmakers and agitators to put through state censorship." Eric Johnston also resisted classification, preferring instead to edit and update the Code. "A rating system will never work in this country," Johnston declared in 1956.

A decade later, however, with the Code a cracked shell, with state censorship under assault from the courts, with television the new consensus medium, and with the studios desperate to lure back the lost millions, classification answered Hollywood's twin needs for product differentiation and self-preservation. It also forestalled state and city boards from devising their own ratings schemes.

On October 7, 1968, after dozens of meetings with motion picture executives and extended huddles with MPAA general counsel Louis Nizer, Valenti proclaimed a revolution in American motion picture spectatorship. A few weeks later, on November 1, 1968, the PCA was officially supplanted by an alphabet rating system whose sliding grade scale evaluated motion pictures along age-appropriate guidelines ranging from family-friendly to adults only. The original ratings were:

G — Suggested for General Audiences, for pictures defined as "acceptable for all ages without consideration of age."

M — Suggested for Mature Audiences, meaning adults and mature young people, for pictures "which because of their theme, content, and treatment might require more mature judgment by viewers, and about which parents should exercise discretion."

R — Restricted—Persons under 16 not admitted unless accompanied by parent or adult guardian.

X — Persons Under 16 Not Admitted, for pictures which "because of treatment of sex, violence, crime, or profanity. Pictures rated X do not qualify for a Code Seal."

When self-regulation became ratings, the personnel holdovers from the old regime fell like tenpins: Jack Vizzard resigned, and by year's end Geoffrey Shurlock had retired. Eugene "Doc" Dougherty was tapped to succeed Shurlock and helm the new Code and Rating Administration, a title whose second noun belied its first. In 1978 the outfit was given the more accurate though redundant name, the Classification and Rating Administration (CARA).[4] Decades later, in a radically transformed media environment, Valenti posted his version of the transition on the MPAA's Web page:

> So, the emergence of the voluntary rating system filled the vacuum provided by dismantling of the Hays Production Code. The movie industry would no longer "approve or disapprove" the content of a film, but we would now see

4. According to film historian Stephen Vaughn, Richard D. Heffner, appointed to head CARA in 1974, insisted on the name change to cast off any lingering confusion with the old Code, "accepting the redundancy to keep the acronym."

our primary task as giving advance cautionary warnings to parents so that parents could make the decision about the movie going of young children.

Where the Breen Office whispered a soothing "Be assured," the Classification and Rating Administration issues a curt "Be warned."

Over the years, the ratings from CARA have been refined, but one practice has remained constant. The new regime is known neither by acronym nor personnel nor document. The grades came handed down anonymously, enigmatically, in the form of blunt letters in a screenlike rectangle imprinted on posters, trailers, and ad mattes: G, PG, PG-13, R, and NC-17, with the slightest of explanations typed in the box: "sexual content," "explicit violence," "brief nudity," "language."[5] CARA is a secret society, guided only by the gut instincts and inchoate feelings of a membership whose names, qualifications, and grade-point scale are a mystery to all save the inner sanctum of the MPAA—a true star chamber.[6]

No matter. The shift from self-regulation to ratings has proven as brilliant a tactical move for contemporary Hollywood as the Code was for Golden Age Hollywood. The MPAA rating system expanded freedom of expression, placated parents, stymied pressure groups, stabilized profit margins, and assured Hollywood's continued dominance over exhibition space. Just as a Code Seal was the entry visa into studio-affiliated theaters during the classical Hollywood era, only an MPAA-rated film bearing a G, PG, PG-13, or R (no NC-17s need apply) will be booked into the multiplex malls that house most of the nearly 38,000 screens in the United States. The closed shop of the new racket is almost as penetration proof as the old. Since 1968, the survival skills and evolutionary adaptability of the American motion picture industry have proven far more impressive than the lumbering reactions of its erstwhile comparison case, the American automobile industry.

In casting off the Code, Hollywood traded up, exchanging its custodial stewardship and presumptive universality for greater screen freedom and continued market domination. "The exhibitors of the United States realize that the age of the picture as mass entertainment unit is passed," said Julian

5. Valenti recalled that after the abolition of the PCA, the MPAA convened a group of learned scholars and moralists to compose a guiding document, but the piffle that resulted was so vague and platitudinous he scrapped it.

6. In *This Movie Is Not Yet Rated* (2006), a documentary exposé on the practices of the top-secret Classification and Rating Administration, director Kirby Dick hired private detectives to track down the membership of the board. Soon afterward, MPAA president Dan Glickman, who succeeded the long-serving Valenti in 2004, pledged to make CARA more transparent and responsive.

Rifkin, president of the National Association of Theatre Owners in 1968, when the ratings were first posted. "Today films are aimed at specialty audiences." Urban upscale, rural downscale, inner-city African American, whitebread suburban, older women, 18- to 34-year-old males, children and, the most special of all specialty audiences, teenagers. Occasionally, what the twenty-first-century descendents of the old studio ad-pub boys call a "four quadrant" film (young/old/male/female) might score across the generations and genders, but Hollywood banks on precision targeting and ancillary marketing aimed at that slice of the demographic pie with hormones to excite and money to burn. Though always more of an imaginative conceit than a reliable statistical model, the idealized moviegoing public that Martin J. Quigley conjured in his never-produced homage to the Code—the extended family of Dad, Mom, Sis, Junior, and Granny trotting off to the local Bijou to see a film suitable for all ages—has been turned away at the doors. Besides, Dad, Mom, and Granny have lost the habit, and Sis and Junior prefer to hang out with their friends.

15

FINAL CUT

Joseph I. Breen and the Auteur Theory

The word *auteur* did not enter the American vernacular until the 1960s, a term of endearment imported from the French. In postwar Paris, clustered around the Cinémathèque Française, a generation of French cinephiles saw what Americans had been blind to. Starved for Hollywood fare after five years of embargo under the Nazi Occupation and besotted by the kinetic energy of studio system craftsmanship, foreign eyes spied priceless masterpieces where the host country nationals had seen only disposable schlock.

In the early 1950s, in the pages of the highbrow fanzine *Cahiers du Cinéma*, a cohort of French film critics and future *nouvelle vague* luminaries concocted a heady brew of polemics and aesthetics known as "la politique des auteurs," a high-stakes gambit dedicated to elevating a lowbrow pastime. Unable to sit still before the bloated literary adaptations and static camera placements of the tiresome French Tradition of Quality, the likes of François Truffaut, Claude Chabrol, Eric Rohmer, and Jean-Luc Godard plotted an artistic defection. "A love of vitality made us love anything that came from Hollywood," remembered Truffaut years later, still in thrall to his *l'amour fou*.

Being French intellectuals, the *Cahiers* crowd argued over everything, but all agreed with the manifesto of group mentor André Bazin: that what made Hollywood "so much better than anything else in the world" was not only the precision engineering of the studio factory ("the genius of the system") but "the quality of certain directors." Throughout the 1950s, Bazin, Truffaut, and their Gaelic coconspirators composed hosannas to a firmament of glittering names above the titles: the old masters John Ford and Alfred Hitchcock, the jacks-of-all-genres Raoul Walsh and Michael Curtiz, the young turks Nicholas Ray and Samuel Fuller, and the one-of-a-kind genius Orson Welles. No longer a sweatshop run by the Lords of Kitsch and the Merchants of Dreck, the Hollywood studio system was lauded as the glorious fount for the greatest art of the twentieth century.

In 1962, auteurism crossed the Atlantic, imported by Andrew Sarris, the American film critic who did more than any other homegrown connoisseur to teach the natives to honor the prophets in their own land. In a pair of essays for the small-circulation but big-impact journal *Film Comment* and later in his synoptic guidebook *The American Cinema: Directors and Directions, 1929–1968*, published in 1968, the first treasure map to the Golden Age of Hollywood, Sarris lent a coherent taxonomy to nearly 10,000 films and composed pithy critiques of precisely 115 directors, assisted only, in those primitive pre-video, pre-cable days, by his prodigious memory and a lifetime spent spellbound in darkness.

According to the Franco-American critical alliance, auteurs were a band apart. "To speak any of their names is to evoke a self-contained world with its own laws and landscapes," Sarris sang in a rhapsodic passage honoring the topmost artists in the "pantheon"—his word—of classical Hollywood cinema. Onto the canvas of celluloid, the true auteur projected a personal set of ideas and images—that is, a consistent moral vision and a unique visual style.

At first, Sarris fought an uphill battle with colleagues who felt more comfortable in the art house than at the drive-in. Pauline Kael, later the doyenne of high-end film criticism at the *New Yorker*, scoffed that the auteur critics "follow the lead of children who also prefer simple action films and westerns and horror films to works that make demands on their understanding." After all, the notion that the studio director moonlighted as a creative visionary was a bold grasp for status. Heretofore considered clever craftsmen at best, hired hacks at worst, Hollywood filmmakers seemed dubious aspirants for admission into the ranks of capital A artists.

The persistence of the auteurists paid off, however, and by the mid-1970s the bookish subtitle-readers were routed. Not only was the language of auteurism spoken fluently by movie fans and critics alike, but the mindset had infiltrated the executive boardrooms of the Hollywood entertainment conglomerates (where the director became a force to be reckoned with) and the corridors of university film schools (where freshly minted graduates from NYU to UCLA assumed the mantle of "auteur" on the strength of a single 16mm student film project). A concept once considered ludicrous on its face—that the names on the studio payroll might be uttered in the same breath as the grand maestros of the finer arts—hardened into an orthodoxy. Fair or not, the directors seized the glory and grabbed the credit. For the savvy moviegoer, the name above the title became the only name that really mattered.

The most cherished emblem of auteur status, the privilege reserved to a select few with the muscle and cunning to reverse the customary hierarchy between moneyman and artist, is the right to final cut. "Final cut" is film industry–speak for the editorial last tag, a legally binding prerogative inked into the written contract between director and studio. To possess final cut is to wrest ownership and assert authorship: to sign off on the film before the negative is duplicated and the prints are circulated. Whatever corporate entity bankrolls the project, the auteur with final cut certifies the film as a finished *objet d'art* stamped with a proprietary credit and personal signature. "Directed by—," "A film by—," "Written for the screen and directed by—."

Joseph I. Breen did not know what an auteur was, much less consider himself one: in his heyday, no one around Hollywood did. "To me, it was always a job of work," snapped John Ford, one of the preeminent auteurs of classical Hollywood cinema, when the critic and future auteur Peter Bogdanovich tried to get the old codger to fess up to an artistic vision. Yet for twenty years, it was Breen—not the studio mogul, not the Oscar-winning director, not the marquee star, and certainly not the lowly screenwriter—who held the right of final cut over Hollywood cinema. It was Breen who approved the blueprint, supervised the construction, and inspected the finished project before stamping it fit for release. "It is not too much to say that Joseph I. Breen has had a greater effect upon the screen than any other one man in pictures," wrote MPPDA vice president Charles Francis Coe in 1944, revealing what people in-the-know already knew. "Joe affects them all." Without his imprimatur, quite literally without the "Breen Seal" of approval, a Hollywood production never left the plant. Breen possessed final cut over more films than anyone in the history of American cinema.

And not just cut. To think of Breen as a bluenose censor, scissors at hand, ripping into a beautiful tapestry to shred what repulsed his eyes, is to miss his method and mission. To be sure, he performed slicing and bleeping aplenty: there was much he did not want to see, or hear, or even whiff, on screen. He expunged dialogue, vetoed scenarios, banned novels, and pronounced projects dead on arrival. However, Breen's enduring legacy lies in what he worked *in* to Hollywood cinema: a moral vision, outlined by the Production Code as read, felt, and interpreted by a Victorian Irish Catholic. In auteurist terms, Breen promulgated a set of laws (the moral universe) and landscapes (the visible images).

The cultural residue from Breen's two decades in Hollywood continues to permeate American culture. Artistically and archivally, the Breen Office is, in a sense, an ongoing operation.

The artistic legacy is ever before the eyes, screened in repertory theaters, telecast on network and cable channels, and sold in DVD packages. The moral universe of classical Hollywood cinema—the world of reticence, constraint, discretion, untruths, and unspokens—comes from out of the past as another country where they do things differently. Packed tight with coded repression, it plays like the cinematic version of a Jane Austen novel, where no one can say what he or she really means and communication depends on decoding tiny gestures and listening for slight inflections of language.

For moviegoers of a certain generation or sensibility, the repressed energy is cherished as the source of the exotic charm and exquisite brinksmanship of Hollywood's Golden Age, an alloy forged not only by the genius of the system but the conscience of the Breen Office. Suffused by a plaintive nostalgia, the affection for the bygone aesthetic bespeaks a longing for the certainty of standards and the security of tradition, an affinity for a mannered time where curse words, nudity, and bloodshed are banished, where bedrooms are for sleeping and bathrooms are unmentioned. "Take three great producers—Irving Thalberg, David Selznick, and Sam Goldwyn—practically all the output of their production activities was made under the rather strict requirements of the Code, and resulted in pictures which are still considered masterpieces," Geoffrey Shurlock pointed out in 1970. "The Code wasn't as much of a tragedy as a lot of liberal writers like to make it out."

Breen's own evaluation of his contribution was not modest. "It seems to be generally agreed that Hollywood, without the Code, just could not exist," he reflected in retirement. "With an occasional exception, no motion pictures made anywhere can begin to compare in artistry, in entertainment, and in beauty with the films which are created in Hollywood and which have brought happiness and immeasurable joy to untold millions throughout the world." Moreover, Hollywood's civic-minded self-discipline kept meddling state czars from mucking up work best left to private business. "And this, mind you, without one penny of subsidy from governments seeking to encourage and expand artistic expression in motion pictures as a cultural part of the nation's pride."

Less self-interested or starry-eyed viewers are more apt to cringe than swoon. Especially in the academic world, where film studies has been a growth industry since Hollywood became a fit vehicle to ride the university tenure track, the judgment on the Breen Office ranges from harsh to vitriolic. The old sneer—that the Breen Office was a nest of hidebound Puritans doing the bidding of the knuckle-dragging *boobus Americanus*—has been replaced by a modern, or postmodern, lexicon of abuse. Hollywood under the Code was variously, cumulatively, and intractably racist, patriarchal, misogynistic, homophobic, capitalistic, and colonialist. A certain artistic sheen and technical expertise is acknowledged, but academic scholars really sink their teeth into exposures and condemnations of the bourgeois, hetero-normative, American-centric values upheld and celebrated from genre to genre, studio to studio. The Code becomes an overarching, billowing, metastasizing "superstructure" and the exegetic action lies in detecting subversive impulses and transgressive undercurrents tugging against the repressive surface calm.

Yet whether submitted for praise or protest, the visible images of Hollywood under the Code reveal an incomplete picture. Harder to focus on is the never seen and might-have-been: the scenarios strangled at birth, the films that failed to bloom, or grew to life stunted and deformed, the issues not raised, the blinders that kept Hollywood from facing the menace of Nazism, the blight of racism, or the other ethical dilemmas and social problems omitted from the Baltimore catechism. Breen saw his mission as a positive force, an active agency for good, but he negated the heretical alternatives and scratched out the wrong answers. The Breen Office files are full of plots rejected as too politically controversial or commercially inconvenient. Motion picture versions of Sinclair Lewis's inflammatory novel *It Can't Happen Here* or Herman J. Mankiewicz's anti-Hitler screenplay *The Mad Dog of Europe* were condemned properties in Breen's Hollywood.

The Code not only smothered worthy studio projects but its stranglehold on independent production and affiliated theaters cut off the creative oxygen available for all cinema. No Code Seal meant no choice exhibition venues. Uncertified "bootleg" motion pictures were squeezed out of respectable neighborhoods and into seedy ghettos of sensationalism and carnival disrepute—marijuana melodramas, sex thrillers, and flesh-baring expeditionary films. In 1940, William Nigh, the producer of *No Greater Sin* (1941), sought desperately and with evident sincerity to obtain a Code Seal for a serious, adult drama about venereal disease. Long negotiations ensued, sustained by the hope that Breen, who was always polite and seemingly sympathetic, would relent. In the end, though, the Code prohibition was nonnegotiable. The glaring title of another film with the same venereal lesson, also denied a Code Seal, sums up the exhibitor attitude to a non-Code film: *Damaged Goods* (1937). Whatever the tone and temper of mainstream Hollywood without the Breen Office, the films outside the margins of the studio system would have been edgier, more dissonant, more diverse—and more accessible at the neighborhood Bijou.

Nonetheless, to imagine that a customer-stroking business like Hollywood would ever have boldly and fearlessly confronted the troubling, alienating, and knotty issues of the day—the Great Depression, World War II, the Cold War—is to lapse into wishful thinking. Code or no Code, the dictates of conventional morality and satisfied patrons would have remained expedient business practice. Without the protective cover of the Code, the pressures from censor boards and bluenose activists might well have made Hollywood *more* craven rather than more courageous. In 1934 the question facing the studio moguls was not whether but what kind of censorship was to be imposed. "It was a miracle that the movies did not become the Government's business," marveled FDR braintruster Raymond Moley, as he began work on his history of the Hays Office in 1944. The creation of a New Deal agency—the National Motion Picture Administration? the Federal Film Review Board?—was a decided possibility, the multiplication of state and city censor boards a certainty. Besieged by the Legion of Decency, intimidated by the New Deal, and unprotected by the First Amendment, the MPPDA held a bad hand and grabbed the best deal on the table.

In fact, the deal was attractive enough to be taken, gladly, by two kindred media tributaries. Having proven so expedient for Hollywood, the template of self-regulation was adopted by both comic books and television for the same reasons the motion picture industry acquiesced: to placate moral guardians, stave off government censorship, and maintain a steady profit stream.

In 1948, when the graphic art of the comic book turned toxically graphic, the newly formed Association of Comics Magazine Publishers announced the adoption of a Comics Code to quell criticism from parents groups and educators appalled by the frightful gore and voluptuous beauties splashed on the covers of material targeted at juvenile innocents. The Comics Code pledged to foreswear "sympathy against law and justice" and eliminate "objectionable 'inspirations'; sadism; sexy wanton comics; femininity indecently exposed; vulgar language; divorce humorously treated; [and] ridicule of racial or religious groups." The language, bragged the proud parent at *Motion Picture Herald*, was "a substantial paraphrase of salient aspects of the Production Code of the motion picture industry."

The evolution of the Comics Code also replicated the time lag between adoption and enforcement undergone by its inspiration: though pledged in 1948, it wasn't until 1954, after investigations by the U.S. Senate into the insidious effects of horror comic books, that the Comics Code Authority enforced the rules. Also, just as on the film frame, the Comics Code Seal, a stamp-like logo reading "Approved by the Comics Code Authority," was imprinted on the front cover of the comic book.

The logical medium to plagiarize the text and lift the blueprint of the Production Code Administration was television. From infancy to the prime time of three-network hegemony, television enforced a video facsimile of the Code. As early as 1950, *TV Guide* founder and media mogul Walter Annenberg urged "the owners and operators of all networks and television stations to join in adopting the Motion Picture Production Code for self-control as a means of living up to the responsibilities of our public franchises." He believed that "since television enjoys the same basic principles of the movies—sight and sound—and since the Code has proved successful during the past 20 years, it is reasonable that the same Code should apply to both mediums."

Before signing on, the networks solicited advice from the leading expert in the field. On April 20, 1950, in a talk to the American Television Society in New York entitled "A Code of Good Taste for the Television Society," Breen explained the philosophy of the Code, reviewed the history of the Production Code Administration, and reminded the network executives of the stupidities, hassles, and expenses of government censorship. "It would be an intolerable presumption on my part to suggest what you should do," Breen said, before suggesting what they should do. "Twenty years' experience has given us license to discuss whether [the Code] has worked," he asserted. "It has worked. It allows for the widest possible variety of entertainment as may be seen from [the] subjects films present. Except for restricted areas like sex perversion, we do not care what producers make. We want good taste and things called by their right name"—by which he meant, of course, that good was called good and evil was called evil. "Take it from me," Breen told the custodians of the future consensus medium, like the moguls of 1934 fearful of federal censorship and eager to strip-mine a golden opportunity, "if we in the picture industry learned one thing, it is this: that people are fair-minded, liberal, broad, but they don't want indecency." The next day, in a closed session, Breen "got down to brass tacks" and bluntly told the television industry to do what the motion picture industry had done exactly twenty years earlier (adopt a Code) and to do immediately what the motion picture industry had done only under duress (enforce it). That same day, the National Association of Broadcasters announced plans to formulate a Television Code. In 1953, when the NAB adopted its own voluntary Television Code, the words of the text and the ethos of self-regulation were borrowed from the Hollywood template.

Television programmers deferred to another Code regulation. In the 1950s, strapped for cash and forced to trade with the enemy, the major studios began selling their film libraries to the networks and independent stations. The stain of the pre-Code era still being too scarlet for the living room, the pre-Breen inventory was excluded from the packages by mutual agreement. When a pre-Code renegade happened to slip by, television stations cut the print to ribbons to suit the Television Code. Only in the age of cable in the 1980s would the lost gems and oddball curios of the pre-Code era be restored and revived for uncensored telecast.

If the artistic legacy of the Breen Office will always spark a lively point-counterpoint, the archival legacy is a case closed. A meticulous administrator and conscientious record-keeper, Breen bequeathed a unique inheritance to film history. "An extensive and well-ordered file is available to facilitate reference to past disputed points," Breen told producers who wanted to research a precedent or appeal a decision. Before Breen, under the Studio Relations Committee, the official record of Hollywood's in-house censorship is hit or miss. After Breen, under the Production Code Administration, the censorship story is exhaustively preserved and readily retrievable, often in a neat tied-up package for each title: from pitch to production and on through the circuits of exhibition, the files are stuffed with reviews, memos, postmortems, charts, enough printed evidence and red-tape residue to warm the heart of a pencil-necked bureaucrat or, for that matter, a film scholar following a paper trail. "Before Breen, the records of the office are a mess," commented Samuel Gill, the longtime archivist at the Margaret Herrick Library of the Academy of Motion Picture Arts and Sciences. "After Breen, the margins on the stationery are the same for the next twenty years."

When the PCA closed up shop in 1968, Hollywood, always careless of its history, buried the files in stockrooms and kept no systematic inventory. When storage space for file cabinets reached critical mass, thousands of copies of blue-penciled scripts—the literary residue of some forty years of American cinema—were tossed into dumpsters. The surviving materials remained behind lock and key for decades, the files unknown or inaccessible. Except to the generation that worked with Breen, his imprint and import receded from memory. Of course, film historians knew about Hollywood censorship and frowned at the bluenose sniffing of "the Hays Office," but the actual process—the protocols of the bureaucracy, the philosophy of the regime, and the character of the man who ran the shop—was a blank slate. Andrew Sarris's landmark 1968 work, *The American Cinema*, the definitive guide for a generation of film buffs and scholars before the dawn of encyclopedic guidebooks and Internet databases, makes not a single mention of Joseph I. Breen. Even today, Breen's name is not listed in the index of many standard histories of American cinema. The surname verb and oft-used pun of so many trade press jibes disappeared from the lingo of Hollywood and slipped under the radar of media historians. "Joseph I. Breen, the best known man to citizens of Hollywood," as the journalist-screenwriter Adela Rogers St. Johns called him in 1941, became the least known man to students of Hollywood.

The cloud of amnesia began to lift in 1983 when film historian Lea Jacobs, then a graduate student in cinema studies at the University of California at Los Angeles, interviewed Albert Van Schmus about the history of Hollywood censorship. Van Schmus's career in the motion picture industry stretched back to 1941, when Breen first hired him as a clerk at RKO, a good cover, he recalled, from which to sneak on to the set of Orson Welles's *The Magnificent Ambersons* (1942) and spy on the engineer with his train set. He later worked at the PCA under Breen from 1949 to 1954, then for Geoffrey Shurlock, and finally at the Classification and Rating Administration (CARA), the successor to the PCA. Soon to retire, Van Schmus lamented the destruction of the script files and revealed to Jacobs the existence of a row of file cabinets stuffed with old PCA material—in-house reports, interoffice memos, reviews, letters from moviegoers, telegrams back and forth from Hollywood to New York. He generously gave the young graduate student access to the records for a project that ultimately became Jacobs's *The Wages of Sin: Censorship and the Fallen Woman Film, 1928–1942*, published in 1995.

A short time after the initial contact with Van Schmus, while doing research at the Margaret Herrick Library, the research arm of the Academy of Motion Picture Arts and Sciences (AMPAS), Jacobs reminded archivist Samuel Gill about the cache of riches whose fate would likely be the literal ash heap of history unless the Academy intervened. Gaining possession of the legendary and seldom-seen files had long been a goal of the Herrick archivists, but the imminent threat spurred the staff to action. Moving with alacrity, Linda Mehr, director of the Herrick Library, contacted Fay Kanin, president of the Academy, who in turn approached Jack Valenti, president of the Motion Picture Association of America. Valenti readily agreed that the PCA's records warranted preservation and approved the transfer of forty-four file cabinets of materials from the MPAA's offices in Los Angeles to the Herrick Library for permanent housing and systematic cataloguing. Better: whereas most industries balk at opening their corporate past to prying eyes, the MPAA granted motion picture researchers generous access to the inside dope. Since 1984, whether seeking raw data or raw emotion, students, scholars, and filmmakers have been able to sift through the case files for a hidden Hollywood backstory.

By then, Breen was not even a dim memory in Hollywood history. The fast fade to black was his own choice: after leaving the stage in 1954, he never returned for a second act. True, his retirement package included a salary of $20,000 for seven years and the title "emeritus advisor," but while the checks were real, the title was honorary. "The fact that I am an advisor around here means that if any of you bastards comes to me for advice, you'll get a punch in the nose," he barked good-naturedly at the PCA staff, before slamming the door on the way out. "I don't think he ever [again] sat in on a meeting or saw a picture," recalled Shurlock. "He had had it."

In 1955, Breen retired with Mary to Arizona, first to a high-rise in Phoenix, and then, in 1960, to the newly built retirement community in Sun City, outside of town. The couple traveled when Breen's health permitted ("Mary would go on a cruise at the drop of a hat," recalled her granddaughter) and returned to Hollywood for the occasional visit with family in the area. Breen was "all too rarely seen in Hollywood nowadays," a society item noted in 1957, when he came back to attend the wedding of actor Pat O'Brien's daughter.

Upon retirement, Breen muttered something about writing a memoir of his newspaper beats, Catholic actions, and Hollywood wars, but in the end the incorrigible raconteur and inveterate wordsmith kept his mouth shut. "Get away from me," he snapped at Shurlock, whenever his friend coaxed him to go to the typewriter. "Don't ever bring up any books to me." Nor did Breen live long enough to be importuned by the young journalists and oral historians bent on resuscitating the waxworks of Hollywood's past, even had he agreed to sit still for an interrogation.

In private, throughout the late 1950s and early 1960s, he would bemoan the sorry state of screen morality and act as in-house censor (literally) for his visiting grandchildren. In 1961 he was furious when Otto Preminger's original, unedited version of *The Moon Is Blue* received a Code Seal from the Shurlock Office, but he limited his rants to the family circle. The once larger-than-life personality and heavy Hollywood hitter stayed out of the public eye with such determination that, by 1961, a premature report of his death was published by Louella Parsons, the wired gossip columnist for the *Los Angeles Examiner*, who referred to "the late Joseph Breen" in an item on the marriage of his granddaughter, Mary Pat Richards. "I am happy to correct this statement," a chagrined Parsons backpedaled the next day. "Mr. Breen is living in retirement with his wife Mary in Phoenix, Arizona."

One Hollywood friend from the old days remembered that Breen was still alive. That same year, the producer and director Stanley Kramer arranged for Breen to attend a private screening of *Judgment at Nuremberg* (1961), his brilliant docudrama, written by Abby Mann, about the second round of Nuremberg trials in 1948. Commenting as a critic, not a censor, Breen composed a warm letter of appreciation to Kramer, both for the film and the gesture. "We thought—my wife and I—that the picture was utterly magnificent," he enthused. "It took us three days to return from the emotional impact of it all. It marks a new high in the development of screen artistry. I shall not easily forget your most distinguished achievement."

In October 1961, Breen's pro forma stint as nominal "advisor" to the Production Code Administration ended. "The twenty years that you devoted to administering the Production Code encompassed the most successful period in Hollywood's history," wrote Eric Johnston, in a kind note marking the transition. "When you assumed this responsibility in 1934, the industry was in deep trouble. Almost single-handed you succeeded in correcting this dangerous threat and got the film business back onto the rails so that it could become the important world force that it is now, and for twenty years you were the conscience of the industry." Johnston signed off with a nice sentiment but a poor prediction: "When history gets ready to sift the wheat from the chaff and to enshrine the names of those who contributed importantly to Hollywood's continued eminence, your name will have to be high on the roll of honor."

When Johnston's letter arrived, Breen was already suffering through the long physical decline that made his final years a purgatory on earth. "I have been seriously ill for most of the past two years," he had confided in his letter to Stanley Kramer. "I have [had] to undergo four major surgical operations at the base of my spine and while I am presently showing some improvement in my general health I still suffer greatly from the pain in my legs and feet. I am still confined pretty much to my bed and unable to walk. *Judgment at Nuremberg* really gave me a lift. I almost forgot the pain in the excitement and entertainment of the picture. God bless you always for your consideration of me."

In 1965, Breen came back to Hollywood for the last time, to visit family and to die. "He had lost the use of both his legs and lower spine and had been confined to a wheel chair for the past two years—then a series of strokes [further disabled him]," wrote his friend the journalist Thomas Pryor, who had covered Breen in his prime. Despite Mary's threats, Breen still stole smokes, even on his deathbed.

Before the final confinement and last rites, his eldest son and daughter-in-law, Joseph, Jr., and Pat Breen, took the frail old man to the movies. The outing was to be Breen's last picture show, and the final print review might have been programmed by a kind Providence. Directed by Robert Wise from the play by Oscar Hammerstein and Richard Rodgers, *The Sound of Music* (1965) was a joyous widescreen musical celebrating the harmonious family values of the Von Trapp Family singers, a chorus of seven well-scrubbed children, a not-really stern patriarch, and a novitiate nun-turned-governess-turned-wife and mother. Set in the late 1930s and shot on location in Salzburg, Austria, a European capital Breen knew well from another lifetime, the old-fashioned throwback to halcyon Hollywood was a huge

The final print review: Angela Cartwright, Julie Andrews, Christopher Plummer, and Charmian Carr in Robert Wise's *The Sound of Music* (1965).

box office hit and proof of the persistence, even in the turbulent 1960s, of an appreciative market for tuneful, wholesome Catholicism. "He was thrilled with it," recalls Pat Breen.

Soon after, on December 5, 1965, forgotten by the industry, a relic of a former age and his former robust self, Breen died at the Brentwood Convalescent Home, aged seventy-seven. He was the last of the men who had engineered the mechanics of Hollywood censorship: Will H. Hays and Rev. Daniel A. Lord, S.J., had both died in 1955, Martin J. Quigley in 1964.

The eulogies from the old guard were also eulogies for a Hollywood forever gone. *Motion Picture Herald* editor Martin S. Quigley remembered Breen as "a man who made for two decades an unequaled contribution to the American motion picture. It was a golden era for Hollywood. Those were the Breen years." More than one mourner remarked on a woeful synchronicity. "It is a strange coincidence that Joseph Ignatius Breen, Knight of St. Gregory, first director of the Production Code Administration of the Motion Picture Association of America, should die in the very week the name of the Legion of Decency is forsaken," grieved his friend Patrick Scanlon, editor of the *Brooklyn Tablet*, who rightly saw in the twin passings the twilight of Catholic stewardship over Hollywood. In praising the fallen warrior of the Church militant, Scanlon implied a martyrdom suffered on the altar of screen entertainment. "In 1954, Mr. Breen, broken in health after working 14 to 16 hours a day and upholding the Code in the face of opposition from some powerful Hollywood moguls, was forced to retire." Scanlon was wrong about Breen's forced departure, but a pastor from Breen's native Philadelphia made the same connection between the death of the man and the end of the Legion. "It was ironic that the same issue of the *Catholic Standard and Times* that reported Joe Breen's death also carried the story of the surrender of the Legion and [executive director] Monsignor Little," he wrote. "Apparently, when Joe died, courage and moral fiber died with him."

More than two hundred friends and a special delegation of religious leaders attended the Solemn High Requiem Mass for Breen at the Church of the Good Shepherd in Beverly Hills. James Cardinal McIntyre, archbishop of Los Angeles, was sidelined by surgery, so Auxiliary Bishop John J. Ward presided. Msgr. John J. Devlin, Hollywood script doctor for the now-defunct Legion of Decency, delivered the funeral eulogy. Father Devlin's remarks quoted at length a heartfelt encomium from Will H. Hays, written in 1954 on the occasion of Breen's retirement dinner:

> What a job: to condemn as well as to praise; to convince as well as cajole; to please, to madden; and to please again; to require as well as to allow; to flatter when necessary and to inspire; to save millions at the expense of hundreds; to preserve a great art-industry and make it in a vast way predominately an agency of the very greatest service; sending individuals and great companies away fighting, to come back in highest esteem and gratitude; to tramp a treadmill endless hours and at all hours day and night, to respond with help and encouragement, seeking always the constructive and not the destructive, but fearlessly to prevent—that promises might be kept, damage avoided, and great good done, enduring devastating weariness in heart sickening strain while radiating good cheer and encouragement; with no evidence of pride amid a unanimous acclamation of gratitude, satisfaction, and praise—what a job, indeed, you have done, what a magnificent job—with everyone benefiting who has come at all within your sphere of influence.

The motion picture industry sent no official representative to pay its respects. Mourners bitterly remarked that Hays himself didn't "get any more industry attention at his funeral." The slight was less an expression of grudges still held—the moguls and producers who had shuffled and scrapped with Breen were mainly long gone, out of power or in their own coffins—than of the indifference of a business not given to classy gestures. The failure of the new generation to pay its respects to the one-time conscience of Hollywood "raised eyebrows," said *Variety* editor Abel Green, speaking of his own eyebrows, disappointed in the short memory of his colleagues. "Film Industry Snubs Joe Breen's Funeral," reported the trade paper in its last Breen headline.

Yet while the new Hollywood ignored Breen's passing, the pageant at his Requiem Mass stuck to an old Hollywood formula. The men who served as Breen's honorary pallbearers were Lou Greenspan, executive secretary of the Screen Producer's Guild; veteran producer Joe Pasternak; MPAA legal counsel Sidney Schreiber; Robert T. Watkins, treasurer of the Association of Motion Picture and Television Producers; and PCA stalwarts Albert Van Schmus and Geoffrey Shurlock—a cast of characters whose melting-pot surnames and diverse lineages better fit the call-out from a Warner Bros. platoon than the tribal solidarity of a Knights of Columbus hall. If Joseph I. Breen had, for a time, converted Hollywood, Hollywood had converted the Victorian Irishman too.

APPENDIX: THE PRODUCTION CODE

Author's Note: Though various texts of the Production Code have been reprinted over the years in trade journals, memoirs, and film histories, the Production Code Administration archives at the Margaret Herrick Library in Los Angeles, California, contain no single copy of the Code deemed definitive and canonical. The extant versions of the Code vary somewhat in typographical details, layout, word choice, and arrangement of the text. Some copies omit the philosophical passages or lack later amendments. Olga J. Martin's *Hollywood's Movie Commandments*, published in 1937, and Jack Vizzard's *See No Evil: Life Inside a Hollywood Censor*, published in 1970, reprint reliable versions of the Code from their respective eras (Martin was Breen's secretary and Vizzard served on the staff of the PCA from 1944 until 1968). The version below, which includes the last major revision of the Code in 1956, is taken from the 1956 edition of *Motion Picture Almanac*, Martin J. Quigley's annual index of motion picture industry facts. As coauthor and custodian of the Code, Quigley kept a sharp eye on the integrity of the text. Of course, Joseph I. Breen was also protective of the body of the Code. Still, like a good Catholic who understands the liturgy of the mass without knowing a word of Latin, he did not need the document at hand to follow along. In 1940 he made a revealing request of Martin J. Quigley. "Once and for all: please send me a *true* and *accurate copy of the Code*—at your convenience."

THE PRODUCTION CODE

Motion picture producers recognize the high trust and confidence which have been placed in them by the people of the world and which have made motion pictures a universal form of entertainment.

They recognize their responsibility to the public because of this trust and because entertainment and art are important influences in the life of a nation.

Hence, though regarding motion pictures primarily as entertainment without any explicit purpose of teaching or propaganda, they know that the motion picture within its own field of entertainment may be directly responsible for spiritual or moral progress, for higher types of social life, and for much correct thinking.

During the rapid transition from silent to talking pictures they realized the necessity and the opportunity of subscribing to a Code to govern the production of talking pictures and of reacknowledging this responsibility.

On their part, they ask from the public and from the public leaders a sympathetic understanding of their purposes and problems and a spirit of cooperation that will allow them the freedom and opportunity necessary to bring the motion picture to a still higher level of wholesome entertainment for all the people.

GENERAL PRINCIPLES

1. No picture shall be produced which will lower the moral standards of those who see it. Hence the sympathy of the audience shall never be thrown to the side of crime, wrongdoing, evil or sin.
2. Correct standards of life, subject only to the requirements of drama and entertainment, shall be presented.
3. Law, natural or human, shall not be ridiculed, nor shall sympathy be created for its violation.

PARTICULAR APPLICATIONS

I. *CRIMES AGAINST THE LAW*

These shall never again be presented in such a way as to throw sympathy with the crime as against law and justice or to inspire others with a desire for imitation.

1. *Murder*
   a. The technique of murder must be presented in a way that will not inspire imitation.
   b. Brutal killings are not to be presented in detail.
   c. Revenge in modern times shall not be justified.
2. *Methods of Crime should not be explicitly presented.*
   a. Theft, robbery, safe-cracking, and dynamiting of trains, mines, buildings, etc., should not be detailed in method.
   b. Arson must be subject to the same safeguards.
   c. The use of firearms should be restricted to essentials.
3. The illegal drug traffic, and drug addiction, must never be presented.[1]

II. *SEX*

The sanctity of the institution of marriage and the home shall be upheld. Pictures shall not infer that low forms of sex relationship are the accepted or common thing.

1. *Adultery and Illicit Sex,* sometimes necessary plot material, must not be explicitly treated, or justified, or presented attractively.
2. *Scenes of Passion*
   a. These should not be introduced except when they are definitely essential to the plot.
   b. Excessive and lustful kissing, lustful embraces, suggestive postures and gestures are not to be shown.

---

1. The original text read: "Illegal drug traffic must never be presented." An amendment adopted by the resolution of the MPAA's Board of Directors on September 11, 1946, read: "The illegal drug traffic must not be portrayed in such a way as to stimulate curiosity concerning the use of, or traffic in, such drugs; nor shall scenes be approved which show the use of illegal drugs, or their effects, in detail." Return to the original was voted by the MPAA Board on March 27, 1951.

   c. In general, passion should be treated in such manner as not to stimulate the lower and baser emotions.
3. *Seduction or Rape*
   a. These should never be more than suggested, and then only when essential for the plot. They must never be shown by explicit method.
   b. They are never the proper subject for comedy.
4. *Sex perversion* or any inference of it is forbidden.
5. *White slavery* shall not be treated.
6. *Abortion, sex hygiene and venereal diseases* are not proper subjects for theatrical motion pictures.[2]
7. Scenes of *actual child birth*, in fact or in silhouette, are never to be presented.
8. *Children's sex organs* are never to be exposed.

III. *VULGARITY*

The treatment of low, disgusting, unpleasant, though not necessarily evil, subjects, should be guided always by the dictates of good taste and a proper regard for the sensibilities of the audience.

IV. *OBSCENITY*

Obscenity in word, gesture, reference, song, joke, or by suggestion (even when likely to be understood only by part of the audience) is forbidden.

V. *PROFANITY*

Pointed profanity and every other profane or vulgar expression, however used, are forbidden.

No approval by the Production Code Administration shall be given to the use of words and phrases in motion pictures including, but not limited to, the following:

"Bronx Cheer" (the sound)
Chippie
God, Lord, Jesus, Christ (unless used reverently)
Nuts (except when meaning crazy)
Cripes
Fairy (in a vulgar sense)
Finger (the)
Fire—cries of
Gawd
Goose (in a vulgar sense)
Hot (as applied to a woman)
Toilet Gags
"In your hat"
Madam (relating to prostitution)
Nance
Pansy
Razzberry (the sound)
S.O.B.
Son-of-a
Tart
Whore

2. The original text read: "Sex hygiene and venereal disease are not subjects for theatrical motion pictures." The amendment was adopted by resolution of the MPAA's Board of Directors on March 27, 1951.

In the administration of Section V of the Production Code, the Production Code Administration may take cognizance of the fact that the following words and phrases are obviously offensive to the patrons of motion pictures in the United States and more particularly to the patrons of motion pictures in foreign countries: Chink, Dago, Frog, Greaser, Hunkie, Kike, Nigger, Spic, Wop, Yid.

It should also be noted that the words "hell" and "damn," if used without moderation, will be considered offensive by many members of the audience. Their use, therefore, should be governed by the discretion and the prudent advice of the Code Administration.

VI. *COSTUMES*

1. *Complete nudity* is never permitted. This includes nudity in fact or in silhouette, or any licentious notice thereof by other characters in the picture.
2. *Undressing scenes* should be avoided, and never used save where essential to the plot.
3. *Indecent or undue exposure* is forbidden.
4. *Dancing costumes* intended to permit undue exposure or indecent movements in the dance are forbidden.

VII. *DANCES*

1. Dances suggesting or representing sexual actions or indecent passion are forbidden.
2. Dances which emphasize indecent movements are to be regarded as obscene.

VIII. *RELIGION*

1. No film or episode may throw *ridicule* on any religious faith.
2. *Ministers of religion* in their character as ministers of religion should not be used as comic characters or as villains.
3. *Ceremonies* of any definite religion should be carefully and respectfully handled.

IX. *LOCATIONS*

The treatment of bedrooms must be governed by good taste and delicacy.

X. *NATIONAL FEELINGS*

1. *The use of the Flag* shall be consistently respectful.
2. *The history*, institutions, prominent people and citizenry of all nations shall be represented fairly.

XI. *TITLES*

The following titles shall not be used:[3]

1. Titles which are salacious, indecent, obscene, profane, or vulgar.

---

3. The original text read: "Salacious, indecent, or obscene titles shall not be used." The revision on titles was adopted by the MPA's Board of Directors on December 3, 1947.

2. Titles which suggest or are currently associated in the public mind with material, characters or occupations unsuitable for the screen.
3. Titles which are otherwise objectionable.

XII. *SPECIAL SUBJECTS*

The following subjects must be treated within the careful limits of good taste.

1. *Actual hangings* or electrocutions as legal punishments for crime.
2. *Third degree* methods.
3. *Brutality* and possible gruesomeness.
4. *The sale of women*, or a woman selling her virtue.
5. *Surgical operations.*
6. *Miscegenation.*
7. *Liquor* and *drinking.*

SPECIAL REGULATIONS ON CRIME IN MOTION PICTURES

RESOLVED (December 20, 1938), that the Board of Directors of the Motion Picture Association of America, Inc., hereby ratifies, approves and confirms the interpretations of The Production Code, the practices thereunder, and the resolutions indicating and confirming such interpretations heretofore adopted by the Association of Motion Picture Producers, Inc., all effectuating regulations relative to the treatment of crime in motion pictures, as follows:

1. Details of crime must never be shown and care should be exercised at all times in discussing such details.
2. Action suggestive of wholesale slaughter of human beings, either by criminals in conflict with police, or as between warring factions of criminals, or in public disorder of any kind, will not be allowed.
3. There must be no suggestion, at any time, of excessive brutality.
4. Because of the increase in the number of films in which murder is frequently committed, action showing the taking of human life, even in the mystery stories, is to be cut to the minimum. These frequent presentations of murder tend to lessen regard for the sacredness for life.
5. Suicide, as a solution of problems occurring in the development of screen drama, is to be discouraged as morally questionable and as bad theatre—unless absolutely necessary for the development of the plot. It should never be justified or glorified, or used to defeat the due process of law.[4]
6. There must be no display, at any time, of machine guns, sub-machine guns or other weapons generally classified as illegal weapons in the hands of gangsters, or other criminals, and there are to be no off-stage sounds of the repercussions of these guns.
7. There must be no new, unique or trick methods shown for concealing guns.
8. The flaunting of weapons by gangsters, or other criminals, will not be allowed.

---

4. As amended by the MPA's Board of Directors on March 27, 1951. The original text did not include the last sentence.

9. All discussions and dialogue on the part of gangsters regarding guns should be cut to the minimum.
10. There must be no scenes, at any time, showing law-enforcing officers dying at the hands of criminals *unless such scenes are absolutely necessary to the development of the plot.* This includes private detectives and guards for banks, motor trucks, etc.[5]
11. With special reference to the crime of kidnapping—or illegal abduction—such stories are acceptable under the Code only when: (a) the kidnapping or abduction is not the main theme of the story; (b) the person kidnapped is not a child; (c) there are no details of the crime of kidnapping; (d) no profit accrues to the abductors or kidnappers; and (e) where the kidnappers are punished.

    It is understood and agreed that the word kidnapping as used in paragraph (11) of these Regulations, is intended to mean abduction, or illegal detention, in modern times, by criminals for ransom.
12. Pictures dealing with criminal activism in which minors participate, or to which minors are related, shall not be approved if they incite demoralizing imitation on the part of youth.
13. No picture shall be approved dealing with the life of a notorious criminal of current or recent times which uses the name, nickname, or alias of such notorious criminal in the film, nor shall a picture be approved if based upon the life of such a notorious criminal unless the character shown in the film be punished for crimes shown in the film as committed by him.[6]

SPECIAL RESOLUTION ON COSTUMES

On October 25, 1939, the Board of Directors of the Motion Picture Association of America Inc., adopted the following resolution:

RESOLVED that the provisions of Paragraphs 1, 3 and 4 of Sub-Division VI of the Production Code, in their application to costumes, nudity, indecent or undue exposure, and dancing costumes, shall not be interpreted to exclude authentically photographed scenes photographed in a foreign land, of natives of such foreign land, showing native life, if such scenes are a necessary and integral part of a motion picture depicting exclusively such land and native life, provided that no such scenes shall be intrinsically objectionable nor made a part of any motion picture produced in any studio, and provided further that no emphasis shall be made in any scenes of the customs or garb of such natives or in the exploitation thereof.

SPECIAL REGULATIONS ON CRUELTY TO ANIMALS

On December 27, 1940, the Board of Directors of the Motion Picture Association of America, Inc., approved a resolution adopted by the Association of Motion Picture Producers, Inc., reaffirming previous resolutions of the California Association concerning brutality and possible gruesomeness and apparent cruelty to animals:

---

5. Italicized material is an amendment adopted by the MPA's Board of Directors on March 27, 1951.
6. Regulation No. 13 was adopted by the MPA's Board of Directors on December 3, 1947.

RESOLVED, by the Board of Directors of the Association of Motion Picture Producers, Inc., that

(1) Hereafter, in the production of motion pictures there shall be no use by the members of the Association of the contrivance or apparatus in connection with animals which is known as the "running W",* nor shall any picture submitted to the Production Code Administration be approved if reasonable grounds exist for believing that use of any similar device by the producer of such picture resulted in apparent cruelty to animals; and

(2) Hereafter, in the production of motion pictures by the members of the Association, such members shall, as to any picture involving the use of animals, invite on the lot during such shooting and consult with the authorized representative of the American Humane Association; and

(3) Steps shall be taken immediately by the members of the Association and by the Production Code Administration to require compliance with these resolutions, which shall bear the same relationship to the sections of the Production Code quoted herein as the Association's special regulations re: Crime in Motion Pictures bear to the sections of the Production Code dealing therewith; and it is

FURTHER RESOLVED, that the resolutions of February 19, 1925, and all other resolutions of this Board establishing its policy to prevent all cruelty to animals in the production of motion pictures and reflecting its determination to prevent any such cruelty, be the same and hereby are in all respects reaffirmed.

REASONS SUPPORTING PREAMBLE OF CODE

1. Theatrical motion pictures, that is, pictures intended for the theatre as distinct from pictures intended for churches, schools, lecture halls, educational movements, social reform movements, etc., are primarily to be regarded as ENTERTAINMENT.

Mankind has always recognized the importance of entertainment and its value in rebuilding the bodies and souls of human beings.

But it has always recognized that entertainment can be a character either HELPFUL or HARMFUL to the human race, and in consequence has clearly distinguished between:

a. Entertainment which tends to improve the race, or at least to re-create and rebuild human beings exhausted with the realities of life; and

b. Entertainment which tends to degrade human beings, or to lower their standards of life and living.

Hence the MORAL IMPORTANCE of entertainment is something which has been universally recognized. It enters intimately into the lives of men and women and affects them closely; it occupies their minds and affections during leisure hours; and ultimately touches the whole of their lives. A man may be judged by his standard of entertainment as easily as by the standard of his work.

So correct entertainment raises the whole standard of a nation.

---

* [A disreputable rodeo and stunt technique whereby wires were attached to a horse's forelegs and pulled to force the horse to the ground in a spectacular fall.—*Author's note.*]

Wrong entertainment lowers the whole living conditions and moral ideas of a race.

Note, for example, the healthy reactions to healthful sports, like baseball, golf; the unhealthy reactions to sports like cockfighting, bullfighting, bear baiting, etc.

Note, too, the effect on ancient nations of gladiatorial combats, the obscene plays of Roman times, etc.

2. Motion pictures are very important as ART.

Though a new art, possibly a combination art, it has the same object as the other arts, the presentation of human thought, emotion, and experience, in terms of an appeal to the soul through the senses.

Here, as in entertainment, Art *enters intimately* into the lives of human beings.

Art can be *morally good*, lifting men to higher levels. This has been done through good music, great painting, authentic fiction, poetry, drama. Art can be *morally evil* in its effects. This is the case clearly enough with unclean art, indecent books, suggestive drama. The effect on the lives of men and women is obvious.

Note: It has often been argued that art in itself is unmoral, neither good nor bad. This is perhaps true of the THING which is music, painting, poetry, etc. But the thing is the PRODUCT of some person's mind and the intention of that mind was either good or bad morally when it produced the thing. Besides the thing it has its EFFECT upon those who come into contact with it. In both these ways, that is, a product of a mind and as the cause of definite effects, it has a deep moral significance and an unmistakable moral quality.

Hence: The motion pictures, which are the most popular of modern arts for the masses, have their moral quality from the intention of the minds which produce them and from their effects on the moral lives and reactions of their audiences. This gives them a most important morality.

1. They *reproduce* the morality of the men who use the pictures as a medium for the expression of their ideas and ideals.
2. They *affect* the moral standards of those who, through the screen, take in these ideas and ideals.

In the case of the motion pictures, this effect may be particularly emphasized because no art has so quick and so widespread an appeal to the masses. It has become in an incredibly short period the *art of the multitudes*.

3. The motion picture, because of its importance as entertainment and because of the trust placed in it by the peoples of the world, has special MORAL OBLIGATIONS:

A. Most arts appeal to the mature. This art appeals at once to *every class*, mature, immature, developed, undeveloped, law abiding, criminal. Music has its grades for different classes; so have literature and drama. This art of the motion picture, combining as it does the two fundamental appeals of looking at a *picture* and *listening to a story* at once reaches every class of society.

B. By reason of the mobility of a film and the ease of picture distribution, and because of the possibility of duplicating positives in large quantities, this art *reaches places* unpenetrated by other forms of art.

C. Because of these two facts, it is difficult to produce films intended for only certain classes of people. The exhibitor's theatres are built for the masses, for the cultivated and the rude, the mature and the immature, the self-respecting and the criminal.

Films, unlike books and music, can with difficulty be confined to certain selected groups.

D. The latitude given to film material cannot, in consequence, be as wide as the latitude given to *book material.* In addition:

   a. A book describes; a film vividly presents. One presents on a cold page; the other by apparently living people.

   b. A book reaches the mind through words merely; a film reaches the eyes and ears through the reproduction of actual events.

   c. The reaction of a reader to a book depends largely on the keenness of the reader's imagination; the reaction to a film depends on the vividness of presentation.

Hence many things which might be described or suggested in a book could not possibly be presented in a film.

E. This is also true when comparing the film with the newspaper.

   a. Newspapers present by description, films by actual presentation.

   b. Newspapers are after the fact and present things as having taken place; the film gives the events in the process of enactment and with the apparent reality of life.

F. Everything possible in a *play* is not possible in a film.

   a. Because of the *larger audience of the film,* and its consequential mixed character. Psychologically, the larger the audience, the lower the moral mass resistance to suggestion.

   b. Because through light, enlargement of character, presentation, scenic emphasis, etc., the screen story is *brought closer* to the audience than the play.

   c. The enthusiasm for an interest in film *actors* and *actresses,* developed beyond anything of the sort in history, makes the audience largely sympathetic toward the characters they portray and the stories in which they figure. Hence the audience is more ready to confuse actor and actress and the characters they portray, and it is most receptive of the emotions and ideals presented by their favorite stars.

G. *Small communities,* remote from sophistication and from the hardening process which often takes place in the ethical and moral standards of groups in larger cities, are easily and readily reached by any sort of film.

H. The grandeur of mass settings, large action, spectacular features, etc., affects and arouses more intensely the emotional side of the audience.

In general, the mobility, popularity, accessibility, emotional appeal, vividness, straight-forward presentation of fact in the film make for more intimate contact with a larger audience and for greater emotional appeal.

Hence the larger moral responsibilities of the motion pictures.

REASONS UNDERLYING THE GENERAL PRINCIPLES

1. No picture shall be produced which will lower the moral standards of those who see it. Hence the sympathy of the audience should never be thrown to the side of crime, wrongdoing, evil or sin.

This is done:

1. When *evil* is made to appear *attractive* or *alluring,* and good is made to appear *unattractive.*

2. When the *sympathy* of the audience is thrown on the side of crime, wrongdoing, evil, sin. The same thing is true of a film that would throw sympathy against goodness, honor, innocence, purity or honesty.

NOTE: Sympathy with a person who sins is not the same the same as sympathy with the sin or crime of which he is guilty. We may feel sorry for the plight of the murderer or even understand the circumstances which led him to his crime. We may not feel sympathy with the wrong which he has done.

The *presentation of evil* is often essential for the art or fiction or drama.

This in itself is not wrong provided:

a. That evil is *not presented alluringly*. Even if later in the film the evil is condemned or punished, it must not be allowed to appear so attractive that the audience's emotions are drawn to desire or approve so strongly that later the condemnation is forgotten and only the apparent joy of the sin remembered.
b. That throughout, the audience feels sure that *evil is wrong* and *good is right.*

2. Correct standards of life shall, as far as possible, be presented. A *wide knowledge of life and of living* is made possible though the film. When right standards are consistently presented, the motion picture exercises the most powerful influences. It builds character, develops right ideals, inculcates correct principles, and all this in attractive story form.

If motion pictures consistently *hold up for admiration high types of characters* and present stories that will affect lives for the better, they can become the most powerful natural force for the improvement of mankind.

3. Law, natural or human, shall not be ridiculed, nor shall sympathy be created for its violation.

By *natural law* is understood the law which is written in the hearts of all mankind, the great underlying principles of right and justice dictated by conscience.

By *human law* is understood the law written by civilized nations.

1. *The presentation of crimes* against the law is *often necessary* for the carrying out of the plot. But the presentation must not throw sympathy with the crime as against the law nor with the criminal as against those who punish him.
2. *The courts of the land* should not be presented as unjust. This does not mean that a single court may not be represented as unjust, much less that a single court official must not be presented this way. But the court system of the country must not suffer as a result of this presentation.

REASONS UNDERLYING PARTICULAR APPLICATIONS

1. *Sin and evil* enter into the story of human beings and hence in themselves *are valid dramatic material.*
2. In the use of this material, it must be distinguished between *sins which repel* by their very nature, and *sins which often attract.*
   a. In the first class come murder, most theft, many legal crimes, lying, hypocrisy, cruelty, etc.
   b. In the second class come sex sins, sins and crimes of apparent heroism, such as banditry, daring thefts, leadership in evil, organized crime, revenge, etc.

The first class needs far less care in treatment, as sins and crimes of this class are naturally unattractive. The audience instinctively condemns all such and is repelled.

Hence the important objective must be to avoid the hardening of the audience, especially of those who are young and impressionable, to the thought and fact of crime. People can become accustomed even to murder, cruelty, brutality and repellent crimes, if these are too frequently repeated.

The second class needs great care in handling, as the response of human nature to their appeal is obvious. This is treated more fully below.

3. A careful distinction can be made between films intended for *general distribution*, and films intended for use in theatres restricted to a *limited audience*. Themes and plots quite appropriate for the latter would be altogether out of place and dangerous in the former.

NOTE: The practice of using a general theatre and limiting its patronage during the showing of a certain film to "Adults Only" is not completely satisfactory and is only partially effective.

However, maturer minds may easily understand and accept without harm subject matter in plots which do younger people positive harm.

Hence: If there should be created a special type of theatre, catering exclusively to an adult audience, for plays of this character (plays with problem themes, difficult discussions and maturer treatment) it would seem to afford an outlet, which does not now exist, for pictures unsuitable for general distribution but permissible for exhibitions to a restricted audience.

I. *CRIMES AGAINST THE LAW*

The *treatment of crimes* against the law must not:

1. *Teach methods* of crime.
2. *Inspire potential criminals* with a desire for imitation.
3. *Make criminals seem heroic* and justified.

Revenge in modern times shall not be justified. In lands and ages of less developed civilization and moral principles, revenge may sometimes be presented. This would be the case especially in places where no law exists to cover the crime because of which revenge is committed.

Because of its evil consequences, the *drug traffic* should not be presented in any form. The existence of the trade should not be brought to the attention of the audiences.

II. *SEX*

Out of regard for the sanctity of marriage and the home, the *triangle*, that is, the love of a third party for one already married, needs careful handling. The treatment should not throw sympathy against marriage as an institution.

Scenes of passion must be treated with an honest acknowledgement of human nature and its normal reactions. Many scenes cannot be presented without arousing dangerous emotions on the part of the immature, the young or the *criminal classes*.

Even within the limits of *pure love*, certain facts have been universally regarded by lawmakers as outside the limits of safe presentation.

In the case of *impure love*, the love which society has always regarded as wrong and which has been banned by divine law, the following are important:

1. Impure love must *not* be presented as *attractive and beautiful*.
2. It must *not* be the subject of *comedy* or farce or treated as material *for laughter*.

3. It must *not* be presented in such a way as *to arouse passion* or morbid curiosity on the part of the audience.
4. It must *not* be made to seem *right and permissible.*
5. In general, it must *not* be *detailed* in method and manner.

III. *Vulgarity*; IV. *Obscenity*; V. *Profanity*
Hardly need further explanation than is contained in the Code.

VI. *COSTUMES*
General principles:

1. *The effect of nudity or semi-nudity* upon the normal man or woman, and much more upon the young and upon immature persons, has been honestly recognized by all lawmakers and moralists.
2. Hence the fact that the nude or semi-nude body may be *beautiful* does not make its use in the films moral. For, in addition to its beauty, the effect of the nude or semi-nude body on the normal individual must be taken into consideration.
3. Nudity or semi-nudity used simply to put a "punch" into a picture comes under the head of immoral actions. It is immoral in its effect on the average audience.
4. Nudity can never be permitted as being *necessary for the plot.* Semi-nudity must not result in undue or indecent exposure.
5. *Transparent* or *translucent materials* and silhouette are frequently more suggestive than actual exposure.

VII. *DANCES*
Dancing in general is recognized as an *art* and as a *beautiful* form of expressing human emotions.

But dances which suggest or represent sexual actions, whether performed solo or with two or more, dances intended to excite the emotional reaction of an audience, dances with movement of the breasts, excessive body movements while the feet are stationary, violate decency and are wrong.

VIII. *RELIGION*
The reason why ministers of religion may not be comic characters or villains is simply because the attitude taken toward them may easily become the attitude taken toward religion in general. Religion is lowered in the minds of the audience because of the lowering of the audience's respect for a minister.

IX. *LOCATIONS*
Certain places are so closely and thoroughly associated with sexual life or with sexual sin that their use must be carefully limited.

X. *NATIONAL FEELINGS*
The just rights, history, and feelings of any nation are entitled to most careful consideration and respectful treatment.

XI. *TITLES*
As the title of a picture is the brand on that particular type of goods, it must conform to the ethical practices of all such honest business.

XII. *SPECIAL SUBJECTS*
Such subjects are occasionally necessary for the plot. Their treatment must never offend good taste nor injure the sensibilities of an audience.

The use of liquor should never be excessively presented. In scenes from American life, the necessities of the plot and proper characterization alone justify its use. And in this case, it should be shown with moderation.

RESOLUTION FOR UNIFORM INTERPRETATION
as amended June 13, 1934

1. When requested by production managers, the Motion Picture Association of America, Incorporated, shall secure any facts, information or suggestions concerning the probable reception of stories or the manner in which in its opinion they may best be treated.
2. Each production manager shall submit in confidence a copy of each or any script to the Production Code Administration of the Motion Picture Association of America, Incorporated (and of the Association of Motion Picture Producers, Inc., California). The Production Code Administration will give the production manager for his guidance such confidential advice and suggestions as experience, research, and information indicate, designating wherein from experience or knowledge it is believed that exception will be taken to the story or treatment.
3. Each production manager of a company belonging to the Motion Picture Association of America, Incorporated, and any producer proposing to distribute and/or distributing his picture through the facilities of any member of the Motion Picture Association of America, Incorporated, shall submit to such Production Code Administration every picture he produces before the negative goes to the laboratory for printing. Said Production Code Administration, having seen the picture, shall inform the production manager in writing whether in its opinion the picture conforms or does not conform to the Code, stating specifically wherein either by theme, treatment or incident, the picture violates the provisions of the Code. In such latter event, the picture shall not be released until the changes indicated by the Production Code Administration have been made; provided, however, that the production manager may appeal from such opinion of said Production Code Administration, so indicated in writing, to the Board of Directors of the Motion Picture Association of America, Inc., whose finding shall be final, and such production manager and company shall be governed accordingly.

NOTES

ABBREVIATIONS USED

ACHRC&UA	The American Catholic History Research Center and University Archives, The Catholic University of America, Washington, D.C.
AC	Archdiocese of Chicago's Joseph Cardinal Bernardin Archives & Records Center, Chicago, Ill.
ALA	Archdiocese of Los Angeles Archival Center, Mission Hills, Calif.
HI	Hoover Institution on War, Revolution, and Peace, Stanford, Calif.
IU	Manuscripts Department, Lilly Library, Indiana University, Bloomington, Ind.
JIB	Joseph I. Breen
MJA	Midwest Jesuit Archives, St. Louis, Mo.
NARA	National Archives and Records Administration, College Park, Md.
PCA	Production Code Administration files, Margaret Herrick Library, Academy of Motion Picture Arts and Sciences, Beverly Hills, Calif.
PP	Papers of Rev. Wilfrid Parsons, S.J., Georgetown University, Washington, D.C.
QP	Papers of Martin J. Quigley, Georgetown University, Washington D.C.
WHP	Papers of Will H. Hays, Indiana State Library, Indianapolis, Ind.

PROLOGUE: HOLLYWOOD, 1954

Page 1. **"Jack Webb of *Dragnet*:** *TV Guide*, March 19, 1954: A-31.

Page 2. **"I rushed home:** Quoted in Sam Rinzler, "Exhib Can't Recall Any Auto Show Plugging the Pix Biz, So Why Should the 'Oscars' Trailerize Oldsmobile?" *Variety*, March 31, 1954: 2.

Page 2. **The second Oscar telecast "marked:** Leo Guild, "Awards Show Makes Topnotch Telecast," *Hollywood Reporter*, March 26, 1954: 7.

Page 2. **"Unlike last year's:** Walter Ames, "Movie Oscar Awards on Radio, TV; Mary McAdoo Previews Show This A.M.," *Los Angeles Times*, March 24, 1954: 28.

Page 2. **"Let me rehearse:** Leisen, quoted in Leo Guild, "On the Air," *Hollywood Reporter*, March 26, 1954: 14.

Page 3. **"The ovation:** "Sinatra's Ovation," *Variety*, March 31, 1954: 2.

1. THE VICTORIAN IRISHMAN

Page 7. **"Unless you are in the motion picture:** Frederick James Smith, "Hollywood's New Purity Tape Measure," *Liberty*, August 15, 1936: 43.

Page 8. **"More than any single individual:** Thomas M. Pryor, "Joe Breen, Sire of Code Ratings, Dies; Long Ill," *Variety*, December 8, 1965: 2.

Page 8. **"It is a mistake:** Hornblow, quoted in William R. Weaver, "Hornblow Cites Producer Responsibility to Decency," *Motion Picture Herald*, May 4, 1946: 39.

Page 9. **In a city lit by flashbulbs:** Media historian Leonard Leff obtained Breen's 12-page FBI file while researching his and Jerold L. Simmons' *The Dame in the Kimono: Hollywood Censorship and the Production Code from the 1920s to the 1960s* (New York: Grove Weidenfeld, 1990). In 2002, when I made my request to the FBI under the Freedom of Information Act for Breen's file, I was informed initially that no file existed and later that it had been destroyed. Leff generously shared his copy of the file with me. With the exception of a 1939 letter from FBI Director J. Edgar Hoover to the Attorney General declaring he intends to write Breen about "an epidemic of 'G-Men' motion pictures," and some reports from the Los Angeles Bureau to the FBI director about the possible appointment of Judge Stephen Jackson to head the PCA in 1947, it contains mostly newspaper clippings mentioning Breen—no revelations or smoking guns.

Page 10. **"Incredible as it may seem:** JIB to Miss Betty Lou Quinn, November 30, 1944 (MJA). Breen had an official MPPDA photo taken in February 1934, which was reprinted for two decades. In 1954, upon retirement, he was coaxed into a formal glamour shot.

Page 11. **Well into the 1950s:** The sharp-eyed Leonard J. Leff and Jerold L. Simmons observed this detail in *The Dame in the Kimono.*

Page 11. **"Nearly everybody in Philadelphia:** Eugene Weare [JIB], "Philadelphia Honors Her Foremost Citizen," *America*, January 7, 1928: 316.

Page 12. **Industrious and ambitious, Hugh Breen:** Eugene Weare [JIB], "Big News from the West," *America*, January 2, 1926: 274.

Page 12. **Settling in the respectable:** "A Citizen of Philadelphia," *Philadelphia Evening Bulletin*, February 26, 1936.

Page 12. **The Irish, the Know-Nothings knew:** Lawrence H. Fuchs, *The American Kaleidoscope: Race, Ethnicity, and the Civic Culture* (Hanover, N.H.: Wesleyan University Press, 1990): 35–53, 500.

Page 12. **"Popery is opposed:** Morse, quoted in Fuchs: 40.

Page 13. **"The Irish Catholics:** Joseph L. J. Kirlin, *Catholicity in Philadelphia: From the Earliest Missionaries Down to the Present Time* (Philadelphia: John Jos. McVey, 1909): 307, 315.

Page 13. **Breen grew up hearing:** Thomas Beer, *The Mauve Decade: American Life at the End of the Nineteenth Century* (New York: Carroll and Graf, [1926] 1997): 159, 153,

152. Written when memories of the 1890s were still fresh, Beer's cultural history devotes a full chapter to prejudice against Irish Catholics.

Page 14. **He played basketball:** Over forty years later, Breen returned to Philadelphia to honor his former coach at the first annual dinner of the William H. Markward Basketball Award Club. "Sportsmen Urge Aid to Youths," *Philadelphia Evening Bulletin*, April 23, 1947: 25.

Page 14. **The Fairmount parish:** JIB to A. J. Dunleavy, March 18, 1927 (AC).

Page 14. **"Whatever formal training:** JIB to Bishop John T. McNicholas, March 22, 1934 (ACHRC&UA).

Page 14. **"Peculiarly Victorian:** Dennis Clark, *The Irish in Philadelphia: Ten Generations of Urban Experience* (Philadelphia: Temple University Press, 1973): 143.

Page 14. **According to its official historian:** David R. Contosta, *St. Joseph's: Philadelphia's Jesuit University: 150 Years* (Philadelphia: St. Joseph's University Press, 2000): 377n.

Page 15. **Breen never lost:** Eugene Weare [JIB], "The Protestant Ambition to Run the Country," *Extension Magazine* (July 1928): 15.

Page 15. **"According to tales:** John J. McCarthy, "Man of Decency," *Esquire* (September 1935): 64, 126–28.

Page 15. **The most oft-told tale:** Glyn Roberts, "Dictator Breen," *Film Weekly*, February 26, 1938: 13; Weare [JIB], "A Citizen of Philadelphia," *Philadelphia Evening Bulletin*, February 26, 1936. The anecdote is also told in McCarthy, above, and the conflagration is verified in "Fierce Fire Wrecks Big Uptown Blocks," *Philadelphia Record*, March 27, 1910: 1, 3.

Page 15. **An index card in:** State Department Name Index, 1910–1919 (NARA).

Page 16. **On April 16, 1917:** Eugene Weare [JIB], "The British Ambassador to the United States," *America*, March 22, 1924: 545.

Page 16. **In 1918, settling:** Eugene Weare [JIB], "When Al Smith Went to University," *Extension Magazine* (October 1928): 27.

Page 16. **He described himself:** Eugene Weare [JIB], "A Criticism and an Answer," *America*, March 17, 1923: 515–16.

Page 17. **"I was there, on the ground:** Eugene Weare [JIB], "A Bit of Polish History," undated MS (PP).

Page 17. **"When I knew the Holy Father:** JIB to Wilfrid Parsons, S.J., November 25, 1929 (PP).

Page 17. **The frustrations of working unbylined:** JIB, "Newsprint: What's Become of News Writers?," *Chicagoan*, June 21, 1930: 42; JIB, "Newsprint: Bigger and Better News Stories," *Chicagoan*, July 5, 1930: 36.

Page 17. **Ever after, he would relish:** Bishop John T. McNicholas to JIB, June 2, 1934 (ACHRC&UA).

Page 17. **In May 1921:** Bruce M. Mohler, Report of the Activities of the Department of Immigration, May 11, 1921 (ACHRC&UA).

Page 17. **Sailing immediately:** "Overseas Commissioner," *National Catholic Welfare Council Bulletin* (June 1921): 4. In 1923, the National Catholic Welfare Council changed its name to the National Catholic Welfare Conference.

Page 17. **He was deeply disturbed:** Eugene Weare [JIB], "The Way to Help Austria," *America*, June 6, 1922: 221.

Page 18. **U.S. Protestant organizations:** Bruce M. Mohler to Countess Jean de Sayve, March 21, 1922 (ACHRA&UA); James M. Ryan to Bruce Mohler, December 23, 1921 (ACHRA&UA).

Page 18. **The Bureau of Immigration:** "European Conditions Described to Delegates," *National Catholic Welfare Council Bulletin* (December 1922): 14.

Page 18. **The two allegiances affirmed:** JIB, "Our Immigrants: What They Need and How We Are Helping Them," *National Catholic Welfare Council Bulletin* (March 1923): 5.

Page 19. **In 1922, Breen returned:** [JIB], "Papal Control of Baseball," *National Catholic Welfare Council Bulletin* (October 1923): 16; [JIB], "The Philosophy of Bolshevism," *National Catholic Welfare Council Bulletin,* (May 1923): 10; [JIB] "Around the Conference Table," *National Catholic Welfare Council Bulletin* (March 1924): 4.

Page 19. **Manning the desk at NCWC:** JIB to Father Tracy, December 12, 1922 (PP).

Page 19. **No more impressed with:** Eugene Weare [JIB], "Washington, A Nest of Schemers," *America,* December 30, 1922: 246.

Page 19. **In April 1924:** "An Announcement," *National Catholic Welfare Council Bulletin* (April 1924): 5.

Page 19. **"The story they tell:** "Catholic Builders of the Nation," *Columbia* (May 1924): 23.

Page 20. **Returning religious prejudice:** Eugene Weare [JIB], "Tammany Hall—et al.," *Extension Magazine* (September 1928): 9–10; Eugene Weare [JIB], "The Protestant Ambition to Run the Country," *Extension Magazine* (July 1928): 15.

Page 20. **Like most intellectuals of the 1920s:** JIB to Will H. Hays, August 29, 1931 (WHP).

Page 20. **He felt heartsick too:** Eugene Weare [JIB], "A Bit of Polish History," undated MS (PP).

Page 20. **After peregrinations:** Eugene Weare [JIB], "What's the Matter with Europe?" *America,* November 10, 1923: 77–78.

Page 20. **"The Irish have been called:** Thomas Cahill, *How the Irish Saved Civilization: The Untold Story of Ireland's Heroic Role from the Fall of Rome to the Rise of Medieval Europe* (New York; Anchor Books, 1995): 214n.

Page 22. **"I'm looking for a job:** JIB to Rev. Wilfrid Parsons, S.J., October 9, 1925 (PP).

Page 22. **"The Holy Father knows:** George Seldes, "Pope Beams When Told Chicago's Eucharistic Congress Plans," *Chicago Daily Tribune,* February 25, 1925: 14.

Page 22. **Not since the storied:** Daniel Sullivan, "Million at Masses Today," *Chicago Daily Tribune,* June 20, 1926: 1, 2.

Page 22. **Local dignitaries feted:** "Chicago Welcomes Eucharist Congress," *Variety,* June 23, 1926: 9.

Page 23. **From the Headquarters Office:** "Six Cardinals Talk to Reporters," *New York Times,* June 19, 1926: 4.

Page 23. **On the payroll:** Eugene Weare [JIB], "His Eminence," *Chicagoan,* December 7, 1929: 28.

Page 23. **"The most impressive religious**: "1,000,000 in Great Eucharistic Demonstration," *Brooklyn Tablet,* June 26, 1926: 1, 9.

Page 23. **"the most colossal prayer meeting:** James O'Donnell Bennett, "Mighty Army of Peace Prays at Mundelein," *Chicago Daily Tribune,* June 25, 1926: 1, 2. For a roundup of press responses, see "Meaning of the Eucharistic Congress," *Literary Digest*, July 17, 1926: 26–28.

Page 23. **No glitches, no fatalities:** JIB, "When a Million People Meet," *Extension Magazine* (April 1927): 14.

Page 24. **Civic-minded Chicagoans:** JIB, "The International Eucharistic Congress," *Extension Magazine* (April 1926): 15.

Page 24. **Patrick Cardinal O'Donnell:** "Fox Had Complete Film Record of Eucharistic Congress," *Moving Picture World*, July 27, 1926: 2; "Cardinals See Eucharistic Film," *Moving Picture World*, July 31, 1926: 299; "Eucharistic Congress Pictures Speeded by International Newsreel," *Exhibitors Herald*, June 26, 1926: 33.

Page 24. **Fox outdid the competition:** "Catholic Church Supports Showing of Congress Film," *Variety*, November 24, 1926: 8.

Page 25. **The deal between Fox:** For an affectionate account of Quigley's life in the motion picture business, see Martin S. Quigley, *Martin J. Quigley and the Glory Days of American Film, 1915–1965* (Groton, Mass.: Quigley, 2006).

Page 25. **Like Breen, Quigley:** Terry Ramsaye, "Martin Quigley's Third of a Century," *Motion Picture Herald*, September 25, 1948: 7.

Page 25. **Quick to recognize:** "The Cardinal's Letter," *New World*, November 19, 1926: 1.

Page 25. **poet Carl Sandburg:** Carl Sandburg, "Classed as a Superpicture," *Chicago Daily News*, November 23, 1926: 24.

Page 26. **A cinematic landmark:** "Eucharistic Picture Is Great Drama of Reality, Says Hall, Who Made It," *Exhibitors Herald*, November 20, 1926: 38.

Page 26. **"There is a great amount:** Martin J. Quigley to Monsignor C. J. Quille, July 12, 1926 (AC).

Page 26. **Breen was equally upbeat:** JIB to Ray Cauwels, October 28, 1926 (AC).

Page 26. **On November 8, 1926:** "Official Eucharistic Picture Opens at Jolson Theater Nov. 8," *Exhibitors Herald*, November 6, 1926: 33; Charles W. McMahon, "A Picture for All Humanity," *Brooklyn Tablet*, November 13, 1926: 17; Will H. Hays, "Remarks of Will H. Hays at Premiere of Eucharistic Congress Film," November 8, 1926 (WHP).

Page 27. **The rapturous audience:** "Congress Crowd Actors in Great Super Picture," *New World*, November 26, 1926: 1.

Page 27. **Commenting on the official:** Quoted in *Literary Digest*, July 17, 1926: 27.

Page 28. **Reviewers and advertisements:** JIB to the *New World*, November 9, 1926 (AC).

Page 28. **Cooperating fully with the campaign:** "Many Branches Send Members to See Films," *New World*, December 10, 1926: 1.

Page 28. **"As absorbing and compelling:** "The Cardinal's Letter," *New World*, November 19, 1926: 1.

Page 28. **In archdioceses across the nation:** "Eucharistic Congress Film a Hit in Newark," *Moving Picture World*, December 18, 1926: 506.

Page 29. **It fell to Breen:** JIB to A. J. Dunleavy, March 18, 1927 (AC).

Page 29. **While peddling *Eucharistic Congress:*** JIB to Ben F. Rosenberg, April 29, 1927 (AC).

Page 29. **Breen also learned:** JIB to Rev. Walter F. Byron, March 24, 1927; JIB to E. C. Grainger, February 18, 1927; A. Teitel to George Cardinal Mundelein, June 5, 1934 (AC).

Page 29. **Surveying the long lines:** "Fox Eucharistic Congress Pictures in Other Cities," *Moving Picture World*, December 4, 1926: 348.

Page 29. ***Variety* agreed, predicting:** "Eucharistic Congress," *Variety*, November 10, 1926: 12; "Eucharistic Congress Film Stirs New York Audience to Enthusiasm," *Moving Picture World*, November 20, 1926: 2; C. S. Sewell, "International Eucharistic Congress," *Moving Picture World*, November 20, 1926: 164.

Page 30. **For Breen, the selling:** JIB to Rev. Wilfrid Parsons, S.J., January 26, 1927 (PP).

Page 30. **Not that Breen didn't sweat:** JIB to Rev. Wilfrid Parsons, S.J., January 26, 1928 (PP).

2: BLUENOSES AGAINST THE SCREEN

Page 31. **In the *American Mercury*:** H. L. Mencken, "Editorial," *American Mercury* (October 1925): 160.

Page 32. **In 1915 in *Mutual Film*:** *Mutual Film Corporation v. Industrial Commission of Ohio*, 236 U.S. 230 (1915).

Page 34. **Born in Sullivan, Indiana:** Will H. Hays, *The Memoirs of Will H. Hays* (New York: Doubleday, 1955): 3, 4.

Page 34. **In 1920, as chairman:** Terry Ramsaye, "Will Hays Dies at 74; Raised Film Stature," *Motion Picture Herald*, March 13, 1954: 23.

Page 35. **For the next twenty-three years:** Will H. Hays, *See and Hear: A Brief History of Motion Pictures and the Development of Sound* (New York: MPPDA, 1929): 26; 25.

Page 35. **For fronting:** "Will Hays's New 10 Year Contract," *Variety*, June 23, 1926: 1, 49; "Some Matters for Mr. Hays," *Variety*, June 13, 1926: 5.

Page 36. **"Will Hays is a politician:** "Inside Stuff—Pictures," *Variety*, June 8, 1927: 10.

Page 37. **The injunctions became known by:** "Curses, Nudity, and Off Titles Ordered Out of A.M.P.P. Films," *Variety*, June 15, 1927: 4.

Page 37. **The *Chicago Tribune* labeled:** "Chicago Tribune on Fool Censoring," *Variety*, July 3, 1929: 9.

Page 38. **In April 1928:** JIB to Rev. Wilfrid Parsons, S.J., April 1, 1928 (PP).

Page 38. **Breen uprooted the family:** Eugene Weare [JIB], "Big News from the West," *America*, January 2, 1926: 274.

Page 38. **Breen sold the World's Fair:** "As a Booster Mr. Breen Is a Great Debater," *Chicago Daily Tribune*, March 1, 1929: 3.

Page 38. **Though employed mainly:** Daniel E. Doran, "Mr. Breen Confronts the Dragons," *The Sign* (January 1942): 328.

Page 38. **"I have more time:** JIB to Rev. Wilfrid Parsons, S.J., October 21, 1929 (PP). For an example of Breen's PR work for the Peabody Coal Company, see JIB, "Work for Smoke Squad," *Chicago Daily Tribune*, October 2, 1929: 14.

Page 39. **One counterintuitive assignment:** Simon L. Rameynn [JIB], "Little Egypt—Stellar Chicagoan," *Chicagoan*, February 23, 1929: 12, 37–38.

Page 39. **Daniel E. Doran:** Doran: 328.

Page 39. **Already a local cause célèbre:** "Big Films Got Big Loop Business," *Variety*, July 10, 1929: 8.

Page 40. **Father Dinneen was livid:** JIB to Rev. Wilfrid Parsons, S.J., October 21, 1929 (PP).

Page 41. **"The more I thought about it:** JIB to Martin J. Quigley, unpublished manuscript: 3 (QP).

Page 41. **According to Quigley:** Quigley's retrospective accounts include "Production Code: A Product of the Industry," *Motion Picture Herald,* November 23, 1946: 22; Martin J. Quigley to Bosley Crowther, Janaury 16, 1955 and January 25, 1955 (QP), and Cynthia Lowry, "AP Tells the Facts About Quigley Code Authorship," *Motion Picture Herald,* November 6, 1948: 22.

Page 41. **Quigley resolved to correct:** Terry Ramsaye, "This Third of a Century," *Motion Picture Herald,* September 25, 1948: 38.

Page 41. **As his friend Terry Ramsaye corroborated:** Terry Ramsaye, "Understanding the Code," *Motion Picture Herald,* October 8, 1949: 7.

Page 42. **In a spirit of compromise:** Document on the origin of the Production Code (QP).

Page 42. **Father Lord:** Father Lord relates his version of the creation of the PCA in his memoir, *Played by Ear: The Autobiography of Daniel A. Lord, S.J.* (Chicago: Loyola University Press, 1955): 303–305.

Page 45. **"I want Martin:** JIB to Rev. Wilfrid Parsons, S.J., October 21, 1929 (PP).

Page 45. **Quigley, Lord, and Breen struck:** "Picture 'Don'ts' for '30," *Variety,* February 19, 1930: 66.

Page 45. **In January 1930:** "Picture 'Don'ts' for '30," *Variety,* February 19, 1930: 9.

Page 45. **"While the assistant moguls:** "Hays' Annual Meet 'Without a Ripple,'" *Variety,* April 2, 1930: 11.

Page 47. **"Studios are more:** "Cycle Wheels Right Over Hays' Code," *Variety,* September 9, 1930: 4. See also Geoffrey Shurlock, "The Motion Picture Production Code," *Annals of the American Academy of Political and Social Science* (November 1947): 141.

Page 47. **"The specific job assigned:** JIB to Maurice McKenzie, February 12, 1931 (WHP).

Page 47. **"Whether Will Hays recognized**: John J. McCarthy, "Man of Decency," *Esquire* (September 1935): 64, 126–28.

Page 47. **"Business is not:** JIB to Rev. Wilfrid Parsons, S.J., October 9, 1930 (PP).

Page 48. **Even "in these hard days:** JIB, "Newsprint: Bigger and Bigger News Stories," *Chicagoan,* July 5, 1930: 36; JIB, "Newsprint: Headlines and Headaches," *Chicagoan,* June 7, 1930: 46; JIB, "Newsprint: Depression's Curious Offspring," *Chicagoan,* August 2, 1930: 30.

Page 48. **Soon after, the adopted Chicagoan:** "Joseph I. Breen Joins Will Hays Organization," *Film Daily,* July 14, 1931: 1.

3. HOLLYWOOD SHOT TO PIECES

Page 49. **Apocalyptic headlines:** "Film Stocks in Sharp Drop," *Variety,* November 26, 1930: 9; "Theater Chains in Red," *Hollywood Reporter,* December 2, 1930, 1.

Page 49. **"The whole town:** JIB to Rev. Wilfrid Parsons, S.J., February 9, 1932 (PP).

Page 49. **Ironically, Breen's personal fortunes:** "Harmon May Succeed Breen," *Daily Variety,* April 25, 1941: 1.

Page 50. **"I must confess:** JIB to Martin J. Quigley, May 1, 1932 (QP).

Page 50. **"I manage to get:** JIB to Martin J. Quigley, May 1, 1932 (QP).

Page 50. **The general condition was discouraging:** JIB to Will H. Hays, August 29, 1931 (WHP).

Page 51. **In 1932, when the kidnap-murder:** Chapin Haze, "Hollywood Happenings," *New York Times*, January 31, 1932, sec. 10: 4.

Page 51. **When the studios tightened:** Muriel Babcock, "Mr. Hays's Green Cards Thwart Fake Reporters," *Los Angeles Times*, November 13, 1932: B13.

Page 51. **"Bear in mind:** JIB to Maurice McKenzie, March 5, 1931 (WHP).

Page 52. **Pre-Code Hollywood:** For a book-length account of the era, indulgent readers may want to consult Thomas Doherty, *Pre-Code Hollywood: Sex, Immorality, and Insurrection in American Cinema, 1930–1934* (New York: Columbia University Press, 1999).

Page 52. **The phrase evokes:** The first use of the phrase "pre-Code" is probably by trade journalist Pete Harrison, who, writing between 1930 and 1934, used the term to refer to the pre-1930 era.

Page 53. **"Warners makes a cheap:** JIB to Rev. FitzGeorge Dinneen, S.J., March 17, 1934 (ACHRC&UA).

Page 54. **"The highlight of this particular story:** JIB to Eric Johnston, March 10, 1949 (QP).

Page 54. **"$100 will be given:** "The Hays Advertising Code of Ethics Thrown in a Trash Can," *Harrison's Reports*, September 17, 1932: 151.

Page 54. **"You can't make a picture:** Rogers, quoted in Hays, *The Memoirs of Will H. Hays* (New York: Doubleday, 1955): 452.

Page 54. **In 1931, Breen reminded:** JIB to Maurice McKenzie, March 5, 1931 (WHP).

Page 55. **The Hays Office condemned:** "Picture 'Don'ts' for 1930," *Variety*, February 19, 1930: 9, 66.

Page 55. **"I hardly know what to say:** JIB to Rev. Wilfrid Parsons, S.J., April 4, 1932 (PP).

Page 55. **"Hays, I am convinced:** JIB to Rev. Wilfrid Parsons, S.J., October 10, 1932 (PP); JIB to Martin J. Quigley, May 1, 1932 (QP).

Page 56. **"It is no longer:** Daniel A. Lord, S.J., *The Motion Pictures Betray America* (St. Louis: The Queen's Work, Inc., 1934): 3, 33.

Page 56. **"The Hays Morality Code:** "Hays' Religious Influence Now Bankrupt," *Harrison's Reports*, June 10, 1933: 91.

Page 57. **the editorial pens:** "Religious War on Movies," *Billboard*, October 14, 1933: 22; Martin J. Quigley to Bishop John T. McNicholas, October 4, 1933 (QP).

Page 57. **"Worn out by promises:** "The Bolt Strikes," *New World*, June 15, 1934: 4.

Page 58. ***Variety* warned that "fully half:** "Church Drive Progresses," *Variety*, May 29, 1934: 5.

Page 59. **"An extraordinary situation:** JIB to Bishop John J. Cantwell, September 20, 1933 (ALA).

Page 59. **"There is no knowledge**: Bishop John J. Cantwell, *The Motion Picture Industry* (Washington, D.C.: National Council of Catholic Men and the National Council of Catholic Women, 1934): 16.

Page 59. **Likening the flood of images:** Henry James Forman, *Our Movie Made Children* (New York: Macmillan, 1933): 140.

Page 60. **"Producers have reduced:** "Deadline for Film Dirt," *Variety*, June 13, 1933: 1, 36.

Page 61. **On February 5, 1934:** "Breen Doubling," *Motion Picture Herald*, December 30, 1933: 8.

Page 61. **"emerged [from the meeting]:** "Can't Be Annoyed by Yelps," *Daily Variety*, December 9, 1933: 1, 3; "Will Study Morality of Films," *Daily Variety*, January 30, 1934: 1, 7.

Page 61. **The "continual talk:** "Putting 'Teeth' in the Code," *Harrison's Reports*, September 15, 1934: 145.

Page 61. **"[The New Deal Motion Picture Code]:** " 'Code Will Be Changed If Wrong,' Says Rosy," *Hollywood Reporter*, January 31, 1934: 1, 6.

Page 62. **"I am opposed to government regulation:** "Doesn't Care for Censors," *Daily Variety*, January 31, 1934: 1, 6.

Page 62. **"Breen was one of the few:** "Kahane Heads Coast Ass'n, Breen Ups," *Variety*, February 6, 1934: 5, 63.

Page 62. **On February 5, 1934:** "Hays Group Stands Pat; Gives Breen New Powers," *Hollywood Reporter*, February 6, 1934: 1.

Page 62. **Breen "was found:** "Breen Censors All Scripts and Pix Under Compact," *Daily Variety*, February 6, 1934: 1, 3.

Page 62. **"Breen's position:** "Kahane Heads Coast Ass'n, Breen Ups," *Variety*, February 6, 1934: 5, 63.

Page 63. **"I tried to evade:** JIB to Bishop John T. McNicholas, March 22, 1934 (ACHRC&UA).

Page 63. **"I am trying:** JIB to Rev. Wilfrid Parsons, S.J., January 2, 1934 (PP).

Page 63. **After only two months:** Victor M. Shapiro, "The Hollywood Scene," *Motion Picture Herald*, March 10, 1934: 21–22; "Fox Vetoes Veto of Hays Veto and Will Veto 'Bottoms' Heat," *Daily Variety*, March 2, 1934: 2.

Page 65. **Breen wanted the entire:** JIB to Louis B. Mayer, January 8, 1934 (*Queen Christina* file, PCA).

Page 65. **"It is quite apparent:** JIB memo, January 8, 1934 (*Queen Christina* file, PCA).

Page 65. **"Joe and I had hoped:** Jason Joy to Earl Bright, January 11, 1934 (*Queen Christina* file, PCA).

Page 65. **"The task is really an impossible one:** JIB to Rev. FitzGeorge Dinneen, S.J., March 17, 1934 (ACHRC&UA).

Page 66. **In Breen's hometown:** "Bad Pictures Condemned by Cardinal," *New World*, June 8, 1934: 7; "Bishops Follow Lead of Cardinals in Film Protests," *New World*, June 15, 1934: 1.

Page 66. **"One of the amazing features:** "Boycott Move Expanding," *Billboard*, July 21, 1934: 19.

Page 66. **The Catholic crusade "has touched:** "Protestantism and Jewry Join Catholics in Movie Ban," *Christian Century*, July 4, 1934: 884.

Page 66. **"A specially gratifying feature:** "Happy Omen," *Catholic Telegraph*, June 21, 1934: 4.

Page 67. **"We have them on the run:** JIB to Bishop John T. McNicholas, May 22, 1934 (ACHRC&UA).

Page 67. **A violation of the rules:** MPPDA Board of Directors Meeting, June 13, 1934 (QP).

Page 67. **Hays told the pair:** Martin J. Quigley to Bishop John T. McNicholas, May 29, 1934 (QP).

Page 67. **"The stage is set:** JIB to Bishop John T. McNicholas, May 22, 1934 (ACHRC&UA).

Page 67. **"a vulgar and highly offensive:** JIB to A. M. Botsford, March 7, 1934 (*The Belle of the Nineties* file, PCA).

Page 68. **Dirty-minded grammarians:** Philip Kinsley, "Will Mae West Survive Movie Uplift Effort?" *Chicago Daily Tribune*, June 14, 1934: 1, 5; "Mae West Movie Delayed by Paramount," *Chicago Daily Tribune*, June 25, 1934: 3.

Page 68. **In cloth and in mufti:** "Film Producers Promise Bishops to Reform," *Catholic Telegraph*, June 28, 1934: 1, 16.

Page 69. **"Certainly, if there is a censorship:** W. R. Wilkerson, "Tradeviews," *Hollywood Reporter*, January 5, 1935: 1.

Page 69. **At the end of the conference:** "Catholic Prelates Give Films One More Chance," *Los Angeles Times*, June 22, 1934: 2; "Cardinal Mundelien Says Process Will Be Given Chance," *Film Daily*, September 22, 1934: 1, 3.

Page 70. **"If Joe Breen tells:** "Censorship at the Source," *Variety*, January 1, 1935: 37.

Page 70. **"We went [to Cincinnati]:** J. D. Spiro, "Ban on 20 Films a Year Proposed," clipping, July 14, 1934 (PP).

Page 70. **"From the bottom of its trunk:** "Hollywood Digs Up Old Code to Govern All Movie Morals, *Philadelphia Record*, July 14, 1934: 1, 2.

Page 70. **"To all intents and purposes:** "Bishops Meet This Week," *Variety*, June 19, 1934: 47.

Page 71. **The campaign opened:** "Will Hays Arrives, Goes into Huddle with Producers," *Film Daily*, July 10, 1934: 7; "Will Hays Starts Clean-up Work," *Film Daily*, July 11, 1934: 2.

Page 71. **In the future, "Hollywood:** "Movie Trade, Feeling Attacks, to Be 'Careful,' Code Head Says," *New York Times*, June 25, 1934: 17. See also "Censor Approves New 'Pure' Movies," *Philadelphia Record*, July 15, 1934, sec. 2: 5.

Page 71. **"Theodore Roosevelt coined:** "Censorship 'Czar' of Films Sees a Rough Road Ahead," *Detroit News*, July 13, 1934: 1, 2.

Page 71. **"Breen talks too much,":** "And the Boycott Has Registered," *Christian Century*, July 4, 1934: 885; "A New Deal in the Movies," *New World*, August 10, 1934: 4.

Page 71. **On August 29, 1934:** "Breen Turns Air Thespian in Hays Drive to Publicize Pic Clean Up," *Variety*, August 28, 1934: 3.

Page 72. **Breen delivered a ten-minute spiel:** Patrick F. Scanlon, "From the Managing Editor's Desk," *Brooklyn Tablet*, September 1, 1934: 7.

Page 72. **He drummed home the same message:** "Breen on Air Today," *Hollywood Reporter*, August 29, 1934: 2; "Breen and Mrs. Winter Broadcast About Pix," *Hollywood Reporter*, September 1, 1934: 5; "12 Stories Rejected by Breen's Office," *Film Daily*, September 7, 1934: 2; "Film Studios' Program," *Variety*, September 4, 1934: 41; "Breen Says New Pix Maintain Virility," *Film Daily*, August 31, 1934: 1, 6.

Page 73. **[The Code's] broad general purpose:** "Motion Picture Official Explains Code," Universal Newsreel vol. 6 #282, September 5, 1934.

Page 73. **"It may interest you:** "Breen and Staff to Be Actors Tomorrow," *Hollywood Reporter*, August 23, 1934: 2; Universal Newsreel vol. 6 #282 lists the release dates as

September 5, 1934, and Universal Newsreel vol. 6 #286, as September 19, 1934. *HR* says the first release appeared on September 12, 1934 (in L.A.): "First Breen Release," *Hollywood Reporter*, September 8, 1934: 4.

Page 74. **"Our job, as I see it:** "Board to Control Pictures," Universal Newsreel vol. 6 #286, September 19, 1934.

Page 74. **Looking at Breen's film debut:** Len Morgan, "True to Form," *Billboard*, September 29, 1934: 21.

Page 75. **"Joe Breen's second subject:** Tom Waller, "Newsreels," *Variety*, September 25, 1934: 12.

Page 75. **"Joe Breen is the banishing:** Patrick F. Scanlon, "From the Managing Editor's Desk," *Brooklyn Tablet*, August 11, 1934: 9.

Page 75. **The visible mark of quality control:** "Hays Meeting Votes Purity Seal for Pix," *Hollywood Reporter*, July 12, 1934: 3.

Page 75. **audiences greeted the emblem:** "Audience Hisses New Purity Seal," *Hollywood Reporter*, August 7, 1934: 1; "Hissing Purity," *Variety*, August 28, 1934: 1; "Hissing the Hays Emblem of Purity," *Harrison's Reports*, September 15, 1934: 145.

Page 75. **The change, insisted the MPPDA:** "Inside Stuff—Pictures," *Variety*, July 31, 1935: 18; "Change in Seal," *Film Daily*, July 24, 1935: 1.

Page 75. **Mrs. Eleanor Roosevelt:** "Movies Discussed by Mrs. Roosevelt," *New York Times*, July 10, 1934: 19.

Page 76. **"The one thing:** Tom Waller, "Newsreels," *Variety*, September 11, 1934: 17.

4: THE BREEN OFFICE

Page 77. **What fueled the studio system:** "U.S. Commerce Dep. Analysis Shows Amusement Biz Hardest Hit in 1932–33," *Variety*, November 18, 1936: 6. By the end of 1934, the motion picture industry "had begun climbing back toward normalcy" after suffering through its "low point of the Depression" during 1932 and 1933.

Page 77. **The baton pass:** Arthur Ungar, "Leading Film Names of '34," *Variety*, January 1, 1935: 1, 36.

Page 78. **"Every producer in this village:** W. R. Wilkerson, "Tradeviews," *Hollywood Reporter*, December 17, 1935: 1.

Page 78. **Agreed Pope:** Frank Pope, "Tradeviews," *Hollywood Reporter*, January 15, 1935: 1, 2.

Page 79. **"Few people realize:** "Thursday," *Harrison's Reports*, December 15, 1934: 200.

Page 79. **"It is difficult today:** "Back to Normalcy Again," *Variety*, November 11, 1936: 4.

Page 79. **"At first, the motion picture:** "Nat'l Body Boosts Pix, Pans Air," *Hollywood Reporter*, July 6, 1938: 1, 4.

Page 79. **"Ever since the Joe Breen office:** "WB Taking a Censorial Rap?" *Variety*, February 15, 1939: 5.

Page 79. **Once a chronic migraine:** See "Any New Censor Measures Seen as Spite Work Against Film Biz Already Self-Purged, at the Source," *Variety*, March 24, 1937: 11; "Chi. Censors So Amiable It's Getting Monotonous," *Variety*, August 8, 1937: 6.

Page 79. **"The greatness of Joseph:** Quoted by W. R. Wilkerson, "Tradeviews," *Hollywood Reporter*, April 16, 1935: 1, 2; Rev. Gerard B. Donnelly, S.J., "The Outstanding

Catholic Achievement," *America*, January 5, 1935: 299. See also Rev. Gerard B. Donnelly, S.J., "'Definitely Cleaner' Films," *America*, July 27, 1935: 366–67.

Page 79. **"You can't kick love:** "Films Realize Need for Sock," *Variety*, July 24, 1934: 1, 2.

Page 81. **Like every department head:** JIB to Martin J. Quigley, August 23, 1935 (QP).

Page 81. **"A written record is essential:** Maurice McKenzie to JIB, June 5, 1934; JIB to Will Hays, June 2, 1934 (*The Belle of the Nineties* file, PCA).

Page 81n. **The PCA was also funded:** "Indies Beefing About High Cost of Haysian and Censorial Okays," *Variety*, May 3, 1939: 5; "Production Code Funds Shrink," *Variety*, September 22, 1954: 7.

Page 83. **He referred to the schoolmarmish:** JIB to Maurice McKenzie, March 5, 1931 (WHP).

Page 84. **"I am looking at pictures:** JIB to Vincent Hart, July 18, 1934 (*Crime Without Passion* file, PCA).

Page 84. **"Once the decision:** JIB to Arthur E. DeBra, November 20, 1944: 2–3. Written in response to an inquiry from DeBra, director of the community relations department of the MPPDA, this 57-page letter is Breen's most eloquent and extensive expression of his philosophy at the Code (PCA).

Page 85. **"Joe has saved the picture companies:** W.R. Wilkerson, "Tradeviews," *Hollywood Reporter*, December 17, 1935: 1.

Page 85. **In 1936, by one reckoning:** Edwin Schallert, "Censors Ban Sex and Gangsters," *Los Angeles Times*, February 7, 1937: C1.

Page 85. **To emphasize the assembly-line setup:** "Drop in British Pix Reflected in Few Seals Issued by Codists," *Variety*, October 14, 1936: 4.

Page 85. **"It may interest you:** JIB to Maurice McKenzie, April 12, 1935 (QP).

Page 86. **Publicly, Breen deferred:** James P. Cunningham, "Issue Not for Code Administration But Hays, Breen Holds," *Motion Picture Herald*, April 24, 1937: 14–15.

Page 86. **a man from the Advertising Council:** "Hays to H'wood on Clean Pix," *Variety*, July 3, 1934: 5.

Page 86. **"They have started working on the Boss:** JIB to Martin J. Quigley, August 23, 1935 (QP).

Page 87. **In 1935, when Hays's:** "Farley Likely to Succeed Hays," *Hollywood Reporter*, March 4, 1935: 1, 2.

Page 87. **"Mr. Breen, despite the difficulty:** "Thursday," *Harrison's Reports*, December 15, 1934: 200.

Page 87. **"Mr. Hays's objections:** Frank Nugent, "Walter Wanger Hurls a Political Bombshell," *New York Times*, December 9, 1934, sec. 10: 5.

Page 88. **Paramount, atypically, pledged:** "Wanger Will Defy Hays," *Billboard*, December 1, 1934: 20.

Page 88. **"In going over Breen's head:** Len Morgan, "Danger," *Billboard*, December 1, 1934: 21; "Hays Reconsiders," *Billboard*, December 8, 1934: 20.

Page 88. **"By the spring of 1934:** "Better Pictures: The Work of the Production Code Administration and the Motion Picture Producers and Distributors of America," August 10, 1936: 5 (WHP). See also "The Hays Office," *Fortune* (December 1938): 142, 140.

Page 89. **Braced by vivid:** "Joe Breen's Newspaper NRA Title Burns Rosy," *Variety*, July 17, 1934: 5.

Page 89. **(Producers Scrub 'Em Clean:** "Producer's Scrub 'Em Clean Before Showing to Breen," *Variety*, July 17, 1934: 5; "Indies Meet on Coast for Hays Censoring Agreement Protests; Investigation on Washington End," *Variety*, August 21, 1934: 5; "Nix Classifying of Pix," *Variety*, August 28, 1934: 7.

Page 89. **"The more I thought:** Statement by JIB (QP).

Page 89. **"rooted in the objective:** JIB to Eric Johnston, March 10, 1949 (QP). Written to MPAA president Eric Johnston in rebuttal to a proposal to liberalize the Production Code, this 12-page letter is another revealing expression of Breen's outlook.

Page 90. **"We refrain from dealing:** JIB to Martin J. Quigley, April 23, 1940 (QP).

Page 91. **Wise to "the subterfuge:** JIB to Vincent Hart, August 7, 1934 (*Crime Without Passion* file, PCA).

Page 91. **The prime directive decreed:** JIB to Arthur E. DeBra, November 20, 1944 (PCA).

Page 92. **must "jealously guard marriage:** JIB to Bishop John T. McNicholas, March 22, 1934 (ACHRC&UA).

Page 92. **"The unacceptability of this story:** JIB to William Burnside, January 8, 1945 (*The Rake's Progress* file, PCA).

Page 93. **"The nude breasts:** JIB to Vincent Hart, July 18, 1934 (*Crime Without Passion* file, PCA).

Page 93. **Beginning in 1934, Breen:** JIB to Frank R. Nostril, April 10, 1946 (*Abie's Irish Rose* file, PCA).

Page 94. **Though acknowledging Fox's arguments:** JIB to Francis Harmon, February 6, 1950 (*Cheaper by the Dozen* file, PCA).

Page 94. **"To my way of thinking:** Eugene Weare [JIB], "A Great National Problem," *America*, January 6, 1923: 273.

Page 95. **Breen credited whatever success:** JIB to Bishop John T. McNicholas, March 22, 1934 (ACHRC&UA).

Page 96. **The "G-Men" pictures:** JIB to Will H. Hays, April 10, 1935 (*Let 'Em Have It* file, PCA).

5. DECODING CLASSICAL HOLLYWOOD CINEMA

Page 97. **"The only thing that's really shocking:** Helen Gwynne, "Not That It Matters," *Hollywood Reporter*, August 6, 1935: 3.

Page 97. **Whereas the switch to talking:** "Readjustment Due to Legion Greatest in Industry: Zanuck," *Motion Picture Herald*, March 16, 1935: 24. See also Douglas W. Churchill, "Hollywood Letter," *New York Times*, May 19, 1935, sec. 10: 3.

Page 100. **"It will be vital:** JIB to John Hammell, October 3, 1935 (*Desire* file, PCA).

Page 100. **At once staid and steamy:** "Set 'Desire' as Model Uncensorable Subtlety," *Hollywood Reporter*, April 22, 1936: 4.

Page 102. **"I love Mr. Chandler:** Quoted in Pete Harrison, "Joe Breen's Temper," *Harrison's Reports*, September 28, 1946: 3. Harrison also noted "the audience roared" at Bacall's racy comeback.

Page 103. **"The boys hereabouts:** JIB to Rev. Daniel A. Lord, S.J., March 1, 1941 (MJA).

Page 106. **"The good spirit:** JIB to Harry Cohn, June 14, 1937; Internal Review by Karl Lischka, September 27, 1937 (*The Awful Truth* file, PCA).

Page 106. **He knew "that Lubitsch:** JIB to Rev. Wilfrid Parsons, S.J., November 23, 1934 (PP).

Page 106. **"The picture as it stands:** JIB to Will H. Hays, October 22, 1934 (*The Merry Widow* file, PCA).

Page 107. ***Angel* is a textbook index:** JIB to Harry Zehner, November 20, 1934; JIB to John Hammell, December 28, 1936; Will H. Hays, December 31, 1936; JIB to John Hammell, February 15, 1937 (all in *Angel* file, PCA).

Page 108. **"*Angel* has come out:** Denis Morrison, "Pix Aim to Please 'Em All," *Variety*, July 28, 1937: 34.

Page 108. **"The pupils, confronted:** Billy Wilder and Charles Bracket, "The Passed Master—In Memoriam," *Hollywood Reporter*, December 3, 1947: 3.

Page 109. **"If at any time you:** Breen, quoted in J. P. McEvoy, "The Back of Me Hand to You," *Saturday Evening Post*, December 24, 1938: 47.

Page 109. **"Breen wants Rebecca:** Hitchcock, quoted in Douglas W. Churchill, "Water Over the Hollywood Dam," *New York Times*, October 1, 1939: 139.

Page 110. **"We were in the business:** James M. Wall, "Interviews with Geoffrey Shurlock," Oral History, Louis B. Mayer Library, American Film Institute, 1970: 261.

Page 110. **"As I told you in my last letter:** JIB to Vincent Hart, February 19, 1936 (*It Can't Happen Here* file, PCA).

Page 110. **Like any shrewd operator:** "A Breen Standoff," *Variety*, January 25, 1939: 5.

Page 110. **"Cooperating with producers:** "Breen Office May Relax Rules a Bit," *Hollywood Reporter*, August 13, 1937: 5.

Page 110. **"Breen today collaborates:** "Censorship at the Source," *Variety*, January 1, 1935: 37. The PCA file on the film basically confirms *Variety*'s account, but the locale and the speaker of the tagline were switched in the final cut. Star Pat O'Brien assures his girlfriend, "Yeah, I'm through with that Millicent dame too, but the cops aren't. They've cabled Paris and they'll be a couple of Gendarmes waiting at the boat." H. J. McCord to JIB, September 7, 1934 (*I Sell Anything* file, PCA).

Page 111. **"Studios say that scarcely a script:** Lucie Neville, "Hollywood Movie-Makers Find Five Years of Hays' Rule Pays Dividends," *Washington Post*, January 27, 1939: A1.

Page 111. **A frequently cited instance:** Douglas W. Churchill, "Hollywood Walks Warily," *New York Times Magazine*, August 23, 1936: 8, 18.

Page 111. **"I have deep regard:** William R. Weaver, "Hornblow Cites Producer Responsibility to Decency," *Motion Picture Herald*, May 4, 1946: 39.

Page 111. **"In the long run:** Hal Wallis and Charles Higham, *Starmaker: The Autobiography of Hal Wallis* (New York: Macmillan, 1980): 100–101.

Page 112. **When screenwriters-turned-producers:** JIB to Vincent Hart, October 5, 1934 (*Crime Without Passion* file, PCA).

Page 112. **"an essential unity:** JIB to Arthur E. DeBra, November 20, 1944: 7 (AMPAS).

Page 112. **It banned titles:** "Too Hot for Hays," *Variety*, June 16, 1937: 7.

Page 112. **Neither *Wayward Girl:*** "Hays Edict Causes Col.'s Hunt for New 'Girl' Tag," *Hollywood Reporter*, April 3, 1937: 3.

Page 112. **The G-String Murders:** "'G-String Murders' Worth $25,000 to Authoress Gypsy Rose Lee from UA," *Variety*, November 12, 1941: 29.

Page 112. **"We are concerned about:** JIB to Hunt Stromberg, December 3, 1942 (*Lady of Burlesque* file, PCA).

Page 113. **Perhaps just as well:** Terry Ramsaye, "Tending Wither," *Motion Picture Herald*, February 6, 1943: 7.

Page 113. **It demanded translations:** "Inside Stuff—Pictures," *Variety*, March 3, 1937: 6.

Page 113. ***Frankie and Johnnie:*** "Frankie and Johnnie Okay," *Film Daily*, May 20, 1935: 3.

Page 113. **"All this dialogue:** JIB to Joseph J. Nolan, September 3, 1940 (*Little Men* file, PCA).

Page 113. **"If your Breen line:** William H. Mooring, "Verbal Oscar to Joe Breen for 20 Years in a Major Role," *Catholic Standard and Times*, October 29, 1954: 14.

Page 113. **"Joe Breen has done:** W. R. Wilkerson, "Tradeviews," *Hollywood Reporter*, May 3, 1935: 1.

Page 114. **"I used always to write:** Donald Ogden Stewart, *By a Stroke of Luck: An Autobiography* (New York: Paddington Press, 1975): 236.

Page 114. **The Breen Office denied blackballing:** "Can't Doctor 'Postman' to Satisfy Joe Breen; Metro Sells to France," *Variety*, August 3, 1938: 6.

Page 114. **Having been kept out of the loop:** James M. Cain, "Postman Rings Thrice," *New York Times*, April 21, 1946: 51.

Page 115. **Six states:** "Heedless of Cost to Industry, Politicians in Nine More States Ask Film Censoring This Year," *Variety*, March 8, 1939: 6.

Page 116. **"The PCA acts:** "Hays Office Clarifies Prod. Code; Realism Up to Individual Producer, But There's Been No Relaxing by PCA," *Variety*, February 22, 1939: 4.

Page 116. **"Gangster Pic Cycle:** "Gangster Pic Cycle Nipped by Hays Ban," *Hollywood Reporter*, February 11, 1937: 3.

Page 116. **Headlined *Hollywood Reporter:*** "Hays Ban on Liquor," *Hollywood Reporter*, February 2, 1937: 1, 3.

Page 117. **"It is a hell:** Terry Ramsaye, "The Code Mystery," *Motion Picture Herald*, February 7, 1942: 7–8.

Page 118. **The sensitivity of the project:** JIB to Louis B. Mayer, January 31, 1936 (*It Can't Happen Here* file, PCA; again, italics in the original).

Page 119. **"are not only joebreened:** Denis Morrison, "Pix Aim to Please 'Em All," *Variety*, July 28, 1937: 1, 34.

Page 119. **Breen's guidance on foreign affairs:** "Foreign Markets Dwindle," *Variety*, May 11, 1938: 13.

Page 119. **Among other quirks:** "Hospital Scenes Draw Heavy Cuts from British Censors, Breen Warns," *Variety*, May 12, 1937: 4.

Page 119. **To placate British sensitivities:** "Britain's Film Act Death Blow for Westerns There," *Hollywood Reporter*, September 21, 1937: 11.

Page 119. **"For your British print:** JIB to David O. Selznick, October 14, 1937 (*Gone With the Wind* file, PCA).

Page 120. **Breen tried to shut off:** "Wanger Ignores Breen's Ruling On 'Cycles,'" Another Alcohol Picture," *Variety*, June 26, 1946: 4.

Page 120. **"The 'use of liquor'**: JIB to Walter Wanger, April 17, 1946 (*Smash-up* file, PCA).

Page 120. **"If only for a social welfare:** JIB to Joyce O'Hara, Mary 26, 1946 (*The Bells of St. Mary's* file, PCA).

6. CONFESSIONAL

Page 121. **As rendered in the purple prose:** "The Hays Office," *Fortune* (December 1938): 140; Thomas M. Pryor, "Joe Breen, Sire of Code Ratings, Dies; Long Ill," *Variety*, December 8, 1965: 2; "Salute to a Warrior for Decency," *Christian Century*, May 28, 1941: 708; Elizabeth Yeaman, "The Catholic Movie Censorship," *New Republic*, October 5, 1938: 233.

Page 121. **His MPPDA colleague Charles Francis "Socker" Coe:** Charles Francis Coe, *Never a Dull Moment* (New York: Hastings House, 1944): 306.

Page 121. **Joe was very:** Albert E. Van Schmus, in Barbara Hall, *An Oral Interview with Albert E. Van Schmus*, Oral History Program, Margaret Herrick Library, Academy of Motion Picture Arts and Sciences, Beverly Hills, Calif., 1993: 14.

Page 121. **"We were with him:** "A Providential Layman!" *Western Catholic*, November 21, 1930: 2.

Page 122. **"He is a newspaperman:** Lemuel F. Parton, "Who's News Today," *Philadelphia Evening Bulletin*, February 5, 1937.

Page 122. **Breen's use of Celtic:** Douglas W. Churchill, "Hollywood Letter," *New York Times*, May 19, 1935, sec. 10: 3; Douglas W. Churchill, "Production Code vs. The Unbelievers," *Motion Picture Herald*, July 20, 1935: 16; J. P. McEvoy, "The Back of Me Hand to You," *Saturday Evening Post*, December 24, 1938: 8.

Page 122. **Tiptoeing around language:** "Censorship at the Source," *Variety*, January 1, 1935: 37.

Page 122. **"What's all this shit?":** Jack Vizzard, *See No Evil: Life Inside a Hollywood Censor* (New York: Simon and Schuster, 1970): 51.

Page 122. **"Breen was not that type:** Shurlock in James M. Wall, "Interviews with Geoffrey Shurlock" (1970): 130–31.

Page 122. **Breen knew that the coarse:** "Hollywood Inside," *Daily Variety*, March 13, 1935: 2.

Page 123. **The talk was backed up by intimidation:** John J. McCarthy, "Man of Decency," *Esquire* (September 1935): 64, 126–28.

Page 123. **That same year:** "Just to Keep the Record Straight!" *Harrison's Reports*, March 30, 1935: 50.

Page 123. **He and "Socker" Coe:** Coe, *Never a Dull Moment*: 307.

Page 123. **"I remember sitting:** Daniel E. Doran, "Mr. Breen Confronts the Dragons," *The Sign* (January 1942): 328.

Page 124. **"If my health is good:** JIB to Rev. Wilfrid Parsons, S.J., December 29, 1925 (PP).

Page 124. **He soldiered on:** Reverend C. F. Donovan, *The Story of the Twenty-Eighth International Eucharistic Congress* (Chicago: The Committee in Charge at Chicago, 1927): ii; JIB to Rev. Wilfrid Parsons, S.J., September 26, 1927 (PP).

Page 124. **Breen spent most of 1927:** JIB to Rev. Wilfrid Parsons, S.J., April 20, 1927 (PP).

Page 124. **"I have been seriously ill:** JIB to Rt. Rev. Msgr. William Quinn, June 4, 1927 (AC).

Page 124. **"Since I took over:** JIB to Rev. FitzGeorge Dinneen, S.J., March 17, 1934 (ACHRC&UA); JIB to Bishop John T. McNicholas, March 22, 1934 (ACHRC&UA).

Page 124. **"The task he has undertaken:** "Just to Keep the Record Straight!" *Harrison's Reports*, March 30, 1935: 50.

Page 125. **"A husky citizen:** Lemuel F. Parton, "Who's News Today," *Philadelphia Evening Bulletin*, February 5, 1937.

Page 125. **"He is a physical:** Howard Hall, "I.H.S. (In Hoc Signo—In His Sacerdotalism)," *Cinema Hall-Marks*, August 6, 1934: 17–18.

Page 125. **"He deliberately keeps:** Frederick James Smith, "Hollywood's New Purity Tape Measure," *Liberty*, August 15, 1936: 43.

Page 125. **Recalled Shurlock:** Shurlock, in Wall, "Interviews" (1970): 347.

Page 125. **"I know Joe Breen:** "The Hitler of Hollywood," *Film Weekly*, August 31, 1934: 11.

Page 125. **"This was my first introduction:** William H. Mooring, "Verbal Oscar to Joe Breen for 20 Years in a Major Role," *Catholic Standard and Times*, October 29, 1954: 14.

Page 125. **Occasionally, Breen was spotted:** "Rambling Reporter," *Hollywood Reporter*, March 16, 1937: 2; "Rambling Reporter," *Hollywood Reporter*, April 4, 1938: 2.

Page 125. **"Clubs, golf, and other diversions:** Bernard J. Nash, "Joseph I. Breen Has Job of Making Movies Behave," *Witness* (unpaginated, undated clipping, circa 1934) (ACHRC&UA).

Page 126. **"The job is a terrific:** JIB to Rev. Wilfrid Parsons, S.J., November 23, 1934 (PP).

Page 126. **"[My] doctor thinks:** JIB to Maurice McKenzie, April 12, 1935 (QP).

Page 126. **"this excellent Christian gentleman:** *Brooklyn Tablet*, April 27, 1935.

Page 126. **"I am simply *flabbergasted:*** JIB to Maurice McKenzie, April 12, 1935 (QP).

Page 126. **"When Joe 'Seal' Breen:** "Inside Stuff—Pictures," *Variety*, May 29, 1935: 6.

Page 127. **On July 30, 1935:** "Joe Breen Returns," *Hollywood Reporter*, July 31, 1935: 1.

Page 127. **"I find the general:** JIB to Martin J. Quigley, August 23, 1935 (QP).

Page 128. **"I think [the trip]:** JIB to Martin J. Quigley, August 23, 1935 (QP).

Page 128. **"Along the first:** JIB to Maurice McKenzie, April 12, 1935 (QP).

Page 128. **"You're not quitting:** Patrick F. Scanlon to JIB, January 11, 1936 (PP).

Page 128. **When Breen blustered:** Martin J. Quigley to JIB, December 30, 1935 (QP).

Page 128. **"Frankly, I'm terribly fed up:** JIB to Martin J. Quigley, September 25, 1937 (QP).

Page 129. **Travel—his preferred restorative:** "Hays Mulls Foreign Gag," *Variety*, August 3, 1938: 6.

Page 130. **As Breen's mood pitched:** Rev. G. B. Donnelly, S.J., to Rev. Wilfrid Parsons, S.J., undated letter (1936). All subsequent quotations are taken from this report (PP).

7. INTERMISSION AT RKO

Page 132. **"Taking the industry entirely:** "Breen Quits Hays Office Post," *Hollywood Reporter*, April 25, 1941: 1, 2.

Page 132. **"The story of Mr. Breen's:** Daniel E. Doran, "Mr. Breen Confronts the Dragons," *The Sign* (January 1942): 330.

Page 132. **Later, in a better mood:** "Passing of a 'No' Man," *Newsweek*, May 12, 1941: 61.

Page 132. **Ultimately, his resignation:** "Attended RKO Convention," *Variety*, June 25, 1941: 5.

Page 132. **Lured by nearly double:** "Breen Extends Vacash," *Variety*, April 1, 1942: 5, 50.

Page 133. **"a backdrop of management:** "History of RKO Goes Back to 1883," *Variety*, May 12, 1948: 4; Betty Lasky, *RKO: The Biggest Little Major of Them All* (Santa Monica, Calif.: Roundtable, 1989): 1, 165.

Page 133. **"During the past five years:** Harold Heffernan, "Breen Seen Returning to Mend Film Fences," December 2, 1941 (unpaginated clipping) (ACHRC&UA).

Page 134. **"This word as used:** Rudy Behlmer, ed., *Memo from David O. Selznick* (New York: Viking, 1972): 229–31.

Page 134n. **As Breen Office files noted:** Douglas W. Churchill, "A 'Damn' Breaks," *New York Times*, December 19, 1937: 153.

Page 135. **"However many Oscars *GWTW:*** W. R. Wilkerson, "Tradeviews," *Hollywood Reporter*, October 18, 1939: 1, 2.

Page 135. **"When Hays office purists:** Jimmie Fidler, "In Hollywood," *Los Angeles Times*, December 25, 1939: 16.

Page 135. **The statement, an angry Breen:** JIB to Will H. Hays, October 21, 1939; memo to Francis Harmon, October 25, 1939; JIB to Jimmie Fidler, December 26, 1939 (all from *Gone With the Wind* file, PCA).

Page 135. **Pressing the advantage:** Thomas M. Pryor, "Mr. Selznick Proposes a New Purity Code," *New York Times*, April 21, 1940, sec. 9: 4.

Page 136. **"In recent months:** Pete Harrison, "Has the Industry Further Use of the Hays Seal?—No. 3," *Harrison's Reports*, April 19, 1941: 61.

Page 136. **"sweaters that are too revealing:** "Breen Notifies Studios Against Sweaters in Pix," *Film Daily*, April 4, 1941: 1, 6.

Page 136. **Joining in the "barrage:** "Passing of a 'No' Man," *Newsweek*, May 12, 1941: 61.

Page 136. **At *Motion Picture Herald:*** Terry Ramsaye, "Accent on Sweaters," *Motion Picture Herald*, April 19, 1941: 7.

Page 137. **By playing the postproduction change-up:** JIB to Mat O'Brien, February 14, 1940; JIB to Mat O'Brien, February 22, 1940; JIB to Francis Harmon, June 11, 1940 (all from *Turnabout* file, PCA).

Page 139. **Breen lectured Roach:** JIB to Martin J. Quigley, June 24, 1940 (QP).

Page 139. **"Breen, in an effort:** Ivan Spear, "Spearheads," *Box Office*, May 3, 1941: 41.

Page 140. **That spring, two films:** "Hughes' Outlaw Refused Seal by the Hays Office," *Hollywood Reporter*, May 1, 1941: 1, 4.

Page 140. **"This type of maneuvering:** "Shurlock May Succeed Joe Breen; Hays Purity Coder Adamant on Resigning," *Variety*, April 30, 1941: 4, 22.

Page 140. **Soon afterward, rumors:** "No RKO Bid—Breen; May Visit So. America," *Film Daily*, April 30, 1941: 2; "Uncertainty at RKO on Production Head," *Box Office*, May 3, 1941: 39.

Page 140. **"In trade circles:** "RKO's Revamp, East-West," *Variety*, April 30, 1941: 5, 22.

Page 140. **"Mr. Breen will take over:** "Breen Signs," *Motion Picture Herald*, May 17, 1941: 8.

Page 140. **"Washington is said:** "Hays Out, Breen In—N.Y. Tip," *Hollywood Reporter*, June 17, 1941: 1, 2; "Breen Definitely Out of Hays Post," *Hollywood Reporter*, June 18, 1941: 1, 9.

Page 140. **Breen's "signal ability:** "Hays Pays Tribute to Breen as PCA Director," *Film Daily*, June 18, 1941: 1, 6.

Page 141. **"Wherever Breen goes:** W.R. Wilkerson, "Tradeviews," *Hollywood Reporter*, April 28, 1941: 1.

Page 141. **As news of Breen's defection:** "Who'll Succeed Breen Occupying Hollywood?" *Box Office*, May 3, 1941: 30.

Page 141. **"Now Hollywood *really:*** Adela Rogers St. Johns, "Why Breen Resigned from the Hays Office," *Liberty*, July 5, 1941: 14–15, 43–44.

Page 141. **"No matter who is chosen:** "Hays Illness Stalls Breen Successor," *Variety*, May 7, 1941: 5, 27.

Page 141. **"Without the guidance:** "Has the Industry Further Use of the Hays Seal?—No. 5," *Harrison's Reports*, May 3, 1941: 69, 74.

Page 142. **To calm the jittery moguls:** "Hays Pays Tribute to Breen as PCA Director," *Film Daily*, June 18, 1941: 1, 6.

Page 142. **This was news to Harmon:** "Harmon to Succeed Breen at PCA?" *Film Daily*, April 28, 1941: 1, 3; "Harmon Unaware of Move to Name Him Head of PCA," *Film Daily*, April 29, 1941: 1, 5.

Page 142. **As a potential Code chieftain:** "Cong. Costello May Succeed Joe Breen," *Variety*, June 11, 1941: 5; "Outside 'Name' to Succeed Joe Breen?" *Variety*, May 28, 1941: 5.

Page 142. **"Mr. Warner is alleged:** "Nye on Warner," *Variety*, September 10, 1941: 5.

Page 143. **Nervously eyeing the situation:** "South America, Breen's Successor and Labor Up Before Prods. on Coast," *Variety*, November 26, 1941: 7.

Page 143. **"As yet, we do not know:** Bishop Joseph T. McGucken to Michael Ready, May 12, 1941 (ACHRC&UA).

Page 143. **A mere four months:** "Pix Penciled in for Another Blast?" *Variety*, November 12, 1941: 5.

Page 143. **"Do I remember it?":** Shurlock, in James M. Wall, "Interviews with Geoffrey Shurlock" (1970): 240.

Page 144. **Later, a confidential PCA report:** Internal Memo, November 21, 1941 (*Two-Faced Woman* file, PCA).

Page 144. **"There is no exact science:** "Here and There," *Harrison's Reports*, December 6, 1941: 193.

Page 144. **Folding immediately, MGM cut:** Robert Rubin to E. J. Mannix, December 5, 1941 (*Two-Faced Woman* file, PCA).

Page 145. **After the face-lift:** "Metro-Goldwyn Mayer," *Harrison's Reports*, January 3, 1942: 3.

Page 145. **To signal the change:** "Production Code Now a Composite Administration," *Variety*, July 9, 1941: 5.

Page 145. **"Shurlock can't be pushed around:** "Better Press Relations the Major Objective of Hays Organization Right Now; Also Tiffs on the Code," *Variety*, March 11, 1942: 7.

Pages 145–46. **On the West Coast:** "Harmon's Full War Job Means Upping for G. Shurlock," *Variety*, December 24, 1941: 14.

Page 146. **Asked if he wanted the job:** Daniel E. Doran, "Mr. Breen Confronts the Dragons," *The Sign* (January 1942): 330.

Page 146. **"Further proof of the sagacity:** Phil M. Daily, "Along the Rialto," *Film Daily*, June 20, 1941: 3.

Page 146. **As RKO's general manager:** "Schaefer Still Struggling with RKO Revamp; Breen's Studio Bid," and "RKO Unit Idea," *Variety*, May 7, 1941: 5.

Page 146. **RKO would never "swerve:** "Indecent Pix No Slump Weapon—Schaefer," *Film Daily*, June 19, 1941: 1, 8.

Page 147. **"One thing wrong:** "New RKO Talent Drive Under Breen Regime," *Box Office*, June 28, 1941: 21; "Breen Cues RKO Studio Staff Reshuffle," *Variety*, June 25, 1941: 5.

Page 147. **"Those guys hadn't better:** "Breen Cues RKO Studio Staff Reshuffle," *Variety*, June 25, 1941: 5.

Page 147. **Reporters were impressed:** Douglas W. Churchill, "Tales from Hollywood," *New York Times*, June 29, 1941, sec. 10: 3.

Page 148. **Breen's press conference:** Ivan Spear, "Spearheads," *Box Office*, April 28, 1941: 39.

Page 148. **"I have not been so impressed:** JIB to Orson Welles, December 2, 1941 (Welles Papers, IU).

Page 148. **Breen also courted director John Ford:** "Rambling Reporter," *Hollywood Reporter*, May 15, 1941: 2.

Page 148. **"Going through the script in detail:** Production Code Administration to JIB, July 22, 1941 (*Four Jacks and a Jill* file, PCA).

Page 148. **Still, Shurlock and his boys:** Production Code Administration to JIB, September 8, 1941 (*Joan of Paris* file, PCA).

Page 148. **By November 1941:** "Clarify RKO Studio Set Up," *Variety*, November 12, 1941: 5.

Page 149. **"Don't be surprised:** Harold Heffernan, "Breen Seen Returning to Mend Film Fences," December 2, 1941 (ACHRC&UA).

Page 149. **On December 16, 1941:** "Rathvon V.P. of RKO in General Exec Reorg; Kingsberg's Titles," *Variety*, December 17, 1941: 5.

Page 149. **RKO was still "the problem child:** "Top Money Stars, Pix in '41," *Variety*, December 31, 1941: 23.

Page 149. **First, Sol Lesser and J. R. McDonough:** "Sol Lesser, McDonough Quit RKO; Studio Prod. Reorg Awaits Schaefer," *Variety*, February 4, 1942: 5.

Page 149. **Accustomed to a large measure:** "Lesser Leaving RKO Studio," *Motion Picture Herald*, February 7, 1942: 24.

Page 149. **By the end of February 1942:** "Koerner May Succeed Breen at RKO Studio," *Box Office*, February 28, 1942: 21.

Page 149. **In a last-ditch effort:** "RKO Conclave," *Motion Picture Herald*, February 21, 1942: 9.

Page 150. **"I am very much under par:** JIB to Bishop McGucken, February 5, 1942; Bishop Joseph T. McGucken to JIB, February 5, 1942 (ALA).

Page 150. **On March 9, 1942:** "RKO May Copy Universal in Culling Studio Manpower from Theater Execs; Charles Koerner Up," *Variety*, March 4, 1942: 5.

Page 150. **"[Koerner] was endowed:** Pat O'Brien, *The Wind at My Back: The Life and Times of Pat O'Brien* (New York: Doubleday, 1964): 261–62.

Page 150. **The next week:** "RKO Directors Strong for Koerner," *Variety*, March 11, 1942: 5.

Page 150. **With competent Charles Koerner:** Ivan Spear, "Spearheads," *Box Office*, April 18, 1942: 45.

Page 150. **As far back as 1935:** Martin J. Quigley to JIB, December 30, 1935 (QP).

Page 151. **"I asked [Breen] about:** Albert E. Van Schmus, in Barbara Hall, *An Oral Interview* (1993): 12.

Page 151. **Initially, as the dream job:** "RKO May Copy Universal in Culling Studio Manpower from Theater Execs; Charles Koerner Up," *Variety*, March 4, 1942: 5.

Page 151. **As Breen angled:** "Not Jackson, Now Breen," *Motion Picture Herald*, April 4, 1942: 9.

Page 151. **"[It is] understood:** "Sarnoff Angry Over McDonough Shift, Threatens Action Blocking RKO Deal with Schaefer; Wants New Exec Line Up," *Variety*, March 25, 1942: 5.

Page 151. **On May 15, 1942:** "Breen Returns as Head of Code Administration," *Motion Picture Herald*, May 16, 1942: 18.

Page 151. **"He might have been:** Shurlock, in Wall, "Interviews" (1970): 213.

8. AT WAR WITH THE BREEN OFFICE

Page 152. **From Pearl Harbor to V-J Day:** A more extensive discussion of Hollywood at war appears in Thomas Doherty, *Projections of War: Hollywood, American Culture, and World War II* (New York: Columbia University Press, 1993).

Page 154. **"To reflect contemporary thought:** "Keeping 'Messages' Out," *Variety*, November 9, 1938: 3.

Page 154. **"that serves the important purpose:** "Hays' Annual Report Reviews Film Biz Problems; Starts His 18th Yr.," *Variety*, March 29, 1939: 4.

Page 154. **The "wholesome function:** "Keep Propaganda Out of Films," *Film Daily*, July 21, 1941: 1, 8.

Page 154. **Hollywood, he promised:** "Pix Biz's War Rally," *Variety*, December 10, 1941: 5.

Page 154. **"Under the circumstances:** Philip K. Scheuer, "Industry Leaders View Crisis with Optimism," *Los Angeles Times*, January 2, 1942: 13.

Page 155. **In June 1942:** "Code Stands in War, Too, Says Breen," *Motion Picture Herald*, June 27, 1942: 40.

Page 156. **The official MPPDA line:** "Gathering of Biggies in H'wood Proves Masterpiece of Privacy," *Variety*, February 24, 1943: 6.

Page 156. **In 1943, Charles Francis ("Socker") Coe:** "Coe Sees Production Code Industry 'Constitution,'" *Motion Picture Herald*, February 20, 1943: 34.

Page 156. **From this vantage:** "Better Press Relations the Major Objective of Hays Organization Right Now; Also Tiffs on the Code," *Variety*, March 11, 1942: 7.

Page 157. **Being on site:** "Brief in Re: *In Which We Serve*" (*In Which We Serve* file, PCA).

Page 158. **Astonishingly, the Breen Office:** "Pix Prexies Caution 'Don't Say Naughty Words,'" *Variety*, February 17, 1943: 3.

Page 158. **The GI attitude:** *In Which We Serve* file (PCA).

Page 158. **While acknowledging that soldiers:** JIB to Lt. O. D. Edwards, January 14, 1943 (*In Which We Serve* file, PCA).

Page 158. **"The use of the words 'hell':** Charles Francis Coe to JIB, December 12, 1942 (*We Are the Marines* file, PCA).

Page 158. **"We went through 'hell':** Bill Fromby, "Hell of a Fuss," *Box Office*, January 1, 1943: 18.

Page 160. **At Warner Bros. the crew:** Hal Wallis and Charles Higham, *Starmaker: The Autobiography of Hal Wallis* (New York: MacMillan, 1980): 80.

Page 161. **A mild joke:** JIB to Jack Warner, October 9, 1942; JIB to Jack Warner, November 11, 1942 (both in *Air Force* file, PCA).

Page 161. **Jack Warner intervened:** Jack Warner to JIB, November 25, 1942; JIB to Lt. Col. J.L. Warner, December 9, 1942 (both in *Air Force* file, PCA).

Page 161. **"We had taken the risk:** Wallis and Higham, *Starmaker*: 91.

Page 161. **The playwright Lillian Hellman:** "Hollywood in Wartime," *Yank*, September 24, 1943: 21.

Page 161. **"If any censor should interpose:** Pete Harrison, "Let There Be No More 'Sissy' Stuff in War Pictures!" *Harrison's Reports*, July 11, 1942: 109.

Page 162. **"There is no need further to sugarcoat:** "War Shorts Program Renewed for Year; More Grim Details," *Hollywood Reporter*, March 2, 1944: 1, 19.

Page 163. **"Dead bodies of Marines:** "What This Picture Did for Me," *Motion Picture Herald*, May 27, 1944: 58; John Stuart, Jr., "*With the Marines at Tarawa*," *Motion Picture Herald*, February 26, 1944: 1774.

Page 163. **"It is doubtful that:** "Battle Scenes of Tarawa Hit As Hard As Marines Did," *Hollywood Reporter*, February 18, 1944: 4.

Page 163. **"In the 1940s:** Paul Fussell, *Wartime: Understanding and Behavior in the Second World War* (New York: Oxford University Press, 1989): 189.

Page 164. **"The public is in no mood:** "Let Us Spare the Public's Feelings," *Harrison's Reports*, January 13, 1945: 8.

Page 165. **"I lost my own:** "More on Sparing the Public's Feelings," *Harrison's Reports*, February 3, 1945: 20.

Page 165. **"We continue to have serious:** JIB to Rev. Daniel A. Lord, S.J., April 2, 1943 (MJA).

Page 166. **After being approached directly:** Confidential Memorandum, Re: Latin America, February 10, 1943 (ACHRC&UA).

Page 167. **The "clever, insidious and incessant":** Eugene Weare [JIB], "Propaganda Run Wild," *Extension Magazine* (May 1928): 19, 20. This is the first in a series of three consecutive articles on propaganda.

Page 167. **In 1937:** Bob LaBonge, "Graduation Day," *Loyola Alumnus* (June 1937): 19.

Page 167. **In 1943 his animosity:** Marcia Winn, "Films Spared Regimentation by Curb on OWI," *Chicago Daily Tribune*, August 1, 1943: 16.

Page 168. **Ultimately, though, not even Breen:** JIB to Rev. Daniel A. Lord, S.J., June 3, 1943 (MJA).

Page 168. **Upon assuming office, Breen:** JIB to Francis Alstock, June 30, 1943; Francis Alstock to JIB, undated, RG 229.6.1, box 952, Council of Inter-American Affairs (NARA).

Page 168. **C.O. Rowe:** C.O. Rowe to JIB, September 3, 1943 (NARA).

Page 168. **Breen's service:** Edwin Schallert, "Millions Spent to Make Films Tasty for Latins," *Los Angeles Times*, June 6, 1943: C3.

Page 169. **Breen's hands-on attention:** JIB to Gerald Smith, November 16, 1943 (NARA).

Page 169. **Even the Victorian Breen:** JIB to Rev. Daniel A. Lord, S.J., October 5, 1943 (MJA).

Page 169. **Meanwhile, on his own home front:** JIB to Bishop John T. McNicholas, January 22, 1943 (ACHRC&UA).

Page 170. **Later, a form letter:** Lt. R. W. Heog to Mrs. J. R. Breen, November 1, 1944 (JIB personal file, PCA).

Page 170. **"We have two of our Marines:** JIB to Rev. Daniel A. Lord, S.J., January 3, 1945 (MJA).

Page 170. **Bishop McGucken expressed:** Bishop Joseph T. McGucken to JIB, August 14, 1944 (ALA).

9. *IN HIS SACERDOTALISM*

Page 172. **"You know, I don't:** Albert E. Van Schmus in Barbara Hall, *An Oral Interview* (1993): 99, 100.

Page 173. **"We could get the Cardinal:** JIB to Martin J. Quigley, June 21, 1930 (QP).

Page 173. **Lord's role:** "Church Drive Progresses," *Variety*, May 29, 1934: 23.

Page 174. **Later, Quigley sought to allay:** Martin J. Quigley to Rev. Daniel A. Lord, S.J., October 25, 1946 (QP).

Page 174. **For the record, Quigley stated:** Martin J. Quigley to Bosley Crowther, January 25, 1955 (QP).

Page 174. **"I asked to be kept out of it":** Quigley, quoted in Cynthia Lowry, "AP Tells the Facts About Quigley Code Authorship," *Motion Picture Herald*, November 6, 1948: 22.

Page 174. **As he told Rev. FitzGeorge Dinneen:** JIB to Rev. FitzGeorge Dinneen, S.J., April 1, 1934 (MJA).

Page 174. **When Breen cozily referred:** JIB to Bishop John T. McNicholas, March 22, 1934 (ACHRC&UA).

Page 174. **The official Hollywood line:** Rev. Daniel A. Lord, S.J., "Production Code: A Product of the Industry," *Motion Picture Herald*, November 23, 1946: 22; reprinted from Father Lord's letter, *Hollywood Reporter*, November 8, 1946.

Page 175. **"So great is the power:** "Catholic Prelates Give Films One More Chance," *Los Angeles Times*, June 22, 1934: 2.

Page 175. **"one dirty film:** JIB to Bishop John T. McNicholas, March 22, 1934 (ACHRC&UA).

Page 175. **"Herod is abroad!":** "Parents and the Moving Picture," *America*, December 20, 1919: 182.

Page 176. **"Censorship is just as stupid:** Arthur James, "The Enemy," *Billboard*, November 4, 1933: 19.

Page 176. **"In 1929:** F. Scott Fitzgerald, "My Lost City" [1932], in *The Crack Up* (New York: New Directions, 1945): 30, 31.

Page 177. **Breen had railed:** Eugene Weare [JIB], "The Protestant Ambition to Run the Country," *Extension Magazine* (July 1928): 43–44; JIB to Rev. Wilfrid Parsons, S.J., January 26, 1927 (PP).

Page 177. **"This philosophical theory:** JIB to Martin J. Quigley, undated 12-page document, circa 1956: 3, 6 (QP). See also Llewellyn Jones, "Cardinal Mundelein Attacks," *Christian Century*, July 18, 1934: 946.

Page 177. **"Here was a program:** Statement by JIB (QP).

Page 178. **"Official censorship has never:** "Censorship 'Czar' of Films Sees a Rough Road Ahead," *Detroit News*, July 13, 1934: 1, 2.

Page 178. **In 1930, after Quigley:** JIB to Martin J. Quigley, June 10, 1937 (QP).

Page 178. **Hays "was prone:** Rev. Gerard B. Donnelly, S.J., "The Outstanding Catholic Achievement," *America*, January 5, 1935: 299.

Page 178. **"Satisfying one church group:** "Hays Plagued by Religionists But Issues 'Don'ts' On Schedule," *Variety*, April 2, 1930: 2.

Page 178n. **"I don't think:** Quoted in Vizzard, *See No Evil* (1970): 56.

Page 179. **Breen warns a mogul:** J. P. McEvoy, "The Back of Me Hand to You," *Saturday Evening Post*, December 24, 1938: 46.

Page 179. **A Catholic journalist:** "A Providential Layman!" *Western Catholic*, November 21, 1930: 2.

Page 179. **Assuming the overdetermined nom de plume Walter White:** [JIB], "Talks About the Talkies," *Catholic Standard and Times*, January 2, 1931: 6.

Page 180. **The editorial did the trick:** "Protests Effect Revision of Film Version of 'Seed,'" *Catholic Standard and Times*, January 30, 1931: 1.

Page 180. **In 1934:** Report by Rev. FitzGeorge Dinneen, S.J., to the Episcopal Committee, March 1934 (ACHRC&UA).

Page 180. **While urging his fellow Catholics:** JIB to Bishop John T. McNicholas, October 27, 1933 (ACHRC&UA).

Page 181. **"The initials *I.H.S.*:** Howard Hall, "I.H.S. (In Hoc Signo—In His Sacerdotalism)," *Cinema Hall-Marks*, August 6, 1934: 17–18.

Page 181. **"Joe picked one:** Albert E. Van Schmus, interview with author, July 21, 2004.

Page 181. **Father Lord boasted:** Lord, *Played by Ear: The Autobiography of Daniel A. Lord, S.J.* (Chicago: Loyola University Press, 1955): 312.

Page 181. **Whenever priests visited:** See, for example, "Inside Stuff—Pictures," *Variety*, April 1, 1936: 6.

Page 181. **"Any request:** JIB to Bishop John T. Cantwell, January 18, 1935 (ALA).

Page 182. **"To attempt to assert myself:** JIB to Bishop John T. Cantwell, September 3, 1937 (ALA).

Page 182. **After 1934 he often:** JIB to Martin J. Quigley, June 22, 1935 (QP).

Page 183. **Thus bookended by printed and spoken:** "Legion Changes 'Amber' Rating," *Motion Picture Herald*, December 13, 1947: 26.

Page 183. **"While the head of the Code:** Terry Ramsaye, "Terry Ramsaye Says," *Motion Picture Herald*, August 9, 1952: 16.

Page 184. **On July 14, 1938:** "Breen a Papal Knight," *Hollywood Reporter*, July 15, 1938: 1.

Page 184. **However, Breen declined:** JIB to Miss Betty Lou Quinn, November 30, 1944 (MJA).

Page 184. **"The minority control:** Donald Kirkley, "Breen—Super Censor," *Protestant Digest* (June-July, 1940): 47.

Page 184. **Secular critics were no less vexed:** Elizabeth Yeaman, "The Catholic Movie Censorship," *New Republic*, October 5, 1938: 233–35; Otis Ferguson, "The Legion Rides Again," *New Republic*, December 22, 1941: 861.

Page 184. **Sometimes the tones of nineteenth-century:** "Censorship and Self Censorship," *America*, March 23, 1935: 560; "Harvard and the Filthy Films," *Catholic Standard and Times*, May 4, 1934: 6.

Page 184. **In a letter of complaint to Eric Johnston:** Don M. Chase to Eric Johnston, May 13, 1947 (PCA files).

Page 185. **"I am constantly:** JIB to Rev. Daniel A. Lord, S.J., December 5, 1937 (MJA).

Page 185. **"The truth is Mr. Breen:** "Correspondence," *New Republic*, November 9, 1938: 20–21.

Page 185. **On September 14, 1936:** George Bernard Shaw, "George Bernard Shaw on Film Censorship," *New York Times*, September 14, 1936: 26.

Page 186. **Will Hayes denied:** "Inside Stuff—Pictures," *Variety*, September 16, 1936: 6.

Page 186. **Interviewed by the *New York Times*:** "Shaw Stands Firm on Censor Charge," *New York Times*, September 27, 1936, sec. N: 14.

Page 187. **"A visitor from Mars:** Kirkley, "Breen—Super Censor": 52.

Page 187. **"It's just that the Catholic:** "Legion of Decency in New Steps to Force 'Cleanup' of H'wood Pix," *Variety*, April 3, 1946: 1, 26.

Page 187. **"Nearly everyone in Hollywood:** John C. Moffitt, "Critic on the Hearth," *Cinema Hall-Marks*, August 6, 1934: 19.

Page 187. **Throughout the 1920s:** Eugene Weare [JIB], "Washington, A Nest of Schemers," *America*, December 30, 1922: 248.

Page 187. **"The great need of the Church:** Eugene Weare [JIB], "Enter: The 'Hick Town' Parish," *America*, October 26, 1929: 61.

Page 188. **In conversations and correspondence:** JIB to Bishop John T. McNicholas, March 22, 1934 (ACHRC&UA).

Page 188. **Breen urged Bishop Cantwell:** JIB to Rev. Joseph T. McGucken, May 28, 1931 (ALA).

Page 188. **Paramount's *Cradle Song* (1933):** JIB to Rev. Daniel A. Lord, S.J., undated (circa 1933) (MJA).

Page 189n4. **Monsignor C. J. Quille:** Shan Van Vocht [JIB], "Father Quille," *Chicagoan*, February 23, 1929: 27–29.

Page 191. **Yet Breen couldn't resist:** JIB to Jason Joy, January 29, 1943 (*The Song of Bernadette* file, PCA).

Page 191. **"We strongly urge:** JIB to Luigi Luraschi, August 12, 1943 (*Going My Way* file, PCA).

Page 191. **"I'm sure you have:** Father Hugh Calkins to JIB, June 17, 1942; JIB to Father Hugh Calkins, June 23, 1942 (both in *Joan of Paris* file, PCA).

Page 192. **Breen assured the bishop:** JIB to Bishop Joseph T. McGucken, August 21, 1943 (ALA).

Page 192. **Just to be sure:** JIB to Luigi Luraschi, August 12, 1943 (*Going My Way* file, PCA).

Page 192. **The extraordinary ecumenical success:** "Bing, Bergman, 'Bells' 46 Boffo," *Variety*, January 8, 1947: 1, 8.

Page 194. **"A must for Catholics:** Archie Winsten, *New York Post*, quoted in *Motion Picture Herald*, May 13, 1944: 21.

Page 196. **Leaving a preview screening:** William R. Weaver, "*The Bells of St. Mary's*," *Motion Picture Herald*, November 24, 1945: 36.

Page 197. **Wary of being typecast:** "Crosby Typed?" *Variety*, April 3, 1946: 26.

Page 197. **"For years now:** Thomas Bledsoe, "Hierarchy over Hollywood," *Protestant Digest* (June-July 1946): 8–18.

Page 197. **Heeding the Protestant outcry:** W.R. Wilkerson, "Tradeviews," *Hollywood Reporter*, October 16, 1946: 1, 15.

Page 197. **"The Roman Catholic Church:** "H'wood Sluffing Protestant Themes, Sez 'Martin Luther' Exec; Time Is Ripe," *Variety*, September 22, 1954: 5, 18.

Page 198. **"Anybody else in the job:** Rev. G.B. Donnelly, S.J., to Rev. Wilfrid Parsons, S. J., undated letter (1936) (PP).

10. "OUR SEMITIC BRETHREN"

Page 199. **"These Jews seem:** JIB to Rev. Wilfrid Parsons, S.J., October 10, 1932 (PP).

Page 199. **"The fact is these damn Jews:** JIB to Martin J. Quigley, May 1, 1932 (QP).

Page 201. **"The names of William Fox:** Quoted in John C. Moffitt, "Critic on the Hearth," *Cinema Hall-Marks*, September 17, 1934: 44.

Page 201. **"Pants pressers:** Karl K. Kitchen, "What's the Matter with the Movies?" *Columbia* (April 1922): 6.

Page 201. **In 1930 Major Frank Pease:** "Self-styled 'Hollywood Technical Directors Institute' Also Wants Eisenstein Ousted from Country," *Exhibitors Herald-World*, June 28, 1930: 11.

Page 201. **"Certain bigots:** "H.M. Warner Condemns All Isms," *Variety*, September 21, 1938: 2.

Page 202. **Father Daniel Lord:** Rev. Daniel A. Lord, S.J., *The Motion Pictures Betray America* (St. Louis: The Queen's Work, Inc., 1934): 11, 12–13, 36–37, 44.

Page 202. **Even the Legion of Decency:** "Join Attack on Movies," *New York Times*, July 7, 1934: 15; Mary Harden Looram, "The Movies Slide Down Toward the Condemned Class," *America*, October 18, 1941: 39. See also Arthur D. Maguire, "An Epistle to the Hierarchy on the Movies," October 26, 1935 (ACHRC&UA).

Page 202. **The "school of vice":** "A School of Vice for All Nations," *Catholic Standard and Times*, March 23, 1934: 23.

Page 202. **"Jewish executives:** Bishop John J. Cantwell, *The Motion Picture Industry* (Washington, D.C.: National Council of Catholic Men and the National Council of Catholic Women, 1934): 11.

Page 202. **Accused by a Jewish correspondent:** Bishop John J. Cantwell to Dr. Carlton J. Hayes, May 19, 1934 (ACHRC&UA).

Page 203. **Culled from private letters:** JIB to Bishop John T. McNicholas, May 22, 1934; JIB to Rev. FitzGeorge Dinneen, S.J., March 17, 1934 (both in ACHRC&UA).

Page 203. **In a two-page proposal:** JIB to Rev. Gerard Donnelly, S.J., March 20, 1934 (MJA).

Page 203. **Today, film historians routinely label:** Gregory D. Black, *Hollywood Censored: Morality Codes, Catholics, and the Movies* (Cambridge: Cambridge University Press, 1994): 172; Michael E. Birdwell, *Celluloid Soldiers: Warner Bros.'s Campaign Against Nazism* (New York: New York University Press, 1991): 21; Anne Morey, *Hollywood Outsiders: The Adaptation of the Film Industry, 1913–1934* (Minneapolis: University of Minnesota Press, 2003): 135.

Page 204. **According to Pete Harrison:** *Harrison's Reports*, October 7, 1933: 160; "The Most Serious Attack on Filthy Pictures," *Harrison's Reports*, March 10, 1934: 40.

Page 205. **"The Jews, of course:** Eugene Weare [JIB], "Proselytizing Europe," *America*, September 30, 1922: 559.

Page 205. **He rebukes American Catholics:** Eugene Weare [JIB], "The Way to Help Austria," *America*, June 4, 1922: 221–22.

Page 205. **"[Catholic] places:** "European Conditions Described to Delegates," *National Catholic Welfare Council Bulletin* (December 1922): 15.

Page 205. **For the Immigration Act of 1924:** Eugene Weare [JIB], "Our Immigration Problem," *America*, April 21, 1923: 7–8; Eugene Weare [JIB], "Our Immigration Problem," *America*, April 28, 1923: 31–33.

Page 206. **"These babies out here:** JIB to Maurice McKenzie, April 12, 1935 (QP).

Page 206. **On the evening of April 26, 1936:** "Films' Anti-Nazi Dinner," *Variety*, April 22, 1936: 2; "Dinner Reservation Rush," *Hollywood Reporter*, April 25, 1936: 2; "Rambling Reporter," *Hollywood Reporter*, April 27, 1936: 2; "Rambling Reporter," *Hollywood Reporter*, April 28, 1936: 2.

Page 207. **Nonetheless, he continued to lend:** "Million Dollar Floor Show Is Gay Spectacle," *Hollywood Now*, August 7, 1937: 1, 6.

Page 207. **"Catholic means universal:** "Pope Warns Italy Not to Hit Church in Race Campaign," *New York Times*, July 30, 1938: 1.

Page 207. **"I note what you tell:** JIB to Rev. Daniel A. Lord, S.J., September 18, 1938; JIB to Rev. Daniel A. Lord, S.J., October 15, 1938 (both in MJA).

Page 208. **"I have myself received:** "Breen 'Ready to Go the Limit,'" *Box Office*, October 15, 1938: 11.

Page 210. **"The Nazi outrages:** "'Quarantine Hitler' Meeting Friday at Philharmonic," *Hollywood Now*, November 17, 1938: 1, 2; "Dr. Smith, Frank Capra Denounce Nazi Pogroms," *Hollywood Now*, November 25, 1938: 2.

Page 210. **According to its statement of purpose:** *Statement and Program of Purpose*, Committee of Catholics to Fight Anti-Semitism (1939) (QP); "Catholic Leaders Band to Fight Race Bigotry," *Hollywood Now*, June 16, 1939: 3.

Page 211. **The committee also issued:** JIB to Martin J. Quigley, June 21, 1939; Martin Quigley to JIB, June 9, 1939 (both in QP).

Page 211. **"It is my judgment:** "Catholics Join in Drive Against Anti-Semitism," *Hollywood Now*, July 7, 1939: 1.

Page 211. **"Outstanding leaders:** "Coughlin Hits Catholics for Bigotry Fight," *Hollywood Now*, September 1, 1939: 2.

Page 211. **Breen also contributed:** Edwin Schallert, "Pageant of the Film World," *Los Angeles Times*, April 11, 1939: 13.

Page 212. **"It is unrealistic:** Martin S. Quigley, interview with author, June 2, 2004.

Page 212. **Former PCA staffer Albert E. Van Schmus:** Albert E. Van Schmus, interview with author, July 21, 2004.

Page 212. **In 1934, writing to Father Lord:** JIB to Rev. Daniel A. Lord, S.J., May 23, 1934 (MJA).

Page 214. **In 1936, commenting on the wisdom:** *The Mad Dog of Europe* file (PCA).

Page 214. **By the late 1930s:** "Hays Preps Political Pix Ban," *Hollywood Reporter*, July 26, 1938: 1, 3.

Page 215. **"I feel sure that:** Luigi Luraschi to JIB, December 10, 1938; JIB to Jack Warner, December 30, 1938 (both in *Confessions of a Nazi Spy* file, PCA).

Page 216. **"Your picture is so fine:** JIB to Al Reeves, September 6, 1940 (*The Great Dictator* file, PCA).

Page 218. **No less evenhandedly:** JIB to Frank R. Nastroly, April 10, 1946 (*Abie's Irish Rose* file, PCA).

Page 219. **Viewing *Abie's Irish Rose:*** William R. Weaver, "Abie's Irish Rose," *Motion Picture Herald*, November 30, 1946: 3334; "'Worst Caricature of Jews, Catholics' Charged to UA's 'Abie's Irish Rose,'" *Variety*, November 6, 1946: 1; Pete Harrison. "A Thoughtless Degradation of Racial Minorities," *Harrison's Reports*, November 30, 1946: 189.

Page 219. **"In the purely escapist:** Red Kahn, "On the March," *Motion Picture Herald*, June 28, 1947: 16.

Page 220. **A minicycle of two:** Ray Lanning, "*Crossfire*," *Motion Picture Herald*, June 28: 1947: 3701.

Page 220. **Having rejected:** JIB to Harold Melniker, February 27, 1947 (*Crossfire* file, PCA).

Page 221. **Though reconciled to the racial:** JIB to Jason Joy, March 21, 1947; Darryl F. Zanuck to JIB, March 27, 1947 (both in *Gentleman's Agreement* file, PCA).

Page 222. **"We assume, of course:** JIB to Reginald Allen, May 13, 1947 (*Oliver Twist* file, PCA).

Page 223. **"a grotesque Jewish caricature:** Francis Harmon to Eric Johnston, September 7, 1948 (*Oliver Twist* file, PCA).

Page 223. **"In a world still:** "Inside Stuff—Pictures," *Variety*, April 27, 1949: 18.

Page 223. **On November 22, 1950:** JIB to Jock Lawrence, November 22, 1950 (*Oliver Twist* file, PCA).

Page 223. **Eagle Lion Classics appealed:** "Code Seal Denied for Rank's 'Oliver Twist,'" *Motion Picture Herald*, December 2, 1950: 15; "Appeal for 'Twist' Seal," *Motion Picture Herald*, December 9, 1950: 35.

Page 224. **He was not overruled:** "'Twist' Back to Breen for New Study," *Motion Picture Herald*, January 13, 1951: 30; "MPAA Board Delays Decision on 'Twist,'" *Motion Picture Herald*, February 17, 1951: 35; "MPAA Board Approves Seal for 'Oliver

Twist,'" *Motion Picture Herald*, February 24, 1951: 28. Willard Johnson to Eric Johnston, January 5, 1951 (*Oliver Twist* file, PCA).

Page 224. **Breen's compromise:** "Breen Softens on 'Twist' Ban; PCA Seal Likely," *Variety*, January 24, 1951: 3, 14.

Page 224. **Afterward, looking back:** JIB to Jock Lawrence, December 1, 1950 (*Oliver Twist* file, PCA).

Page 224. **Guinness's Fagin:** "Despite Its MPAA Seal 'Twist' Faces Exhib Chill as Pic Begins Release," *Variety*, February 28, 1951: 5, 15; Red Kahn, "'Oliver Twist,'" *Motion Picture Herald*, May 5, 1951: 825.

Page 224. **"No Jew or group:** "'Oliver Twist' to Get Another O.O. for PCA Seal," *Variety*, January 10, 1951: 14.

11. SOCIAL PROBLEMS, EXISTENTIAL DILEMMAS, AND OUTSIZE ANATOMIES

Page 226. **On September 19, 1945:** "As Forecast, Eric Johnston Now New Film Czar; Hays Stays as Consultant; Harmon Head Man in N.Y., Breen Coast," *Variety*, September 26, 1945: 3, 22.

Page 226. **"Call us progressives:** Eric Johnston, *American Unlimited* (New York: Doubleday, Doran, 1944): 232.

Page 226. **Nodding in approval, *Variety*:** "Eric A. Johnston," *Variety*, September 26, 1945: 3.

Page 227. **"Industry interests elsewhere:** William R. Weaver, "Johnston Studio Trip 'No Lecture,'" *Motion Picture Herald*, March 29, 1947: 20.

Page 227. **"The Production Code:** "Easing of Production Code Will Not Be Permitted by MPAA," *Box Office*, March 16, 1946: 8.

Page 227. **"An America divided:** "Eric A. Johnston Takes the Helm," *Harrison's Reports*, September 29, 1945: 153, 156.

Page 228. **Pressured by panicky moguls:** "Film Industry's Policy Defined," *Variety*, November 26, 1947: 3.

Page 228. **Neither the Production Code Administration:** Edith Gwynn, "Rambling Reporter," *Hollywood Reporter*, December 22, 1947: 2.

Page 228. **In 1946, 90,000,000:** Jack Alicoate, ed., *The 1952 Film Daily Year Book of Motion Pictures (* New York: Wid's Films and Film Folk, Inc, 1952): 127. Accountants being, reputably, the most creative people in Hollywood, audience attendance figures for the classical Hollywood era are ballpark estimates. *The Film Daily* recalibrated its estimates almost with each successive year-end volume, and pumped the numbers on the high side. The figures given here are a rough calculation and fair sampling of Hollywood's own estimate of its depleting audience.

Page 229. **Significantly, a condition:** "Johnston Reshuffles MPPDA," *Variety*, December 5, 1945: 24.

Page 229. **From his vice presidential perch:** "MPAA's Pitch on Hollywood," *Variety*, August 3, 1949: 4, 22; "Hollywood Making 'Best Films in Years,' Says Breen," *Motion Picture Herald*, August 6, 1949: 32.

Page 231. **Though the Code "has nothing:** William R. Weaver, "Studios Turn to Psychiatry As New Picture Theme," *Motion Picture Herald*, June 3, 1944: 28.

Page 231. **On March 20, 1946:** "Code Refresher," *Motion Picture Herald*, March 23, 1946: 8; "Breen Warns Prod to Keep Code Spirit," *Daily Variety*, April 2, 1946: 1, 7.

Page 233. **"The idea that pictures:** "Anti-Bigotry Pix Snare $5,000,000 Domestic Profits," *Variety*, July 7, 1948: 1, 40.

Page 234. **The Haysians, Quigley:** Martin J. Quigley to JIB, April 13, 1940 (QP).

Page 234. **Quigley was "absolutely infuriated:** Shurlock, in James M. Wall, "Interviews with Geoffrey Shurlock" (1970): 74.

Page 235. **In 1933, when MGM:** "Breen Bars Twain's 'Pudd'nhead Wilson,'" *Hollywood Reporter*, August 20, 1934: 1.

Page 235. **Yet because race was deemed:** Will H. Hays to JIB, February 14, 1936; JIB to Jack Warner, August 2, 1935 (both in *Green Pastures* file, PCA).

Page 235. **"With respect to the portrayal:** JIB to Allen Wilson, May 12, 1950 (John Ford Manuscripts, IU).

Page 236. **In director Dudley Murphy's:** "Negro Societies Object," *Billboard*, October 21, 1933: 21.

Page 236. **Appropriately, the Civil War super-production:** Francis Harmon to Mart Everlyn Mickens, February 16, 1939; JIB to David O. Selznick, October 14, 1937; Islin Auster to JIB, February 9, 1939 (all in *Gone With the Wind* file, PCA).

Page 237. **By 1949:** Red Kahn, "On the March," *Motion Picture Herald*, April 23, 1949: 22.

Page 238. **"There was a lot of discussion:** Lillian Scott, "A Hollywood Independent Shows Big Studios How It's Done," *Chicago Defender*, May 14, 1949: 16.

Page 239. **Breen cautioned Kramer:** JIB to George Class, February 16, 1949 (*Home of the Brave* file, PCA).

Page 240. **"It is in fact startling:** Charles J. Lazarus, "*Home of the Brave*," *Motion Picture Herald*, April 30, 1949: 4590.

Page 240. **"One thing is certain:** Walter White, "Do Race Pictures Denote New Hollywood Attitude?" *Chicago Defender*, June 25, 1949: 7.

Page 241. **"Joe Breen says:** Herb Stein, "Rambling Reporter," *Hollywood Reporter*, August 2, 1949: 2.

Page 241. **When critics carped:** Wayne G. Dowdy, "Censoring Popular Culture: Political and Social Control in Segregated Memphis," *The West Tennessee Historical Society Papers* (2001): 98–117.

Page 242. **Binford became more notorious:** Lester Velie, "You Can't See That Movie: Censorship in Action," *Collier's*, May 6, 1950: 11–12, 66.

Page 242. **"Binfordized":** "'Home of the Brave' Passed by Censor in Memphis," *Motion Picture Herald*, August 6, 1949: 32; "*Home of the Brave* in Dallas, Houston Without Tension," *Motion Picture Herald*, July 16, 1949: 21.

Page 242. **Of all the Binfordizations:** "Screen Goes to Mat with Binford, Memphis Censor," *Motion Picture Herald*, September 27, 1947: 26.

Page 243. **"We are against political censorship:** Ezra Goodman, "The Censorship Bugaboo: Breen Suggests a Way Out," *New York Herald Tribune*, July 10, 1949, sec. 5: 3.

Page 243. **(Despite the best efforts:** "High Court Will Not Act on 'Curley,'" *Motion Picture Herald*, May 13, 1950: 40.

Page 243. **Smith was smart enough:** "Decision Is Reserved on 'Boundaries,'" *Motion Picture Herald,* June 10, 1950: 32.

Page 243. **"I think the picture:** "Censor Strikes Again at Screen's Freedom," *Motion Picture Herald,* November 5, 1949: 14.

Page 243. **"It's a peculiar kind of picture:** "Memphis Board of Censors Approves 'Pinky' Showings," *Motion Picture Herald,* December 10, 1949: 43.

Page 243. **A Hollywood film bearing:** "Bids Press Join Pix in Censorship Fight," *Film Daily,* February 9, 1951: 6.

Page 246. **Film noir was encrusted:** "Violence in Films Hits Femme B.O., Wald-Krasna Find," *Variety,* January 10, 1951: 1, 56. For exhibitor response, see "What This Picture Did for Me," *Motion Picture Herald,* November 20, 1948: 42; "What This Picture Did for Me," *Motion Picture Herald,* March 26, 1949: 46.

Page 248. **"Sadism ... has been increasing:** Terry Ramsaye, "Shudders & Horrors," *Motion Picture Herald,* August 20, 1949: 7.

Page 248. **Fed on "a steady diet:** Fred Hift, "Code Works, Says Schary," *Motion Picture Herald,* September 24, 1949: 18.

Page 248. **William H. Mooring:** "Legion of Decency in New Steps to Force 'Cleanup' of H'wood Pix," *Variety,* April 3, 1946: 1, 26.

Page 248. **"More will have to be done:** JIB to Harold Melniker, July 7, 1947, July 18, 1947, and August 24, 1947 (*The Set-Up* file, PCA).

Page 248. **Breen had passed:** "*Scarlet Street,*" *Harrison's Reports,* January 19, 1946: 10.

Page 249. **She banned *Scarlet Street:*** "Atlanta Bans Scarlet," *Variety,* February 6, 1946: 4.

Page 249. **"We shall spare no effort:** " 'Scarlet' May Free Southeast Screen," *Hollywood Reporter,* February 15, 1946: 17.

Page 249. **The producer and the censor:** JIB to Walter Wanger, March 26, 1946 (*Scarlet Street* file, PCA).

Page 249. **In an affidavit for Wanger's:** JIB affidavit, March 25, 1946 (*Scarlet Street* file, PCA).

Page 250. **(Atlantans won the right:** " 'Street' in Atlanta Opening Tomorrow," *Hollywood Reporter,* April 30, 1946: 1, 4.

Page 250. **"There has been growing criticism:** "Legion Changes 'Amber' Rating," *Motion Picture Herald,* December 13, 1947: 26.

Page 250. **"For all practical purposes:** "Breen, in Reply to Allied, Cites Legion Figures," *Motion Picture Herald,* November 22, 1947: 24.

Page 251. **"If you are unaware of this:** "Myers Scores Breen Defense of Studio Code," *Motion Picture Herald,* December 6, 1947: 36.

Page 251. **On June 28, 1949:** "Joe Breen Asks Flacks to Help Curb Brutality," *Variety,* June 29, 1949: 3.

Page 251. **Attending for MGM, Robert Vogel reported:** Robert Vogel to Dore Schary, June 29, 1949 (PCA).

Page 251. **Reflecting on the atmospheric shifts:** Breen quoted in Ezra Goodman, "The Censorship Bugaboo: Breen Suggests a Way Out," *New York Herald Tribune,* July 10, 1949, sec. 5: 3. See also Thomas J. Fitzmorris, "Films," *America,* November 23, 1946: 222; and Thomas J. Fitzmorris, "Films," *America,* January 4, 1947: 391. For a full discussion of the wartime roots of the genre, see Sheri Chinen Biesen, *Black-*

out: World War II and the Origins of Film Noir (Baltimore: Johns Hopkins University Press, 2005).

Page 252. **Hughes reveled in playing:** "Hughes May Appeal Code Decision on Coast to Hays' Full Board East," *Variety*, January 5, 1932: 6.

Page 253. **"We direct your particular attention:** JIB to Col. Jason S. Joy, May 3, 1947 (Darryl F. Zanuck Manuscripts, IU).

Page 254. **"In my more than ten years:** JIB to Will H. Hays, March 28, 1941 (*The Outlaw* file, PCA).

Page 254. **the MPAA Board blinked:** "Haysites in N.Y. OK 'The Outlaw' Finally," *Variety*, May 21, 1941: 4; "PCA Seal for 'Outlaw' Following Changes," *Film Daily*, May 16, 1941: 10.

Page 256. **Caught in a moment of unprofessional:** "Russell Birdwell," *Variety*, December 28, 1977: 62. See also Dwight Whitney, "'The Outlaw': A Lavish Western," *San Francisco Chronicle*, February 8, 1943: 8; William R. Weaver, "*The Outlaw*," *Motion Picture Herald*, February 13, 1943: 1157.

Page 256. **The Hughes-Birdwell ballyhoo:** "Hughes Press Junket for 'Outlaw' Comes Off OK Despite Wartime Travel," *Variety*, February 10, 1943: 16.

Page 256. **"Chiefly atrocious:** Red Kahn, "On the March," *Motion Picture Herald*, February 20, 1943: 14; William R. Weaver, "Mr. Hughes Unveils His Maverick—and How," *Motion Picture Herald*, February 13, 1943: 23.

Page 258. **"The whole campaign of this picture:** Darryl F. Zanuck to JIB, April 2, 1946 (*The Outlaw* file, PCA).

Page 259. **When Hughes refused:** "MPAA Calls 'Outlaw' Hearing on Advertising Code Changes," and "Hughes in Brief Comment on Johnston's Charges," *Box Office*, April 13, 1946: 8.

Page 259. **With a deep stubborn streak:** "MPAA vs Hughes Goes to Court; 'Outlaw' to Jail," *Motion Picture Herald*, April 27, 1946: 15.

Page 260. **He then resigned:** "Hughes Suit Against MPAA Is Ended," *Motion Picture Herald*, June 16, 1951: 16.

Page 260. **"Have you read the ads:** W. R. Wilkerson, "Tradeviews," *Hollywood Reporter*, April 30, 1946: 1, 2. See also "The Case of Howard Hughes Versus Eric Johnston," *Harrison's Reports*, May 11, 1946: 74.

Page 260. **Replied the MPAA:** "'Outlaw' Star's 'Outsize Anatomy' Main Basis of MPA's Spotlight on Hughes Picture; Meantime Some Calculations," *Variety*, May 1, 1946: 21.

Page 260. **For the multimillionaire:** "Rambling Reporter," *Hollywood Reporter*, May 12, 1941: 2.

Page 260. **When tabloid headlines:** "'Outlaw' Sours Censorship Drive," *Variety*, May 22, 1946: 5.

Page 260. **"It's not good showmanship:** "MPA Surprised at Sympathy with It," *Variety*, April 24, 1946: 5; Abel Green, "Hughes Is Wrong," *Variety*, April 17, 1946: 6.

Page 261. **"The [MPAA] must protect:** W. R. Wilkerson, "Tradeviews," *Hollywood Reporter*, April 25, 1946: 1, 2.

Page 261. **"It takes something like *The Outlaw:*** Bryson, quoted in "Ban Outlaw in Boston; Causes N.J. Censor Bid," *Motion Picture Herald*, October 5, 1946: 27.

Page 261. **Fortunately for Hollywood:** "Move to Decency No 'Conspiracy,'" *Motion Picture Herald,* May 4, 1946: 22.

Page 261. **On June 14, 1946:** "U.S. Court Rebukes Hughes, Rejects 'Outlaw' Plea," *Motion Picture Herald,* June 22, 1946: 15.

Page 262. **"It is obvious:** Terry Ramsaye, "'Outlaw Seal,'" *Motion Picture Herald,* June 22, 1946: 7; Terry Ramsaye, "'Outlaw' Waits," *Motion Picture Herald,* June 29, 1946: 7.

Page 262. **On September 13, 1946:** Hughes, quoted in "MPA Revokes PCA Certificate for 'The Outlaw,'" *Motion Picture Herald,* September 14, 1946: 26.

Page 263. **Backed by Hughes's checkbook:** "Outlaw Getting Plenty Coin on Repeat Dates," *Variety,* July 23, 1947: 6, 25; "'The Outlaw' Joins 'GWTW,' 'Jolson' As Champ Reissue," *Variety,* June 4, 1947: 4; "Jane Russell, The Bard, and GBS Also Among Unusual Grossers," *Variety,* January 8, 1947: 3.

Page 263. **In October 1949:** "Production Code Reinstates Code Seal for 'The Outlaw,'" *Motion Picture Herald,* October 29, 1949: 36; Red Kahn, "*The Outlaw,*" *Motion Picture Herald,* December 3, 1949: 138.

Page 263. **"If we stay within the boundaries:** "Johnston Asks East-West Unity on Code and Labor," *Motion Picture Herald,* June 29, 1946: 23.

12. INVASION OF THE ART FILMS

Page 264. **"I do hope:** "Breen Accepts Rank's London Invite; Johnston on Films' Foreign Problems," *Variety,* May 15, 1946: 5, 22.

Page 264. **Basking in the glow:** "Breen and the Lady," *Motion Picture Herald,* August 10, 1946: 9; JIB to Eric Johnston, March 22, 1946, and "Results of JIB viewing of *The Wicked Lady*" (*The Wicked Lady* file, PCA).

Page 265. **Pointing to Code-stretching:** "Breen Talks and Listens," *Motion Picture Herald,* July 20, 1946: 26.

Page 265. **Rank himself:** "Joe Breen Will Rule on Rank's 'Bedelia' Finale," *Variety,* June 5, 1946: 11.

Page 265. **He bantered good-naturedly:** Gwen Morgan, "British Critics Pounce on U.S. Movie Censor," *Chicago Daily Tribune,* July 16, 1946: 14. For the British reaction, see "'Don't Call Us a Censorship,' Says Mr. Breen," *Picture Post,* August 3, 1946: 7-8.

Page 265. **Despite the coyness:** "Breen Reports British Visit on Code a Success," *Motion Picture Herald,* August 17, 1946: 19.

Page 266. **Back in the States:** "'Notorious Gent' Belies Breen Has Any Anti-British Bluenose Ideas," *Variety,* November 6, 1946: 3, 30; JIB to William Burnside, January 26, 1945 (*The Rake's Progress* file, PCA).

Page 267. **Summing up his trip:** Thomas M. Pryor, "Breen's Mission to London," *New York Times,* August 18, 1946, sec. 2: 3. See also Peter Burnuop, "Breen Mission Is Termed Triumph," *Motion Picture Herald,* August 3, 1946: 78.

Page 267. **"Since last November:** JIB to Eric Johnston, October 3, 1947 (QP).

Page 267. **Breen requested a three-month:** "Jackson Reported in Line for Breen Spot," *Hollywood Reporter,* December 15, 1947: 1.

Page 267. **On paper, Judge Jackson:** "N.Y. Judge Named Aide to Breen," *Variety*, March 26, 1947: 4; Edwin Schallert, "Breen May Retire from Film Code Post; Jackson Hinted as Possible Successor," *Los Angeles Times*, June 13, 1948: C1.

Page 268. **Breen offered formal support:** JIB to Eric Johnston, October 3, 1947 (QP).

Page 268. **The point was *Letter:*** Stephen S. Jackson, Memo, February 18, 1948; Stephen S. Jackson to William Gordon, March 13, 1948 (both in *Letter from an Unknown Woman* file, PCA). See also Jack Vizzard, *See No Evil* (1970): 142–44.

Page 268. **Cornered by a *Variety* reporter:** "Breen Denies He's Quitting," *Variety*, June 16, 1948: 2.

Page 269. **By 1949:** "Art Houses Grow A-Pace," *Motion Picture Herald*, February 16, 1952: 24; "More Foreign Product Due in U.S. This Year," *Motion Picture Herald*, January 1, 1949: 21.

Page 270. **The art house was "built on:** Terry Ramsaye, "Terry Ramsaye Says," *Motion Picture Herald*, January 10, 1953: 18; Al Sherman, "The Art Theatre," *Motion Picture Herald*, January 31, 1953: 8.

Page 270. **An estimated 25,000,000:** "Sureseaters Now Surefire B.O.," *Variety*, March 26, 1947: 5, 22; "Certain Producers Urge Code Be Changed to Sidestep Constant Criticism U.S. Pix Are 'Stereotyped,'" *Variety*, May 28, 1947: 2.

Page 271. **"Times are certainly changing:** James M. Jerauld, "Men and Events," *Box Office*, April 5, 1947: 22.

Page 271. **"Certainly the *Hamlet* award:** W. R. Wilkerson, "Tradeviews," *Hollywood Reporter*, May 3, 1949: 1.

Page 272. **"The Code [should] be adopted:** JIB to Rev. Daniel A. Lord, S.J., October 26, 1937 (MJA).

Page 272. **In 1935 the MPPDA:** "Expect Hays Code Branch for East," *Film Daily*, May 25, 1935: 1; "Inside Stuff—Pictures," *Variety*, April 29, 1936: 6.

Page 272. **A two-man shop:** "N.Y. Counterpart to Breen-Hays Office to Service British Films," *Variety*, June 19, 1935: 4; "Inside Stuff-Pictures," *Variety*, July 10, 1935: 19; "Hays Purity Stamps on 2,371 Pictures on Coast; 500 in N.Y.," *Variety*, September 2, 1936: 3.

Page 272. **From a Breen Office perspective:** "Call for Linguist," *Variety*, April 29, 1936: 29.

Page 273. **"Usual close-ups:** "Extase," *Variety*, April 11, 1933: 20.

Page 273. **British producer John Maxwell:** "As Maxwell Sees Production Code," *Motion Picture Herald*, August 31, 1935: 43.

Page 273. **Not until 1950, under the title *My Life:*** "Herb Stein, "Rambling Reporter," *Hollywood Reporter*, November 17, 1948: 2; "New 'My Life' Is Still Same Old 'Ecstasy,'" *Motion Picture Herald*, February 4, 1950: 35.

Page 273. **"The scene of the husband:** JIB to Jason Joy, February 26, 1943 (*The Song of Bernadette* file, PCA).

Page 273. **As late as 1947:** "Inside Stuff—Motion Pictures," *Variety*, May 7, 1947: 26.

Page 274. **Nonetheless, the postwar Brits:** "Breen's Nix on a Number of British Films Straining Anglo-U.S. Entente," *Variety*, May 7, 1947: 9, 29.

Page 274. **On March 30, 1942:** Eric Johnston to Paul Graetz, April 17, 1950 (*The Devil and the Flesh* file, PCA).

Page 275. **"If foreign producers:** "Say Italians Ought to Follow Own 'When in Rome Do as Romans Do' and Accept Hollywood's Code," *Variety*, October 13, 1954: 7.

Page 275. **"In the case of foreign pictures:** JIB to Eric Johnston, March 10, 1949 (QP).

Page 275. **"As an independent distributor:** "Reverberations from the Articles on the Hays Seal," *Harrison's Reports*, May 31, 1941: 85.

Page 276. **"We must blush:** Kenneth Macgowen, "And So Into the Sunset . . . ," *New Republic*, January 31, 1949: 23.

Page 276. **Reviewing *Open City*:** "*Open City*," *Variety*, February 27, 1946: 8.

Page 277. **Trying to account for the lucrative:** "Unusual Grosses of British and Italo Pix, Both War Themes, Surprise B'way," *Variety*, March 6, 1946: 29.

Page 278. **As any experienced Breen watcher:** "Breen Fights Code Attack," *Motion Picture Herald*, March 11, 1950: 41.

Page 279. **Bosley Crowther:** Bosley Crowther, "Unkindest Cut," *New York Times*, April 2, 1950, sec. 2: 1.

Page 280. **Fed up with all the squawking:** Terry Ramsaye, "Manners and Morals," *Motion Picture Herald*, April 8, 1950: 7; Terry Ramsaye, "Spot on the Wall," *Motion Picture Herald*, March 11, 1950: 7.

Page 280. **In the end:** This précis is taken from JIB to Francis S. Harmon, February 6, 1950; Vittorio De Sica to Joseph Burstyn, February 27, 1950; Joseph Burstyn to JIB, February 27, 1950; JIB to Joseph Burstyn, March 8, 1950; Fred Niblo to JIB, March 21, 1950; JIB to MPAA Board, March 21, 1950 (all in *The Bicycle Thief* file, PCA). See also "'Bicycle Thief' Refused Seal, Cuts Not Made," *Motion Picture Herald*, March 4, 1950: 14; "MPAA Board Sustains Rejection of 'Bicycle,'" *Motion Picture Herald*, April 1, 1950: 13.

Page 281. **"As a result [of having:** Arthur Mayer, "A Movie Exhibitor Looks at Censorship," *Reporter*, March 2, 1954: 39.

Page 282. **"All regulatory codes:** "See Tighter Censorship of Pix," *Variety*, February 28, 1951: 54.

Page 282. **In calmer moments, Breen appreciated:** Ezra Goodman, "The Censorship Bugaboo: Breen Suggests a Way Out," *New York Herald Tribune*, July 10, 1949, sec. 5: 3.

Page 282. **"Young Tom, the baby—:** JIB to Rev. Daniel A. Lord, S.J., August 9, 1950 (MJA).

Page 282n. **Despite "deceit sympathetically treated: "**Legion of Decency Reviews Twelve New Productions," *Motion Picture Herald*, March 23, 1946: 64.

Page 283. **"She possesses that:** Richard Watts, Jr., "Ingrid Bergman Is Starred in Maxwell Anderson Play," *New York Post*, November 19, 1946.

Page 284. **Breen was thrilled:** JIB to Rev. Daniel A. Lord, S.J., July 22, 1947 (MJA).

Page 284. **Also, in what was both a coup:** "'Joan' Preem on B'Way Will Be Telecast Wed," *Hollywood Reporter*, November 8, 1948: 1.

Page 284. ***Joan of Arc*, boasted Wanger:** "Inside Stuff—Pictures," *Variety*, October 20, 1948: 15.

Page 284. **Unfortunately, when the reviews:** Irving Hoffman, "'Joan of Arc' Runs Gamut of Reviews in New York," *Hollywood Reporter*," November 16, 1948: 5, 9; "Inside Stuff—Pictures," *Variety*, November 24, 1948: 14.

Page 285. **"Walter Wanger has:** JIB to George Sokolsky, October 5, 1948 (HI).

Page 285. **"As I cannot contain:** George Sokolsky, "These Days," *Washington Times Herald*, October 26, 1948: 13.

Page 285. **"Simply magnificent!":** JIB to George Sokolsky, November 1, 1948 (HI).

Page 287. **"The star and the director:** "Stromboli Idyll," *Life,* May 2, 1949: 48; "Letters to the Editor," *Life,* May 23, 1949: 16.

Page 287. **Walter Wanger was more concerned:** "Bergman-Rossellini Idyll Seen as B.O. Boost for 'Stromboli,' NG for 'Joan,'" *Variety,* August 10, 1949: 63.

Page 287. **"One thing:** Herb Stein, "Rambling Reporter," *Hollywood Reporter,* May 3, 1949: 2.

Page 287. **Certainly not Breen:** JIB to Rev. Paul Dancouer, S.J., April 22, 1949 (HI).

Page 288. **On April 22, 1949:** JIB to Ingrid Bergman, April 22, 1949 (HI).

Page 288. **In a brief note of reply:** Ingrid Bergman to JIB, May 8, 1949 (HI).

Page 288. **By the time Bergman's letter:** Robert Conway, "Ingrid Bergman Confirms Romance with Film Director Rossellini," *Los Angeles Times,* May 3, 1949: 1. For a full account of the Bergman-Rossellini cultural contretemps, see Adrienne L. McLean, "The Cinderella Princess and the Instrument of Evil: Revisiting Two Postwar Hollywood Scandals," in David A. Cook and Adrienne L. McLean, eds., *Headline Hollywood: A Century of Film Scandal* (New Brunswick, N.J.: Rutgers University Press, 2001), 163–89.

Page 289. **Despite a sense:** "NAB Moves Towards Establishing Code," *The Daily Compass,* April 21, 1950: 16.

Page 289. **RKO president:** "'Stomboli' Gross Fair in Openings," *Motion Picture Herald,* February 25, 1950: 28.

Page 289. **Meanwhile, Bergman:** "Johnson Has More Steam; Rankin Helps," *Motion Picture Herald,* April 1, 1950: 34.

Page 289. **"We are getting our ears:** "NAB Moves Towards Establishing Code," *The Daily Compass,* April 21, 1950: 16.

Page 290. **On June 22, 1950:** "Revise Ad Code on Misconduct," *Motion Picture Herald,* June 25, 1950: 24.

Page 290. **Not being party:** "Senator Calls Off the Dog But Holds Fast to Leash," and "Johnson Gets Name in Theater Ad," *Motion Picture Herald,* May 6, 1950: 28; "What This Picture Did For Me," *Motion Picture Herald,* October 14, 1950: 41.

Page 290. **Bergman was expunged:** "Battle Rages on 'Stromboli,'" *Motion Picture Herald,* February 18, 1950: 20.

Page 290. **Bergman's imported work:** "Any Bergman-Rossellini Pic Will Get MPAA Nix, Mex Backers Told," *Variety,* December 27, 1950: 1, 47.

Page 290. **Breen had no authority:** The distributor, Italian Film Export (I.F.E.), did not apply for a Code Seal (*The Greatest Love* file, PCA).

Page 291. **"I have never regretted:** Murray Schumach, "Ingrid Bergman Returns to U.S.," *New York Times,* January 20, 1957: 76.

13. AMENDING THE TEN COMMANDMENTS

Page 292. **The tally:** For a typical trend line see Jack Alicoate, ed., *The 1956 Film Daily Year Book of Motion Pictures* (New York: Wid's Film and Film Folk, 1956): 107.

Page 292. **"The swimming pools:** Lewis, quoted in Thomas F. Brady, "This Is Where the Money Went," *New Republic,* January 31, 1949: 12.

Page 293. **In December 1951:** "Joe Breen's Operation," *Variety*, January 2, 1952: 7.

Page 293. **The scrappy Sam Goldwyn:** "TOA Gives Hollywood Slant on Exhibition," *Motion Picture Herald*, September 17, 1949: 14.

Page 294. **"I was here, on the ground:** JIB to Eric Johnston, March 10, 1949 (QP).

Page 294. **"One does not consider:** Terry Ramsaye, "Amending the Ten Commandants," *Motion Picture Herald*, September 24, 1949: 7, 9.

Page 294. **"Not only has:** "Freedom and the Code," *Motion Picture Herald*, September 13, 1952: 7.

Page 294. **"Please bear in mind:** JIB to William Feeder, March 25, 1953 (*The French Line* file, PCA).

Page 294. **Insisted Inglis:** Ruth A. Inglis, "Need for Voluntary Self-Regulation," *Annals of the American Academy of Political and Social Science* (November 1947): 158.

Page 295. **"The Hollywood taboos:** Hortense Powdermaker, *Hollywood, the Dream Factory: An Anthropologist Looks at the Movie-Makers* (Boston: Little, Brown, 1950): 55, 78.

Page 295. **"I believe that:** Gilbert Seldes, *The Great Audience* (New York: Viking, 1950): 73–74.

Page 296. **"I would like:** Eric Hodgins, "What's with the Movies?" *Life*, May 16, 1949: 97–106.

Page 296. **"Never before have moviemen:** "What's Right with Hollywood?" *Parade*, May 29, 1949: 5–7; "Parade Round Table Finds What's Right with Screen," *Motion Picture Herald*, May 28, 1949: 32.

Page 296. **"It has been my experience:** JIB to Jock Lawrence, September 4, 1946 (*The Wicked Lady* file, PCA).

Page 297. **Breen sized him up:** JIB to Rev. Daniel A. Lord, S.J., January 3, 1945 (MJA).

Page 297. **The Code, he told audiences:** "Vizzard Defends Production Code in U.S.C. Lecture," *Motion Picture Herald*, November 14, 1953: 12.

Page 297. **When director William Wyler:** "PCA Replies to Wyler," *Motion Picture Herald*, February 16, 1952: 37. See also "PCA Defends Industry on Narcotics Charge," *Motion Picture Herald*, April 12, 1952: 26.

Page 297. **Trying to calm ruffled filmmakers:** Fred Hift, "Code Works, Schary Says," *Motion Picture Herald*, September 24, 1949: 18.

Page 297. **"I have seemingly:** JIB to Rev. Daniel A. Lord, S.J., April 9, 1950 (MJA).

Page 297. **Breen had good reason:** JIB to Rev. Daniel A. Lord, S.J., April 9, 1950 (MJA).

Page 298. **Quizzed by Martin J. Quigley:** JIB to Martin J. Quigley, September 13, 1946 (QP).

Page 299. **Unappeased, Quigley:** Terry Ramsaye, "Dope and Compromise," *Motion Picture Herald*, September 21, 1946: 7.

Page 299. **"In effect, [the revision]:** "New Teeth in Production Code Kills Any Devices to Cash in on Lurid Sex Sellers; K.O. to the Gangster Cycle," *Variety*, December 3, 1947: 18.

Page 300. **undertaken on March 27, 1951:** The 1951 Code revisions are chronicled in "MPAA Board Tightens Regulations on Industry Production Code," *Variety*, March 28, 1951: 3, 13; "MPAA Restores Ban on Drugs," *Motion Picture Herald*, March 31, 1951: 22.

Page 300. **"Who can tell:** JIB to Arthur E. DeBra, November 20, 1944: 35 (PCA).

Page 300. **As he wrote in 1944:** JIB to Arthur E. DeBra, November 20, 1944: 35 (PCA).

Page 301. **At that, Martin S. Quigley:** "The Screen and 'Dope,'" *Motion Picture Herald*, June 23, 1951: 7.

Page 302. **"This whole business:** JIB to Kenneth Clark, November 11, 1951 (*The Miracle* file, PCA).

Page 302. **On March 26, 1952:** Justice Clark, quoted in J. A. Otten, "Court Breaks Trail to Freedom of the Screen," *Motion Picture Herald*, May 31, 1952: 13, 16; "Industry Leaders See Hope in 'Freedom' Protection," *Motion Picture Herald*, May 31, 1952: 16.

Page 303. **"Irrespective of how the winds:** Martin J. Quigley, "The Court Rules—Yes and No!" *Motion Picture Herald*, May 31, 1952: 7.

Page 303. **"Wanted, An Idea:** Quoted in Eric Hodgins, "A Roundtable on the Movies," *Life*, June 6, 1949: 100.

Page 303. **"There is some sinister:** JIB to Martin J. Quigley, November 29, 1949 (*Beyond the Forest* file, PCA).

Page 304. **"As you go along:** JIB to Vincent Hart, August 7, 1934 (*Crime Without Passion* file, PCA).

Page 305. **"The big strength of the Code:** W. R. Wilkerson, "Tradeviews," *Hollywood Reporter*, March 2, 1954: 1.

Page 305. **"When we have committed:** Terry Ramsaye, "Terry Ramsaye Says," *Motion Picture Herald*, January 10, 1953: 18.

Page 305. **Even after 1948:** "Attack on Purity Seal Expected at Allied Meet," *Film Daily*, May 21, 1935: 6.

Page 305. **"What right has Will Hays:** "Has the Industry Further Use of the Hays Seal?—No. 2," *Harrison's Reports*, April 12, 1941: 57, 60.

Page 306. **In 1946, Harrison:** "The Case of Howard Hughes Versus Eric Johnston," *Harrison's Reports*, May 11, 1946: 74, 76.

Page 306. **Incensed, Breen lashed back:** Pete Harrison, "Joe Breen's Temper," *Harrison's Reports*, September 28, 1946 (unnumbered).

Page 307. **The rebel was United Artists:** Tino Balio, *United Artists: The Company That Changed the Film Industry* (Madison: University of Wisconsin Press, 1987).

Page 307. **As a creature of the majors:** Arthur L. Mayer, "A Movie Exhibitor Looks at Censorship," *Reporter*, March 2, 1954: 38.

Page 307. **UA's vice president Max E. Youngstein:** "A Strong Indictment of the Code Administration," *Harrison's Reports*, January 30, 1954: 20.

Page 307. **In 1953, after what UA:** Martin J. Quigley, "Playing with Fire," *Motion Picture Herald*, August 1, 1953: 7; James D. Ivers, "The Moon Is Blue," *Motion Picture Herald*, June 13, 1953: 1869.

Page 308. **To its editorial dismay:** "A Sober Suggestion," *Harrison Reports*, September 5, 1953: 143; "*The Moon Is Blue*," *Harrison's Reports*, June 6, 1953: 90.

Page 308. **The grown-ups agreed:** Jack Alicoate, ed., *The 1953 Film Daily Year Book* of Motion Pictures (New York: Wid's Film and Film Folk, 1953): 67.

Page 308. **"The judgments of the Code's:** Bosley Crowther, "Decoding the Code," *New York Times*, January 10, 1954, sec. 10: 1.

Page 308. **"If the Production Code:** "Modernization of Production Code Advocated by Goldwyn," *Harrison's Reports*, January 2, 1954: 1, 4.

Page 309. **However, the statement Johnston:** "MPAA Reaffirms Code As 'Contract with Public,'" *Motion Picture Herald*, August 15, 1953: 9.

Page 310. **"Re-examination of the Production Code:** "3-D May Require Code Changes," *Hollywood Reporter*, February 23, 1953: 1, 4.

Page 310. **"We assume the best:** JIB to William Feeder, May 29, 1953; JIB to James R. Grainger, January 6, 1954; Internal PCA Memorandum, January 13, 1954 (all in *The French Line* file, PCA).

Page 310. **"If within the Code:** Kenneth Clark to JIB, February 19, 1954 (*The French Line* file, PCA).

Page 311. **"The Breen edicts:** W. R. Wilkerson, "Tradeviews," *Hollywood Reporter*, March 2, 1954: 1.

Page 311. **Perhaps: but the truculent Hughes:** "Hughes Gives In on Code Issue," *Variety*, April 6, 1955: 4.

Page 312. **As the designated defender:** "'French Line' Opens in St. L. Minus Seal," *Hollywood Reporter*, December 24, 1953: 1, 4; "'French Line' Opening Sets St. L. Box Record," *Hollywood Reporter*, December 30, 1953: 1.

Page 312. **"After twenty years:** JIB to Sidney Schreiber, December 13, 1950 (*Oliver Twist* file, PCA).

Page 312. **Breen had never bounced back:** JIB to Rev. Daniel A. Lord, S.J., August 16, 1954 (MJA).

Page 312. **"Hollywood is taking:** "Code Unrevised, But Studios Now Say: How, Not What, Keys Story 'Morality,'" *Variety*, August 11, 1954: 4, 22.

14. NOT THE BREEN OFFICE

Page 313. **In 1950 the irrepressible:** Martin J. Quigley Papers, January 5, 1950 (QP).

Page 314. **Geoffrey Shurlock recalled:** Shurlock, in James M. Wall "Interviews with Geoffrey Shurlock" (1970): 145, 217.

Page 314. **"I am anxious:** JIB to Rev. Daniel A. Lord, S.J., August 16, 1954 (MJA).

Page 314. **Along with the golden statue:** "Breen's $20,000 Yearly Till '61," *Variety*, October 20, 1954: 20.

Page 314. **In announcing the succession:** "Name Shurlock to Succeed Breen as PC Administrator," *Film Daily*, October 15, 1954: 1.

Page 314. **Wags joshed:** "Shurlock's Background: Laundry, Literary, Sec'y," *Variety*, October 20, 1954: 20.

Page 314n. **Breen's annual salary:** "Breen's Economy," *Variety*, October 27, 1954: 22.

Page 315. **"While Breen held:** "Breen Almost Became Generic Name for Code; What Now with Shurlock?" *Variety*, October 20, 1954: 20.

Page 315. **"The trade will:** Abel Green, "1954 in Biz There's None Like," *Variety*, January 5, 1955: 70.

Page 315. **No fool, Shurlock:** Geoffrey M. Shurlock, "Code Administrator Reiterates Values of the 'Breen' Principle," *Variety*, January 5, 1955: 7.

Page 315. **Even Breen's honorary Oscar:** "Col., Par, 20th Top Oscars," *Hollywood Reporter*, March 26, 1954: 12. See also "Code's Value Is Lauded by Keough," *Motion Picture Herald*, April 17, 1954: 16.

Page 316. **"The world has moved:** "Goldwyn Asks on Code—Again," *Motion Picture Herald,* March 6, 1954: 22.

Page 316. **In 1954 the syndicated columnist:** Arthur Schlesinger, Jr., "History of the Week," *New York Post,* January 10, 1954: 3M.

Page 317. **Gaily throttling his paymasters:** Ben Hecht, *A Child of the Century* (New York: Donald A. Fine, 1954): 468–69.

Page 317. **In 1954, the tipping-point year:** "A Free Screen," *Life,* February 8, 1954: 28.

Page 318. **Again, the court chose:** "Censors: 'We've Been Censored!'" *Variety,* January 20, 1954: 5, 20.

Page 318. **"The Code is as necessary:** Jerry Cotter, "Stage and Screen," *The Sign* (March 1954): 25.

Page 318. **On September 13, 1954:** "Revised Pix Code OKs Miscegenation, Drinking, Smuggling, If 'In Good Taste,'" *Variety,* September 15, 1954: 3, 16.

Page 319. **Labeled "technical or clarifying":** "MPA Board Amends Production Code," *Motion Picture Herald,* September 18, 1954: 12; "MPAA Approves Code Revisions," *Hollywood Reporter,* September 14, 1954: 1, 8.

Page 320. **When Wallis appealed:** "Wallis Eliminates 'Cease Fire' Controversial Words," *Motion Picture Herald,* November 21, 1953: 35.

Page 320. **The dialogue in question:** JIB to Eric Johnston, April 23, 1954 (*On the Waterfront* file, PCA).

Page 321. **Understandably, Hal Wallis:** Hal Wallis to JIB, May 18, 1954 (*On the Waterfront* file, PCA).

Page 322. **"The energies of the PCA:** Martin J. Quigley, "Latest Code Changes," *Motion Picture Herald,* September 18, 1954: 17; Martin J. Quigley, "Hell, Damn, and the Code," *Motion Picture Herald,* November 21, 1953: 7.

Page 322. **"The Code's strength:** Virginia van Upp, "Pro and Con," *Film Daily,* October 4, 1954: 4.

Page 322. **The boss was not gone:** "New Wages of Sin: Remorse," *Variety,* April 25, 1956: 7, 22.

Page 323. **MGM appealed to the MPAA Board:** "TV Liberal, Screen Strict," *Variety,* April 27, 1955: 3.

Page 324. **Similarly, Twentieth Century-Fox:** "Fox Nixes 'Hatful' If No Seal," *Hollywood Reporter,* December 9, 1955: 1.

Page 324. **At the *Hollywood Reporter,* Billy Wilkerson:** W. R. Wilkerson, "Tradeviews," *Hollywood Reporter,* December 9, 1955: 1.

Page 324. **On December 11, 1956:** "Dope, Kidnapping, and Other Tabu Plots OK Under Revised Film Code," *Variety,* December 12, 1956: 1, 20; "Production Code Liberalized," *Hollywood Reporter,* December 12, 1956: 1, 6.

Page 326. ***Baby Doll* had already been condemned:** "'Baby's' Code in Headlines," *Variety,* December 19, 1956: 11.

Page 326n. **Episcopalian Shurlock was away:** Vizzard, *See No Evil*: 207, 210.

Page 327. **"In this country:** Kazan, quoted in "'Baby's' Code in Headlines," *Variety,* December 19, 1956: 11.

Page 327. **"It's open season:** Youngstein, quoted in "No Rest for the Weary," *Variety,* May 1, 1957: 17.

Page 330. **"There are now no taboos:** Shurlock, quoted in "Inside Stuff—Pictures," *Variety*, October 2, 1963: 30.

Page 330. **"I did not become president:** Valenti, quoted in Frank Barron, "Valenti Plans Creative Push," *Hollywood Reporter*, June 21, 1966: 1, 3.

Page 331. **Bare breasts:** Monsignor Little, quoted in Ronald Gold, "Film Art Requires No Bra," *Variety*, March 31, 1965: 5, 22.

Page 331. **Knowing better,** *Variety:* Ronald Gold, "Film Art Requires No Bra," *Variety*, March 31, 1965: 5, 22.

Page 331. **Confronted with a fait accompli:** "'Woolf' Gets Code Exemption," *Hollywood Reporter*, June 13, 1966: 1, 4; "Review Board Okays 'Woolf,'" *Film Daily*, June 13, 1966: 1, 8.

Page 332. **On September 20, 1966:** "Valenti Plans Info Campaign to Point 'Mature' Pictures," *Hollywood Reporter*, September 22, 1966: 1, 4.

Page 333. **The headline in *Variety:*** Ben Kaufman, "New Pic Code 'For Adults Only,'" *Hollywood Reporter*, September 21, 1966: 1, 4; "New Code Suggests Rather Than Directs," *Hollywood Reporter*, September 21, 1966: 4; Vincent Canby, "A New Movie Code Ends Some Taboos," *New York Times*, September 21, 1966: 1, 42; "Pious Platitudes Take It on Chin As Film Biz Rewrites Moral Code," *Variety*, September 21, 1966: 1, 21.

Page 333. **"It is dangerous:** "Nix Classifying of Pix," *Variety*, August 28, 1934: 51.

Page 333. **"A rating system:** "'Forbid and You Attract'—Elmer Rice; Talk Again Heard of Value of U.S. 'Adults Only' Film Category," *Variety*, December 19, 1956: 16.

Page 334. **The original ratings were:** "Mom-Pop Code: G-M-R-X," *Variety*, October 9, 1968: 3, 9.

Page 334. **"So, the emergence:** Jack Valenti, "The Voluntary Movie Rating System" (December 1996; from the Web page). See also Jack Valenti, "Ratings Born of Conflict," *Variety*, December 4, 2006: 6, 82.

Page 334n. **According to film historian Stephen Vaughn:** Stephen Vaughn, *Freedom and Entertainment: Rating the Movies in an Age of New Media* (New York: Cambridge University Press, 2006), 35.

Page 335. **Over the years, the ratings:** Vaughn's *Freedom and Entertainment* offers a marvelous scholarly exposé of the inner workings of CARA. The other required reading on the topic is Jon Lewis, *Hollywood v. Hardcore: How the Struggle Over Censorship Saved the Modern Film Industry* (New York: New York University Press, 2000).

Page 335. **"The exhibitors of the United States:** Rifkin, quoted in "Mom-Pop Code: G-M-R-X," *Variety*, October 9, 1968: 3, 9.

15. FINAL CUT: JOSEPH I. BREEN AND THE AUTEUR THEORY

Page 337. **"A love of vitality:** François Truffaut, *The Films in My Life*, trans. Leonard Mayhew (New York: Simon and Schuster, 1975): 278–79.

Page 337. **Being French intellectuals:** André Bazin, "La politique des auteurs," (1962), in Peter Graham, *The New Wave* (London: British Film Institute, 1968): 142–43.

Page 338. **In 1962, auteurism:** Emanuel Levy, *Citizen Sarris, American Film Critic: Essays in Honor of Andrew Sarris* (Lanham, Md.: Scarecrow Press, 2001).

Page 338. **"To speak any:** Andrew Sarris, *The American Cinema: Directors and Directions, 1929–1968* (New York: Dutton, 1968): 39.

Page 338. **Pauline Kael:** Pauline Kael, "Circles and Squares," reprinted in Gerald Mast and Marshall Cohen, eds., *Film Theory and Criticism: Introductory Readings* (New York: Oxford University Press, 1974): 520.

Page 339. **"To me, it was:** Ford, quoted in Peter Bogdanovich, *John Ford* (Berkeley: University of California Press, 1978): 108. In an amusing exchange with the flinty director in Bogdanovich's documentary, *Directed by John Ford* (1971), Ford is terse, taciturn, and good-naturedly vulgar when the word "art" comes up in the conversation.

Page 339. **"It is not too much:** Charles Francis Coe, *Never a Dull Moment* (New York: Hastings House, 1944): 306.

Page 340. **"Take three great producers:** Shurlock, in James M. Wall, "Interviews with Geoffrey Shurlock" (1970): 127.

Page 340. **Breen's own evaluation:** JIB statement (QP).

Page 342. **"It was a miracle:** "Mr. Moley Writes," *Motion Picture Herald*, February 12, 1944: 8.

Page 342. **The Comics Code pledged:** Terry Ramsaye, "Code for Comics," *Motion Picture Herald*, July 31, 1948: 7. See also Cynthia Lowry, "AP Tells the Facts About Quigley Code Authorship," *Motion Picture Herald*, November 6, 1948: 22.

Page 342. **As early as 1950:** "Television Urged to Adopt Screen's Production Code," *Motion Picture Herald*, April 8, 1950: 37.

Page 343. **On April 20, 1950:** "Advise TV on Code," *Motion Picture Herald*, April 29, 1950: 27.

Page 343. **The same day:** "Convention Notes," *Television Digest*, April 22, 1950: 6; "NAB Moves Towards Establishing TV Code," *The Daily Compass*, April 21, 1950: 16.

Page 344. **"An extensive and well-ordered file:** JIB to Arthur E. DeBra, November 20, 1944: 7 (PCA).

Page 344. **"Before Breen, the records:** Samuel Gill, correspondence with author, June 7, 2002.

Page 345. **A short time after:** Lea Jacobs, interview with author, March 21, 2006.

Page 345. **Better: whereas most:** Linda Mehr, interview with author, January 11, 2007.

Page 345. **"The fact that I am an advisor:** Shurlock, in Wall, "Interviews" (1970): 107.

Page 346. **Breen was "all too rarely seen:** "Option Impending for John Wilder," *Los Angeles Times*, July 2, 1957: B7.

Page 346. **"Get away from me:** Shurlock, in Wall, "Interviews" (1970): 108.

Page 346. **"I am happy to correct:** Louella Parsons, "Gay Reunion," *Los Angeles Examiner*, April 14, 1961: 7.

Page 346. **"We thought—my wife and I:** JIB to Stanley Kramer, undated (circa Christmas 1961). (Courtesy of Mary Pat Dorr)

Page 347. **"The twenty years:** Eric A. Johnston to JIB, September 18, 1961. (Courtesy of Mary Pat Dorr)

Page 348. **"He was thrilled with it:** Pat Breen, interview with author, June 17, 2006.

Page 348. **The eulogies:** Martin S. Quigley, "Breen—The Man and His Cause," *Motion Picture Herald*, December 22, 1965: 8.

Page 349. **"In 1954, Mr. Breen:** Patrick F. Scanlon, "From the Managing Editor's Desk," *Brooklyn Tablet*, December 9, 1965: 22.

Page 349: **"It was ironic:** "Legion Official's Views Draw Fire," *Catholic Standard and Times*, December 17, 1965: 6.

Page 349. **The failure of the new generation:** "Film Industry Snubs Joe Breen's Funeral," *Variety*, December 15, 1965: 13; Abel Green, "Toward New Super-Show Biz," *Variety*, January 5, 1966: 69.

FILM INDEX

INDEX